Military Sexual Slavery by Imperial Japan

Military Sexual Slavery
by Imperial Japan

First edition published by Seoul National University Press in 2024

Seoul National University Press
1 Gwanak-ro, Gwanak-gu, Seoul 08826, Republic of Korea
Tel: +82-2-880-5252
Fax: +82-2-889-0785
Homepage: http://www.snupress.com
Facebook: @snupress1947
Instagram: @snupress
E-mail: snubook@snu.ac.kr

ISBN 978-89-521-1525-6 93330

Military Sexual Slavery by Imperial Japan

Historical Realities and Social Movements for Resolution

Chung Chinsung

Translated by Kim Yoo-suk

SNUPRESS
Seoul National University Press

Table of Contents

Chapter 3 The Forced Mobilization of Women as Japanese Military Sex Slaves

Chapter 4 The Social Structural Background and Reality of Japanese Military Sexual Slavery

Part II The Social Movements to Resolve the Issue of Japanese Military Sexual Slavery

Chapter 5 The Movement to Resolve the Issue of Japanese Military Sexual Slavery

Chapter 6 The Issue of Japanese Military Sexual Slavery at the UN

Chapter 7 The Issue of Japanese Military Sexual Slavery at the ILO

Supplements

I. Research on Japanese Corporate Sexual Slavery

II. The Reality of the Women's Labor Volunteer Corps

A Note on the Text, Translation, and Transliteration

- This volume is an English translation of Chung Chinsung [鄭鎭星], *Military Sexual Slavery by Imperial Japan: Historical Realities and Social Movements for Resolution* [日本軍性奴隷制—日本軍慰安婦問題의 實像과 그 解決을 爲한 運動] (Seoul: Seoul National University Press [서울大學校出版文化院], 2016), which is a revised edition of the author's work of the same title published by the same publisher in 2004.
- For the sake of clarity and brevity, apostrophes have been omitted from plural forms of acronyms/initialisms and years, as in "NGOs" and "1940s," respectively.
- Throughout this work, all translatable terms including the titles of publications, titles of posts, names of organizations, and concepts have been rendered into English, employing official or established translations when available, with transliterations provided only sparingly for the sake of brevity and convenience.
- In transliterating Korean, the Revised Romanization system used by the South Korean government has been adopted, as in "Seo-gu." However, in the case of surnames such as 姜 (강), 吉 (길), 金 (김), 高 (고), and 具 (구), the spellings "Kang," "Kil," "Kim," "Ko," and "Ku" have been chosen instead of "Gang," "Gil," "Gim," "Go," and "Gu," respectively, because they are more widespread and preclude unnecessary confusion with the English words *gang*, *kill*, *gym*, *go*, and *goo*. Another exception has been made for the names of places in and figures from what is North Korea today, in which case the modified McCune-Reischauer system used by the North Korean government up to 1992 has been adopted for convenience's sake, as it is still widely used in the international community.
- In transliterating Japanese, while the Revised Hepburn system has been adopted, the macron indicating long vowels has been omitted for the sake of simplicity, as in "*ochonin*."
- In transliterating Mandarin Chinese, while the Hanyu Pinyin system has been adopted, all diacritical marks including tone marks and the umlaut over "u" in certain words have been omitted.
- For the sake of historical accuracy and consistency, the names of places in China have been transliterated using the Postal Map Romanization system when references to them date from before the establishment of the People's Republic of China, as in "Kiukiang." The same principle has been applied to the names of former Western and Japanese colonies and occupied territories and locations in them, as in "Batavia."
- All diacritical marks including tone marks have been omitted from the names of Vietnamese figures and places, as in "Tien Yen." Also, as in this example, the Vietnamese custom of placing spaces between syllables in toponyms has been followed.
- As for the names of Korean, Japanese, Chinese, and Vietnamese figures, in accordance with the tradition common to these countries, the surname has been placed before the forename, omitting the comma separating the two throughout the main body (but not in the bibliography and the index) for the sake of brevity and convenience, as in "Manabe

Motoyuki." An exception has been made for the names of Anglicized or Westernized figures, however, as in "Michael 'Mike' Makoto Honda."

- To avoid possible confusion due to homophonous or identical surnames, full names have been provided for Asian figures at all times, even in parenthetical references, as in "(Chung Chinsung, 1995: 179)." An exception has been made for the names of Anglicized or Westernized figures, however, as in "(Chen, 1968: 71-90)."
- When a figure is known by two or more names including nicknames, all of them have been provided in the index, as in "Pillay, Navanethem 'Navi.'"
- Except for cases of personal preference, all multisyllabic Chinese, Korean, and Japanese surnames and forenames have been written as single words without intervening hyphens, as in "Chungmoo."
- Notwithstanding the virtual absence of grammatical gender in English, in keeping with the local custom, gender-inflected ethnonyms/demonyms have been used in references to people of or from the Philippines, as in "Lunas—Let's Walk Hand in Hand with Filipina Former 'Comfort Women.'"
- When necessary, important terms have been presented in the original languages alongside their English translations. This has been indispensable especially for disparate Asian terms that have the same English rendition, as in "prostitutes" for 賣淫婦, 賣春婦, 娼妓, and 娼婦. In such cases as well as in the index and the bibliography, Chinese characters in their traditional forms rather than the simplified forms used in China, Singapore, and Malaysia (*Jianhuazi*) and Japan (*Shinjitai*), respectively, have been provided for all applicable names or titles of figures, places, organizations, publications, and concepts when possible. This is because the traditional forms were universally used both before and during World War II and also to avoid the cumbersomeness of having to provide all variant forms for each term.
- Intervening spaces have not been used in Japanese- and Chinese-language entries as words are customarily run together in these languages. Likewise, the spacing between words has been minimized in Korean-language entries, as in "朝鮮新報."
- When the names of historical events in or involving Asia, especially political and military ones, differ by country, only terms generally used in South Korea have been provided in addition to their common Western designators, with the corresponding Japanese and Chinese names given in the footnotes, as in "中日戰爭" (Korean) over both "日中戰爭" (Japanese) and "中國抗日戰爭" (Chinese) for the "Second Sino-Japanese War."

Abbreviations

Because this volume covers considerable time and space and, in particular, alludes to a multitude of organizations, the bulk of which no longer exist, the use of acronyms and initialisms has been minimized in order to prevent confusion. In such cases, official or customary acronyms/initialisms, if existent, have been included in the first appearances of the full names of organizations but not used afterwards (excluded from this list). While non-acronymic abbreviations have been used more often, many of their full forms have been repeated in each new section or chapter, notwithstanding established editorial practices, in order to aid readers who may be unfamiliar with Asian history.

4th Geneva Convention	Convention Relative to the Protection of Civilian Persons in Time of War; Geneva Convention of 1949 [1949]
4th Hague Convention	Convention Respecting the Laws and Customs of War on Land; 4th Hague Convention of 1907 [1907]
2000 Women's Tribunal	Women's International War Crimes Tribunal on Japan's Military Sexual Slavery in 2000 [2000]
Asian Solidarity Conference	Asian Solidarity Conference for the Issue of Military Sexual Slavery by Japan; 日本軍'慰安婦'問題解決을 爲한 아시아連帶會議; 日本軍'慰安婦'問題 아시아連帶會議; 아시아連帶會議; 日本軍「慰安婦」問題解決のためのアジア連帶會議; 日本軍「慰安婦」問題アジア連帶會議; アジア 連帶會議 [1992-]
Asian Women's Fund	Asian Peace and People's Fund for Women; AWF 女性のためのアジア平和國民基金; アジア女性基金; 國民基金 [1995-2007]
ATIS	Allied Translator and Interpreter Section [1942-1945]
Batavia War Criminal Court	Temporary Court Martial Tribunal of Batavia [1946 1948]
Geneva Convention on Slavery	Convention to Suppress the Slave Trade and Slavery; 1926 Slavery Convention [1926]
GHQ/SCAP	General Headquarters, Supreme Commander for the Allied Powers [1945-1952]
ILO	International Labour Organization [1919-]

ILO Committee of Experts	International Labour Organization Committee of Experts on the Application of Conventions and Recommendations; CEACR
ILO Conference Committee	International Labour Organization Conference Committee on the Application of Standards; CAS
ILO Forced Labour Convention	International Labour Organization Convention Concerning Forced or Compulsory Labour; ILO Convention No. 29 [1930]
International Criminal Tribunal for the Former Yugoslavia	International Tribunal for the Prosecution of Persons Responsible for Serious Violations of International Humanitarian Law Committed in the Territory of the Former Yugoslavia since 1991; ICTY [1993-2017]
Jichiro	All-Japan Prefectural and Municipal Workers Union; AJPMWU 全日本自治團體勞動組合; 自治勞 [1954-]
Kono Statement	Statement by Chief Cabinet Secretary Kono Yohei on the Result of the Study on the Issue of "Comfort Women" 慰安婦關係調查結果發表に關する河野內閣官房長官談話; 河野談話 [1993]
Korean Council	Korean Council for the Women Drafted for Military Sexual Slavery by Japan 韓國挺身隊問題對策協議會; 挺對協 [1990-2018]
Korean Organizing Committee	Korean Organizing Committee for the 2000 Women's Tribunal [1998-2000]
Korean Research Group	Korean Chongshindae Research Group 韓國挺身隊研究會 [1990-1997]
Korean Research Institute	Korean Research Institute for the Women Drafted for Military Sexual Slavery by Japan 韓國挺身隊研究所 [1997-]
Meiji Constitution	Constitution of the Empire of Japan 大日本帝國憲法 [1889-1947]
NEFIS	Netherlands Forces Intelligence Service [1941-1948]
NGOs	non-governmental organizations
OFSET Union	Osaka Fu Special English Teachers' Union 大阪府特別英語教員組合
Public Hearing	Public Hearing on Crimes against Women in Recent Wars and Conflicts [2000]

Rengo	Japanese Trade Union Confederation; JTUC; JTUC-Rengo 日本勞動組合總聯合會; 聯合 [1989-]
Russell Tribunal on Vietnam	International War Crimes Tribunal on Vietnam [1967]
San Francisco Treaty	Treaty of Peace with Japan [1951]
SEATIC	South East Asia Translation and Interrogation Center [1943 or 1944-1946?]
South Korean-Japanese Claims Agreement	Agreement on the Settlement of Problem Concerning Property and Claims and the Economic Cooperation between the Republic of Korea and Japan; Agreement between Japan and the Republic of Korea Concerning the Settlement of Problems in Regard to Property and Claims and Economic Cooperation 大韓民國과 日本國間의 財産 및 請求權에 關한 問題의 解決과 經濟協力에 關한 協定; 韓日請求權協定; 財産及び請求權に關する問題の解決竝びに經濟協力に關する日本國と大韓民國との間の協定; 日韓請求權竝びに經濟協力協定 [1965]
South Seas Mandate	Japanese Mandate for the Governance of the South Seas Islands 日本委任統治領南洋群島; 南洋群島; 南洋諸島; 內南洋 [1920-1945]
STDs; VDs	sexually transmitted diseases; venereal diseases
Students' Tribunal	Students' Tribunal on Japan's Military Sexual Slavery in 2000 2000年日本軍性奴隸戰犯學生法廷 [2000]
Tokyo Chihyo	Tokyo Regional Council of Trade Unions 東京地方勞動組合評議會; 東京地評 [1951-]
Treaty of Versailles	Treaty of Peace between the Allied and Associated Powers and Germany [1919]
UN	United Nations [1945-]
UN Commission on Human Rights	United Nations Commission on Human Rights; UNCHR [1946-2006]
UN Committee on the Elimination of Discrimination against Women	United Nations Committee on the Elimination of All Forms of Discrimination against Women; CEDAW [1981-]
UN Committee on the Elimination of Racial Discrimination	United Nations Committee on the Elimination of All Forms of Racial Discrimination; CERD [1970-]

UN Human Rights Committee	United Nations Human Rights Committee; UNHRC [1976-]
UN Human Rights Council	United Nations Human Rights Council; UNHRC [2006-]
UN Human Rights Council Advisory Committee	United Nations Human Rights Council Advisory Committee; UNHRCAC [2007-]
UN Special Rapporteur on Systematic Rape, Sexual Slavery and Slavery-like Practices during Armed Conflict	United Nations Special Rapporteur on the Situation of Systematic Rape, Sexual Slavery and Slavery-like Practices during Periods of Armed Conflict [1993-1995 or 1997]; United Nations Special Rapporteur on Systematic Rape, Sexual Slavery and Slavery-like Practices during Armed Conflict [1995 or 1997-2000]
UN Special Rapporteur on the Right to Reparation	United Nations Special Rapporteur on the Right to Restitution, Compensation and Rehabilitation for Victims of Gross Violations of Human Rights and Fundamental Freedoms [1989-1993]
UN Special Rapporteur on Violence against Women	United Nations Special Rapporteur on Violence against Women and Girls, Its Causes and Consequences [1994-]
UN Sub-Commission on Human Rights	United Nations Sub-Commission on the Promotion and Protection of Human Rights [1999-2006]
VAWW-Net Japan	Violence against Women in War Network Japan 「戦争と女性への暴力」日本ネットワーク; バウネット·ジャパン [1998-2011]
VAWW RAC	Violence against Women in War Research Action Center 「戦争と女性への暴力」リサーチ·アクション·センター; バウラック [2011-2021]
Zenroren	National Confederation of Trade Unions; NCTU 全國勞動組合總連合; 全勞連 [1989-]
Zenzosen	All Japan Shipbuilding and Engineering Union; AJSEU; SEU; Zenzosen Kikai 全日本造船機械勞動組合; 全造船機械; 全造船 [1946-2016]

Tables and Diagrams

Preface

Although it is an utterly unconscionable violation of the most basic human rights, females of diverse ages have been subjected to violence, especially of the sexual kind, by soldiers and militiamen during armed conflicts worldwide since time immemorial. It would be safe to say that awareness of the sheer gravity of the issue—and, indeed, of human rights themselves—has become strong enough to lead to the creation of various relevant laws and agencies, both domestic and international, only in the 20th century, which witnessed the destruction and carnage wreaked by no fewer than two world wars.

In relation to the last world war, one instance of such wartime sexual violation of women's human rights stands out in particular: Japanese military sexual slavery. This was the Japanese armed forces' uniquely systematic and coercive sexual enslavement of a vast number of girls and women for the "morale" of the soldiers during the nation's prolonged military expansion overseas encompassing the Second Sino-Japanese War 中日戰爭[1] (1937-1945) and the Pacific War (1941-1945). Consisting mainly of lower-class women from the Japanese empire's colonies and occupied territories in Asia, these victims of sexual exploitation were mobilized through diverse means including employment fraud and forced taking 強制連行 by civilians, police officers, and soldiers.

Euphemistically called the military "comfort women" system by the Japanese government, the very fact lay dormant for decades following

---

1 [Translator's note (henceforth "TN")] This is the customary Korean name for this war. Common designators for the historical event in Japanese and Chinese are 日中戰爭 and 中國抗日戰爭, respectively.

World War II due to: Japan's intentional destruction and concealment of official documents both toward and since the end of the war and postwar denial of its legal responsibility for the creation and maintenance of the institution per se and forced transfer of women; the failure of the Allied Powers, especially the United States, fully to indict the former empire for its crimes immediately after the war and subsequently during the Cold War, thus raising the issue of impunity; and a patriarchal social climate that shamed and silenced the survivors, especially in the victim nations. Though the war itself had ended long before, Japanese military sexual slavery thus remained an unfinished ordeal, still all too real and raw for the survivors and their families.

It was only in 1991, when South Korean survivor Kim Hak-Soon 金學順 came forward and spoke up about her long-buried past, that the issue truly became public, notwithstanding a rather tenuous postwar current of social activism, studies, press coverage, memoirs, and artistic recreations in South Korea, Japan, and elsewhere. This courageous revelation was partly a fruit of continued efforts by South Korean women's movements working on violence against women, which discovered a commonality between the use of rape as a tool in the "ethnic cleansing" that was committed in Europe in the 1990s and Japanese military sexual slavery. In the fact that violence against women was not only an outcome but also an instrument of armed conflicts throughout the world including civil wars, they discovered the fundamental meaning of the Japanese empire's wartime sexual enslavement of women. Kim Hak-Soon's disclosure prompted other survivors around the globe to come forth as well, thus leading to the expansion of and cooperation within the movement to resolve the issue to Japan, other Asian victim nations, and the world.

Thanks to the endeavors of women's organizations, in the 1990s, the United Nations (UN) Sub-Commission on the Promotion and Protection of Human Rights (henceforth "Sub-Commission on Human Rights"; reformed as the UN Human Rights Council Advisory Committee (UNHRCAC) in 2007) started to discuss Japanese military sexual slavery in depth under the more general title of "systematic rape, sexual slavery and slavery-like practices during armed conflict," and the UN Commission on Human Rights (UNCHR; reformed as the

UN Human Rights Council (UNHRC) in 2006), too, dealt with this issue through the Special Rapporteur on Violence against Women and Girls, Its Causes and Consequences (henceforth "Special Rapporteur on Violence against Women"). The International Labour Organization (ILO) likewise discussed Japanese military sexual slavery as a violation of the Convention Concerning Forced or Compulsory Labour (ILO Convention No. 29; henceforth "Forced Labour Convention"), and, later, major UN treaty bodies including the UN Committee on the Elimination of All Forms of Discrimination against Women (CEDAW; henceforth "Committee on the Elimination of Discrimination against Women"), UN Human Rights Committee, and UN Committee on the Elimination of All Forms of Racial Discrimination (CERD; henceforth "Committee on the Elimination of Racial Discrimination") also addressed the issue as a violation of their respective conventions. Having been horrified by the genocide of the Jewish people at the hands of the Nazis during World War II, the international community was greatly shocked by the fact that the issue of sexual slavery, a human rights violation on a comparable level, had occurred and, moreover, that it had been disclosed to the world only after 60 years. The global community agreed that the continued violation of women's human rights in wartime stemmed from the failure strictly to convict such a tremendous human rights violation.

While it is increasingly common knowledge around the globe, Japanese military sexual slavery nevertheless remains an unresolved issue, and the historical fact itself has yet to be thoroughly elucidated. Many documents were destroyed, remaining ones have not been fully disclosed, and the Japanese government refuses to admit legal responsibility. Some say that we should stop holding onto this history after so many decades and move forward instead. However, the present and the future cannot stand firmly on a distorted past. Moreover, true reconciliation is possible only when the victims—with their honor restored and their hearts set at ease at last based on the Japanese government's full disclosure of relevant materials, heartfelt official apology, material compensation, and inclusion of the history in public education—willingly hold out their hands first. In this respect, I am very happy to publish this volume, which is the English translation of *Military Sexual Slavery by Imperial Japan: Historical Realities and Social Movements for Resolution*

日本軍性奴隷制—日本軍慰安婦問題의 實像과 그 解決을 爲한 運動, a study that I published in Korean in 2004 and 2016 (both Seoul National University Press, with the latter a revision) and in Japanese, with updates, in 2008 (日本軍の性奴隷制—日本軍慰安婦問題の實像とその解決の爲の運動; Ronsosha Publishing Co., Ltd.), respectively. The continued, multilingual publication of this work reflects all the more the fact that Japanese military sexual slavery has come to be perceived as a human rights issue of not only Asia but also the world.

By training, I am a social scientist, who must endeavor to conduct objective analysis based on accurate materials. At the same time, I am an activist, who makes appeals to the international community including the UN regarding this issue, visiting other countries when necessary. Although I have striven to perform objective analysis in this book based on all documentary evidence obtainable and the testimonies of both victims and experiencers of the military comfort station system, a strong desire for human rights and peace will be evident at times. I hope and believe that readers who are pained by this issue will understand and empathize with glimpses of such a passion.

Since the publication of the original Korean edition in 2004, there have been many changes to the issue of Japanese military sexual slavery. A large number of materials such as military documents, photographs, and video recordings illuminating historical facts have been discovered, and, following the passing of a resolution on Japanese military sexual slavery in the US House of Representatives, legislatures in diverse countries and regions including the European Union (EU) have adopted similar resolutions. In nations such as Japan, South Korea, and United States, academic works and collections of commentaries on Japanese military sexual slavery have been published. In publishing this English translation, I have endeavored to reflect such changes.

A word of caution regarding the terminology is necessary here. The expression "comfort women 慰安婦," first coined and consistently used by the Japanese to this day, is deeply problematic for numerous reasons. First, with the word "comfort 慰安," this euphemism simultaneously degrades women with its inherent sexism and phallocentrism and conceals the grim reality of sexual services forced on women, of both Japanese and foreign origins, by the Japanese military and private corporations for the "morale" and "productivity" of their personnel until the end of World War II. In other words, in both presupposing and perpetuating exploitation on multiple levels—i.e., of women by men; of individual citizens by powerful collective bodies such as the government and private corporations; of civilians by the military; and of colonized/occupied peoples by colonizers/ occupiers—the comfort women system was profoundly dehumanizing, which makes it all the more unjustifiable. In consideration of the historical reality and ideological implications, terms such as "sex slaves," "sexual slavery," "sexual slavery policies," and "sexual slavery facilities" have been used together with "comfort women," "comfort women system," "comfort women policies," and "comfort facilities" throughout this volume. Due to its cumbersomeness and rare use in English-language media, however, the expression "sexual slavery stations" has been dropped in favor of "comfort stations." Nevertheless, all terms that include the word "comfort" should eventually be replaced by more accurate designators such as "sexual slavery" and "sex slaves."

This work consists of three parts: historical facts, social movements, and theoretical discussions. Based on the latest, revised Korean, edition, this volume includes additional information in new subheadings and footnotes to reflect more recent developments regarding Japanese military sexual slavery and the movements to redress it both in South Korea and around the world. In the process, I have enlisted the help of Mr. Kim Yoo-suk, who studied English literature in the United States, as the translator. Working with a sense of personal dedication to the causes of peace and human rights, he has created the explanatory note on the translation and transliteration, translator's notes, and list of abbreviations and updated the author's notes and the index in addition to translating the entire book, all of which I have reviewed and approved. Providing partial support for the translation, Seoul National University Press has decided to publish this version. I would like to thank all of them.

Chung Chinsung

Part I

The Reality of the Issue of Japanese Military Sexual Slavery

Chapter 1

The Concept of Japanese Military Sex Slaves

1. The Many Names for Japanese Military Sex Slaves

As the issue of Japanese military sexual slavery began to gain public attention in South Korean society at the end of the 1980s, the term "comfort women 慰安婦" led to considerable confusion. With public discussions on the fact that the Japanese authorities had forcibly taken innumerable Korean women during the Japanese colonial era (1910-1945) yet to begin and with the confused coexistence of concepts in the minds of the public such as the Volunteer Corps 挺身隊, supply of unmarried women to the government 處女供出, and Patriotic Corps 報國隊, this issue suddenly surfaced as that of the "Volunteer Corps." Not only the press and the media including newspapers but also organizations created specifically to address the issue—for example, the Korean Chongshindae Research Group 韓國挺身隊研究會 (henceforth "Korean Research Group"; renamed the Korean Research Institute for the Women Drafted for Military Sexual Slavery by Japan 韓國挺身隊研究所 (henceforth "Korean Research Institute") in 1997), Korean Council for the Women Drafted for Military Sexual Slavery by Japan 韓國挺身隊問題對策協議會[1] (挺對協; henceforth

1 [TN] In 2018, the Korean Council merged with the Foundation for Justice and Remembrance for the Issue of Military Sexual Slavery by Japan 日本軍性奴隷制問題解決을 爲한 正義記憶財團, which it had established in 2016 for the struggle to annul the 2015 agreement between Seoul and Tokyo on Japanese military sexual slavery, and was renamed the Korean Council for Justice and Remembrance for the Issue of Military Sexual Slavery by Japan 日本軍性奴隷制問題解決을 爲한 正義記憶連帶 (正義連).

"Korean Council"), etc.—alike used the term "Volunteer Corps" in Korean. At the same time in Japan, however, this issue began to attract public attention as that of "comfort women accompanying the military 從軍慰安婦." The Women's Labor Volunteer Corps 女子勤勞挺身隊[2] system, whereby unmarried women had been mobilized as munitions factory laborers, and the military comfort women system, whereby women had been mobilized as soldiers' sex slaves, had been clearly separate in Japan in the 1940s. As a result, when this issue became a social one, the Japanese criticized the South Koreans for "ignorantly" failing to distinguish between the concepts of the Volunteer Corps and military comfort women. However, this, in fact, was ignorant criticism unaware of what had actually happened in colonial Korea during the period. Nevertheless, daunted by such criticism, members of South Korean society—most of whom probably were hearing the term "comfort women accompanying the military" for the first time—including even organizations created specifically to address this issue suddenly began to waver between the concepts of the Volunteer Corps and "comfort women accompanying the military," finally settling on the term "Japanese military comfort women 日本軍慰安婦."

The Japanese armed forces' comfort women system thus led to confusion in the terminology because this system had been implemented clandestinely without being discussed officially, mentioned only surreptitiously. Moreover, "military comfort women 軍慰安婦" had not been an official term used in proclaimed laws such as the Ordinance on Women's Voluntary Labor 女子挺身勤勞令[3] but had been a term used sporadically in Japanese military documents together with others such as "shameful female workers 醜業婦," "female workers 從業婦," and "bar

---

In order to avoid confusion, however, all future references to the organization will use its older name.

2 [TN] Though this was the official designation, the institution has been known also as 女子挺身勤勞隊, or "Women's Volunteer Labor Corps." Both the erroneous but widespread Japanese name and its English translation—and, by extension, the terms 挺身勤勞隊 and "Volunteer Labor Corps"—are included in the index to aid readers of this volume.

3 [TN] Though this was the official designation, the law has been known also as 女子勤勞挺身令, or "Ordinance on Women's Labor Volunteering." Both the erroneous but widespread Japanese name and its English translation are included in the index to aid readers.

girls 酌婦," thereby adding to the confusion. Furthermore, because even the Women's Labor Volunteer Corps, which had been based on officially proclaimed laws, had actually been mobilized in colonial Korea arbitrarily in many cases, regardless of law, this name had been widely misused also for purposes other than labor. Even more confusing was the fact that, in the memories of the former victimizers, experiencers, and victims of Japanese military sexual slavery, who included not only Koreans but also Japanese, the Volunteer Corps and military comfort women had not been clearly distinguished both as institutions and in actual operation. The most important point above all was the fact that most South Koreans who had been alive at the time had perceived the sexual damage inflicted on women as the Volunteer Corps system. Consequently, despite all such historical facts, distinguishing between the Volunteer Corps and military comfort women simplistically as official institutions can be yet another historical error.

However, the decision made by the Korean Research Group and the Korean Council, despite their own names in Korean, to use the term "(Japanese) military comfort women (日本)軍慰安婦" in distinction from the Volunteer Corps was brought about by the need to distinguish, from among the victims, between those who had been subjected to forced labor at factories and those who had been exploited as Japanese soldiers' sex slaves. When the Korean Council began to receive reports from the victims in 1990, a large number of forced labor victims and sexual victims alike filed reports. This clearly reveals the fact that, in the minds of the South Koreans, "Volunteer Corps" is a concept encompassing both types of victimization and, at the same time, also raises the need to distinguish between the two.

However, it was not through a simple process that the Korean Research Group and the Korean Council decided to use the term "(Japanese) military comfort women." Objections to the acceptance of the term "comfort women accompanying the military" as it was, which Japan had first used and continues to use even now and which is used in North Korea as well, were made from diverse perspectives. First, there was criticism that the term "comfort women" itself had been created from a male perspective, and this was raised from early on in not only South Korea but also Japan. In other words, it was not possible to accept this term, which conceptualized the clear sexual damage inflicted by men as the act of providing them with sexual "comfort 慰安." The argument that, instead of this term, it was correct to use the term "sex slaves 性奴隸,"[4] which expressed the slavelike circumstances of Japanese military comfort women, was raised. However, the use of this alternative term could not be broadened further because of concern about causing confusion in a situation where the issue was already perceived widely as one of "military comfort women." Instead, it was decided that the term "comfort women" would be used as it was because it was difficult to eradicate now, but with quotation marks. Although these quotation marks are sometimes omitted for the sake of convenience, the general consensus seems to have reached this term for the time being. The claim that the term "sex slaves" most appropriately reflects the actual situation has been raised ceaselessly, however, and recent years have seen the emergence of a strong argument among scholars and activists to overcome confusion and to expand the use of this term into a movement.

In addition, another objection was raised to the modifier 從軍, which means "accompanying the military." Presumably used to coin the term "comfort women accompanying the military 從軍慰安婦" based on already existing ones such as "military nurses 從軍看護婦" and "war correspondents 從軍記者," this word was opposed because it implied that, like nurses and correspondents, these sex slaves had followed the Japanese armed forces voluntarily and therefore was unacceptable. The same criticism was raised in Japan as well (Takagi Ken'ichi, 1992: 3). The Asian organizations that participated in the 1st Asian Solidarity Conference for the Issue of Military Sexual Slavery by Japan 日本軍'慰安婦'問題解決을 爲한 아시아連帶會議[5] (henceforth "Asian Solidarity Conference"),[6] which

4 Kang Man-gil, "A Historiographical Approach to the Issue of Japanese Military Sex Slaves," presented in December 1993 at the 2nd Joint Symposium by the Center for Research and Documentation on Japan's War Responsibility 日本の戰爭責任資料センター and the Korean Council. Professor Yoshimi Yoshiaki claimed at the 1st Joint Symposium by the Center for Research and Documentation on Japan's War Responsibility and the Korean Council, held in August 1993, that "war slaves 戰爭奴隷" was the correct term.

5 [TN] This is the Korean name for the conference. The Japanese designator is 日本軍「慰安婦」問題解決のためのアジア連帶會議.

6 This conference was organized by Japan and Asian victim nations including South Korea and Taiwan to forge solidarity for the resolution of the issue of Japanese military

was held in August 1992, created the concept of "comfort women forcibly accompanying the military 强制從軍慰安婦" to restrict the connotation of voluntariness in the modifier "accompanying the military." This new coinage was used only for a short period following the conference and discarded, however. There were reasons for such discontinuation. In South Korea, some criticized that it was wrong to combine the two contradictory ideas of coercion ("forcibly") and volition ("accompanying") in the same term. In Japan, the term "comfort women accompanying the military" was already widespread in society and therefore difficult to change. Subsequently, while the South Koreans further struggled with the terminology on several occasions, in Japan, the term "comfort women accompanying the military" has continued to be used without change even by scholars and non-governmental organizations (NGOs) working to resolve this issue,[7] which has held true also for North Korea.

Based on the strong problematics that the modifier "accompanying the military," which connoted voluntariness, could not be used verbatim in a situation where the Japanese government was claiming that "comfort women accompanying the military" had been impoverished Korean women who had voluntarily applied to earn money, the South Korean government, in an interim report presented in July 1992, used the term "military comfort women 軍隊慰安婦."[8] Amid such confusion, noting the use of the term "military comfort stations 軍慰安所" in wartime Japanese military documents (Ministry of War, 1943, etc.) and an advertisement that read, "Urgent recruitment of military comfort women 軍慰安婦" in the *Maeil Sinbo* 每日申報,[9] [10] a newspaper published in Korea during

sexual slavery.

7 Though he argued for the use of the term "war slaves" in 1993, Yoshimi Yoshiaki still titled his 1995 book *Military Comfort Women* 從軍慰安婦 ("Comfort Women Accompanying the Military," to be exact).

8 Working Group on the Issue of Military Sexual Slavery, South Korean Ministry of Foreign Affairs, "Investigations on the Reality of Military Comfort Women under Japanese Colonial Rule: Interim Report," July 31, 1992.

9 October 27 and November 1, 1944.

10 [TN] The Government-General of Korea (and the Residency-General of Korea 統監府 preceding it, to a lesser extent) had three official mouthpieces, all dailies: the *Maeil Sinbo* (1910-1945; Korean), *Keijo Nippo* 京城日報 (1906-1945; Japanese only from 1907 onward), and *Seoul Press* (1905-1937; English; under Japanese control from 1906 onward). In celebration of the *Maeil Sinbo's* independence from the *Keijo Nippo*, the

the Japanese colonial era, the Korean Research Group argued that it was appropriate to use the term "military comfort women 軍慰安婦" because it best approximated contemporary usage. Consequently, *Forcibly Taken Korean Military Comfort Women* 强制로 끌려간 朝鮮人軍慰安婦들, a collection of victims' testimonies published by the Korean Research Group in early 1993,[11] and a law enacted by the South Korean government in June 1993 to provide support to the victims both used the term "military comfort women."[12] Afterwards, the Korean Council likewise decided to use the term "(Japanese) military comfort women (日本)軍慰安婦," thus leading this expression to take root in South Korean society.

On the other hand, in arenas of international activities including the UN, the terms "military sex slaves" and "military sexual slavery" have been in use.[13] When the Korean Council and Japanese NGOs first raised this issue at the UN in 1992, the English term "comfort women," a literal translation of the term "(military) comfort women (軍)慰安婦," was used. As will be discussed later, the Allied Forces, too, had used terms such as "comfort girls," "comfort stations," and "military brothels" during World War II to designate both the victims and the facilities.[14] Likewise,

---

Chinese characters for the former's title were changed to 每日新報 (no difference in the Korean pronunciation) in 1938 and remained so until the discontinuation of the newspaper in 1945 after Japan's defeat in the war. To avoid unnecessary complication and confusion, however, the better-known 每日申報 will be used throughout this volume.

11 [TN] Though an English translation of this first volume in the Korean-language series bears the title *True Stories of the Korean Comfort Women* (1995, ed. Keith Howard, trans. Young Joo Lee, Cassell Global Issues Ser., London: Cassell), texts in the series will be referred to as *Forcibly Taken Korean Military Comfort Women*, a literal translation of the original Korean title.

12 Korean Council for the Women Drafted for Military Sexual Slavery by Japan and the Korean Chongshindae Research Group, eds., *Forcibly Taken Korean Military Comfort Women*, vol. 1 (Seoul: Hanul, 1993); and the Act on the Support of Livelihood Stability for Former Comfort Women Drafted into the Japanese Forces under Japanese Colonial Rule 日帝下日本軍慰安婦에 對한 生活安定支援法.

13 [TN] These two terms are in English in the original text. In addition, the English expressions "military sexual slaves" and "military sex slavery" are in use as well.

14 For example, "The 'comfort girls' have been found wherever it was necessary for the Japanese Army to fight," Psychological Warfare Team, United States Army Forces India-Burma Theater, United States Office of War Information, "Japanese Prisoner of War Interrogation Report No. 49" (Record Group 208, Entry 366A, Box 231 [also classified as Record Group 208, Entry 378, Box 446 or Record Group 208, Box 226]), October 1, 1944.

the report on the issue of military sexual slavery that the International Commission of Jurists (ICJ) created and announced on the basis of investigations in North and South Koreas, Japan, and Philippines used the English term "comfort women."[15] However, as the Korean Council brought this issue to the UN Working Group on Contemporary Forms of Slavery and, more specifically, urged the UN Sub-Commission on Human Rights to appoint a Special Rapporteur on Systematic Rape, Sexual Slavery and Slavery-like Practices during Wartime, Including Internal Conflict so that the UN would investigate it more systematically and create recommendations, the issue naturally began to be called one of "military sexual slavery" in English. The report[16] submitted to the UN Commission on Human Rights in 1996 by Radhika Coomaraswamy clearly defined this issue as one of "military sexual slavery in wartime." In addition, in her report,[17] Special Rapporteur Gay Johnson McDougall of the UN Sub-Commission on Human Rights called what had been known earlier as "comfort stations" "rape centres." Indeed, the Korean Council, which led such an international situation, early on decided on "Korean Council for the Women Drafted for the Military Sexual Slavery by Japan" as its English name.

Whether the decision, amid such unclarity regarding the official name of the institution, to use the terms "Labor Volunteer Corps" and "military comfort women" to distinguish between labor exploitation and sexual exploitation was faithful to colonial and wartime circumstances cannot be stated clearly. In other words, it cannot be ascertained that the Volunteer Corps and military sexual slavery were institutions implemented in colonial Korea in the 1930s-1940s with an actual and clear distinction indeed. On the contrary, they may not have been differentiated.

---

15 International Commission of Jurists, *Comfort Women: An Unfinished Ordeal—Report of a Mission*, 1994.

16 Radhika Coomaraswamy, "Addendum: Report of the Special Rapporteur on Violence against Women, Its Causes and Consequences, Ms. Radhika Coomaraswamy, in Accordance with Commission on Human Rights Resolution 1994/45: Report on the Mission to the Democratic People's Republic of Korea, the Republic of Korea and Japan on the Issue of Military Sexual Slavery in Wartime" (UN Doc. E/CN. 4/1996/53/Add. 1).

17 Gay McDougall, "Systematic Rape, Sexual Slavery and Slavery-like Practices during Armed Conflict: Final Report Submitted by Ms. Gay J. McDougall, Special Rapporteur" (UN Doc. E/CN. 4/Sub. 2/1998/13).

This chapter therefore will examine how the Volunteer Corps and military comfort women were distinguished both institutionally and in actual operation and how they existed in the memories of the victimizers, victims, and experiencers of military comfort stations through documents and testimonies. In addition, to explore the situation of social perception regarding the concepts through which South Koreans who were alive at the time understood the issue of military sexual slavery, it will include an analysis of surveys of those aged 70 or above.

While I have thus focused mainly on the relationship between "military comfort women 軍慰安婦" and the "Volunteer Corps," which are terms used in the documents and practices of imperial Japan, on the other hand, the need to use the concept of "sex slaves," which describes the actual contents of this institution, has been strongly raised in recent years. In other words, because the term "sex slaves" has already been established in English, the problematics that its use must be initiated in South Korean society from now on as a movement and spread to Japan, North Korea, and China has been discussed persuasively.

2. The Terminology of the Official Institution

1) The Labor Mobilization of Women: The Patriotic Labor Corps, Women's Promotion Corps, and Women's Volunteer Corps

While names for military sexual slavery recounted by the victimizers, victims, and other experiencers of military comfort stations as well as members of the public who remember the 1930s-1940s include those such as "supply of unmarried women to the government 處女供出," "Women's Patriotic Service Corps 女子愛國奉仕隊," and "Labor Corps 勤勞隊," names confirmed to have been used for the official institution include the "Patriotic Labor Corps 勤勞報國隊," "Women's Promotion Corps 女子推進隊," and "Women's (Labor) Volunteer Corps 女子(勤勞)挺身隊."

With the Manchurian Incident[18] 滿洲事變[19] of 1931 as the starting

18 [TN] Also known in English as "Mukden Incident."

point, Japan entered a semi-wartime system and began to strengthen the labor mobilization of Koreans including women. Women in rural areas were forced to work outdoors or to hold side jobs, and the Japanese colonial authorities implemented a policy of relocating *en masse* farming households from southern Korea to Manchuria in order to develop the latter region. With the initiation of the National Mobilization 國家總動員 system starting in 1937, the labor mobilization of women likewise became even more active so that the Government-General of Korea (GGK) 朝鮮總督府 established a policy of seeking ways to strengthen women's labor. In 1941, it repealed laws that hitherto had prohibited women from working in mines by proclaiming the Exceptions to the Permission System for Women Miners' Employment in Mines 女子鑛夫坑內就業許可制特例 and established the Policy on the Adjustment of Agricultural Manpower 農村勞動力調整方針, issuing guidelines on its implementation to provincial governors 道知事 (see Supplement II).

On the other hand, labor mobilization through both specific laws and official mediation 官斡旋 occurred under many names. The Patriotic Labor Corps consisted of both men and women, and the Government-General of Korea calculated the number of possible recruits for this institution as 3 million in June 1938 and classified provincial populations into students, youths, women, and farmers, thus focusing on the use of manpower through labor adjustment (*Maeil Sinbo*, June 29, 1938). Accordingly, it enacted the Item Regarding the Patriotic Labor Movement under National Spiritual Mobilization 國民精神總動員勤勞報國運動ニ關スル件 in July 1938 to mobilize the Patriotic Labor Corps and enacted the Ordinance on National Cooperation with Patriotic Labor 國民勤勞報國協力令 in November 1941, thereby completing the legalization of the institution (Kim Yoon Mi, 2008: 122). In the process, women aged 20-40 began to be mobilized for the Patriotic Labor Corps, and unmarried women aged 14-24 became the objects of mobilization starting in September 1941. The law was revised once in December 1943 as the Item Regarding the Legislation of the Guidelines on the Implementation of the Ordinance on National Cooperation with Patriotic Labor 國民勤勞報國協力令實施

19 [TN] This is the common name for the historical event in both Korean and Japanese. The corresponding designator in Chinese is 九·一八事變.

要綱制定ニ關スル件 to increase the duration of mobilization for unmarried women aged 14-24 from 30 days to 50 days and revised again in November 1944 to expand the scope of the objects of mobilization to spouseless women aged 14-40. The statistics that the number of those mobilized as members of the Patriotic Labor Corps amounted to 1,925,272 in 1944 alone (Park Kyung-Sik, 1986: 361) reveals the fact that many women were mobilized through this institution.

The Women's Promotion Corps were mobilized through official mediation, without laws. Women aged 20-30 with at least primary school diplomas were selected and organized into the Women's Promotion Corps on town and township levels, with local branches of the National League of Total Effort in Korea 國民總力朝鮮聯盟[20] playing central roles in most cases, and these corps seem to have been used for the movement to promote women's labor and for the implementation of Japanization 皇國臣民化 policy (*Maeil Sinbo*, August 2, 1942 and March 9 and August 29, 1944).

The Volunteer Corps were an institution that mobilized women in colonial Korea in the 1940s with immense force. Denoting "voluntary physical self-sacrifice (for the nation) 挺身," the Volunteer Corps were an institution created by the Japanese authorities to mobilize manpower without monetary compensation and implemented in colonial Korea as well. According to what has been elucidated so far, the Volunteer Corps encompassed both men and women and implemented mobilization across diverse fields including news coverage, medical service, and labor. The earliest documentarily verifiable Volunteer Corps were the case of the Agricultural Volunteer Corps 農村挺身隊, which selected 60-100 people from each county in Hamhung, South Hamgyong Province in November 1939 and mobilized them for state construction projects for 2-3 months starting in December (*Maeil Sinbo*, November 13,

20 In 1938, the Japanese colonial authorities created the National League for Spiritual Mobilization in Korea 國民精神總動員朝鮮聯盟 as well as branches on lower levels and, as the terminal organs of praxis, the Patriotic Units 愛國班, each of which consisted of ten households. In 1940, the National League for Spiritual Mobilization in Korea was reorganized as the National League of Total Effort in Korea, and, in 1943, the Patriotic Units, which were the basic organizations of workplace leagues 職場聯盟 including those at mines and factories, were renamed the Service Corps 仕奉隊 (Yeo Soon-joo, 1994: 32).

1940; and Yeo Soon-joo, 1994: 2). There existed the Japanese-Korean Unity Volunteer Corps 內鮮一體挺身隊, which were discussed by the Government-General of Korea and the Japanese Ministry of Commerce and Industry 商工省 at around the same time, in the fall of 1940, and started to be implemented in March 1941. This was an institution where 600 adolescents with diplomas from 6-year primary schools were selected and sent to factories or businesses in Japan possessing branches in colonial Korea and technically trained for 2-3 years and then assigned to branches in the colony (*Maeil Sinbo*, February 18, 1941; and Yeo Soon-joo, 1994: 3). In 1941, the *Maeil Sinbo* often published articles on the Volunteer Corps, some of which read (Kang Man-gil, 1997: 13-14): "53,000 mobilized, organized into the Agricultural Volunteer Corps, and begin drills in each county in South Hamgyong Province" (*Maeil Sinbo*, February 12, 1941); "A reinforcement of 10 million students, even primary schoolers, [engages in] patriotic labor 勤勞報國 as the Production Increase Movement Volunteer Corps 增産運動挺身隊" (*Maeil Sinbo*, February 14, 1941); "The Women's Agricultural Volunteer Corps 婦人農業挺身隊 selected from each county to visit rural areas in mainland Japan" (*Maeil Sinbo*, March 4, 1941); "Volunteer Corps of loyalty, bravery, and service to the nation 義勇奉公" (*Maeil Sinbo*, September 4, 1941); and "Full of zeal, the Patriotic Labor Volunteer Corps 勤勞報國挺身隊 finally to be organized in units of neighborhood leagues 町聯盟" (*Maeil Sinbo*, November 23, 1941). In addition, the Students' Volunteer Corps 學徒挺身隊 and the Patriotic Volunteer Corps 報國挺身隊 were organized in March 1941 and January 1943, respectively (Chung Jae-Chul, 1985: 415; requoted from Yeo Soon-joo, 1994: 3). Diverse types of the Volunteer Corps including the National Language [i.e., Japanese] Promotion Volunteer Corps 國語普及挺身隊, News Volunteer Corps 報道挺身隊, and Medical Volunteer Corps 仁術挺身隊 were organized, mobilizing men and women from colonial Korea. Targeting only women, the Young Women's Special Volunteer Corps 特別女子青年挺身隊 were created in January 1944 for cooking duties. There are also records that the Women's Relief Volunteer Corps 女子救護挺身隊 were organized in December 1944 for relief work.[21] Because news coverage by the *Maeil Sinbo* alone, nearly the

21 On January 17, 1944, the Yongsan Police Station [in Seoul] created the "Young Women's

sole publication available in this period, amounts to so much, it is easy to presume that the "Volunteer Corps," in fact, were used synonymously with forced mobilization.

In mobilizing women, the names "Women's Volunteer Corps 女子挺身隊" and "Women's Labor Volunteer Corps 女子勤労挺身隊" were used extensively. Used for mobilization mainly for labor at munitions factories, these corps were officialized by the Ordinance on Women's Voluntary Labor, an edict signed by the Japanese emperor and proclaimed on August 23, 1944, and sometimes abbreviated as the "Women's Volunteer Corps," as stipulated by Article 1 of the Ordinance on Women's Voluntary Labor.[22] Although, according to this ordinance, one could become a member of the "Women's Volunteer Corps" by volunteering (Article 3), mobilization was basically directed at those required to report for national registration, who would have included graduates of secondary schools related to the mining and manufacturing industries and were extremely limited in number in colonial Korea.[23] However, as will be discussed later, because members of the Women's Volunteer Corps were mobilized through various methods and extensively in colonial Korea even years before the proclamation of this ordinance and regardless of the scope delimited in the ordinance, unlike in Japan, the Women's Labor Volunteer Corps were not implemented as a clear, official institution in Korea at the time.

Special Volunteer Corps" with 150 female employees (aged 16 or above) of restaurants within its jurisdiction to prompt them to embody their duty as female imperial subjects and to practice voluntary physical self-sacrifice for service to the nation 奉公 through cooking and relief work in times of emergency, and, in December 1944, the Patriotic Units throughout Daesin-jeong in Seo-gu [in Busan] each selected an individual to create the "Women's Relief Volunteer Corps" for relief work in times of emergency (*Maeil Sinbo*, January 18 and December 18, 1944; requoted from Yeo Soon-joo, 1994: 3).

22 It stipulates, "Henceforth to be termed the 'Women's Volunteer Corps 女子挺身隊.'" Bureau of Printing, Ministry of Finance, ed., *The Official Gazette List*, August 1944.

23 Women who underwent national registration were: "only vocational technicians between the ages of 12 and 39 who [had] graduated from secondary or similar schools related to the mining and manufacturing industries or who [were] currently or previously employed as mining technicians, electric technicians, electric communication technicians, mechanical technicians, aviation technicians, shipbuilding technicians, chemical technicians, ceramics technicians, carpentry technicians, civil engineering technicians, construction technicians, meteorological technicians, and the like through ability and experience" (National League of Total Effort in Korea, 1944: 66; and *Maeil Sinbo*, August 26, 1944).

Already in September 1943, the *Maeil Sinbo* reported that the Women's Voluntary Labor Corps system had been organized in Japan and that the Government-General of Korea planned to implement this institution in colonial Korea in full consideration of the local circumstances (*Maeil Sinbo*, September 21, 1943). In November 1943, the Korean magazine *Morning Light* 朝光 published an article on the Women's Labor Volunteer Corps. In March 1944, the *Maeil Sinbo* reported that the Women's Volunteer Corps 女子挺身隊 had been mobilized *en masse* in places including Pyongyang, Pohang, Daegu, Yeosu, and Mokpo, to be sent to factories in Japan. In June of the same year, the newspaper started to publish numerous articles publicizing the Women's Labor Volunteer Corps more actively (Chung Chinsung, 1996a: 173-174). As has thus been shown, the Ordinance on Women's Voluntary Labor was, in fact, proclaimed after the mobilization of the Women's Volunteer Corps had already begun to take place.

2) The Sexual Mobilization of Women: "Bar Girls," "Shameful Female Workers," "Female Workers," and "Comfort Women"

While labor mobilization can thus be confirmed in various official institutions, cases of sexual mobilization can be found only sporadically in Japanese military documents. A document issued in 1932 by the Japanese Consulate-General in Shanghai uses the term navy "comfort stations 慰安所" (Japanese Consulate-General in Shanghai, 1932), and the North Korean newspaper *Rodong Sinmun* 勞動新聞 has stated that the 19th Division 師團 of the Japanese army stationed in present-day Ranam installed "soldiers' comfort stations 軍人慰安所" in 1928, thus showing the widespread use of the term "comfort stations" from early on (Yonhap News Agency, March 12, 2001). However, the name "comfort stations" was not an official one uniformly used everywhere. Terms such as "clubs 俱樂部" and "soldiers' halls 軍人會館" are found at times in Japanese military documents from the same era as well.[24]

---

24 See Yoshimi Yoshiaki, 1992b.

The names for women who worked at these facilities as sex slaves were even more diverse. While the term "bar girls 酌婦" is found most frequently, other such as "comfort station female workers 慰安所從業婦," "shameful comfort station female workers 慰安所醜業婦," "comfort station women 慰安所婦女," "professional entertainers 藝妓," "prostitutes 娼妓," "special women 特種婦女," and "hostesses 接客婦女" were used also. The term "comfort women" began to be used often around 1939 and was subsequently established as the most common one. In addition, the term "military comfort women 軍慰安婦" is found at times, too. As has been mentioned above, it was near the end of the war that newspapers published advertisements recruiting "military comfort women."

The use of such terminology in official Japanese documents implies that the term "comfort women" was not the official name for the military comfort station policy that the Japanese government implemented in the strictest secrecy. Moreover, it is difficult to find traces of the use of the term "comfort women accompanying the military 從軍慰安婦" during the same period.

3. Problems with the Actual Operation of the Volunteer Corps/Military Sexual Slavery

Despite the relative unclarity of the terminology in the official institutions, it is plausible that, in general, the Volunteer Corps were for labor mobilization and "comfort women" were for sexual mobilization, respectively. The situation of their respective and actual operation, however, already and amply included a possibility for the mutual intermixture of these two institutions.

1) Problems with the Methods of Mobilizing the Women's Labor Volunteer Corps

Judging from the objects and methods, the mobilization of the Women's Volunteer Corps in colonial Korea occurred without a clear connection to the Ordinance on Women's Voluntary Labor and even before its proclamation. First, as for the objects of mobilization, they extended beyond the abovementioned scope stipulated in the ordinance. According to articles in the *Maeil Sinbo*, depending on the location of recruitment, the ages of the women mobilized ranged from 16-22 to 13-21 and 16-20, thus being irregular. Likewise, although highly educated women were preferred, primary school graduates and even enrollees were mobilized, thus being irregular again. As for the mobilization methods, mobilization through means including schools, Patriotic Units 愛國班, and women's organizations as well as official mediation were important, rather than recruitment and voluntary enlistment. To mobilize the Women's Labor Volunteer Corps, the Government-General of Korea announced in October 1943 that it would consign school principals to mediate mobilization actively and would also make use of the Patriotic Units, women's organizations, and other organizations closely related to the National League of Total Effort in Korea (*Maeil Sinbo*, October 7, 1943). In addition, explaining the meaning of "official mediation" as "guiding those acknowledged to be fit for labor through administrative measures and encouraging them to report to work," the Government-General of Korea made it clear that, in the colony, the Women's Volunteer Corps had been mobilized through official mediation even before the proclamation of the Ordinance on Women's Voluntary Labor and that the same would continue in the future.[25]

The fact that, at the time, the National League of Total Effort in Korea, which the Government-General of Korea had established for national mobilization, thus served as an important actor in mobilization and that official mediation was an important mobilization method demonstrates that the mobilization of the Women's Volunteer Corps was implemented in a largely arbitrary manner and based on the compelling power of the colonial government rather than on law. Consequently, it is highly problematic to include the Women's Labor Volunteer Corps in the legal category in accordance with a clearly legal mobilization system, as in Japan. Moreover, it is a fact that there are many unclear points in drawing

25 Tahara Minoru, then a junior official in the Department of Labor 勞務課 in the Government-General of Korea, thus stated: "...All Women's Volunteer Corps in colonial Korea hitherto have been based on official guidance and mediation and... the intention is to continue official guidance and mediation in the future as well" (National League of Total Effort in Korea, 1944: 12 and 66).

a boundary between the mobilization of these corps from that of women as military sex slaves, which occurred through employment fraud and violence, with its nature as an official institution concealed.

2) Wartime and Postwar Records: The Volunteer Corps Used as a Pretext for Mobilizing Military Sex Slaves

As the mobilization of the Volunteer Corps became widespread, there is ample possibility for the mobilization of military sex slaves to have intruded into this arbitrary space. An official mouthpiece of the Government-General of Korea, the daily *Maeil Sinbo* repeatedly stressed that the Koreans' concern about the Women's Labor Volunteer Corps was misguided: "...All kinds of groundless, senseless, and malicious mad rumors... that women are to be supplied to the government 供出... are rampant" (March 7, 1944); "Do not marry early; [unmarried] women will not be drafted [for labor]" (May 16, 1944); and "There seem to be some who are inadequate in the understanding of the Women's Volunteer Corps" (June 15, 1944). However, this can be seen, instead, as proving the fact that such confusion actually existed back then. In addition, the fact that, at the end of 1944, by which indiscriminate fraud regarding and violent mobilization of military sex slaves had intensified, advertisements reading, "Military comfort women 軍慰安婦 urgently wanted" and even including the destinations (military units) and age restrictions were published only a few times in the *Maeil Sinbo* (October 27 and November 1, 1944) can be interpreted as a ploy intended to show the distinction between the Women's Volunteer Corps and military comfort women.

The majority of records published immediately after the war, when free testimonies finally became possible, clearly show what the wartime mobilization of the Volunteer Corps had been: "I was forcibly taken away across the Genkai Sea under the pretext of the Women's Volunteer Corps... and trapped in a munitions factory... I ran away from the dormitory... but was caught... in the course... and sold as a bar girl" (Um Kwang-Sup, 1946: 2); and "We can point out the fact that our daughters were forcibly or fraudulently sent not only to Japan but also to distant places such as China and the South Seas [Islands][26] 南洋[群島] under the pretext of the Women's Volunteer Corps or the Consolation Units

慰安部隊" (*Seoul Shinmun*, May 12, 1946).

The following reminiscences of the era of the wartime system that were published in the 1970s, a period before public discussions on the issue of Japanese military sexual slavery, likewise reveal the fact that military sex slaves had been mobilized in the name of the "Women's Volunteer Corps": "The Japanese colonial authorities mobilized countless women in the name of the 'Women's Volunteer Corps', sacrificing them as workers at munitions factories or comfort women at forward units" (*Seoul Shinmun*, August 14, 1970); "Although I was still unaware that the Volunteer Corps system had been established in Korea and that fellow Korean women were being brought by force, I felt endless compassion for those unknown compatriots at comfort stations" (Bak Duseok, 1977); and "A large number of those taken away in the name of the 'Women's Volunteer Corps' were turned into the Japanese military's comfort women" (Kim Dae Sang, 1978).

Such facts can be discovered also in Japanese publications dating from the 1970s. Yoshida Seiji (Yoshida Seiji, 1977) clearly stated, "[members of] the Volunteer Corps were brought away from colonial Korea, taken to comfort stations, and used as comfort women." This holds true also of works by Korean residents in Japan. Kim Il-myon (or Kimu Irumyoun) 金一勉, who published *The Emperor's Armed Forces and Korean Comfort Women* 天皇の軍隊と朝鮮人慰安婦[27] in Japanese in 1976, corroborated: "Although it was in January 1942 that unmarried Korean women began to be drafted in earnest as members of the 'Volunteer Corps', no one even imagined that they would become the 'comfort women' of the Japanese military" (Im Jongguk, 1981: 196). He thus explained this confusion: "The term 'Volunteer Corps' virtually flooded the colony [i.e., Korea]" (Im Jongguk, 1981: 200); and, "[i]n fact, [the

26 [TN] The Japanese Mandate for the Governance of the South Seas Islands 日本委任統治領南洋群島 to be exact, it will henceforth be referred to as "South Seas Mandate." Originally a group of German colonies in Micronesia, this territory was given to Japan following World War I as a League of Nations mandate. Subsequently, it was captured during World War II and administered for several decades by the United States as the Trust Territory of the Pacific Islands (TTPI), a UN trust territory.

27 [TN] Im Jongguk's edited Korean translations of this book were published in South Korea in 1981, 1990, and 1992, the earliest of which is included in the bibliography of this volume.

public in] South Korea is not even aware of the term 'comfort women'... [It is because] they [i.e., Japanese colonial authorities] never mobilized [comfort women] in the name of 'military comfort women'" (Im Jongguk, 1981: 301). In other words, he is stating the fact that the Volunteer Corps were used as a pretext for mobilizing military sex slaves.

4. Institutional Confusion in the Testimonies of the Victims, Victimizers, and Investigators

In determining historical facts of the past including the issue of Japanese military sexual slavery, the dominant atmosphere is to acknowledge the value only of official documents as materials. However, it is already widely accepted in historiography that history does not consist solely of records and documents. If one agrees that "[h]istory... is a test of our ability imaginatively to place ourselves in the positions of other people, so that we can understand the reasons for their actions," because history based only on inevitably and highly limited documentary materials can be seriously distorted, the daily lives, housing styles, tombs, drawings and paintings, extant diaries, and letters of contemporaries become important materials. Moreover, if direct accounts of experiencers of such historical facts can be collected, they will place one in a highly advantageous position in illuminating history (Hoopes, 1995).

In cases such as Japanese military sexual slavery, where documents have been purposely destroyed, it is extremely dangerous to reconstruct history with reliance only on documentary materials. Indeed, a Japanese military document states, "Because most of the materials on the 48th Division were disposed of by the order of superiors upon the cessation of hostilities and the remainder has been submitted to the Australian armed forces, most of the accurate materials are lacking. The memories of soldiers have therefore been combined..." (48th Division, *War History Materials and Postwar Conditions of the 48th Division*, July 1946), thus implying the limitations of records and the importance of testimonies in the issue of military sexual slavery.

Regarding the concept of Japanese "military comfort women," the discussions below will examine in succession the testimonies of the mobilizers, military sexual slavery victims, and experiencers (soldiers in the Japanese armed forces) of military comfort stations. The perception of "military comfort women" held by South Koreans who lived during the colonial and wartime periods, too, will be discussed in a separate section based on survey data.

1) Testimonies of the Victimizers (Mobilizers)

In Japan, where, unlike colonial Korea, the concept of "comfort women" was widespread from early on and the institutions of the Labor Volunteer Corps and military sexual slavery were clearly distinguished, there does not seem to be conceptual confusion about "military comfort women 軍慰安婦" and the "Volunteer Corps" even after the emergence of this issue decades later. It is surprising, however, that the Japanese have failed to notice the fact that the wartime system of mobilizing military sex slaves officially used the term "Volunteer Corps."

In his book published in Japan in 1977, *Korean Comfort Women and the Japanese People: The Memoir of the Former Labor Conscription Manager of the Shimonoseki Patriotic Labor Society* 朝鮮人慰安婦と日本人—元下關勞報動員部長の手記, Yoshida Seiji confessed that he, as the Labor Conscription Manager 勞務動員部長 of the Patriotic Labor Society 勞務報國會 of Yamaguchi Prefecture in Japan, had forcibly taken Korean women from Jeju Island as the Korean Women's Volunteer Corps for the Consolation of the [Japanese] Imperial Armed Forces 皇軍慰問朝鮮人女子挺身隊 in 1944. This testimony created a great stir in Japan and led to debates regarding its veracity. Subsequently, there was a commotion, with the *Asahi Shimbun* retracting in 2014 its earlier coverage of his testimony (see Chapter 9). Setting aside the issue of the truthfulness of Yoshida Seiji's testimony, this section will focus on the term "Women's Volunteer Corps 女子挺身隊," which appears in his testimony. According to his testimony, mobilization orders read, "Korean Women's Volunteer Corps for the Consolation of the Imperial Armed Forces" but were actually intended to draft women to be sent to military comfort stations (Yoshida Seiji, 1977: 151-156). That he states that he took women away as members of the Volunteer Corps in his book while using the term "Korean comfort women 朝鮮人慰安婦" in its title betrays the fact that the

Volunteer Corps were used as a pretext for mobilizing military sex slaves. Even if there are problems with its reliability, his personal testimony undeniably has important implications regarding the concept and institution of the "Volunteer Corps."

2) Testimonies of Experiencers of Military Comfort Stations (Japanese Soldiers)

Just as the Korean Council accepted the victims' statements, in Japan, several organizations including the Group for Considering the Issue of Korean Military Comfort Women (also known as "Association for Thinking about the Issue of Korean Comfort Women") 朝鮮人従軍慰安婦問題を考える會 (present-day Mirine「在日」女性の集まり「ミリネ」; 미리내) likewise gathered and created "Military Comfort Women #110 従軍慰安婦110番" (hotline) in January 1992 and began to collect reports by those who had experienced military comfort stations. Here, many former soldiers who had experienced comfort stations filed reports, providing numerous testimonies of comfort stations and sex slaves, especially of Korean ones. There were many testimonies, too, that employment as "civilian employees of the military 軍屬" was used as a pretext to mobilize military sex slaves (Editorial Board of *Military Comfort Women #110*, ed., 1992).

An interesting fact is that a number of former Japanese soldiers have testified the recruitment of military sex slaves sent to the Kwantung Army 關東軍 in 1944. According to their testimonies, the Sanitation Department 衛生部 of Unit 3100, a rear unit of the Kwantung Army, recruited 2,000 well-educated Korean women, transporting them from Seoul Station to Hsinking (present-day Changchun) in Manchuria by train and stationing them in various locations. There are several studies on the mobilization of Korean sex slaves in relation to the Kwantung Army Special Exercises 關東軍特種演習 (see Chapter 3), and what must be noted here is that the terms "comfort women" and the "Volunteer Corps" were used interchangeably. Sex slave management regulations were recorded in a thick book titled *Regulations on the Service of Special Female Civilian Employees of the Kwantung Army* 關東軍女子特殊軍屬服務規定, and one former Japanese soldier has testified that "Special Female Civilian

Employees of the [Japanese] Military 女子特殊軍屬" here designated Korean sex slaves. Another former soldier has testified that these women wept and told him that they had originally been recruited under the name of the "Special Wartime Women's Volunteer Corps for the Kwantung Army 關東軍戰時特別女子挺身隊" but, upon arrival, had turned out to be sex slaves (Editorial Board of *Military Comfort Women #110*, ed., 1992: 23 and 43). This betrays the fact that the "Volunteer Corps" were used as a pretext for mobilizing military sex slaves.

3) Testimonies of the Victims of Military Sexual Slavery

Most victims of military sexual slavery have designated themselves as former members of the "Volunteer Corps." When the Korean Council began to accept statements regarding the "Volunteer Corps" in 1990, former members of the Labor Volunteer Corps and military sexual slavery victims alike filed reports, which demonstrates the fact that military sexual slavery victims saw themselves as having been taken away in the name of the "Volunteer Corps."

What must be discussed here is that the testimonies of military sexual slavery victims confirm the "institutional confusion" where women, in fact, had been mobilized in the name of the "Labor Volunteer Corps" but then sent to military comfort stations. The South Korean government legislated the Act on the Support of Livelihood Stability for Former Comfort Women Drafted into the Japanese Forces under Japanese Colonial Rule[28] in June 1993, and the Ministry of Health and Welfare began to receive victims' reports.[29] In reports filed to the South Korean Ministry of Health and Welfare by 175 victims as of December 1993, eight of them were confirmed to have testified that they had been mobilized clearly as members of the Labor Volunteer Corps but then been turned into military sex slaves.[30] Despite differences in clarity and reliability

---

28 This law was revised as the Act on Livelihood Stability and Memorial Services, Etc. for Sexual Slavery Victims for the Japanese Imperial Army 日帝下日本軍被害者에 對한 生活安定支援 및 紀念事業等에 關한 法律 in December 2002.

29 With the new establishment of the Ministry of Gender Equality and Family in 2001, this duty was transferred to the Women's Rights Planning Division within the same ministry.

30 This is based on my synthesis of the basic information while participating as a

according to the individual, the testimonies of these eight victims are adequate for implying the fact that, in colonial Korea, the mobilization of the Labor Volunteer Corps and of military sex slaves was not clearly distinguished institutionally, either.

Keenly interested in these eight testifiers, the Korean Research Group attempted more in-depth research on them. While two of them could not be contacted and therefore were unavailable for research, the investigation of three others showed progress, thus leading to a considerably in-depth understanding of the wartime circumstances and gaining trust as to the truthfulness of their testimonies. However, due to the time needed to supplement lacunae, the testimonies of these three testifiers have yet to be published in the Korean Research Group's *Forcibly Taken Korean Military Comfort Women* (5 vols.; 1993-2001). First, let us examine the testimonies of the three other testifiers included in *Forcibly Taken Korean Military Comfort Women* published by the Korean Research Group.

One testifier was initially mobilized as a member of the Labor Volunteer Corps and worked at a factory. Unable to bear the hunger and the workload, she fled, only to be caught and sent to a military comfort station.[31] Consequently, this is a case of mobilization through a type of abduction not directly related to the Labor Volunteer Corps system. However, considering the fact that many thus fled due to the poor conditions of the Labor Volunteer Corps, the institution, too, can be seen as having been an indirect channel for mobilizing military sex slaves.

Another testifier worked at a factory in Japan, but, after the bombing of the factory, was sent to military comfort stations together with all other surviving women.[32] It is a well-known fact that the factories in Toyama

---

deliberative committee member. Because the external disclosure of these reports is strictly prohibited, only the contents of the reports were analyzed while excluding personal information such as names and addresses for most of the victims, with the exception of those who have disclosed their identities.

31 Kang Duk-kyung 姜德景 in *Forcibly Taken Korean Military Comfort Women*, vol. 1. She was mobilized as a member of the Labor Volunteer Corps while in the 1st grade in the Advanced Program of primary school and escaped while working at a factory in Toyama Prefecture, Japan, only to be caught by the Military Police Corps (*Kempeitai* 憲兵隊) and to be taken to the comfort station of a Japanese military base.

32 Kim Eunjin 金은진 in *Forcibly Taken Korean Military Comfort Women*, vol. 2. The Korean Research Group visited the primary school in question, reviewed the school registers, secured documentary materials proving that she had indeed departed as a

Prefecture, Japan for which the Labor Volunteer Corps were mobilized had close ties with the Japanese military. Because Toyama Prefecture did, in fact, have military bases and experienced bombings as well, cases like this would have occurred on numerous occasions.

Yet another testifier was mobilized as a member of the Labor Volunteer Corps while still in the 6th grade at primary school, taught simple military drills and calisthenics in Toyama Prefecture for two weeks, stationed to the comfort station attached to a local military unit without ever having set foot in a factory, and then moved to military comfort stations in Hiroshima and Kyushu.[33] The testimony that the official mobilization of the Labor Volunteer Corps through primary schools thus led directly to military comfort stations has been corroborated also by two other testifiers still being studied by the Korean Research Group. These latter two victims likewise have testified that they were mobilized as members of the Labor Volunteer Corps but sent directly to military comfort stations instead of factories.

The one remaining testifier, too, was mobilized as a member of the Labor Volunteer Corps and repeatedly raped while working at a factory. After many interviews, the Korean Research Group decided that this testifier had been a victim of military sexual slavery and suggested that the South Korean Ministry of Health and Welfare provide financial support. Although this is not applicable to everyone mobilized as members of the Labor Volunteer Corps, many of them could have been sexual victims like this last testifier.

Such research results show the fact not only that Japanese military comfort women and the Volunteer Corps were confounded in the minds of contemporaries but also that the institution of the Labor Volunteer Corps itself was related both directly and indirectly to the suffering of military comfort women.

---

member of the Labor Volunteer Corps, and also investigated others from the same school who had departed together as members of the Labor Volunteer Corps.

33 Bak Suni 朴順伊 in *Forcibly Taken Korean Military Comfort Women*, vol. 2. In her case, a school register recording her departure as a member of the Labor Volunteer Corps likewise has been confirmed.

4) The Perception of the Allied Forces

Investigative reports on the Japanese military created by the Allied Forces during World War II generally referred to military sex slaves as "comfort girls" and "comfort women" (Allied Translator and Interpreter Section (ATIS); and South East Asia Translation and Interrogation Center (SEATIC)), with the expression "enforced prostitutes" used by others as well (Netherlands Forces Intelligence Service[34] (NEFIS)). The acts imposed on these women were termed "enforced prostitution" ([NEFIS] "Interrogation Report No. 409"; October 23, 1944), and the facilities were called by names including "brothels" (ATIS), "houses of prostitution" (SEATIC Psychological Warfare Bulletin No. 186; July 12, 1945), "comfort houses" (SEATIC Topographical Bulletin No. 197; July 26, 1945), and "comfort stations" (SEATIC Psychological Warfare Bulletin No. 116; March 31, 1945). The Japanese armed forces created guidelines instructing the translation of military sex slaves and comfort stations in Japanese military documents into English as "licensed prostitutes" and "army brothels," respectively, as well (Kang Sunghyun, 2016: 314).

What is interesting is that Cpt. Won-Loy Chan (Chinese-American serviceman) of the Allied Forces, who interrogated the prisoners of war after the August 3, 1944 fall of Myitkyina, Burma (present-day Myanmar), an area hitherto occupied by the Japanese military, uses the term "Women's Volunteer Labor Corps" in his book *Burma: The Untold Story* (Chan, 1986). He states, "Estimates [of Korean women and girls mobilized as sex slaves for the Japanese armed forces] run as high as 200,000... between 1935 and 1945 they were rounded up by the Kempei Tai [i.e., Japanese Military Police Corps]... The comfort girls were organized by the Japanese into what they euphemistically called the Women's Volunteer Labor Corps" and "As members of the Women's Volunteer Corps they [i.e., military sex slaves at comfort stations] had been paid and also received tips." In addition, he points out, "The Japanese destroyed all records of this chapter in the history of the Imperial forces" (Chan, 1986: 93-96).

34 [TN] Also known, erroneously, as "Netherlands East Indies Forces Intelligence Service."

5. The Perception of South Koreans Who Experienced the Japanese Colonial Era: Survey Results

I and fellow researchers and activists have encountered, close at hand, numerous accounts of Korean women's hurried and haphazard marriages to strangers or refuge at relatives' homes to avoid being taken away as members of the "Volunteer Corps." Likewise, it is common knowledge in South Korea that township office 面事務所 clerks and police officers led the roundup of victims. For members of the South Korean public who had lived during the colonial era, they all too clearly had never heard the term "comfort women" until its recent use in Japan. To verify this commonsensical fact, in 2000, I interviewed 50 male and female respondents aged 70 or above at the time regarding their perceptions of both the Volunteer Corps and Japanese military comfort women.

1) The Characteristics of the Testifiers

Based on the given framework that the subjects were aged 70 or above (born in 1930 or before) and included 30 men and 20 women and on the sole principle that they should come from diverse educational and residential backgrounds (urban/rural areas), interviews were conducted with easily accessible respondents (see <Table 1-1>).

⟨Table 1-1⟩ The characteristics of the interviewees (Unit: 1 person)

	Rural areas				Urban areas				Total
	Unedu-cated	Pri-mary	Sec-ondary	Univer-sity	Unedu-cated	Pri-mary	Sec-ondary	Univer-sity	
Men	5	11	6	2	1		3	2	30
Women	12	4	1		1		1	1	20
Total	41				9				50

2) The Testifiers' Perceptions of Military Comfort Women/ Women's Volunteer Corps

The testifiers' respective positions were determined by complex combinations of diverse factors across many categories. According to the results of this research, the quality and contents of the responses were significantly different depending on the respondents' respective genders, educational attainments, and degrees of closeness to the Japanese. The respondents' domiciles and social classes, however, made no marked difference to their responses.

(1) Differences in Perceptions According to Gender

According to the responses, female testifiers tended to have been less well aware of the situation as it had been at the time in comparison with male testifiers. Few had heard the term "Volunteer Corps" itself (three out of 20 female respondents), and one who had heard this term even testified, "People who took others away rather than those taken away were called [members of] the Volunteer Corps." Even among those who had heard the term "Volunteer Corps," only one out of 20 female testifiers had been clearly aware of how members of these corps had been mobilized and what activities they had engaged in afterwards, but this individual had studied in Japan and experienced public life, which had made her position exceptional in the era.

While female testifiers thus had had only a vague understanding of the mobilization of the Volunteer Corps, relatively more male testifiers had heard the term "Volunteer Corps" (18 out of 30 male testifiers), and a larger number of these respondents had already been aware, at the time, of the lives of the members of these corps as military sex slaves than had been female respondents (six out of 30 male testifiers).

These responses on one hand reflect the fact that the sphere of women's daily lives was restricted to the home. On the other hand, however, they seem to be related also to the point that the average level of educational attainment was lower for women than for men.

(2) Differences in Perceptions According to Educational Attainment

Differences in educational attainment even more clearly showed differences in the respondents' ways of understanding the issue of military sexual slavery. Nearly all respondents with no education remembered women in the Volunteer Corps simply as the "supply of women to the government 女子供出" (10 out of 19 uneducated testifiers) and answered that they had thought that the work engaged in by these women in the locations of supply likewise had been labor mobilization. Among male respondents, some had even thought that the wartime mobilization of manpower had been an experience restricted to men only. There was one exceptional uneducated testifier who had been aware of both of the terms "Volunteer Corps" and "military comfort women 軍慰安婦" and of the work for which these women had been mobilized. However, this respondent revealed in passing that he had had special relationships with the Japanese.[35]

The higher the educational level attained, the more likely the testifiers were to have heard the term "Volunteer Corps," in its Korean or Japanese pronunciation, and even to have been aware of the daily lives of members of these corps as military comfort women. In particular, respondents who had received higher education (withdrawal or graduation from high school or above) said, without exception, that they had known of the term "Volunteer Corps." However, to the question "Did you know about the kind of work that women in the Volunteer Corps were engaged in?" even those belonging to this group mainly responded, "I did not know at the time," and the two respondents who were comparatively knowledgeable had had especially close relationships with the Japanese.

(3) The Degree of Closeness to the Japanese

Testifiers who seemed to have had close relationships with the Japanese exhibited a depth of understanding of the mobilization of the Volunteer Corps far surpassing that of other South Korean survivors of the colonial era. Most of these respondents had heard the expression "military comfort women" and testified that they had been aware of the work engaged in by these women. For example, one male testifier (high school graduate) testified that he, as a friend of a county prefect 郡守, had been in a position to be aware of current affairs and heard of the existence of comfort women from Korean students in Japan but also that people had inevitably "hushed up" about the issue at the time. Another male testifier

35 "In Seoul, many [Korean women] were taken as [members of] the Patriotic Corps. I, too, went and worked as a substitute for a Japanese..."

(high school graduate) testified, "I was on good terms with the Japanese military in China and actually saw women deal [sexually] with Japanese soldiers, too."

(4) Differences in Perceptions According to Social Class/Region

While the respondents' genders, educational attainments, and degrees of close relationships with the Japanese led to differences in their knowledge of the Volunteer Corps, their social classes and city/country differences were insignificant in comparison. This is partly because the low level of social development at the time did not lead to adequate class differentiation and urbanization but also can be seen as stemming from the fact that the mobilization of military comfort women occurred indiscriminately, regardless of social class and geographical area (see Chapter 3).

3) Contemporaries' Perceptions of the Volunteer Corps/Military Comfort Women

When the testifiers' accounts were synthesized, the degree of contemporaries' understanding of the issue of the Volunteer Corps could be classified into several stages. The first stage involved those who had been unaware of or denied the mobilization of women itself. They consisted mostly of uneducated men, and those belonging to this group were the smallest in number. Those belonging to the next stage recalled the wartime mobilization of women only as the "supply of women to the government" or, even worse, simply as "women being taken away." They stated that they had come to hear the term "Volunteer Corps" itself only recently. While some of them had been aware of the women's lives as military comfort women, most had understood the women's mobilization simply as labor mobilization, with most female respondents as well as male respondents with little education belonging to this group. Respondents belonging to the next group had been aware of the term "Volunteer Corps." However, they likewise had had no clear concept of the work engaged in by the women thus mobilized. Factory labor, caregiving to soldiers, and work as military comfort women were all lumped together and remembered in terms of the expression "Volunteer Corps." Those belonging to this group had received education to a certain extent or lived near people with learning. Having hard the terms "Volunteer Corps" and "military comfort women" alike, most of those belonging to the next group of respondents had either had close relationships with the Japanese or lived in Japan or Manchuria and generally had attained considerable education also. Members of this group, who had even known the term "Japanese military comfort women 日本軍慰安婦," had, of course, been aware of the fact that the Japanese armed forces had forcibly mobilized women to operate military comfort stations (see <Table 1-2>).

〈Table 1-2〉 South Korean survivors' perceptions of the Volunteer Corps/military comfort women during the Japanese colonial era (per gender/educational attainment)

(Unit: No. of people)

	Men				Women				Total
	Unedu-cated	Pri-mary	Sec-ondary	Univer-sity	Unedu-cated	Pri-mary	Sec-ondary	Univer-sity	
Unaware of the fact of the mobilization of women itself	3				3				6
Unaware of the term "Volunteer Corps 挺身隊" but aware of the fact of the mobilization of women (remembered as the "supply of unmarried women to the government 處女供出," etc.)	2	9	1		8	4	2		26
Unaware of "military comfort women 軍慰安婦" but aware of "Volunteer Corps"		1	5	4	2				12
Aware of the terms "Volunteer Corps" and "military comfort women" alike	1	1	3					1	6
Total	6	11	9	4	13	4	2	1	50

Notes) Primary: Withdrawal or graduation from a primary school
Secondary: Withdrawal or graduation from a secondary school higher than a primary school
University: Withdrawal or graduation from a college/university or study in Japan

When contemporaries' use and understanding of the terminology related to the issue of the Volunteer Corps are reconstructed based on the data obtained from these interviews, the more plebeian expression at the time had been the "supply of women to the government," and the respondents tended to remember accurately the term "Voluntary Corps," in its Korean or Japanese pronunciation, as their educational attainment rose. For this latter group, however, this term had comprehended everything related to mobilization for labor and military sexual slavery. The term "military comfort women" had been used within restricted groups directly related to Japan and therefore had been very unfamiliar to the public in colonial Korea then.

6. Conclusion

From the discussions above, the general contour of the ways in which the Volunteer Corps and military comfort women were mobilized in colonial Korea becomes clear. Mobilized extensively across fields including not only factory labor but also agricultural labor, news coverage, and medical service from the end of the 1930s onwards and institutionalized by law, the Volunteer Corps were perceived by contemporaries to be synonymous with the mobilization of women. On the contrary, it is difficult to find clear legal grounds for Japanese military sex slaves because these women were mobilized according to top secret policy. Nor did the ensuing confusion stop at being only conceptual. In colonial Korea, the mobilization of the Labor Volunteer Corps depended on official mediation, which was highly arbitrary. Numerous were cases where, through this gap, the mobilization of military comfort women was implemented using the pretext of the Volunteer Corps. Cases in which the mobilization of the Volunteer Corps more directly led to the mobilization of military comfort women can be confirmed through victims' testimonies, but they require more detailed investigation. Newspaper articles and memoirs dating from the period from the years immediately after the war to the 1980s, before this issue became a public one, without exception describe the victims as having been "mobilized as the Volunteer Corps but used as military comfort women." Even among the Japanese, some remember the Volunteer

Corps as the name of an institution used to mobilize military sex slaves. Surprisingly, according to the results of research on members of the South Korean public aged 70 or above, not a few had been unaware even of the "Volunteer Corps," and nearly none reported actually having heard the term "(Japanese) military comfort women" during the Japanese colonial era.

It is clear that the Volunteer Corps and military sex slaves were not clearly distinguished institutions. If so, then even as a distinction is made in the designation between the "Labor Volunteer Corps" and "military comfort women" according to the contents of the exploitation imposed on the victims after forced mobilization, it must be recognized that these two were by no means institutions implemented in strict distinction. In addition, it is necessary at present to pay attention to the process through which the name of this institution has been established in South Korean society as "sexual slavery 性奴隸制."

Chapter 2

The Process of Establishing Japanese Military Comfort Stations

1. The Periodization of the Implementation of Japanese Military Sexual Slavery

Committed during the 1930s-1940s, the crime of the forced taking 强制連行 of women as Japanese military sex slaves was gradually brought to light only in the 1990s. However, many aspects of this issue still are not known clearly, thus leading to numerous debates. One of these problems concerns the period in which comfort stations were established. Although Japanese military comfort stations are generally said to have been established in earnest with the Nanking (present-day Nanjing) Massacre[1] 南京大虐殺[2] in 1937 as the occasion, materials proving the operation of military comfort stations in Manchuria and Shanghai in the early 1930s have been discovered, and documents showing the fact that comfort stations existed even earlier as well have been discovered. With the continued discovery of documentary materials and testimonies by victims and other experiencers of comfort stations on one hand, studies on the establishment of policies on Japanese military comfort stations and on the process through which the installation of these facilities was expanded have reached a considerable number, too. These studies divide the relevant era into several periods based on the number of sex slaves or

1 [TN] Also and formerly referred to in English as "Rape of Nanking."

2 [TN] This is the common name for the historical event in Korean. The corresponding designators in Japanese and Chinese are 南京事件 and 南京大屠殺, respectively.

historical events, which have important implications for grasping changes in the form of comfort stations.

In their petition, the group of lawyers who raised a lawsuit for the compensation of damages with the Tokyo District Court argues: military comfort stations began to be established at the request of the Japanese armed forces garrisoned in Shanghai to the Japanese government for sex slaves dispatched from Japan proper due to numerous incidences of rape by Japanese soldiers during the Shanghai Incident[3] 一次上海事變[4] of 1932; and policies on military sexual slavery were implemented in earnest following the Japanese occupation of Nanking in December 1937. According to this petition, at the beginning, the recruitment of sex slaves relied on operators of "pleasure quarters 遊廓," or brothels, but because such a recruitment method alone could not supply an adequate number of sex slaves in response to demands due to the expansion of the battlefront in early 1938, the military came to play a central role in taking Korean women forcibly. This group of lawyers thus sees the expansion of war by the Japanese armed forces and the taking of Korean women as important occasions for the establishment and expansion of Japanese military comfort stations.[5]

Geum Byeongdong, a Korean scholar in Japan who early on published a sourcebook of materials on Japanese military sexual slavery, further highlights these two aspects. First, he points out as the impetus for Japan's establishment of military comfort stations the experience where, during the Siberian Intervention in 1918-1922, numerous Japanese soldiers suffered from sexually transmitted diseases (STDs), thereby leading to a serious weakening of military power. Military comfort stations were established in earnest between the end of 1937 and early 1938, which is a period that spans the Japanese occupation of Nanking in December 1937 and the proclamation of the National Mobilization Law 國家總動員法 in 1938. In other words, it was at the juncture of the two following points that comfort stations began to be installed in earnest:

3 [TN] Also known as "Shanghai War of 1932" in English.

4 [TN] This is a common name for the historical event in Korean. The corresponding designators in Chinese and Japanese are 一·二八事變 and 第一次上海事變, respectively.

5 See the lawsuit seeking compensation for the Korean victims of the Asia-Pacific War, *Petition*, 2nd ed., 1992, 24-27.

demands for military sex slaves, which arose due to numerous incidences of rape during the Japanese occupation of Nanking and the consequent installation of military comfort stations under the pretext of preventing such incidents; and the condition for supply, where a basis for the mobilization of manpower was established with the implementation of the National Mobilization Law in colonial Korea (Geum Byeongdong, 1992: 3-4).

According to explanations by Professor Yoshimi Yoshiaki, who is one of the most active scholars of the issue of Japanese military comfort stations, and the research group created around him, military comfort stations were founded by Japanese army and navy units dispatched to Shanghai in early 1932 and, from then on, generally established in keeping with historical events that caused the expansion of territories occupied by Japan. From the outbreak of a full-fledged war with China in July 1937 to the end of the same year, Japan began to install military comfort stations in occupied areas in China, and, following the empire's provocation of war against nations including the United States, United Kingdom, and Netherlands in December 1941 and occupation of Southeast Asia and the Pacific region, the Japanese armed forces led the direct and successive establishment of comfort stations in these occupied areas (Yoshimi Yoshiaki and Hayashi Hirofumi, eds., 1995: 3-4 and 71-142). While studies by the lawyers' group and Geum Byeongdong above clearly distinguish between the early form of military comfort stations as of 1932 and the systematic expansion of these facilities in 1937-1938 and onwards, Yoshimi Yoshiaki's joint research group, which has performed a closer positivistic examination, surveys the overall establishment and development of military comfort stations in 1932 and onwards according to the development of historical events without specific periodization. This latter group fundamentally questions the assumption that the overwhelming majority of sex slaves consisted of Koreans[6] and therefore does not focus on the Japanese government's overall mobilization of manpower during the war including its mobilization of manpower in

6 "The claim that Koreans were the vast majority of Japanese military comfort women requires reconsideration" (Yoshimi Yoshiaki and Hayashi Hirofumi, eds., 1995: 89, etc.).

colonial Korea as an important aspect of the process of establishing the military comfort station system. In addition, it does not present a clear view of the effect, on the process of establishing comfort stations, of aspects such as the number of sex slaves, the degree of the Japanese armed forces' intervention, and the forms in which sex slaves were recruited.

One later study based on research on the social history of unlicensed (i.e., private) prostitution 私娼制 and licensed (i.e., state-authorized) prostitution 公娼制 in Japan clearly distinguishes between civilian-led and military-led comfort stations and between prostitution-type and sexual slavery-type comfort stations in the process through which Japanese military comfort stations developed, with the agents of the establishment and management of these facilities and the forms of recruiting sex slaves as the standards. According to this study, while comfort stations for soldiers began to be established in 1894, these facilities were led by civilians. After going through a transitional form from 1918-1922 to 1932-1933, they came to take a primitive form of military sexual slavery from 1931-1933 onwards, with the initiation of Korean women's participation. From 1937-1938 and onwards, Korean women came to occupy the overwhelming majority of sex slaves as comfort stations expanded considerably in number, and, starting in 1940, the forced taking of women as sex slaves became mainstream (Kurahashi Masanao, 1994). Contrary to research by Yoshimi Yoshiaki's team, which is very positivistic yet lacks a specific viewpoint, this study attempts unreasonable abstraction that is not supported by positivistic data.

The report presented by the South Korean government in 1992 likewise argues, without discussions in particular, that the fact that STDs were rampant among Japanese soldiers during the Siberian Intervention in 1918 was the main reason for the Japanese government's subsequent establishment of military comfort stations. In addition, it states that military comfort stations were first installed during the Shanghai Incident of 1932 and that full-fledged military comfort station policies were adopted following the Second Sino-Japanese War of 1937 (Working Group on the Issue of Military Sexual Slavery, 1992: 21-24).

In-depth interviews of 19 former military sex slaves by the Korean Council and the Korean Research Group have revealed that, from among these women, one was taken in 1936 and the rest were taken in or after

1937.[7] In addition, all of the 175 survivors who reported to the South Korean Ministry of Health and Welfare as of 1994 were revealed to have been taken in or after 1932, with 93% of them taken in or after 1937.[8] Such information on the victims shows the fact that, as far as Korean women are concerned, victims began to be taken to military comfort stations in 1932 and that 1937 was a qualitative turning point. Although many other studies summarize the process through which Japanese military comfort stations developed, they generally agree that the Manchurian Incident of 1931, the Shanghai Incident of 1932, and the Second Sino-Japanese War of 1937 were the major points in terms of changes to these facilities.

In reference to such studies, this chapter will seek to review the process through which Japanese military comfort stations were established by more closely scrutinizing documentary evidence and testimonies of experiencers of these facilities. In conclusion, this chapter will verify the several following points. First, the Japanese armed forces seem to have installed military comfort stations for the first time around 1905. Second, the form of military comfort stations under discussion here seems to have begun to be established in approximately 1932. Third, policies for establishing more systematic and organized military comfort stations were created at the end of 1937, and the military comfort stations formed at the time exhibited important and essential changes that differentiated them from those installed earlier. These changes were: military comfort stations were established throughout regions garrisoned by the Japanese armed forces based on the military's systematic command according to the central command's policies; and, basically, sex slaves were supplied through the mobilization of women in colonial Korea. Fourth, although there were changes in military comfort station policies, forms of comfort stations, and methods of mobilizing sex slaves from the end of 1937 onwards as well, they generally consisted of quantitative changes stemming from the expansion of occupied territories and can be seen essentially as

7 See the Korean Council for the Women Drafted for Military Sexual Slavery by Japan and the Korean Chongshindae Research Group, eds., *Forcibly Taken Korean Military Comfort Women*, vol. 1 (Seoul: Hanul, 1993).

8 The total number of victims who have reported to the South Korean Ministry of Health and Welfare as of December 1994. It was decided that, from among these, only 169 would receive government funding.

continuations of policies implemented in 1937. Finally, there were some differences even within the same period depending on the region and the time elapsed since occupation by the Japanese armed forces.

2. The Primitive Form of Military Comfort Stations: Approximately 1905

Japan early on established a licensed prostitution system where the state managed prostitution and performed systematic and regular medical examinations on prostitutes 娼妓, and important users of licensed prostitution were warriors (*samurai*) and, later, soldiers. It is therefore amply possible to presume that comfort stations whose main users would be soldiers were established near the Japanese armed forces whenever the latter were dispatched to the battlefield. A form of military comfort stations led by civilians can be confirmed from the First Sino-Japanese War 淸日戰爭[9] in 1894 (Kurahashi Masanao, 1994: 52-54), and the general argument is that, until the installation of military comfort stations by Japanese army and navy units dispatched to Shanghai in 1932, only such civilian-led comfort stations existed.

However, former Japanese soldiers' testimonies that the Japanese military already established comfort stations at the time of the Russo-Japanese War 露日戰爭[10] (1904-1905) can be found. Judging from testimonies such as "brothels 淫婦賣買屋 were established... communication was impossible because most were Chinese women," "while they were lodgings authorized by the military, it was nearly impossible for soldiers to make use of the brothels 娼妓屋 due to their economic situations," and "they were contracted to work there for two years and to receive a monthly wage of 30 yen, which makes it unlikely that they were Chinese prostitutes," it is clear that, during this period, the Japanese armed forces either established comfort stations at the Chinese

9 [TN] This is the common Korean name for the historical event. The corresponding designators in Japanese and Chinese are 日淸戰爭 and 甲午戰爭, respectively.

10 [TN] This is the common Korean name for the historical event. The corresponding designators in Japanese and Chinese are 日露戰爭 and 日俄戰爭, respectively.

battlefront, mobilizing Chinese and Japanese women as sex slaves, or authorized existing comfort stations for military use only, thus allowing soldiers to make use of them (Oe Shinobu, ed., 1988).

Such military comfort stations do not seem to have been established systematically and continuously during later wars as well. There is only a report that, during Japan's Siberian Intervention in 1918-1922, from among 72,000 soldiers, 2,012 suffered from serious STDs and that this number would have increased fivefold or sixfold if benign cases, too, had been included (Geum Byeongdong, 1992: 3). There is no record, however, that military comfort stations were installed to prevent STDs.

3. The Formation of Military Comfort Stations: Approximately 1932

When numerous incidences of rape by Japanese soldiers occurred in early 1932 during the Shanghai Incident, Lt. Gen. Okamura Yasuji, the Vice Chief of Staff 參謀副長 of the Shanghai Expeditionary Army 上海派遣軍, requested the governor of Nagasaki Prefecture to send military comfort women. Later, he was to reminisce that he had been happy because, following the overseas dispatch of sex slaves, incidences of rape had disappeared. Judging from the fact that Lt. Gen. Okamura Yasuji thus requested sex slaves in imitation of the Japanese navy likewise garrisoned in Shanghai,[11] navy comfort stations 海軍慰安所 apparently were established even earlier.[12] Similarly, Gen. Okabe Naozaburo recorded that Japanese army and navy units dispatched to Shanghai in early 1932 installed military comfort stations (Okabe Naozaburo, 1982: 23). The

11 Inaba Masao, ed., *General Okamura Yasuji Materials, Vol. 1: Reminiscences of the Battlefield* (Tokyo: Hara Shobo, 1970); requoted from the lawsuit seeking compensation for the Korean victims of the Asia-Pacific War, 1992: 24-25.

12 At the outbreak of the Manchurian Incident, the Japanese navy deployed the 1st Expeditionary Fleet 遣外艦隊 to Central and South China and the 2nd Expeditionary Fleet to North China, additionally dispatching battleships in October 1931 and January 1932. In January 1932, battles between the Shanghai Special Naval Landing Force 上海海軍特別陸戰隊 and the Chinese army began, and, in February of the same year, the 9th Division and the 12th Division of the Japanese army dispatched one mixed brigade to Shanghai (Fujiwara Akira, 1994: 209-210).

Japanese Consulate-General in Shanghai recorded in December 1932 that there were 17 navy comfort stations and, furthermore, specified that this statistics followed numerous incidences of the earlier opening and closing of comfort stations, thus implying that the establishment of navy comfort stations occurred even earlier (Japanese Consulate-General in Shanghai, 1932). Materials from the same consulate-general from 1935 and 1936 likewise show that navy comfort stations existed. According to these records, the sex slaves at these military comfort stations were forbidden to service clients other than soldiers and were subjected to medical examinations by medical specialists twice a week in the presence of members of the Special Naval Landing Forces 海軍特別陸戰隊 and the competent police officers, and strict control was exercised based on cooperation from the navy. In addition, these materials demonstrate the fact that members of the general public other than the military participated in the operation of comfort stations.[13]

On the other hand, 1933 records of the Kwantung Army 關東軍 stationed in Pingchuan (present-day Pingquan), China closely and strictly stipulate the performance of medical examinations on professional entertainers and prostitutes 藝娼妓 and bar girls 酌婦 at least once a week to prevent STDs among soldiers and order the management of hygiene facilities in brothels 妓樓 and the prevention of STDs among the troops. In addition, it can be confirmed that, here, Koreans already occupied the overwhelming majority of the sex slaves (Headquarters, 14th Mixed Brigade, 1933: 3-8). Although it is difficult to say that they were established by or solely for the Japanese armed forces, these comfort stations can be seen as an early form of military comfort stations in the fact that the military actively controlled professional entertainers and prostitutes and bar girls whose users were soldiers.

13 Japanese Consulate-General in Shanghai, "The State of Police Affairs of the Consulate-General in Shanghai in 1935," 1935 and "The State of Police Affairs of the Consulate-General in Shanghai in 1936," 1936.

4. The Establishment and Implementation of Full-fledged Military Comfort Station Policies: The End of 1937 and Onwards

It seems to have been from around the end of 1937 that the establishment of military comfort stations, hitherto executed sporadically in each area, began to be systematically implemented throughout the Japanese armed forces as a policy led by the Ministry of War 陸軍省. From this point onwards, the entire process from the establishment and management of comfort stations to the recruitment and shipment of sex slaves was mainly led by the military, with the active and systematized cooperation of the Government-General of Korea 朝鮮總督府 and the Government-General of Taiwan (GGT) 臺灣總督府 as well as Japanese government organs such as the Ministry of Home Affairs 內務省 and the Ministry of Foreign Affairs 外務省.

The direct background of such changes, above all, was the expansion and prolongation of war, and the policy of the total mobilization of manpower not only in Japan itself but also throughout its colonies implemented against this backdrop, in turn, buttressed the changes. Japan initiated an all-out war against China in July 1937 and occupied Nanking in December of the same year. As the Second Sino-Japanese War expanded and continued further than expected, Japan entered a full-fledged war system and went on to reorganize its industrial structures on the mainland and in the colonies alike in order to wage war and to consolidate structures of the general mobilization of goods and manpower.

1) The Ministry of War's Policies, Planning, and Implementation on and of Military Comfort Stations

Dating from the end of 1937 and onwards, numerous and clear records on military comfort stations have been discovered. From this period until the end of the war, Japan's comfort station policies differed fundamentally from earlier ones, developing for the systematic and mass-scale installation of these facilities and mobilization of sex slaves under state leadership. Based on a Ministry of War document discovered in 2005,[14] Professor Nagai Kazu of Japan has argued that the Japanese army established the grounds for the installation of comfort stations as military logistics facilities by modifying field canteens in September 1937. According to this document, the Ministry of War revised its Regulations on Field Canteens 野戰酒保規程 in order to turn military comfort stations into the armed forces' rear facilities (Han Hye-in, 2015: 4). Subsequent actions can be confirmed below.

(1) Instructions from Each Dispatched Segment of the Military for the Establishment of Military Comfort Stations

In December 1937, the Central China Area Army 中支那方面軍 ordered the establishment of military comfort stations. The 2nd Department of Staff 參謀第二課 had drawn up a plan and requested Lt. Col. Cho Isamu, a staff officer, for the installation of military comfort stations in Nanking. In the same period, the 10th Army Staff 軍參謀 instructed the Military Police Corps to establish military comfort stations in Huchow (present-day Huzhou).[15]

(2) Direct Orders from the Ministry of War

Numerous records from the period that started in March 1938 demonstrate direct orders from the Ministry of War. In March 1938, the Department of Military Affairs 兵務課 in the Bureau of Military Affairs 兵務局 in the Ministry of War thus ordered the Chiefs of Staff 參謀長 of both the North China Area Army 北支那方面軍 and the Central China Expeditionary Army 中支那派遣軍: "the recruitment of comfort women is to be controlled by expeditionary armies for the selection of appropriate persons, and close cooperation with the Military Police Corps and the police is to be maintained."[16] The decisions made at a meeting of the

---

14 Ministry of War, "Item Regarding the Revision of the Regulations on Field Canteens," September 18, 1937.

15 Editorial Board of the *History of the War in Nanking*, ed., *A Sourcebook on the History of the War in Nanking* (Tokyo: Kaikosha, 1989), 211, 220, 280, and 411; requoted from Yoshimi Yoshiaki and Hayashi Hirofumi, eds., 1995: 16-17.

16 Drafted by the Department of Military Affairs, Bureau of Military Affairs, Ministry of War, "Item Regarding the Recruitment of Female Workers for Military Comfort Stations, Etc.," March 4, 1938.

relevant personnel from the three ministries of the Ministry of War, Ministry of the Navy 海軍省, and Ministry of Foreign Affairs held in Nanking in April 1938 stated that comfort stations belonging exclusively to the army and the navy, respectively, were directly managed and supervised by these two branches of the armed forces and therefore were not to be interfered with by Japanese consulates,[17] and this was reconfirmed by the Japanese Consul-General in Shanghai in July of the same year.[18] This clearly demonstrates that the Ministry of War and the Ministry of the Navy directly controlled comfort stations.

Compiled in May 1938 by the Japanese Inspectorate-General of Military Training 教育總監部, "Wartime Service Manual 戰時服務提要" thus stipulates: "while methods for the active prevention of sexually transmitted diseases are to be established and comfort stations are to be fully equipped with hygiene facilities, at the same time, contact with prostitutes 賣春婦 and locals other than those designated by the armed forces is to be strictly prohibited."[19] In the *Bulletin of the Department Chiefs of the Bureau of Medical Affairs in the Ministry of War* 陸軍省醫務局課長會報 dated April 1939, chief of the Division of Medical Officers 軍醫部 Matsumura of the 21st Army 軍 reported, "To prevent sexually transmitted diseases, comfort women are to be imported, one per 100 soldiers… the medical fees for the [comfort women's] treatment are to be paid by the [comfort station] managers. Medical examinations are [to be performed] twice a week."[20] Similarly, in September 1940, the Ministry of War ordered special attention to the guidance and regulation of military discipline and morals.[21] These records clearly demonstrate the fact that the

17 Japanese Consulate-General in Nanking, "Decisions of the Meeting of the Personnel from the Ministry of War, Ministry of the Navy, and Ministry of Foreign Affairs Regarding the Permission and Regulation of Diverse Business Operations of Japanese Abroad," April 16, 1938.

18 Sent by the Japanese Consul-General in Shanghai, "A Summary of the Notification Dispatched to the [Japanese] Consulate-General in Nanking by the [Japanese] Consulate-General in Shanghai Dated July 5, 1938," July 5, 1938.

19 Inspectorate-General of Military Training, "Wartime Service Manual," May 25, 1938.

20 Kinbara Setsuzo, 1939-1941, *A Summary of the Main Points of the Work Logs of the Ministry of War*, vol. I, 1-I (April 15, 1939).

21 Sent by the Ministry of War Adjutant, Headquarters, Gunnery Unit, "Measures for Arousing Soldiers' Morale as Observed in the Experience of the Second Sino-Japanese War," September 19, 1940.

Ministry of War was the center of control over military comfort stations.

Even during periods in which the Ministry of War central's control over comfort stations was thus achieved, tasks including the installation of military comfort stations, legislation of comfort station regulations, and reporting of the operation of comfort stations were performed also on levels including those of area armies, armies, battalions, and regiments. Numerous military documents show that diverse levels of the Japanese armed forces participated in multifaceted ways in military comfort stations: for example, the North China Area Army Chief of Staff stated in June 1938 that it was crucial to establish sexual comfort facilities at the earliest date possible;[22] and there is a record that regiment headquarters orally gave instructions regarding comfort stations to each unit commander.[23] In the end, these individual units must be seen as having been controlled and ordered by the Ministry of War central.

(3) Early Plans of the Ministry of War for the Establishment of Military Comfort Stations

A record proving that, from as early as around July 1941, the Ministry of War planned to establish military comfort stations throughout territories garrisoned by the Japanese armed forces has been discovered. According to this document, as Japan prepared for full-fledged war against nations including the United States, United Kingdom, and Netherlands in 1941, the Ministry of War clearly and early on planned to install military comfort stations in regions garrisoned by the Japanese armed forces. Using this plan, which, in turn, was based on the nation's experience in China, Japan, in fact, established military comfort stations immediately, without delay, in diverse areas in Southeast Asia once they were garrisoned by its military forces.[24] "A Report on the Inspection of the Hygiene Situation in the Netherlands East Indies by Medical Officer

22 Okabe Naozaburo, Chief of Staff, North China Area Army, "Notification on the Item Regarding Caution with the Behavior of [Japanese] Soldiers and Units to Locals," June 27, 1938.

23 Headquarters, 3rd Independent Mountain Artillery Regiment, "Instructions to Each Unit Commander, Etc.," June 1939.

24 Allied Translator and Interpreter Section, South West Pacific Area, "Interrogation Report No. 28, Terada, K." (serial no. 40), January 30, 1943; and Yoshimi Yoshiaki, 1992b: 465-487.

Major Fukada 深田軍醫少佐蘭印衛生狀況視察報告" of July 1941 states that, due to problems of hygiene caused by the Netherlands East Indies Campaign (1941-1942), comfort stations must be installed under strict medical examinations.[25]

On the other hand, it has been revealed that, in the same period, the Kwantung Army established and implemented a plan to install military comfort stations on a massive scale and, for the operation of these facilities, to take an enormous number of Korean women as military sex slaves. In reaction to the former Soviet Union's reinforcement of military power in East Asia, the Japanese armed forces had already executed a wholesale reinforcement of the army and, in approximately July 1941, performed the Kwantung Army Special Exercises 關東軍特種演習. According to his later testimony, Kwantung Army Staff Officer 關東軍參謀 Lt. Col. Harayoshi Nishiro, who was in charge of logistics at this time, calculated that, based on experience in the Second Sino-Japanese War, over 20,000 military sex slaves would be needed and sought to draft them through the Government-General of Korea but only obtained 8,000 women in the end. This fact is corroborated also by the testimonies of those who had experience with military comfort stations and subsequently reported to Military Comfort Women #110 從軍慰安婦110番, a Japanese NGO. There are testimonies, too, that Korean women were taken in the name of the "Special Wartime Women's Volunteer Corps for the Kwantung Army 關東軍戰時特別女子挺身隊," not knowing that they would be made to work as military sex slaves (Senda Kakou, 1978: 104; Editorial Board of *Military Comfort Women #110*, ed., 1992; and Yoshimi Yoshiaki and Hayashi Hirofumi, eds., 1995: 89-90). Barely known through testimonies in the absence of official documents, such facts have been confirmed by materials recently disclosed by the Heilongjiang Province branch of the State Archives Administration 國家檔案局, China's national archives agency. Based on a report from the commander of the Nantienmen Unit 南天門隊 in the Suiyang County Border Police Corps 綏陽縣國境警察隊, the commander of the Hantsungho Unit 寒葱河隊 in the same corps thus reported to the commander of the Suifenho Unit 綏芬河隊 on October 20,

25 Kinbara Setsuzo, 1939-1941, 3-Ha (July 26, 1941).

1941: "Approximately ten out of the 2,000 women recruited from Korea as comfort women exclusively for units of the Japanese armed forces dispatched to the [Asian] continent 日本軍大陸派遣部隊專用慰安婦 have arrived in Nantienmen [present-day Nantianmen]." In addition, Special Operations Section Assisting Police Officer 特務係警補 Takayama Akane, too, reported to the commander of the Suifenho Unit on October 30 of the same year: "Through police stations and the Military Police Corps in diverse areas in Korea, the armed forces recently recruit[ed] volunteers to operate restaurants with Korean hostesses exclusively for the Japanese military 日軍專用鮮人接待料理店 in Manchuria."[26]

The Pacific War broke out in December 1941, and the Japanese armed forces successively occupied Southeast Asia and the South Seas Mandate. The Ministry of War continued to stress that, to prevent STDs among soldiers, comfort station facilities must be sufficient and thorough.[27] In this period, military comfort stations continued to increase in China on one hand and were established in rapid succession in areas such as Hong Kong, Malaya, Singapore,[28] Netherlands East Indies, and Philippines. According to one record, because of a request from the Southern Expeditionary Army Group 南方總軍 (or 南方軍) for the dispatch of 50 native women to Borneo as prospective sex slaves, the Taiwan Army Commander 臺灣軍司令官 decided that three managers who had been investigated and selected by the Military Police Corps should be allowed to travel and thus needed permission. On March 12, 1942, the commander therefore requested the Minister of War permission for these managers' travel, and the Ministry of War granted it on March 16.[29] Subsequently, in

---

26 "Suiyang County Border Police Corps Suifenho-Hantsungho Top Secret No. 890 綏國警綏寒特秘第八九零號" (also titled "Item Regarding the Installation of Korean Restaurants Exclusively for the Japanese Military 日軍專用鮮人料理店開設ニ關スル件"; housed in the Heilongjiang Province Archives Administration 黑龍江省檔案局); and Special Operations Section Assisting Police Officer Takayama Akane, "Item Regarding the Installation of Restaurants Designated for Units of the Japanese Armed Forces 日本軍部隊指定料理店開設ニ關スル件," October 30, 1941 (housed in the Heilongjiang Province Archives Administration). Both requoted from Seo Hyun-ju, 2015: 247.

27 Drafted by the Department of Hygiene, Bureau of Medical Affairs, Ministry of War, "Item Regarding the Treatment of the Sexually Transmitted Diseases of Soldiers Related to the Greater East Asia War," June 18, 1942; and "The Proceedings of [the Meeting of] Bureau Chiefs on July 30, 1942," Kinbara Setsuzo, 1941-1943, *A Summary of the Main Points of the Work Logs of the Ministry of War*, vol. II, 4-Ro (July 30, 1942).

28 [TN] Referred to at the time by the Japanese as "Syonan Island" (*Shonan-to*) 昭南島.

June, the Ministry of War instructed the Taiwan Army Chief of Staff 臺灣軍參謀長 appropriately to process the replacement of a small number of the personnel as a supplement.[30] Such materials demonstrate that the Ministry of War oversaw the entire process including the travel of sex slaves.

(4) The Total Plan of the Ministry of War

In September 1942, when territories occupied by Japan were expanding in areas in Southeast Asia and the South Seas Mandate, the Ministry of War, from a more total viewpoint, presented a plan for the establishment of military comfort stations throughout regions garrisoned by the Japanese armed forces. In the *Bulletin of Department Chiefs* 課長會報 dated September 3, 1942, the chief of the Department of Awards and Recognitions 恩賞課 in the Bureau of Personnel 人事局 in the Ministry of War stated that he wished to install a total of 400 comfort stations for officers and soldiers: 100 in North China; 140 in Central China; 40 in South China; 100 in Southeast Asia; ten in the South Seas Mandate; and ten on Sakhalin.[31] [32] In addition, the Ministry of War systematically shipped condoms for comfort stations attached to each of the military forces[33] and provided funds for the import of sex slaves.[34]

While the Ministry of War thus controlled military comfort stations based on a total vision of their actual establishment, in each region in the occupied territories, military organizations on diverse levels actively performed the instruction and supervision of comfort stations. The China Expeditionary Army General Headquarters 支那派遣軍總司令部 controlled the issue of supplying condoms;[35] in the Philippines, the

29 Drafted by the Taiwan Army, "Item Regarding Travelers Dispatched to the South," March 1942.

30 Higuchi Keishichiro, Chief of Staff, Taiwan Army, "Taiwan Army Telegram No. 935," June 13, 1942.

31 Kinbara Setsuzo, 1941-1943, 5-I (September 3, 1942).

32 [TN] Referred to as "Karafuto" 樺太 in Japanese since the modern era.

33 Department of Construction, Bureau of Intendance, Ministry of War, *Great Log of Army Secrets in Asia*, 1942; and Center for Research and Documentation on Japan's War Responsibility, 1993: 25-28.

34 National Archives and Records Administration, 1944-1945; and Center for Research and Documentation on Japan's War Responsibility, 1993: 34-36.

35 General Headquarters, China Expeditionary Army, "Opinions, Questions, and Answers

Philippines Military Administration 比島軍政監部 took charge of the instruction and supervision of military comfort stations;[36] in Mandalay, Burma, the Garrison Commander 駐屯司令官 took charge of the establishment of comfort stations and the legislation of the regulations;[37] in Malaya, the Malaya Military Administration 馬來軍政監部 did so;[38] and, in the Netherlands East Indies, the Civil Administration Governor 民政部長官 was responsible for the installation and supervision of comfort stations.[39] A 1943 report created by the NEFIS states that comfort stations were established as soon as the Japanese armed forces were stationed anywhere.[40]

According to information collected by the NEFIS in the Netherlands East Indies during 1944-1945, the Japanese military forces occupied buildings that previously had been used as hotels or inhabited by Europeans, establishing and operating comfort stations there.[41] From May 1944 to February 1945, the Japanese armed forces directly constructed comfort stations in Okinawa on the levels of the Southern Area Garrison Headquarters 南地區駐屯地司令部, divisions, battalions, and companies, and numerous records of discussions on other general issues related to comfort stations have been discovered.[42] These materials show that

---

from Meetings of Adjutants (General Affairs Officers) in September 1942 (Addenda)," September 1942.

36 Iloilo Office, Visaya Branch, Philippines Military Administration, "Item Regarding the Forwarding of Regulations on Comfort Stations (Asia Hall, Comfort Station No. 1)," November 22, 1942.

37 Headquarters, 5th Field Transport, "Regulations on the Garrison Duties of the 5th Field Transport Headquarters," October 31, 1943. As for the situation in Burma, also see Won-Loy Chan, *Burma: The Untold Story* (Novato, CA: Presidio Press, 1986).

38 Legislated by the Malaya Military Administration, "Regulations on the Regulation of the Operation of Comfort Facilities and Inns," November 1943; and Hayashi Hirofumi, 1993: 73.

39 Chief, 2nd Demobilization Unit (Navy Auditor and Inspector), Celebes Civil Administration, "A Report on the Item Regarding the Demobilization of Members of the 2nd Demobilization Unit in the Celebes Civil Administration," June 20, 1946.

40 Here is one example: "Whenever troops were stationed in a locality in numbers, brothels were immediately established by both the Army & [the] Navy," Allied Translator and Interpreter Section, South West Pacific Area, "Interrogation Report No. 37 Kumagae, S." (serial no. 55), February 23, 1943.

41 Netherlands Forces Intelligence Service, "Compilation of NEFIS Interrogation Reports Nos. 295, 330 and 334 (Not Issued Separately)" (October 14, 1944), etc. Requoted from Baek Jaeye, 2016: 56-57.

42 Headquarters, Southern Area Garrison, "The Proceedings of the Meeting of Adjutants

the Japanese military's comfort station policies became increasingly systematic and that the armed forces' direct intervention was increasingly strengthened.

2) The Participation of Other Japanese Government Organs

From among Japanese government organs, those that intervened deeply in military comfort stations other than the Ministry of War were the Ministry of Foreign Affairs and the Ministry of Home Affairs. Because military comfort stations basically were established on foreign territories occupied by the Japanese armed forces, departments in the Ministry of Foreign Affairs in charge of managing Japanese citizens abroad such as consulates inevitably intervened in the management of these facilities. While military comfort stations themselves were under the responsibility of the Japanese military, cooperation from the Ministry of Foreign Affairs was necessary for the immigration control of sex slaves and comfort station managers. For example, in September 1940, the chief of the Division of Foreign Affairs 外事部 in the Government-General of Taiwan notified the chief of the 3rd Department 課 in the Bureau of American Affairs 亞米利加局 in the Ministry of Foreign Affairs that "Although passengers would need certificates of purpose of travel [overseas], the passage of 'comfort station workers 慰安所從業員' is urgent and therefore has been specially allowed and must be understood."[43] In addition, it is possible to confirm the fact that the Ministry of Foreign Affairs intervened in military comfort stations both directly and indirectly from the following: Japanese consulates reported to the Minister for Foreign Affairs the entry of women and investigated and reported the occupations of the Japanese, Koreans, and Formosans (i.e., Taiwanese), particularly with respect to the circumstances of comfort station managers and sex slaves and information on comfort stations.

The intervention also of the Ministry of Home Affairs is apparent

---

in the Armies and the Brigades," January 13, 1945, etc.

43 Chiba Hoichi, Chief, Division of Foreign Affairs, Government-General of Taiwan, "Item Regarding the Treatment of Travelers to Opposite Areas Acknowledged as Impossible to Regulate through Certificates of Purpose of Travel to China, Etc.," 1940.

mainly from the departure of sex slaves and comfort station managers. In February 1938, reporting the passage of women whose purpose was "shameful work 醜業" as indispensable due to the local situation, the chief of the Bureau of Police and Public Security 警保局 in the Ministry of Home Affairs decided that, for the time being, these women's departure for China was to be condoned and ordered that circumstances surrounding the recruitment and brokerage of such women be carefully regulated.[44] Likewise, according to a material from 1940, the Ministry of Home Affairs instructed that the purpose of "special women's 特殊婦女" passage abroad was to be recorded as "For settlement."[45]

3) Cooperation from the Government-General of Korea and the Government-General of Taiwan

Numerous materials show that Korean women constituted the bulk of Japanese military sex slaves. At the time, departure from colonial Korea required without fail a written permission from the police station in charge of one's place of abode, and the qualifications for such a permission consisted of both proof of the guarantee of a definite occupation in the destination and the possession of a certain sum of money.[46] Begun in the 1920s, this overseas departure permission system became increasingly strict in its requirements and even more stringent with the implementation of manpower mobilization policies in 1938 and onwards. Consequently, it is unthinkable for the mobilization of Korean women to have been implemented without the intervention of the Government-General of Korea.

Materials related to the Government-General of Korea show that,

---

44 Chief, Bureau of Police and Public Security, Ministry of Home Affairs, "Item Regarding the Treatment of Women Traveling to China" (Material No. 5), February 23, 1938. As with the Allied Forces' World War II documents, contemporary Japanese documents alluded to in this volume have been presented with their official document numbers. However, materials with designators that begin "Material No." have been cited from Yoshimi Yoshiaki, 1992b.

45 Ministry of Home Affairs, "Points of Consultation on 'Item Regarding the Provisional Treatment of Japanese Nationals Traveling to China,'" May 1940.

46 Bureau of Police and Public Security, Ministry of Home Affairs, "Notification by Order on the Item Regarding the Recruitment of Korean Laborers"; and Park Kyung-Sik, 1975.

starting in early 1938, this organ was well aware of the circumstances surrounding the passage of military sex slaves and the comfort station personnel to China (Yoshimi Yoshiaki, 1994: 32-35). I have mentioned earlier that, in July 1941, the Kwantung Army came to use 8,000 sex slaves with help from the Government-General of Korea. There is a material from the chief of the Bureau of Police Affairs 警務局 in the Government-General of Korea that similarly, in 1942, reports to the chief of the Division of Shipbuilding 造船部 in the Ministry of Colonial Affairs 拓務省, the chief of the Division of Police 警察部 in each Korean province, and each delegate in China on the circumstances surrounding travel abroad per occupation including "professional entertainers and prostitutes 藝娼妓."[47] The testimonies of South Korean victims reveal that, in many cases, officials in the Government-General of Korea including police officers, unit heads 班長, township heads 面長, and township office 面事務所 staff workers intervened in the mobilization of sex slaves. Indeed, from among those who reported to the South Korean Ministry of Health and Welfare as of December 1994, 157 former sex slaves identified their main mobilizers. Out of these, 51 (32.4%) testified that they had been taken by police officers or colonial government officials.

Widespread is the perception among South Koreans who have lived through the Japanese colonial period that some members of the Labor Volunteer Corps 勤勞挺身隊 recruited by the Government-General of Korea using schools or by lower colonial government organs themselves were sent as military sex slaves. Indeed, recently, an individual testified that she had been mobilized as a member of the Labor Volunteer Corps but then exploited as a military sex slave, thus requiring a closer study of the issue.

Also noteworthy are materials showing the intervention of the Government-General of Taiwan. The role of the Government-General of Taiwan likewise was related mainly to passage abroad. In particular, in the case of Formosa, there were numerous items regarding the treatment of comfort station managers who were to establish comfort facilities in the

47 Chief, Bureau of Police Affairs, Government-General of Korea, "Item Regarding the Regulation of Persons Traveling to China," March 19, 1942 and August 29, 1942 (Material Nos. 24 and 25).

South Seas Mandate.[48] As demonstrated in the abovementioned report by the Taiwan Army Commander on comfort station managers who were headed to Borneo, there seem to have been many cases where the colonial authorities in Formosa were responsible for passage to the South Seas Mandate.

The 1937 revision of the Regulations on Field Canteens mentioned earlier includes "The fulfillment of goods for canteens is to be performed by the supplying organs," which can be seen as having served as a legal basis for the construction of a system of cooperation among colonial administrative organs in the mobilization and transport of military sex slaves (Han Hye-in, 2015: 4).

5. Changes in the Establishment and Form of Management of Military Comfort Stations

Following their rather sporadic installation at the early stage, Japanese military comfort stations began to take a particular form and to be established in a stable manner with the full-fledged intervention of the Japanese armed forces and government from the end of 1937 and onwards. The patterns in the installation and management of these facilities likewise exhibited certain changes according to the formation of the empire's military comfort station policies and their implementation in occupied territories.

1) The Nature of Military Comfort Stations

As they took on a fixed system, Japanese military comfort stations came to exhibit the following characteristics. First, with extremely rare exceptions,[49] these facilities were formed solely for soldiers based on a

48 Government-General of Taiwan, "Item Regarding the Establishment of Comfort Stations in Occupied Territories in the South Seas," January 10, 1942.

49 In Hankow (present-day Hankou, a part of Wuhan) and Nanchang, China, in 1940, prostitutes' districts 娼區 (i.e., licensed prostitution) were established, existing prostitution regulations were applied, the payment of business taxes was performed within a licensed prostitution system, and these districts substituted as organs created

system separate from brothels 遊廓, which followed the existing licensed prostitution system. Second, as a result, with extremely rare exceptions, military comfort stations could be used only by soldiers and civilian employees of the military 軍屬, and, conversely, soldiers could not use comfort stations other than military ones. Third, military sex slaves were subjected to regular examinations for STDs by physicians designated by the armed forces. Fourth, all tasks related to comfort stations including the relocation of sex slaves were placed under strict military control.

2) The Establishment and Management of Military Comfort Stations

While sharing the characteristics examined above, Japanese military comfort stations at times differed slightly from one another in their establishment and management. Indeed, these facilities could be classified into diverse forms: those established and managed directly by the armed forces; those established by the military but entrusted to civilians for their management; those entrusted by the military to civilians for their installation and management, which, in turn, were permitted and supervised by the military; existing unlicensed brothels 私娼 incorporated into military comfort stations; and the dispatch of sex slaves to occupied territories mainly in remote areas lacking comfort stations. When Japanese military comfort stations are examined in terms of the two extremes of those established and managed directly by the armed forces and those relying on civilians, it becomes possible to discern a current according to the process through which military comfort station policies were formed and implemented in occupied territories.

(1) The Initial Stage: The Japanese Military's Direct Establishment and Management of Comfort Stations

At the stage when military comfort stations first began to be installed in China, most of them took the form of direct establishment and

to aid the "comfort 慰安" of soldiers. In terms of all of the materials that have hitherto been uncovered, this case is nearly the only one of its kind. Division of Special Affairs, Ro Group, *Monthly Bulletin of the Ro Group Division of Special Affairs*, April 1940.

management by the Japanese armed forces. One report from January 1938 records, "As for comfort facilities, there are two types: those managed by logistics units and those managed directly by military units."[50] The excerpt "Comfort facilities… arranged in… [and] brothel 遊廓 owners…" from "Regulations on Internal Duties during the Occupation of Changchow [present-day Changzhou] 常州駐屯間內務規定" (Government Announcement Materials: Material No. 41), dating from March of the same year, makes it possible to surmise that, while the military comfort stations in question were managed by civilians, their establishment was implemented by the armed forces.[51] Similarly, the material from the Japanese Consulate-General in Nanking dated April 1938 quoted above records that comfort stations belonging exclusively to the army and the navy, respectively, were to be managed and supervised directly by these two branches of the military. Even in this period, the recruitment of sex slaves seems to have been entrusted to civilians. The Japanese armed forces also ordered caution in the selection of those who were to recruit sex slaves.[52] At the early stage, the recruitment of sex slaves seems to have occurred mainly in Japan and colonial Korea.[53] Many materials record that Koreans constituted the vast majority of sex slaves and that there were some Japanese women as well.[54] Some records say, however, that there were numerous Chinese women depending on the region,[55] and one tells of cases where, in regions such as Southeast Asia and the South Seas

---

50 Commander, 2nd Independent Heavy Siege Artillery Battalion, "A Report on the State of Affairs," January 20, 1938.

51 2nd Independent Heavy Siege Artillery Battalion, "Regulations on Internal Duties during the Occupation of Changchow," March 16, 1938 (Government Announcement Materials: Material No. 41).

52 Drafted by the Department of Military Affairs, Bureau of Military Affairs, Ministry of War, "Item Regarding the Recruitment of Female Workers for Military Comfort Stations, Etc.," March 4, 1938.

53 Many extant records dating from early 1938 and onwards concern both the passage of sex slaves and people "returning home" to Japan to recruit sex slaves. See Chief, Bureau of Police and Public Security, Ministry of Home Affairs, "Item Regarding the Treatment of Women Traveling to China" (Material No. 5), February 23, 1938; Senda Kakou, 1978, etc.

54 See medical officer 2nd Lt. Aso Tetsuo, "Methods for the Active Prevention of Venereal Diseases," June 26, 1939.

55 For example, Governor of Taipei Prefecture Hu Shuisheng, "Item Regarding the Regulation of [Japanese Subjects'] Travel to China," March 2, 1939.

Mandate, to which the battlefront expanded from the end of the 1930s to 1940, "locals" were used as well.[56]

(2) The Massive Influx of Civilians as Comfort Station Managers

The brief early stage of the Japanese military's systematic intervention was soon followed by a massive influx of civilians. In general, starting around the end of 1939, numerous records begin to mention those who wished to establish comfort stations and requests for the installation of these facilities.[57] Prior to the abovementioned revision of the Regulations on Field Canteens in September 1937, in principle, comfort stations were to be managed directly by the armed forces. With the modification of the regulations, these facilities were to be managed on their own but, when inevitable, could be managed by contractors with permission from the military officers in charge (army commanders, division commanders, quartermaster-generals, and army corps commanders), thus greatly facilitating the influx of civilians. Even in such cases, however, the transport costs came from government expenses, and both management and the receipt and disbursement of money and goods were overseen by chiefs of the Division of Accounts 經理部 (Han Hye-in, 2015: 4-5). This situation continued into the 1940s as well. While the military began directly to establish comfort stations in China at first, in regions such as Pacific islands and Southeast Asia, these facilities seem to have been installed, based on the experience in China, by civilians from the start. In many cases, civilians requested and received permission from the armed forces to manage comfort stations,[58] and, even in such cases, the military seems to have helped in diverse ways including leasing buildings. At this time, the recruitment of sex slaves seems to have targeted Koreans the most.

Because this was a period of the great expansion of military comfort

---

56 Headquarters, 21st Army, *Wartime Thrice-monthly (Rear Relations)*, April 11-20, 1939.

57 Minister of War Nomura Kichisaburo/Consul-General in Hankow Hanawa Yoshitaka, "Regarding the Travel to China of Women at the Comfort Station of the Amaya Unit of the Army in Hankow," December 22 and 27, 1939, etc.

58 Iloilo Office, Visaya Branch, Philippines Military Administration, "Item Regarding the Forwarding of Regulations on Comfort Stations (Asia Hall, Comfort Station No. 1)," November 22, 1942.

stations, in general, a large number of civilians participated in the establishment of these facilities. Nevertheless, there also existed not a few exceptional forms of comfort stations. The Kwantung Army mobilized sex slaves on a mass scale in July 1941, and the Japanese armed forces irregularly ordered sex slaves or entire military comfort stations to travel to areas without such facilities in order to provide service.[59]

(3) The Later Period: The Military's Resumption of the Direct Establishment of Comfort Stations

The latter half of 1943 saw a tendency of the Japanese military once again to be directly involved in the installation of comfort stations. In particular, the cases of the Netherlands East Indies during the latter half of 1943 (Van Poelgeest, trans. Yasuhara Keiko, 1994: 49-53) and Okinawa in 1944 undeniably demonstrate the circumstances surrounding the establishment of comfort stations by the armed forces.[60] Such direct installation of comfort stations by the Japanese military seems to have stemmed not only from the systemization of the armed forces' intervention but also from the difficulty of having civilians establish and manage comfort stations due to the increasing difficulty of mobilizing goods and manpower. This was the context in which the coerciveness of the mobilization of sex slaves, too, was strengthened. Indeed, it was in this period that the forced mobilization of sex slaves not only in colonial Korea but also other regions occupied by the Japanese military occurred extensively. It was mostly at this time that not only local but also Dutch women were mobilized in the Netherlands East Indies.[61]

---

59 Squad Leader, Cebu Military Police, and Squad Leader, Tacloban Military Police, "Item Regarding the Investigation of the State of Military Comfort and Recreation Facilities," August 1943 (Material No. 72). This was the case of the former sex slave Kim Bok-dong 金福童.

60 6th Garrison Construction Labor Company, *Field Diary*, May-June 1944.

61 During this period, in colonial Korea, advertisements to recruit military sex slaves were published a few times in the *Maeil Sinbo* 每日申報 and the *Keijo Nippo* 京城日報. While they ostensibly cite civilians as the recruiters, it is doubtful whether such recruitments were actually implemented by civilians. Although a recruitment advertisement published earlier, in March 1942, in Southeast Asia likewise cites civilians as the recruiters, Hayashi Hirofumi has proven that it was, in fact, implemented by the Japanese military (Hayashi Hirofumi, 1994: 34-35). It is implausible, too, that similar advertisements should have been published only a few times in colonial Korea. Rather,

(4) Immediately before Japan's Defeat in the War: Confusion

With impending Japanese defeat in the war, military comfort stations reacted in a diverse and confused manner according to the regions in which they were located. While the Japanese armed forces continued to establish comfort stations in Okinawa, in the case of Southeast Asia, they relied on local comfort station managers for all operations related to these facilities including the recruitment of sex slaves due to the increasing difficulty of shipping women from colonial Korea (Hayashi Hirofumi, 1994: 42; and Yoshimi Yoshiaki, 1994: 54). As for places such as Burma, in numerous cases, comfort station managers who had been entrusted by the Japanese military in colonial Korea mobilized women *en masse* and operated comfort stations deep in the battlefield with the aid of the armed forces.[62]

6. Conclusion

This chapter has thus examined the process of the formation and development of Japanese military comfort station policies mainly based on Japanese military documents and victims' testimonies. Sporadically in existence from 1905 and established in regions occupied by the Japanese armed forces starting around 1932, Japanese military comfort stations underwent a qualitative transformation at the end of 1937 and continued until the end of the war. As demands for sex slaves increased with the expansion of occupied territories and the prolongation of war, the Japanese military and the Ministry of War came to implement systematic policies. Accordingly, the level of systemization rose from orders by expeditionary armies to direct orders from the Ministry of War, then to total planning by the same ministry. In addition to the Japanesearmed forces and the Ministry of War, other government organs such as the Ministry of Foreign Affairs, Ministry of Home Affairs, Government-General of Korea, and Government-General of Taiwan cooperated with

such attempts most likely were made to conceal the fact that women were being taken forcibly.

62 See Ahn Byung Jik, trans., 2013.

the implementation of policies on military comfort stations.

Although they reveal differences in the recruitment of sex slaves and their own establishment and management according to the region and the lapse of time following Japan's occupation of the region in question, in general, military comfort stations tended largely to rely on the armed forces or the government central or to be installed and managed directly by the military at the initial stage, soon to witness a massive influx of civilians. It is possible to discern a current in the changes surrounding the establishment and management of these facilities: in the later period, the degree to which the military directly intervened once again rose, only to exhibit considerable confusion near the end of the war. In the early period, when the armed forces led the installation and management of military comfort stations, both Japanese and Korean women were mobilized. With the mass influx of civilians as comfort station managers, however, an overwhelming number of Koreans were taken. It was at this time that prospective sex slaves were recruited through fraud and human trafficking. During the later period, when the military's intervention once again became strong, coercion and violence were added to the process of taking sex slaves from colonial Korea, and a large number of women from occupied territories were introduced as well. In other words, as the shipment of sex slaves from Korea became difficult amid the chaos near the end of the war, the use of local women increased further.

Chapter 3

The Forced Mobilization of Women as Japanese Military Sex Slaves

1. The Debate Surrounding Forced Mobilization

The forced mobilization of women as Japanese military sex slaves is the most controversial issue in relation to Japanese military sexual slavery. While the forced taking of women as military sex slaves has established itself as an obvious fact in South Koreans' minds, the Japanese right wing has argued that "forced mobilization" is a tale fabricated by South Korean victims. In addition, the Japanese government's report on the issue released in 1993 states that, while there was some forced mobilization, this was implemented by civilians and unrelated to the government (Cabinet Councilors' Office on External Affairs, Cabinet Secretariat, 1993). Such claims by Japan have continued on the basis of the premise that documentary materials on the forced taking of women as military sex slaves are lacking and that victims' testimonies are false. However, this premise, harbored by both the Japanese right wing and government, is problematic in many ways. First, the argument that there was no forced mobilization because no documentary material proving it is extant is not one that can be presented by the Japanese government, which ordered the systematic destruction of documents after the war and has refused to disclose relevant documents ever since. Though this will be discussed later, numerous documents recording the fact that the Japanese government or military mobilized women as sex slaves through the use of violence in China and Southeast Asia have been discovered, and, in the case of colonial Korea, materials showing that the Japanese government indirectly condoned forced mobilization by civilians[1] have been found as well. In addition, innumerable victims from diverse countries who are isolated and therefore cannot affect one another's testimonies have testified that they were taken through violent coercion. Not only victims but also victimizers, experiencers, and investigators including members of the Allied Forces likewise have testified the forced taking of women as sex slaves.

This chapter will conduct largely two kinds of analysis of the forced taking of women as military sex slaves. Broadly referencing hitherto discovered materials and the fruits of research, the first will consist of the analysis of the mobilization of women as sex slaves, with a focus on both the results of in-depth interviews conducted by the Korean Research Group[2] and statistical data on the contents of the testimonies of over 170 former sex slaves who have reported to the South Korean Ministry of Health and Welfare in order to receive supplementary living allowances.[3] The second will consist of the analysis of numerous other testimonies and

1 This can be surmised from facts such as the Japanese government's instruction that the sex slaves' purpose of travel abroad be recorded as "For settlement" (Ministry of Home Affairs, 1940) and a document instructing the careful control of the recruitment and recommendation of the women (Chief, Bureau of Police and Public Security, Ministry of Home Affairs, 1938).

2 Including *Forcibly Taken Korean Military Comfort Women* 强制로 끌려간 朝鮮人軍慰安婦들, vol. 1 (1993), which encompasses testimonies by 19 former sex slaves, the Korean Council and the Korean Research Institute have published collections of testimonies by victims. As of 2016, these collections amount to six volumes of testimonies by Korean victims and two volumes of testimonies by victims living in China.

3 The South Korean government legislated in June 1993 the Act on the Support of Livelihood Stability for Former Comfort Women Drafted into the Japanese Forces under Japanese Colonial Rule 日帝下日本軍慰安婦에 對한 生活安定支援法 and began to accept reports by former sex slaves. The statistical data used in this chapter consist of basic information that I, as a member of the deliberative committee, synthesized while reviewing the investigative data on the 175 victims who reported to the South Korean Ministry of Health and Welfare as of December 1993. In the process of analyzing reports by the 175 women, victims with insufficient information were excluded depending on the item analyzed, thus resulting, at times, in a decrease in the total number of cases analyzed. Immediately after the enactment of the abovementioned law, reports from survivors flooded in, with the number gradually decreasing. Considering the fact that a total of 238 women were registered with the South Korean government as victims of Japanese military sexual slavery through victim reports and government deliberations as of 2016, approximately 73.5% of them turned out to have filed victim reports in 1993. Consequently, the initial 175 reporters can be said to reflect reasonably the circumstances of the entire victims. Because these materials on victim reports are strictly restricted from disclosure, only the contents of the reports are presented, with personal information on the victims such as their names and addresses omitted. I am grateful to researcher Yi Sang-Hwa at the Korean Research Institute for aiding the analysis of the statistics.

documents, obtained both at home and abroad, on the violent and forced mobilization of women as sex slaves implemented by the Japanese military.

1) The Coerciveness of Japanese Military Sexual Slavery

Before going into the analysis, it is necessary briefly to mention the concept of "forced mobilization." "Forced mobilization" is limited, in the narrow sense, to taking a victim by physical violence and, more broadly, also signifies the entire situation where a victim is taken against her wishes and, due to coercive control, cannot return according to her wishes. However, not only women who were mobilized by physical force but also all those who were turned into Japanese military sex slaves through means such as human trafficking, kidnapping, and employment fraud were taken unaware of the fact that they would be made to serve as sex slaves, were strictly watched during the process of being taken, and were so closely watched at comfort stations as to make escape impossible. In this respect, all cases of Japanese military sexual slavery must be defined as having been based on coercion in the wide sense.

Likewise, the Japanese military comfort women system is called "Japanese military sexual slavery" because of the coercion involved in this institution. Special Rapporteur McDougall, who submitted a report on the system to the UN Sub-Commission on Human Rights in 1998, points out: "The 1926 Slavery Convention [i.e., Convention to Suppress the Slave Trade and Slavery; henceforth "Geneva Convention on Slavery"] sets out the first comprehensive and now the most widely recognized definition of slavery. As adapted from the 1926 Slavery Convention, 'slavery' should be understood to be the status or condition of a person over whom any or all of the powers attaching to the right of ownership are exercised." That is, "slavery" refers to limitations on autonomy, freedom of movement, and power to decide matters relating to one's sexual activities and also includes situations involving rape or other forms of sexual violence.[4]

In addition, the UN's 1956 Supplementary Convention on the Abolition of Slavery, the Slave Trade, and Institutions and Practices

4 The abolishment of such slavery is described in customary international law as "*jus cogens*" (McDougall, 1998: paras. 27-29).

Similar to Slavery (also known as "Supplementary Convention on the Abolition of Slavery") defines "Any institution or practice whereby... [a] woman, without the right to refuse, is promised or given... on payment of a consideration in money or in kind to her parents, guardian, family or any other person or group..." as a practice of slavery to be abolished.[5] In other words, this convention already negates the claim of the Japanese government and right wing that the mobilization of women as military sex slaves was legal or voluntary because cash advances (loans) were paid to their families.

Here, "military comfort women system" (sexual slavery) refers to the overall mobilization and exploitation of sex slaves committed by the Japanese armed forces in both Japan and diverse areas in Asia. In other words, as is apparent from the analysis of South Korean victims below, diverse other forms of comfort women existed in addition to women who were mobilized to typical comfort stations, where the victims were forcibly mobilized from their respective locations, transported over long distances by the Japanese military, lived for prolonged periods in confinement at comfort stations, and moved together with the Japanese armed forces, with entire comfort stations moving together beyond national borders in some cases.[6] Likewise, there were cases of Korean women who were not only made to work at comfort stations but also dispatched to remote areas lacking comfort stations to provide "outcall comfort 出張慰安" (Kim Bok-dong's 金福童 case). As for women in occupied territories such as China, Philippines, Southeast Asia, and South Seas Mandate, the duration of their exploitation as sex slaves was generally short, and there existed not only forms of comfort stations but also forms of temporary exploitation as sex slaves such as gang rape centers. For example, numerous cases in the Philippines where women were confined to hotels and gang raped for weeks

5 (c)(i), Supplementary Convention on the Abolition of Slavery, the Slave Trade, and Institutions and Practices Similar to Slavery, Adopted by a Conference of Plenipotentiaries Convened by Economic and Social Council Resolution 608 (XXI) of 30 April 1956, and Done at Geneva on 7 September 1956; Entry into Force 30 April 1957.

6 Surrounding 1) sex slaves at comfort stations, 2) prostitutes at brothels under the wartime system, and 3) victims of sexual violence in territories occupied by the Japanese armed forces (i.e., cases where women were subjected to sexual violence by Japanese soldiers in certain periods and in certain areas), there have been debates on the extent to which these women can be seen as Japanese military sex slaves (Park Jung-ae, 2015).

by Japanese soldiers have been reported. When also added here is even the mobilization of Japanese women, who, in many cases, were mobilized on a small scale and from existing licensed brothels, with violent and forced taking nearly absent, and are reported to have been madeto provide sexual services mainly to officers, these various forms of the exploitation of women can be understood within the larger framework of the Japanese military comfort women system. That is, the institution was forced sexual slavery implemented through the power of the Japanese armed forces.

Judging from this, the countless one-time rapes that were committed during the war, too, must be understood as extensions of the Japanese military comfort women system in the context of war and coercion by the Japanese armed forces. This is because while women are subjected to serious sexual damage in most wars, the Japanese military, which implemented the comfort women system widely, can be said to have exhibited particularity in the scale and degree of its own institution. In the abovementioned report, though McDougall calls the facilities "comfort women stations" in the title of the appendix, she describes them as "rape camps" and "rape centres" in the main body and the appendix (McDougall, 1998, Appendix: paras. 7-62). In the end, "comfort stations" were places where rape was committed on a daily basis, and, in this sense, one-time and successive rapes can all be interpreted in the same context as Japanese military sexual slavery, too.

2) The Fictiveness of "Coercion in the Narrow Sense"

In the process through which the US House of Representatives House Resolution 121 (H. Res. 121) was discussed and passed in the American House of Representatives in 2007,[7] the then Japanese premier Abe Shinzo

7 Although the incident is discussed in Chapter 9, a brief summary of it will be presented here. Ever since Daniel William Lipinski, a Congressman from Illinois, first proposed a resolution on Japanese military sexual slavery to the US House of Representatives Committee on Foreign Affairs in 1997, for the first time in the United States, Congressman Lane Allen Evans, also from Illinois, proposed this resolution on five occasions starting in 2000, only to be frustrated each time. In January 2007, however, Michael "Mike" Makoto Honda, a Congressman from California, made an attempt once again, which led to a public hearing on the issue including testimonies by victims, for the first time in the history of the US Congress, in February of the same year, and

strongly argued that there had been no "coercion in the narrow sense." Indeed, he had maintained the stance that there had been no coercion in the narrow sense since as early as 1997 (*Choson Sinbo*, March 20, 2007).[8]

This was repeated in the advertisement that 60 Japanese National Diet members, professors, and critics published in the *Washington Post* on June 14, 2007 under the title of "The Facts" as well. In other words, there had been no forced mobilization of sex slaves using physical violence by Japanese government officials. Such an obsession with so-called coercion in the narrow sense is pervasive among all conservative groups in Japan. *The Yomiuri Shimbun* has argued that the "key to the issue of military comfort women lies in whether there was forced taking by Japanese government officials" (*Yomiuri Shimbun*, March 5 and August 1, 2007).

As will be mentioned later, most South Korean survivors were taken through fraud and violence. In other words, they were made to go to Japanese military comfort stations against their wishes. Even in cases of taking through fraud, the majority of these victims were either placed under control during movement via means such as ships and trains or confined to comfort stations by Japanese soldiers or military police officers when they tried to return home after realizing that they were being sent to comfort stations. That is, taking through employment fraud, too, was only a starting stage of the larger category of violent taking by the Japanese armed forces. Countless documents on the overall coerciveness of Japanese military sexual slavery thus including the transport of women and the situation of control at comfort stations and the Japanese government's systematic intervention including the planning of the comfort station system and the establishment and operation of these facilities have been discovered, and records showing that women were violently taken from diverse areas in Asia have been discovered.

Even more noteworthy is the fact that the mobilization of Japanese

---

the resolution passed the US House of Representatives Committee on Foreign Affairs in June. Finally, on July 30, a resolution demanding the Japanese government's official apology was unanimously passed in the House of Representatives.

8 His remarks at a subcommittee of the Committee on Budget, House of Representatives on May 27, 1997; his written contribution to the Group of National Diet Members Who Consider the Future of Japan and History Education 日本の前途と歴史教育を考える議員の會 in December 1997; his remarks at the House of Representatives Committee on Budget on December 6, 2006, etc.

military sex slaves through fraud, not so-called coercion in the narrow sense, was acknowledged as unlawful and punishable by the Japanese Penal Code as well. Regarding a case where Japanese women were abducted by deception from Nagasaki, Japan to a Japanese navy-designated comfort station in 1932, during the Shanghai Incident, the Nagasaki District Court of Appeals 長崎地方裁判所控訴院 punished the mobilizers in 1936 by applying the then current Japanese Penal Code. Although the defendants appealed, in 1937, the Supreme Court of Judicature 大審院 dismissed this and confirmed the original sentence of guilty. The original verdict of this criminal case was discovered later, in 2004, by Japanese scholar Totsuka Etsuro. Presented after a Cabinet meeting decision, Prime Minister Abe Shinzo's written reply to "Statement of Questions on the Issue of 'Comfort Women' 「慰安婦」問題に關する質問主意書," which was submitted three times in 2014 by Councilor Fujita Yukihisa, acknowledged: a provision in the Japanese Penal Code at the time had defined the transport of victims from mainland Japan to abroad (not only by violence but also) by deception as the crime of abduction, and this provision had been applicable also to the commitment of the same crime even in Japanese territories outside Japan proper (e.g., Korean Peninsula).[9] In other words, employment fraud committed against countless victims of Japanese military sexual slavery, too, had constituted the crime of abduction.[10]

2. An Analysis of the Testimonies of South Korean Victims

As mentioned earlier, the Japanese right wing has questioned the credibility of testimonies by former military sex slaves, and even conscientious scholars have tended to view such testimonies only as

9 As for Japanese newspaper articles, statements of questions from the National Diet and the Japanese government's written replies to them, and research papers containing detailed accounts of this, see Totsuka Etsuro, 2015: 30-32.

10 In Japan, too, there is a case where damage due to abduction based on civilians' cajolery is understood as abduction by the victimizing nation. The Japanese National Police Agency defined and announced the case where Tanaka Minoru, a restaurant employee, was sent to North Korea in 1978 through the restaurant owner's cajolery as "abduction by North Korea" (Yoshimi Yoshiaki, 2013: 29-30).

supplements to documentary materials. As for the value of testimonies in terms of social history, the new historiography has already and amply reached a consensus.[11] Conducted here is a statistical analysis of the contents of the testimonies of over 170 former military sex slaves in addition to the results of in-depth interviews of a smaller number of victims, which will be highly valid for judging the general trend in the forced mobilization of women as sex slaves. Because, from among this sheer number of former sex slaves, most survivors are separated in their respective spaces of daily life without any contact with activist organizations or other victims except for the some 50 who either are devoted to the movement to redress the issue or maintain contact with the Korean Council, it is very unlikely for the survivors to testify falsely about experiences from over 50 years ago with the same phrasing. It must be noted that, in the statistical analysis below, the total number of the cases analyzed differs for each category because of differences in the information obtainable from the data based on the victims' reports to the South Korean Ministry of Health and Welfare.

1) The Periods in Which Women Were Taken and the Victims' Characteristics

Women were taken from colonial Korea through methods including employment fraud, human trafficking, kidnapping, threats, and violence. The distribution of such methods of taking women as Japanese military sex slaves differed somewhat according to the period. The general perception is that the women thus taken inevitably must have been from the lower classes in order to minimize the social controversy that would have been caused by such criminal ways of taking the victims. However, when the characteristics of the victims from the analysis of testimonies presented in this section are compared with the overall social circumstances in the era, the taking of women seems to have been committed indiscriminately against all Korean women instead of being

11 One example is a work by James Hoopes (1995), where he thus stresses the importance of testimonies: "History… is a test of our ability imaginatively to place ourselves in the positions of other people."

directed at particular classes. Before discussing the methods by which women were taken, the periods in which women were taken and the characteristics of these victims will be examined.

(1) The Periods in Which Women Were Taken

Begun in approximately 1932, when Japan invaded Manchuria and began to station occupation forces in locations including Shanghai, the establishment of Japanese military comfort stations became full-fledged in 1937, when Japan invaded mainland China, and continued until the end of the war. The eras in which women were taken as sex slaves wholly reflect such trends in the establishment of military comfort stations. In other words, women were taken throughout the period from 1932 to 1945, with their number drastically increasing from 1937 onwards. While there were some changes from 1937 to 1945 in Japan's military comfort station policy and the circumstances of the subjects who established these facilities (see Chapter 2), the taking of women as sex slaves continued to increase (see <Table 3-1>). In order to examine more closely changes

⟨Table 3-1⟩ The number of victims taken per period

Year	No. of victims	Period	No. of victims
1932	1	1932-36	16
1933	2		
1934	1		
1935	5		
1936	7		
1937	16	1937-39	45
1938	14		
1939	15		
1940	24	1940-41	45
1941	21		
1942	27	1942-43	43
1943	16		
1944	23	1944-45	26
1945	3		
Total	175	Total	175

during the era beginning in 1937, when the war was urgently expanded and the number of military sex slaves rose drastically, this section will divide the period further into the years 1937-1939, 1940-1941, 1942-1943, and 1944-1945 for the sake of convenience.

(2) Family and Educational Backgrounds

Nearly without exception, the victims were from family backgrounds of impoverished agricultural households and very low educational levels. However, such backgrounds do not mean that the taking of women as Japanese military sex slaves took place in colonial Korea with a focus on the lowest socioeconomic class. This is because former sex slaves' circumstances were not much removed from the average economic and educational levels of the entire population of colonial Korea. Indeed, at the time, over 80% of the population in colonial Korea was engaged in agriculture and fishery (as of 1933, 80.5% of the Koreans were farmers and 1.5% were fishers; Yi Yeoseong and Kim Se-yong, 1933: 62), and even the agricultural population consisted mostly of impoverished tenant farmers, semi-tenant farmers, and small-income independent farmers.[12] When almost the entire population except for a very small minority is thus seen to have been indigent, it becomes difficult to argue that the taking of Korean women as Japanese military sex slaves was concentrated on any particular class. The same holds true of the educational level also. Because 19.9% of school age children were enrolled in "ordinary schools" (primary schools) as of 1931 (Yi Yeoseong and Kim Se-yong, 1931: 82-83), the victims' educational level was, in fact, close to the average for the entire colonial Korea (see <Table 3-2>).

〈Table 3-2〉 The educational levels of victims at the time that they were taken

Educational level	No education	Night school	Primary school dropout	Primary school graduate	Middle school or above	Total
No. of victims	11	5	18	4	3	41

12 There are many studies on poverty in Korea during this period. For example, in 1930, 48% of all agricultural households in the colony suffered from food shortage in spring (Park Kyung-Sik, 1986).

In other words, although the victims of the Japanese military comfort station system came from an extremely impoverished and nearly uneducated class, they were not concentrated in the lowest class so that the taking of Korean women as Japanese military sex slaves must be seen not as having been carefully directed at the lowest class in colonial Korea but as having been directed indiscriminately at all Korean women, with the exception only of a small number of the uppermost class.

(3) The Ages at Which Women Were Taken

While the minimal legal age at which a woman could become a prostitute 娼婦 as a part of licensed prostitution 公娼制 was 18 or above in Japan and 17 or above in colonial Korea (Yamashita Yeong-Ae, 1991), the minimal legal age restriction does not seem to have been uniformly set in the case of Japanese military sex slaves. Available thus far are a document from 1938 stating that women who wish to travel to China for employment must be aged at least 21 (Chief, Bureau of Police and Public Security, Ministry of Home Affairs, 1938) and the regulations of the Japanese army in China from 1940 stipulating that prostitutes 娼妓 must be aged at least 16 (Division of Special Affairs, Ro Group, 1940), and most regulations on comfort stations in Japanese military documents do not mention the sex slaves' ages. In fact, the 1938 document cited above records that even such age restrictions were not observed (Yoshimi Yoshiaki, 1998: 106-107).

Amid such circumstances, the youngest age at which women were taken as military sex slaves was 11. While one out of the 175 victims who have reported was taken at the age of 27, the greatest number of these women was taken at an age between 14 and 19, especially between 16 and 17. The 1993 investigations of 19 victims interviewed in depth by the Korean Research Group have yielded the same results (Korean Council for the Women Drafted for Military Sexual Slavery by Japan and the Korean Chongshindae Research Group, eds., 1993: 18-19).

One interesting fact is that, from 1932 to 1936, when military comfort stations had yet to be expanded considerably, the ages of the victims were concentrated in the 14-19 range, but the highest and lowest limits of the victims' ages expanded greatly as demands for sex slaves increased considerably afterwards (see <Table 3-3>).

〈Table 3-3〉 The periods in and the ages at which victims were taken

(Unit: No. of people)

Age \ Period of taking	1932-36	1937-39	1940-41	1942-43	1944-45	Total
11		1		2		3
12		3	1	1		5
13		1	1	3	1	6
14	6	2		2	7	17
15	2	8	3	4	3	20
16	4	7	13	9	5	38
17	1	11	10	7	3	32
18	2	3	6	6	2	19
19	1	3	4	1	1	10
20		1	3	1	1	6
21		1	1	4	1	7
22			1	2	1	4
23		1	1			2
24		2	1	1	1	5
27		1				1
Total	16	45	45	43	26	175

(4) The Places from Which Women Were Taken

Although the victims were generally taken from rural areas, the mobilization of women as military sex slaves occurred on a wide scale in urban areas including Seoul, Busan, Gwangju, and Daegu also. As for urban areas, employment agencies 職業紹介所, which began to be established for labor mobilization in the 1920s, and business establishments such as eating houses 飮食店 and *gisaengs*' 妓生[13] unions

13 [TN] These were traditional Korean female professional entertainers similar to geishas in Japan.

券番,[14] which continued to increase in number during the Japanese colonial era, occasionally served as channels for the mobilization of Korean women as Japanese military sex slaves. Nevertheless, the forms of mobilization consisted mostly of fraud, kidnapping, and violence committed by civilians, police officers, soldiers, and government officials and therefore differed little from those used in rural areas. However, let us examine mobilization through employment agencies briefly here. In the 1930s, employment agencies functioned as the lowest organs in transferring and deploying laborers from colonial Korea to Japan as well as other areas within Korea. In 1940, with the proclamation of the Ordinance on Employment Agencies in Korea 朝鮮職業紹介所令, these agencies were switched from municipal management to state management, thus strengthening state control much further (Kim Min-Young, 1995: 58-63). The fact that, in cities, the majority of former victims were taken through employment agencies further ascertains state involvement in the mobilization of women as military sex slaves.

As for regions from which former sex slaves were taken, North and South Gyeongsang Provinces ranked overwhelmingly high, with North and South Jeolla Provinces coming next. Even when taking into consideration the fact that the survivors making reports are likely to have come from southern Korea because they are residents of South Korea, Gyeongsang Provinces took up a far greater share than did other regions. In addition, such a high proportion of Gyeongsang Provinces held true also of all Korean residents in Japan including men (see <Table 3-4>).[15] Nor have records proving that the targets of mobilization were assigned discriminately per region been found. As has been mentioned above, when the taking of women is considered to have been committed indiscriminately, without distinction among the victims, it is difficult to view such taking as having been planned differentially according to the area.

Even if not planned, a large number of Korean women would have

14 [TN] Also written as 券班, 檢番, or 見番, these organizations were Korean adaptations of geishas' unions in Japan.

15 As of 1942, the ratio of Korean residents in Japan by the province of their origin was, in the following order: South Gyeongsang Province, 34.4%; North Gyeongsang Province, 23.8%; and South Jeolla Province, 17.3% (Bureau of Police and Public Security, Ministry of Home Affairs, 1942).

〈Table 3-4〉 The places from which victims were taken

Starting point	No. of victims
Seoul	14
Busan	10
Gwangju	1
Daegu	8
South Gyeongsang Province	43
North Gyeongsang Province	36
South Jeolla Province	13
North Jeolla Province	13
North and South Chungcheong Provinces	10
Gangwon Province	2
Gyeonggi Province	4
North and South Hamgyong Provinces	5
North and South Pyongan Provinces	5
Hwanghae Province	1
Manchuria	3
China	2
Total	170

been taken from Gyeongsang Provinces, especially South Gyeongsang Province, to become Japanese military sex slaves for geographical reasons above all. Because the destination of both labor mobilization and migration was Japan, South Gyeongsang Province, due to its physical proximity, would have given rise to many mobilizers as well as migrants. In the case of Japanese military sexual slavery, however, because many victims were taken not only to Japan but also to China and the South Seas Mandate, yet another reason besides the provinces' closeness to Japan can be cited. This second reason is that Busan frequently played the role of a midpoint in the process of deploying women to military comfort stations. Because former sex slaves were first collected in Busan and then shipped elsewhere by sea in numerous cases, North and South Gyeongsang

Provinces, close to this city, were convenient places from which to take women. Of course, the fact that the absolute number of people in and the population density of Gyeongsang Provinces were higher than those of other provinces,[16] too, seems to have been an important reason.

(5) The Places to Which Women Were Taken

The places to which the victims were taken as Japanese military sex slaves included colonial Korea, Japan, Manchuria, Formosa, China, Southeast Asia, and South Seas Mandate, extending throughout territories occupied by the Japanese armed forces (see <Table 3-5>). In other words, women from colonial Korea were taken "wherever it was necessary for the Japanese Army to fight."[17] Though it will be discussed later, this was possible because the Japanese armed forces were in charge of transporting military sex slaves. While Japanese soldiers' morale and rape of local women as a result of the prolongation of the nation's military presence abroad have been known as the direct reasons for mobilizing women as

〈Table 3-5〉 The places to which victims were taken

Destination	Korea	Japan	Formosa	Manchuria	China	Southeast Asia	South Seas Mandate	Total
No. of victims	1	20	12	15	27	8	6	89

16 In 1940, the most populous provinces throughout colonial Korea were, in the following order: Gyeonggi Province, 2,864,389 people; South Jeolla Province, 2,638,969 people; North Gyeongsang Province, 2,472,211 people; and South Gyeongsang Province, 2,241,902 people. As for the population density, the highest provinces were, in the following order: Gyeonggi Province, 223 people/km^2; South Chungcheong Province, 195 people/km^2; South Jeolla Province, 190 people/km^2; North Jeolla Province, 186 people/km^2; South Gyeongsang Province, 182 people/km^2; and North Gyeongsang Province, 130 people/km^2 (Government-General of Korea, 1940b: 20-21). The situation was slightly different for the agricultural population, for whom the order was, in 1930: North Gyeongsang Province, 1,946,324 people; South Jeolla Province, 1,826,923 people; and South Gyeongsang Province, 1,547,044 people (Lee Hoon Koo, 1936: 50).

17 "The 'comfort girls' have been found wherever it was necessary for the Japanese Army to fight," Psychological Warfare Team, United States Army Forces India-Burma Theater, United States Office of War Information, "Japanese Prisoner of War Interrogation Report No. 49" (Record Group 208, Entry 366A, Box 231), October 1, 1944.

military sex slaves,[18] the fact that a considerable number of sex slaves were deployed even to comfort stations within Japan demonstrates that the reason for the establishment of military comfort stations lay more fundamentally in the Japanese armed forces' need for women. The fact that military comfort stations in Japan proper used women taken from colonial Korea, not Japanese women, demonstrates well the following: the basic policy of annihilating Korean women's motherhood, which contrasted with the policy of protecting Japanese women's motherhood implemented in the 1930s-1940s (see Chapter 4), was one background of the establishment of Japanese military comfort station policies; and the mobilization of military sex slaves in colonial Korea was implemented in the context of the general mobilization system together with labor mobilization and military mobilization.

2) The Methods of Taking Women

According to materials on reports made by former Japanese military sex slaves to the South Korean government, these women were taken most often through employment fraud, with violence and threats coming next. This pattern shows that the mobilization of women as sex slaves occurred against the backdrop of poverty and through the active intervention of the Japanese government and military. As has been mentioned above, the number of cases where mobilization methods such as human trafficking and kidnapping were used is unexpectedly small even when the possibility of their combination with employment fraud is taken into consideration. Some victims have recalled and stated pretexts for mobilization such as "supply to the government 供出," "Service Corps 奉仕隊," and "Labor Corps 勤労隊," which, in the end, signifies that these women left due to coercion from the Japanese colonial authorities even when they were suspicious of the accuracy of such pretexts. Other former sex slaves have been found to have been sent to military comfort stations through the Labor Volunteer Corps 勤労挺身隊 system (see <Table 3-6>).

---

18 Materials such as the Headquarters, Gunnery Unit, "Measures for Arousing Soldiers' Morale as Observed in the Experience of the Second Sino-Japanese War," September 19, 1940; and 9th Infantry Brigade, *Field Diary*, July 1-31, 1938 state such direct purposes.

〈Table 3-6〉 The methods of taking women per period (Unit: No. of people)

Periods of taking / Method of taking	1932-36	1937-39	1940-41	1942-43	1944-45	Total
Employment fraud	9	24	21	16	12	82
Threats and violence	7	12	20	20	3	62
Human trafficking		4				4
Kidnapping and abduction		2	1	2		5
Labor Volunteer Corps 勤労挺身隊					6	6
Escape from the Labor Volunteer Corps					2	2
Supply to the government 供出, Service Corps 奉仕隊, Labor Corps 勤労隊, etc.		3	3	5	3	14

(1) Employment Fraud

According to the testimonies of former Japanese military sex slaves who followed mobilizers because of promises that they would secure employment at "good [work]places," only to end up in military comfort stations, these supposedly desirable destinations were diverse. The most frequently cited workplaces were factories in Japan. These women could earn money if they worked hard for several years, the mobilizers claimed, and return to Korea whenever they wished. Slightly closer to the reality yet nevertheless attractive to the victims were promises of employment such as working with injured soldiers at hospitals and working as military nurses.[19]

19 Segments of the American military that investigated the Japanese armed forces likewise discovered numerous Korean women and thus reported: "…Japanese agents arrived in Korea for the purpose of enlisting Korean girls for 'comfort service' in newly conquered Japanese territories in Southeast Asia. The nature of this 'service' was not specified but it was assumed to be work connected with visiting the wounded in hospitals, rolling bandages, and generally making the soldiers happy. The inducement used by these agents was plenty of money, an opportunity to pay off the family debts, easy work… On the basis of these false representations many girls enlisted for overseas duty…" (Psychological Warfare Team, United States Army Forces India-Burma Theater, United States Office of War Information, "Japanese Prisoner of War Interrogation Report No. 49" (Record Group 208, Entry 366A, Box 231), October 1, 1944).

Although the majority of the victims set out, thus lured by mobilizers, without even informing their families in order to shake free the yoke of poverty, some of them have testified that a sum of money was given to their families under the pretext of "emergency funds" or "advance payments." It is unclear just how general this was. Nor were the amounts paid uniform. According to interrogations of prisoners of war conducted by the Allied Forces in 1944 in Burma, the women reported that they had received cash advances of a few hundred yen and left their homes due to mobilizers' fraudulent claims that they would be engaged in work such as treating injured Japanese soldiers. Allied interrogators reported that these women, the majority of whom were ignorant and impoverished, had received the cash advances in order to appropriate the money for the repayment of their families' debts and that the cash advances had bound the women to military regulations and comfort station managers for durations of 6 months-1 year.[20]

Such prepayments are reminiscent of numerous cases where, in the mobilization of laborers, anyone was grabbed and taken by mobilizers like beaters on hunts at the level of townships 面, the lowest administrative unit, and paid emergency funds even though "official mediation 官斡旋" was the pretext and of the customary practice where the Labor Section 勞務係 in a township office 面事務所 would request the Vocation Section 職業係 for the supply to the government 供出, of manpower, presenting approximately 50-100 yen as advance payments (Kim Min-Young, 1995: 88). While the Japanese colonial authorities' intervention is clear in labor mobilization, in most cases of the mobilization of women as military sex slaves, in general, only civilians' intervention is apparent on the surface. Nevertheless, a considerable number of people have testified that Japanese soldiers, police officers, and government officials directly led employment fraud as well. However, the fact that, in addition to exhibiting many similarities to labor mobilization through official mediation, the procurement of large sums of money for the provision of

20 Psychological Warfare Team, United States Army Forces India-Burma Theater, United States Office of War Information, "Japanese Prisoner of War Interrogation Report No. 49" (Record Group 208, Entry 366A, Box 231), October 1, 1944; requoted from Ahn Byung Jik, trans., 2013: 408.

advance payments would have been difficult for civilians clearly shows that, even if the majority of individuals who committed employment fraud on the lowest level were civilians, employment fraud was ultimately committed under the supervision of the Japanese armed forces and government and that the Government-General of Korea intervened as well. In fact, there are documents that can prove this. Extant are records showing that, on May 1, 1945, "[t]he [Japanese] Army" sent 76,000 yen as "money for the importation of prostitutes [i.e., comfort women]" from the Bank of Mengchiang [i.e., Mengkiang] 蒙疆銀行 in Kalgan (present-day Zhangjiakou) to the Naikoku Bank 內國銀行[21] in Seoul. On June 4 of the same year, the Japanese armed forces made a request for the return of this amount, in response to which the chief of the Bureau of Financial Affairs 財務局 in the Government-General of Korea sent a reply stating that, although it was difficult to render the money according to the regulations of the Japanese Ministry of the Treasury 大藏省, efforts were being made.[22] These documents clearly show that Japanese military sexual slavery was implemented through the general mobilization of the Japanese armed forces and government, Government-General of Korea, banks, and comfort women mobilizers.

21 [TN] The US military decodes the name of the receiving bank in the Japanese army's encrypted radio communication (https://archives.seoul.go.kr/item/17) as both "?KEIJŌ [i.e., Seoul] NATIONAL BANK?" and "KEIJŌ (?NAIKOKU?) GINKŌ [i.e., Bank]." The question marks here perhaps imply the uncertainty of such interpretations, a point overlooked by Pang Sun-joo's study on this document and the reply to it (https://archives.seoul.go.kr/item/46) mentioned in the next footnote. According to the Japanese Bankers Association's 全國銀行協會 database of the history of changes to Japanese banks at https://s-opac.net/Opac/search.htm?s=OuE-_cBuDY2FFDpl1TgIkz-R2Co, however, there was no Japanese bank with the word 國家 or 國立 (both translatable as "national") in its name in this period. It is also unclear whether or not the decoded name refers to the Naikoku Chokin ("Domestic Savings") Bank 內國貯金銀行 (1912-1945). See the War Department, "S-11414" (Record Group 457, Entry A1 9032, Box 900; June 15, 1945) and "S-12382" (Record Group 457, Entry A1 9032, Box 900; June 29, 1945).

22 These are Japanese army and navy documents deciphered by the US armed forces currently stored at the National Archives and Records Administration: "S-11414" (decoded: June 15, 1945) WS 13674 6/4/1945; and "S-12382" (decoded: June 29, 1945) WS 15211 6/13/1945 from the S-Series (SJM). They are stamped, "TOP SECRET ULTRA." Requoted from Pang Sun-joo, 1992: 237-238.

(2) Threats and Violence

Literally violent taking was nearly as frequent as employment fraud. Many former sex slaves have testified that they were loaded on trucks by force. Some have testified that they were forcibly taken to police stations while walking in the street. Though this will be discussed later, such violent taking was committed, in most cases, by Japanese soldiers and police officers, especially by the latter. On the contrary, civilians resorted to violence in very few cases. The Japanese government's report (1993) claiming that while forced taking did occur in some cases, it was committed by civilians and unrelated to the government itself directly contradicts the testimonies of the victims. It must be noted that, according to a considerable number of testimonies, violent taking was directly committed by the Government-General of Korea and the Japanese military, with civilians resorting to this method occasionally.

(3) Human Trafficking and Kidnapping

Although not numerous, still notable are cases of the mobilization of women for Japanese military comfort stations based on human trafficking without advance payments. These include women who were sold off: by their adoptive families after having been sent to other families as stepdaughters due to poverty; by the owners of restaurants or stores where they were working; and, most tragically, by their own fathers. Out of the 175 victims who have made reports, however, only four were sent to military comfort stations through human trafficking. Even when diverse errors are taken into consideration, this is a very small number. As one reason for this rarity of human trafficking, it is possible to cite, above all, the near absence of a custom of parents selling off their own daughters in Korea, unlike in some other countries. In fact, even in the poorest rural communities, only one case of selling one's own daughter has been discovered, and, in most cases, former sex slaves have testified of the utter wretchedness of their parents at losing their daughters through employment fraud or violence. If there had been a custom of parents selling off their own daughters, the mobilization of Japanese military sex slaves in colonial Korea would have been far easier, and the number of women mobilized would have increased as well. The relatively low degree of the spread of prostitution in the colony, too, can be seen as a backdrop of the comparative rarity of human trafficking. This also explains the fact that while many cases of prostitution in Korea stemmed from kidnapping in this period, the number of women taken as Japanese military sex slaves from the territory through kidnapping was very small. There is also a record that, during the first half of 1943, the Japanese armed forces committed the "forced abduction" of five young local women in Solo (also known as "Soerakarta"; present-day Surakarta) in the Netherlands East Indies.[23]

(4) Mobilization through the Labor Volunteer Corps System

The common perception among those who have lived through the colonial and wartime eras is that the concept of the "Volunteer Corps 挺身隊" comprehensively designated the mobilization of laborers and military sex slaves alike.[24] Because "Volunteer Corps," literally signifying "corps for sacrificing oneself physically and voluntarily (for the nation)," was a concept used to mobilize people in various fields including medical service and news coverage, military comfort women mobilizers likewise may have misappropriated the name of these corps when mobilizing women. However, there is, in fact, considerable possibility for the institution of the "Volunteer Corps" to have encompassed the mobilization of military sex slaves in addition to mobilization for diverse other purposes. It must be noted that, notwithstanding suspicion cast in Japan over the credibility of the contents of his testimonies, Yoshida Seiji (Yoshida Seiji, 1989) uses the term "Korean Women's Volunteer Corps for the Consolation of the Imperial Armed Forces 皇軍慰問朝鮮人女子挺身隊." One former Japanese soldier who was a member of the Communication Education Corps 通信教育隊 in Fuchin (present-day Fujin) in Heilungkiang Province (present-day Heilongjiang Province), China in 1944 has testified that he encountered Japanese military sex slaves who had been brought

23 Netherlands Forces Intelligence Service, "Compilation of NEFIS Interrogation Reports Nos. 418-425 Inclusive (Not Issued Separately)" (October 23, 1944).

24 The fact that the *Maeil Sinbo* 每日申報 (March 7, 1944, etc.), a mouthpiece of the Government-General of Korea, often published articles lamenting the Koreans' tendency at the time to view the Volunteer Corps 挺身隊 as a means of either mobilization for labor or human trafficking paradoxically reveals colonial Koreans' perception of this institution.

as members of the "Special Wartime Women's Volunteer Corps for the Kwantung Army 關東軍戰時特別女子挺身隊" (Editorial Board of *Military Comfort Women #110*, ed., 1992: 44-45).

More specifically, widespread among those who have lived during this era is the idea that the Labor Volunteer Corps system, which had already been implemented through official mediation but was subsequently officialized by an imperial edict in 1944, was used as a means of mobilizing women as military sex slaves as well. Kawaoka, a Japanese teacher who, at the time, worked at a primary school in colonial Korea, has testified that all of the eight students who left to be members of the Labor Volunteer Corps at her recommendation later became military sex slaves (*Hankook Ilbo*, January 17, 1992). Another teacher named Ikeda Masae, too, has stated that the number of students from her school who left to be members of the Labor Volunteer Corps and that of students who subsequently and actually worked at factories in Japan did not agree (*Dong-A Ilbo*, January 15, 1992), thus implying that the students who represented the difference between these two figures most likely were sent to military comfort stations.

From among the over 170 former sex slaves who have reported to the South Korean Ministry of Health and Welfare, six victims have testified that they were mobilized as members of the Labor Volunteer Corps but later taken to military comfort stations.[25] These women have testified that they were mobilized, while still at school, as members of the Labor Volunteer Corps at their teachers' recommendation, then taken to military comfort stations after only receiving training at factories or after working there for some time. One of them has testified that she was shipped to a military comfort station while working at a factory, together with many other fellow workers, after the destruction of the factory building due to bombing.

On the other hand, two of the victims have testified that, while working as members of the Labor Volunteer Corps at factories in Japan, they escaped, unable to bear the duress of the labor, only to be captured and forcibly taken to military comfort stations. Of course, these

25 Besides the six individuals in the statistics as of December 1993, used in this study, two more individuals were discovered later.

testimonies do not mean that women became military sex slaves through the institution of the Labor Volunteer Corps itself. Nevertheless, if there were many cases where, regardless of the reasons, women were mobilized as members of the Labor Volunteer Corps and sent to Japan and then became military sex slaves, it is possible to say that the Labor Volunteer Corps system served as one channel in the mobilization of women as military sex slaves (see Chapter 1).

(5) Others: Under the Pretexts of Supply to the Government, Service Corps, and Labor Corps

Not a few of the victims have testified that they were taken under the pretext of supply to the government, Volunteer Corps, or Labor Corps, then sent to military comfort stations. Under the National Mobilization 國家總動員 system, numerous institutions were created for the mobilization of women's labor. They included the Patriotic Labor Corps 勤勞報國隊, Women's Promotion Corps 女子推進隊, and the mobilization of students. The Patriotic Labor Corps and the mobilization of students were institutions established, respectively, through the Ordinance on National Cooperation with Patriotic Labor 國民勤勞報國協力令 of 1941 and the Ordinance on Students' Labor 學徒勤勞令 of 1944, and the recruitment of members of the Women's Promotion Corps was implemented through government organs' mediation and recommendation. On the other hand, in colonial Korea, the expression "supply of unmarried women to the government 處女供出" was widespread during this era, and the terms "Service Corps 奉仕隊" and "Labor Corps 勤勞隊" likewise seem to have been used in the mobilization of women. It is likely that former military sex slaves were drafted through the official institutions mentioned above but do not remember the precise names of these institutions or that mobilizers took women as sex slaves while using arbitrary expressions such as the "supply to the government 供出" of women. In addition, not a few women were taken as military sex slaves through employment fraud or violence, as with the victims mentioned above, but are likely to have imprinted on their memories expressions that were pervasive during the era including the "supply of women to the government" and now remember their past situations as such. For example, one former military sex slave who made a report to the South Korean Ministry of Health and Welfare in the mid-1990s had been taken to a military base in Japan by the police probably in 1944 and then typically raped during relocation with the military unit. At present, however, the survivor herself and her family state that she "went as [a member of] the Unmarried Women's Patriotic Corps 處女報國隊 and was ruined by those Japanese bastards."

The fact that former sex slaves remember such pretexts in any case and that, as will be discussed later, mobilization under these pretexts was implemented mainly by Japanese police officers and government officials clearly demonstrates that this was mobilization through official intervention.

3) The Mobilizers

Regarding the creation of the policy on Japanese military comfort stations and the management of these facilities, while the clear chain of command can only be conjectured in terms of the structures of imperial Japan's armed forces and government, partly discovered documentary materials indubitably demonstrate the leading roles of the Japanese military and government and the Government-General of Korea (Yoshimi Yoshiaki and Hayashi Hirofumi, eds., 1995: 16-19). Moreover, regardless of the question of at whose orders mobilizers on the lowest level resorted to methods such as fraud and violence mentioned above, these individuals' characteristics clearly show the central roles of the Japanese military and government and the Government-General of Korea. Although the victims' testimonies confirm that the vast majority of the mobilizers were civilians, Koreans in particular, they demonstrate that Japanese police officers, soldiers, and government officials, too, were very important direct mobilizers. The results of research that while civilians generally took the victims through the method of employment fraud, soldiers and police officers took the women through violence, and officials took the victims based on pretexts such as "supply to the government" confirm general predictions, thus highly strengthening the credibility of the victims' statements (see <Table 3-7>).

〈Table 3-7〉 The mobilizers and the methods of taking victims

(Unit: No. of people)

Mobilizers \ Method of taking	Employment fraud	Violence	Threats	Human trafficking	Kidnapping	Labor Volunteer Corps 勤勞挺身隊	Supply to the government 供出, Service Corps 奉仕隊, Labor Corps 勤勞隊, etc.	Total
Korean civilians	38	3	1	1	2		2	47
Japanese civilians	17	6		1		3		27
Soldiers	4	18					2	24
Civilian employees of the military 軍屬	1						1	2
Military police	2	3						5
Police	6	26	1		3		3	39
Officials	4	2				2	4	12
Others		1						1

(1) Civilians

As can be seen from a Japanese military document that stipulates, "To prevent disturbances in the recruitment process, care must be taken in the selection of those who are to execute [the] recruitment [of comfort women]" (Department of Military Affairs, Bureau of Military Affairs, Ministry of War, March 4, 1938), in the plans of the Japanese armed forces, the principal and lowest mobilizers in the recruitment of Japanese military sex slaves were civilians. According to the military document above, these civilian mobilizers were selected by the Japanese military and in charge solely of recruiting women. In fact, many former sex slaves have testified that the civilians who had taken them disappeared at one point, after handing them over to other civilians or Japanese soldiers. As will be discussed in the following section, the Japanese armed forces were responsible for the transport of military sex slaves. Judging from the fact that there was a considerable number of civilians also among Japanese military comfort station managers,[26] it is apparent that the civilians in charge of recruiting sex slaves and those in charge of managing comfort stations were separate and that the entire process encompassing not only the selection of both recruiters and station managers but also the recruitment and deployment of sex slaves was supervised by the military.

As investigations by Senda Kakou (Senda Kakou, 1978) demonstrate, however, in not a few cases, military comfort station managers themselves recruited sex slaves. Likewise, in investigations by the Korean Research Group, there is a case where the same individual not only accompanied a victim from the moment she was taken from colonial Korea to the moment she arrived at a comfort station but also managed the same facility. As <Table 3-8> shows, regardless of whether comfort stations

〈Table 3-8〉 The relationship between mobilizers and comfort station managers

(Unit: No. of people)

Mobilizers / Managers	Korean civilians	Japanese civilians	Soldiers	Civilian employees of the military 軍屬
Civilians	17	7	1	1
Soldiers	10	11	12	1
Mobilizers / Managers	**Military Police**	**Police**	**Officials**	**Total**
Civilians	2	2		30
Soldiers	1	13	6	54

26 When the forms of the establishment and management of military comfort stations are classified, there is information on comfort station managers in the data on 90 former sex slaves from among those who have reported to the South Korean Ministry of Health and Welfare. 30 of these victims have testified that civilians managed comfort stations while the remaining 60 have testified that soldiers were comfort station managers.

managers themselves were civilians or soldiers, the majority of the mobilizers were civilians at any rate. However, the fact that when women were taken by Japanese soldiers or police officers to be turned into sex slaves, they were sent, in most cases, to comfort stations managed by soldiers and that women taken by civilian mobilizers more often tended to end up in stations managed by civilians rather than soldiers implies that, in not a few cases, the same individuals took women as sex slaves and managed comfort stations.

The fact that more Koreans than Japanese constituted civilians participating in the mobilization of women as military sex slaves and the management of comfort stations left delicate emotional scars on the victims. It is possible to grasp that this larger proportion of Koreans among the civilian mobilizers and comfort station managers stemmed from the Japanese armed forces' consistent policy at the time of placing Koreans in positions of direct war criminals on the lowest level such as prisoner of war camp wardens in addition to the greater ease for Koreans to take women from colonial Korea.

(2) Soldiers, Civilian Employees of the Military, and the Military Police Corps

Also considerable are cases where Korean women were taken by members of the Japanese armed forces including soldiers, civilian employees of the military 軍屬, and military police officers. Many victims have testified that they were forcibly loaded on trucks and taken somewhere by soldiers, stopping in the course to load many other women. As <Table 3-6> demonstrates, violent taking became more frequent and serious later, which can be interpreted as the direct and violent intervention of Japanese soldiers in the recruitment of sex slaves, hitherto consigned mainly to civilians, due to a drastic rise in the demand for sex slaves. As has been discussed above, when taken by soldiers, the victims were sent to comfort stations managed by the military. This likewise shows that, with an increase in the Japanese armed forces' demand for sex slaves in the later period, soldiers established comfort stations and directly procured sex slaves to these facilities.[27]

27 Japanese military comfort stations tended to be directly established and managed by

(3) Police Officers and Government Officials

Also constituting a considerable portion of the total, the mobilization of Korean women as military sex slaves by Japanese police officers and government officials confirms the intervention of the Government-General of Korea in the taking of Korean women as sex slaves. Indeed, as has been demonstrated in many foregoing sections, the intervention of the Japanese government and armed forces was clear from the beginning regardless of who the direct mobilizers were. As <Table 3-6> shows, it can be said that Japanese police officers and government officials became direct mobilizers in many cases during the later period, when the demand for sex slaves rose, as with the use of violent recruitment methods. In addition, as with cases where Japanese soldiers took Korean women, when Japanese police officers and government officials directly took these women as military sex slaves, the victims were linked to comfort stations managed by Japanese soldiers.

4) The Transportation and Deployment of Women

Not only victims taken by Japanese soldiers but also most other victims have testified that they were transferred to soldiers when long-distance transportation using trains, trucks, or ships began. Subsequently, these women were shipped to their destinations under soldiers' strict surveillance. One victim taken to Manchuria by train has testified that Japanese soldiers kept watch at either ends of each car and that, in some areas, the windows were closed during transportation so that one could not see what was outside.

In addition to the fact that Japanese soldiers thus oversaw the transportation of military sex slaves, it is noteworthy that means of transportation such as trucks, trains, and ships were provided by the Japanese armed forces. According to the victims' testimonies, trucks, of course, were military trucks, and ships, in most cases, were large battleships. Indeed, when military sex slaves were sent to the battlefront by sea, conscription ships of Japanese registration managed by the

---

the armed forces in the initial stage. This shifted to the massive influx of civilians, only to revert to the military's initiative from 1943-1944 (see Chapter 2).

Japanese army were used. In the case of trains, it is even clearer that they were provided by the Japanese military. In particular, the railroads in mainland China were under the de facto control of the Japanese armed forces (Yoshimi Yoshiaki, 1998: 51-52). One Japanese comfort station manager interrogated by the Allied Forces in 1944 stated that he had departed from Busan on July 10, 1942 with 22 Korean women and sailed to Singapore via Formosa on a 4,000-ton passenger ship escorted by seven Japanese battleships. The Japanese army headquarters had provided free passage tickets.[28]

In fact, the Japanese military was in charge of the transportation of sex slaves not only from their starting points in colonial Korea to comfort stations but also from one comfort station to another. Only approximately half of the victims who have reported to the South Korean Ministry of Health and Welfare stayed in one place, and not a few were transferred three times or more.[29] Such relocation occurred either as relocation with the military unit to which a comfort station belonged or as relocation only of sex slaves, *in toto* or in part. In all of these cases, the Japanese armed forces were responsible for the transportation. In other words, the relocation of military comfort stations occurred on the basis of the Japanese military's needs and through the latter's means of transportation. Angus McDougall, an Australian soldier, was captured by the Japanese armed forces in the early stage of the Pacific War and interned in the Changi prisoner of war camp in Singapore and then sent to the Ban Pong (i.e., Nong Pladuk) prisoner of war camp in Thailand on a freight car. He has testified that, at the time, young girls likewise were transported along with the prisoners of war, accompanied by Japanese guards. The journey was like "hell," he has stated (Morris-Suzuki, 2015).

As for remote areas where it was difficult to establish military comfort stations, using their own trucks, the Japanese armed forces regularly transported sex slaves from nearby stations and returned them

28 Allied Translator and Interpreter Section, [General Headquarters,] Supreme Commander for the Allied Powers, "Research Report No. 120: Amenities in the Japanese Armed Forces" (Record Group 407, Entry A1-427, Box 913), November 15, 1945.

29 Of the 170 individuals, 96 were made to stay in the same places, 33 were relocated once, 12 were relocated twice, and 29 were relocated thrice or more, respectively (data reported to the South Korean Ministry of Health and Welfare).

to their respective stations after use for some time. Former victim Kim Bok-dong 金福童 has testified that, during such "outcall comfort," so many soldiers would rush at her that she was like a frog (Korean Chongshindae Research Group, ed., 1997: 93). Former British Commonwealth soldiers who were Japanese prisoners of war in Southeast Asia have testified that military sex slaves were regularly shipped to Japanese guards' bases. In other words, it was a system of mobile comfort stations circulating around Japanese military camps in the area (Morris-Suzuki, 2015).

All of these testimonies demonstrate the fact that the Japanese military led and supervised the transportation and deployment of sex slaves.

3. The Testimonies of Other Victims and Experiencers of Comfort Stations and Documentary Materials

1) Multiple Testimonies of Victims and Experiencers of Comfort Stations from Diverse Countries

Before elucidating documentary materials, it is necessary to discuss the testimonies. The Japanese right wing's argument mentioned earlier is that forced taking cannot be acknowledged because there only are testimonies, not documentary materials. This is based on the idea that testimonies are untrustworthy. If countless South Korean victims' testimonies that they were taken to comfort stations from the streets, homes, and villages by government officials, soldiers, and police officers are lies, it means that their testimonies have been constructed to be identical, influencing one another.

How, then, are we to understand the same testimonies coming from victims from many other countries? Already at the Women's International War Crimes Tribunal on Japan's Military Sexual Slavery in 2000 (henceforth "2000 Women's Tribunal"; see Chapter 8), victims from 11 nations testified to forced taking. In particular, I will elucidate testimonies that I personally heard during investigations conducted in Indonesia. A South Korean research team including me was able to meet two former Japanese sex slaves in Balikpapan,[30] Indonesia during January

31-February 6, 2004. One testified that she had followed the manager of an Indonesian theater troupe, deceived that she would be made an actress, only to end up at a comfort station. The other testified that she had been grabbed by her hair in the street and loaded on a small truck, on which had been four other young women already. The forms of forced taking in these testimonies were nearly identical to those in the testimonies by over 170 South Korean women discussed above. Indeed, the research team was astounded that the subsequent transportation to comfort stations, examinations for STDs, and the situation at comfort stations as recounted by these Indonesian women had been nearly identical to those in South Korean victims' testimonies.

There are numerous testimonies by former Japanese soldiers as well. In 1992, when the issue of Japanese military sexual slavery began to be known in Japanese society, *Military Comfort Women #110: The Voice of History from across the Telephone* 従軍慰安婦110番—電話の向こうから歴史の聲が, a collection of testimonies by former Japanese soldiers, was published, and this book includes diverse testimonies including those on the forced taking of women as sex slaves. Furthermore, however, it is not difficult to find passages recounting such forced taking in memoirs by former Japanese soldiers published earlier, since the 1960s. Recounting his experience of visiting a comfort station in Burma, one former soldier thus transmitted the words of a sex slave: "There was a recruitment, supposedly for workers at a munitions factory in Tokyo… I got on the ship at Incheon, but we sailed south, south… and ended up in Burma. Because I can't return [home] on foot or run away, I've given up [on returning to Korea]" (Omata Yukio, 1967: 56). Another former soldier, also recounting his experience in Burma, stated: "…Korean women aged approximately 19-20 were hunted by the hundreds under the pretext of typists, waitresses, and office clerks and were brought [to Burma] on [Japanese] government ships… Some were unmarried women from good families who had received higher education… but said that they had been forcibly brought as a group" (Hamamura Ikusaburo, 1987: 102). One

30 This is where former Japanese premier Nakasone Yasuhiro reminisced that he had established a comfort station for his subordinate soldiers during the war while working as a naval paymaster lieutenant (Nakasone Yasuhiro, 1978: 90-98).

former Japanese soldier who had participated in the war in the Territory of New Guinea (present-day Papua New Guinea) testified: "In Rabaul, there were three comfort stations for [Japanese] soldiers. I heard that young Korean women had been put on ships and brought [to the Territory of New Guinea] regardless of their wishes, utterly forcibly" (Ichikawa Yasuto, 1989: 46).

Even more vivid is the testimony of a former Japanese soldier who had an experience with a comfort station in Pingyangchen (present-day Pingyangzhen) in Mishan County (present-day Mishan (City)) in Tung'an Province (present-day eastern Heilongjiang Province), China. "The comfort woman I was familiar with used the professional Japanese name of 'Masao'. Her family was the poorest peasant family in Gangwon Province [in colonial Korea]. One day, the village elder suddenly visited them and said, 'It's an order from the military. As service to the nation, surrender your daughter'. Because they quickly understood the meaning of 'service to the nation', her parents repeatedly cried out, 'Oh, woe is me!' rubbing their hands in supplication, but the village elder did not heed them. Although this township had been assigned to supply eight unmarried women [as military sex slaves], because there were only five unmarried in the township, he said, not a single one was to be let slip. Standing behind the village elder was a Japanese police officer armed with a sword. Loaded on a truck along with rocks, the five unmarried women from the village crossed the bridge that served as the boundary of the village, never to return home again… She said, 'I receive 15 soldiers every day. My body can't take it any more. It's a wonder I'm still alive'" (Manabe Motoyuki, 1981: 129-130).

2) The Investigative Reports of the Allied Forces

Many of the Allied Forces' reports on prisoners of war record that, when the Allied Forces advanced into numerous nations in East Asia, they were puzzled by the women who were among the defeated Japanese soldiers. Since then, reports drawn up by the Allied Forces during and after the war have been discovered one after another in government archives in Western Europe as well as the National Archives and Records Administration (NARA) in the United States, and, out of these, many elucidating so-called coercion in the narrow sense have been unearthed as well. Completed as a result of the Allied Forces' multifaceted investigations including interrogations of former Japanese soldiers and sex slaves and investigations on relevant parties, many of these reports were submitted to war crime tribunals such as the Temporary Court Martial Tribunal of Batavia (present-day Jakarta; henceforth "Batavia War Criminal Court") and the International Military Tribunal for the Far East (IMTFE; also known as "Tokyo War Crimes Tribunal") immediately after the war and are, as such, trustworthy documents.

Drawn up by the American military in 1945 in Kunming, China and discovered in 2002 at the National Archives and Records Administration, the document "Attached Memorandum: Korean and Japanese Prisoners of War in Kunming: 28 April, 1945" thus records: "…all of the 23 [Korean] women became 'comfort girls', apparently under compulsion and misrepresentation."[31] Cpt. Chan of the Allied Forces, who interrogated Korean military sex slaves in Burma in 1944, reported, "Taken forcibly for the most part from their families' farms and homes in far-off Korea, they were there only for the pleasure of the Imperial Japanese troops."[32]

Although partly presented by Omura Tetsuo in the magazine *Sekai* in 1993, "Report on Enforced Prostitution in Western Borneo, N. E. I. during Japanese Naval Occupation" (IMTFE Exhibit No. 1702), a document drawn up by the NEFIS in both Dutch and English, was unearthed in the National Archives of the Netherlands and fully disclosed in 2007 by a research team from South Korea. Here, recorded very clearly is the indiscriminate and forced taking of women as sex slaves by Japanese soldiers. This document records that, in West Borneo, Netherlands East Indies, the Special Naval Police Corps 海軍特別警察隊 (abbreviated as the *Tokkeitai* 特警隊), a segment of the Japanese navy, was responsible for the establishment of comfort stations and the supply of sex slaves, indiscriminately arrested women in the streets, subjected them to physical examinations, and then placed them in comfort stations, arresting and

31 Office of Strategic Services, "Attached Memorandum: Korean and Japanese Prisoners of War in Kunming: 28 April, 1945," Kunming-REG-OP-3, Field Station Files, Records of the Office of Strategic Services (Record Group 226, Entry 154, Box 185), April 28, 1945.

32 Chan, 1986: 97.

severely ill-treating, even killing in extreme cases, the families of women who escaped from these facilities.[33]

Numerous NEFIS interrogation reports from 1944-1945 often mention Japanese military sex slaves, with the institution described as "enforced prostitution" and "forced abduction of young girls."[34] As for methods of mobilizing the women, these documents overwhelmingly report violent coercion. According to Baek Jaeye's analysis of eight NEFIS reports that describe mobilization methods (Baek Jaeye, 2016: 64-65), one mentions fraud while six mention coercion. There are allusions including: "On the order of the Assistant *Wedana* [i.e., District Head]... a number of young girls were assembled, selected and forcibly taken [by the Japanese]" (nos. 418-425; compilation); "[forcibly] taken from their homes... and installed in brothels" (nos. 455-469; compilation); "the Japanese systematically [took local] girls and unmarried women from... homes" (no. 554); "taken to Pontianak for immoral purpose" (nos. 661-669; compilation); "young unmarried native girls were sought from the villages and taken to hotels" (nos. 103, 106-138, 141-159, 161-171, 173, 175-178, and 193-194; compilation); and "Local young women were forcibly conscripted" (nos. 1590-1630; compilation).

Describing, "Brothels were started by civilians but were subject to military control," one Allied Forces report drawn up in 1943 in Rabaul states that, "The girls [at these facilities] were procured from all sources."[35]

Discovered in the University of Tokyo library and disclosed by Japanese scholars in 2007, the documents submitted to the International

33 "The Special Naval Police [Corps] (Tokei Tai [*sic*]) had orders to keep the brothels supplied with women: to this end they arrested women on the streets, enforced medical examination, and placed them in the brothels... During the first half of 1943 the Naval garrison Commander of Pontianak, Lt. Cdr. xxxxxx... issued the order for the establishment of official brothels... Women did not dare to escape from the brothels as members of their family [*sic*] were then immediately arrested and maltreated by the Tokei Tai. In one case it is known that this caused the death of the mother of the girl concerned." This document was drawn up by Cpt. J. N. Heybroek in the NEFIS on July 5, 1946 in Batavia (IMTFE Exhibit No. 1702).

34 Netherlands Forces Intelligence Service, "Interrogation Report No. 409" (October 23, 1944), "Compilation of NEFIS Interrogation Reports Nos. 418-425 Inclusive (Not Issued Separately)" (October 23, 1944), etc. Requoted from Baek Jaeye, 2015: 50.

35 Allied Translator and Interpreter Section, South West Pacific Area, "Interrogation Report No. 47, Yoshikawa, S." (Record Group 3, Box 111, Records of Headquarters South West Pacific Area, 1942-1945; serial no. 79), April 1, 1943.

Military Tribunal for the Far East by the public prosecutors of the respective nations likewise record vividly the forced taking of women as sex slaves by the Japanese armed forces in countries and territories in East Asia including China, Netherlands East Indies, and Indochinese Union.[36] In "Statement by Lt. Ohara Seidai, 13 January, 1946" (IMTFE Exhibit No. 1794), which the NEFIS drew up in Batavia, there is the following testimony: "[In September 1944, on Moa Island, Netherlands East Indies,] I organized a brothel for the soldiers... They were daughters of the men who attacked the KEM PEI TAI [*sic*; i.e., Japanese Military Police Corps]... Then these [five] women were forced into the brothel as a punishment for the deeds of their fathers." In another document of the NEFIS, "Report on Interrogation of Hayashi Shuichi Dated March 13th 1946 on Pontianak Massacre" (IMTFE Exhibit No. 1701-A), there is the following testimony: "...their arrest... was only a pretext in order to put them in a brothel." NEFIS documents include statements by victims of sexual slavery as well. "Affidavit of Interrogation: Summary of Examination of J. Beelman-v. Ballegooyen, 16 May, 1946" (IMTFE Exhibit No. 1725-A) shows how the women detained at the Moentilan (present-day Muntilan) Internment Camp were taken to a comfort station in January 1944 and forced to become sex slaves. Here, these women state that when they resisted, members of the Japanese military threatened to have their husbands be responsible for it and sexually assaulted them after tearing off their clothes and twisting their arms.[37]

"Summary of Examination of Lois Antonio Numes Rodreigues, 26 June, 1946" (IMTFE Exhibit No. 1792-A) shows the atrocity of the Japanese armed forces' forced taking of women as sex slaves by using influential figures in villages. Rodreigues,[38] a Portuguese, thus stated: "[In

36 The full Japanese text of these seven documents is included in the Research and Executive Bureau, Center for Research and Documentation on Japan's War Responsibility, 2007, "Presentation of Materials: The Japanese Military Comfort Women System, Adjudged at the Tokyo Tribunal," ed. Center for Research and Documentation on Japan's War Responsibility, *Report on Japan's War Responsibility* 56 (summer).

37 "...I was told... to appear at the Japanese Camp Office... We were medically examined by the Japanese doctors... a KEMPEI-official [i.e., an official in the Military Police Corps]... told me that we had to receive the Japs, for if we were not willing, our husbands... would be held responsible... he tore my clothes from my body and twisted my arms on my back... whereafter he compelled me to have sexual intercourse with him."

Díli [present-day Dili], Portuguese Timor [present-day Timor-Leste], in February 1942,] I know of a lot of places where the Japanese forced the chiefs to send native girls to Japanese brothels, by threatening the native chiefs by telling them that if they did not send the girls, they, the Japanese, would go to the chiefs' houses and take away their near[est] female relatives for this purpose." Another deposition demonstrates the forced taking of women as sex slaves in the Indochinese Union. According to "Affidavit of Nguyen-thi-Thong" (September 6, 1946; IMTFE Exhibit No. 2120), the Japanese forcibly took Vietnamese women who were living with French soldiers to a comfort station established in Tien Yen.[39]

3) The Trial Records of the Allied Forces

As of date, only two Allied Forces' trials regarding Japanese military sexual slavery are known to have occurred: the Batavia War Criminal Court and the US Navy War Crimes Commission on Guam (also known as "Guam War Crimes Trials"). A military tribunal held in Batavia, Netherlands East Indies in 1946, the Batavia War Criminal Court partly concerned cases related to Japanese military comfort women and gave decisions in 1948. Twelve former Japanese soldiers were tried on the charge of having forcibly taken 35 Dutch women detained at an internment camp in Samarang (present-day Semarang) to comfort stations in February 1944 and used them as sex slaves, and, from among them, an officer, who ranked the highest, was executed.[40] At the signing of the Treaty of Peace with Japan (henceforth "San Francisco Treaty") in 1951, Japan acquiesced in the rulings of numerous war crime tribunals. In other words, the factuality of the Japanese armed forces' forced taking of women as sex slaves was admitted by the Japanese government as well as the Allied Powers. Considering that such coercion was imposed on Dutch women at

38 [TN] Also spelled "Lois Antonio Nunes Rodrigues," "Luis Antonio Nunes Rodrigues," etc. in various documents.

39 "...the Japanese forced several of my fellow-countrywomen who were living with French soldiers, to follow them to a brothel which they had set up at Tien Yen."

40 The ruling is explained in detail in Ni'imi Takashi, 1994, "Judgment on the Case of Forced Dutch Comfort Women by the Temporary Court Martial Tribunal of Batavia," ed. Center for Research and Documentation on Japan's War Responsibility, *Report on Japan's War Responsibility* 3 (spring).

the time, it is not difficult to surmise that even more ruthless forced taking was imposed on Asian women by the Japanese military.

An American territory, Guam[41] was occupied by Japan in December 1941. After recovering the region, the United States held a military commission in July 1945. According to "Samuel T. Shinohara: Trial by Military Commission at Agana, Guam, 28 July, 1945" (Record Group 125, Entry A1-12, Box 7), an extensive record of the US navy's trials in Guam discovered in the National Archives and Records Administration, in February 1942, Sakai, a Japanese officer, armed with a sword and with Shinohara, the head of the Japanese residents' association, as a guide, went to the home of a 17-year-old female named Alfonsina Flores, threatened the family, and took this young woman to the home of one Mercedes Kerner, keeping her there and using her as a sex slave.[42] After thus being forcibly taken by force of arms, Flores was forced into providing sexual services through continuous violence (e.g., the threat that she would "be beheaded"). Continued for six months, this life of sexual slavery ended with Sakai's return to Japan. This incident was put on trial along with other, non-sexual charges, on July 28, 1945 and judged on August 27. However, because Sakai had already returned to Japan, only Shinohara was sentenced to capital punishment.[43] Added to the list of Shinohara's crimes was his abetment, during the same period, in having a woman named Nicholasa P. Mendiola be forcibly taken and used as a sex slave.[44]

One of the few cases where trial records are extant, this one can be seen as evidence demonstrating so-called coercion in the narrow sense because, though a civilian was punished, the contents involved the

41 [TN] Referred to at the time by the Japanese as "Omiya Island" (*Omiya-to*) 大宮島.

42 Kerner's husband was absent because he had been shipped to Japan as a prisoner of war of the Japanese military, and, after being brought to this house, Flores was visited by not only Sakai but also, occasionally, Hayashi Hiroshi, the Japanese governor of the territory.

43 [TN] This sentence was commuted to 15 years of imprisonment on August 24, 1948, however. "Case of Samuel T. Shinohara," *Record of Proceedings of a Military Commission Convened at Agana, Guam, by Order of the Island Commander* (July 28, 1945), WWII JAG Case Files, Pacific-Navy.

44 Here, the nature of the offense was: "Did unlawfully take Alfonsina Flores, a female person, for the purpose of prostitution, procuring her consent thereto by misrepresentation" and "Did unlawfully take Nicholasa P. Mendiola, a female person, against her will and without her consent, for the purpose of prostitution."

mobilization of women by force and their use as sex slaves by a Japanese military officer. In addition, the case is likely to receive attention newly as the victims were American citizens. On May 2, 2007, the Legislature of Guam proposed a resolution demanding an official apology from the Japanese government for its past taking of women from Guam, the only American territory occupied by the Japanese armed forces during the war, as sex slaves (*Korea Times*, July 4, 2007).

In 2014, Hayashi Hirofumi unearthed and disclosed even more compelling materials on the forced taking of women as Japanese military sex slaves.[45] These materials concern a member of the Japanese Special Naval Police Corps who was tried in 1947 in the Batavia War Criminal Court. Aged 38 at the time, he was indicted on the charge of having forcibly mobilized women as both sex slaves and Japanese military officers' sex partners, and a sentence of 12 years of imprisonment with labor for him was requested. Interestingly, a 1962 document titled "A Report on Business Trips to the Osaka and Kobe Areas (In Relation to War Trials) 大阪, 神戶地方出張調査報告書(戰爭裁判關係)" contains various materials including the contents of the incident and the testimonies of both the defendant himself and the victims. The interrogation reports feature the testimonies of eight victims. These victims consisted of both military sex slaves and sexually coerced women (aged 20, 15, 19, 18, and 23), two fathers of these women, and one individual ordered by the Japanese armed forces to manage a comfort station. The women had been brought through the defendant's violence, threats (with a pistol), and fraud, which the comfort station manager, too, admitted. When interrogated by the official in charge from the Japanese Ministry of Justice in 1962, the defendant, a former Japanese soldier, stated that he had directly mobilized military sex slaves by force and subsequently avoided being overtaken as a war criminal because of the Japanese armed forces' concealment of the crime through the use of funds. Although these materials are in the possession of the Japanese Ministry of Justice, they were omitted from the Japanese government's second report on the military comfort women system from 1993 (Hayashi Hirofumi, 2014a: 17-29).

45 Hayashi Hirofumi, 2014b.

Hayashi Hirofumi then disclosed yet another, similar material. A record from the Batavia War Criminal Court, it concerns acts of the forced prostitution of women of Dutch nationality from April 1942 to September 1945 by those including Cpt. Wada Kunishige, the commander of the Japanese Military Police Corps garrisoned in Djember (present-day Jember) on eastern Djawa (present-day Java). Described in interrogation reports on ten victims are the circumstances in which the Japanese military police forcibly took the women and exploited them as military sex slaves. One woman was captured together with her younger sister. While being subjected to violence, the latter was forced to have sexual relations and "threatened to choose between cohabiting with one Japanese [man] or letting all Japanese [men] use her as their wife." Another woman testified, "I was taken to a hotel by the Japanese police station chief, and that hotel later became a [Japanese military] comfort station... I [later] gave birth to a child by a Japanese [man]" (Hayashi Hirofumi, 2014b: 44-50).

4) The Report of the Dutch Government

A synthesis of documents housed in the National Archives of the Netherlands published by the Dutch government in 1993, *Forced Prostitution of Dutch Women in the Former Netherlands East Indies* (*Gedwongen Prostitutie van Nederlandse Vrouwen in Voormalig Nederlands-Indië*) likewise confirms in numerous passages the factuality of the forced taking of women as sex slaves by the Japanese military.[46] Several passages have been excerpted below.

The Japanese military landed on Djawa in March 1942 and conquered the Netherlands East Indies a week later. The Japanese armed forces saw the establishment of comfort stations as a matter of course, and officers in charge of logistics were responsible for issuing comfort

46 As for the Dutch government's 1993 report, a Japanese translation was published, along with Yoshimi Yoshiaki's explanation, as "[Material] Report of a Study of Dutch Government Documents on the Forced Prostitution of Dutch Women in the Dutch East Indies during the Japanese Occupation," in the Center for Research and Documentation on Japan's War Responsibility, ed., 1994, *Report on Japan's War Responsibility* 4 (summer), 6. This section has made use of this Japanese translation.

station permits and supervising the permission conditions. Subsequently, numerous incidences of rape occurred in various areas. For instance, the rape incident that occurred in Blora, near Samarang, Djawa, was especially heinous: over 20 European women were confined to two houses and raped. For three weeks, at least 15 women including many mothers and daughters were raped several times a day by Japanese soldiers as diverse regiments passed through the area. In September 1943, the segment of the Japanese navy on Borneo directly managed comfort stations while the Special Naval Police Corps (Japanese navy's segment corresponding to the army's Military Police Corps) were responsible for recruiting women.

On Djawa, in the early days of their invasion of the island, the Japanese armed forces exerted pressure on officials in the government of the Netherlands East Indies to find appropriate women as sex slaves. During the latter half of 1943, however, the Japanese army and military police used force to abduct and bring women from detention centers and other locations. In other words, they set out directly to recruit Djawanese women and a small number of European women to send them to comfort stations on the numerous surrounding islands.

In Magelang, the Japanese military decided to take European women from the nearby Moentilan Civilian Detention Center to the comfort station in Magelang. Consequently, in January 1944, 13 women were taken to Magelang, subjected to violent examinations, raped, and forced to work as sex slaves.

In Samarang, in February 1944, Japanese soldiers visited seven women's detention centers nearby for a massive woman hunt. While they had to give up at three of the detention centers due to strong resistance, from the remaining four facilities, they took at least 24 women despite resistance and used them as sex slaves (the standards by which the victims were selected remain unknown). These women were violently examined, raped, and beaten.

In Samarang (Flores Island), in April 1944, Japanese police officers and military police officers arrested some hundred European and native women living outside the detention centers in Samarang, took them to the comfort station at the Samarang Club, selected over 20 of these women, subjected them to violent examinations, and then shipped them to Soerabaja (present-day Surabaya) on the train the following day. Two months later, 17 of the women (seven of them Europeans) were forced to work as sex slaves at a comfort station on Flores Island.

In Bondowoso, using a list drawn up by several European women, the Japanese police and military police forced resident European women to work as sex slaves at a hotel in the area for several months in early 1943. In August 1943, Japanese police officers and military police officers threatened four European women to work at a bar and, after taking them to a hotel, raped them for two days. Two of these women subsequently attempted suicide. At the end of October of the same year, Japanese military police officers took to this hotel two sisters and two cousins other than the two remaining women (sisters). In addition, at least eight other European women were taken. From late August 1943 to January 1944, at least ten other women were made to work at the same hotel. One of them later testified that she had been raped by a military police officer and made to work as a sex slave throughout November 1943. According to the testimony of yet another woman, many Japanese military police officers in Malang confined three European women in a house near the military police headquarters and raped and forced prostitution on them.

On central Djawa, in December 1943, Japanese soldiers attempted to take women to the comfort station in Solo but were thwarted by courageous local leaders.

In Padang, approximately 20 European women were forced into prostitution at Sakario Restaurant (comfort station).

5) The Rulings of Japanese Courts[47]

Although the plaintiffs have been defeated in nearly all trials regarding former Japanese military sex slaves conducted in Japan, there are not a few cases in which the factuality of the damage has been admitted. In the first case of the lawsuit seeking compensation for damages to Chinese comfort women, the Tokyo High Court's ruling (July 28, 2004) clearly admitted: "In 1942 [during the implementation of the so-called Three Alls Strategy 三光作戦], there was an incident in which members of the Japanese state

47 This section has been excerpted from Yoshimi Yoshiaki, 2007.

forcibly kidnapped, took, and raped Chinese women living near the garrison and then daily raped them while under confinement, relegating them to the status of so-called comfort women."

In the second case of the lawsuit seeking compensation for damages to Chinese comfort women, the rulings of the Tokyo District Court (March 29, 2003) and the Tokyo High Court (March 18, 2005), respectively, admitted the fact that, "in 1942 in Shanxi Province, Japanese soldiers kidnapped, confined, and gang raped the two of the female plaintiffs." Likewise, in the lawsuit seeking compensation for damages from sexual violence in Shanxi Province, etc., the rulings of the Tokyo District Court (April 24, 2003) and the Tokyo High Court (March 31, 2005), respectively, admitted the damage claimed by some ten female plaintiffs from Shanxi Province as true. In the lawsuit seeking compensation for damages from wartime sexual violence on Hainan Island, the Tokyo District Court's ruling (August 30, 2005) admitted that eight women had been raped and then kidnapped, confined, and raped by Japanese soldiers.

6) The Wartime Rulings of Government-General of Korea Courts

There are other documentary materials indirectly showing that the forced mobilization of military sex slaves was implemented *en masse* on the Korean Peninsula in 1938, when the Japanese armed forced occupied parts of China and began to expand military comfort stations systematically. They are the rulings of Government-General of Korea courts. From 1938 to 1944, numerous courts including the Daegu Court of Review, Daegu District Court, Miryang Branch of the Busan District Court, and Ganggyeong Branch of the Daejeon District Court and many other branch courts including the Jangheung Branch of the Gwangju District Court, Jeonju District Court, and Gwangju District Court punished innumerable people on charges of the propagation of groundless rumors, and the contents of these groundless rumors were that government authorities were capturing young women and sending them to comfort stations in China. Below are some examples of such rumors:

> "The Sunchang Police Station has investigated the daughter (aged 17-18) of one Yang living in Tong'an in Sunchang to take her to the front so that,

worried, the said female has been unable even to eat for three months, only crying" (Jeonju District Court, ruling no.: 1938 criminal trial no. 998, Jeon Haksun (aged 38), occupation: day laborer, four months' imprisonment demanded).

"To comfort the soldiers who are campaigning in the Second Sino-Japanese War, unmarried women aged 16-20 and widows aged 16-30 are being collected forcibly and sent to the front, made to cook and do the laundry by day and to have sexual relations with soldiers by night" (Miryang Branch, Busan District Court, ruling no.: 1938 criminal trial no. 376, Jang Insik, occupation: none, four months' imprisonment demanded).

"Lately, the [Japanese colonial] government authorities have been planning to recruit unmarried women aged 17-18, take them to Northern Manchuria, and have them cook or provide comfort to Japanese soldiers, who are at war right now. So you should quickly marry off your daughter Seoksun (aged 16)" (Daegu Court of Review, ruling no.: 1941 criminal trial no. 240, Ha Chagi, occupation: liquor seller, four months' imprisonment demanded).

"Because of the [political] situation, there has been the supply of unmarried women to the [Japanese colonial] government as of late so that the youngest daughter of old man Choe, a neighbor, likewise has been supplied without even knowing the destination. It's so sad and pitiful that she should have been supplied without even being able to get married" (Daegu District Court, ruling no.: 1943 criminal trial no. 377, Bak Bongnye, occupation: agriculture, a fine of 70 yen demanded).

"From the village next to mine, three unmarried women have been supplied to the [Japanese colonial] government and are to be sent to Manchuria... If you have a daughter, marry her off" (Gimcheon Branch, Daegu District Court, ruling no.: 1943 criminal trial no. 209, Yoshimoto Kasuke, occupation: agriculture, four months' penal servitude demanded). "In Gwangju, South Jeolla Province and Jeong'eup, the supply of unmarried women to the [Japanese colonial] government is prevalent,

> and, from Chilbo Township, two unmarried women likewise have been supplied. As a result, many unmarried women are getting married so that my sister, who lives in Chilbo Township, too, got married early" (Jeonju District Court, ruling no.: 1944 criminal trial no. 171, Han Gyucheol, a fine of 50 yen demanded).
>
> "I went to Jeonju and saw that all unmarried women had been supplied to the [Japanese colonial] government. They say that all unmarried women in Gimje, too, will be supplied soon. So you should all quickly go back to your home villages and get married" (Jeonju District Court, ruling no.: 1944 criminal trial no. 214, Yi Jin'gyu, occupation: restaurant cook, a fine of 50 yen demanded).

The examples above were punished according to laws including Article 99 of the Japanese Army Penal Code, Article 100 of the Japanese Navy Penal Code, and the Provisional Ordinance on Security in Korea 朝鮮臨時保安令. Besides these, many other court rulings can be found. Judging from the fact that such rulings emerged and expanded in 1938 and that the same things were said in diverse areas, all of this can be seen as reflecting the actual and forced mobilization of sex slaves, which increased drastically starting in 1938.

4. Conclusion

In addition to those mentioned above, materials demonstrating the forced taking of women as Japanese military sex slaves continue to be unearthed. By now, the denial of forced taking by the Japanese government and right wing has become nonsensical. More importantly, however, it is necessary to overcome the discursive framework of "forced taking (in the narrow sense)," as discussed earlier, and to develop more fundamental discussions on the coerciveness of Japanese military sexual slavery itself. In South Korea, Japan, and China, efforts have been under way to acknowledge the value of testimonies of not only victims but also comfort station managers, Japanese soldiers, and Allied prisoners of war and to shed light on the historical fact multifacetedly by incorporating into such testimonies contemporary administrative procedures and the circumstances surrounding the armed forces and the war. Thanks to the lone efforts and accomplishments of the Center for Research and Documentation on Japan's War Responsibility (JWRC) 日本の戰爭責任資料センタ-, which was launched immediately after the issue began to be highlighted in the early 1990s, and South Korean historians, jurists, and women scholars as well as the achievements of organizations that have endeavored much to unearth Allied Forces materials in recent years such as South Korea's National Institute of Korean History (former National History Compilation Committee) 國史編纂委員會 and the research team in the Human Rights Center at Seoul National University, the truth of the forced mobilization of women as Japanese military sex slaves can be expected to be elucidated further. Moreover, the efforts that scholars in nations and regions worldwide including the United States, Europe, and Australia have started in order to shed light on the shocking historical fact of Japanese military sexual slavery will become increasingly important.

Chapter 4

The Social Structural Background and Reality of Japanese Military Sexual Slavery

1. The Formative Background and Coloniality of Japanese Military Sexual Slavery

It is widely known that the Japanese military early on went to battlefields along with prostitutes 娼妓 called *karayukisan* 唐行きさん (literally, "people going abroad") during the First Sino-Japanese War (1894-1895), Russo-Japanese War (1904-1905), and Siberian Intervention (1918-1922) (Geum Byeongdong, 1992: 2). There is also a record that, during World War I, the British military brought along women to battlegrounds (Igeta Jun, 1992). It is true, too, that prostitution flourishes near military troops worldwide. However, the military sexual slavery policy implemented by the Japanese armed forces during the so-called Asia-Pacific War is unique and unprecedented in world history in the sense that it was a crime committed under the government's plan on an immense scale and in an organized and systematic manner, whereby women mainly from Japan's colonies and occupied territories were forcibly taken. Having widely studied accumulated research accomplishments and reviewed the testimonial records housed in both the Australian War Memorial and the Imperial War Museum in the United Kingdom, Tessa Morris-Suzuki thus concluded in 2015: though many armed forces including those of the United States are closely related to prostitution during wars and "military camp towns 基地村" in South Korea exploit women as well, the massive and forced mobilization, vastly long-distance transport, and postwar abandonment in the battlegrounds of women as military sex slaves found in the Japanese military comfort women system have not occurred (Morris-Suzuki, 2015). Indeed, Japanese military sexual slavery was a result of the intersection of the universal social conditions of the oppression of women, ethnic[1] discrimination, and wartime state violence. Nevertheless, the context of the unique social structure of imperial Japan at the time and the particularity of colonial Korea, which was a wide site of the mobilization of women, cannot be disregarded, either. In other words, a complex combination of such universality and particularity created Japanese military sexual slavery, an institution unprecedented around the globe.

1) Japan's Emperor System and Strengthening of Militarism

The Meiji government (1868-1912) consolidated the emperor system, absolutist in both name and deed, by proclaiming in 1889 the Constitution of the Empire of Japan 大日本帝國憲法 (henceforth "Meiji Constitution").[2] According to this constitution, it became possible for the Japanese emperor, as the overseer of all sovereignty and as His Majesty the Generalissimo, in the highest position in the Japanese army and navy, to

1 [TN] In this volume, the Sinoxenic cognates 民族 and 民族的 have been translated into English as "ethnicity" (or, depending on the context, "ethnic group(s)") and "ethnic," respectively. However, 民族主義 has been rendered as "ethnic nationalism" only in its initial appearance, subsequently abbreviated as "nationalism" in order to avoid the cumbersome "ethnic nationalism" and "ethnonationalism." Derivates of this last term, 民族主義的 and 民族主義者 likewise have been shortened as "nationalist(ic)" and "nationalist(s)," respectively, throughout in order to avoid "ethnic nationalist(ic)," "ethnonationalist(ic)," "ethnic nationalist(s)," and "ethnonationalist(s)."

2 Although the emperor system of Japan had existed since antiquity, most emperors had been excluded from direct political involvement. However, in the Edo or Tokugawa period (1603-1868), which began with the unification of diverse forces, the emperor, who hitherto had been neglected and abandoned, started to be used as a symbol of unified power and, at the end of the Tokugawa shogunate, led to emperor centralism. This is because warriors, among the ruling class, demanded an ideology justifying their own rule due to confusion in the existing medieval class hierarchy brought about by the development of capitalism and peasant rebellions and because there arose the need to establish an absolutist regime that would foreground the emperor, who embodied legitimacy in terms of the world of myth based on folk religion. Established through this process, the Meiji government consolidated the ideology of the emperor system as an economic and military impetus so as to implement downward modernization policy more forcefully and promptly and sought to inculcate the entire nation with this ideology even more thoroughly.

declare both war and martial law. In addition, all Japanese nationals were the emperor's subjects and forced to render absolute loyalty to him, and public education indoctrinated the people with such an imperialistic view of history (Suzuki Yuko, 1989a: 7-16). With the emperor at the center, the Japanese government led modernization (capitalization), and, also in the process through which capitalism developed in Japan, the state continued to have absolute ascendancy over civil society (class situation). Thus established, the emperor system led to a very strict class society with the emperor at the top and was characterized mainly by severe discrimination. Discrimination against women and colonized peoples alike was a representative form of the creation of an order of discrimination under the emperor system. In the process of Japan's militarization, the emperor system easily became fascist and, unlike Western fascism, came to exhibit a patriarchal tendency (familistic state ideology) and a regionalistic ideology (Pan-Asianism 大亞細亞主義) (Maruyama Masao, 1964: 29-87).

During the war, Japan revealed both a standpoint where the state was seen as an extension of the family and, in fact, the tendency of a family-state that consisted of the imperial family as the head family (*honke* 本家) and the people's families as collateral families, which was an expansion of the patriarchal nature of the emperor system that had been developed since the Meiji era. In addition, Japanese militarism proclaimed Pan-Asianism as a pretext for expelling Western imperialist forces from various countries in Asia and developed this more specifically into the idea of constructing the "Greater East Asia Co-Prosperity Sphere 大東亞共榮圈," with Japan at the center. Such ideas, in turn, served as the direct impetus for war and led to a policy of the cultural genocide 民族文化抹殺 of the peoples colonized by Japan (Maruyama Masao, 1964: 29-87). As is well known, starting in the latter half of the 1930s, Japan aggressively implemented in colonial Korea Japanization 皇國臣民化 policy, whose ultimate goal lay in cultural genocide, and forced on the Korean people measures including the use of the Japanese language, adoption of Japanese names 創氏改名, and worship at Shinto shrines 神社參拜 in the name of "Japanese-Korean unity 內鮮一體" and "impartiality and equal favor 一視同仁" (Suzuki Yuko, 1991a: 19).

Continued since the Meiji era, this militaristic system suppressed the Freedom and People's Rights Movement in Japan itself and expanded war abroad. Japan entered a quasi-wartime system with the Manchurian Incident (1931) as the turning point and entered a full-fledged war system with the Second Sino-Japanese War as the turning point, respectively. In this process, the Japanese government expanded the emperor's prerogative of supreme command and, at the same time, formulated a highly developed military state, unlike the system consisting of the Cabinet, National Diet, and Privy Council 樞密院 established in the Meiji Constitution, and reorganized the government structure accordingly. In addition, it infiltrated into all spheres of the people's lives the ideology of the theocratic and military emperor as the Generalissimo (Miyachi Masato, 1988: 98-100) and integrated into government administration residents' self-government organizations such as village associations 部落會 and neighborhood associations 町内會 (Kurasawa Susumu and Akimoto Ritsuro, 1990).

The Japanese government implemented a series of economic control, labor mobilization, and military mobilization policies including the National Mobilization Law 國家總動員法 of 1938. As the war progressed, the scope of mobilization increasingly expanded so that, by the end of the war, the number of people mobilized for war reached 7,193,000 and the number of people mobilized for labor reached 13,104,269 (Saito Yasuaki, 1964: 23-26). It was to raise the battle strength and productivity, respectively, of forcibly mobilized soldiers and laborers, who included Koreans and Chinese as well, that the need for sexual slavery facilities was raised.

2) Japan's Patriarchy and Wartime Mobilization of Women

The emperor system can be seen as an immense patriarchy with the emperor at the top. What buttressed this patriarchal system were the *ie* 家 (household) system, which structured a patriarchal order in individual homes, and licensed prostitution 公娼制, which functioned to absorb men's licentious sexual acts and to protect and maintain the *ie* system from such acts.

With the patriarch's rights over his wife and children made absolute and with authority and obedience established as the basic principles, the *ie* system started to develop in the mid-Edo period and continued to be established until the end of the same era. Subsequently, both the constitution and civil law even came to determine its contents in the Meiji era (Nakane Chie, 1983: 7). According to these laws, a woman in the position of a wife was legally considered incapable and therefore prohibited from economic activities and legally meaningful decision making and, as her husband's possession, could not act without the latter's permission[3] (Tsunoda Yukiko, 1989: 197).

While Japan's patriarchal social system thus consisted of the *ie* system, licensed prostitution was developed as a supplement. Licensed prostitution, or state-authorized prostitution, where the state received taxes in return for issuing permission (licenses) to procurers and prostitutes, was established during the Edo era and spread nationwide in the Meiji era. Prostitution had come into being even earlier as a result of the commercialization of sex in line with the development of capitalism.[4] However, the direct reason for the establishment and expansion of licensed prostitution centering on brothels 遊廓 was to provide an official arena in which warriors, who were anxious due to continuing wars, could satisfy their sexual desire, thus preventing disorder in the *ie* system that could arise from such desire, and to contain these warriors' rebellious tendencies by thus securing their psychological stability (Fukae Masako, 1989: 202-205). This stemmed from a viewpoint from which men's licentious desire was considered "natural" and prostitution was seen as a "necessary" evil for the protection of the home (Hayashi Chiyo, 1992: 125). The Meiji government implemented syphilis examinations on prostitutes (Yamashita Yeong-Ae, 1991: 6-7), but this was less out of consideration for prostitutes' health and more out of the desire to prevent the infection of these women's male clients with STDs. In other words, the purpose of these examinations lay in protecting the patriarchal household, the warrior class and their homes in particular. In the end,

3 Formed somewhat discriminatorily according to class, such a strict family system was applied mostly to aristocrats, great landlords, great townsmen (*ochonin* 大町人), and gentlemen (*shizoku* 士族). Legally, the *ie* system was abolished with the revision of the Civil Code of Japan in 1947 (Kawashima Takeyoshi, 1950: 7-23).

4 Said to have begun during the Kamakura era (1185-1333), brothels 賣春宿 were encouraged during the Muromachi period (1337-1573) to develop markets and post station towns 宿場町 as commodity economy became active (Hayashi Chiyo, 1992: 124).

licensed prostitution was a reorganization of the "pleasure women 遊女," or courtesan, system from the Edo era in the Meiji government's process of consolidating the emperor system.

In the process of militarization, the Japanese government turned its attention to the education of women, where the basic framework was the integration of the household, state, and motherhood. For this purpose, 1931 saw the establishment of the Coalition of Women's Associations of Greater Japan 大日本聯合婦人會, and the following year saw the establishment of the Women's Association of Greater Japan for National Defense 大日本國防婦人會 (Suzuki Yuko, 1989a: 22-23). As the National Spiritual Mobilization Movement 國民精神總動員運動 arose following the Second Sino-Japanese War, the Japanese government promoted the ideological mobilization of women through motherhood so that books such as *The Mother of Japan* 日本の母, *The Mother of the Military State* 軍國の母, *The Mother of the Pacification of the Nation* 靖國の母, *The Mother of a Healthy Child* 健兒の母, *The Mother of a Healthy Nation* 健民の母, *The Mother of Asian Development* 興亞の母, and *In Praise of the Mother* 母を讚揚する were published as well (Suzuki Yuko, 1989b: 21-23). In 1940, women became members of the Imperial Rule Assistance Association 大政翼贊會, a people's organization created by the government to buttress the fascist wartime system (Suzuki Yuko, 1988: 53-73), and forged a general mobilization system from their own standpoint by creating diverse women's organizations and a confederation of them, and this latter organization stressed the raising of children as Japanese imperial subjects.[5]

Lower-class women alienated from the status granted by such roles, and prostitutes from among these women, were assigned the role of "comforting" the Japanese armed forces. Created under the wartime system as a "gift to the officers and soldiers in the Imperial Armed Forces" (Aso Tetsuo, 1939) to arouse the troops' will to fight in the war system, to prevent the explosion of their discontent and frustration, and to

5 Formed in 1942, the Women's Association of Greater Japan 大日本婦人會 announced the Three Patriotic Platforms for the Home 家庭報國三綱領 and, based on them, the Fourteen Main Points for Practice 實踐十四要目. One of the platforms cites the raising of children as Japanese imperial subjects (Suzuki Yuko, 1989b: 53-60).

prevent rape, Japan's military sexual slavery policy was based on the same patriarchal logic as the initiation of licensed prostitution at the end of the Sengoku (Warring States) era (1467-1573) for warriors and can thus be seen as one variation of licensed prostitution (Suzuki Yuko, 1991a: 18).

However, because the number of soldiers increased explosively due to war, the Japanese military sexual slavery policy was, in fact, impossible to implement from the time of its planning solely with Japanese prostitutes. At this point, women in colonial Korea came to be seen as an unlimited pool of sex slaves, and it was on this foundation that the military sexual slavery policy finally materialized. This was linked, in turn, to Japan's cultural genocide policy, which progressed drastically in colonial Korea following the Second Sino-Japanese War.

3) Japan's Colonial Policies and the General Mobilization System

A latecomer opened up to the world by the United States in 1854, Japan enjoyed a relatively high level of productivity in comparison with other Asian countries yet, like these nations, was nevertheless threatened with the danger of being reduced to a Western colony. However, because of the policy of the Japanese government, which sensitively grasped the riskiness of foreign capital, and a global situation in which Western powers' attention was focused on countries such as India, China, and Dai Nam (present-day Vietnam), the nation was able to avoid the danger (Norman, 1940: 116-127; and Halliday, 1975: 17-55). On the contrary, Japan came to invade and to colonize weak surrounding nations in order to realize its age-old desire for territorial expansion (Harada, 1969: 75) and to mitigate the discontent of its peasants and warriors (Cohen, 1949: 33; and Conroy, 1960: 53). Unlike Western imperialism, Japanese imperialism came into being when the nation was on a low level of capitalist development. Consequently, in contrast to Western countries, Japan perceived the acquisition of colonies as a shortcut to the accumulation of capital (Kiernan, 1975: 44). It is thus possible to presume that Japan's colonial policy was more exploitative and violent than those of its Western counterparts.

By establishing in its colonies Korea and Formosa new land, legal, and currency systems, Japan formed a bloc economy, with itself at the center (Johnston, 1953: 50-51). In the case of colonial Korea, the influx of Japanese products and the Japanese' seizure of land led to the ruination of its rural economy so that many peasants lost arable land, and a broad class of the indigent emerged in cities as well. On the other hand, state organs including the police implemented strong control, to which Japan's colonized peoples were subjected.

In particular, colonial Korea was seen at this time as the stepping stone to Japan's invasion of China (Nelson, 1945: 296; and Crowley, 1966: 4-8) so that a very strong integration policy was implemented from the early years after Japan's annexation (1910), unlike in Formosa, which was treated as a separate entity politically. The goal of annexation itself was the complete absorption of Korea into Japan (Chen, 1968: 71-90). This, in turn, would lead to a violent cultural genocide policy on the Korean people in the process of Japan's militarization. In 1938, Japan announced a plan for facilities to strengthen "Japanese-Korean unity" and, accordingly, sought the complete Japanization of the Korean people and introduced into school education the emperor ideology. Koreans were therefore forced to worship at Shinto shrines, to adopt the language and customs of Japan while being prohibited from using their own, and to adopt Japanese names as a result of the revision of the Civil Ordinance of Korea 朝鮮民事令 in 1939. On the other hand, the Japanese colonial authorities strengthened even further during the war the existing policy of expelling Koreans from their own land and relocating the Japanese to colonial Korea. The plan for facilities for the realization of "Japanese-Korean unity" from 1938 likewise included the stipulation "Promote the increase of the Japanese [in colonial Korea] and devise means of encouraging their settlement."

As an extreme policy of cultural genocide, the Japanese government implemented the policy of Korean-Japanese intermarriage. It revised the Civil Ordinance of Korea in 1930 and established Japanese-style systems for the adoption of both differently surnamed individuals 異姓養子 and sons-in-law (*mukoyoshi* 壻養子), which made possible the adoption of Japanese men into Korean families, thus attempting so-called Japanese-Korean blood intermixture 內鮮血混合. The government began actively to implement the Korean-Japanese intermarriage policy in 1937, and the

Government-General of Korea Investigative Meeting for Plans against the Present Situation 朝鮮總督府時局對策調査會 held in September 1938 resolved that "Appropriate measures for encouraging Japanese-Korean intermarriage are to be devised" as a policy for strengthening and thoroughly implementing "Japanese-Korean unity."[6] In other words, the Government-General of Korea noted Korean-Japanese intermarriage as an ultimate means to bring about not only mental and cultural assimilation but also consanguineous assimilation, thus realizing "Japanese-Korean unity" in everyday life (Lee Jeong-Seon, 2015: 261). Likewise, the 1938 plan to implement "Japanese-Korean unity" included "Appropriate measures for encouraging Japanese-Korean intermarriage are to be devised." This policy immediately led to results so that, during the five years from 1937 to 1942, Korean-Japanese intermarriage increased by nearly 100%.

Initiated by the National Mobilization Law of 1938, the military and labor mobilization of Koreans was implemented, on one hand, for its need in wartime but, on the other hand, led to an extremely severe situation when combined with such cultural genocide policy. Military mobilization was de facto forced taking even from the voluntary stage, before the implementation of a conscription system (Ordinance on Special Volunteers to the Army 陸軍特別志願兵令 of 1938, Regulations on the Temporary Appointment of Special Volunteers to the Army 陸軍特別志願兵臨時採用規則 of 1943, and conscription system of 1944),[7] and most of those thus mobilized were dispatched to the forefront as cannon fodder. Indeed, in countless cases, Koreans were dispatched even to locations where Japan's defeat was already certain (Miyata Setsuko, 1989). The same held true of labor mobilization so that it was actually implemented through coercion by the Japanese colonial authorities even from the stage of voluntary application (recruitment in 1939, official mediation 官斡旋 in 1942, and the draft 徵用 in 1944) (Ichihara Hiroshi, 1992). As for labor in coal mines, unlike their Japanese peers, the

6 Government-General of Korea, *Written Reply to the Consultation of the Government-General of Korea Investigative Meeting for Plans against the Present Situation*, 1938 (republication; Seoul: Minsokwon, 1998), 3.

7 Kinbara Setsuzo, 1939-1941, 3-Ha (March 1-April 27, 1941).

overwhelming majority of Korean laborers were made to work in mine shafts and mobilized for dangerous construction work, which led to innumerable injuries and deaths (Shirato Hitoyasu, 1992). In addition, the fact that a tremendous number of Korean women were mobilized as Japanese military sex slaves, most of them killed in battlefields or becoming infertile even if they managed to survive, can be seen as a "natural" consequence of Japan's cultural genocide policy.

In both military and labor mobilization, the exercise of coercion through official intervention was evident in cases not only of mobilization for work and conscription for war but also of recruitment, voluntary application, and official mediation. Threats and violence were used often.[8] Moreover, such exercise of coercion by the Japanese colonial authorities occurred through a very tight network of organizations throughout colonial Korea from the Patriotic Units 愛國班 at the very bottom to neighborhood and village leagues 町洞里部落聯盟, town and township leagues 邑面聯盟, prefectural, county, and provincial leagues 府郡道聯盟, provincial leagues 道聯盟, and, ultimately, the center (Yi Mahn-yol, 1997: 86-89). Launched in 1940, the National League of Total Effort in Korea 國民總力朝鮮聯盟 thus organized Koreans *en masse*, and, in a situation where the entire colony had been thus scrupulously organized, it would have been impossible to mobilize so many women without the intervention of the Government-General of Korea including petty clerks in the respective areas.

Furthermore, all cases of travel abroad required certificates of travel issued by police stations within each jurisdiction. In 1925, the Government-General of Korea started to control the departure of Koreans to Japan, beginning with applicants in South Gyeongsang Province, in accordance with the orders of the Ministry of Home Affairs in Japan.[9] Thus initiated, the regulatory policy was strengthened until the period of

---

8 As for the reality of recruitment and official mediation in the mobilization of labor, see Kim Min-Young, 1995.

9 Overseas departure permits were issued only to those with the following qualifications: (1) securement of definite employment; (2) possession of 10 yen or more in addition to travel expenses; (3) no alcoholism; (4) ability to understand Japanese; and (5) no supplementation of the personnel by labor brokers. Applicants had to apply to the police stations in their respective places of abode (Park Kyung-Sik, 1975: 12).

forced mobilization, which began in 1939, with the continued addition of new regulatory clauses.[10] Amid such a situation, over half of applicants in colonial Korea failed to obtain permission for departure,[11] and many who tried to leave the territory illegally were stopped at the diverse ports of the colony. Both at sea on the way to Japan and at Japanese ports, illegal migrants likewise were arrested one after another (Bureau of Police Affairs, Government-General of Korea, 1931-1939). Japanese military sex slaves' overseas travel therefore would have been condoned without certificates of travel abroad or performed with the issuance of such certificates from police stations and, in either case, was impossible without the intervention of the Japanese colonial authorities including the police.

4) The Impoverishment of Colonial Korea and the Establishment of Licensed Prostitution

With land surveys by the Government-General of Korea and the infiltration of Japanese capital, the rural communities of colonial Korea

10 In 1927, the Government-General of Korea ordered every Korean applicant for an overseas departure permit to submit a certified copy of his or her household register 戶籍 and a signature from the police station in charge of his or her place of abode. In 1929, the Japanese government began to issue certificates of reentry to those who were temporarily returning to colonial Korea. In 1932, the military and the mobile police were mobilized to control entry into Japan, and Korean migrants were now to receive special letters from the police in the Korean cities or towns of their abode. After receiving confirmation from the police stations in the areas in Japan where Korean migrants were to work, the police in colonial Korea itself was to record in detail the background information on these migrants on the back of the copies of their household registers. When temporarily returning to colonial Korea, Korean students studying in Japan had to obtain certificates of enrollment from their respective schools, and the police had to describe the students' background information on the back of the certificates (Bureau of Police and Public Security, Ministry of Home Affairs, 1932). In addition, the Japanese government established strict rules regarding Japanese recruiters of Korean workers and arrested those who violated these rules (Bureau of Police and Public Security, Ministry of Home Affairs, 1926).

11 According to the Bureau of Police Affairs in the Government-General of Korea (1939), the number of overseas departure permit applicants and the number of overseas departure permit rejects amounted to 300,052 people and 169,121 cases, respectively, in 1933; 294,947 people and 188,600 cases in 1934; 200,650 people and 135,528 cases in 1935; 161,477 people and 87,070 cases in 1936; 130,430 people and 71,559 cases in 1937; and 129,205 people and 75,216 cases in 1938.

collapsed so that the number of Japanese landlords increased and the ratio of Korean independent farmers decreased considerably. While the ratios of independent farmers, semi-independent farmers, and tenant farmers among Korean agricultural households were 23%, 37%, and 40%, respectively, in 1920, the figures changed to 18%, 23%, and 59%, respectively, by 1940 (Toyo Keizai, ed., 1980). Thus ruined, Korean farmers accumulated as surplus population in rural areas, leading to a vicious circle where competition for tenancy worsened. In this process, a broad class of farmers left the countryside for livelihood, either in entire households or select family member groups. According to estimates by the Division of Investigation 調査部 of the Chosen Industrial Bank 朝鮮殖産銀行, approximately 40,000 left rural areas each year during 1925-1930, approximately 60,000 did so during 1930-1935, and approximately 220,000 did so during 1935-1940 (*Monthly Investigation Bulletin of the Industrial Bank*, 1947).[12] Such displacement from rural areas, too, formed one background of the mobilization of women as military sex slaves. This is because nearly all of the women taken not only from the countryside but also from cities were from impoverished rural communities originally and, in the case of the latter, were taken while working as maidservants or going from one workplace to another such as factories and restaurants, having left home villages alone. The lower the rungs of the social ladder that agricultural households occupied, the more marked was departure from rural areas (Society for the Investigation of Hygiene in the Rural Society of Korea, 1949: 134-135), and the same was especially true for young women.[13] In other words, it was to lessen one mouth to feed in

12 Judging from the fact that the ratio of labor population aged 15-49 or above was much higher in urban areas than in rural areas, it is possible to surmise that, while entire families migrated, there were also many cases of solitary migration for employment (Chang, 1967: 139).

13 One newspaper article from this period thus describes, rather exaggeratedly, the phenomenon of women's departure from their rural homes: "Departure of women in the prime of youth from homes in succession. To factories, to prostitutes' districts 花巷. Remaining in rural areas are widowers and unmarried men" (*Dong-A Ilbo*, December 23, 1936). The fact that the ratio of women without spouses was far higher in urban areas than in rural areas, too, explains such migration for employment. In 1930, the ratio of unmarried women amounted to 64.18% in urban areas and 31.22% in rural areas, respectively, for women aged 15-19 and 15.61% in urban areas and 1.39% in rural areas, respectively, for those aged 20-24 (Chang, 1967: 257).

impoverished families, to escape from hopeless environments, to earn money to buy medicine for ailing fathers, or to pay off family debts that these women followed mobilizers, dreaming of "good" workplaces where they could earn money.

With Korea's opening of its ports to the world in 1876, licensed prostitution began to be established, with Japanese enclaves as the center, and this, in turn, led to the development not only of licensed prostitution but also of unlicensed prostitution 私娼制 so that prostitution came to spread extensively throughout the country (Yamashita Yeong-Ae, 1991; and Song Eoun-ok, 1998). Consequently, fraud, human trafficking, and kidnapping surrounding prostitution became serious social problems in Korea (Kang Man-gil, 1997; and Park Jung-Ae, 2010). Such social conditions clearly facilitated the taking of Korean women as Japanese military sex slaves. Nevertheless, in terms of the entire Korea, the scale was not yet considerable, and although the number of Korean prostitutes gradually increased, from the beginning to a certain point, the majority of prostitutes in Korea were Japanese. In 1927, the *Dong-A Ilbo* reported that, throughout colonial Korea, there were 2,178 Japanese prostitutes and 1,034 Korean prostitutes, respectively (*Dong-A Ilbo*, September 28, 1927). The fact that forms of taking occurring in relation to prostitution such as trafficking, kidnapping, and abduction did not constitute a large portion of the methods used to take Korean women as Japanese military sex slaves, too, reflects such circumstances. In addition, nearly no case has been discovered where women from existing "pleasure quarters" were taken as military sex slaves. This demonstrates the fact that, in the process through which the taking of Korean women as military sex slaves occurred against a broad backdrop of poverty, the environment of prostitution only formed a part.

5) Colonial Institutions That Made Massive Forced Mobilization Possible

More importantly, diverse colonial institutions created a structure that facilitated the taking of women as military sex slaves. As has been examined in the previous chapter as well, many former comfort women have testified that Japanese police officers and government officials directly mobilized the victims (see Chapter 3), and the intervention of the Government-General of Korea, too, has been examined (see Chapter 2). More specifically, there are more recent studies on Japanese colonial laws regarding employment agents who gathered women through employment fraud and sent them to military comfort stations. In Japan proper and colonial Korea alike, the managers of business establishments such as eating houses 飲食店, restaurants 料理屋, brothels 貸座敷, and *gisaengs'* unions 券番 were prohibited by regulation from engaging in job brokerage.[14] However, while regulation punishing violations of this prohibition was legislated as well in Japan, there was no such punitive regulation in Korea.[15] It is therefore possible to say that, in the colony, the mobilization of women as Japanese military sex slaves was far easier under such loose legal regulation.

In addition, in Japan, there was a notification 通達 stating, "As for the passage of women for the purpose of shameful work 醜業, [women] aged 21 or above currently engaged [as] prostitutes 娼妓 or in other de facto shameful work in mainland Japan... are to [be] issue[d] identity documents through notifications 通牒 from the Vice Minister for Foreign Affairs... women who seek to travel for the purpose of shameful work must present themselves at police stations and apply for the issuance of identity documents[;] in the passage of women for the purpose of shameful work, when applying for identity documents, [they] must obtain approval from the nearest parents or ascendants 尊族親 on the same household registers, [or] household heads 戶主 in the absence of parents or ascendants..."[16] In contrast, there were no such restrictions for the Koreans. Consequently, children and women lacking experience with licensed prostitution were mobilized from the colony *en masse* as military sex slaves, without their consent.

This massive and forced mobilization of women from Korea as

---

14 Government-General of Korea, "Government-General of Korea Ordinance on South Jeolla Province No. 39: Regulations on the Regulation of Brokerage," *The Official Gazette of the Government-General of Korea*, June 11, 1940, etc. Requoted from Seo Hyun-ju, 2015: 249.

15 Han Hye-in, 2013; and Seo Hyun-ju, 2015: 248-251.

16 Chief, Bureau of Police and Public Security, Ministry of Home Affairs, "Item Regarding the Treatment of Women Traveling to China" (Material No. 5), February 23, 1938. Requoted from Totsuka Etsuro, 2015: 33.

Japanese military sex slaves was such that it became a cause of social confusion in the colony. Documents showing that the United States was already aware of the situation have been discovered. A US Department of State document dated 1942 based on reports from American consul-generals, vice consuls, and missionaries who worked in Korea records that the Japanese authorities were "procuring of a variety of methods of large numbers of Korean girls, to be shipped to Manchurian and Chinese brothels," thus leading the Koreans to bear deep grudges. Victimized families were loath to disclose the fact in many cases, and those not victimized knew nothing of the institution. This situation was occurring throughout the colony, however, and providing a "fertile cause of hate" for Japan.[17]

Interrogations of Korean prisoners of war conducted in 1945 at Camp Tracy in California, where major prisoners of war were transported and interned, consisted of 30 questions based on a very detailed awareness of the situation in Korea including personal names (including those before the adoption of Japanese names 創氏改名), Korea's regional administrative system, draft 徵用, collective migration to locations including Manchuria, conscription 徵兵, pro-Japanese/anti-Japanese tendencies, resistance against Japan, and Koreans' attitudes toward pro-Japanese collaborators. Very surprisingly, the 18th item concerned the mobilization of women as military sex slaves, consisting of the questions "Do Koreans generally know about the recruitment of Korean girls by the Japanese Army to serve as prostitutes? What is the attitude of the average Korean toward this program? Does the P/W know of any disturbances or friction which has grown out of this program?"[18] It is thus clear that the United States already knew of the Japanese armed forces' mobilization of military sex slaves in Korea and was aware that the institution was enough to cause confusion in Korean society. In other words, although these questions do not reflect

---

17 Harold B. Quarton, "Survey of Current Political Thought and Temper of the Korean People," August 15, 1942, 11d, US Department of State, Records of the Department of State Relating to the Internal Affairs of Korea (Chosen), 1940-1944 (Department of State Decimal File 895 (document 895.01/162 PS/ET [also classified as 895.01/157-1/2])). Requoted from Pang Sun-joo, 1992: 218-219.

18 Military Intelligence Service, United States Army, Department of War, "Special Questions for Korean PWS," April 4, 1945.

the fact that Japanese corporations likewise mobilized corporate sex slaves *en masse* together with the mobilization of laborers (see Supplement I), the American government perceived the seriousness of the mobilization of military sex slaves alone.

6) The Direct Purposes of Establishing Military Comfort Stations

According to diverse Japanese military documents that simultaneously discussed the need for military comfort stations in the process of their establishment, the direct reasons for founding these facilities can be summarized as follows. First, comfort stations were needed to boost Japanese troops' morale. Because soldiers' morale dropped as the war continued and this had a very serious mental effect, leading to many problems, especially in Japan's occupied territories, the expansion of sexual slavery facilities was viewed as one important way of controlling the situation.[19] This can be seen as stemming from the same idea as the establishment of licensed prostitution during the Edo period earlier to promote psychological stability among warriors, who were highly anxious due to continuing wars (Fukae Masako, 1989). In other words, according to this way of thinking, men's sexual desire was "natural," especially in anxiety-arousing situations, and prostitution was a "necessary" evil (Kamisaka Fuyuko, 1992).

Second, the prevention of STDs among Japanese troops was an important reason that Japanese soldiers were prohibited from using sexual slavery facilities outside garrisons and were to use military comfort stations separately created only for them. As is well known, when Japanese military forces were dispatched to Siberia (1918-1922), STDs among the soldiers became a considerable problem, and the argument that this experience became an important motive for the establishment of military comfort stations is persuasive (Geum Byeongdong, 1992). This is related, in turn, to the fact that regular examinations of sex slaves for STDs constituted a very important part of the Japanese armed forces' control and supervision of military comfort stations. In a similar vein, the Meiji

19 Headquarters, Gunnery Unit, "Measures for Arousing Soldiers' Morale as Observed in the Experience of the Second Sino-Japanese War," September 19, 1940.

government implemented regular examinations of prostitutes for syphilis (Yamashita Yeong-Ae, 1991: 7).

Third, the most direct reason for the expansion of the establishment of military comfort stations during the war was the incidences of rape committed by Japanese soldiers in occupied territories. Indeed, in occupied territories, Japanese soldiers caused trouble with plunder, rape, arson, and murder of prisoners of war, and rape in particular led to an explosion of unexpectedly serious anti-Japanese sentiments among the locals.[20] Because such problems led to difficulty in governing occupied territories, the Japanese military ordered the "strict regulation of individual soldiers' acts and, at the same time, the prompt consolidation of sexual comfort facilities [for the soldiers]."[21]

In addition, judging from the fact that Japanese military comfort stations that were not directly established and managed by the armed forces but were managed by civilians were taxed under the pretext of "business tax" or "special monopoly tax,"[22] some have pointed out that the Japanese military was more enthusiastic in establishing military comfort stations because it could thus secure an independent source of revenue.[23]

As has been discussed above, the emperor system, *ie* system, licensed prostitution, situation in the colonies, and capitalist development were closely related and formed the background of the social structure against which Japanese military sexual slavery policies were formulated. Under such a social structure, the strengthening of militarism and war itself formed the specific conditions for the establishment of military sexual slavery policies, and direct reasons such as a drop in Japanese soldiers' morale and the occurrence of rape incidents led to the establishment of military comfort stations (see <Diagram 4-1>).

---

20 Headquarters, Gunnery Unit, "Measures for Arousing Soldiers' Morale as Observed in the Experience of the Second Sino-Japanese War," September 19, 1940; 9th Infantry Brigade, *Field Diary*, July 1-31, 1938, etc.

21 9th Infantry Brigade, *Field Diary*, July 1-31, 1938.

22 Division of Special Affairs, Ro Group, *Monthly Bulletin of the Ro Group Division of Special Affairs*, April 1940.

23 *Minutes of the Meetings of the House of Councilors Committee on Budget*, April 8, 1992.

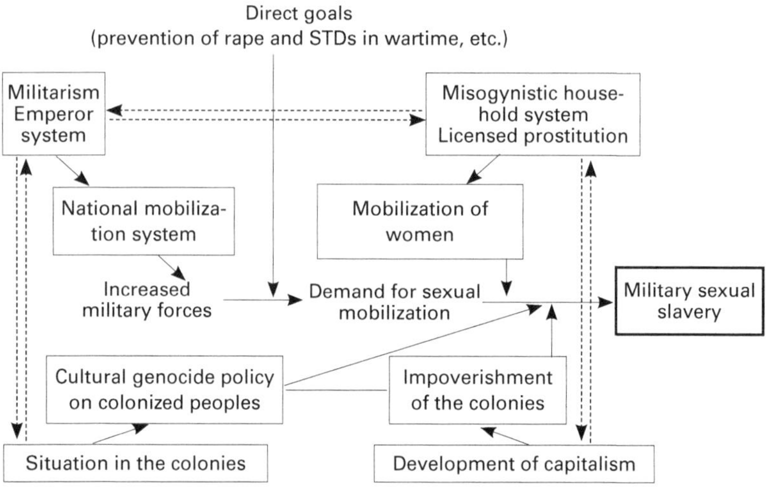

〈Diagram 4-1〉 The social structural background of Japanese military sexual slavery

2. The Reality of Japanese Military Sexual Slavery

Because materials on Japanese military sexual slavery are still being discovered, the reality of the institution continues to be unearthed. First, there is still no consensus on whether or not the term "military comfort women" itself is accurate and appropriate, and materials clearly demonstrating the overall scale and national origins of military sex slaves, the taking of these women, and the chain of command that implemented policies on the institution have not been discovered, either. As the terminology of military sex slaves, the establishment of military comfort stations, and the forced mobilization of women have been discussed in other chapters (see Chapters 1-3), this section will review the reality of the system with a focus on the circumstances at comfort stations.

1) The National Origins and Ages of Military Sex Slaves

The national origins of Japanese military sex slaves constitute a topic on which it is difficult to obtain accurate information yet one that has attracted considerable attention. During the war, Korean military sex slaves constituted the majority of the total and were found everywhere Japanese troops were present. This has been clarified by former medical officer Aso Tetsuo's testimony of the circumstances in a Shanghai comfort station,[24] which is one of the earliest discovered materials on Japanese military comfort stations, and investigations by Senda Kakou (Senda Kakou, 1991), who is a pioneer in the study of Japanese military sexual slavery. The fact that Koreans took up the overwhelming ratio of over 90% of the total military sex slaves has been corroborated also by a Japanese military document disclosed by the Japanese government in July 1993[25] and a material from the Manchurian Army 滿州軍 discovered and disclosed by the Fact-finding Team on the Truth about Forced Korean Laborers in Japan 朝鮮人强制連行眞相調查團 on December 6, 1992.[26] In addition, former Japanese soldiers who have reported to Military Comfort Women #110 從軍慰安婦110番, a hotline established by a Japanese civilian organization, likewise have testified that the vast majority of sex slaves at Japanese military comfort stations in Southeast Asia, South Seas Mandate, and remote areas in the Philippines were Koreans. On the other hand, there are occasional materials elucidating the fact that, out of military sex slaves who underwent medical examinations in places in China including Nanking and Wuhu, the Japanese and the Chinese outnumbered the Koreans,[27] and numerous materials show that, in many regions occupied by the Japanese armed forces, a considerable number of local women were forcibly mobilized as military comfort women as well.[28] Nevertheless, most materials mention the presence of Korean military sex slaves throughout occupied territories along with local women. Many ATIS interrogation

24 Medical officer 2nd Lt. Aso Tetsuo, "Methods for the Active Prevention of Venereal Diseases," June 26, 1939.

25 Ministry of Foreign Affairs, "Item Regarding Reporting on Population Statistics on Japanese Abroad per Occupation," April-September 1939.

26 According to the results of medical examinations, "out of 38 [Japanese military comfort women], 35 were Koreans." Headquarters, 14th Mixed Brigade, "Guidelines on the Implementation of the Medical Examination of Professional Entertainers and Prostitutes and Bar Girls," *Hygiene Duties Thrice-monthly*, May 1-10, 1933. Requoted from the *Asahi Shimbun*, December 6, 1992.

27 Division of Medical Officers, 15th Division, "A Summary Report on Hygiene Duties," December 1942-February 1943.

28 Squad, Tacloban Military Police, and Squad, Baguio Military Police, *The Monthly Military Police Bulletin of the 14th Army Military Police Corps*, 1943.

reports mention the national origins of military comfort women, the vast majority of whom were Koreans, and military comfort stations consisting solely of Japanese women were extremely small in number:[29] Koreans (nos. 34, 46, and 67); Koreans and Japanese (nos. 24, 25, 27, and 48); Koreans, Chinese, and Filipinas (no. 28); and Koreans, Formosans, and locals (no. 31). Allied Forces documents discovered in the National Archives and Records Administration by a South Korean investigation team in January 2015 report of the presence of Koreans in each area, as in: "Japanese, Chinese, and Koreans (Rabaul)"; "Japanese and Koreans (Rabaul)"; "Chinese and Koreans (Canton [present-day Guangdong], Singapore)"; "Koreans and Dutch East Indians (Malang)"; "Koreans and Formosans (Malang)"; "Koreans and Japanese (Sungshan [present-day Songshan;[30] also known as "Mt. Sung"])"; "Koreans (Myitkyina)"; "Koreans, Chinese, and Malayans (Singapore)"; and "Koreans, Formosans, Japanese, and Filipinas (Manila)," etc.[31] Koreans were found nearly everywhere. This situation is found in materials including those of the US Office of War Information (US OWI) and the SEATIC as well. More specifically, the Allied Forces' report on Kunming mentioned above elucidates that all 23 women were Koreans,[32] and there is also a document showing that the absolute majority of women sent to Myitkyina, Burma in 1942 were Koreans.[33] A prisoner of war interrogation report created by the US Office of War Information in 1944 in Assam states that all Japanese military sex slaves there were Koreans.[34] As for Miyako Island (*Miyako-jima*), a

29 Though the NEFIS classified all women as "Japanese" without distinguishing among the Japanese, Koreans, and Formosans so that the Japanese seem to have been in the majority at a glance, it is a fact that the Koreans were actually numerous (Baek Jaeye, 2015: 58-63).

30 [TN] Referred to at the time by the Japanese as "Lameng" (*Ramo*) 拉孟.

31 Human Rights Center, Seoul National University, 2016.

32 Office of Strategic Services, "Attached Memorandum: Korean and Japanese Prisoners of War in Kunming: 28 April, 1945," Kunming-REG-OP-3, Field Station Files, Records of the Office of Strategic Services (Record Group 226, Entry 154, Box 185), April 28, 1945.

33 Allied Translator and Interpreter Section, [General Headquarters,] Supreme Commander for the Allied Powers, "Research Report No. 120: Amenities in the Japanese Armed Forces" (Record Group 407, Entry A1-427, Box 913), November 15, 1945.

34 United States Office of War Information, "Investigation Reports, Directives and Other Records Relating to Captured Personnel and Materials, 1940-1946" (Record Group 165, Entry 177, Box 915, OWI Outpost Report No. WDC406), April 18, 1944.

small island in Okinawa Prefecture, 10,000 out of the 40,000 locals were evacuated to nearby Formosa toward the end of the war so that it came to be occupied by the remaining residents and the same number of (30,000) soldiers. At this time, Korean comfort women reportedly were brought along by the armed forces. To date, a total of 17 comfort stations have been found on this island. Consequently, the number of military sex slaves, though inexact, likewise would have been considerable. According to the locals, all of these women were Koreans.[35]

On the other hand, former Japanese soldiers have also testified that while ethnic Japanese sex slaves were for officers, Korean sex slaves were for soldiers or that while Japanese sex slaves were for officers, Korean sex slaves were for soldiers and Formosan sex slaves were for civilian employees of the military 軍屬, respectively (Editorial Board of *Military Comfort Women #110*, ed., 1992). However, because regulations on comfort stations found in most military documents had both officers and soldiers use the same sex slaves, with differences only in the time slots,[36] such regulations depending on sex slaves' respective national origins do not seem to have been implemented in general at Japanese military comfort stations.

According to regulations, the minimum age for prostitutes in licensed prostitution was 18 or above and 17 or above in Japan and colonial Korea, respectively (Yamashita Yeong-Ae, 1991: 50). As for military sex slaves, however, there does not seem to have been a uniformly prescribed age restriction. Although, according to one document from a Japanese military unit stationed in China in 1940, prostitutes were to be aged 16 or above,[37] regulations on comfort stations generally did not mention sex slaves' ages. While some of the victims who have reported to the South

---

35 See Hong Yunshin, 2016. In September 2015, I participated in a ceremony held on Miyako Island to commemorate the 7th anniversary of the erection of the Monument of Arirang アリランの碑. That is, the Japanese who remembered *Arirang* 아리랑, a Korean folk song, from wartime had erected the monument in order to remember Korean women who had been brought as Japanese military sex slaves.

36 Many including the Headquarters, 3rd Independent Mountain Artillery Regiment, *Field Diary*, April 1-6 and April 30, 1941; and the 35th Independent Defense Infantry Battalion, *Field Diary*, April 1-June 30, 1942.

37 Division of Special Affairs, Ro Group, *Monthly Bulletin of the Ro Group Division of Special Affairs*, 1940.

Korean government were taken as sex slaves at the ages of 11-13 and 20 or above, most were taken at the ages of 14-19. This shows that regulations on the restriction of military sex slaves' ages were implemented only in certain areas and that, in general, young women were forcibly taken regardless of their ages.

2) The Establishment and Management of Comfort Stations

• **Establishment:** It is no exaggeration to say that, from the early 1930s to the end of the war, Japanese military comfort stations were established "wherever it was necessary for the Japanese Army to fight."[38] The testimonies of former Japanese soldiers who disclosed their experiences decades later likewise show that military comfort stations existed very extensively (Editorial Board of *Military Comfort Women #110*, ed., 1992). Indeed, these facilities existed not only in regions occupied by the Japanese armed forces such as China and Manchuria but also Japanese colonies such as Formosa and Korea and even within mainland Japan. A record stating that 50 Korean sex slaves and relevant personnel were to be found even on Soembawa (present-day Sumbawa) Island,[39] one of the southernmost islands of Indonesia today, makes it possible to surmise the sheer extent of the regions to which Korean women were mobilized as Japanese military sex slaves. Similarly, victims who have reported to the South Korean government were taken to every corner of territories occupied by the Japanese armed forces as well as Japan itself, Formosa, and Korea. Furthermore, many of them did not stay in single locations but were transferred as Japanese troops moved on.

• **Use only by soldiers:** Existing during the warring period from the Manchurian Incident to World War II, Japanese military comfort stations could be used only by Japanese soldiers and civilian employees of the military according to the forcible regulations of the armed forces.[40] Local

38 "The 'comfort girls' have been found wherever it was necessary for the Japanese Army to fight," Psychological Warfare Team, United States Army Forces India-Burma Theater, United States Office of War Information, "Japanese Prisoner of War Interrogation Report No. 49" (Record Group 208, Entry 366A, Box 231), October 1, 1944.

39 48th Division, *War History Materials and Postwar Conditions of the 48th Division*, July 1946.

officials and civilians could in no way use these Japanese military comfort stations.[41] On the other hand, Japanese soldiers and civilian employees of the military were strictly prohibited from using comfort stations other than military comfort stations and from contacting prostitutes 賣淫婦 and "natives."[42]

• **Management:** Although Japanese military comfort stations exhibited diverse forms in their establishment and management and the recruitment of sex slaves such as direct intervention by the military or consignment to civilians according to the time and location, they were subjected to protection, supervision, and strict control by the Japanese armed forces in all cases. The establishment of comfort stations can be classified into establishment by the Japanese military, civilian establishment authorized by the military,[43] and designation, incorporation, and reorganization of existing civilian stations as military stations by the armed forces.[44]

---

40 "The use of comfort stations is to be restricted to uniformed soldiers and civilian employees of the military." Iloilo Office, Visaya Branch, Philippines Military Administration, "Item Regarding the Forwarding of Regulations on Comfort Stations (Asia Hall, Comfort Station No. 1)," November 22, 1942.

41 "...Local users absolutely may not be received [by Japanese military comfort women]," Japanese Consulate-General in Shanghai, "History of the Ministry of Foreign Affairs Police, Section on China: The State of Special Women from Japan and Their Regulation and the State of the Regulation of Unlicensed Prostitution by the Concession Authorities in 1938"; and "...Local officials and civilians absolutely may not use [Japanese military comfort stations]," 3475th Yama Unit [i.e., 32nd Infantry Regiment], "Regulations on Soldiers' Clubs," December 1944.

42 "...Soldiers and civilian employees of the military are strictly prohibited from using other [i.e., non-military] comfort stations," 3475th Yama Unit, "Regulations on Soldiers' Clubs," December 1944; and "...Contact with prostitutes, natives, and the like other than those designated by the military is to be strictly eradicated," compiled by the Inspectorate-General of Military Training, "Wartime Service Guidelines," 1938.

43 "[Military comfort station] establishment applicants are to visit and apply to the Department of Medical Affairs 醫務課 in the present division." Division of Special Affairs, Ro Group, *Monthly Bulletin of the Ro Group Division of Special Affairs*, May 1940.

44 "The [Japanese] Navy authorities are to inspect and examine the pleasure quarters and designate six establishments in a satisfactory state of hygiene as comfort stations for the military personnel... and give lectures on hygiene," 3rd Torpedo Boat Unit, *The Wartime Diary of the 3rd Torpedo Boat Unit*, July 1944 (Japan Defense Agency National Institute for Defense Studies Materials: Material No. 85); and "...As for already established [military] comfort stations,... while also taking into consideration the convenience of settlers in general, some are to be integrated and reorganized into special comfort stations 特種慰安所...," Japanese Consulate-General in Nanking, "History of the Ministry of Foreign Affairs Police, Section on China: The State of Special Women from Japan and Their Regulation and the State of the Regulation of

Numerous are Japanese military documents demonstrating the fact that the armed forced directly constructed comfort stations,[45] and there also are testimonies that prisoners of war were made to build or repair these facilities.[46]

Here, civilians who wished to manage military comfort stations had to submit an application form, a written plan, a written pledge, and employees' personal dossiers to the Japanese armed forces.[47] For comfort stations established by civilians to be operated as military comfort stations, both permission and licenses from the military were indispensable.[48] Civilian managers paid a certain sum of money each month as a business tax.[49]

As for the management of comfort stations established by the Japanese armed forces, it can be classified into direct management by the military[50] and consigned management by civilians. As for comfort stations established by civilians, they seem to have been managed by civilians in most cases. Even military comfort stations established and managed by civilians were provided with sanitary equipment and medical officers' regular examinations by the Japanese military, had to adhere strictly to the

---

Unlicensed Prostitution by the Concession Authorities in 1938," April 16, 1938.

45 "In establishing comfort stations, each unit is to report the following promptly," file of the bulletins of the 62nd Division, *Bulletin of the Ishi Corps*, no. 56, September 17, 1944; "Order: On the 5th, the company must urgently construct a temporary comfort station facility in the designated house," 6th Garrison Construction Labor Company, *Field Diary*, June 1-30, 1944; and "Five including Sgt. Yamaguchi of the Management Unit 管理班 are to perform the task of providing a comfort station," Division of Adjutants, 62nd Division, *Field Diary*, January-February 1945.

46 The testimony of a British prisoner of war. Morris-Suzuki, 2015.

47 The information was to be written on forms created by the Japanese military. Allied Translator and Interpreter Section, [General Headquarters,] Supreme Commander for the Allied Powers, "Research Report No. 120: Amenities in the Japanese Armed Forces" (Record Group 165, Entry 79, Box 342), November 15, 1945.

48 "[Military comfort station] managers are to renew their licenses every three months." Division of Special Affairs, Ro Group, *Monthly Bulletin of the Ro Group Division of Special Affairs*, April 1940.

49 "License fees 50 sen, monthly business tax 7 yen," from the material above.

50 "The adjutant of the unit must supervise and direct the operations of the soldiers' club 軍人俱樂部 and manage it smoothly and certainly... The medical officer attached to the unit is to be responsible for hygiene facilities... The paymaster of the unit is to be responsible for tasks regarding accounts and supply..." See the table of the division of the duties of the Soldiers' Hall of the 3475th Yama Unit in the Nakayama Guard Forces, "Regulations on the Use of Soldiers' Clubs," May 1944; and "Regulations on Soldiers' Clubs," December 1944.

guidelines for hygiene and cleanliness stipulated by the military, and were obliged to follow the many clauses in the regulations on comfort stations established by the military. They also had to make regular business reports to the Japanese military,[51] and even the transportation of sex slaves took place at military orders.[52] According to an Allied Forces report drawn up in the Philippines, civilian comfort station managers had to submit daily reports and monthly business reports and, even in cases of temporary business suspension or closure, had to obtain permission from the Japanese armed forces.[53] There is also a concrete report that a Japanese who managed a comfort station in Myitkyina, Burma with Korean women did so under the supervision and regulation of the 114th Infantry Regiment.[54]

• **Comfort station regulations:** Each Japanese military comfort station was managed according to station regulations established by the Japanese armed forces. These station regulations stipulated the time slots and fees for each military rank as well as medical examinations for STDs and other clauses regarding hygiene. While the specific contents differed for each comfort station, there seem to have been, in general, stipulated regulations covering the clauses and categories above. Although such regulations were to be "strictly observed,"[55] it is unclear just how faithfully they were

51 "...Comfort station managers... must report their business conditions to the [Philippines] Military Administration [比島]軍政監部." Iloilo Office, Visaya Branch, Philippines Military Administration, "Item Regarding the Forwarding of Regulations on Comfort Stations (Asia Hall, Comfort Station No. 1)," November 22, 1942.

52 "...'special women 特種婦女' are being transferred at military orders." Japanese Consulate in Kiukiang [present-day Jiujiang], "History of the Ministry of Foreign Affairs Police, Section on China: The State of Special Women from Japan and Their Regulation and the State of the Regulation of Unlicensed Prostitution by the Concession Authorities in 1938," December 1, 1938.

53 The report forms, too, were created by the Japanese military. See the Allied Translator and Interpreter Section, [General Headquarters,] Supreme Commander for the Allied Powers, "Research Report No. 120: Amenities in the Japanese Armed Forces" (Record Group 407, Entry A1-427, Box 913), November 15, 1945.

54 Allied Translator and Interpreter Section, [General Headquarters,] Supreme Commander for the Allied Powers, "Research Report No. 120: Amenities in the Japanese Armed Forces" (Record Group 407, Entry A1-427, Box 913), November 15, 1945.

55 "The regulations on the use of military comfort stations in occupied territories are to be strictly observed." Headquarters, 15th Independent Mixed Regiment, *Field Diary,* October 1-31, 1945.

followed in reality.

• **Hours of use:** The hours at which Japanese military comfort stations could be used were stipulated and to be strictly observed.[56] When many units shared one comfort station, each unit was designated a particular day of the week on which it could use the station.[57] Although the actual hours differed for each comfort station, soldiers, non-commissioned officers, and officers were restricted in the time slots in which they could respectively use a station as well.[58] Even the duration at which an individual could use a comfort station was limited, too.[59] However, many former Japanese soldiers have testified that there was no need to limit the time to use a military comfort station because there were far too many users in most cases,[60] and approximately half of the victims have testified that although time restrictions existed at comfort stations, they were not strictly observed in most cases.

• **Fees:** Regulations on Japanese military comfort stations stipulated fees in accordance with soldiers' ranks and the time spent at a station.[61] The

56 Headquarters, 15th Independent Mixed Regiment, *Field Diary*, January 1-31, 1945.

57 2nd Independent Heavy Siege Artillery Battalion, "Regulations on the Use of Comfort Stations," "Regulations on Internal Duties during the Occupation of Changchow," March 16, 1938 records, among other things, "[as for the use of the comfort station,] the Hoshi Unit 星部隊, on Sundays, the Kuri'iwa Unit 栗岩部隊, on Mondays, and the Matsumura Unit 松村部隊, on Wednesdays… as for [the] use [of the station] by other temporarily stationed units, separate instructions will be given."

58 For example: soldiers, 10 AM-5 PM, 1 yen 50 sen, 20-30 minutes/non-commissioned officers, 5-9 PM, 3 yen, 30-40 minutes/officers, 9 PM-12 AM (mistakenly written "12 PM" in the following source document), 5 yen, 30-40 minutes. Psychological Warfare Team, United States Army Forces India-Burma Theater, United States Office of War Information, "Japanese Prisoner of War Interrogation Report No. 49" (Record Group 208, Entry 366A, Box 231), October 1, 1944. Requoted from Ahn Byung Jik, trans., 2013: 410. Only officers were allowed to stay overnight. Headquarters, 3rd Independent Mountain Artillery Regiment, *Field Diary*, April 1-6 and April 30, 1941, etc.

59 The time for the use of a Japanese military comfort station was limited to 30 minutes or 1 hour per person, and an overnight stay at a station after regular hours was permitted with the payment of an additional fee. 35th Independent Defense Infantry Battalion, *Field Diary*, April 1-June 30, 1942, etc.

60 Because there were too many soldiers, each one had only 2-3 minutes to use a military comfort station, and 20-30 soldiers waited outside the door in lines (Editorial Board of *Military Comfort Women #110*, ed., 1992).

61 For example, according to the regulations of a Japanese military comfort station from 1942, for 30 minutes and 1 hour, respectively, soldiers were charged 1 yen and 2 yen, non-commissioned officers were charged 1 yen 50 sen and 2 yen 50 sen, and officers were charged 3 yen and 4 yen, and an overnight stay cost 8 yen. 35th Independent Defense Infantry Battalion, *Field Diary*, April 1-June 30, 1942.

fees thus stipulated differed according to time and place and were to be paid, in most cases, with tickets to prevent congestion.[62] Despite such regulations, however, the payment of wages to sex slaves does not seem to have occurred properly in nearly all cases. In fact, most victims either received no wage whatsoever or received tickets from soldiers but did not receive money from station managers later in return for these tickets.[63] Cpt. Chan of the Allied Forces, who interrogated some 20 Korean women sexually enslaved by the Japanese military after the fall of Myitkyina, an area previously occupied by the Japanese armed forces, on August 3, 1944, stated in his 1986 book, "when I thought of what these girls had endured to earn this worthless scrip [i.e., ticket] I was heartsick" (Chan, 1986: 97).

The regulations of many military comfort stations stipulated different fees according to sex slaves' national origins.[64] Among former Japanese soldiers who have reported to Military Comfort Women #110, some have testified that the fees were the highest for ethnic Japanese sex slaves, followed by Korean and Chinese sex slaves, in this order. However, such a system of charging different fees according to sex slaves' national origins was not imposed on any of the victims who have reported to the South Korean government.

• **STD tests:** Regular examinations of sex slaves for STDs were a very important aspect of the Japanese military comfort station system. Indeed, comfort station regulations stipulating the examination of sex slaves by medical officers once a week, every two weeks, or every month have been found in numerous military documents and studies.[65] In addition, many materials reporting the results of such examinations of sex slaves have been found.[66] Medical officers conducting STD tests were supposed

62 See, for example, "Prevent confusion due to the ticket system," Headquarters, 2nd Army, "A Summary of the State of the 2nd Army," December 10, 1938, etc.

63 A very small number of former sex slaves have testified that the tickets they had received from soldiers were settled and paid in money once every 1-3 months or that they received tips.

64 For example, in the case of non-commissioned officers, the amount was 2 yen for Japanese, 1 yen 50 sen for Koreans, and 1 yen for Chinese. 2nd Company, 2nd Independent Heavy Siege Artillery Battalion, *Field Diary*, January 1-April 30, 1938.

65 2nd Independent Heavy Siege Artillery Battalion, "Regulations on the Use of Comfort Stations," "Regulations on Internal Duties during the Occupation of Changchow," March 16, 1938; 35th Independent Defense Infantry Battalion, *Information Thrice-monthly*, no. 19, *Field Diary*, December 1942, etc.

to report the test results to their commanders each time.[67] Likewise, most victims have testified that they were tested for STDs every week or month at hospitals or by medical officers visiting comfort stations. To prevent the spread of STDs among soldiers, the Japanese military provided male contraceptives to soldiers or comfort stations,[68] ordering that they be used without fail. In fact, according to victims' testimonies, condoms were insufficient so that, in many cases, they were washed and reused. In addition, Japanese military documents stressing strict hygiene management including disinfection have been discovered.[69] However, despite all such hygiene regulations, STDs were prevalent among Japanese military sex slaves. Records reporting examinations of sex slaves for STDs show that many of these women contracted STDs[70] and were hospitalized for treatment.[71] Amid such a situation, some even argued that medical examinations were useless.[72] In addition, sex slaves judged to have STDs

---

66 Special Service Ship Unit, "File of the 8th Summary Table of Achievements in the Second Sino-Japanese War, Investigation of the Meritorious Service of the Navy," April-November 1940, etc.

67 An already prepared report form was presented as well. Combat Intelligence Center, South Pacific Force [i.e., South Pacific Area Command (SOPAC)], "Translation of Captured Japanese Document: Regulations Governing the Use of the Special South Sector Brothel and Regulations Governing the Operation Thereof," item no. 1033 (Record Group 165, Entry 79, Box 404), December 10, 1942.

68 "Hygiene sacks 衛生サック [i.e., condoms] collectively issued to units in charge of rear facilities…," file of the bulletins of the 62nd Division, *Bulletin of the Ishi Corps*, no. 64, October 2, 1944; and "Although the military currently issues hygiene sacks to each soldier once every two months, they [i.e., hygiene sacks] are to be disposed of by sale to each comfort station manager for the following reasons… In cases where individual soldiers do not bear [hygiene] sacks [to comfort stations], [hygiene sacks are] used in locations other than military comfort stations, and there is a danger of causing accidents [by bearing and using the hygiene sacks] in locations other than military comfort stations," Ministry of War, *Great Log of Army Secrets in China in 1942, No. 39*, October 2, 1942.

69 Iloilo Office, Visaya Branch, Philippines Military Administration, "Item Regarding the Forwarding of Regulations on Comfort Stations (Asia Hall, Comfort Station No. 1)," November 22, 1942; 3475th Yama Unit, "Regulations on Soldiers' Clubs," December 1944, etc.

70 See the Headquarters, Nami Group [i.e., 23rd Army], *Wartime Thrice-monthly (Rear Relations)*, April 11-20, 1939; Division of Medical Officers, 15th Division, "A Summary Report on Hygiene Duties," December 1942-February 1943, etc.

71 Special Service Ship Unit, "File of the 8th Summary Table of Achievements in the Second Sino-Japanese War, Investigation of the Meritorious Service of the Navy," April-November 1940.

72 Medical officer 2nd Lt. Aso Tetsuo, "Methods for the Active Prevention of Venereal Diseases," June 26, 1939.

were forbidden to receive users until they were fully treated.[73] NEFIS reports reported that girls who had contracted STDs were immediately dismissed and replaced.[74] According to victims' testimonies, they were given injection "no. 606"[75] when they contracted STDs and, in severe cases, treated in isolation. Some have also testified of fellow sex slaves who, due to severe STDs, were treated in isolation but never returned to comfort stations in the end.

Regulations on Japanese military comfort stations also included clauses such as the prohibition of alcohol within these facilities and of entry by users under the influence of alcohol. In addition, regulatory clauses forbidding violence by station managers have been found.[76] Such regulations were but mere formalities, however, and experiencers and victims of Japanese military comfort stations have testified, without exception, that Japanese soldiers and managers treated sex slaves very cruelly, without reserve.

3) The Abandonment of Military Sex Slaves

Though Japanese military sex slaves supposedly were free once they paid off all of their cash advances according to the Allied Forces' prisoner of war interrogation records, no one reportedly was allowed to leave comfort stations.[77] Women who managed to return home before the end of the war were very exceptional cases. Out of the victims interviewed by the Korean

---

73 3475th Yama Unit, "Regulations on Soldiers' Clubs," December 1944.

74 Netherlands Forces Intelligence Service, "Compilation of NEFIS Interrogation Reports Nos. 103, 106-138, 141-159, 161-171, 173, 175-178 and 193-194 (Not Issued [Separately])" (August 28, 1944); and "Compilation of NEFIS Interrogation Reports Nos: 534, 552, 567, 568, 579, 586, 587, 588 and 592 (Not issued separately)" (December 6, 1944).

75 Currently used only on animals due to its high potency, this injection caused in military sex slaves not only the treatment of STDs but also abortions in cases of pregnancies, and repeated injections led to infertility.

76 2nd Independent Heavy Siege Artillery Battalion, "Regulations on the Use of Comfort Stations," "Regulations on Internal Duties during the Occupation of Changchow," March 16, 1938.

77 Allied Translator and Interpreter Section, [General Headquarters,] Supreme Commander for the Allied Powers, "Research Report No. 120: Amenities in the Japanese Armed Forces" (Record Group 407, Entry A1-427, Box 913), November 15, 1945.

Research Group, Kim Soon-duk 金順德 returned to Korea with the aid of the military officer who had kept her as his personal comfort woman; and Mun Ok-ju 文玉珠, who had been mobilized to Tung'an Province (present-day eastern Heilongjiang Province) in Manchuria, likewise was able to come back after promising a Japanese military officer in charge of supply management who was fond of her that she would live with him after a visit to the colony and receiving a certificate.

Japanese military units rarely returned home along with military sex slaves when the war ended. According to the testimonies of many former Japanese soldiers, these women were abandoned at comfort stations, forced to commit suicide together with Japanese soldiers, or killed after being driven into caves or placed inside submarines (Yun Chung-Ok, 1991a). The Japanese military abandoned sex slaves on the battlegrounds or treated them cruelly upon the nation's defeat, which was even more serious than the forced mobilization of these women and their coercive treatment at comfort stations and which must be redressed.

Many survivors have testified that, one day, Japanese soldiers stopped coming to comfort stations. Most of them returned home either on their own amid extreme hardships or after having been interned in the Allied Forces' internment camps. There are investigations and testimonies by the Allied Forces in addition to testimonies by victims of Japanese military sexual slavery as well. There is a report that women previously at a comfort station in Myitkyina, Burma were discovered by the Allied Forces while following the footsteps of the departed Japanese troops together.[78] A second-generation Japanese-American Military Intelligence Service (MIS) member of the Allied Forces, Karl Gozo Yoneda wrote in his diary that, after the fall of Myitkyina in early August 1944, "114th Regiment commander Col. Maruyama Fusayasu secretly ran away last night, taking healthy subordinates and abandoning these men and these women [i.e., injured soldiers and Korean comfort women]" (Yoneda, 1989). An Australian member of the United Kingdom's Royal Regiment of Artillery

78 Allied Translator and Interpreter Section, [General Headquarters,] Supreme Commander for the Allied Powers, "Research Report No. 120: Amenities in the Japanese Armed Forces" (Record Group 407, Entry A1-427, Box 913), November 15, 1945.

deployed to the Burmese front testified of military comfort women shot to death by Japanese soldiers who had retreated from the jungle in the country, and there is also a testimony that five Korean sex slaves who had escaped from a comfort station at the end of the war during the Japanese armed forces' withdrawal entered a British base along the Thai-Burmese border. There is a record on Korean military comfort women who fled from a comfort station in Ubon Ratchathani, Thailand and one in Syriam (present-day Thanlyin), Burma, respectively, and sought out the British troops' aid as well.

Many Japanese military sex slaves discovered by the Allied Forces had been disguised as nurses as well. Upon arriving in Koepang (present-day Kupang) on Timor Island, Netherlands East Indies, Allied troops found 26 women, who had been issued with Red Cross armbands by the Japanese military on the eve of the latter's surrender (Morris-Suzuki, 2015). Five Korean women captured alive by American soldiers on May 19, 1945 were reported to have been abandoned by the Japanese armed forces and to be quite feeble, having subsisted solely on grass for the past 10 days.[79]

With Japanese defeat, the bodies of countless[80] military comfort women were discovered in Myitkyina as well as Sungshan and Tengchung (present-day Tengchong)[81] in China, along the Burmese border—all strategic points on the Burma Road toward the end of the war—at times including those of babies. According to materials unearthed and provided to the South Korean press by Dr. Pang Sun-joo, the Chinese Expeditionary Force (Y Force), which occupied Sungshan on September 7, 1944 and captured Tengchung on September 14, recorded in the September 15 entry in its field diary (*G-3 Daily Diary*), "Night of the 13th the Japs shot 30 Korean girls in the city."[82] Pang Sun-joo has also conducted pioneering research on the return of former Japanese military sex slaves from the

79 Headquarters, 1st Corps, Office of the Assistant Chief of Staff, G-2 (Intelligence), 163rd Language Detachment, APO 301 (Record Group 338, Box 443), May 21, 1945. Requoted from Chang, 2003.

80 The number of Japanese military sex slaves in the area is estimated to have amounted to 1,500.

81 [TN] Referred to at the time by the Japanese as "Tengyue" (*Toetsu*) 騰越.

82 Covered on Munhwa Broadcasting Corporation, *MBC Newsdesk*, August 15, 1997.

Philippines as well as regions in the Pacific Ocean and the Indian Ocean, demonstrating the women's wretched circumstances (Pang Sun-joo, 1997: 236-244).

Following their return to Korea, survivors were unable to lead ordinary lives due to factors including guilt for their past as Japanese military comfort women, diseases contracted during their period as sex slaves, and the prejudice of those around them. Consequently, most of them currently live alone and suffer from considerable difficulty in both finance and health.

3. Concealment

After being nearly forgotten following the end of war, such an immense fact finally started to be publicized for the first time in the 1990s. Initiated in South Korea, discussions on Japanese military sexual slavery soon spread to Japan and Asian victim nations, and the issue began to be discussed in earnest in the international community as well, through organs such as the UN.

Why, then, was Japanese military sexual slavery concealed until then? The answer to this question will be one also to the question of why the issue became a social one only in the 1990s, after 50 years. It was due first and foremost to the concealment of the relevant materials by the Japanese government and military. Indeed, military documents confirm that the Japanese armed forces not only implemented policy on sex slaves in extreme secrecy[83] but also ordered the soldiers in charge to dispose of the relevant materials immediately after the war.[84] When the issue was raised in the 1990s, scholars began in earnest to search for materials, and imperial Japanese military documents began to be discovered at Japanese government organs including the library of the former Japan Defense

83 Most Japanese wartime documents on military sex slaves are classified as "Top Secret."

84 One recently discovered document states, "Because most of the materials from the 48th Division were disposed of at superiors' orders at the armistice and the remainder was submitted to the Australian forces, most accurate materials are missing. Consequently, gathering [former] soldiers' memories..." 48th Division, *War History Materials and Postwar Conditions of the 48th Division*, July 1946.

Agency. Basically, most of the relevant documents can be seen as having been destroyed, however, and such absolute concealment of materials led to the concealment of this historical fact.

Second, the fact that, in the case of Japan, unlike Germany, the task of shedding light on the truth and postwar settlement including compensations and punishments were hardly performed, too, blocked the path for Japanese military sexual slavery to be raised as an issue. This can be seen as stemming, in turn, from the Japanese government's patronizing attitude toward Asian countries and, simultaneously, the inability of the victim nations in Asia, unlike in the case of Germany, strongly to demand just postwar settlement due to their own weak economic and political circumstances and underdeveloped social movements. Indeed, the fact that while Japan's wartime crimes against Asian women went completely unpunished afterwards, the Batavia War Criminal Court held by the Dutch government in 1946 executed sentences on nine former Japanese soldiers on charges of having forcibly mobilized Dutch women living in the Netherlands East Indies as Japanese military sex slaves (McDougall, 1998: 92) clearly shows the weakness of Asian victim nations.

At the same time, the American response to Japan, whose role in the implantation of capitalism in Asia was a consideration of the United States, can be said to have contributed considerably to the situation as well. During the Cold War against the former Soviet Union, the United States prioritized above all the bringing over of Japan as an ally and hence neglected to convict the latter of its injustices, thus contributing to the securement, once again, of Japan's domination over Asian countries (Takagi Ken'ichi, 1992: 56-57). Cpt. James Gowing Godwin, who conducted investigators at the General Headquarters of the Supreme Commander for the Allied Powers (GHQ/SCAP) in Tokyo as a member of the Australian War Crimes Section of the International Military Tribunal for the Far East, recorded that although there was a debate among investigators on the serious issue of Japanese military sexual slavery, investigations were discontinued due to pressure from the upper ranks of the GHQ/SCAP.[85]

85 James MacKay, *Betrayal in High Places* (Stockport, UK: A Lane Publishing, 1996); requoted from Hayashi Hirofumi, 2005: 147.

Overcoming oblivion and silence, Japanese military sexual slavery survivors have disclosed the damage that they have suffered and raised their voices so that human rights and peace may be established worldwide.

The most important reason was a patriarchal social climate. A situation where those who had experienced Japanese military comfort stations including both victimizers and victims maintained silence due to guilt or shame prevented the fact from surfacing. Moreover, a patriarchal social climate that socially stigmatized the victims instead of criticizing the victimizers' violence in such issues regarding the outright violation of women's human rights can be seen to have functioned as the most fatal factor in the concealment of Japanese military sexual slavery.[86]

In addition, the fact that Japanese intellectuals and social movements failed to turn their attention to Japan's postwar responsibility to Asia

86 The influence of Confucian culture is clear in the difference between former military sex slaves in the Philippines and those in South Korea and Taiwan in their lives following return to their respective countries. According to an investigation conducted by the International Commission of Jurists in May 2002, while former sex slaves in the Philippines generally lead ordinary married lives following their return home, nearly all of their counterparts in South Korea and Taiwan live in wretched conditions (International Commission of Jurists, 1994).

(Takagi Ken'ichi, 1992: 56-58) and that research on the history of damages inflicted during Japan's forced occupation, especially women's history in this period, was meager, too, was a major factor that delayed the discovery of the issue.

Because changes, big and small, took place despite all such obstacles, it has been possible to give voice to the issue of Japanese military sexual slavery after 50 years of silence. Above all, the economic development of South Korean society and the growth of women's movements for the transformation of a patriarchal society have served as the most important basis for making military sexual slavery public. In other words, first raising their voices at the end of the 1980s, when economic development and democratization rapidly accelerated, women's movements in South Korea turned to the hitherto buried issue of Japanese military sexual slavery and began to see it as one of their important tasks. The discovery at the end of 1991 and in early 1992 in the United States and Japan of military documents on military sex slaves and the public testimonies of victims in South Korea in 1991 served to gather public attention considerably. Also important were factors such as: the rise of a certain sense of wariness among Western countries including the United States toward Japan, which began to wield immense influence as a major economic power; the beginning of public attention to new social movements including those demanding compensation from Japan for its war crimes in Asian countries such as South Korea and Taiwan as they recovered economically from war to a certain degree; and the participation of NGOs in Japan, which were already well established, in this issue.

Part II

The Social Movements to Resolve the Issue of Japanese Military Sexual Slavery

Chapter 5

The Movement to Resolve the Issue of Japanese Military Sexual Slavery

Japanese military sexual slavery began to receive public attention only at the end of the 1980s, over 50 years after the end of World War II, and came to be highlighted as an important issue in social movements both in South Korea and abroad. Because the relevant documents on the institution, which had been established through top-secret policies, were destroyed by the Japanese armed forces following the war, relevant materials themselves have been extremely rare. Moreover, due to the United States' postwar Asian policy, the pursuit of the question of Japan's war responsibilities took place only on a minimal level so that the issue of military sexual slavery was not mentioned at the International Military Tribunal for the Far East held during 1946-1948. Subsequently, experiencers and victims of the institution alike firmly maintained silence in a patriarchal society. Nevertheless, this issue, which had violated the human rights of countless people, did not lie utterly forgotten and untouched in the mean time, either.

This chapter will summarize discussions on Japanese military sexual slavery before the rise of movements to resolve it, the formation of the movements during the latter half of the 1980s and their subsequent development, and the state of these movements since 2000 and, at the same time, analyze the ways in which diverse subjects cooperated with one another in the process through which the movements developed. Activities at the UN and the ILO and the movement for the 2000 Women's Tribunal, which occurred in the context of the overall movements, will be discussed in detail in separate chapters (Chapters 6-8). Added to the end of this chapter is a summary of changes to the positions of the South Korean and Japanese governments according to currents in the movements.

This chapter has been written in reference to primary materials including pamphlets published by various organizations and documents of international organs. More importantly, broad use has been made of in-depth interviews of members of diverse activist groups and the participatory observations that I myself have made as a participant in the movements.

1. The Issue of Japanese Military Sexual Slavery before Social Movements

From the end of the war to the 1980s, the issue of Japanese military sexual slavery was sporadically raised in both South Korea and Japan in the forms of newspaper articles, novels, films, and scholarly research. However, such academic and cultural activities were buried in an overwhelmingly patriarchal social climate, failing to gain public attention in South Korea and Japan alike, both of which were focused on economic development.

It must be pointed out that unceasing research and movements continuing from earlier eras lay in the background against which Japanese military sexual slavery became a major social issue at the end of the 1980s through the voices of South Korean women's movements. Indeed, following World War II, many records on Japanese military sex slaves were to be found in South Korea alone (*Seoul Shinmun*, May 12, 1946; and Um Kwang-Sup, 1946), and this issue was already made public in Japan through films and prose fiction. One example concerns *Shunpuden* 春婦傳 (known in English as *Story of a Prostitute* or *Joy Girls*; written by Tamura Taijiro 田村泰次郎), a Japanese novel published in 1947 that depicts an ethnic Korean woman taken as a Japanese military sexual slave, with the Second Sino-Japanese War as the backdrop. This work was subsequently turned into a movie titled *Akatsuki-no Dasso* 暁の脱走 (known in English as *Escape at Dawn* or *Desertion at Dawn*) in 1950, then once again made into a movie in 1965 under the title of *Shunpuden*, this time, with the heroine's ethnicity changed to Japanese. What is interesting is that Japanese records mentioning military sex slaves circulated even within Japanese-American communities. For instance, it is said that, from time to time, a Japanese weekly titled *Shukan Taishu* 週刊大衆 published articles such as "0012 A Report from the Extremes: The Midopa Internment Camp in Seoul That Supplied [Food] to 40,000 Comfort Women—Women Who Starved amid Concrete, with Soybean Meal as the Staple 0012 極限からのレポ-ト: 四萬人の慰安婦を供給したソウルの美都波收容所—豆カスを主食にコンクリ-トの中で飢えていた女たち" (December 27, 1971).[1]

The 1970s and 1980s likewise saw the occasional publication of works on this issue in both South Korea and Japan (*Seoul Shinmun*, August 14, 1970; Bak Duseok, 1977; Yoshida Seiji, 1977; Senda Kakou, 1978; Kim Dae Sang, 1978; and Im Jongguk, 1981), and some works are considerably in depth. Figures such as Professor Yun Chung-Ok have steadily made an issue of Japanese military sexual slavery, and the continued problematization today of the issues of atomic bomb survivors (*hibakusha*) since the early 1960s and of Japan's conscription and mobilization for labor during its colonial rule of Korea since the 1970s, too, has formed the basis for the transformation of the issue of Japanese military sexual slavery into a social movement.

2. The Development and Periodization of the Movement

It was when the Korea Church Women United (KCWU) 韓國教會女性聯合會 and researchers including Professor Yun Chung-Ok came together and began to cooperate with one another at the end of the 1980s, with the Korea Women's Associations United (KWAU) 韓國女性團體聯合 as a medium, that the issue of Japanese military sexual slavery started to be approached as a social movement in South Korea. With the launch

1 Dr. Pang Sun-joo, who has unearthed many materials on Japanese military sex slaves in the National Archives and Records Administration, states that, during her study in the United States in the 1960s, Japanese weeklies occasionally published articles on Korean victims of the institution (Pang Sun-joo, 1992: 2).

in November 1990 of the Korean Council, which encompassed nearly all major women's organizations nationwide, the movement came to proceed more systematically and actively. Subsequently, the movement in South Korea has been implemented with a focus on the Korean Council, and the Korean Research Group, House of Sharing 나눔의 집 managed by the Jogye Order of Korean Buddhism, Daegu Citizen's Forum for Halmuni 挺身隊할머니와 함께 하는 市民모임 in Daegu, Busan Council for the Women Drafted for Military Sexual Slavery by Japan 挺身隊問題對策釜山協議會,[2] Tongyeong and Geoje Citizen's Forum for Halmuni "Dagagagi" 日本軍'慰安婦'할머니와 함께 하는 統營·巨濟市民모임 '다가가기', Masan, Changwon, and Jinhae Citizen's Forum for Halmuni 日本軍'慰安婦'할머니와 함께 하는 馬·昌·鎭市民모임 as well as ethnic Koreans in countries including the United States, Japan, Germany, and Australia have formed solidarity, actively engaging in activities to resolve the issue of Japanese military sexual slavery.

Based on the contents of the *20-Year History of the Korean Council for the Women Drafted for Military Sexual Slavery by Japan* 韓國挺身隊問題對策協議會二十年史 (Hanul Academy, 2014) and in consideration of subsequent changes, it is possible to divide the movement to resolve Japanese military sexual slavery into the several following stages: (1) end of the 1980s-1990: period of preparations; (2) 1991-1995: period of establishment; (3) 1996-1998: the UN's presentation of recommendations and diverse groups' and individuals' opposition to the Asian Peace and People's Fund for Women (AWF) 女性のためのアジア平和國民基金 (also known as "アジア女性基金" and "國民基金"; henceforth "Asian Women's Fund"); (4) 1999-2000: period of the movement for the 2000 Women's Tribunal; (5) 2001-2007: period of the development of commemorative projects; (6) 2007-2011: period of the reactivation of the movement following the US House of Representatives House Resolution 121; (7) 2011-2014: new developments following a verdict of the Constitutional Court of Korea (CCK) 憲法裁判所; and (8) 2015-present: period since the agreement between the South Korean and Japanese foreign ministers on December 28, 2015.

A brief survey of the formation and development of the movement

2 [TN] Despite the similarity of its names in both Korean and English, this organization is not affiliated with the Korean Council.

is as follows. (1) As the democratization of South Korea at the end of the 1980s led to an explosion of women's movements, the issue of Japanese military sexual slavery came to receive considerable public attention. The Korean Research Group was founded in July 1990, and the Korean Council was founded in November, respectively, thus launching full-fledged research and activism. These organizations demanded from both the South Korean and Japanese governments fact-finding investigations, apologies, support for and compensations to the victims, education of the public, and erection of monuments. (2) Former victim Kim Hak-Soon 金學順 disclosed herself to the world in August 1991, Japanese military documents mentioning military sexual slavery were discovered in January 1992, and the Korean Council raised the issue at the UN in 1992. The South Korean government legislated a special law in 1993 and started to provide support to survivors, and the Korean Council raised the issue at the ILO along with labor unions in 1995. Lawsuits against the Japanese government were filed at diverse district courts in Japan as well as the Permanent Court of Arbitration (PCA), and bills of indictment and complaint were submitted to the Japanese Public Prosecutors Office. Although all of them were frustrated due to the Japanese government's rejection, such indictments and complaints greatly expanded the movement and led the South Korean and Japanese governments to release their respective investigations on Japanese military sexual slavery. (3) The UN and the ILO issued major reports encompassing recommendations that Tokyo make apologies and compensations to the victims, and the history of the institution was included in Japanese middle school history textbooks. Amid increasing expectations of resolution, however, the Japanese government blocked the prospects of legal resolution on the government level by announcing the creation of the Asian Women's Fund based on private donations. Subsequently, the movement focused on opposing this fund. The Asian Women's Fund caused not only diverse conflicts among activist groups but also distrust among the victims, thus leading to considerable confusion. (4) A people's tribunal on the issue was proposed at the Asian Solidarity Conference in 1998, and efforts were focused on preparations up to the 2000 Women's Tribunal. (5) The outcome of the 2000 Women's Tribunal, which encompassed accumulated records on the victims, legal judgments, and materials on international solidarity, was gathered. Subsequently, the movement seemed temporarily to turn to memorial projects, with a focus on South Korea and Japan. Scholars from both countries worked together to publish a book on the modern and contemporary history of the two nations from a gender perspective that included Japanese military sexual slavery as well. Museums were erected, too. (6) Initiated earlier, efforts to bring about the passage of a resolution on Japanese military sexual slavery in the US Congress dramatically bore fruit in the US House of Representatives in 2007. This had a considerable political effect, thus succeeding in the passage of similar resolutions in the legislatures of various European nations, Australia, and Canada, which, in turn, served to activate the participation of overseas Koreans and major international NGOs in the movement. (7) Amid such a situation, South Korean activist groups centering on the Korean Council submitted a petition to the Constitutional Court of Korea on the unconstitutionality of the South Korean government's failure to take measures regarding Japanese military sexual slavery. Intended to urge the government to take active measures, this successfully led to a verdict pointing out the government's unconstitutional nonfeasance (omission) in 2011. Consequently, the South Korean government's attitude inevitably changed, which, in turn, led to changes in the country's relations with Japan, considerably heightened public interest in the issue, and noteworthily activated research. The erection of a Statue of Peace 平和碑[3] (comfort girl statue) in front of the Japanese embassy in Seoul occurred in 2011 as well. (8) As the South Korean government's actions became noticeable and both activism and research were energized, public anticipation of the resolution of the issue of Japanese military sexual

3 [TN] A realistic, life-size bronze statue of a girl dressed in traditional Korean clothing and sitting on a chair, this monument is also known as the 平和의 少女像 ("Statue of a Girl of Peace"), 少女像 ("Statue of a Girl"), 慰安婦少女像 ("Comfort Girl Statue"), and 慰安婦像 ("Comfort Woman Statue") in Korean and the "Peace Monument," "Comfort Girl Statue," and "Comfort Woman Statue" in English, respectively. Though not necessarily figural like this one, commemorative or memorial works have been erected also in Japan, China (including Hong Kong), Taiwan, Philippines, Australia, Canada, United States, Germany, and Italy as of July 2024 according to the Korean Council's website at https://womenandwar.net/remembrance and https://womenandwar.net/article/?q=YToxOntzOjEyOiJrZXl3b3JkX3R5cGUiO3M6MzoiYWxsIjt9&bmode=view&idx=28456807&t= board (both in Korean).

slavery heightened. Amid such a situation, however, the South Korean and Japanese governments announced a political resolution of the issue on December 28, 2015. The gist was that the issue was to be considered finally and irreversibly resolved with the establishment of a foundation with funds from the Japanese government. South Korean civil society, which has learned of Japanese military sexual slavery over the past 25 years, has continued tremendously to oppose the agreement to this day.

3. The Raising of the Issue by South Korean Women's Movements and the Establishment of the Korean Council

1) The Formation and Development of the Movement to Resolve the Issue of Japanese Military Sexual Slavery

What turned the issue of Japanese military sexual slavery, which had lain buried in silence for over half a century, into a public one was South Korean women's movements, which grew considerably during the latter half of the 1980s. Because Korea had started to experience modernization during the Japanese colonial era, women's movements had been obliged to bear the burden also of national liberation from the very beginning, and, even after the Liberation (1945), it was difficult to separate from these movements the problematics of democratization and economic development under prolonged dictatorship.[4] Having thus borne and

4 Modern Korean women's movements are said to have started during the Enlightenment period 開化期 (1876-1910), with the spread of enlightenment thought. Mainly begun with a focus on the expansion of education, the women's movements of the Enlightenment period became more multifaceted during the Japanese colonial era. After developing as a part of overall social reform movements, which also included nationalist, socialist, and labor movements, and as independent movements such as the "New Women 新女性" movement, they became somewhat inactive following the Liberation. Having grown among labor and student movements in a turbulently changing society, South Korean women's movements declared independence from such movements and sought to extend women's human rights but, after thus removing themselves from mainstream social reform movements, supported the government at times and therefore were evaluated as having failed properly to establish their position as well. In the 1970s, women's movements that went hand in hand with the

grown as a part of the overall development of social movements in South Korea, women's movements gradually began to have the presence of mind and time to turn their attention to their own issues and grew into independent movements as democratization progressed throughout society during the latter half of the 1980s, becoming capable of resolving issues on their own in the 1990s (Lee Hyo Chae, 1989; Lee Seung-hee, 1990; Chung Chinsung, 1996a, etc.). In other words, through this process, the issue of Japanese military sexual slavery surfaced as an important task for South Korean women's movements.

More specifically, the movement regarding the issue of Japanese military sexual slavery was born at the intersection of three slightly different currents.[5] At the end of the 1980s, there was one woman researcher (Professor Yun Chung-Ok at Ewha Womans [*sic*] University) who, remembering that she herself had barely escaped being taken as a member of the "Volunteer Corps 挺身隊,"[6] continued to collect materials on this issue. There was also the Korea Church Women United, which, since the 1970s, had continued to work to resolve the issue of Japanese men's sex tourism in South Korea (so-called *gisaeng* tourism). Finally, there were women's movements, which, during the latter half of the 1980s, created a national coalition (Korea Women's Associations United). In other words, the movement to resolve Japanese military sexual slavery was born as a result of the encounter of these three parties. Yun Chung-Ok had already visited Bae Bong-gi 裵奉奇, a Korean victim living in Okinawa Prefecture, Japan, on her own and published an article titled "People Taken: The Path to Find Potters and [Members of] the Volunteer Corps [i.e., Japanese military sex slaves] 끌려간 사람들—陶工과 挺身隊를 찾아가는 길" in the daily *Hankook Ilbo* (September 3, 1981). It was amid

---

democratization movement such as women's labor movements, the issue of American military camp towns, and opposition to sex tourism began undoubtedly to develop, and these movements flourished even further in the 1980s.

5 The process up to the foundation of the Korean Council is recorded in great detail in Chapter 1 of the Compilation Committee of the *20-Year History of the Korean Council for the Women Drafted for Military*, ed., 2014.

6 After a rather complicated process, it was finally agreed that the issue would be called one of "Japanese military comfort women 日本軍慰安婦." This is because those who had lived during the Japanese colonial era remembered the forced mobilization of these women as mobilization for the "Volunteer Corps 挺身隊." Regarding the issue of this concept, see Chapter 1.

little public response, however, that she encountered the Korea Church Women United. In other words, South Korean women's movements discovered and turned into a social movement the fact that the issue of Japanese military sexual slavery was the root of currently continuing sex tourism and therefore was not only a past issue but also a present one that must be resolved immediately. Members of the Korea Church Women United and Professor Yun Chung-Ok explored various places across Japan, held international seminars, and organized the Committee for Research on the Issue of the Chongshindae 挺身隊問題硏究委員會 within the coalition. In January 1990, she published in four installments a feature titled "An Investigative Record of Footsteps Fraught with the Resentful Spirits of [Members of] the 'Volunteer Corps' [i.e., Japanese military sex slaves] '挺身隊'寃魂서린 발자취取材記" in the daily *Hankyoreh*, which aroused tremendous public responses. In May 1990, upon President Roh Tae-woo's visit to Japan, the Korea Church Women United, Korea Women's Associations United, and National Council of Women University Student Representatives 全國女子大學生代表者協議會 held a press conference and raised to the South Korean and Japanese governments alike the issue of Japanese military sexual slavery. Meanwhile, in July 1990, Yun Chung-Ok created the Korean Research Group, composed mainly of students in the Department of Women's Studies at Ewha Womans University, and promoted research. Together with the Korean Council, the group subsequently went on to publish numerous collections of testimonies by former Japanese military sex slaves.

At a session of the Committee on Budget in the Japanese House of Councilors held in June 1990, regarding a request from National Diet member Moto'oka Shoji of the Japan Socialist Party for investigations on "comfort women accompanying the military 從軍慰安婦," Shimizu Tsutao, the chief of the Employment Security Bureau in the Ministry of Labor, replied, "comfort women accompanying the military seem to have been under the charge of civilian managers, and fact-finding investigations [on the government level] are not possible" (June 6). In response to this, in October of the same year, 37 South Korean women's organizations held a press conference and announced their demands to the Japanese government including an acknowledgement of its forcible taking of women as military sex slaves, official apologies, fact-finding investigations, erection of memorials, compensations, and inclusion of Japanese military sexual slavery in the nation's history education. These organizations demanded that the South Korean government likewise receive apologies from Tokyo, conduct fact-finding investigations, construct memorials, practice independent and equal diplomacy with Japan, demand Japan to correct distortions in the latter's history education, and include Japanese military sexual slavery in its own educational curricula and materials. In other words, these 37 women's organizations, which included the Korean Research Group, Korea Women's Associations United, and Korea Church Women United, launched the Korean Council on November 16, 1990.

The Korean Council's efforts to find victims of Japanese military sexual slavery bore fruit so that, on August 14, 1991, Kim Hak-Soon (aged 67 at the time) held a press conference and made the first survivor's testimony, which immensely shocked South Korean society. Then the organization established a hotline for former military sex slaves on September 18 of the same year so that former victims including Mun Ok-ju and Kim Bok-sun 金福善 began to make reports. Because the Republic of Korea National Red Cross (Korean Red Cross) started to receive reports in January 1992 and the South Korean government legislated the Act on the Support of Livelihood Stability for Former Comfort Women Drafted into the Japanese Forces under Japanese Colonial Rule in June 1993 and started to receive reports from and to review survivors in August of the same year, the Korean Council closed its own hotline. The government went on to support former Japanese military sex slaves after reviews.[7] As of August 15, 2016, a total of 238 were registered with the South Korean government, with 40 of them alive.[8] In order to receive reports from

7 The reception of reports by former victims of Japanese military sexual slavery was initiated by the Ministry of Health and Welfare but transferred later to the Ministry of Gender Equality, which was created in 2001. The Special Committee for the Investigation of Forced Labor under the Japanese Colonialism 日帝強占下強制動員被害眞相糾明委員會 was created on November 10, 2004 (renamed the Commission on Verification and Support for the Victims of Forced Mobilization under Japanese Colonialism in Korea 對日抗爭期強制動員被害調査 및 國外強制動員犧牲者等支援委員會 on March 22, 2010) and temporarily received survivors' reports until its abolishment at the end of 2012, following which the duty was transferred back to the Ministry of Gender Equality and Family (renamed from the Ministry of Gender Equality in 2005).

8 In May 2016 alone, two passed away. Both 95 years old, they were quite advanced in age. At the time of first reports by former Japanese military sex slaves in 1991, both

former victims and victimizers alike, Military Comfort Women #110 (hotline) was opened in January 1992 in Japan as well.

With the discovery of a large number of military documents from the end of 1991 to early 1992 in the United States and Japan, not only the movement but also research started to proceed by leaps and bounds. In November 1991, American military investigative documents on Japanese military sexual slavery were released.[9] In January 1992, Professor Yoshimi Yoshiaki of Chuo University in Japan unearthed numerous documents related to the institution housed in the library of the former Japan Defense Agency. The movement was strengthened as official documents thus supported survivors' testimonies and shed light on the historical fact of Japanese military sexual slavery.

The Wednesday Demonstration, which has established itself as a key activity of the Korean Council, was begun in front of the Japanese embassy in Seoul at noon on January 8, 1992 with Japanese prime minister Miyazawa Ki'ichi's visit to South Korea as the impetus. Except for the one week skipped in 1995 as an expression of sympathy and condolences for the victims and sufferers of the Great Hanshin (Kobe) Earthquake in Japan,[10] the Wednesday Demonstration has continued to this day without any exception and marked its 1,243rd occasion on August 10, 2016. The Korean Council's installation of a Statue of Peace 平和碑 (comfort girl statue) on the site of the Wednesday Demonstration in front of the Japanese embassy on December 14, 2011 upon the 1,000th Wednesday Demonstration came to serve as a new spark for the movement. The fact that the removal of this Statue of Peace was discussed during negotiations leading to the agreement between the South Korean

---

Kim Hak-Soon and Mun Ok-ju had been aged 67. Currently, most of the survivors are in their 90s.

9 Headquarters, United States Naval Military Government, Okinawa, "Pictorial Supplement to Report of Military Government Activities for November 1945" (Record Group 313, Entry P31, Box 19), November 1945 was discovered, and the Psychological Warfare Team, United States Army Forces India-Burma Theater, United States Office of War Information, "Japanese Prisoner of War Interrogation Report No. 49" (Record Group 208, Entry 366A, Box 231), October 1, 1944 was discovered in December.

10 Similarly, in 2011, those who had gathered for the Wednesday Demonstration held a silent memorial rally, instead of staging the usual protest, as an expression of sympathy and condolences for the victims and sufferers of the Great Tohoku (East Japan) Earthquake.

The 1st Wednesday Demonstration (Jan. 16, 1991)

and Japanese foreign ministers announced on December 28, 2015[11] demonstrates the monument's symbolic role in the movement to resolve Japanese military sexual slavery. Following this announcement, countless citizens participated in the South Korean civil society's movement against the agreement in order to protect the comfort girl statue and to oppose its removal.

2) The Orientation of the Movement to Resolve the Issue of Japanese Military Sexual Slavery

Initiated with the Korean Council at the center, this movement began with a strong sense of problematics regarding imperialism and colonialism, as can be observed in most ways of understanding women's issues in the last years of the Empire of Korea 大韓帝國 (1897-1910) and during the

11 In the written statement of the joint press conference held after the talk between the South Korean and Japanese foreign ministers, the Japanese side mentioned: (1) Prime Minister Abe Shinzo's apology and expression of remorse; (2) the establishment of a foundation; and (3) the final and irreversible solution and restraint from mutual criticism. The South Korean side alluded to: (1) the final and irreversible solution; (2) concern about the Statue of Peace and the need to find an appropriate solution; and (3) restraint from mutual criticism (*Dong-A Ilbo*, Internet edition, December 28, 2015).

The 1,000th Wednesday Demonstration (Dec. 14, 2011)

Japanese colonial era, along with the feminist consciousness that South Korean women's movements started to espouse clearly in the 1990s. The document that the Korean Council presented to the UN Sub-Commission on Human Rights for the first time, in 1992, begins with the following sentences, which clearly show that the organization understood Japanese military sexual slavery as an issue of the violation of women's human rights within the social contexts of war and colonialism:

> "Annexed by Japan in 1910, Korea suffered from Japan's ruthless and oppressive rule until 1945, when World War II ended. While the Korean people were inflicted with diverse forms of exploitation and oppression during this period, the forced mobilization of Korean women as sex slaves of the Japanese military, which was spread throughout the Asia-Pacific region, was the gravest and cruelest of them"[12] (Korean Council for the Women Drafted for Military Sexual Slavery by Japan, ed., 1992: 16).

In addition, judging from the public statements and many other documents issued by the Korean Council,[13] this movement can be

12 [TN] Though this is a back translation of a Korean translation of the English original, it reflects the essential meaning.

viewed above all as having started first from an awareness of damages to women. The fact that the Korean Council was very careful about male members' participation in its organization in the early days[14] can be seen as an expression of the will of South Korean women's organizations not to damage a feminist viewpoint in interpreting and resolving this issue.[15] Solidarity with Japanese women's organizations and organizations in Asian victim nations, which soon ensued, was based on such feminism.

In fact, women who suffered under the Japanese armed forces can be classified into three disparate groups. The largest of the three groups, the first consisted of women from colonial Korea and Formosa. The second consisted of women in territories occupied by the Japanese military such as the Philippines, China, and Netherlands East Indies. The third group consisted of Japanese women themselves. If Japanese women were the victims of the state of Japan and women in occupied territories were the victims of a "wartime enemy," then Korean and Formosan women were the victims of imperialism/colonialism. Consequently, as very different social variables intervened in these three groups, who shared damages to women as the commonality, these women suffered from extreme but somewhat distinct damages.[16] In other words, even though the orientations of these three groups differed due to such disparate social variables, feminism basically has served as the strongest basis unifying them all.

On the other hand, participants in the movement regarding Japanese military sexual slavery agree that it becomes possible to approach the contemporary reality more closely only when the issue of damages

---

13 See the Korean Council for the Women Drafted for Military Sexual Slavery by Japan, ed., 1991-1997.

14 With a few exceptions, most of the member organizations have been limited to women's organizations, and the Board of Executive Members and staff members as well as the co-representatives are all women.

15 Of course, the view that men's participation directly leads to damages to feminism is seriously problematic. Although there was much debate regarding this issue within the Korean Council, the decision seems to have stemmed, to a certain degree, from the actual experiences of women's movements.

16 In this respect, the remark from Japanese woman scholar Ueno Chizuko 上野千鶴子 (1998) that, at the time, the victimized women could be classified legally into Japanese/Koreans and those in occupied territories can be seen as an analysis lacking sensitivity to the issue.

suffered by Korea is understood within the context of imperialism/colonialism. In other words, they focus on the fact that the mobilization of Korean women as military sex slaves was sexual mobilization implemented in the same context as military mobilization and labor mobilization implemented by the Japanese colonial authorities from 1938 under the general mobilization system established in accordance with the National Mobilization Law 國家總動員法 and was also a part of the cultural genocide 民族文化抹殺 committed by Japan along with the Koreans' forced worship at Shinto shrines 神社參拜 and adoption of Japanese names 創氏改名. On the level of research, this issue has been approached comparatively objectively as double damage due to the combination of the variables of gender and ethnicity,[17] and the need for theoretical discussions on the ways in which colonialism and discrimination against women were combined has been raised. On the level of activism, a nationalistic tendency has at times surfaced, which has combined very naturally with feminism, as in the cases of many other forms of damages to women that can easily arise in concert with ethnic conflict, especially damages to women during wartime.

South Korean women's movements have been capable of espousing feminism and a critical stance toward colonialism because, from the last years of the Empire of Korea and the Japanese colonial era to the mid-1980s, they have had to bear the burden of social change as well. It is precisely in this respect that they have been able to expand the issue of Japanese military sexual slavery as an international women's movement abroad and a citizens' movement at home, respectively. It is possible to say that feminism has served as the basis of international solidarity and nationalism has served as the foundation of the domestic movement. Of course, these two orientations did not surface separately according to the objects of solidarity. Rather, the smooth combination and contribution of feminism and nationalism to a more comprehensive understanding of Japanese military sexual slavery can be viewed as a strength of the South Korean movement regarding the issue in its early years. More specifically,

17 However, some see the "combination" of the variables of gender and ethnicity itself as the weakening of a feminist standpoint and argue that ethnicity, colonialism, and imperialism must be approached as subordinate variables of patriarchy and misogyny.

the movement set as its goals support for victims, investigation of distorted history, and, ultimately, prevention of violence inflicted by powerful nations on women in weak countries and, under these goals, went on to expand solidarity with diverse organizations.

4. The Participation of Other South Korean NGOs, North Korea, and Overseas Koreans

While the social movement to resolve Japanese military sexual slavery at the end of the 1980s first stemmed from the growth of South Korean women's movements, it soon forged solidarity with Japanese women's movements, and solidarity with Japanese organizations continues to be very important to this day. Subsequently, cooperation from diverse citizens and groups in South Korea was secured, overseas Koreans came to take part actively, and North Korea's participation became another important aspect of this movement. Japanese NGOs and women's organizations and NGOs from Asian victim nations as well as Japanese NGOs joined the movement, too, and various NGOs worldwide soon came to provide support, thus expanding the movement. While participants thus increased, the movement placed weight on supporting the victims and expanded the scope of its activities not only within South Korea but also to the international community including Japan, United States, UN, and ILO in order to resolve Japanese military sexual slavery legally.

1) The Spread of the Movement among Other NGOs in South Korea

While firmly maintaining a women-centered method of operating the organization, the Korean Council included male international law experts and historians by creating external organs such as the Legal Expert Committee and the Truth Investigation and Research Committee and formed ad hoc organs consisting of renowned figures who included men when nationwide efforts such as donation drives were necessary. The Truth Investigation and Research Committee, which had exchange with Japanese historians such as Yoshimi Yoshiaki, included respected male historians in South Korea,[18] and the Legal Expert Committee, which aided the Korean Council's overseas activities such as those at the UN, included numerous international law experts and lawyers in South Korea.[19] The Truth Investigation and Research Committee practically disbanded following its publication in 1997 of *The Truth about the Issue of "Comfort Women" in the Japanese Military* 日本軍'慰安婦'問題의 眞相 based on joint symposia held twice with Japanese scholars, in August and December 1993, and the Legal Expert Committee likewise naturally disbanded after irregularly meeting to provide advice and penning the legal portions of the book above. To collect donations, in 1992, the Headquarters of the National Movement for the Collection of Living Allowances for Former Members of the Volunteer Corps 挺身隊할머니生活基金募金國民運動本部 was established separately from the Korean Council, and, as its main officers including the co-chairs and the Steering Committee head, men were appointed.[20] Such methods of obtaining male experts' cooperation have continued to be employed so that men have temporarily participated in diverse activities such as the October 1996 collection of donations against the Asian Women's Fund by the Citizens' Coalition against the Asian Women's Fund and for the Resolution of the Issue of Forcibly Taken Japanese Military Comfort Women 日本國民基金을 反對하는 强制連行當한 日本軍慰安婦問題解決을 爲한 市民連帶 as well as the 2000 Women's Tribunal.[21]

---

18 Kang Man-gil, Yi Mahn-yol, Cho Dong-geol, et al.

19 Lee Janghie, Kim Chan'gyu, Park Won Soon, Kim Chang-Rok, Chang Wan-Ick, Jeong Inseop, Cho Si-Hyun, et al.

20 The co-chairs were Seo Yeonghun and Yun Chung-Ok; the chair of the Steering Committee was Yi Suseong; and many other men including Kang Wollyong and Song Wolju participated (Lee Hyo Chae, 1997: 342-343).

21 Begun with the opening ceremony, which was held on the evening of December 7, 2000, and consisting of the main tribunal, held during the three days of December 8-10, the Public Hearing, held on December 11, and the judgment, held on December 12, the 2000 Women's Tribunal was a people's tribunal organized by South Korean, Japanese, and other Asian organizations with help from international NGOs after defeat in actual lawsuits in Japan and the Japanese government's refusal to execute recommendations from international organs such as the UN and the ILO. Appointed as the judges for this tribunal, renowned legal experts from around the world found the worst war criminals of Japanese imperialism including the emperor himself guilty and clearly stated that the Japanese government had an obligation to make compensations and to punish those responsible for military sexual slavery (see Chapter 8).

On the other hand, the issue of Japanese military sexual slavery spread to various NGOs in South Korea in addition to women's organizations. The Association for the Pacific War Victims 太平洋戰爭犧牲者遺族會,[22] which had been established in the 1970s and focused on the issues of the draft of the Koreans for labor and conscription by the Japanese government, began to address the issue of Japanese military sexual slavery. In addition, Lawyers for a Democratic Society (Minbyun) 民主社會를 爲한 辯護士會 (民辯) participated in UN activities and hearings together with the Korean Council. The Buddhism Human Rights Committee 佛教人權委員會 established the House of Sharing, which is collective housing for victims. Buddhist intellectuals and historians created the Headquarters of the National Movement for the Settlement of the Past between South Korea and Japan upon the 50th Anniversary of the Liberation 光復五十年韓日過去清算國民運動本部, partly addressing Japanese military sexual slavery. Hospitals such as Asan Jung'ang Hospital in Seoul and Kwak's Hospital in Daegu examined former sex slaves free of charge, and many other civilians began to help in large and small ways.

Such expansion of the movement within South Korea signifies that the perspective on Japanese military sexual slavery broadened from one of women's human rights to one of more universal human rights, and nationalistic sentiments can be seen as tying the two together. It was on such a foundation that both public interest in the victims of the Korean people's suffering and movements to correct distorted history, which began to spread from the end of the 1980s, naturally converged with the movement regarding Japanese military sexual slavery. Even though there was at times conflict with anti-feminist nationalistic organizations,[23] solidarity has been generally forged without trouble, and, in a joint task force created in more recent years to address the issue of distortions in Japanese history textbooks,[24] the Korean Council has cooperated and

22 [TN] Though the organization was renamed the Association for Requesting Compensation for the Pacific War Victims 太平洋戰爭被害者補償推進協議會 in 2000, all references to it will use the older name in order to avoid confusion.

23 For example, organizations of figures who had engaged in nationalistic movements during the Japanese colonial era were discontent because they were being classified into one same category as former Japanese military sex slaves. The frustration of the Korean Council's efforts to win a separate space for military sex slaves in the Independence Hall of Korea 獨立記念館 in 1991, too, can be understood in this context.

worked together with other NGOs as well. In addition, increasingly important is the participation of legal experts' organizations such as Lawyers for a Democratic Society, which have provided legal assistance, a very important aspect of Japanese military sexual slavery.

2) The Participation of North Korea

Prompted by shock at the internationalization of the South Korean movement, North Korea's participation began with its wholesale accommodation of the research results and viewpoints of South Korea. Because direct contact between the people of the two Koreas is impossible, North Koreans have been linked to South Korean organizations generally through the mediation of Japanese organizations and Korean residents in Japan.[25] It was at an international public hearing held in Tokyo in 1992 that North Korea came face to face with South Korean activist groups for the first time.[26] At the time, presentations by North Korean representatives and victims demonstrated that the North Korean awareness of the issue of Japanese military sexual slavery was identical to its South Korean counterpart. Since then, North Korean representatives have participated in conferences on Japanese military sexual slavery held around the world including the UN, and, in addition to official statements, North and South Koreans have organized NGO forums together also. At the 2000 Women's Tribunal, North and South Koreans came together to form a single team of prosecutors.[27]

---

24 The Civilian Movement for Correcting Japan-distorted Textbook 教科書바로잡기運動本部 (formed in April 2001).

25 Following its first participation in the UN Sub-Commission on Human Rights in 1992, the Korean Council began to collaborate with the Fact-finding Team on the Truth about Forced Korean Laborers in Japan 朝鮮人强制連行眞相調査團, which is a Korean-Japanese group affiliated with the General Association of Korean Residents in Japan (Chongryon) 在日本朝鮮人總聯合會 (總聯). Subsequently, links to women affiliated with the Korean Residents Union in Japan (Mindan) 在日本大韓民國民團 (民團), too, became important so that connection among South Korea, North Korea, Korean Residents Union in Japan, and General Association of Korean Residents in Japan at the 2000 Women's Tribunal was the veritable reunification of all ethnic Koreans.

26 Held on December 9, 1992 in Tokyo, the international public hearing was attended by UN experts as well as activists and victims from nations including the Philippines, Netherlands, and China, thus being the first large-scale global conference on the issue of Japanese military sexual slavery (Executive Committee of the International Public Hearing, 1993).

Such strong solidarity between North and South Koreans is based, above all, on nationalism. What is interesting is that, in comparison with South Korea, North Korea has demonstrated nationalism more strongly than feminism. This is related to Pyongyang's method of activism as well: in order to resolve Japanese military sexual slavery, the North Koreans established in 1992 the Committee on Measures for Compensation to the "Former Comfort Women for Japanese Army" and Pacific War Victims (COCOPA) '從軍慰安婦' 및 太平洋戰爭被害者補償對策委員會 (從對委; present-day 朝鮮日本軍性奴隸 및 强制連行被害者問題對策委員會; 朝對委), which formally is not a government organ but can be seen as a de facto part of the government, and has accepted victims' reports and engaged in activities. It is no exaggeration to say that this has determined the nature of the country's activism. Unlike South Korean organizations, North Korea's Committee on Measures for Compensation to the "Former Comfort Women for Japanese Army" and Pacific War Victims consists of similar numbers of men and women and, in fact, gives the impression of being led by men. In addition, this committee's participation in NGOs' meetings and presentation of opinions are decided according to the North Korean government's policies. There were cases where representatives of the Committee on Measures for Compensation to the "Former Comfort Women for Japanese Army" and Pacific War Victims suddenly announced that they would be absent from occasions such as the Asian Solidarity Conference or denied South Korean delegates' participation in a meeting held in Pyongyang. In other words, these were decisions made by the North Korean government in accordance with changes in inter-Korean relations. Whereas the Korean Council and the South Korean government occasionally clash at the UN, the Committee on Measures for Compensation to the "Former Comfort Women for Japanese Army" and Pacific War Victims and Pyongyang act in unison. Without exception, North Korea makes strong remarks stressing Japan's responsibility at the UN.[28]

---

27 The single team of prosecutors was named "North and South of Korea," thus reflecting the will that Korea is a single nation (see Chapter 8).

28 After making a statement on Japanese military sexual slavery at the UN Working Group on Contemporary Forms of Slavery for the first time in May 1993, the North Korean government went on to present strong remarks at most sessions of the UN Commission on Human Rights, UN Sub-Commission on Human Rights, and working groups. The South Korean government likewise spoke out actively at diverse UN

Found in many places are examples of North Korea's stronger manifestation of nationalism than of feminism. Written announcements prepared by either Pyongyang or the Committee on Measures for Compensation to the "Former Comfort Women for Japanese Army" and Pacific War Victims overall use very strong language expressing hostility against Japan, and North Korea locates the essence of Japanese military sexual slavery mainly in the Japanese empire's policy of cultural genocide 民族文化抹殺. It was also in this context that, when penning the joint North-South Korean indictment at the 2000 Women's Tribunal, the North Koreans placed an excess focus on Japan's colonial policies (see Chapter 8).

3) The Activities of Overseas Koreans

Overseas Koreans' activities have occupied a very important position in the movement regarding Japanese military sexual slavery. As in the case of solidarity with Japanese women's movements mentioned above, Korean residents in Japan have engaged in the movement in diverse ways, both independently and together with the Japanese, and groups centering on Tokyo and Osaka have been established separately as well. Cooperative activities with Japanese organizations including the Group for Supporting a Korean Resident's Comfort Women Lawsuit (also known as "Support Group for the Comfort Women Lawsuit of the Resident Korean" and "Support Group for Lawsuit of Korean Former Comfort Women in Japan") 在日の慰安婦裁判を支える會 (present-day Group for Preserving Thoughts of Ms. Song Sin-do 宋神道さんの思いをつなぐ會) have continued. Created in more recent years, the Japan Nationwide Action for the Resolution of the Japanese Military "Comfort Women" Issue 日本軍「慰安婦」問題解決全國行動 has responded to major issues under a close relationship with the Korean Council (Compilation Committee of the *20-Year History of the Korean Council for the Women*

organs and aided the activities of representatives of the Korean Council, at times standing opposed to the Japanese government's rebuttals. Following the instatement of the Kim Dae-jung administration, however, the South Korean government refrained completely from speaking officially on the issue in the international arena together with the Japanese government. Amid such a situation, the North Korean government alone continued to issue strong remarks (see Chapter 8).

Drafted for Military Sexual Slavery by Japan, ed., 2014: Part II, Chapters 1, 2, and 7). The Korean-Americans, too, have been very active from the early years. They have created organizations in places such as New York City, Washington, DC, and Los Angeles and been active and, in particular, played decisive roles by organizing the Pan-Korean Community Alliance on the Comfort Women Issue 軍隊慰安婦決議案採擇을 爲한 워싱턴地域汎同胞對策委員會 in Washington, DC (present-day Washington Coalition for Comfort Women Issues, Inc. (WCCW) 워싱턴挺身隊問題對策委員會) in order to bring about the passage of the US House of Representatives House Resolution 121 in 2007. In addition, despite defeat in courts, the Korean-Americans have filed lawsuits concerning former victims of Japanese military sexual slavery by winning support from American lawyers (Compilation Committee of the *20-Year History of the Korean Council for the Women Drafted for Military Sexual Slavery by Japan*, ed., 2014: Part II, Chapters 3-5 and 7). Ethnic Koreans in Germany including members of the Korean Women's Organization in Germany 在獨韓國女性모임 (*Koreanische Frauengruppe in Deutschland*), an organization formed by South Korean nurses dispatched to West Germany in the 1960s-1970s, likewise have been concerned with the issue and been active since the early years of the movement (Compilation Committee of the *20-Year History of the Korean Council for the Women Drafted for Military Sexual Slavery by Japan*, ed., 2014: Part II, Chapter 6). Also active have been Korean-Australians, whose activities began comparatively late through the medium of Amnesty International (AI). While women's activities have formed the mainstream in countries including Japan and Germany, it is noteworthy that men's participation has been as active as women's in the United States.

5. Solidarity with Civil Society in Japan and Asian Victim Nations and around the World

1) The Active Participation of Japanese Women's Organizations

When the issue of Japanese military sexual slavery was raised in South Korea, Japanese women's organizations promptly began to respond.

The Korea Church Women United in South Korea and the Japan Anti-Prostitution Association (JAPA) 賣買春問題ととりくむ會, a Japanese organization that had worked to resolve the issue of Japanese men's sex tourism abroad, started to collaborate even before the creation of the Korean Council. Subsequently, several women's organizations in Japan together formed, in 1992, the Action Network for the Resolution of the Japanese Military "Comfort Women" Issue (also known as "Action Network for the Military 'Comfort Women' Issue," "Japan Action Network for the 'Comfort Women' Issue," and "Action Network") 従軍「慰安婦」問題行動ネットワーク (present-day Japan Action Network for the Military Sexual Slavery Issue (also known as "Action Network for the Issue of Japanese Military 'Comfort Women'" and "Action Network") 日本軍「慰安婦」問題行動ネットワーク), and many women's organizations went on to collaborate concretely with the Korean Council (see Chapter 10).

However, there have been subtle conflicts due to South Korean organizations' nationalistic tendency, and the nationalistic tendency of Japanese women's groups has led to the dissolution of solidarity at times as well. For example, at the 1st Asian Solidarity Conference held in 1992, one Japanese woman activist said that it would be difficult to forge solidarity if the South Korean side strongly raised the issue of ethnicity. In addition, in a commentary on Tokyo's announcement in August 1993 of its second investigations on Japanese military sexual slavery, the Korean Council rebuked the Japanese government for its motive for disregarding the discriminatory and forced mobilization and exploitation of women from the colonies and occupied territories, to which Japanese women's groups reacted negatively. Meanwhile, many Japanese women's organizations expressed discomfort at the Korean Council's movement as it began, around 1993, to turn from the issue of compensations to that of the punishment of the liable parties. In other words, these groups asked how already deceased or elderly people were to be punished and, moreover, were anxious about what would be said of the Japanese emperor, the highest-ranking individual responsible. The fissures that appeared at this time would lead to complete severance later with respect to the issue of the Asian Women's Fund.[29] In the end, many Japanese organizations would come to participate in this

29 As for the Asian Women's Fund, see Chapter 9.

fund and turn their backs on the Korean Council.

Organizations of female Korean residents in Japan such as the Military Comfort Women Issue Network Uri Yosong (Yosong Net) 從軍慰安婦問題ウリヨソンネットワ-ク (ヨソンネット) and the Association of Democratic Korean Women in Japan (also known as "Association of Korean Democratic Women in Japan" and "Democratic Women's Association of Resident Korean Women") 在日韓國民主女性會 and individual Korean-Japanese active in Japanese organizations played important roles in linking South Korean groups, Japanese groups, and the North Korean group created to resolve Japanese military sexual slavery. While women's activities regarding this issue were concentrated on the single women's organization of the Korean Council in South Korea itself, Korean-Japanese women worked to resolve Japanese military sexual slavery within not only women's groups but also a variety of NGOs together with men. This seems to be because their position as Korean residents in Japan allowed them to have a more open perspective.

As in South Korea, Japan saw the spread of the movement initiated by women's organizations to other NGOs. Groups including lawyers' organizations engaged in the movement against the revision of the postwar Constitution of Japan (also known as "Peace Constitution"), local NGOs engaged in diverse local movements (e.g., Fukuyama Group for Considering the Issue of Japanese Military "Comfort Women" 日本軍「慰安婦」問題を考える會·福山), nationwide organizations for the peace movement (e.g., Japan Asia Africa Latin America Solidarity Committee 日本アジア·アフリカ·ラテンアメリカ連帶委員會), and the newly formed Center for Research and Documentation on Japan's War Responsibility joined the movement to address this issue. In that they espouse the goals of prompting Japan to face its war responsibilities and preventing the recurrence of such atrocities, these groups can be said to be peace-oriented. Meanwhile, various victim relief organizations such as the Balloon Flower Society ききょうの會 and the Group for Supporting a Korean Resident's Comfort Women Lawsuit 在日の慰安婦裁判を支える會 include a large number of men in addition to women based on the perspective of universal human rights. In order to address the broader issue of Japan's war responsibilities instead of limiting themselves to that of Japanese military sexual slavery, many of them have engaged in activism independently of the Korean Council.

In addition, some Japanese groups and individuals espouse "to make Japan a better society" as the motive of their activism. In the end, it is natural for this motive, however large or small, to inform Japanese citizens' participation in the movement. However, it is also evident that organizations and individuals espousing such "progressive" nationalism more directly have generally created fissures with their South Korean counterparts regarding delicate issues. This holds true of most groups and individuals joining the Asian Women's Fund. According to such organizations and individuals, while the Japanese government's compensations and punishment of the liable parties are ultimately important as the assumption of responsibility for its own war crimes, providing support even, at least, on the civilian level in itself is important as an expression of the Japanese conscience (interview of a relevant figure).

While the movement to resolve Japanese military sexual slavery spread within Japan in a multifaceted manner, a strong countermovement formed, thus leading to the expansion of right-wing ideology across society at a frightening rate instead. Represented by the movement for a "liberal" view of history 自由主義史觀, or by the Japanese Society for History Textbook Reform (Tsukurukai) 新しい歴史教科書をつくる會 as more specific praxis, this countermovement has led the conservatization of the entire Japanese society while encompassing existing right-wing movements. With the country's war responsibilities as the axis, such an opposition between movements critical of Japan and neo-nationalism is a new phenomenon in contemporary Japanese social movements.[30]

2) The Participation of NGOs in Other Asian Victim Nations

Following Japanese organizations, victim support organizations soon emerged in other Asian victim nations as well and began to accept reports from former sex slaves. The earliest and the most active have been organizations in the Philippines, followed by those in Taiwan. Having joined the movement regarding the issue of Japanese military sexual slavery relatively late, China has actively conducted research and

30 Regarding this, see Chung Chinsung, 2001c: Chapters 1 and 5.

The 4th Asian Solidarity Conference (Mar. 28-29, 1996)

engaged in activism, and Indonesia has participated sporadically. As for the Philippines, which took part in the movement immediately, existing women's organizations such as the Asian Center for Women's Human Rights (ASCENT), which had very actively forged an international network, took on this issue. As in South Korea, the movement in the Philippines has been led by women, and male experts have been allowed to participate on special occasions such as the 2000 Women's Tribunal. Organizations in the nation have been important participants in the Asian Solidarity Conference,[31] begun in 1992, and were among the key members taking charge of international solidarity in the 2000 Women's Tribunal, held in Tokyo in December 2000. Because the forced mobilization of Filipinas as military sex slaves was committed not under Japanese colonial rule but during Japan's invasion, the duration of victims' suffering was generally shorter than the case of victims from Korea (International Commission of Jurists, 1994), and the Philippine criticism of Japan has not been based on imperialism/colonialism but been directly related to

31 First held in August 1992, the Asian Solidarity Conference was held annually or biannually up to the session in Tokyo in 2003, with the participation of activists from Japan and Asian victim nations. As for a detailed record on the conference, see the Compilation Committee of the *20-Year History of the Korean Council for the Women Drafted for Military Sexual Slavery by Japan*, ed., 2014: 84-99.

war. In this respect, the case of victims in the Philippines forms a pattern of damages typically suffered in relation to the issue of violence against women in wartime, the context in which the issue of Japanese military sexual slavery has been positioned in the international community.[32]

The case of Taiwan differs from those of both Korea and the Philippines. Although it, too, was a Japanese colony like Korea, the nature of Japanese colonial rule differed, and the Taiwanese' view of Japan differs as well.[33] Just as mobilization for labor occurred in concentration in Korea, the forced mobilization of women as Japanese military sex slaves mainly occurred in the same colony, too. Consequently, in the case of Taiwan, while the damages are similar to those of Korea in nature, there is a large difference in the degree. Perhaps for this reason, the Taiwanese movement has not shown clear signs of feminism or nationalism. Here, women lawyers have been central, creating a new organization to help victims and mainly engaging in relief work (Taipei Women's Rescue Foundation (TWRF) 臺北市婦女救援社會福利事業基金會), with the active participation of male lawyers. Thanks to a continued relationship with the Taiwanese government, victims, who opposed the Asian Women's Fund, were provided with a government subsidy equal to the amount that would have been provided by the Japanese fund, which happened in 1997, even before similar measures were taken in South Korea. While criticism of the Japanese government and an awareness of women's suffering are naturally evident, the movement in Taiwan overall can be seen as one mainly to support former sex slaves from the perspective of human rights.

As for China, although it joined the movement relatively late, it has been very active since then. This is closely related to Beijing's attitude. Having established a policy of not pressing Japan about its war

32 Of course, in comparison with the sexual violence that has been committed in areas such as the former Yugoslavia, Rwanda, and Indonesia, the issue of Japanese military sexual slavery is clearly unique because of the systematic intervention of the state.

33 In the case of Korea, Japan implemented a policy of comparatively more thorough integration so that not only cultural coercion but also economic pressure were stronger in the colony. Formosa, which experienced foreign rule for a long duration, differs from Korea historically as well. Such general differences have led to considerable differences in the Koreans' and the Taiwanese' anti-Japanese sentiments. Indeed, nationalistic movements were far stronger in Korea than in Formosa during the Japanese colonial era, and postwar attitudes toward Japan likewise have not been so negative among the Taiwanese (Gold, 1981; Chung Chinsung, 1984, etc.).

responsibilities at first, the Chinese government had internally suppressed even research on the issue of Japanese military sexual slavery.[34] However, as Beijing's attitude toward Japan changed as a result of its recovered confidence thanks to the success of the open door policy in bringing about economic development, research on the issue has become active as well. Interestingly, the movement in China has developed as a part of the research process centering on Professor Su Zhiliang 蘇智良, a male scholar at Shanghai Normal University (Research Center for Chinese "Comfort Women" 中國'慰安婦'研究中心 at the same university (also known in English as "Shanghai Research Center on Comfort Women"), etc.). While many women do participate in it, the movement in China basically focuses on unearthing and publicizing victims and former comfort stations and relies on solidarity mainly with its counterparts in Japan and South Korea for other activities. Also characteristic has been China's approach to Japanese military sexual slavery not as an independent issue but as one within the overall context of Japan's war responsibilities including those such as the Nanking Massacre (1937-1938). The symposium that the Chinese held in March 2000 in Shanghai, to which hundreds of scholars and activists including those working with this issue not only in Asia but also in the United States were invited, characteristically demonstrated the nature of the movement in the nation. Chinese activist groups actively participated in the 2000 Women's Tribunal and have continued to address the issue of Japanese military sexual slavery since then.

Similarly, from Indonesia, male lawyers have participated a few times in the Asian Solidarity Conference, and there are NGOs that receive reports from victims and provides them with support. Organizations in victim nations such as the Netherlands and Timor-Leste have participated also.

3) Solidarity with International NGOs

One important factor to exert pressure on the Japanese government regarding the issue of military sexual slavery has been international

34 In the early 1990s, there was one Chinese scholar who very cautiously provided information to the Korean Council and inquired about the situation. Citing fear of the Chinese government's oppression, however, this individual soon cut off contact.

pressure. Indeed, what agitates the Japanese right wing the most is the doubt cast on their nation's ethicality by international organs such as the UN and the ILO and Western (not Asian) countries.[35]

When the Korean Council and Japanese organizations first raised Japanese military sexual slavery at the UN in 1992, groups that cooperated were Canadian organizations of prisoners of war who had suffered at the hands of Japan during World War II. However, solidarity with these organizations, which presumably were based on pacifism, did not last long (see Chapter 6). This is because, as the movement defined Japanese military sexual slavery as an issue of women's human rights, especially of the violation of women's human rights during wartime, and proceeded with its activities, it grew distant from the Canadian organizations and, instead, strengthened solidarity with women's organizations. As the gravity of the violation of women's human rights in the international wars and civil wars that coincidentally were occurring all over the world was exposed, Japanese military sexual slavery came to win attention as an unpunished historical origin of such recent issues. As a result, the Korean Council naturally went on to form solidarity with organizations addressing those issues.

The International Commission of Jurists, which has expanded its activities with the UN as the backdrop, took considerable interest in Japanese military sexual slavery ever since it was first raised at the UN in 1992 and, after dispatching two lawyers to South Korea, Japan, and Philippines to conduct careful investigations, published a report in 1994. Titled *Comfort Women: An Unfinished Ordeal—Report of a Mission*, this book served as an important basis for the interpretation of the issue in terms of international law. Another important support basis was the World Council of Churches (WCC), which obtained for the Korean Council a right to speak when the latter raised Japanese military sexual slavery at the UN for the first time, while still lacking this right officially, and aided various preparatory processes. Based on such solidarity,

35 For example, one individual from the Japanese Society for History Textbook Reform has angrily described the international criticism of Japan due to the issue of military sexual slavery as a "new war where numerous nations unite and attack a single nation" (Eto Jun, 1998: 102).

South Korean women's movements succeeded in prompting the UN Commission on Human Rights and the UN Sub-Commission on Human Rights to publish important reports on the issue, based on which they further strengthened solidarity. When Special Rapporteur on Violence against Women Coomaraswamy submitted a detailed report on Japanese military sexual slavery to the UN Commission on Human Rights in 1996, countless women's organizations active at the UN together expressed support for it, which clearly demonstrates the sheer breadth of the solidarity regarding the issue forged by South Korean activist groups with feminism-based international NGOs.

Solidarity with labor unions around the globe has been crucial for raising Japanese military sexual slavery at the ILO. Although this solidarity has not continued outside the ILO, without solidarity with such labor unions, it would have been impossible for the Federation of Korean Trade Unions (FKTU) 韓國勞動組合總聯盟 and the Korean Confederation of Trade Unions (KCTU) 全國民主勞動組合總聯盟 to raise the issue continuously amid Japanese labor unions' opposition and for the movement to obtain from the ILO Committee of Experts on the Application of Conventions and Recommendations (CEACR; henceforth "Committee of Experts") the judgment that Japanese military sexual slavery had constituted a violation of the Forced Labour Convention (ILO Convention No. 29) (see Chapter 7).

Meanwhile, in the process of preparing for the 2000 Women's Tribunal, a network with countless international law scholars and women's movement activists worldwide was formed. Held on the final day of the tribunal, the Public Hearing on Crimes against Women in Recent Wars and Conflicts (henceforth "Public Hearing") was organized by the Women's Caucus for Gender Justice (WCGJ), an international NGO (see Chapter 8).

The largest global NGO, Amnesty International distanced itself somewhat in the early years of the movement for the resolution of Japanese military sexual slavery. However, in 2005, it released a report titled "Still Waiting after 60 Years: Justice for Survivors of Japan's Military Sexual Slavery System" based on research in South Korea and Japan, which went on to serve as a great stimulus to the international movement addressing the issue. Amnesty International held a solidarity campaign regarding Japanese military sexual slavery at an Asia-Pacific regional conference held in Hong Kong in 2006 and did so again in Australia in the same year. Indeed, solidarity with this organization had a strong effect on the adoption of resolutions on the issue in legislatures in regions around the world including Europe (European Parliament (EP)) and Australia following the passage of the House Resolution 121 in the US House of Representatives in 2007 (Compilation Committee of the *20-Year History of the Korean Council for the Women Drafted for Military Sexual Slavery by Japan*, ed., 2014: 1 and 21-125).

The diverse organizations that intervened in the movement can be summarized as in <Diagram 5-1>:

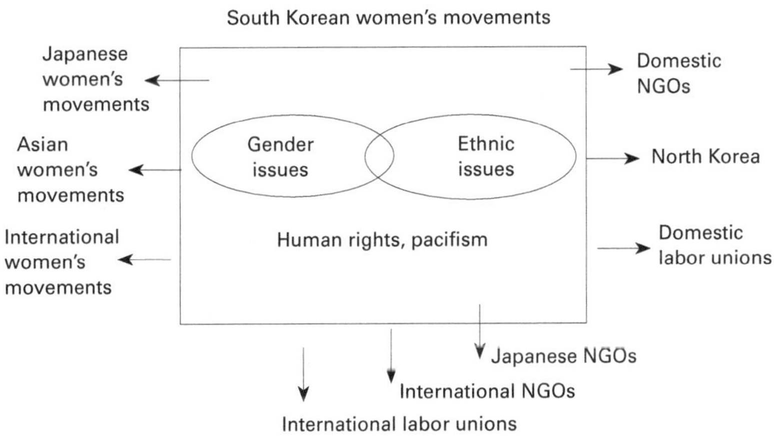

⟨Diagram 5-1⟩ The agendas of domestic and overseas organizations participating in the movement to resolve Japanese military sexual slavery

6. The Movement since the 2000 Women's Tribunal

1) Progress in Educational and Commemorative Projects

After the 2000 Women's Tribunal, activist groups in South Korea and Japan alike began to devote efforts to commemorative projects. In Japan, such projects were accelerated mainly by women's organizations that had led the tribunal. Thus founded was the Women's Active Museum on War and Peace (WAM) アクティブ·ミュ-ジアム女たちの戰爭と平和資料館, which has collected and exhibited materials on Japanese military sexual slavery. In 2013, the Violence against Women in War Research Action Center (VAWW RAC) 「戰爭と女性への暴力」リサ-チ·アクション·センタ- (バウラック; former Violence against Women in War Network Japan (VAWW-Net Japan) 戰爭と女性への暴力日本ネットワ-ク (バウネット·ジャパン)), the manager of this museum, and the Center for Research and Documentation on Japan's War Responsibility, which had been established in 1993 and focused on research, created a website titled "Fight for Justice: The Japanese Military 'Comfort Women'—Resistance to Forgetting & Responsibility for the Future 日本軍「慰安婦」—忘却への抵抗·未來の責任"[36] to display relevant materials.

From its early days, the Korean Council devoted efforts to the publication of Japanese military sexual slavery survivors' testimonies as well as academic research, education of the public, and activities involving archives. Following the 2000 Women's Tribunal, it focused even more on such activities. Immediately afterwards, women scholars in both South Korea and Japan who had engaged in activities to resolve the issue agreed to create a single book that would retell the modern and contemporary histories of the two nations with a focus on bilateral relations and from the perspective of women in order to shed light on Japanese military sexual slavery historically. Based on collaboration, the outcome was simultaneously published in both countries in 2005.[37] In addition, the Korean Council earnestly set about building its own archives. It created the Construction Committee in 2004 and, at last, opened the War and Women's Human Rights Museum 戰爭과 女性人權博物館 on May 5, 2012.

The 2011 erection of the Statue of Peace (comfort girl statue) mentioned earlier, too, was implemented in this context. After this statue was built in front of the Japanese embassy in Seoul, diverse memorials were constructed in a variety of places including the United States and Japan as well as Changwon and other areas within South Korea.[38]

---

36 http://fightforjustice.info.

37 It was published in South Korea as *Modern and Contemporary Korean-Japanese History as Seen through Women's Eyes* 女性의 눈으로 본 韓日近現代史 and in Japan as *Modern and Contemporary Japanese-Korean History as Seen from the Perspective of Gender* ジェンダ-の視點から見る日韓近現代史, respectively.

The Statue of Peace, Suwon, South Korea (press release, Korean Council homepage, May 5, 2014)

The South Korean government has partly revised the 1993 Act on the Support of Livelihood Stability for Former Comfort Women Drafted into the Japanese Forces under Japanese Colonial Rule 日帝下日本軍慰安婦에 對한 生活安定支援法 on a number of occasions. In 2002, it renamed this law the Act on Livelihood Stability and Memorial Services, Etc. for Sexual Slavery Victims for the Japanese Imperial Army 日帝下日本軍被害者에 對한 生活安定支援 및 紀念事業等에 關한 法律 and specified the implementation of commemorative projects in addition to support for the victims. Accordingly, the e-History Museum of Victims of the Japanese Military "Comfort Women" 日本軍'慰安婦'被害者e-歷史館 was created on the homepage of the Ministry of Gender Equality and Family and has been in service, and the exhibition hall on Japanese military sexual slavery within the Independence Hall of Korea 獨立記念館 was expanded.

38 The construction of the War and Women's Archives 戰爭과 女性史料館, War and Women's Human Rights Center 戰爭과 女性人權센터, etc. (Compilation Committee of the *20-Year History of the Korean Council for the Women Drafted for Military Sexual Slavery by Japan*, ed., 2014: Chapter 7).

2) The 2007 Passage of the US House of Representative Resolution, 2011 Verdict of the Constitutional Court of Korea, and 2015 Agreement between Seoul and Tokyo and Changes in the Movement

What newly activated the movement to resolve Japanese military sexual slavery, which thus turned to commemorative projects after the 2000 Women's Tribunal, was the passage of a resolution on comfort women in the US House of Representatives in 2007. After the release of recommendations on the issue to the Japanese government from the UN and the ILO in the 1990s and the clear definition and analysis of the issue in terms of international law at the tribunal, international activities dulled somewhat. Thanks to the efforts of Korean-Americans including the Washington Coalition for Comfort Women Issues, however, the passage of a resolution on Japanese military sexual slavery in the US Congress started to become visible.[39]

After Congressman Daniel William Lipinski (Illinois) of the Democratic Party first proposed a resolution on Japanese military sexual slavery in the House of Representatives in 1997, Congressman Lane Allen Evans (Illinois) introduced the bill five times, starting in 2000 (2000, 2001, 2003, 2005, and 2006). In 2006, the resolution (H. Res. 759) was adopted by the House of Representatives Committee on Foreign Affairs but not presented to the main session of the House of Representatives and abrogated. This was taken up and presented by Congressman Michael "Mike" Makoto Honda (California) in 2007. In fact, Congressman Honda had presented and brought about the adoption of a resolution on Japanese military sexual slavery (Assembly Joint Resolution 27 on War Crimes: Japanese Military during World War (AJR 27)) to the California State Legislature in 1999.

In January 2007, Congressman Honda submitted the resolution to the House of Representatives Subcommittee on Asia, the Pacific, and the

39 As for the movement to bring about the passage of the resolution on Japanese military sexual slavery in the US House of Representatives, see the Compilation Committee of the *20-Year History of the Korean Council for the Women Drafted for Military Sexual Slavery by Japan*, ed., 2014: Part II, Chapters 3-5.

Global Environment under the House of Representatives Committee on Foreign Affairs, and a public hearing was held in the House of Representatives on February 15. On June 26, 2007, this resolution (H. Res. 121)[40] was officially adopted by the House of Representatives Committee on Foreign Affairs, with 39 assenting votes and two dissenting votes, and, at last, passed unanimously by the House of Representatives on July 30, 2007.

In order to bring about the passage of this resolution, the Korean Council actively pursued activities for international solidarity, which, in turn, went on to serve as a new impetus for the organization's activities such as solidarity with Amnesty International. After the passage of the resolution in the US House of Representatives in 2007,[41] similar resolutions were adopted by the European Parliament as well as the legislatures of nations including the Netherlands, Australia, and Canada and of American states including New York (upper house), Illinois (both houses), and New Jersey (both houses). In 2008, South Korea's National Assembly (legislature) likewise saw the passage of the Resolution Urging [the Japanese Government's] Official Apologies and Compensations for the Restoration of the Honor of Victims of [the] Japanese Military Comfort Women [System] 日本軍慰安婦[制度]被害者名譽回復을 爲한

40 "...it is the sense of the House of Representatives that the Government of Japan—
(1) should formally acknowledge, apologize, and accept historical responsibility in a clear and unequivocal manner for its Imperial Armed Force's coercion of young women into sexual slavery, known to the world as 'comfort women', during its colonial and wartime occupation of Asia and the Pacific Islands from the 1930s through the duration of World War II;
(2) should have this official apology given as a public statement presented by the Prime Minister of Japan in his official capacity;
(3) should clearly and publicly refute any claims that the sexual enslavement and trafficking of the 'comfort women' for the Japanese Imperial Armed Forces never occurred; and
(4) should educate current and future generations about this horrible crime while following the recommendations of the international community with respect to the 'comfort women'" (January 31, 2007).

41 Congressman Honda submitted the resolution to the Subcommittee on Asia, the Pacific and the Global Environment under the US House of Representatives Committee on Foreign Affairs, and a public hearing was held on February 15, 2007. This resolution (H. Res. 121) was officially adopted on June 26 in the same committee, with 39 assenting votes and two dissenting votes, and, on July 30, passed unanimously in the House of Representatives at last.

[日本政府의] 公式謝過 및 賠償促求決議案 in the main session (Compilation Committee of the *20-Year History of the Korean Council for the Women Drafted for Military Sexual Slavery by Japan*, ed., 2014: 115-126).

Meanwhile, Japanese military sexual slavery victims and support groups submitted a constitutional petition to the Constitutional Court of Korea and succeeded in obtaining a verdict of unconstitutionality in 2011, which became another groundbreaking occasion for the movement. On July 5, 2006, 109 survivors submitted to the Constitutional Court of Korea a constitutional complaint requesting adjudication on whether or not the South Korean government's nonfeasance—i.e., its failure to determine whether or not compensations to victims of Japanese military sexual slavery had been annulled by the 1965 Agreement on the Settlement of Problem Concerning Property and Claims and the Economic Cooperation between the Republic of Korea and Japan 大韓民國과 日本國間의 財産 및 請求權에 關한 問題의 解決과 經濟協力에 關한 協定 (henceforth "South Korean-Japanese Claims Agreement")[42]—violated the victims' basic rights. On August 30, 2011, the Constitutional Court of Korea ruled that the South Korean government's nonfeasance was unconstitutional. This had an immense effect on the South Korean movement to resolve Japanese military sexual slavery. In other words, Seoul initiated negotiations on the issue with Tokyo (Compilation Committee of the *20-Year History of the Korean Council for the Women Drafted for Military Sexual Slavery by Japan*, ed., 2014: 209-213). After having refrained from stating a clear position, the South Korean government now changed its attitude and came to express active determination to resolve the issue during the subsequent Lee Myung-bak and Park Geun-hye administrations, which would ultimately lead to the December 28, 2015 agreement between the South Korean and Japanese foreign ministers. As Seoul began to raise its voice to Tokyo as a result of the ruling of the Constitutional Court of Korea, South Korean NGOs' international activities increased considerably, and diverse organs under the UN came to discuss the issue

42 [TN] Known as the Agreement between Japan and the Republic of Korea Concerning the Settlement of Problems in Regard to Property and Claims and Economic Cooperation 財産及び請求權に關する問題の解決竝びに經濟協力に關する日本國と大韓民國との間の協定 in Japanese.

during 2014-2015 (see Chapter 6).

Amid a standstill between South Korea and Japan regarding diverse current issues such as the economy and national defense and a sense of crisis that Japanese military sexual slavery victims were increasingly passing away due to their advanced ages, the December 28, 2015 agreement following talks between the foreign ministers of the two countries dramatically changed the direction of the movement. According to the joint press release published in the media, the Japanese side stated: (1) Prime Minister Abe Shinzo was to make apologies and to express remorse; (2) a foundation for South Korean victims was to be created; and (3) the agreement was to be the final and irreversible resolution of the issue. The South Korean side stated: (1) the agreement was to be the final and irreversible resolution; (2) there was concern about the prospects of the Statue of Peace; and (3) both nations were to refrain from mutual criticism.[43] This greatly dispirited survivors and activist groups who had striven to resolve the issue for nearly 30 years. Though Prime Minister Abe Shinzo did apologize, it was through the Japanese foreign minister.[44] In addition, the foundation was to be built by the South Korean government, and the money sent by Tokyo for this purpose was very insufficient. Moreover, the stipulation that the implementation of this agreement was to constitute the final and irreversible resolution of Japanese military sexual slavery was utterly unacceptable to survivors and activist groups alike. In particular, the suspicion that the Japanese government had demanded the removal of the Statue of Peace from its current location in front of the Japanese embassy in Seoul angered countless South Korean citizens. Consequently, young citizens would stay up all night even in extreme cold in order to safeguard the statue for a considerable period. In a survey of South Korean and Japanese citizens jointly conducted by the *Yomiuri Shimbun* and the *Hankook Ilbo* in May 2016, 73.4% of the South Korean

---

43 *Dong-A Ilbo*, Internet edition, December 28, 2015.

44 Prime Minister Abe Shinzo rejected a demand from a National Diet member affiliated with the Democratic Party of Japan that he apologize again in his own voice. Moreover, in the National Diet on October 3, 2016, he stated that he had "not even an iota" of wish to express his apology, as stipulated in the agreement made between the South Korean and Japanese foreign ministers on December 28, 2015, in a letter and convey it to the surviving victims, thus revealing the lack of sincerity in his apology.

respondents were negative toward the agreement, and 87.2% opposed the removal of the statue. In addition, 75.4% stated that discussions on Japanese military sexual slavery must continue.[45] UN Special Rapporteurs likewise expressed regret regarding the agreement.[46] In addition, in its review of the Japanese government's Universal Periodic Review (UPR) in March 2016, the UN Committee on the Elimination of Discrimination against Women criticized the December 28, 2015 agreement between the South Korean and Japanese foreign ministers as failing to reflect adequately recommendations hitherto presented by diverse UN organs and to adopt a victim-centered approach and recommended Tokyo to take measures for redress for survivors in not only South Korea but also other victim nations (UN Doc. CEDAW/C/JPN/CO/7-8, paras. 28-29). Amid such a situation, the number of participants in the Wednesday Demonstration increased explosively, and the Korean Council established the Foundation for Justice and Remembrance for the Issue of Military Sexual Slavery by Japan 日本軍性奴隸制問題解決을 爲한 正義記憶財團 with support from countless citizens. Since then, this movement has focused on annulling the agreement and reinitiating discussions on Japanese military sexual slavery.

3) Progress in Research and Solidarity in the International Academia

While differences of opinion between the South Korean and Japanese governments manifested themselves glaringly, historical revisionism was having a considerable impact in Japan. Amid a somewhat chaotic situation where the number of researchers increased and ensuing social debates came to be highlighted in South Korea, international solidarity, previously limited to activism, spread into the sphere of research as well. While international academic conferences or research projects centering

45 *Hankook Ilbo*, Internet edition, May 12, 2016.

46 Office of the United Nations High Commissioner for Human Rights, "Japan/S. Korea: 'The long awaited apology to "comfort women" victims is yet to come'—UN rights experts," March 11, 2016. https://www.ohchr.org/en/press-releases/2016/03/japan-s-korea-long-awaited-apology-comfort-women-victims-yet-come-un-rights?LangID=E&NewsID=17209.

on specific research topics are common, it is rare to witness scholars from diverse countries who share the same position to announce a statement in solidarity. This is noteworthy as yet another important occasion in the process through which the movement to redress Japanese military sexual slavery has proceeded.

On October 15, 2014, the Historical Science Society of Japan (HSSJ) 歷史學硏究會, a Japanese academic organization composed of historians, issued a statement titled "A Critique of the Japanese Government's Stance on the Wartime 'Comfort Women' Issue and Its Coverage in the Media 政府首脳と一部マスメディアによる日本軍「慰安婦」問題についての不當な見解を批判する." Regarding this, on May 5, 2015, 187 figures[47] consisting mainly of US-based scholars of Japan and historians released in their names a document titled "Open Letter in Support of Historians in Japan." In addition, on May 25, 16 history-related Japanese organizations including the Historical Science Society of Japan presented a statement ending, "We renew our demand for all concerned politicians and media outlets to squarely face up to the damage that Japan inflicted in the past, as well as to the victims 當該政治家やメディアに對し, 過去の加害の事實, およびその被害者と眞摯に向き合うことを, あらためて求める."

The international academic symposium on Japanese military sexual slavery held in South Korea in August 2015 in commemoration of the 70th anniversary of Korea's liberation from Japanese colonial rule, too, was based on such international solidarity in research. Founded in January 2016, the Research Network on Japanese Military Sexual Slavery 日本軍'慰安婦'硏究會 likewise encompasses researchers on the issue in countries including South Korea, Japan, and United States.

7. Beyond a Movement for Victims

With the prolongation of the movement to resolve Japanese military sexual slavery for over 20 years, the methods of activism likewise have become diverse, with the addition of new demands to existing ones

47 464 additional Japan scholars signed the open letter, thus leading to a total of 651 by May 11, 2015. https://apjjf.org/-Asia-Pacific-Journal-Feature/4828/article.html.

including the implementation of compensations, punishment of the liable parties, education of the Japanese public, and commemorative projects by the Japanese government. Noteworthy among such new demands are a movement that, going beyond one for the victims of the institution, more universally opposes war and violence directed at women and activities to support victims of similar violence and exploitation worldwide. In addition, the victims of Japanese military sexual slavery themselves have personally led and encouraged these activities.

1) The Universal Orientation Opposing War and Violence against Women

As has been examined above, in accordance with the nature of Japanese military sexual slavery, which occurred at the intersection of the universality of wartime damages to women and the historicity of colonialism, the movement to resolve this issue has proceeded in collaboration with diverse NGOs domestically and in solidarity with the international community. When the idea that it was necessary to delve deeper into the more fundamental issue of war and violence against women became stronger in the course of the movement, the Korean Council established the War and Women's Human Rights Center 戰爭과 女性人權센터 within itself in 2001 and thus began to broaden its horizons. The War and Women's Archives 戰爭과 女性史料館 and the War and Women's Human Rights Museum 戰爭과 女性人權博物館, created in 1999 and 2012, respectively, likewise have been used as spaces for publicizing and teaching about the issue of war and women overall beyond that of Japanese military sexual slavery (Compilation Committee of the *20-Year History of the Korean Council for the Women Drafted for Military Sexual Slavery by Japan*, ed., 2014: 244-258).

While acknowledging the particularity of Japanese military sexual slavery, the movement led by the Korean Council began to forge solidarity with diverse women's movements. The 2012 creation of the Butterfly Fund 나비基金, which will be discussed later, more clearly shows this direction of the movement and was founded under the goal of working for victims of wartime sexual violence around the globe. Within South Korea, representative of such new solidarity is that with women in American military camp towns 基地村. In 2014, the Korean Council mediated a meeting between Japanese military sexual slavery survivors and women in military camp towns, thus sharing the awareness that both groups were victims of the same injustice. In addition, as the first recipients of the Butterfly Peace Prize 나비平和賞 established in 2016, Durebang 두레房, Saeumteo 새움터, and Sunlit Sisters' Center 햇살社會福祉會, all three organizations providing support to women in military camp towns, were selected. The Korean Council has formed solidarity also with overseas organizations for victims of wartime sexual violence, providing support to those for victims of the Congolese civil wars since 2012.

2) A Unique Way of Implementing the Movement That Transforms Victims into Subjects

The movement to resolve Japanese military sexual slavery has established a very unique direction of activism where, going beyond feminism and nationalism, it transforms the victims into subjects. Indeed, the survivors have participated in the Wednesday Demonstration without fail from the start and personally conducted lectures to students visiting the Korean Council's Education Hall or the Museum of Sexual Slavery by Japanese Military 日本軍慰安婦歷史館 at the House of Sharing. Such activities have served as occasions for the victims not only to heal their wounds but also to transform themselves into active peace activists and women activists.

In 2000, Japanese military sexual slavery survivors Moon Myung-keum 文明今 and Kim Okju 金玉珠 donated 70 million won as a construction fund for the Korea-Vietnam Peace Memorial Museum 한베平和歷史館. With this amount as seed money, the construction of the Peace Museum 平和博物館 has been pursued, and a corporation for the purpose was launched in 2003 (*Hankyoreh*, May 16, 2016). Also former victims, Kim Bok-dong 金福童 and Kil Won-Ok 吉元玉 stated on March 8, 2012, or the International Women's Day, that if and when they received legal compensations from the Japanese government, they would use the money to help women subjected to wartime sexual violence. In commemoration of this wish, the Korean Council established the Butterfly Fund. Even before any legal compensation from Tokyo, Kim Bok-dong then donated the 50 million won that she had saved to this fund. Indeed, survivors including Lee Yong-soo 李容洙, who testified in the US House of Representatives in 2007 before the passage of the House Resolution 121, define themselves as activists.[48]

8. The Movements Demanding Measures from the South Korean and Japanese Governments and the South Korean Government's Position

Finally, this section will summarize the attitudes of the South Korean and Japanese governments toward such citizens' movements. It will focus on the South Korean government because the stance of the Japanese government will be discussed in detail in Chapter 9. The most important part of the movement to resolve Japanese military sexual slavery has been demands to the Japanese government, and the movement has made clear its demands to the South Korean government as well. Because the issue basically concerns state violence (more specifically, violence inflicted on colonized peoples by an empire), it could be raised amid the growth of South Korean civil society in the 1990s. One of the most crucial aspects of the movement is this growth of civil society as it implemented campaigns to make demands to the government. When the issue gained public attention for the first time, not a few people in South Korea rebuked the survivors and activists for exposing a humiliating national past. Such voices have decreased with the passage of time, however, and the view that the issue must be faced squarely has become central. This education of civil society can be seen as the greatest achievement of the movement. Likewise, awareness of the issue seems to have expanded gradually in Japan (see Chapter 10). Unlike such continued growth of civil society, however, both Seoul and Tokyo have proceeded toward political and diplomatic "settlements" instead of the clarification of the historical truth or a resolution based on international law, thus continuously clashing

---

48 Kim Bok-dong was presented with the grand prize in the Seoul Women's Prize by the Seoul Metropolitan Government and with the Korea Human Rights Award (Human Rights Order) by the National Human Rights Commission of Korea (NHRCK), both in 2015. When receiving the grand prize from the Seoul Metropolitan Government, she was called a "women's human rights and peace activist."

against activism.

As many survivors of Japanese military sexual slavery revealed themselves in diverse Asian countries and official documents related to the institution were unearthed in places including Japan and the United States, Tokyo came to acknowledge partly the intervention of the government and the armed forces and the forced taking of the victims as comfort women. Nevertheless, it steadfastly maintains the position that its duty in terms of international law has been fully performed through the 1951 San Francisco Treaty and Japan's bilateral treaties with Asian nations. Although the Japanese government sought to resolve the issue conclusively by launching in 1995 the Asian Women's Fund, which consisted of civilians' donations and the government's support fund in order to avoid a legal resolution, it failed because of opposition from survivors and support groups across Asia. Subsequently, as will be discussed later, Tokyo came to attempt a "final and irreversible resolution" through the 2015 agreement between the South Korean and Japanese governments. The position of the Japanese government and the arguments of the Japanese right wing supporting it will be discussed again in Chapter 9.

While the South Korean government continued to demonstrate a commitment to support the victims, it maintained an ambiguous stance regarding the legal resolution of Japanese military sexual slavery. Through the Korean Council's efforts, a petition sponsored by legislator Bak Yeongsook 朴英淑 alone was submitted to the National Assembly on July 18, 1991. This petition requested that the South Korean government create a special task force for the investigation of Japanese military sexual slavery and build a monument commemorating the victims on the site of the Independence Hall of Korea. Seoul then announced on January 15, 1992 that it would establish a fact-finding committee consisting of the working-level staff from the relevant ministries and created the Working Group on the Issue of Military Sexual Slavery 挺身隊問題實務對策班, which consisted of members from 17 ministries, on January 24.

At the summit talk held on January 16, 1992 during Japanese prime minister Miyazawa Ki'ichi's visit to South Korea, President Roh Tae-woo requested Tokyo to investigate the truth of Japanese military sexual slavery more actively and to take appropriate measures based on the results. In response, Prime Minister Miyazawa Ki'ichi stated, "It is an unmovable fact that the Japanese army was involved in the recruiting of comfort women and managing of comfort stations." He apologized both during the summit and before the South Korean legislature, said, "Concerning the comfort women, I apologize from the bottom of my heart and feel remorse for those people who suffered indescribable hardships" at a press conference, and stated that fact-finding investigations would be conducted and appropriate measures would be taken as soon as possible (Cho Sei-young, 2015: 67).

On July 6, 1992, the Japanese government released a report on Japanese military sexual slavery based on investigations of the relevant materials housed in the six ministries and offices of the National Police Agency, former Japan Defense Agency, Ministry of Foreign Affairs, former Ministry of Education, Science, Sports and Culture, former Ministry of Health and Welfare, and former Ministry of Labor.[49] In his announcement, Chief Cabinet Secretary Kato Koichi denied coercion in the process of recruiting comfort women and stated that compensations had been resolved through the 1965 South Korean-Japanese Claims Agreement. On July 31, 1992, the Working Group on the Issue of Military Sexual Slavery within the South Korean government released "Investigations on the Reality of Military Comfort Women under Japanese Colonial Rule: Interim Report 日帝下軍隊慰安婦實態調查—中間報告書." Despite the subtitle of "Interim Report," however, no final or other version of the report has been released since then. In fact, this report was criticized by South Korean civil society because of its failure to present a wealth of contents such as newly unearthed facts or legal interpretations. Nevertheless, as a material clarifying Seoul's position on Japanese military sexual slavery to this day, it supposedly was used as the main framework in the process through which the South Korean government worked on a white paper on the issue in 2015.[50]

49 "On the Issue of the So-called Wartime Comfort Women from the Korean Peninsula 朝鮮半島出身のいわゆる従軍慰安婦問題について" announced by the Cabinet Councilors' Office on External Affairs in the Cabinet Secretariat on July 6, 1992.

50 Though Seoul began work on this white paper in 2014 with the aid of scholars, it cancelled the publication of an officially endorsed report on Japanese military sexual slavery following the December 28, 2015 agreement on the issue between the South

Though successive South Korean administrations did not clearly state their respective positions on Japanese military sexual slavery to the Japanese government, they made efforts to support former victims. Stating on March 13, 1993 that it was "Having the moral upper hand [over Japan]," the Kim Young-sam administration said that it would not demand monetary compensations from Tokyo and would directly support the survivors. Nevertheless, it demanded the Japanese government to conduct fact-finding investigations and to implement public education on the history of the institution. At a provisional session held on May 18, 1993, the South Korean legislature passed the bill for the Act on the Support of Livelihood Stability for Former Comfort Women Drafted into the Japanese Forces under Japanese Colonial Rule 日帝下日本軍慰安婦에 對한 生活安定支援法 prepared by the government, according to which survivors were to be paid a livelihood allowance of 5 million won besides being provided with livelihood protection and medical protection in accordance with the former Protection of Minimum Living Standards Act 生活保護法 and the former Medical Care Act 醫療保護法, respectively, and to be granted priority in moving into permanent rental housing if they so wished.

Meanwhile, on August 4, 1993, the Japanese government announced the results of investigations of materials housed in the Ministry of Justice, National Archives of Japan, National Diet Library, and National Archives and Records Administration in addition to the six ministries and offices mentioned above and interviews of surviving victims. However, Tokyo continues to keep important materials from major ministries classified, disclosing only the minimum.[51] In the August 1993 announcement, the Japanese government acknowledged forced taking 强制連行 but stated

---

Korean and Japanese foreign ministers. Consequently, "A Report on the Issue of Victims of [the] Japanese Military 'Comfort Women' [System] 日本軍'慰安婦'被害者問題에 關한 報告書," the product of the research released at last in May 2017, came to be a civilian report even including statements against the views of many of the contributing scholars themselves (Yonhap News, May 3, 2017; and *Hankyoreh*, May 3, 2017).

51 A considerable portion of materials housed in the former Japan Defense Agency as well as those safeguarded by the National Police Agency, former Ministry of Labor, former Ministry of Health and Welfare, and former Ministry of Finance are classified, and materials from the former Ministry of Colonial Affairs and Ministry of Home Affairs have been barely disclosed (Yoshimi Yoshiaki, 1993).

that it had been committed mostly by civilian mobilizers or comfort station managers and that "officials, too, [had taken] part in some cases," thus concluding that, at any rate, the imperial Japanese government had not been the agent or subject behind forced taking. Based on these results, Chief Cabinet Secretary Kono Yohei apologized that such acts had seriously damaged the honor and dignity of women who had been turned into comfort women against their wishes, and Prime Minister Hosokawa Morihiro likewise admitted that the Asia-Pacific War waged by Japan had been a war of aggression (August 10, 1993). In response, the South Korean government announced the policy that it would no longer raise Japanese military sexual slavery as a current diplomatic agenda between the two countries. However, when Tokyo sought to solve the issue in 1995 through the Asian Women's Fund, which evaded legal resolution by the Japanese government, and South Korean survivors and support groups strongly opposed the fund, Seoul, too, came to adopt an oppositional stance.

Protesting against the publication of a full-page advertisement in the South Korean dailies *Hankyoreh* and *Hankook Ilbo* on January 6, 1998 by the Asian Women's Fund,[52] the Kim Dae-jung administration demanded the fund to stop paying consolation money to the survivors. In addition, in opposition to the Asian Women's Fund, Seoul came to accept activist groups' demand for support and to provide compensations corresponding to the amount paid by the Japanese fund. The payment from the Asian Women's Fund amounted to approximately 43 million won per victim at the time. Separately from the initial lumpsum payment of 5 million won out of this amount, the South Korean government resolved to pay 38 million won to each survivor at a State Council (cabinet) meeting held on April 21, 1998. Then on May 7, with the exception of some 6.5 million won fundraised and presented by the Korean Council, 31.5 million won were paid *en bloc* to each survivor who had reported to government, and this amount (38 million won) has been paid to each survivor who reported afterwards (Yoon Meehyang, 2007).

What is noteworthy here is that the South Korean government, in

---

52 The contents were that South Korean victims of Japanese military sexual slavery would each be provided with 5 million yen as consolation money and a medical welfare support fund together with a letter of apology from the Japanese prime minister.

providing lump sums, demanded the following statement from each of the former Japanese military sex slaves. This statement is an example of South Korea's strong expression of its clear position against all measures from Japan evading legal compensations:

> I, the person named above, accept the support fund of 43 million won paid by the government of the Republic of Korea for the livelihood stability of the victims of the Japanese military comfort women system during Japanese colonial rule under the following conditions:
>
> 1. From now on, I will not accept money from Japan's Asian Peace and People's Fund for Women or other sources.
> 2. In case I accept money from Japan's Fund or other sources against the above [condition], I will return it to the Japanese side through the Korean Council for the Women Drafted for Military Sexual Slavery by Japan.
>
> Recipient: Minister of Gender Equality and Family

However, with the announcement of the South Korean-Japanese joint declaration "A New Japan-Korea Partnership towards the 21st Century" by President Kim Dae-jung and Prime Minister Obuchi Keizo on October 8, 1998, Japanese military sexual slavery was removed from Seoul's agendas.[53]

Subsequently, Japanese military sexual slavery would be included in comprehensive references to historical problems overall whenever there was conflict between the two nations due to issues such as Japanese textbooks, only to have bilateral relations return to a politically "stable" state. The situation encountered a change with Seoul's release in 2005 of documents related to the 1965 South Korean-Japanese Claims Agreement. After reviewing the documents, the Roh Moo-hyun administration concluded that the issues of Japanese military sex slaves, forcibly mobilized Koreans left in parts of Sakhalin previously occupied by Japan, and atomic bomb survivors had not been covered by the South Korean-

53 Even in the international arena including the UN, the South Korean government did not mention the issue of Japanese military sexual slavery.

Japanese Claims Agreement. Even at this time, however, Seoul did not demand compensations from Tokyo.

As has been mentioned earlier, 109 survivors of Japanese military sexual slavery filed a lawsuit against the South Korean government in the Constitutional Court of Korea in 2006 regarding the contradiction where Seoul did not hold Tokyo to account even after having confirmed the latter's legal responsibility. When the court ruled in 2011 that the government's nonfeasance violated the victims' basic rights, the Lee Myung-bak administration immediately created the Task Force to Resolve the Issue of Japanese Military "Comfort Women" 日本軍'慰安婦'問題解決을 爲한 태스크포스. When South Korean NGOs erected the Statue of Peace in front of the Japanese embassy in Seoul on December 14, 2011 to commemorate the 1,000th Wednesday Demonstration, Tokyo expressed displeasure and demanded the removal of the statue. The South Korean government then responded that it could not intervene because the monument had been erected by a civilian organization. At the South Korean-Japanese summit talk held on December 18 in Kyoto, President Lee Myung-bak urged Prime Minister Noda Yoshihiko to resolve Japanese military sexual slavery. However, the latter replied that legal resolution of the issue had been completed and demanded the removal of the statue. President Lee Myung-bak then responded that, without Tokyo's sincere measures, second and third such monuments could very well be erected. During his visit to South Korea in March 2012, Vice Minister for Foreign Affairs Sasae Ken'ichiro unofficially presented the so-called Sasae proposal, whose gist was: (1) the Japanese ambassador to South Korea would visit and console the survivors; (2) the Japanese prime minister would express his sentiments regarding Japanese military sexual slavery; and (3) humanitarian measures would be taken with the Japanese government's budget. However, Seoul rejected this, stating that Japan's admission of state responsibility was needed. Victims and support groups opposed the proposal as well.

Strongly impacting South Korean NGOs' activism and the government alike together with the judgment by the Constitutional Court of Korea discussed above, the verdict on a case involving Korean laborers forcibly drafted to Japan before or during World War II was announced by the South Korean Supreme Court on May 24, 2012. In other words, in a lawsuit filed by South Korean victims of forcible mobilization against Japanese corporations including Mitsubishi Heavy Industries, Ltd. 三菱重工業株式會社, the Supreme Court saw imperial Japan's colonial rule over Korea as illegal and ruled that illegally and forcibly drafted Korean laborers' right to request compensations for damages from the Japanese government and companies had not been annulled by the South Korean-Japanese Claims Agreement.[54] Efforts by both Seoul and Tokyo to improve the deteriorated bilateral relations failed to bear fruit, and the issue was transferred to the succeeding Park Geun-hye administration.

Stating in 2014 that "the issue of comfort women is the first step in the new beginning of South Korean-Japanese relations,"[55] President Park Geun-hye expressed the determination for the proper resolution of Japanese military sexual slavery, and South Korean NGOs likewise were highly encouraged so that there were signs of the great activation of research on the issue as well as activism. Amid the Japanese government's unyielding position that the legal resolution of the issue was already over, however, the situation in the end led to the agreement between the South Korean and Japanese foreign ministers on December 28, 2015. As has been mentioned earlier, in this agreement, Tokyo stated: (1) Prime Minister Abe Shinzo was to express apologies and remorse; (2) the Japanese government was to provide 1 billion yen, which the South Korean government was to manage by establishing a foundation; and (3) these measures were to constitute the final and irreversible resolution of the issue, and both countries were to refrain from mutual criticism in the future. Meanwhile, Seoul stated: (1) the agreement was to constitute the final and irreversible resolution of the issue; (2) the South Korean government was concerned about the prospects of the Statue of Peace and was to seek an appropriate solution; and (3) both nations were to refrain from mutual criticism in the international arena.[56] South Korean NGOs have continued to oppose the agreement vehemently, and such antagonism has spread further in South Korean civil society. In addition,

---

54 See Kim Chang-Rok, 2015.

55 During a reception with members of the Korea-Japan Parliamentarians' Union 韓日議員聯盟 on October 24, 2014. Requoted from Cho Sei-young, 2015: 76.

56 Press release (*Dong-A Ilbo*, Internet edition, December 28, 2015).

a new form of activism where South Korean citizens shocked by the inclusion of the possible removal of the Statue of Peace in the agreement voluntarily guard the statue has arisen as well.

Chapter 6

The Issue of Japanese Military Sexual Slavery at the UN

1. The Internationalization of the Issue of Japanese Military Sexual Slavery

At the end of the 1980s, Japanese military sexual slavery surfaced in earnest in South Korean society after a long silence. However, this issue, which constitutes the violation of women's human rights on an immense scale, did not lie utterly forgotten before then. In fact, it continued to be discussed in both South Korea and Japan following the Liberation and, in the 1970s, was addressed through publications and films. It was only that the issue lay outside society's attention. The background of such public oblivion included, domestically, the patriarchy and oppressive political structure of South Korean society and, internationally, abnormal South Korean-Japanese relations, global Cold War system, and American policies on East Asia, weighing heavily on the issue. When Japanese military sexual slavery penetrated these barriers thanks to the democratization of South Korean society and the expansion of women's movements, both of which occurred from the end of the 1980s, it was hoped that the Japanese government would resolve the issue properly.

However, South Korean women's organizations felt the limitations of demanding resolution from the Japanese government, which denied the existence of the issue itself. This led them to bring the issue to the human rights organs of the UN. In a situation where overall social movements in South Korea had yet to turn to the international community, it was a pioneering idea indeed. However, social movements worldwide were, in fact, already changing swiftly in a transnational direction, and human rights norms had become global so that cases where any particular nation could not avoid international criticism because it had violated those norms were becoming frequent. It was based on an understanding of such an already established international climate that the Korean Council raised the issue of Japanese military sexual slavery at the UN. The Korean Council stressed to the global community that such violation of women's human rights must never recur and increasingly gained sympathetic responses from the international community by linking this issue to that of the wartime violation of women's human rights, which coincidentally were being committed in places including Rwanda and the former Yugoslavia.

At the UN, the issue of Japanese military sexual slavery garnered global attention and led to diverse important judgments and recommendations in terms of international law. Even though the Japanese government ultimately has continued to ignore recommendations from UN human rights organs to this day, pressure from the international community has brought about many other developments regarding the resolution of this issue. In the process of presenting to the international community important criteria regarding the issues of violence against women, wartime violation of women's human rights, and impunity, the Korean Council also came to present South Korean civil movements with the important method of making use of international human rights norms and the UN's human rights mechanisms for activism.

Focusing on discussions on Japanese military sexual slavery at the UN Sub-Commission on Human Rights, this chapter will summarize UN records and my experience of direct participation in the processes.

2. The UN's Human Rights-related Organs

Feeling the need to secure the safety of weak nations following World War I, the international community created the League of Nations. After experiencing genocide during World War II, it once again established the UN as a stronger human rights organ. However, when ethnic conflict broke out around the world as globalization became full-fledged in the 1990s and gaps among countries widened uncontrollably, in-depth discussions on international regimes or global governance began to be conducted.[1] The norm of international regimes came to be highlighted as the most effective form more in the sphere of human rights than in those of politics and economics, which is also resistance against international systems centering on superpowers or the world economic system since the Bretton Woods system.

It is very interesting that, in the process through which these discussions have sought after practical alternatives, the UN once again has become the focus of attention. While the UN will seek diverse institutional reforms in order to become an effective organ of correct global governance, considerable expansion of NGOs' participation in the basic, nation-centered system has been under discussion. Also noteworthy is the gradual consolidation of regional human rights organs and national human rights institutions (NHRIs) in diverse regions worldwide while forming relations with the UN. This demonstrates the immense influence of the UN, which encompasses not only human rights organs but also economic functional agencies such as the World Trade Organization (WTO) and the International Monetary Fund (IMF) and organs addressing political issues such as the UN Security Council (UNSC). However, it must also be kept in mind that one must proceed while embracing, to a certain degree, the UN's limitations including its state- and superpower-centered system and restricted compelling power.

In the transformation of norms regarding human rights into a concrete political reality in the international community, the UN has played a decisive role. In fact, it can be said that a human rights regime has been able to possess reality and to impose certain standards on violations of human rights norms because of the UN's existence despite its many flaws (Apodaca, et al., 1998: 186). The UN's human rights-related

1 Assuming a rather normative and loose organization, global governance on one hand represents the ideal of international civil society rather than being an international regime. Although it is etymologically identical to "government," "governance" is a concept that began to be used, for the sake of convenience, to explain the collective influence of the numerous, diverse, and pervasive quasi-governments that spread during the previous century (Brown, 2001: 130). International regimes are defined as the norms and decision-making processes that have been accepted by various nations and that have binding power in certain spheres (Donnelly, 1989: 205).

organs can largely be divided into the following several groups. Consisting of commissions within the UN Economic and Social Council (ECOSOC), the first group includes organs such as the UN Commission on Human Rights (UNCHR), UN Commission on the Status of Women (CSW), and UN Commission on Crime Prevention and Criminal Justice (CCPCJ). The UN Sub-Commission on Human Rights belongs to none other than the UN Commission on Human Rights here and, in turn, oversees several working groups. While the main task of UN commissions, which will be discussed later, lies in monitoring signatories' observance of treaties and expert organs limit their discussions to specific issues such as labor and health, the UN Commission on Human Rights and the UN Sub-Commission on Human Rights inclusively and intensively address all human rights issues worldwide and form the center of the international human rights system. In other words, although the UN General Assembly (UNGA) and the Office of the UN High Commissioner for Human Rights (UNHCHR) (OHCHR) comprehensively deal with human rights issues, they do so based on the practical discussions of the UN Commission on Human Rights and the UN Sub-Commission on Human Rights. With the expansion of the international community's awareness of the importance of human rights, the UN Commission on Human Rights was elevated to the UN Human Rights Council (UNHRC) in 2006. Consequently, the UN Sub-Commission on Human Rights likewise was newly reorganized as the UN Human Rights Council Advisory Committee (UNHRCAC).

Second, treaty bodies monitoring the observance of major treaties related to human rights include the UN Human Rights Committee (HRC), UN Committee on Economic, Social and Cultural Rights (CESCR), UN Committee on the Elimination of Racial Discrimination, UN Committee on the Elimination of Discrimination against Women, UN Committee on the Rights of the Child (CRC), UN Committee against Torture (CAT), UN Committee on Migrant Workers (CMW), Committee on the Rights of Persons with Disabilities (CRPD), and Committee on Enforced Disappearances (CED), and signatories of these treaties must submit reports to the relevant committees periodically.

There also are: specialized agencies focusing on specific issues such as the ILO, World Health Organization (WHO), and UN Educational, Scientific, and Cultural Organization (UNESCO); funds or programs under the UN General Assembly such as the UN Children's Fund (UNICEF); and organs such as the UN High Commissioner for Refugees (UNHCR). In addition, specific human rights issues are discussed intensively through UN world conferences including: the UN World Conference on Human Rights (UNWCHR), which was held in Vienna in 1993; the UN World Conference on Women (UNWCW), which is held every five years; and the UN World Conference against Racism, Racial Discrimination, Xenophobia and Related Intolerance (UNWCAR; also known as "World Conference against Racism" and "Conference on Racism"), which has been held every year in South Africa since 2001. The most important organ, naturally, is the UN General Assembly, which reviews issues related to human rights and takes measures according to the recommendations of the UN Economic and Social Council. In addition, the Office of the UN High Commissioner for Human Rights was established in 1994 with the mission of overseeing and coordinating human rights organs within the UN (Apodaca, et al., 1998: 196-203; and Joo Sungsoo, et al., 2000: 91-96).

While the issue of Japanese military sexual slavery has been raised in working groups-UN Sub-Commission on Human Rights-UN Commission on Human Rights since 1992, it has been discussed by treaty bodies such as the UN Human Rights Committee and the UN Committee on the Elimination of Discrimination against Women and nearly all UN apparatuses such as the 1993 World Conference on Human Rights held in Vienna, World Conference on Women, Office of the UN High Commissioner for Human Rights, and ILO and has led to reports including strong recommendations to the Japanese government.

Also worth mentioning are NGOs, which, though neither UN organs nor formal members of UN human rights organs such as national governments and individual experts, have played equally important roles and whose importance has been stressed even more as of late. The UN Charter grants the UN Economic and Social Council the authority to consult NGOs (Article 71). Any NGO that satisfies the qualifications for NGOs stipulated by the UN Economic and Social Council[2] is granted

2 In UN Doc. ECOSOC 1296 (1968), the UN Economic and Social Council defined NGOs as organizations not created through consultation between nations and, as their

consultative status and can participate in meetings within the Economic and Social Council including the UN Commission on Human Rights and the UN Sub-Commission on Human Rights and submit written statements or make oral statements.

3. The Issue of Japanese Military Sexual Slavery at the UN Sub-Commission on Human Rights

Before their reorganization into the UN Human Rights Council (2006) and the UN Human Rights Council Advisory Committee (2007), respectively, the UN Commission on Human Rights[3] and the UN Sub-Commission on Human Rights[4] were organs within the UN Economic and Social Council having subordinate links in the form of working groups.[5] Consequently, discussions at the UN Commission on Human

---

qualifications, stipulated that NGOs must: exist for and be involved in economic and social activities; not support the use of violence; not represent political parties; and be international. NGOs must submit to the UN Economic and Social Council materials on their budgets and financial sources (Apodaca, et al., 1998: 199-200).

3 Established in 1946 through a resolution by the UN Economic and Social Council, the UN Commission on Human Rights held its first session in 1947. Consisting of government representatives from 53 nations, the UN Commission on Human Rights proposed at its first meeting the establishment of sub-commissions composed of experts to analyze and to make recommendations regarding diverse human rights issues. At this time, three sub-commissions were established: the UN Sub-Commission on the Status of Women; the UN Sub-Commission on Freedom of Information and of the Press; and the UN Sub-Commission on Prevention of Discrimination and Protection of Minorities. From among them, the UN Sub-Commission on the Status of Women developed into the UN Commission on the Status of Women, and the UN Sub-Commission on Freedom of Information and of the Press was abolished in 1952. Consequently, the Sub-Commission on Prevention of Discrimination and Protection of Minorities, which, in accordance with its name, focused on the rights of minorities, was left as the only sub-commission under the UN Commission on Human Rights and came to be a comprehensive human rights organ that made proposals to the UN Commission on Human Rights regarding human rights issues in general based on research and analysis. It is for this reason that, in 1999, the UN Economic and Social Council renamed the sub-commission the Sub-Commission on the Promotion and Protection of Human Rights.

4 Unlike the UN Commission on Human Rights, which consisted of representatives of national governments, the UN Sub-Commission on Human Rights consisted of 26 individual experts and therefore could be expected to approach human rights issues comparatively independently, free from national interest.

5 As its subordinate organs, the UN Sub-Commission on Human Rights had several

Rights, UN Sub-Commission on Human Rights, and working groups were held in close relations with one another. Despite the formal structure, however, these three organs did not, in fact, form strictly hierarchical structures or links and, instead, acted independently or overlapped in discussions in many cases. As a result, Japanese military sexual slavery, too, was discussed in disparate contexts by the three organs.[6] The issue was separately raised to these agencies in 1992, almost at the same time, and both the UN Commission on Human Rights and the UN Sub-Commission on Human Rights produced very important reports during 1996-1998.

1) The Presentation of the Issue at the UN Sub-Commission on Human Rights: 1992

When South Korean and Japanese NGOs began to engage in activities at the UN, their initial goal seems to have been to create a tribunal at the UN regarding Japanese military sexual slavery like the International Tribunal for the Prosecution of Persons Responsible for Serious Violations of International Humanitarian Law Committed in the Territory of the Former Yugoslavia since 1991 (ICTY; henceforth "International Criminal Tribunal for the Former Yugoslavia"). In the end, however, such efforts concluded with the adoption of resolutions on the issue by the

working groups including the Working Group on Contemporary Forms of Slavery, which met both before and during its sessions and discussed in greater depth and in advance diverse human rights issues addressed by the sub-commission itself. As has been discussed above, the general structure of discussion consisted of the following cycle: working groups-UN Sub-Commission on Human Rights-UN Commission on Human Rights-UN Economic and Social Council-UN General Assembly (Hannum, 1965: 61).

6 Such a structure for discussion led to the frequent overlapping of functions and activities between the UN Commission on Human Rights and the UN Sub-Commission on Human Rights because the latter was the sole sub-commission under the former. Begun in 2000, the functional reduction of the UN Sub-Commission on Human Rights was a foregone conclusion stemming from this structural problem. In 2000, the UN Commission on Human Rights reduced the sessions of the UN Sub-Commission on Human Rights from four weeks to three weeks and transferred to itself the right and control over discussions on human rights violations per nation (1503 procedure), which hitherto had been within the domain of the UN Sub-Commission on Human Rights.

UN Commission on Human Rights, UN Sub-Commission on Human Rights, and Working Group on Contemporary Forms of Slavery and the appointment of and the submission of reports by Special Rapporteurs.

At the UN, Japanese military sexual slavery was raised by South Korean and Japanese NGOs independently of each other. Disappointed by the Japanese government's lack of sincerity, the Korean Council decided to raise this issue at the UN and obtained advice from diverse parties. It then participated in the UN Sub-Commission on Human Rights for the first time in August 1992 and, here, made an oral statement on Japanese military sexual slavery in the name of the World Council of Churches, which had consultative status. On the other hand, Japanese NGOs raised the issue of military sexual slavery along with that of forcibly taken laborers at the UN Commission on Human Rights in February and at the Working Group on Contemporary Forms of Slavery in May of the same year. Having thus begun to raise the issue at the UN unaware of each other, these two parties subsequently cooperated and engaged in activities together, participating in the Working Group on Contemporary Forms of Slavery-UN Sub-Commission on Human Rights-UN Commission on Human Rights.

In 1992 sessions of the UN Sub-Commission on Human Rights, the Korean Council made oral statements regarding the two agenda items of "Contemporary Forms of Slavery" and "Reparation to Victims of Gross Violations of Human Rights" and held press conferences and open forums for NGOs, thus appealing to the international community. In addition, it lobbied members of the sub-commission and succeeded in lobbying and inviting to South Korea the UN Special Rapporteur on the Right to Restitution, Compensation and Rehabilitation for Victims of Gross Violations of Human Rights and Fundamental Freedoms (henceforth "Special Rapporteur on the Right to Reparation"), who was already working on the issue of Japanese military sexual slavery.[7] The results of such efforts were immediate so that a resolution encompassing the issue of reparation already raised at the Working Group on Contemporary Forms

7 In November 1992, the Korean Council invited Professor Theodoor "Theo" Cornelis van Boven, the Special Rapporteur on the Right to Reparation, and held a seminar titled "International Human Rights Treaties and Forced Military Comfort Women."

The Korean Council's press conference at the UN Sub-Commission on Human Rights (Aug. 18, 1992)

of Slavery was adopted at the UN Sub-Commission on Human Rights,[8] and the Special Rapporteur on the Right to Reparation stated that he would obtain information on Japanese military sexual slavery and reflect it in his report in the following year.[9]

When they first raised Japanese military sexual slavery at the UN Sub-Commission on Human Rights, South Korean and Japanese NGOs aimed at publicizing the issue simply as one of human rights violation to the international community and demanding the Japanese government to take appropriate measures. Consequently, at this time, the Korean Council forged broad solidarity with Japanese NGOs and Korean residents' organizations addressing the issue of forced taking by Japan during wartime, North Korean organizations, and Canadian organizations for

8 The resolution on contemporary forms of slavery (UN Doc. E/CN. 4/Sub. 2/1992/L. 3) includes a "request to the Secretary-General that he submit to the Special Rapporteur [on the Right to Restitution, Compensation and Rehabilitation for Victims of Gross Violations of Human Rights and Fundamental Freedoms] information received by the Sub-Commission [on Prevention of Discrimination and Protection of Minorities] and by the Working Group [on Contemporary Forms of Slavery] regarding the situation of women forced to engage in prostitution during wartime."

9 As for specific figures and further details on the foregoing discussion, see Shin Heisoo, 1997: 363-369.

former prisoners of war of Japan during World War II.

2) The Adoption of a Resolution on the Issue of the Wartime Violation of Women's Human Rights: 1993-1999

The activities engaged in during 1993-1999 at the UN Sub-Commission on Human Rights focused on situating Japanese military sexual slavery within the category of "systematic rape, sexual slavery and slavery-like practices during armed conflict" and, under this title, bringing about the appointment of a Special Rapporteur and the submission of a report. The definition of this issue as a wartime violation of women's human rights, which subsequently determined not only the nature of the issue itself but also the scope of solidarity, was, in fact, not intended from the beginning. At the UN Sub-Commission on Human Rights in 1993, South Korean and Japanese NGOs attempted lobbying to bring about the appointment of van Boven, the Special Rapporteur on the Right to Reparation mentioned above, as the Special Rapporteur on the issue of Japanese military sexual slavery (Shin Heisoo, 1997: 374). If these activities had proceeded smoothly, the issue perhaps would have been discussed as one of general human rights violations, with a focus on reparation. According to a citizen activist who participated in the lobbying, van Boven was unavailable then so that Linda Lou Chavez, an American member of the UN Sub-Commission on Human Rights, was approached, and, in the course, the activists strategically came to focus more on wartime sexual slavery than on reparation per se, in consideration of the conflict in Bosnia, which coincidentally shocked the world at the time. In 1993, the UN Sub-Commission on Human Rights finally adopted a resolution appointing Chavez as a Special Rapporteur and instructing her to submit a special report titled "Systematic Rape, Sexual Slavery and Slavery-like Practices during Wartime, Including Internal Conflict" (UN Doc. E/CN. 4/Sub. 2/1993/L. 12/Rev. 1). Although this resolution of the UN Sub-Commission on Human Rights was rejected at the UN Commission on Human Rights in 1994, the following year, the sub-commission adopted a resolution to create an investigative report on its own level. After the submission of Chavez's investigative report (UN Doc. E/CN. 4/Sub. 2/1995/38) in 1995, the UN Sub-Commission on Human Rights adopted a resolution to reappoint her as a Special Rapporteur, and this resolution was finally adopted at the UN Commission on Human Rights in the following year. Chavez visited South Korea, Philippines, and Japan and submitted the preliminary report (UN Doc. E/CN. 4/Sub. 2/1996/26) in 1996 but stopped the submission of the subsequent and final report, which was supposed to occur in 1997, due to her withdrawal from the office (Shin Heisoo, 1997: 372-376).

In 1997, the UN Sub-Commission on Human Rights adopted a resolution newly appointing McDougall, an American alternate member, as the Special Rapporteur on Systematic Rape, Sexual Slavery and Slavery-like Practices during Armed Conflict. In 1998, Special Rapporteur McDougall submitted a report of the same title (UN Doc. E/CN. 4/Sub. 2/1998/13). Together with the report submitted to the UN Commission on Human Rights in 1996 by UN Special Rapporteur on Violence against Women Coomaraswamy, which will be discussed later, this report is a memorable accomplishment regarding the issue of Japanese military sexual slavery. Indeed, McDougall's report is a very careful study that calls to account not only the Japanese government for compensation but also the relevant individuals for their criminal liability in its appendix, titled "An analysis of the legal liability of the Government of Japan for 'comfort women stations' established during the Second World War," following a theoretical discussion on systematic rape, sexual slavery, and slavery-like practices during armed conflict. In addition, it stresses that because the Asian Women's Fund, while being "'atonement' money," does not in any sense provide official, legal compensation, another appropriate mechanism must be created.

3) The Adoption of a Resolution for the Annual Reports of the UN High Commissioner for Human Rights: 1999-2006

With 1996 as the apex, the voice of the reports of the UN Commission on Human Rights gradually weakened. With the 2003 report as the final one, it became difficult to envision new prospects. Nor was it possible to anticipate the revival of discussions on Japanese military sexual slavery in the working groups. Amid such a situation, the UN Sub-Commission on Human Rights likewise demonstrated few prospects of activities after

McDougall's final report of 2000 (including supplements; UN Doc. E/CN. 4/Sub. 2/2000/21), whose coverage of the issue was much smaller than in the 1999 version of the report. Even Western NGOs that had taken interest in Japanese military sexual slavery began to express fatigue, implying that enough had been done to resolve the issue. In addition, the interest of the international community in the issue of violence against women in wartime, which had been sparked by that of Japanese military sexual slavery, seemed to shift to current problems occurring in areas including the former Yugoslavia, Kosovo, Timor-Leste, and Maluku Islands (also and formerly known as "Molucca Islands").

Amid such a situation, a new breakthrough was necessary in order to sustain discussions on Japanese military sexual slavery at the UN Sub-Commission on Human Rights from 2000 and onwards. Unexpectedly, however, the issue once again came under considerable attention at the UN Sub-Commission on Human Rights in 1999 thanks to the activities of NGOs. Regarding "Agenda Item 6. Contemporary Forms of Slavery," the Korean Council made a strong statement urging the resolution of Japanese military sexual slavery, and, from among subsequent statements by a total of ten NGOs, those from six NGOs including Japanese organizations mentioned the issue as their main or subsidiary topic. These groups criticized the Japanese government for having continuously ignored the recommendations of both the UN Commission on Human Rights and the UN Sub-Commission on Human Rights and the legal interpretation and recommendations of the ILO. These were followed also by supportive statements from members of the UN Sub-Commission on Human Rights. In particular, some newly appointed members very directly urged the Japanese government's responsible treatment of the issue. The South Korean government had maintained silence on Japanese military sexual slavery at the UN since its signing of a cooperation agreement with Japan in 1997, and, as if by proxy, the North Korean government attracted notice with its strong statements. During the sessions of the UN Sub-Commission on Human Rights, the Korean Council held the NGO Forum jointly with the Fact-finding Team on the Truth about Forced Korean Laborers in Japan 朝鮮人强制連行眞相調查團, a pro-Pyongyang Korean-Japanese organization, North Korea's Committee on Measures for Compensation to the "Former Comfort Women for Japanese Army" and Pacific War Victims, and International Fellowship of Reconciliation (IFOR), an international NGO. Unlike in the previous year, the forum attracted many participants and much attention. Held before the 2000 Women's Tribunal, it contributed considerably to the promotion of the former event as well.

Encouraged by such an atmosphere, the Korean Council[10] visited and discussed plans after the completion of McDougall's final report with human rights experts including Professor van Boven, a Dutch scholar of international law and a member of numerous UN committees who had actively provided aid for the resolution of Japanese military sexual slavery since 1992, when the Korean Council had first become active at the UN, as well as McDougall herself. In the process, an idea was raised: the Office of the UN High Commissioner for Human Rights would submit annual reports on the issue of the wartime violation of women's human rights to the UN Sub-Commission on Human Rights. A draft of a new resolution that included this proposal was subsequently drawn up and used to persuade members of the UN Sub-Commission on Human Rights while contacting them individually.

This resolution, which newly included diverse clauses such as states' responsibilities, underwent a very heated debate that lasted for hours due to opposition from many members such as those from Japan and Morocco but was finally adopted. Assistance and supportive statements from members from countries such as the United Kingdom and Uganda from the drafting stage and onwards played an important role in this successful adoption of the resolution. Due to strong proposals from Japanese commissioners, however, the resolution came to be limited, with the insertion of the following expression: all contents related to wartime sexual slavery to be reviewed by the Office of the UN High Commissioner for Human Rights in the future would be restricted to "ongoing conflict."[11]

10 I and Professor Cho Si-Hyun participated as the representatives.

11 "Calls upon the High Commissioner for Human Rights to monitor the implementation of the present resolution and to submit a report to the Sub-Commission at its fifty-second session on the issue of systematic rape, sexual slavery and slavery-like practices in situations of ongoing conflict, including information on the status of the recommendations made by the Special Rapporteur" (UN Doc. E/CN. 4/Sub. 2/1999/16).

Nevertheless, this resolution opened an important channel for maintaining Japanese military sexual slavery alive at the UN Sub-Commission on Human Rights both in and after 2000. In other words, in a situation where there was no prospect of solving the issue either in working groups or at the UN Commission on Human Rights, the resolution made it possible for the issue at least to be pending at the UN until it was solved.

A report authored by the Office of the UN High Commissioner for Human Rights in 2000 and submitted to the UN Sub-Commission on Human Rights for the first time (UN Doc. E/CN. 4/Sub. 2/2000/20) comprehensively reported how UN human rights organs currently dealt with the issue of the wartime violation of women's human rights. Because of the word "ongoing" in this report, however, the issue of Japanese military sexual slavery was not addressed. South Korean and Japanese NGOs participating in the UN Sub-Commission on Human Rights in August 2000 criticized this omission, stressing that the issue had to be seen as a current one as long as victims were still alive. Other NGOs likewise emphasized the UN's responsibility to resolve Japanese military sexual slavery, and, moreover, British and Chinese members stated that the Office of the UN High Commissioner for Human Rights report must include this issue. The Korean Council separately contacted the personnel responsible for the Office of the UN High Commissioner for Human Rights report on the issue of the wartime violation of women's human rights, informed them of this atmosphere at the UN Sub-Commission on Human Rights in 2000, and sent reference materials, beseeching their attention to the issue of Japanese military sexual slavery.

First proposed in 1993 and newly revised in 1999, the resolution on systematic rape, sexual slavery and slavery-like practices during wartime, including internal conflict was adopted once again in 2000, with contents nearly identical to those of the previous year. An American member who remembered that, in the preceding year, a very heated debate had taken place for a long time before the eventual adoption of the resolution, devised a compromise plan by going between South Korean and Japanese commissioners, the directly affected parties, and proposed the resolution. Due to Japanese members' strong opposition against the South Korean proposal to delete "ongoing," however, the word was left intact in the end.[12] Nevertheless, thanks to this resolution, a channel through which the issue of Japanese military sexual slavery can be raised has been retained.

Like the version from the previous year, the 2001 Office of the UN High Commissioner for Human Rights report comprehensively described the ways in which the issue of currently occurring wartime sexual slavery was addressed by UN human rights organs (UN Doc. E/CN. 4/Sub. 2/2001/29). However, to revive this resolution, which faced oblivion because no one had taken the initiative, South Korean and Japanese NGOs and South Korean members of the UN Sub-Commission on Human Rights set out diligently to persuade members of other nationalities of the sub-commission. As a result, the situation reversed itself thanks to reproach, during sessions on the agenda of contemporary forms of slavery, by members from countries including China, South Korea, and Norway regarding the issue of Japanese military sexual slavery. The Korean Council, which, until the previous year, had spoken in the name of foreign NGOs, participated in the name of the Korea Women's Associations United 韓國女性團體聯合, which had consultative status at the UN, for the first time in 2001. Coincidentally, the issue of distorted Japanese history textbooks, too, surfaced at the time, thus leading to stronger statements by Japanese, Korean-Japanese, and South Korean NGOs. After statements from Pyongyang, Seoul made comments on the issues of Japanese textbooks and military sexual slavery, thus breaking its silence since 1997, all of which served to change the atmosphere as well. The 2001 resolution included the issue of distorted Japanese textbooks and omitted the word "ongoing," which had been included in resolutions from the two previous years, thus implying that the Office of the UN High Commissioner for Human Rights report from the following year would address Japanese military sexual slavery.[13] Because the resolution from the previous year

---

12 "Calls upon the High Commissioner... to submit a report to the Sub-Commission... on systematic rape, sexual slavery and slavery-like practices during ongoing armed conflicts" (UN Doc. E/CN. 4/Sub. 2/2000/13).

13 "Encourages States to promote human rights education on the issues of systematic rape, sexual slavery and slavery-like practices during armed conflict, ensuring the accuracy of accounts of historical events, in the educational curricula," "Calls upon the High Commissioner for Human Rights to monitor the implementation of the resolution, as well as of resolutions 2000/13 of 17 August 2000 and 1999/16 of 26 August 1999, and

had thus omitted the word "ongoing," the 2002 annual report from the Office of the UN High Commissioner for Human Rights mentioned the issue in its conclusion. Here, it firmly stated in the conclusion, "The use of sexual slavery in any form during times of armed conflict—rape camps,[14] 'comfort stations', or other forms of sexual abuse—constitutes a grave breach of international human rights and humanitarian law" (UN Doc. E/CN. 4/Sub. 2/2002/28). Subsequently, nearly identical resolutions were adopted until the reorganization of the UN Sub-Commission on Human Rights in 2006, and the reports of the Office of the UN High Commissioner for Human Rights were annually submitted to the UN Sub-Commission on Human Rights until the latter's reorganization into the UN Human Rights Council Advisory Committee in 2007.

4. The Issue of Japanese Military Sexual Slavery at the UN Commission on Human Rights/Human Rights Council

Meanwhile, the UN Commission on Human Rights appointed Coomaraswamy in 1994 as the Special Rapporteur on Violence against Women. She submitted a preliminary report in 1995 and "Addendum: Report of the Special Rapporteur on Violence against Women, Its Causes and Consequences, Ms. Radhika Coomaraswamy, in Accordance with Commission on Human Rights Resolution 1994/45: Report on the Mission to the Democratic People's Republic of Korea, the Republic of Korea and Japan on the Issue of Military Sexual Slavery in Wartime" (UN Doc. E/CN. 4/1996/53/Add. 1)[15] to the 52nd session of the UN Commission on Human Rights in 1996, respectively. This latter report consists of the definition of sexual slavery, historical background, victims'

---

to submit a report to the Sub-Commission at its fifty-fourth session on the issues of systematic rape, sexual slavery and slavery-like practices during armed conflict" (UN Doc. E/CN. 4/Sub. 2/2001/20).

14 In her own report submitted to the UN Sub-Commission on Human Rights, McDougall dubbed Japanese military comfort stations "rape camps."

15 A Korean translation of this latter report is included in Lee Mikyung, ed., *Sourcebook on Assemblyperson Lee Mikyung's Legislative Activities 1*, February 1997.

South Korean survivors in a dialogue with Coomaraswamy during her visit to the House of Sharing (Jul. 20, 1995)

testimonies, positions of the three nations, and recommendations to the Japanese government. As is apparent from the title of the report, Coomaraswamy viewed the Japanese military comfort women system as military sexual slavery and, while welcoming the Asian Women's Fund as a humanitarian measure, argued that the legal resolution of violations of international law still remained unrealized. She demanded that the Japanese government: (1) admit that the installation of military comfort stations was a violation of international law and take legal responsibility for it; (2) compensate individual victims in accordance with the principles presented by the Special Rapporteur on the Right to Reparation; (3) disclose all relevant documents and materials; (4) apologize publicly and in writing to individual victims; (5) reorganize Japanese curricula to reflect the historical fact so as to raise the Japanese public's awareness; and (6) seek out and punish the liable parties as much as possible. In addition, as for the international community, she recommended: (1) NGOs should continue to raise the issue at the UN and make efforts to seek advice from either the International Court of Justice or the Permanent Court of Arbitration; (2) the North and South Korean governments should consider inquiring the International Court of Justice about legal issues such as Japan's liability and compensations; and (3) Tokyo should resolve the issue at the earliest date possible in consideration of the advanced ages of the victims[16] (Compilation Committee of the *20-Year History of the Korean Council for the Women Drafted for Military Sexual Slavery by Japan*, ed., 2014: 102-103).

There was little discussion on Japanese military sexual slavery for some time at the UN Human Rights Council[17] after the submission of Coomaraswamy's report. However, in the Universal Periodic Review of Japan,[18] the council recommended Tokyo to take measures that were acceptable to women who had been taken as military sex slaves by the Japanese armed forces during World War II.[19] In a report dated April 23, 2010 (UN Doc. A/HRC/14/22), Rashida Manjoo, then the UN Special Rapporteur on Violence against Women, stressed Tokyo's responsibility to compensate the victims.

On March 11, 2016, the working groups and Special Rapporteurs[20] of the UN Human Rights Council expressed concern about the December 28, 2015 agreement between the South Korean and Japanese foreign

---

16 A member state of the UN Commission on Human Rights at this time, the Japanese government submitted to the same organ, before the initiation of its sessions, a written statement urging the rejection of a resolution to adopt Coomaraswamy's report. It also sent copies of this statement to the relevant diplomats from major countries, seeking their support. But because no government would support Japan, the latter retracted its written rejection of the report and did not oppose the adoption of the resolution, thus leading to the unanimous adoption of the report. In October 2014, however, delegates from the Japanese government visited Coomaraswamy and demanded that she revise her 1996 report. Sankei News, October 16, 2014. Requoted from Totsuka Etsuro, 2015: 24-27.

17 As has been mentioned above, the UN made the UN Commission on Human Rights independent from the UN Economic and Social Council and reorganized it into the UN Human Rights Council, an agency on an equal footing, in order to respond to explosively increasing human rights issues worldwide.

18 Established following the reorganization of the UN Commission on Human Rights into the UN Human Rights Council, this is a system whereby all member states of the UN are reviewed every four years for their respective human rights circumstances.

19 https://www.ohchr.org/en/hr-bodies/upr/highlights31-october2012pm.

20 Eleonora Zielinska, Chair-Rapporteur of the Working Group on the Issue of Discrimination against Women in Law and Practice; Pablo de Greiff, Special Rapporteur on the Promotion of Truth, Justice, Reparation and Guarantees of Non-recurrence; and Juan E. Méndez, Special Rapporteur on Torture and Other Cruel, Inhuman or Degrading Treatment or Punishment. https://www.ohchr.org/en/press-releases/2016/03/japan-s-korea-long-awaited-apology-comfort-women-victims-yet-come-un-rights?LangID=E&NewsID=17209.

ministers on Japanese military sexual slavery and urged Tokyo faithfully to implement the recommendations presented by the UN Committee on the Elimination of Discrimination against Women earlier in the same week. Pointing out that this agreement did not adequately reflect the victims' views, they expressed both concern about the possible removal of the Statue of Peace and hope for the realization of justice for the victims.

5. The Issue of Japanese Military Sexual Slavery at Treaty Bodies

While discussions on Japanese military sexual slavery thus focused on working groups-UN Sub-Commission on Human Rights-UN Commission on Human Rights, attempts were made to raise the issue at nearly all of the UN human rights organs mentioned above. Together with Lawyers for a Democratic Society (Minbyun) 民主社會를 爲한 辯護士會, the Korean Council submitted to the UN Human Rights Committee, which monitors signatories' observance and violation of the UN International Covenant on Civil and Political Rights (ICCPR), a report on the Japanese government's crimes in relation to military sexual slavery. Member states of this covenant must submit reports to the UN Commission on Human Rights and be subjected to investigations by the commission every five years.[21] In other words, the Korean Council and Lawyers for a Democratic Society sent materials critical of the Japanese government for review by the commission in 1993, the year in which the Japanese government was to undergo investigations (Lawyers for a Democratic Society and the Korean Council for the Women Drafted for Military Sexual Slavery by Japan, 1993). However, because only the report was sent and, unlike with the UN Commission on Human Rights itself, no lobbying in particular was done and, moreover, a follow-up report was not sent five years later,

21 http://www.unhchr.ch/html/menu2/6/a/introhrc.htm [defunct since 2009]. [TN] Since a change made to the rule in 1997, however, states parties now had to report, after their accession to the covenant and the ensuing first report, at individually specified times (usually every 4-5 years). For the current regulation, see https://www.ohchr.org/en/treaty-bodies/ccpr/introduction-committee and http://www.ohchr.org/Documents/Publications/FactSheet15rev.1en.pdf.

the action did not yield any result such as recommendations by the UN Commission on Human Rights.

In December 2008, the UN Human Rights Committee criticized the Japanese government for still failing to provide appropriate compensations for and history education on Japanese military sexual slavery and Japanese politicians and media for damaging the victims' dignity and denying the relevant facts. The committee thus recommended Tokyo to admit its legal responsibility, to make apologies that were acceptable to the majority of the victims and would restore their dignity, to punish the liable parties who were still alive, and to compensate survivors, as their right as victims, through immediately effective legal and administrative measures. In addition, it pointed out that the Japanese government must educate students and the public in the nation regarding this issue and bridle all efforts to damage the victims' dignity or to deny facts related to the institution (UN Doc. CCPR/C/JPN/CO/5, para. 22).

In August 2014, the UN Human Rights Committee issued strong recommendations regarding Japanese military sexual slavery. Pointing out that the Japanese government had a direct legal responsibility, it demanded that Tokyo implement independent and fair investigations, punishment of the liable parties, compensations to the victims and their families, disclosure of the relevant materials, history education for the Japanese public including descriptions of the institution in school textbooks, public apologies, official admission of the state's responsibility, and restraint from damaging the victims' dignity or denying facts related to Japanese military sexual slavery (UN Doc. CCPR/C/JPN/CO/6, para. 14).

After reviewing the Japanese government's report, in May 2013, the UN Committee against Torture issued strong recommendations in a separate section on Japan. Viewing Tokyo as having rejected recommendations hitherto presented by various UN organs, the committee pointed out that private donations were inappropriate as compensations to victims of Japanese military sexual slavery and stated that definitions of acts including torture must be adopted. In addition, it expressed regret about the concealment of the relevant facts and materials, the retraumatization of the victims due to the denial of facts related to the military comfort women system, and a failure properly to implement education in Japan on the history of the institution. The committee recommended the implementation of the following victim-centered measures: Tokyo must admit its legal responsibility for the crime of military sexual slavery and punish the liable parties; both the government and major politicians must stop retraumatizing the victims by repeatedly denying facts related to the institution; Japan must disclose the relevant materials and thoroughly investigate the facts; the government must take measures to redress the victims including compensations; and the history of military sexual slavery must be described in school textbooks and taught to the Japanese public (UN Doc. CAT/C/JPN/CO/2, paras. 19-20).

In its review of the Japanese government's report in September 2014, the UN Committee on the Elimination of Racial Discrimination likewise stated that justice for and compensations to the victims of Japanese military sexual slavery did not end with the Asian Women's Fund and recommended Tokyo promptly to conduct fact-finding investigations, to issue earnest apologies, to provide compensations to the victims and their families, and to prohibit damages to the victims' dignity and denials of the factuality of the institution (UN Doc. CERD/C/JPN/CO/7-9, paras. 18-19).

Expressing concern in 2009 about the Japanese government's failure to devise a resolution regarding Japanese military sexual slavery and its deletion of passages on the institution from Japanese school textbooks, the UN Committee on the Elimination of Discrimination against Women recommended Tokyo promptly to devise a solution including compensations to the victims, punishment of the liable parties, and education of the Japanese public (UN Doc. CEDAW/C/JPN/CO/6, paras. 37-38). Having reviewed the Japanese government's report, in March 2016, the committee criticized the December 28, 2015 agreement between the South Korean and Japanese foreign ministers on Japanese military sexual slavery as a solution neither fully incorporating past recommendations from diverse UN organs nor centering on the victims themselves and recommended Tokyo to implement compensations, apologies, fact-finding investigations, and restoration of justice to and for the victims, to teach students and the public in Japan about the historical fact of Japanese military sexual slavery, and to include descriptions of the institution in school textbooks (UN Doc. CEDAW/C/JPN/CO/7-8, paras. 28-29).

In 2013, after reviewing the Japanese government's report, the UN Committee on Economic, Social and Cultural Rights likewise expressed concern that victims of Japanese military sexual slavery failed to enjoy economic, social, and cultural rights and to be compensated. It thus recommended the Japanese government to take measures promptly so that the survivors could enjoy these rights and to educate the Japanese public so that these women would not suffer from abuses such as hate speech (UN Doc. E/C. 12/JPN/CO/3, para. 26).

6. Discussions on Japanese Military Sexual Slavery at Global Conferences and by International NGOs

In addition, one of other important activities has been to participate in the UN's major special meetings and to appeal to the international community regarding the issue of Japanese military sexual slavery. Diverse South Korean human rights NGOs participated *en masse* in the 1993 UN World Conference on Human Rights held in Vienna, creating a special preparatory group. Here, organizations related to Japanese military sexual slavery that had already worked with the UN played an important role. From among these meetings, the Korean Council presented the issue of Japanese military sexual slavery at the Global Tribunal on Violations of Women's Human Rights, which was created by women's organizations worldwide (Shin Heisoo, 1997: 382-384). At the 4th World Conference on Women held in Beijing in 1995, all South Korean participants addressed the issue as the main one and engaged in activities together. At the 2001 World Conference against Racism, Racial Discrimination, Xenophobia and Related Intolerance (also known as "World Conference against Racism") held in South Africa, South Korean NGOs likewise participated and raised the issue of military sexual slavery along with that of distorted Japanese history textbooks, which surfaced as a major issue at the time. More importantly, South Korean organizations have continued to raise Japanese military sexual slavery from the perspective of forced labor at the ILO, a specialized UN organ, since 1995, and, in December 2000, women's organizations from Asian nations including South Korea and Japan established a people's tribunal together with their counterparts worldwide in criticism of existing legal systems and to discuss the issue.[22]

Another accomplishment of activities thus engaged in at the UN

South Korean human rights groups took part in the 1993 World Conference on Human Rights and discussed Japanese military sexual slavery.

was that the International Commission of Jurists, an international NGO globally acknowledged for its authority, coming to learn of Japanese military sexual slavery in the process of discussions at the UN, went on to visit South Korea, North Korea, Philippines, and Japan and to conduct research, publishing in 1994 a report presenting a very in-depth interpretation of the issue in terms of international law (International Commission of Jurists, 1994). Organizations such as the World Council of Churches and Amnesty International provided considerable help as well.

While serving as the UN High Commissioner for Human Rights, whose responsibility is to oversee the human rights-related duties of UN agencies including the UN Human Rights Council and treaty bodies

---

22 As for the ILO and the people's tribunal, see Chapters 7 and 8, respectively. In addition, attempts to resolve the issue of Japanese military sexual slavery in the international arena included activities to file lawsuits at the Permanent Court of Arbitration (1994) and those to submit bills of complaint and indictment to the Japanese Public Prosecutors Office (1994). Although frustrated by the Japanese government and the Public Prosecutors Office, respectively, these two sets of activities served to maintain public interest in the issue and to reactivate the movement to resolve it.

from the UN Secretariat, Navanethem "Navi" Pillay mentioned Japanese military sexual slavery a few times in 2014 (Office of the United Nations High Commissioner for Human Rights, 2014b). Stating that the Japanese government had failed to implement a "comprehensive, impartial and lasting resolution" of Japanese military sexual slavery, thus causing further violations of the victims' human rights and rendering the issue a "current" one (Office of the United Nations High Commissioner for Human Rights, 2014a). Even after the termination of her term of office, she has continued to express interest in the issue. At an invitational lecture she gave at Seoul National University in 2015, she likewise mentioned Japanese military sexual slavery. Inaugurated in 2015, her successor, Zeid Ra'ad Al-Hussein, visited the War and Women's Human Rights Museum 戰爭과女性人權博物館 in Seoul and had a meeting with former Japanese military sex slavers during his South Korean trip in the same year. He promised the UN's sustained efforts to address the issue and also urged Tokyo to implement a resolution desired by the survivors (New Delhi Television, June 25, 2015; and *Hankyoreh*, June 25, 2015).

7. Conclusion

Although the fact that Japanese military sexual slavery has been discussed at the UN for over 20 years signifies that the international community has continued to be interested in this issue, on the other hand, it also reveals the limitations of UN human rights organs, which lack the ability for forced execution. Nevertheless, especially in the face of countless human rights violations committed around the globe today, there is a most urgent need to highlight the importance of Japanese military sexual slavery newly, in ways different from those of the past 20 years. Amid weakened interest in the issue in both South Korean and Japanese societies now, it is necessary to make efforts so that discussions on the issue will continue at UN organs such as the UN Human Rights Council and the ILO. This is because, without pressure from the global community, the Japanese government will immediately stop feeling tension regarding military sexual slavery. In other words, the internationalization of human rights issues is proof of advances in the international community that can squarely face such logic of power among governments. In addition, it is necessary also to go beyond a fixed view of Japanese military sexual slavery as a wartime violation of women's human rights and to turn the diverse aspects of the institution into current issues anew. For example, human trafficking, which was a key method of mobilizing women as Japanese military sex slaves, can be linked to human trafficking today, which is one of the most serious human rights violations worldwide, thus newly underscoring the issue of impunity. It is important also to search for ways of forging solidarity with groups in Africa and Latin America despite current difficulties and of highlighting the issue of colonial rule, which is a very important aspect of the issue of Japanese military sexual slavery.

Chapter 7

The Issue of Japanese Military Sexual Slavery at the ILO

1. International Activities for the Resolution of the Issue of Japanese Military Sexual Slavery

Following World War I, the international community initiated efforts to create a common order so as to protect the human rights of ethnic minorities. Since World War II, it has forged a basis for human rights protection in the forms of charters and conventions and established international organs such as the UN, thus developing in earnest diverse countries' common efforts to protect human rights. Human rights not only have become an issue raised in multinational relations through international agencies but also are considered an important issue in diplomatic relations between countries. Meanwhile, human rights within individual nations have begun to be discussed in the international arena as well. Despite opposition based on cultural particularity and economic development, the so-called universality and internationalization of human rights seem to be forming an irreversible current. In this process, the participation of not only national governments but also NGOs has started to take on great importance.

The movement to resolve Japanese military sexual slavery provides important implications to other social movements within South Korea in that it has very effectively adjusted to this climate of the international community and attempted to resolve this issue in the global arena. Of course, in a reality where international agencies still lack compelling power, international activities to resolve military sexual slavery have faced great difficulties in yielding actual fruits in comparison with their tremendous efforts. Nevertheless, they have played a considerable role in shaping pressure on the Japanese government through public opinion and, moreover, prompting the international community to address the wartime violation of women's human rights as an important human rights issue. Established in 1990 by numerous women's organizations and individual women, the Korean Council initiated solidarity with Japan and Asian victim nations from the beginning, has succeeded in obtaining cooperation from major international NGOs such as the International Commission of Jurists, and has engaged in joint activities with North Korea by building trust. Since 1992, the Korean Council has raised the issue at the UN as a major case of human rights violations, thus inducing major sectors of this organization including the UN Commission on Human Rights and the UN Sub-Commission on Human Rights to issue important resolutions and reports. Since 1996, the Korean Council has raised the issue at the ILO as well, thereby bringing about strong recommendations to the Japanese government on many occasions. To date, the UN and the ILO have served as important arenas of international activities as global organs that are effective for exerting pressure on Tokyo in order to resolve the issue.

Military sexual slavery continued during Japan's "Fifteen Years War," from 1931 until the end of World War II in 1945. Planned by the Japanese government and armed forces, this large-scale forced mobilization of women from the colonies and, subsequently, even those from occupied territories, who were then sexually enslaved by Japanese troops, constitutes a war crime and a crime against humanity. It is therefore an issue not only concerning both women during wartime and ethnicity but also encompassing that of imperialism/colonialism in a complex manner. The international solidarity hitherto forged by South Korean NGOs with Asian victim nations at the UN to bring about a resolution has been based on an awareness that approaches this issue as a wartime violation of women's human rights. As for North Korea, South Korean organizations have forged solidarity by focusing on the aspect of ethnic/colonial exploitation inherent in the issue.

In contrast, the presentation of Japanese military sexual slavery at the ILO can be viewed as a very refreshing idea, approaching the issue from the perspective of forced labor. Established decades before the UN, the ILO has performed the role of creating and safeguarding the labor order around the globe and was incorporated as a specialized agency of the UN after the latter's establishment. Though it is an agency for negotiations among laborers, employers, and governments, the ILO is basically headed by trade unions. Consequently, for the Korean Council's activities at this organization, it is important to obtain cooperation from labor unions both in South Korea and across the world. Such activities at the ILO must be importantly evaluated also as the expansion of both the perspective for understanding and the support basis for Japanese military sexual slavery through international activities so far.

While it was in March 1995 that the Federation of Korean Trade Unions (FKTU) 韓國勞動組合總聯盟 first launched activities at the ILO by specifically submitting documents, NGOs and activists in Japan had already been gauging the possibility of raising Japanese military sexual slavery at this international organization since around 1992. Ever since a trade union in Japan presented the issue in 1995 after several years of preparation, participation in the activities has spread to the Federation of Korean Trade Unions and the Korean Confederation of Trade Unions (KCTU) 全國民主勞動組合總聯盟 in South Korea and many other labor unions in Japan. Likewise, legal judgments on the issue in the Committee of Experts' reports and special mentions of the issue by the Conference Committee on the Application of Standards (CAS; henceforth "Conference Committee") have become increasingly detailed and strong. In addition, with the further participation of Japanese trade unions and the Association for the Pacific War Victims 太平洋戰爭犧牲者遺族會 in South Korea, the scope of the issue, too, has expanded to encompass forced taking in general.

This chapter will summarize activities at the ILO, with a focus on the Korean Council. I have referred to numerous reports issued by the international organization and documents sent to it by the Federation of Korean Trade Unions, Korean Confederation of Trade Unions, and Korean Council. Major materials used in this chapter include records of my personal participation in and observation of the International Labour Conference (ILC) and interviews with members of South Korean labor unions, delegates of trade unions from various nations participating in the conference, and members of the International Labour Office.

2. The ILO, the Arena of the Presentation of Japanese Military Sexual Slavery

1) The ILO and Its Forced Labour Convention

Major international organs at which South Korean NGOs have been active in order to resolve Japanese military sexual slavery, the UN and the ILO hold important meanings in at least two aspects. The first is that judgments on the issue can be derived based on these agencies' own power to create conventions, to conduct investigations, to issue legal judgments, and to make recommendations. Even in a reality where they lack the power to enforce the execution of measures, authoritative international organs can exert considerable pressure through their judgments. In particular, such international agencies' judgments immediately influence similar discussions, thus strengthening interrelationships among international organs. The second is that solidarity can be forged with diverse NGOs around the world that engage in activities in these international organs. In other words, such solidarity situates Japanese military sexual slavery within the larger framework of women's human rights, thus simultaneously promoting the resolution of this issue and contributing to the resolution of other relevant human rights issues.

Like the UN Educational, Scientific, and Cultural Organization and the World Health Organization, the ILO is a specialized agency of the UN now but was founded before the latter, in 1919. Following the idea that the improvement of workers' position is indispensable to lasting world peace, the ILO was established through the Treaty of Peace between the Allied and Associated Powers and Germany (henceforth "Treaty of Versailles") immediately after World War I. The ILO, in which workers, employers, and government representatives participate on an equal footing, is the only international organ whose members are NGOs.

The ILO has numerous labor-related conventions as well as channels through which it can raise, determine, and make strong recommendations regarding violations of these conventions. In addition, it is also an arena for trade unions in countries around the globe to forge solidarity. As of 2024, the organization produced 191 conventions and 208 recommendations on international labor standards, with a membership numbering 187 countries.[1] In contrast to conventions, which, as international laws, must be complied with when ratified and entail monitoring as well, recommendations are guidelines lacking compelling power.

Of the ILO's basic conventions, Convention No. 29, or the Forced Labour Convention, is one of the most important, as it transcends the sphere of labor to have a broad impact on the protection of basic human rights. Influenced by the international dialogue on the issue of forced labor, which, in turn, was set off by the abolition of slavery (Geneva Convention on Slavery was adopted in 1926), the ILO adopted Convention No. 29 in 1930 (effective from 1932), which has been ratified by 181 states as of date. Articles 1 and 11 of this convention prohibit the forced labor of women, and persons who are called up for forced labor are entitled to be paid compensation under Articles 14 and 15. Article 25 stipulates that those responsible for the imposition of forced labor must be criminally punished. In addition, while Article 2 specifies the conditions of emergencies that can allow exemption from the prohibition on forced labor, the ILO Committee of Experts has ruled that the forced mobilization of women for Japanese military sexual slavery did not take place under such exceptional conditions.[2]

---

1 http://www.ilo.org and https://normlex.ilo.org/dyn/normlex/en/f?p=NORMLEXPUB:1:0::NO:::.

2 **Article 1**

1. Each Member of the International Labour Organization which ratifies this Convention undertakes to suppress the use of forced or compulsory labour in all its forms within the shortest possible period…

Article 2

1. For the purposes of this Convention the term forced or compulsory labour shall mean all work or service which is exacted from any person under the menace of any penalty and for which the said person has not offered himself voluntarily.

2. Nevertheless, for the purposes of this Convention, the term forced or compulsory labour shall not include--

(a) any work or service exacted in virtue of compulsory military service laws for work of a purely military character;

(b) any work or service which forms part of the normal civic obligations of the citizens of a fully self-governing country;

(c) any work or service exacted from any person as a consequence of a conviction

Japan ratified the Forced Labour Convention on November 21, 1932 as Treaty No. 10, and the convention took effect on November 21, 1933. Once the Forced Labour Convention comes into effect, it cannot

---

in a court of law, provided that the said work or service is carried out under the supervision and control of a public authority and that the said person is not hired to or placed at the disposal of private individuals, companies or associations;

(d) any work or service exacted in cases of emergency, that is to say, in the event of war or of a calamity or threatened calamity, such as fire, flood, famine, earthquake, violent epidemic or epizootic diseases, invasion by animal, insect or vegetable pests, and in general any circumstance that would endanger the existence or the well-being of the whole or part of the population;

(e) minor communal services of a kind which, being performed by the members of the community in the direct interest of the said community, can therefore be considered as normal civic obligations incumbent upon the members of the community, provided that the members of the community or their direct representatives shall have the right to be consulted in regard to the need for such services.

Article 11

1. Only adult able-bodied males who are of an apparent age of not less than 18 and not more than 45 years may be called upon for forced or compulsory labour. Except in respect of the kinds of labour provided for in Article 10 of this Convention, the following limitations and conditions shall apply:

(a) whenever possible prior determination by a medical officer appointed by the administration that the persons concerned are not suffering from any infectious or contagious disease and that they are physically fit for the work required and for the conditions under which it is to be carried out;

(b) exemption of school teachers and pupils and officials of the administration in general;

(c) the maintenance in each community of the number of adult able-bodied men indispensable for family and social life;

(d) respect for conjugal and family ties.

2. For the purposes of subparagraph (c) of the preceding paragraph, the regulations provided for in Article 23 of this Convention shall fix the proportion of the resident adult able-bodied males who may be taken at any one time for forced or compulsory labour, provided always that this proportion shall in no case exceed 25 per cent...

Article 12

1. The maximum period for which any person may be taken for forced or compulsory labour of all kinds in any one period of twelve months shall not exceed sixty days, including the time spent in going to and from the place of work...

Article 14

1. With the exception of the forced or compulsory labour provided for in Article 10 of this Convention, forced or compulsory labour of all kinds shall be remunerated in cash at rates not less than those prevailing for similar kinds of work either in the district in which the labour is employed or in the district from which the labour is recruited, whichever may be the higher...

Article 25

The illegal exaction of forced or compulsory labour shall be punishable as a penal offence, and it shall be an obligation on any Member ratifying this Convention to ensure that the penalties imposed by law are really adequate and are strictly enforced.

be repealed for ten years. If and when made after those ten years through a notification to the ILO Director-General, repeal comes into effect one year following the notification (Article 30 Clause 1 of the Forced Labour Convention). Consequently, Japan, having ratified the Forced Labour Convention in 1932, was bound to uphold the convention's effectiveness in all cases until November 21, 1944 (Park Won Soon, 1995: 30-31). NGOs and labor unions in both South Korea and Japan have raised the issue of Japanese military sexual slavery as a violation of the Forced Labour Convention and, through cooperation from many labor unions, striven to induce the International Labour Conference to issue strong recommendations.

2) The Channels for Raising Issues

While there are numerous organs and channels installed within the ILO for raising labor-related issues, what organizations such as the Korean Council attempted in relation to the issue of Japanese military sexual slavery were the methods of going through the Governing Body and the Committee of Experts. Because two channels may not be used simultaneously for a particular case at a given time, when the first method of going through the Governing Body was not effective, the organizations immediately switched to the method of going through the Committee of Experts.

The method of going through the Governing Body refers to the ILO's allowance, in Article 24 of its constitution, for the Workers' or Employers' Group to file lawsuits, called "representations," against a member state that has ratified but does not comply with an ILO convention. Once the International Labour Office, the ILO's secretariat, receives a representation, it informs the government concerned and forwards the fact to the Governing Body. After determining the representation's receivability and accepting it, the Governing Body then creates an ad hoc committee consisting of workers, employers, and government representatives in order to investigate the issue. This committee investigates the issue and, after contacting the government concerned, prepares a report for review by the Governing Body, requesting the dispatch of a representative from the government concerned at times as well. The Governing Body then determines the publication of the ruling on the representation.[3]

The Federation of Korean Trade Unions raised the issue of Japanese military sexual slavery in spring 1995 through these procedures but withdrew it in the following year. Ever since the Osaka Fu Special English Teachers' Union 大阪府特別英語教員組合 (henceforth "OFSET Union") in Japan subsequently raised the issue in 1995, yet another channel through which the Korean Council has raised the issue together with the Federation of Korean Trade Unions and the Korean Confederation of Trade Unions to this day is the Committee of Experts. This is the regular system that supervises compliance with ILO conventions. Consisting of 20 labor law experts, the Committee of Experts conducts reviews of issues raised in relation to the implementation of conventions and recommendations for each nation and publishes reports. Issues can be raised at the committee only by labor unions and are generally accepted until July or August. The Committee of Experts notifies the governments concerned of the representations that have been brought forward and prompts them to submit their respective opinions. It then convenes in November or December to review the submitted materials comprehensively and publishes a report in March of the following year. Including legal judgments on innumerable issues regarding countries around the world, this report in itself holds the significance and functions of a case law and therefore can exert important influence. From among the many cases presented in the report, 20-30 of the more important ones are selected, intensively discussed at the Conference Committee during the International Labour Conference[4] in June, created into a report, submitted to the International Labour Conference, and adopted (International Labour Organization, 1995: 22-24).

3 See https://www.ilo.org/international-labour-standards.

4 The ILO's top decision-making body, the International Labour Conference meets during the first three weeks of June every year. It is operated based on the Conference Committee, which is a permanent body, and 3-4 topical committees. Together with the Committee on Freedom of Association (CFA), the Conference Committee is the ILO's monitoring and supervisory organ. The Committee on Freedom of Association monitors and supervises cases of violations by member nations that have not ratified the Freedom of Association and Protection of the Right to Organize Convention (ILO Convention No. 87) and the Right to Organize and Collective Bargaining Convention (ILO Convention No. 98), and the Conference Committee is an organ that monitors violations of all ratified conventions (Yoon Young Mo, 1999).

The Conference Committee consists of a total of over 500 members, attended by one representative each of workers, employers, and the government in an ILO member state. The major agendas to be discussed intensively at the International Labour Conference are determined at the Workers' Meeting, which is held earlier than the conference itself. The important fact, however, is that those main agendas are largely decided at sessions of the International Confederation of Free Trade Unions (ICFTU),[5] whose membership numbers over 140 nations.[6] The International Confederation of Free Trade Unions, of which both the Federation of Korean Trade Unions and the Korean Confederation of Trade Unions are members as well, holds executive committee meetings four times a year (March, June, September, and December). The March session, which coincides with the period in which the Committee of Experts' report is published, can be viewed as a meeting important for the determination of the International Labour Conference's major agendas. In other words, the agendas created at the International Confederation of Free Trade Unions are discussed at the Worker's Meeting and largely accepted by both the Employers' Group and the Government Group at the Conference Committee.

In consideration of both the time necessary for reviewing compliance with decisions including recommendations made at the June International Labour Conference and the timing of the presentation of issues, which must be received by the Committee of Experts by July, it is customary for the same agenda to be addressed in the Committee of Experts' report every other year. As will be discussed later, Japanese military sexual slavery has been dealt with at the Committee of Experts on numerous occasions but has yet to be discussed as the Conference Committee's major agenda. This is known to be considerably due to lobbying by the Japanese Trade Union Confederation (JTUC; also known as "JTUC-

5 [TN] This federation was combined with the World Confederation of Labour (WCL) and reorganized into the International Trade Union Confederation (ITUC) in 2006. In order to avoid confusion, however, all references to the organization will use the older name.

6 As for international labor union federations, besides the International Confederation of Free Trade Unions, which is the largest organization, there are the World Confederation of Labour and the Confederation of Christian Trade Unions (ACV-CSC), both largely Catholic labor union federations, and the World Federation of Trade Unions (WFTU), a federation mainly of Eastern European labor unions at one time, among others.

Rengo") 日本勞動組合總聯合會 (聯合; henceforth "Rengo"), a Japanese labor union federation that wields strong influence on the International Confederation of Free Trade Unions.

3. Raising the Issue of Japanese Military Sexual Slavery at the ILO: 1995-1996

1) The Preparatory Stage: 1992-1994

It was at a session of the UN Working Group on Contemporary Forms of Slavery held in May 1992 that the Forced Labour Convention and Japanese military sexual slavery were raised in conjunction.[7] This was after speaking out about both the military comfort women system and forced taking at the UN Commission on Human Rights for the first time, in February of the same year. However, legal discussions on whether or not military sexual slavery had constituted a violation of ILO Convention No. 29 did not continue for some time afterwards. Considerable advances began to be made as the International Human Rights Research Society 國際人權硏究會, Japan Federation of Bar Associations (JFBA) 日本辯護士聯合會, and Fact-finding Team on the Truth about Forced Korean Laborers in Japan 朝鮮人强制連行眞相調査團 in Japan invited judge Prafullachandra Natwarlal Bhagwati from India, a member of the ILO's Committee of Experts, to Tokyo and held a seminar at the end of September 1994 (September 23-24).[8] Determining that military sexual slavery had been a serious human rights violation, judge Bhagwati criticized the Allied Forces for not having punished the liable parties after World War II despite their knowledge of the institution. In addition, defining the issue as a case of forced labor, she ascertained that it had constituted a violation

7 It was at an August 1992 session of the UN Sub-Commission on Human Rights that the Korean Council raised Japanese military sexual slavery at the UN, after some preparation. Around this time, Totsuka Etsuro, a Japanese lawyer, started to raise the issue at the UN Commission on Human Rights and the Working Group on Contemporary Forms of Slavery as well. Following the August 1992 session of the sub-commission, he went on to engage in international activities for the resolution of the issue in cooperation with the Korean Council.

8 As for this seminar, see Totsuka Etsuro, 1999 (Chapter 7).

of the Forced Labour Convention, or ILO Convention No. 29, discussing diverse legal grounds. In January 1995, the Korean Bar Association (KBA) 大韓辯護士協會 and the Japan Federation of Bar Associations announced their legal opinion that military sexual slavery had been a violation of the Forced Labour Convention. Encouraged by this, Japanese NGOs immediately began to contact the Korean Council and, at the same time, to persuade trade unions in both countries that could raise the issue at the ILO.

2) The Federation of Korean Trade Unions' Presentation of the Issue to the Governing Body and Frustration

It was the Federation of Korean Trade Unions that first formally raised Japanese militarysexual slavery at the ILO. The trade union confederation held a seminar on February 9, 1995 as a preparation for submitting a representation on the issue to the ILO and participated in a symposium on military sexual slavery sponsored by the Japan Federation of Bar Associations in Tokyo during March 10-12, where it made a presentation arguing that military sexual slavery had been a violation of the Forced Labour Convention. On March 20, it submitted a formal representation to the International Labour Office requesting that a committee based on Article 24 of the ILO's constitution be established and investigate the issue as a violation of Convention No. 29 (Federation of Korean Trade Unions, 1995). Receiving no response to this, the organization sent another letter on July 5. On August 11, it finally received a reply in the Director-General's name stating that the issue would be addressed by the Governing Body in November.[9] According to the Federation of Korean Trade Unions' report (Federation of Korean Trade Unions, 1995b), on November 8, the Governing Body held a session of a subcommittee of three members, one each from the Workers' Group, Employers' Group, and government organizations, to discuss Japanese military sexual slavery.

9 Apologizing for the delayed reply, the Director-General stated in this letter: the officers had finally begun discussions only before the early part of the 82nd International Labour Conference and the 263rd session of the Governing Body's meetings but been unable to finish reviews. Consequently, reviews would be completed by the Governing Body's November meeting and materials would be submitted to that session (Federation of Korean Trade Unions, 1995a).

Here, it was stated, "The issue will be reviewed by legal experts in the Governing Body. After supplementary materials have been received from the Federation of Korean Trade Unions regarding legally ambiguous aspects and the general purport of the representation, it will be processed at the forthcoming Governing Body meeting scheduled for March of next year."[10]

However, the Governing Body did not address this issue at its meeting in March of the following year and went on to hold the International Labour Conference in June without having taken any action whatsoever. In its 1997 report, the Committee of Experts clearly stated that the Governing Body had neither investigated the contents of the Federation of Korean Trade Unions' presentation of the issue in 1995 nor determined the receivability of the issue even up to the Federation of Korean Trade Unions' withdrawal of its representation in a letter dated May 30, 1996[11] (International Labour Organization, 1997a: 83).[12]

3) The OFSET Union's Presentation of the Issue through the Committee of Experts and the Committee of Experts Report

Meanwhile, spurred on by social movements in Japan, the OFSET Union sent a letter on February 24, 1995 to the ILO urging the organization to

---

10 At this subcommittee, William "Bill" Brett (United Kingdom), Jean-Jacques Oechslin (France), and Yvon Chotard (chairperson; France) represented the workers, employers, and governments, respectively. The subcommittee stated that this representation was unprecedented, and, in consideration of the fact that its results would affect not only South Korea but also China and certain Southeast Asian countries including the Philippines, it had been agreed that an internationally acceptable and reasonable conclusion must be derived. It also said that, at present, recommendations to Japan, the object of the petition, would consist mainly of compensations for damages, and, in relation to this, Japan was known to be preparing a fund (i.e., Asian Women's Fund) as well (Federation of Korean Trade Unions, 1995b).

11 As the Federation of Korean Trade Unions' letter that I obtained is dated June 10, 1996, it is uncertain whether a second one was sent. In this letter, the Federation of Korean Trade Unions stated that although the OFSET Union had raised the same issue at a session of the Committee of Experts, the Governing Body had not taken any measure, as addressed in the committee's 1996 report. Expressing deep regret, the federation said that it was withdrawing its representation (Federation of Korean Trade Unions, 1996).

12 The failure of the Governing Body thus to adopt any measure has been seen as due to the lobbying of both the Japanese government and the Rengo (Totsuka Etsuro, 1997). At the time, a Swiss newspaper supposedly reported pressure from the Japanese government and the Governing Body's conduct as a scandal.

investigate the issues of Japanese military sexual slavery and the Japanese government's wartime forced labor as violations of the Forced Labour Convention.[13] While the Governing Body was postponing the processing of the issue raised by the Federation of Korean Trade Unions, the OFSET Union's observation was received by the Committee of Experts on June 12, 1995. Regarding this observation, at its session held in November of the same year, the Committee of Experts judged that the institution must be defined as sexual slavery and had constituted a violation of the Forced Labour Convention, concluding that it hoped Tokyo would promptly prepare compensatory measures for it. This report was published in March of the following year (International Labour Organization, 1996a).

When an issue is submitted, the Committee of Experts reviews it and conveys the relevant documents to the government in question to hear the latter's opinions. According to its report, the Committee of Experts sent the OFSET Union's letter to the Japanese government on August 31, 1995, but the latter did not issue any comment (International Labour Organization, 1996a). In the following year, Tokyo claimed that it had not received the OFSET Union's letter from the Committee of Experts and retorted that this was a deviation from existing procedures. However, the committee strongly reiterated that it had sent the letter (International Labour Organization, 1997a). While such conduct on the part of the Japanese government possibly warranted criticism for undermining the authority of the Committee of Experts, there was no further exchange between the two parties.

The fact that the Committee of Experts passed such a judgment and published the report meant that no measure had been taken regarding the issue submitted to the Governing Body by the Federation of Korean Trade Unions earlier. If the Governing Body had determined the receivability of the issue raised by the Federation of Korean Trade Unions and, based on

---

13 Osaka Fu Special English Teachers' Union co-representative Robert Millard, "Letter Sent to the ILO," February 24, 1995. Though the union's observation was supposedly received by the Committee of Experts on June 12, the relationship between the letter and the observation is unclear. Nevertheless, because the Committee of Experts' report published in March 1996 addresses Japanese military sexual slavery alone, it is possible to assume that an observation only mentioning this issue was submitted separately from the letter.

it, installed an investigation committee and made investigations, because these procedures take precedence over those of the Committee of Experts, the latter would have been stopped (Totsuka Etsuro, 1997).

4) The Federation of Korean Trade Unions' Change of Direction to the Channel of the Committee of Experts and the Conference Committee Report

Once the Federation of Korean Trade Unions became aware that the Committee of Experts had addressed the issue of military sexual slavery at the request of the OFSET Union, it sent a letter to the Governing Body withdrawing its representation and changed the direction of its efforts to a focus on the Committee of Experts. At the 1996 International Labour Conference held during June 5-6, the Federation of Korean Trade Unions went to the Workers' Meeting and strongly pushed for the selection of the issue of Japanese military sexual slavery as a major agenda to be presented for deliberation by the Conference Committee,[14] with support from labor union federations in Belgium, Netherlands, China, New Zealand, Pakistan, Singapore, and Indonesia. Although the issue failed to be included among the some 30 main agendas at the Workers' Meeting, this was discussed: while military sexual slavery would not be adopted for discussion at the Conference Committee during the International Labour Conference, it would be addressed at the next conference if the Japanese government failed to establish an appropriate policy.[15] This was made clear by the spokesperson of the Workers' Group at the Conference Committee during the International Labour Conference and included in the committee's report.[16]

14 The Federation of Korean Trade Unions mentioned Japanese military sexual slavery also in President Park In Sang's keynote speech on June 13, 1996.

15 As the Conference Committee was passing the list of major agendas, the Workers' Group chair obtained a right to speak and stated that though there were cases that had to be discussed within the year, they had been omitted due to the reduced duration of the International Labour Conference. Mentioning Japan's violations of the Forced Labour Convention first out of those cases, the chair suggested that if Tokyo failed to take satisfactory measures by the next conference, the participants should formally resolve to discuss the omitted items at the International Labour Conference in the following year without fail. The Employers' Group agreed with this proposal from the Workers' Group as well (Federation of Korean Trade Unions, 1996).

The Korean Council's demonstration at the ILO (1996)

4. The Initiation of Active Activities through the Channel of the Committee of Experts and the Committee of Experts and Conference Committee Reports: 1996-1997

The publication of the Committee of Experts' report in March 1996 confirming Japan's violations of the Forced Labour Convention served as an impetus to begin action in earnest at the ILO. The Japanese government, which had not reacted to the OFSET Union's observations in 1995, expressed strong objection to the report this time, and the Rengo, the nation's representative labor union federation and a major supporter of the Asian Women's Fund,[17] sent a letter of protest as well.

---

16 "The Worker members stated that they would wish, in principle, to consider including in the list of cases for discussion next year the following: Bangladesh (Convention No. 107), Indonesia (Convention No. 98), Japan (Convention No. 29), Morocco (Convention No. 98), Pakistan (Conventions Nos. 98 and 111), Romania (Convention No. 111), and Saudi Arabia (Convention No. 111). They hoped that positive reports from the governments in question concerning changes made would avoid the necessity of discussing those cases in fact next year" (International Labour Organization, 1996b).

17 This is an organ that the Japanese government prompted Japanese NGOs to create in order to avoid its own legal responsibility and to mitigate the victims' complaints.

Meanwhile, the Federation of Korean Trade Unions, too, had been working steadily on this issue since the previous year and was joined by the Korean Confederation of Trade Unions. The Korean Council actively made efforts, and Asian NGOs began to pay attention to the issue as well. In addition, it is noteworthy that minority labor unions in Japan, in opposition to the Rengo, started activities at the ILO for the resolution of the issues of military sexual slavery and the forced mobilization of industrial labor.

The November 1996 meeting of the Committee of Experts seems to have consisted of a review of the opinions of both the Japanese government (May 31 and October 30) and the Rengo (September 30) regarding the committee's report published in March. In other words, though the customary practice is not to deal with the same issue in two consecutive years, the Committee of Experts made an exception in order to readdress the issue of Japanese military sexual slavery this year, too, after 1995.

The judgment of the Committee of Experts published in March 1997 conveyed an even more detailed legal interpretation of Japanese military sexual slavery in accordance with specific provisions in the Forced Labour Convention. In other words, citing Article 1 Clause 2 and Articles 14 and 15, it confirmed the need for compensation and clearly elucidated that the exemption from the prohibition on forced labor stipulated in Article 2 Clause 2 Nos. a and d was not applicable to the issue. In addition, based on Article 25, the judgment expressly stated that this illegal exaction of forced or compulsory labor should be punishable as a penal offence and that punishment was possible also under the Penal Code of Japan (Act No. 45, April 24, 1907; Articles 176 and 177).[18]

Another important point was that, with respect to claims by the Japanese government and the Rengo alike that Tokyo had already conveyed an apology to former Japanese military sex slaves and that compensations had been replaced with the Asian Women's Fund, the

---

Regarding this organization, see Chapters 9-10.

18 On June 22, 1994, in response to a question from Shimizu Sumiko, a Councilor in the Japanese National Diet Committee on Foreign Affairs, the Japanese government answered that the Forced Labour Convention had not applied in wartime. Tokyo seems to have conveyed this position to the ILO as well (Totsuka Etsuro, 1997).

Committee of Experts urged the continued implementation of measures meeting the expectations of the victims. This meant that in cases where the victims refused compensation from the Asian Women's Fund, the fund must be discontinued and other measures that satisfied the victims must be adopted.

Meanwhile, Japanese NGOs that were engaged in activities to resolve Japanese military sexual slavery together with the Korean Council started to respond actively, placing great importance on the resolution of the issue through the Committee of Experts. The Korean Council sent additional materials to the committee through the Federation of Korean Trade Unions in November 1996 and, after the publication of the committee's report in March 1997, began the task of informing both the ILO and worldwide labor unions of the reality of the Asian Women's Fund.[19] Japanese NGOs, too, cooperated with the Korean Council or separately pursued similar activities.[20] The Korean Council also sent a representative to the International Labour Conference in June 1997 and engaged in activities with the Federation of Korean Trade Unions and the Korean Confederation of Trade Unions. Although unable to participate officially due to the Rengo's monopoly and therefore lacking speaking rights, minor Japanese labor unions including the Tokyo Regional Council of Trade Unions 東京地方勞動組合評議會 (東京地評; henceforth "Tokyo Chihyo") and the Kanto Regional Council 關東地方聯合會 of the All Japan Shipbuilding and Engineering Union (AJSEU) 全日本造船機械勞動組合 (全造船; henceforth "Zenzosen") likewise began their activities at the International Labour Conference.

The list of major agendas for the Workers' Meeting, which opened before the Conference Committee, had already been determined by

19 For example, in April, the Korean Council sent letters explaining the Asian Women's Fund to the ILO Workers' Group chairperson Willy Peirens and Dutch labor unions, which were the most actively cooperative regarding the issue of Japanese military sexual slavery at the ILO. In May, in cooperation with organizations from Taiwan and the Philippines as well as many from Japan, it sent a detailed report on the fund to the ILO.

20 For example, organizations such as the United Church of Christ in Japan (UCCJ) 日本基督教團 and the National Christian Council in Japan (NCC) 日本基督教協議會 sent letters to members of the ILO urging an appropriate review of the issue of Japanese military sexual slavery.

the International Confederation of Free Trade Unions. This was due to the powerful activities of the Rengo, which had strong influence on the confederation (Totsuka Etsuro, 1997). Japan's violations of Convention No. 29, not included on the list, became the focus of intense debate at this Workers' Meeting. Objection to listing the issue as a main agenda of the Conference Committee was based on several grounds: with many current issues requiring urgent attention, dealing with one that had occurred 50 years before was inappropriate; it was difficult for the ILO to deal with a case that had occurred during wartime; and this issue would be better addressed at the UN rather than at the ILO. The Federation of Korean Trade Unions, Korean Confederation of Trade Unions, and unions from the Netherlands, which had victims of Japanese military sexual slavery, opposed these points. A labor union from Turkey (present-day Türkiye) charged that this was an example of the failure intensively to pursue cases involving developed countries at the ILO.[21]

In the end, attempts to prompt the Conference Committee to address Japanese military sexual slavery were frustrated once again. Nevertheless, as in the previous year, the chair of the Workers' Group brought up the issue at the committee and stated that it would be dealt with in the following year if no measures were taken by Tokyo. The report prepared by the Conference Committee clearly stated that the Committee of Experts should monitor whether the Japanese government implemented appropriate compensatory measures in consultation with groups representing the victims.[22] The Committee of Experts' report passed a more detailed legal judgment on the issue compared to the preceding year. Likewise, the report from the Conference Committee was more strongly worded than in the year before.

21 In addition, Education International (EI) and a labor union from Afghanistan expressed their support in selecting military sexual slavery as a major agenda of the Conference Committee (Son Hijoo, 1997).

22 "In approving the draft list, the Worker members wished to make certain important remarks for the Committee of Experts, the ILO, the governments concerned and the present Committee… the Committee of Experts should monitor the implementation of compensatory measures, which should be taken by the Government preferably in consultation with organizations representing the victims (Japan, Convention No. 29)" (International Labour Organization, 1997b).

5. The Committee of Experts' Judgment and the Repeated Frustration of the Adoption of Japanese Military Sexual Slavery as an International Labour Conference Agenda: 1998-2000

Since the inclusion of Japanese military sexual slavery in the Committee of Experts' 1996 report, labor unions in South Korea, Japan, and Netherlands have cooperated with NGOs to send annual statements to the same committee. Solidarity with labor unions around the world and the united efforts of the Federation of Korean Trade Unions and the Korean Confederation of Trade Unions, which have often been in conflict with each other on many other issues, must be seen as especially important fruits of this movement. In accordance with established practices, the Committee of Experts heard and discussed the position of the Japanese government and published a report after a year. The committee made judgments on the issues of both military sexual slavery and conscripted labor (this one has been included in the committee's reports since 1999) in 1996, 1997, 1999, and 2001-2003 including the unprecedented publication of two consecutive reports dealing with the same issue in the first two years. In fact identical to the judgments of the Committee of Experts, which is composed of labor law experts, the ILO's legal judgments have authority and are conclusive. However, the issue of Japanese military sexual slavery has been continuously frustrated in the somewhat political process of annually selecting 20-30 major agendas, out of hundreds of issues according to their importance, to be discussed within the limited time of the International Labour Conference.

1) Strong Recommendations from the Committee of Experts and the Conference Committee in 1999

Amid heightened interest among labor unions and NGOs in both South Korea and Japan, the Committee of Experts' report published in March 1998 failed to include Japanese military sexual slavery. In October 1997, the Federation of Korean Trade Unions and the Korean Confederation of Trade Unions as well as the National Confederation of Trade Unions (NCTU) 全國勞動組合總連合 (全勞連; also known as and henceforth

"Zenroren") in Japan had sent statements to the Committee of Experts, but the issue had not been discussed at the committee's November session. This was because these organizations had sent their statements too late, thus leaving insufficient time for the Committee of Experts to hear the Japanese government's responses. At the same time, this seems to have been due also to the application of the established practice of not dealing with the same issue in two consecutive years. Because the issue thus was not included in the committee's report, it was automatically left out from discussions at the International Labour Conference held in June.

Nevertheless, the Korean Council, which had newly noted the importance of the ILO, took part in the International Labour Conference held in June 1998 in order to prepare for discussions in the following year and met with members of the International Labour Office and labor union representatives from diverse countries to explain Japanese military sexual slavery. Owing to discussions on the issue in international arenas such as the UN, the level of recognition of the issue among the staff responsible for the Forced Labour Convention was relatively high despite the aggressive activities of both the Japanese government and the Rengo. As in the previous year, the International Labour Conference was attended by many members of minor Japanese labor unions that maintained positions different from that of the Rengo such as the Zenroren, engaging in activities to raise the issue of wartime forced industrial labor.[23] At the Workers' Meeting held before the Conference Committee, a representative from the Federation of Korean Trade Unions noted the need continuously to monitor violations of the Forced Labour Convention and, in particular, to conduct a careful review of wartime instances of forced labor.[24] Anyhow, because issues not included in the Committee of Experts' reports are not discussed at the International Labour Conference, military sexual slavery failed to be presented at the 1998 conference.

23 Although participants from Japanese labor unions had come prepared to demonstrate, the ILO did not allow demonstrations. As the UN likewise allowed demonstrations only outside the actual time of the meetings, they staged a protest against Japan's violations of the Forced Labour Convention in the morning outside the UN building. South Korean participants in the conference joined as well.

24 My personal observation at the conference.

Right after the 1998 International Labour Conference, the Korean Council and the Korean Confederation of Trade Unions[25] prepared a report and sent them it to the Committee of Experts. The OFSET Union, which had first raised Japanese military sexual slavery in 1995, once again presented a statement urging the resolution of the issue. The Tokyo Chihyo and the Kanto Regional Council of the Zenzosen, too, submitted statements on conscripted labor. It is noteworthy that, in connection with conscripted labor, South Korea's Association for the Pacific War Victims worked in cooperation on the issue with the Japanese labor unions mentioned above. The Japanese government and the Rengo likewise submitted statements claiming the substitution of compensations with the Asian Women's Fund. Based on all of these materials, the Committee of Experts passed down a very strong recommendation to the Japanese government on top of reconfirming its legal judgment from the previous year. It is worth noting the following points made in the committee's report published in March 1999. First, the report clearly stated that Asian Women's Fund, claimed by the Japanese government and the Rengo alike to substitute for compensation, did not meet the expectations of the majority of the victims. Second, as the victims were advancing in age, the Japanese government was requested to adopt appropriate measures expeditiously. Third, the issue of forced labor was addressed for the first time, and the report recognized conscripted labor also as a violation of the Forced Labour Convention and requested the Japanese government to submit a report on its implementation of appropriate measures (International Labour Organization, 1999a).

Encouraged by the Committee of Experts' report, which included unprecedentedly strong recommendations, the Korean Council and labor unions from both South Korea and Japan made preliminary preparations in April and May for the June International Labour Conference and participated in the conference in large numbers. The Federation of Korean Trade Unions, Korean Confederation of Trade Unions, Korean

25 Having sent a statement in collaboration with the Federation of Korean Trade Unions in the previous year, the Korean Council decided to send a statement in the name of the Korean Confederation of Trade Unions in order to demonstrate to the ILO cooperation from yet another organization.

Council, and Association for the Pacific War Victims jointly wrote a letter and sent it to labor unions in major countries, explaining the issue and requesting their cooperation. Japanese labor unions visited international organizations such as the International Confederation of Free Trade Unions, World Confederation of Labour, Confederation of Christian Trade Unions, Education International, and International Federation of Journalists (IFJ) and requested cooperation in resolving the issue of Japan's violations of the Forced Labour Convention (Association for the Pacific War Victims, 1999). Many from the Federation of Korean Trade Unions, Korean Confederation of Trade Unions, and Japanese labor unions participated in the June International Labour Conference, and the Korean Council likewise sent representatives including one survivor. A representative and a former victim from a Philippine organization joined as well. At the Workers' Meeting (June 3) held before the Conference Committee's June session, heated discussions broke out on Japanese military sexual slavery. However, as in the previous year, the list of major agendas had already been determined at the International Confederation of Free Trade Unions. Emphasizing that this issue had to be firmly brought to justice in order to stop continuing violence against women in wartime, the Korean Confederation of Trade Unions criticized that the frequent omission of cases involving developed countries from the list of main agendas reflected the ILO's neglect of its duty. The chief of the Federation of Korean Trade Unions' international bureau likewise argued that the issue had to be included on the list. In response to these assertions by South Korean labor union federations, trade unions from the Netherlands, India, Germany, and France made statements of support while those from Japan and Sweden stood in opposition. The grounds of the Swedish labor unions' opposition differed somewhat from the logic of both Japan and trade unions influenced by its lobbying. In other words, these groups were concerned about the danger of political misunderstanding that the issue could entail. They were of the passive position that because having the ILO address the highly controversial issue could provide governments and employers, which were already bent on reducing the monitoring and supervisory authority and functions of the organization, with an excuse to do so in the future, it was better to focus only on issues that could be discussed as labor problems per se without disagreement. Constituting a very defensive response to attacks from governments and employers, this was not right, the Korean Confederation of Trade Unions pointed out in private. Because the International Confederation of Free Trade Unions was in such a situation that it could not disregard the Rengo's stance, it adopted the position that it did not wish conflict to arise among workers. However, many workers including members of American labor unions criticized this as an irresponsible attitude, not attempting actively to mediate among numerous trade unions whose positions differed from that of the Rengo. In addition, the Rengo engaged in lobbying activities that verged on the unreasonable out of anxiety because of the joint letter created by the Korean Confederation of Trade Unions, Federation of Korean Trade Unions, Korean Council, and Association for the Pacific War Victims from South Korea and also stated a plan to hold a joint South Korean-Japanese seminar on the issue of war responsibilities (Yoon Young Mo, 1999).

At the Conference Committee on the following day, June 4, the Workers' Group chair, explaining the adoption of agendas and stating that three items not included on the list had been discussed at the Workers' Meeting, mentioned Japan's violations of Convention No. 29 as one of them. Saying that the Workers' Group respected the judgment of the Committee of Experts regarding this issue, the chair urged Tokyo to hold meetings with parties including the relevant labor unions, organizations representing the victims, and relevant governments for the creation of effective measures demanded by the survivors and to notify the committee of such activities promptly. In addition, both the Committee of Experts and the Conference Committee stated that they would take follow-up measures in accordance with the Japanese government's attitude, all of which was recorded in the Conference Committee's report.[26]

26 "...the Worker members considered that the report of the Committee of Experts rightly emphasized the universal and fundamental principles concerned in the case... The Government should take the initiative of holding meetings with the trade unions concerned, the representative organizations of the victims and the governments of the various countries concerned, in order to find an effective solution responding to the expectation of the majority of the victims. The Worker members urged the government of Japan to rapidly inform the Committee of Experts of the action and initiatives that it would take in this regard. The reaction of the Government would be decisive for the follow-up of this case by the Committee of Experts and this Committee..."

2) The 2001 Committee of Experts Report

Although the issue was not dealt with at the International Labour Conference, the Committee of Experts' strong recommendation and the Conference Committee's special mention greatly boosted the morale of the Korean Council and South Korean and Japanese labor unions alike. The Korean Council and the Korean Confederation of Trade Unions discussed future policy without delay, and Japanese trade unions also visited South Korea, meeting with the Korean Council, Association for the Pacific War Victims, Federation of Korean Trade Unions, and Korean Confederation of Trade Unions to hold solidarity meetings. The report sent to the Committee of Experts in the summer of 1999 had new meaning in many respects. First, it was co-signed by the Korean Confederation of Trade Unions and the Federation of Korean Trade Unions, and it is worth emphasizing the considerable significance of the cooperation between these two labor union federations. Second, unlike reports up to the preceding year, which had been limited to Japanese military sexual slavery, the 1999 one also addressed the issue of forced labor. Accordingly, it was prepared in collaboration with not only the Korean Council but also the Association for the Pacific War Victims, thus becoming the joint product of four groups working together (Korean Confederation of Trade Unions and the Federation of Korean Trade Unions, 2000).

In accordance with established practices, the Committee of Experts' report published in March 2000 did not address the issue. The four organizations above once again submitted an observation to the committee in the summer of the same year (Korean Confederation of Trade Unions and the Federation of Korean Trade Unions, 2000). The Netherlands Trade Union Confederation (*Federatie Nederlandse Vakbeweging*; FNV) likewise submitted an observation regarding the issue of compensations for Dutch victims of Japanese military sexual slavery to the Committee of Experts, and the Kanto Regional Council of the Zenzosen and the Tokyo Chihyo, too, sent observations concerning the issue of conscripted labor. On the other hand, both the Japanese

(International Labour Organization, 1999b).

government and the Rengo submitted observations adopting a position differing from that of the abovementioned organizations. The gist of their statements was that, through the San Francisco Treaty and Japan's bilateral treaties with diverse Asian countries, the rights of the victims and citizens in these countries to demand claims from Tokyo had been fulfilled and that the Japanese government had amply conveyed apologies and aid to the survivors. Arguing that this issue was not appropriate to be addressed by the ILO, the two groups expressed their hope that the issue would no longer be mentioned at the Committee of Experts.

Regarding this, the Committee of Experts took a somewhat ambiguous position—a departure from its strong recommendation to Japan in 1999. While noting Tokyo's claims that the issue of compensation had been resolved through treaties was legally correct, at the same time, it acknowledged the point discussed in the report of the UN Sub-Commission on Human Rights on "Systematic Rape, Sexual Slavery and Slavery-like Practices: Sub-Commission Resolution 1999/16" (UN Doc. E/CN. 4/Sub. 2/RES/1999/16): "the rights and obligations of States and individuals with respect to the violations referred to in the present resolution [of the Sub-Commission] cannot, as a matter of international law, be extinguished by peace treaty, peace agreement… or by any other means." In addition, the committee expressed its hope that, before it was too late, the Japanese government would confer with the victims of military sexual slavery and the organizations representing them and compensate the survivors in a manner that accorded with their expectations instead of the Asian Women's Fund, which went against their wishes. With respect to forced labor, it likewise mentioned its wish that Tokyo would urgently meet the victims' demands in consideration of their advanced ages. On the other hand, the Committee of Experts expressed its wish that going through these tasks again would become unnecessary at the next round (International Labour Organization, 2001a). While this report did not differ markedly from previous ones, it was the first instance of the committee taking such an ambiguous stance.

6. A Partial Victory—The Adoption of the Issue at the Workers' Meeting: 2001-2003

While the Committee of Experts' report thus signaled a slight retreat, there was a great advance at the 2001 International Labour Conference. A decision was made at the Worker's Meeting to modify the list of major agendas, already prepared at the International Confederation of Free Trade Unions, to include Japan's violations of the Forced Labour Convention. However, the issue was voted down at the Employers' Meeting, thus frustrating its inclusion among main agendas in the end.

1) The Adoption of the Issue at the Workers' Meeting

The Korean Council initiated preparations such as sending a letter to the International Confederation of Free Trade Unions together with the Korean Confederation of Trade Unions and the Federation of Korean Trade Unions before going to the International Labour Conference and, in order to appeal to both other labor unions and members of the International Labour Office, created documents refuting Tokyo's position that the issue had been resolved through the South Korean-Japanese claims agreement of 1965.

At the Workers' Meeting, from the onset, representatives of the Rengo aggressively brought forward an agenda criticizing Tokyo for its treatment of the issue of the right of Japanese laborers in the public sector to organize. This was a matter of ILO Convention No. 87 (Freedom of Association and Protection of the Right to Organize Convention). Because the principle is to deal with only one issue as a Conference Committee agenda for each country, this move was intended to prevent Japan's violations of the Forced Labour Convention from being addressed as the nation's agenda. Such an intention on the part of the Rengo immediately aroused opposition from labor union representatives from diverse countries. Though a list of some 20 main agendas had already been created at the International Confederation of Free Trade Unions, as was customary, various trade union delegates argued that Japan's violations of the Forced Labour Convention, which was an old unresolved issue for the ILO, had to be dealt with this time. Representatives of labor unions in the Netherlands, Greece, France, Italy, Germany, Portugal, United States, and United Kingdom spoke of the importance of Japanese military sexual slavery. More importantly, delegates from American and British trade unions, which had previously maintained silence on this issue, exposed the lobbying activities hitherto engaged in by Tokyo and the Rengo alike. With the exception of the Pakistani representatives solely expressing support for Japan, even the Swedish labor union delegates, who had opposed discussions on the issue up to the previous year out of concern over the politicization of the ILO, remained silent. The Workers' Group chair newly appointed in this session[27] concluded that Japan's violations of the Forced Labour Convention would be included among the agendas for intensive discussions instead of the issue of Japanese laborers in the public sector. This was a great victory for the movement, six years after first approaching the ILO with the issue in 1995.

2) Opposition from the Employers' Meeting

Though it is an established practice at the ILO for decisions reached at the Workers' Meeting to be passed at the Employers' Meeting without modification, a turnaround occurred during the 24 hours following this decision made at the Workers' Meeting. In other words, due to strong opposition from Japanese employers, Japan's violations of the Forced Labour Convention were voted down as an agenda at the Employers' Meeting, which was exceptional. Japanese employers' group emphasized that, in the current situation, where there was no sign of yet another war whatsoever in Japan, it was wrong once again to take up this issue, which had occurred during World War II. They were supported by the majority of the Employers' Group.

While chairs of the Workers' and Employers' Groups gathered in an attempt to reach a compromise, due to differences of opinion between the two groups, they seemed to have provisionally agreed not to present this issue to the Conference Committee. Two days later, the Workers' Group convened in the morning for an unscheduled 30-minute meeting.

---

27 Luc Cortebeeck from Belgium.

The Workers' Group chair announced a compromise with the Employers' Group chair based on the outcome of discussions within the latter group. Because labor union representatives strongly voiced dissatisfaction with this, however, the meeting continued into the afternoon. The atmosphere of the afternoon meeting was somewhat depressed but finally led to the ponderous conclusion that, as conflict between the Workers' and Employers' Groups was undesirable, the issue of forced labor imposed by Japan, for the moment, would not be dealt with this time.

Expressing regret that the Workers' Group had not been able to reach an agreement with the Employers' Group regarding Japan's violations of the Forced Labour Convention, the Conference Committee's 2001 report (International Labour Organization, 2001b) stated that whether or not Tokyo took appropriate measures regarding the issue would continue to be closely monitored.

3) Attempts at a Dangerous Compromise

Published in March 2002, the Committee of Experts' report discussed Japan's violations of the Forced Labour Convention again, continuing from the preceding year. Because of the debate between the Workers' and Employers' Groups at the Conference Committee in the previous year, the report thus came to address the issue in two consecutive years, contrary to established practices. The Committee of Experts recommended the Japanese government to meet the victims' demands.[28]

Because Japan's violations of Convention No. 29 were thus included in the Committee of Experts' report and had been decided as a major agenda by the Workers' Group in the preceding year, labor unions and NGOs all came to entertain the hope that the issue would be selected and discussed as a main agenda at the 2002 International Labour Conference. Due to Japanese trade unions' proposal for a compromise made before the conference in June, however, the movement for the resolution of Japanese

---

28 "...One year later, the Committee hopes that the (Japanese) Government will be in a position to supply particulars to the Conference... and action taken to respond to the claims of wartime 'comfort women' and industrial forced labor" (International Labour Organization, 2002a).

military sexual slavery at the ILO once again came to undergo a distortion.

Japanese labor unions requested their South Korean counterparts to raise the right of Japanese laborers in the public sector to organize (ILO Convention No. 87) as Japan's issue at the International Labour Conference to be held in June 2002. This was the reasoning: because Tokyo was trying to amend the relevant law within 2002, if the ILO could make an appropriate recommendation regarding the issue to the Japanese government, that would serve as very strong pressure. Because of the urgency of the situation, the Rengo hoped that South Korean labor unions would agree to raise this issue in 2002. If this could be brought about, the Japanese trade union federation promised, it would then cooperate to raise Japan's violations of the Forced Labour Convention in 2003.

Regarding this proposal, the Federation of Korean Trade Unions and the Korean Confederation of Trade Unions exhibited divergent reactions. Strongly arguing that it could not forsake its principle, the Federation of Korean Trade Unions rejected the suggestion. In contrast, the Korean Confederation of Trade Unions adopted a stance inclined to compromise: one should understand the situation in Japan as a fellow labor union confederation, and the wise thing would be to obtain even more concessions by first showing such a cooperative attitude instead.[29] The Korean Council held a meeting of the Board of Executive Members and, after reviewing the Japanese trade unions' proposal, consolidated its principle that the suggestion was unacceptable.

Amid this ascendancy of the principle against accepting the proposal, the Federation of Korean Trade Unions and the Korean Confederation of Trade Unions continued discussions and began to search for a compromise. It was: Japanese labor unions must secure a firm answer from the Employers' Group that it would agree to discuss Japan's violations of the Forced Labour Convention as an individual agenda at the next

29 There was also an interpretation that such differences of opinion between the two labor union federations reflected these organizations' divergent stances toward the issue of public sector labor unions within South Korea. In other words, while the Federation of Korean Trade Unions had bridged differences of opinion with the South Korean government to a considerable extent, the Korean Confederation of Trade Unions was in a state of strong tension with the central government regarding this issue so that its solidarity with Japanese trade unions was able to play an important role.

International Labour Conference. This was a strategy of "a step backward for two steps forward": because the Employers' Group, as in the previous year, could once again oppose the decision of the Workers' Group in the current year, the matter should be postponed to the following year in order to secure certainty. Unable to delve into the internal circumstances of the ILO in detail, the Board of Executive Members of the Korean Council could not strongly oppose the decision of the two trade union confederations even as it espoused the stance of adhering to the principle of no compromise.

Before the official Workers' and Employers' Meetings were held at the International Labour Conference in June, South Korean and Japanese labor unions unofficially contacted delegates from trade unions around the world and discussed the issue of Japan's violations of the Forced Labour Convention at the conference. Regarding the compromise between labor unions from the two nations, representatives of trade unions in the Netherlands, France, Germany, and United States expressed opposition at first. Under the condition that a firm pledge to discuss the issue at the International Labour Conference in the following year could be obtained, they eventually approved of the compromise. Japanese labor unions claimed to have received a pledge from the Japanese employers' group certainly to cooperate on discussing the issue at the conference in the following year, and the Employers' Group chair confirmed this as well. All of this came about during unofficial negotiations.

At the Conference Committee, the chairs of the Workers' and Employers' Groups said that they "jointly declared" to address Japan's violations of the Forced Labour Convention at the International Labour Conference in the following year. When the representative of French labor unions still expressed dissatisfaction with the committee for not dealing with the issue in the current year, the Workers' Group chair once again ascertained that it would be addressed in the following year.

However, there were signs that the circumstances would not be simple. At the Employers' Meeting, representatives of employers in disparate countries understood this issue somewhat differently. At the Conference Committee, the Japanese government stated that it had never come to an agreement with labor unions regarding the issue. In the end, the "joint declaration" strongly espoused by the Workers' and

Employers' Groups at the International Labour Conference came to be documented in a drastically reduced form. The Conference Committee's 2002 report strongly expressed only the stance of the Workers' Group. In contrast, it recorded differing positions for the Employers' Group and the Government Group. In other words, according to the report: the Workers' Group said that it would, along with the Employers' Group, address the issue as an agenda of the Conference Committee in the following year; the Employers' Group, on the other hand, stated that it would deal with the issue if agreed on by the Japanese laborers, employers, and government. Meanwhile, according to the report: the Japanese government expressed its hope that the Committee of Experts would consider the opinions of not only minority labor unions from Japan but also Tokyo itself in a balanced manner and stressed that, contrary to the words of the Workers' and Employers' Groups chairs, the Japanese laborers, employers, and government had not reached an agreement on the issue at all.[30]

7. Repeated Conflict between the Workers' and Employers' Groups: Since 2004

Despite the compromise made earlier, in 2002, attempts to adopt the Forced Labour Convention and the issue of Japanese military sexual slavery as an individual agenda at the 2003 International Labour Conference failed. This was due to differences of opinion between the Workers' and Employers' Groups. The conflict where the Workers' Group's decision regarding the issue as an individual agenda at the ILO is rejected by the Employers' Group has continued since 2004.

30 "The Worker members deplored the fact that the [Japanese] Government had still not taken the necessary measures. Together with the Employer members, they undertook to include the application of Convention No. 29 in Japan on the agenda of the Committee the next year. The Employer members said that if there were an agreement among the Japanese tripartite constituents for the examination of the case by the Conference Committee in 2003, they could support it. The Government member of Japan... called on the Committee of Experts not to prejudice the future course of discussions on the case and made clear that there was no agreement among the three parties of Japan to revisit this case next year as referred to by the previous speakers" (International Labour Organization, 2002b).

Chapter 8

The 2000 Women's International War Crimes Tribunal on Japan's Military Sexual Slavery

1. The 2000 Women's Tribunal as a New Movement

The 2000 Women's Tribunal began with an opening ceremony held on the evening of December 7, 2000 in Tokyo as the first step, followed by the 3-day main trial during December 8-10 and the Public Hearing on December 11 and closing with the judgment on December 12. Based on a thorough review following the preliminary judgment passed during the tribunal period, it concluded with the final judgment issued in the Hague, Netherlands in December 2001. As a people's tribunal, organized by civilian organizations without any relationship to intergovernmental organs such as the UN, the 2000 Women's Tribunal consisted of both a civil trial charging the Japanese government with responsibility for compensations and a criminal trial demanding the punishment of individuals responsible for crimes related to Japanese military sexual slavery. In addition, held after the tribunal was the Public Hearing, where the issue of diverse forms of current violations of women's human rights in areas of conflict such as the former Yugoslavia was discussed, thus publicizing the issue as a current one. In particular, it is noteworthy that the tribunal included Emperor Hirohito among the individuals indicted. At the tribunal, prosecution teams consisting of people working to resolve the issue from ten countries—South Korea, North Korea, China, Japan, Philippines, Indonesia, Taiwan, Malaysia, Timor-Leste, and Netherlands—filed indictments separately. As for the Public Hearing, NGOs from regions with current armed conflict such as Kosovo and Colombia[1] participated and denounced the issue of the violation of women's human rights.

In this way, the 2000 Women's Tribunal served as a testing ground for more systematic judgment on the still unresolved criminality of the issue of Japanese military sexual slavery from the perspective of international law. Despite conflicting views about the legal binding force of people's tribunals, the 2000 Women's Tribunal has been acknowledged for the legal value and moral binding force of its ruling, and the judgment of this tribunal has already begun to be used as a judicial case. At the same time, this tribunal also served as an arena bringing together existing international (transnational) movement, as evinced by the participation of citizens from countries worldwide including 75 victims. The background of the creation of and the process of the preparation for the 2000 Women's Tribunal summarize the movement hitherto engaged in regarding this issue and the circumstances under which it was problematized, and the fruits and limitations left by the tribunal present the direction of the movement in the future.

What most discussions on the 2000 Women's Tribunal miss but must be noted is the development of the movement in South Korea accomplished as an effect of both the process of preparation and the tribunal itself. Many international law scholars and historians newly joined the movement to bring about the court indictments, and the expansion of the movement not only to civic movements but also among university students was a very important outcome. Joint indictment with North Korean representatives was a major fruit of inter-Korean cohesion achieved on the level of civil society. As detailed discussions have already been performed on the tribunal's legal effects (Yokota Yuichi, 2001; Chang Wan-Ick, 2001; Higashizawa Yasushi, 2001; and Chinkin, 2001) and procedures (Shim Young-Hee, 2001), this chapter will examine its overall process, supplementing information on items not addressed in the abovementioned discussions such as the South Korean movement and the preparatory process.

The 2000 Women's Tribunal was a new type of solution pursued as a

---

1 Chiapas, Colombia, Guatemala, Algeria, Sierra Leone, UN Peacekeeping Somalia, Kosovo, United States, Palestine, Afghanistan, Myanmar, Burundi, Vietnam, Timor-Leste, and Okinawa.

result of the movement engaged in for over a decade. Launched with the establishment of the Korean Council in 1990, the movement regarding the issue of Japanese military sexual slavery raised citizens' awareness domestically, making various demands to the South Korean government while performing many activities including fund raising for the victims, research, and demonstrations. As for the Japanese government, participants in the movement in South Korea directly sent written requests, called Tokyo to account through organs such as the UN and the ILO, and continued lawsuits in Japan and the United States. In the midst of this, diverse activities to help the survivors were performed on the level of the private sector, and the South Korean government likewise legislated the Act on the Support of Livelihood Stability for Former Comfort Women Drafted into the Japanese Forces under Japanese Colonial Rule 日帝下日本軍慰安婦에 對한 生活安定支援法 in 1993 and provided special subsidies to the victims. What is important above all is that the social climate at first, where the tendency to seek to avoid discussions on this issue had been strong, changed and an active historical consciousness that painful history had to be faced and overcome became widespread, thus leading the movement to be diffused among a variety of groups including scholars, jurists, teachers, and students. The international community's interest grew considerably as well. However, neither the South Korean nor the Japanese government, both of which must assume the responsibility to implement official procedures for the restoration of the victims' honor, found a clue to resolution. The South Korean government continued to exhibit divergent stances to domestic NGOs and the Japanese government, and the latter did not budge at all despite multifaceted international pressure. With the prolongation of the movement, a shift in the direction to research and education began to be discussed in South Korea, and the view that lawsuits and the movement for legislation were the only remaining paths was gaining strength. Legal resolution, political pressure, and moral demands through social movements all failed in this way to find actual solutions for the victims, and, in particular, the limitations of intergovernmental organs such as the UN were revealed. It was against this background that NGOs working for the resolution of the issue discovered people's tribunals as a measure.

It was as an occasion for supplying new energy to the movement that the 2000 Women's Tribunal was proposed regarding the issue of Japanese military sexual slavery, in relation to which there still remains much to be done such as education, research, and commemorative projects besides direct solutions such as compensations and apologies to the victims. Admittedly, none of the members who agreed to the establishment of the 2000 Women's Tribunal happened to possess a clear, long-term vision of the ways in which the tribunal, a single event when seen in terms of the trials themselves, could be continued. Nevertheless, in the process of actually preparing for the tribunal, many new figures from home and abroad alike took part, thus expanding the scope of the movement.

2. The Factors That Made the 2000 Women's Tribunal Possible

Women's organizations from victim nations across Asia, which hitherto had proceeded with the movement by combining their strength, decided to hold the 2000 Women's Tribunal in Tokyo in December 2000. The intention was precisely to bring to justice the still unresolved issue of Japanese military sexual slavery by women's efforts through a formal process before the end of the 20th century. It was modeled on the International War Crimes Tribunal on Vietnam (henceforth "Russell Tribunal on Vietnam"),[2] held in Europe in 1967. However, unlike the Russell Tribunal on Vietnam, which had been led mainly by European intellectuals, the 2000 Women's Tribunal may be said to have gone a step further because it was realized through the efforts of women from the victim nations.

At the 5th Asian Solidarity Conference held in Seoul during April 15-17, 1998, women's organizations from the victim nations and Japan gathered their determination and swiftly began the preparations. While a proposal for the 2000 Women's Tribunal had been made for the first time by Matsui Yayori, a Japanese women's movement activist, at a Violence against Women in War Network International (VAWW-Net International)

2 In addition to the Russell Tribunal on Vietnam, there was a Permanent People's Tribunal in Italy during the 1970s as an early case of a people's tribunal (Chinkin, trans. Chang Bok-Hee, 2001: 300).

meeting held in Geneva several days before, an official agreement to hold it was reached at this conference. More broadly, however, the tribunal must be seen as a result of the numerous conditions realized by the movement regarding the issue of Japanese military sexual slavery begun in the early 1990s. Because there already existed an accumulation of interpretations in terms of international law made by international organs including the UN and the ILO and Japanese and American courts (whether positive or negative), women's organizations across Asia were able to hold a concept of the tribunal. In addition, these organizations were confident that they could draw worldwide attention because of growing global concern over the issue of wartime violence against women such as the International Criminal Court (ICC or ICCt) and the International Criminal Tribunal for the Former Yugoslavia. Because there existed networks with NGOs and figures related to human rights not only within Asia but also around the world including the West, they had the capacity that would enable them to hold the 2000 Women's Tribunal.

1) The Accumulation of Interpretation in Terms of International Law and the Frustration of Resolution

In 1992, the Korean Council began its efforts to raise the issue of Japanese military sexual slavery at the UN Sub-Commission on Human Rights and, in the process, obtained the interpretation of van Boven, an important expert within the UN, in terms of international law. In 1994, the International Commission of Jurists investigated military sexual slavery victims and relevant figures in North and South Koreas, Japan, and Philippines and produced a very meticulous analysis in terms of international law. Holding the Japanese government accountable for war crimes and crimes against humanity alike, this analysis is an important reference material in discussions on the issue even today.[3] The Korean Council's activities at the UN led the UN Commission on Human Rights to prompt Coomaraswamy, the UN Special Rapporteur on Violence against Women, to submit an in-depth report on Japanese military sexual

3 [TN] The results of the analysis were published in 1994 as a book, *Comfort Women: An Unfinished Ordeal—Report of a Mission.*

slavery in 1996 and the UN Commission on Human Rights to prompt McDougall, the Special Rapporteur on Systematic Rape, Sexual Slavery and Slavery-like Practices during Armed Conflict, to include contents calling Tokyo to account for military sexual slavery in her 1998-2000 reports. In 1995, the ILO began to address the issue of military sexual slavery as it had been raised by the Federation of Korean Trade Unions and the OFSET Union. Producing the judgment that the Japanese government had violated ILO Convention No. 29 (convention prohibiting forced labor), the ILO Committee of Experts recommended the former promptly to make adequate compensations to the victims. However, such numerous legal judgments and recommendations by international organs have failed to cause Tokyo to budge (see Chapters 6 and 7).

On the other hand, while many lawsuits regarding damages to former military sex slaves are under way in Japanese district courts, most of them either have been defeated or are pending. Even though it was not a judgment on the crime of military sexual slavery per se, the 1996 verdict on the lawsuit seeking official apology, etc. to former military sex slaves and members of the Women's Labor Volunteer Corps in Busan (henceforth "Shimonoseki court case") ordered the Japanese government to pay 300,000 yen to each plaintiff/victim for its fault of not having taken appropriate legislative measures following the admission of its own responsibility in 1993, thus presenting the first and only positive interpretation concerning this issue. However, it, too, was defeated at both a high court and the Supreme Court of Japan. A lawsuit brought to an American court in 1997 is now under way in the form of pursuing the responsibility of Japanese corporations (Han Woosung, 2000). In addition to this, the separate attempts made in 1994 to file a lawsuit at the Permanent Court of Arbitration and to submit a written indictment to the Japanese Public Prosecutors Office were frustrated because they failed to obtain consent from the Japanese government.

If such legal interpretations, recommendations, and judgments had been implemented as they were, there would have been no need to form the 2000 Women's Tribunal. In other words, such conflicting outcomes—i.e., the accumulation of numerous legal interpretations and the frustration of the resolution of the issue through official organs—led to the birth of the tribunal on the level of the private sector.

2) The Arousal of the International Community's Awareness of Wartime Violence against Women

As the 20th century drew to a close, war and internal conflict broke out in diverse places around the globe, and, in those areas, violence against women was committed without exception. Its representative examples are the violation of women's human rights amid ethnic cleansing in the former Yugoslavia and armed conflict in Kosovo, Timor-Leste, Rwanda, and others. Japanese military sexual slavery, which began to be raised at the UN in 1992, was posited as a historical predecessor of such diverse women's issues during wartime, and its importance came to be recognized by the international community. While plans for the practical resolution of the issue could not be found because of the Japanese government's powerful lobbying, 1998 saw the adoption of the Rome Statute for the establishment of the International Criminal Court, where it would be possible to bring charges against states for crimes on individual, not governmental, levels, unlike the International Commission of Jurists, which allowed indictments only by governments. With this statute, the International Criminal Court began to function in 2002. Though Japanese military sexual slavery could not be raised at this court due to the principle that past issues were not to be addressed, it now became possible to address wartime violence against women effectively in the international community. A situation where even as such international courts were gathering the attention of the world, military sexual slavery, which had served as an important basis in the process of their establishment, could not be addressed at these institutions ripened the atmosphere for the creation of a new tribunal, regardless of its form, for the resolution of the issue. Here, the Russell Tribunal on Vietnam emerged as a model.

3) Networks among International NGOs

For it to move global public opinion, as had the Russell Tribunal on Vietnam, the 2000 Women's Tribunal needed an array of conscientious and competent figures acknowledged by the international community and the formation of international solidarity capable of smoothly proceeding with the practicalities and possessing a common will. Japan and victim nations in Asia were able to dare to establish the tribunal because of confidence in the international solidarity that had formed over the past decade.

From the time they joined hands to address Japanese military sexual slavery at the end of the 1980s, Professor Yun Chung-Ok and the Korea Church Women United in South Korea immediately started to cooperate with Japanese women's organizations and subsequently expanded solidarity with women's organizations and NGOs as well as Korean residents in Japan. After holding the 1st Asian Solidarity Conference in Seoul in August 1992 with the participation of women from Taiwan, Hong Kong, and Thailand as well as Filipinas' organizations, which had a wealth of experience with international activities, the conference was continued with the addition of organizations from China, North Korea, and Indonesia, thus forming solidarity in arenas of diverse international activities (see Chapter 5).

The movement for former military sex slaves built networks of individuals and organizations working for human rights not only in Asia but also around the world. Since it had begun its activities regarding the UN in 1992, the Korean Council formed networks with figures directly and indirectly related to the UN including van Boven, a renowned international law scholar and the UN's Special Rapporteur on the Right to Reparation, and McDougall, an American human rights lawyer and an alternate member of the UN Sub-Commission on Human Rights.[4] With the addition of connections forged by activists in countries including Japan and the Philippines, broad international networks came to be formed. It was because of the existence of such a foundation that the 2000 Women's Tribunal was able to mobilize numerous figures.

In addition, as has been mentioned above, in international arenas such as the UN, women from Asian countries including South Korea positioned Japanese military sexual slavery as an issue of violence against women during times of armed conflict and formed links with movements for the resolution of many issues arising in various places around the world today. In the midst of this, they came to gain widespread support

4 These figures visited South Korea many times for symposia and investigations.

from human rights and women's organizations across the globe. In support of Coomaraswamy's report submitted to the UN Commission on Human Rights in 1996, women's organizations worldwide established the International Alliance Supporting Radhika Coomaraswamy's Report on Military Sexual Slavery in Wartime as well. Military sexual slavery was presented before the Global Tribunal on Violations of Women's Human Rights, held at the NGO Forum on Human Rights during the UN World Conference on Human Rights in Vienna in 1993, and solidarity with women's organizations from dozens of nations was formed. A forum for the issue was opened at the World Conference on Women held in Beijing, and solidarity with other women's organizations was forged. The formation of such extensive solidarity with women's organizations around the globe was an important foundation for the 2000 Women's Tribunal. In particular, the Public Hearing held during the tribunal, which highlighted military sexual slavery as an issue of the present, was made possible by such solidarity with women's organizations across the world.

As has been stated above, however, it must also be pointed out that such global solidarity, which made possible the attempt to hold the 2000 Women's Tribunal, was limited in that it restricted Japanese military sexual slavery only to an issue of wartime violence against women. Although the point that the issue of colonialism must be supplemented was discussed several times in the process of preparing for the tribunal, discussions could not be further developed due to the limitations of such international solidarity. For one thing, strong solidarity with Japanese women's organizations and NGOs restricted in-depth discussions on coloniality to a certain extent. Another major factor was that other Asian victim nations, because they were in positions differing from that of South Korea, could not move further together with respect to the issue of imperialism.

3. The Movement in South Korea in the Process of Preparing for the 2000 Women's Tribunal

Gathered in Seoul for the 5th Asian Solidarity Conference, which was to be held in April 1998, representatives from the five countries of South

Korea, Philippines, Indonesia, Taiwan, and Japan confirmed the fruits and limitations of the joint movement described above, decided thenceforth, in close collaboration, to urge the Japanese government's fulfillment of its responsibilities and to engage in multifaceted activities for the determination of the truth and the punishment of those responsible. In addition, they agreed on the inauguration of the 2000 Women's Tribunal as an activity to achieve these goals.[5] The South Korean and Japanese sides promptly began preparations. South Korean participants formed the Preparatory Committee on April 25, immediately after the 5th Asian Solidarity Conference, and, after several preparatory sessions, inaugurated the Korean Organizing Committee for the 2000 Women's Tribunal (henceforth "Korean Organizing Committee") on December 7 of the same year. Japanese counterparts established the VAWW-Net Japan[6] in June and began preparatory activities in earnest. After gathering in Seoul and founding the International Organizing Committee in February 1999, representatives from Japan, Taiwan, and Philippines held

5 The contents of the resolution made by all participants in the 5th Asian Solidarity Conference on April 17, 1998 are as follows:
① We urge the Japanese government to act upon the recommendation made by the UN Commission on Human Rights.
② We will once again spur on our efforts for the investigation of the truth and the punishment of responsible persons.
Specifically, we will proceed with the following movements:
First, we will uncover lists of criminals related to the issue of comfort women.
Second, we will urge countries around the world including Asian victim nations to legislate laws prohibiting Japanese war criminals' entry into and departure from their respective territories.
Third, we urge the UN to establish an international criminal court.
Fourth, we will make 2-year preparations for the opening of the Women's Tribunal.
Fifth, we will build a network for the investigation of the truth and the punishment of responsible persons.
③ We urge the Japanese government to perform legal compensations and demand the dissolution of the Asian Women's Fund, created by the Japanese government to avoid its legal responsibility.
④ We urge the legislation of a special law for the investigation of the truth currently under way in Japan.
(from "The Joint Resolution of the 5th Asian Solidarity Conference for the Issue of Military Sexual Slavery by Japan")

6 An international network of women created during the International Conference on Violence against Women in War and Armed Conflict Situations held in Tokyo in November 1997, the VAWW-Net Japan also held a meeting during the session of the UN Commission on Human Rights in April 1998, where the 2000 Women's Tribunal was first proposed.

several meetings to coordinate each country's preparation process and formulated the framework of the 2000 Women's Tribunal. In the process of contacting each other through Korean residents in Japan and Japanese representatives, North and South Koreas successfully performed joint tasks after meeting in person at the Shanghai conference in March 1999.

1) The Korean Organizing Committee

After the decision to hold the 2000 Women's Tribunal was made in April 1998, it is no exaggeration to say that the activities of the Korean Council focused on preparations for the tribunal. In addition, in the process of actually preparing for the 2000 Women's Tribunal, many new figures were recruited, thus expanding the scope of activities. With three sessions of the Preparatory Committee (May 20, November 6, and November 20, 1998) and visits to the VAWW-Net Japan in Tokyo (June 6-7 and July 30-31, 1998) as the footing, the Korean Council inaugurated the Korean Organizing Committee on December 7, 1998. The committee comprised not only members of the Korean Council but also a large number of jurists, lawyers, researchers, legislators, writers, journalists, dancers, and members of other activist organizations.[7] It is noteworthy, too, that not only women but also men participated actively. The Korean Organizing Committee was initiated with the following structure: the Legal Committee, which consisted mainly of jurists and lawyers; the Fact-finding Committee, which centered on researchers; the Planning and Public Relations Committee, which centered on the Executive Members of the Korean Council; the External Cooperation Committee; the Financial Committee; and the Secretariat, which was taken charge of by the Korean Council. It then went on to review the preparatory activities while holding several meetings.

7 The Sarangbang Group for Human Rights 人權運動舍廊房, Korea Sexual Violence Relief Center 韓國性暴力相談所, Association for the Pacific War Victims 太平洋戰爭犧牲者遺族會, House of Sharing 나눔의 집, Docufactory Vista 記錄映畵製作所보임, etc.

2) The Students' Tribunal on Japan's Military Sexual Slavery in 2000

One of the important fruits reaped during the preparation for the 2000 Women's Tribunal was the expansion of participation by university students. With preparations begun in early 1999, the Students' Tribunal on Japan's Military Sexual Slavery in 2000 2000年日本軍性奴隷戰犯學生法廷 (henceforth "Students' Tribunal") held during April 28-29, 2000 at Ewha Womans University became yet another version of the 2000 Women's Tribunal.[8] There were several opportunities to hold exchange with Japanese university students in the process, and, from September and onwards, when the 2000 Women's Tribunal itself became imminent, the Students' Tribunal was held at universities in Daegu and Busan as well as those in Seoul including Kyung Hee University. Besides the Students' Tribunal, cultural festivals related to former military sex slaves were held at many universities such as the Korea Maritime University and Wonkwang University, and events including the relay Wednesday Demonstration and signature campaigns in support of the 2000 Women's Tribunal spread also to universities in places such as Jeju Island, Masan, and Daegu.

3) Research and Investigative Activities and Symposia

Numerous studies and investigations were newly conducted for the 2000 Women's Tribunal. As a part of the activities of the Fact-finding Committee, the Testimony Team was established anew, and sociologists, psychologists, and women scholars conducted intensive research on the victims' social and psychological repercussions. As for the physical

8 The Students' Tribunal was first suggested on January 8, 1999 during the educational program for the Wednesday Demonstration Participation Group from Ewha Womans University and underwent discussions and approval by the National Council of Women University Student Representatives on January 13. The proposal was agreed on and taken up also by students from Kwanak Feminists (Seoul National University), Seoul Women's University, and Hongik University on February 3 so that preparations began in earnest in March. After the inauguration ceremony at Hongik University on September 29, the Students' Tribunal was held during April 28-29, 2000 at Ewha Womans University.

repercussions, young physicians conducted systematic investigations in addition to records from hospitals already in charge of examining and treating the survivors. In addition, the Historians' Team carefully investigated evidence materials, and the Jurists-Lawyers' Team held in-depth discussions on the issue of legal application. The fruits of such studies were published in 2001, a year after the 2000 Women's Tribunal.

From the time the Korean Organizing Committee began preparations for the 2000 Women's Tribunal, the sense that the tribunal must not end as a one-time event held in Tokyo was strong, and proposals were made for a pre-tribunal symposium, where the fruits of the preparation in South Korea would be presented. Consequently, a symposium was held during June 4-5, 1999, to which lawyer McDougall was invited, and a forum titled "The Movement for the Resolution of the Issue of Japanese Military Comfort Women and the 2000 International War Crimes Tribunal on Japan's Military Sexual Slavery" was held during the International Conference of Non-governmental Organizations (ICONGOs) on October 13 of the same year. In addition, the presentation of "Research Accomplishments for the 2000 Women's Tribunal" made at the symposium held on November 16, 2000 to commemorate the 10th anniversary of the foundation of the Korean Council can be viewed as an important achievement of preparatory activities for the tribunal.

In addition, many cultural events took place in South Korea. Local cultural festivals and lectures were held in numerous areas nationwide, and cyber campaigns were implemented as well. Fund-raising events for the 2000 Women's Tribunal were held at home (Yonsei University Alumni Association Building; October 25, 2000) and in countries including Japan, United States, and Germany as well.[9] Through such activities engaged in domestically for the tribunal, the movement expanded considerably.

---

9 To date, the use of all proceeds from fundraising launched by the Korean Council has been limited to support for the survivors.

4. The Main Points of Contention of the International Organizing Committee and the Tribunal

Basically, the 2000 Women's Tribunal was an international activity accomplished through the cooperation of organizations and individuals from numerous countries. After its inauguration was agreed upon at the Asian Solidarity Conference in April 1998, South Korean and Japanese activists exchanged opinions through mutual visits, and representatives of Japanese, Filipino, and Taiwanese NGOs visited Seoul on February 17, 1999 and constructed the framework of the international preparatory gathering for the first time. There were largely three organizations for the tribunal: the victim nations; the victimizer nation; and the International Advisory Committee. The International Organizing Committee was headed by three convenors (co-representatives): Professor Yun Chung-Ok from South Korea, representing the group of victim nations; Matsui Yayori, representing Japan; and Indai Lourdes Sajor from the Philippines, leading the International Advisory Committee. The International Organizing Committee held several meetings in places such as Seoul, Tokyo, Shanghai, Manila, and Taiwan and organized country prosecution teams, holding international prosecutors' meetings. Meanwhile, the International Advisory Committee, which consisted of experts from diverse regions worldwide including North and South Americas, Europe, and Africa, made use of international conferences such as those of the UN in places including New York City, Hague, and Washington, DC, holding meetings before or after them and discussing the many issues of the 2000 Women's Tribunal. The main points of contention that were debated at such meetings can be summed up as follows.

1) The Venue and Official Languages of the Tribunal

As for the venue of the 2000 Women's Tribunal, Seoul and Tokyo were discussed as the main candidates. Points including the fact that South Korea was the country with the largest number of victims and the area that required the expansion of the movement in the future more than any other did as well as the great need to highlight the coloniality of Japanese military sexual slavery were the grounds of the argument that the tribunal had to be held in Seoul. Against this, points including those that the 2000 Women's Tribunal was to supplement the insufficiency of the International Military Tribunal for the Far East held after World War II and that an occasion for giving a stimulus to the Japanese government was necessary were the grounds of the argument that Tokyo had to be the venue.

On the other hand, as for the official language of the 2000 Women's Tribunal, English was decided on in the early stage without much consideration, but some, centering on members of the Korean Organizing Committee, raised a strong objection. It was a persuasive objection that selecting English as the official language when the victimizer nation was Japan and the victim nations were all countries in Asia would reduce the significance of the tribunal, which was being held through the efforts of women across the region. In the end, English, Japanese, Korean, and Chinese were decided on as the official languages of the 2000 Women's Tribunal, with simultaneous interpretation provided.

2) The Nature of the Tribunal and the Issue of the Indictment of Emperor Hirohito

The most basic issue above all was the degree of formality (fairness and reliability) to be assumed. If somewhat strict formality was to be assumed based on existing laws, it would be possible to strengthen the authority of the 2000 Women's Tribunal, but the tribunal itself would remain in a reduced state without being able to overcome the limitations of international law at present. On the contrary, if a more open tribunal that could convey the message of conscience that one wished to were created, it would be possible to present a new direction for international law instead, but there would be a danger of undermining the authority of the 2000 Women's Tribunal as a tribunal. Begun with the awkward stance of coordinating these two positions and preserving the form of the tribunal as much as possible while keeping its openness intact so as not to reduce its significance, the preparation for the tribunal gradually veered toward formality. Unlike the Russell Tribunal on Vietnam, which had comprised the representative conscientious intellectuals of the world, it was decided that the judges and the chief prosecutors would consist entirely of legal experts. Gabrielle Anne Kirk McDonald, the representative of the judges, was an incumbent judge who had served as a chief judge of the International Criminal Tribunal for the Former Yugoslavia. In addition, Carmen María Argibay, an Argentine judge with expertise in criminal law and the president of the International Association of Women Judges (IAWJ), Christine Mary Chinkin, a renowned woman international law scholar and a professor at the University of London, and Willy Munyoki Mutunga, a Kenyan human rights lawyer and a professor at the University of Nairobi, participated in the 2000 Women's Tribunal as judges. At the preparatory meeting held one day before the tribunal, the judge representative McDonald repeatedly stressed the point that the 2000 Women's Tribunal was not simply a mock court but must be equivalent to a serious and actual trial. Although not a few worried to the end whether an emphasis on such jurist-centered composition and form might not lead the 2000 Women's Tribunal in an unintended direction, the tribunal confirmed, after strict material review and discussions by the judges, the guilt of the major war criminals including Emperor Hirohito and the crimes of the state of Japan.

Next, there were continuous discussions on issues such as whether the 2000 Women's Tribunal would address only state responsibility or include criminal trials regarding individual war criminals, what the scope would be if indictments were to be brought against individuals, and whether the specific amount of punishment would be pronounced or the proceedings would stop at judging guilt and innocence. In the end, it was decided that the tribunal would indict both the state and individuals and that individual judgments would verify guilt and innocence. In addition, it was also decided that indictments against the dead, which are not implemented in ordinary courts, would be brought in so as to reveal the nature of military sexual slavery.

The most sensitive issue was that of indicting Emperor Hirohito. Even among those who had actively participated in the preparation for the tribunal from the very first stage, some were hesitant to indict the emperor in consideration of the overall sentiments of the Japanese people. Nevertheless, the strong argument of the South Korean side that avoiding the emperor, who had been the highest-ranking individual responsible for this issue, would seriously reduce the significance of the tribunal finally won international agreement.

3) The Structure of the Tribunal

While it was agreed on early that, with judges and prosecutors at the center, there would be legal advisors, experts, and testifiers, opinions did not reach a consensus regarding several points. At the beginning, it was agreed on that there would be a jury, but the decision was cancelled out of concern about confusion. In addition, the chief prosecutor system, which did not surface in the early days, emerged. This stemmed from the fact that because written indictments were to be prepared separately by the numerous victim nations, it was necessary to synthesize them. It was agreed on that the Japanese government would be placed as the accused and its presence therefore was requested, but the latter did not actually appear at the tribunal. At the end of much ado, five judges were finally decided on in consideration of their regions and genders, but, to ensure fairness here, jurists from victim nations in Asia were excluded.[10] Prosecution teams were to be constructed on a national basis, and it was decided that each country prosecution team would have an hour and a half for indictment time, with the order of indictment by the victim nations decided by the International Organizing Committee and prosecution team meetings. While ten countries including North and South Koreas, China, Japan, and Philippines each constructed prosecution teams, what must be noted is that the two Koreas spent three hours to file a joint indictment. Chinkin, one of the judges of the 2000 Women's Tribunal and a feminist international law scholar, was moved and stated: "A goal common to North and South Koreas that would not have been thinkable on a government level has been achieved and expressed" (Chinkin, trans. Chang Bok-Hee, 2001: 295).

The issue that divided opinions to the very end was that of whether to have the defense counsel. South Korea and Japan disagreed on this from the first International Organizing Committee gathering in Seoul in February 1999. While the Japanese side proposed two lawyers to heighten the authority of the 2000 Women's Tribunal, the South Korean side thought that it was dangerous to present lawyers who would represent the

10 From among them, judge Prafullachandra Natwarlal Bhagwati (former Chief Justice of India and member of the ILO Committee of Experts) did not attend due to illness.

position of the Japanese government. Although this debate was resolved through South Korea's last-minute decision to make a concession and to respect Japan's opinions, this time, the Japanese side failed to recruit lawyers so that, in the end, the tribunal had none. With the Japanese government having refused to participate, the Japanese preparatory team had two Japanese veterans testify as victimizers and two *amici curiae* speak on behalf of Tokyo.

What else must be pointed out is that, without the full understanding of most of the people who had participated in the numerous meetings of the International Organizing Committee, it was decided that a Filipina jurist would be the court clerk (registry) and take charge of the proceedings of the 2000 Women's Tribunal. Against this point, Japanese and South Korean NGOs voiced criticism during the proceedings of the tribunal.

4) The Public Hearing

The Public Hearing was discussed from the early stage of planning the 2000 Women's Tribunal to raise to the surface the fact that this issue was a current one and to form solidarity with women's organizations worldwide. After heated discussions surrounding who was to take charge of it, in the end, it was decided that the Women's Caucus for Gender Justice, an international women's organization established in 1997 to prepare for the International Criminal Court, would be in charge of the clerical duties. Very active internationally, this organization succeeded in prompting 15 nations around the globe including Vietnam and Afghanistan to make presentations on the issue of war and the violation of women's human rights in diverse forms and, as intended by the International Organizing Committee, instilled the awareness that Japanese military sexual slavery was not at all an issue of the past but was one of the violation of women's human rights committed in various places across the world even today and that the 2000 Women's Tribunal was being held to break the vicious cycle of its impunity. However, as has already been pointed out, the fact that the historical particularity of Korea and the particularity of the Japanese armed forces, which cannot be explained solely with the concept of the issue of women during wartime, faded away further because of this public hearing is quite regrettable (Shim Young-Hee, 2001a).

5) The Final Judgment

Because a more detailed legal analysis of the vast amount of materials and testimonies submitted by the prosecution teams from ten countries required time, it was decided that the final judgment would be delivered apart from the preliminary judgment, which would be passed immediately following the completion of the 2000 Women's Tribunal, several months later. While the Legal Advisors[11] were conducting analysis, the International Organizing Committee continued discussions on the venue, nature, and financial sources of the final judgment. Opinions were divided into two sides: whereas some contented that the final judgment should be greatly enlarged in scale and turned into an event that would shock the entire world once again, others argued that it should serve as an occasion to add the significance of bringing the 2000 Women's Tribunal to a conclusion, with a focus on the major figures of the tribunal. As for the venue, New York City, where the attention of the international community and the press could easily be attracted, and the Hague, where the image of peace could be emphasized, were discussed, with the decision opting for the latter in the end. As for the scale, while the final judgment would not be comparable to the 2000 Women's Tribunal, it was decided to create a form that would assort, even if minimally, the framework of judges, chief prosecutors, country prosecution teams, and victims. Originally planned for March 2001, the final judgment was delivered in December of the same year. In a format identical to that of the tribunal a year before, indictments were filed during December 3-4 and the final verdict was declared on December 6. The final judgment differed little from the preliminary judgment passed at the tribunal a year before (Shim Young-Hee, 2001b).

For reference, one point that must be added is the discussions on the issue of where to store the materials submitted by country prosecution teams and reviewed at the final judgment as well as the original tribunal judgments. In the end, it was decided that the Korean Council from South Korea, where the number of victims was the largest, would safeguard

11 Rhonda Copelon, a professor at the City University of New York, was the representative.

the originals and Japanese and Taiwanese organizations would safeguard copies.

5. Cooperation among South Korea, North Korea, and Korean Residents in Japan

One of the most important fruits reaped during the process of preparing for the 2000 Women's Tribunal was cooperation among South Korea, North Korea, and Korean residents in Japan. In October 1998, representatives from the two Koreas and Japan held a trilateral gathering in Beijing and decided to participate together in the tribunal. However, North Korea did not participate in the International Preparatory Meeting held in Tokyo at the end of the year, and it was decided that contact with that country would be made through the Fact-finding Team on the Truth about Forced Korean Laborers in Japan 朝鮮人强制連行眞相調査團, an organization affiliated with the General Association of Korean Residents in Japan 在日本朝鮮人總聯合會 that had engaged in research on and a movement regarding the issue of forced taking since the 1970s. It was at the International Organizing Committee and prosecution team meetings held in Shanghai in March 2000 (March 30-April 1) that the encounter between the two Koreas was accomplished. The North and South Korean representatives agreed to highlight the two sides as a single country at the tribunal. In other words, the former proposed that the two be styled "North and South of Korea," and the latter cheerfully agreed. This time, the South Korean side proposed that the two jointly draw up the written indictment, which was realized at the International Organizing Committee and prosecution team meetings held in Manila at the end of July: they agreed to create a joint written indictment and a joint prosecution team. Subsequently, although the exchange of opinions between the North and South Korean representatives could not be implemented effectively because it could take place only through Japan, preparation for the joint written indictment was made in earnest at the meeting in Taiwan in September. First, the representatives from the two Koreas stressed colonial rule by Japan, discussing the naming of this era as the "forced occupation period," and agreed that while the written indictment would be jointly

After successfully holding the 2000 Women's Tribunal through a joint indictment, the two Koreas held discussions and continued exchange.

drawn up through mutual contact, as for presentations at the tribunal, South Korea would take charge of individual responsibilities and North Korea would take charge of state responsibilities, respectively. Discussions were held on the drawing up not only of the written indictment but also of the courtroom scenario. On the other hand, it was agreed that the two Koreas would cooperate with the team of Korean residents in Japan who had conducted research on Korean victims in the former colonial metropolis since the end of 1998, which led to the exchange of the fruits of research afterwards.

In a situation where the written indictment had yet to be completed due to difficulties in mutual contact, members of the North and South Korean organizing committees and prosecution teams met in a church in Tokyo on December 6, 2000, two days before the 2000 Women's Tribunal. Two days later, after much ado, the structure of the joint indictment was completed. The two days leading up to the tribunal were continuing moments of enormous tension indeed. After briefly discussing the written indictment, the prosecution teams from North and South Koreas reviewed the materials that the other party had prepared for presentation at the tribunal. Separating after first getting a certain degree of feel for each other, the two national teams met again at 9 PM on the same day. They were joined by the team of Korean residents in Japan as well. Upon once again mutually reviewing the contents of the materials to be presented at the tribunal, both sides concluded that it would be realistically impossible for them to execute the 3-hour-long prosecution jointly.[12] The atmosphere was extremely painful and hopeless. It was a moment at which the long-wished-for joint indictment seemed to vanish. The two teams decided to take a short break and to rethink the matter. In addition, they agreed to try to reach a consensus, making small mutual concessions and dividing up roles. Deciding on the contents and order of the indictment on a large blackboard, even down to the details, the two teams determined their respective portions. It was past midnight that the North and South Korean representatives parted, after promising to meet again on the morning of rehearsals. Both sides revised their respective presentation materials, not even begrudging the time to sleep. Meeting precisely at the promised time on the following morning, the two teams began rehearsals amid tension. As they checked each detail during the rehearsals, however, tension began to ease, and smiles gradually spread over their faces by the time they had to move to the Kudan Kaikan, the venue of the tribunal, for the group rehearsals. It was thus decided: the moderation of the overall procedure, by South Korea; the introduction, by North Korea; the forced taking of people, mainly by South Korea; crimes committed at comfort stations, mainly by North Korea; their repercussions, alternately by the two Koreas; state responsibilities, by North Korea; and individual indictments, by South Korea, thereby concluding the tribunal. After the rehearsals, the North and South Korean representatives successfully brought in a 3-hour-long joint indictment in the courtroom.

12 From the perspective of the South Korean representatives, their North Korean counterparts' simplicity in trying to explain everything about military sexual slavery through the Japanese empire's invasion and aggressiveness in exposing damages due to the institution lowered persuasiveness in the international arena. However, the latter was puzzled by this stance instead. The South Korean side proposed the idea of jointly presenting only the initial problematization and the final legal application, with the middle portions addressing forced taking as well as the victims' lives at comfort stations and repercussions after return to Korea to be divided between the two parties over disparate time slots.

6. The Significance and Limitations of the 2000 Women's Tribunal

Created for each country, the prosecution teams exposed the illegality of Japanese military sexual slavery on the basis of the official documents of the Japanese armed forces and government and documentary materials such as the testimonies and diaries of the victims and experiencers of Japanese military sexual slavery as well as the direct courtroom testimonies of the survivors. After the completion of the 3-day-long indictments by the prosecution teams, the Public Hearing was held on the following day. The judges had this interval of one day for study and passed the preliminary judgment the next day. In accordance with his responsibility to give orders from the point that he either had known of such crimes or had not even though it had behooved him to do so, Emperor Hirohito was pronounced guilty (Chinkin, trans. Chang Bok-Hee, 2001: 299). In addition, nine high-ranking officials and generals including Tojo Hideki were found guilty, and the Japanese government was recommended to make compensations to the victims. The 2000 Women's Tribunal drew to a close with the delivery of the final judgment, which presented more detailed legal analysis, in the Hague in December 2001.

What was the legal significance of this tribunal, and with what limitations did it end? What are remaining tasks? First, the legal significance of the 2000 Women's Tribunal is as follows. Chinkin claimed that a people's tribunal "starts with the understanding of law not as belonging to the government but as being a tool of civil society... While it cannot impose punishments or issue orders for compensations, it can make recommendations based on the value of the legal judgment and moral compelling power." Adding to such significance of earlier people's courts such as the Russell Tribunal on Victnam, the 2000 Women's Tribunal is noteworthy because, as has been mentioned already, it was prepared by organizations from the victim nations through women's strength. In addition, it holds very important legal significance for points including: individual criminal responsibility was addressed in addition to state responsibility; historical documents were extensively collected; legal judgments reflected the perspective of gender; and legal judgments

The 2000 Women's Tribunal (Tokyo, Dec. 2000)

were passed based on laws from the 1940s, when these criminal acts had been committed (Chinkin, trans. Chang Bok-Hee, 2001: 300-304). Japanese military sexual slavery came to be perceived in the international community as a bad precedent of both impunity from and the recurrence of the wartime violation of women's human rights so that the judgments of the 2000 Women's Tribunal, as important judicial precedents in international courts, influenced the trial proceedings of the International Criminal Tribunal for the Former Yugoslavia (Yokota Yuichi, 2001).

More specifically, while discussions and recommendations regarding Japanese military sexual slavery in terms of international law hitherto had been limited to the responsibility of the Japanese government, the 2000 Women's Tribunal enumerated the important liable parties and found them guilty, thus producing the first judgments to make clear the loci of responsibility. In particular, the declaration of the guilt of Emperor Hirohito was expected to give the Japanese society a new stimulus.

However, this tribunal also revealed its limitations in indicting individuals' legal responsibilities only as crimes against humanity after all. The judges of the 2000 Women's Tribunal decided not to indict the acts of forcibly mobilizing sex slaves as war crimes, thus, on one hand, removing issues that could arise if the forced mobilization of sex slaves from North and South Koreas and Taiwan were to be indicted as war crime. On the other hand, by avoiding the point raised by the two Koreas, which saw colonial rule as a military occupation, the judges abandoned attempts to overcome the void in international law regarding colonial rule.[13]

Second, it must be pointed out that because it was held by NGOs instead of intergovernmental organs, the 2000 Women's Tribunal considerably developed the strength of civil society in the international community. The international networks of NGOs, which both made the tribunal possible and developed further in the preparatory process, surely will be discussed as an index expressing the growth of international civil society. However, how can these international networks be maintained? How are fissures in the solidarity revealed in the preparatory stage to be addressed after the tribunal? The tribunal ended without clear answers to such questions.

Third, it must be stressed that one of the most important achievements made at this tribunal has been ethnic cohesion among North and South Koreans and Korean residents in Japan. The experience that it is possible to forge close cooperation when the parties have the same goal and trust one another is a noteworthy point not only for the movement in the future but also for the entire South Korean society. The expansion of the domestic movement including the participation of new groups such as men and youths, too, is a considerable fruit of activities for the tribunal.

Finally, together with the failure to address the issue of colonial rule in the judgments mentioned above, the limitation that the tribunal, like previous international activities, was unable to progress from defining

13 Because the two Koreas and Taiwan had not been Japan's opponents in war but had been its colonies during the commitment of the crime of military sexual slavery by the latter, their indictment of Japan's acts as war crime does leave room for controversy. On the other hand, North and South Koreas prosecuted Japan for the crime of military sexual slavery as a war crime based on the judgment that the latter's rule over the Korean Peninsula had been illegal occupation by force, not colonial rule. They intended to resolve the abovementioned controversy with this argument and to overcome the current loophole that there existed no international law whatsoever concerning the crime of colonial rule. Regarding this point, see Chang Wan-Ick, 2001.

Japanese military sexual slavery as an issue of women during wartime must be pointed out. The precise determination of the nature of this issue, which encompasses that of colonial rule, has been left once again as a task to be resolved.

Part III

Japan's Responses

Chapter 9

The Responses of the Japanese Government and Conservative Public

1. Changes in the Position of the Japanese Government in the Process of Raising the Issue of Japanese Military Sexual Slavery

The party ultimately responsible for resolving the issue of Japanese military sexual slavery is the Japanese government. This is because it both was the key agent of the crime and is the executor of punishments on individual criminals. Tokyo is also the implementer of the legal compensation demanded by the victims, agent of genuine apology based on an admission of legal responsibility, and preparer of guidelines on peace education for the Japanese people. It also holds the key to yet undisclosed documentary materials. It is to this Japanese government that the victims and international human rights organs alike have raised their voices in unison, demanding appropriate measures for the resolution of the issue. However, Tokyo has not budged to this date. In addition, right-wing public opinion in the nation has surrounded the inert Japanese government, serving as an increasingly strong shield. This right-wing public opinion has been created by Japanese intellectuals including university professors, in a language at times calm and at times extremely blatant. Though it raised its head when Japanese military sexual slavery became prominent in the 1990s, it is firmly based on Japanese nationalism, which has been formed and taken root deep within Japanese society since the early years of the country's modernization.

When Japanese military sexual slavery first began to gain public attention, Tokyo vehemently denied its and the military's involvement. Although it admitted the fact, albeit gradually, whenever decisive evidence surfaced, it has returned to its original denial of legal responsibility and has been unmovable since its establishment of the Asian Women's Fund in 1995.

1) Denial of the Intervention of the Japanese Government and Military

Upon the South Korean President Roh Tae-woo's visit to Japan in May 1990, the Japanese emperor very ambiguously said that he "cannot help but feel the deepest regret 痛惜の念" regarding the past relationship between the two nations. As for Japanese military sexual slavery, however, the Japanese government stated that it was "something that civilians [had] committed and [that] an investigation on the government level [was] impossible."[1] On October 17, 1990, South Korean women's organizations that would serve as the basis for the establishment of the Korean Council demanded to the Japanese government: an acknowledgment of the forced taking of women as military sex slaves; official apologies; investigations; the erection of monuments to commemorate the victims; compensations to the survivors; and history education for the Japanese public.

To this, on April 24, 1991, counselor Ono Masaiki from the Japanese embassy in Seoul replied, "According to the results of the Japanese government's investigation, there was no forced mobilization of comfort women, and rights and obligations regarding compensations in terms of international law were completed through the South Korean-Japanese Claims Agreement of 1965" (Compilation Committee of the *20-Year History of the Korean Council for the Women Drafted for Military Sexual Slavery by Japan*, ed., 2014: 54). Tokyo repeated similar remarks later on: "the [Japanese] government did not at all intervene in Korean comfort women" (Ministry of Labor, April 1991) and, "as for the question of compensation, it is difficult for the [Japanese] government to take

1 The response of Shimizu Tsutao, the chief of the Employment Security Bureau in the Ministry of Labor, to an inquiry from National Diet member Moto'oka Shoji at a session of the Committee on Budget in the House of Councilors on June 6, 1990.

measures" (Chief Cabinet Secretary Kato Koichi, December 6, 1991).

2) Admission of the Intervention of the Japanese Government and Military

As Kim Hak-Soon emerged and materials on Japanese military sexual slavery were discovered in 1991 and the South Korean movement regarding the issue became active, the Japanese government's attitude began to change. This was especially noticeable immediately before Japanese premier Miyazawa Ki'ichi's visit to South Korea. At a session of the Committee on Budget in the Japanese House of Councilors held on December 12, 1991, Japan's Chief Cabinet Secretary Kato Koichi ordered six relevant government ministries to investigate the facts regarding military sexual slavery, thus elevating the issue to a diplomatic agenda between the two countries. Upon arrival in South Korea in 1992, Prime Minister Miyazawa Ki'ichi stated, "I cannot help feeling acutely distressed over this [i.e., Japanese military sexual slavery], and I express my sincerest apology... our faults [i.e., Japan's acts of aggression]... will never again be repeated" (January 17, 1992). Soon afterwards, he admitted the Japanese government's intervention in military sexual slavery in the Japanese National Diet for the first time, apologizing, "We cannot deny that, in the past, the Japanese military intervened in this issue" (January 29, 1992).

However, as is clear from Japanese Minister for Foreign Affairs Watanabe Michio's statement that military sexual slavery was "not a legal issue but a humanitarian and political one"[2] and the statement of the Northeast Asia Division in the Asian and Oceanian Affairs Bureau, Ministry of Foreign Affairs that "this issue [had] been completely resolved in terms of international law" (*Weekly Post*, March 7, 1992), Tokyo clearly expressed the stance of not admitting its own criminality and legal responsibility as well.

On July 6, 1992, the Japanese government announced the results of an investigation of six ministries and admitted that it had intervened in

2 His response to an inquiry from National Diet member Doi Takako at a session of the Committee on Foreign Affairs in the Japanese House of Representatives on February 26, 1992.

military sexual slavery but denied the existence of materials on the forced taking of the victims.[3]

3) Partial Admission of Forced Taking

After announcing the results of its preliminary investigation based solely on its own documents, the Japanese government announced on August 4, 1993 the outcome of its second investigation, which supplemented the grounds with materials at the National Archives and Records Administration and publications by the Korean Council and referenced victims' testimonies. The gist of the second report was: (1) military comfort stations were installed at the time at the requested of the Japanese military authorities, and the former Japanese armed forces directly or indirectly intervened in both the installation and management of these facilities and the transport of military sex slaves; (2) the recruitment of these women was performed mainly by [private] operators at the request of the military, and, even in such cases, many of the victims were recruited against their wishes through fraudulent promises or coercion; (3) moreover, the fact that figures including officials directly took part in some cases as well has been clearly elucidated; (4) led in a coercive situation, the victims' lives at comfort stations were wretched; and, (5) as for the areas of origin of sex slaves transported to the battlegrounds, excepting Japan, the Korean Peninsula took up a large share, and the mobilization, transport, and management of victims from the colony likewise were based on fraudulent promises or coercion, implemented against the women's wishes overall.[4] Here, while admitting forced taking, Tokyo stated that this had been committed mostly by private operators and that "there [had been] even cases where administrative/military personnel [had] directly [taken] part in the recruitments," thus concluding that the government itself had not been an agent of forced taking. Based on these results, Chief Cabinet Secretary Kono Yohei apologized, stating that such acts had

3 The results of this investigation led to suspicion of the concealment of materials due to the fact that no materials whatsoever had been discovered at the Japanese National Police Agency and the Ministry of Labor, and the investigation was criticized by South Korean organizations as a careless one altogether.

4 Based on the summary in Nam Sang Gu, 2014.

seriously damaged the honor and dignity of the numerous women who had become military comfort women against their wishes.[5] In addition, Prime Minister Hosokawa Morihiro admitted that, as far as Japan was concerned, World War II had been a war of aggression (August 10, 1993). In all such statements, progress in the Japanese government's awareness of its own responsibility can be observed.

4) The Announcement of a Solution Evading Legal Responsibility

With fierce attacks from right-wing Japanese public opinion and countless abusive remarks by high-ranking officials during the period from the latter half of 1993 to the first half of 1994, the series of processes above finally led to the reversion of Tokyo's stance to the starting point. In other words, even disregarding pressure from international organs such as the UN and the International Commission of Jurists, the Japanese government consolidated the stance of categorically denying its legal responsibility and seeking to resolve the issue through the establishment of the Asian Women's Fund, no longer issuing apologies.

In February 1994, the Korean Council and victims attempted to submit a written accusation demanding the punishment of those responsible for military sexual slavery to the Japanese Public Prosecutors Office, only to be rejected. In May of the same year, Japanese Minister of Justice Nagano Shigeto defined the Pacific War as a "war of liberation" and stated that sex slaves could not be seen negatively because they had been members of "licensed brothels 公娼" at the time. In the same vein, Japanese Minister of the Environment Sakurai Shin absurdly remarked in August that Japan had "liberated" Asia through the war. While other prominent Japanese figures such as Minister of International Trade and Industry Hashimoto Ryutaro and Chief Cabinet Secretary Igarashi

5 Although the South Korean government assessed this investigation somewhat positively, organizations such as the Korean Council pointed out its many shortcomings including: its refusal to admit that the Japanese government had been the subject of forced taking; and its failure to mention that the process through which Korean women had been mobilized had been forced taking and thus different from that through which Japanese women had been mobilized.

Kozo were saying that Japan had no need to apologize, the Japanese government and the opposition parties announced their final solution to military sexual slavery notwithstanding the International Commission of Jurists' repeated recommendations for compensation (September 2 and November 22, 1994). In August (August 31, 1994), Japanese premier Murayama Tomi'ichi expressed "[his] profound remorse for these acts of aggression, colonial rule, and the like[, which] caused such unbearable suffering and sorrow for so many people," and stated that, "[o]n the issue of wartime 'comfort women', which seriously stained the honor and dignity of many women, [he] would like to take this opportunity once again to express [his] profound and sincere remorse and apologies," but shifted the logic in the direction of carefully avoiding the characterization of the war as a war of aggression (Yoshida Yutaka, 1996: 54). Instead, he announced the inauguration of the so-called Peace, Friendship, and Exchange Initiative 平和友好交流計劃. The gist of this plan was that the Japanese government would reject direct compensation to victims of military sexual slavery but, instead, conclude the issue by implementing investigations, research, and exchange amounting to approximately 100 billion yen with the victim nations of Asia over the next ten years. At this point, he hinted at Tokyo's intention of raising a civilian fund by saying that "[he] would like to find out, together with [the] Japanese people, an appropriate way which enables a wide participation of people."

This position on the part of Tokyo was reconfirmed in December (December 7, 1994) by the Liberal Democratic Party of Japan. The Subcommittee to Address the Wartime Comfort Women Issue 從軍慰安婦問題等小委員會 within this party, which was one of the ruling parties then, thus announced its final solution to the issue of military sexual slavery: "With regard to the question of restitution or the right to demand material compensation as a result of issues arising from the past war, including the so-called wartime comfort women issue, the Japanese Government has always acted in good faith and in view of international law and the practice of diplomacy in accordance with the stipulations of the San Francisco Peace Treaty, bilateral peace treaties and other relevant accords. But… from a moral standpoint,… from a wide spectrum of the population," a fund would be raised and disbursed to former sex slaves as consolation money, and the government would cooperate. In January

1995, in response to demands from NGOs in both South Korea and Japan for Tokyo's consent in order to bring the issue to the Permanent Court of Arbitration, the Ministry of Foreign Affairs flatly denied the possibility of legal compensation, officially replying that it could not consent because the issue had already been resolved through treaties including the San Francisco Treaty. Then, in the end, the Japanese government officially inaugurated the Asian Women's Fund in July 1995. In other words, Tokyo was attempting to resolve the commotion through consolation money on a civilian level instead of compensation on the government level, without admitting its own criminality and legal responsibility. Unlike his three predecessors, Prime Minister Hashimoto Ryutaro, who succeeded Murayama Tomi'ichi, did not allude to the issue of historical consciousness (Yoshida Yutaka, 1996: 54).

The following characteristics can be extracted from the process through which the Japanese government responded, thus arriving at a conclusion that ultimately denied state responsibility after undergoing several stages. First, though Tokyo seemed to acknowledge the facts gradually whenever incontrovertible evidence surfaced, the essence of its position—i.e., denial of its own criminality and legal responsibility—has never for once budged. Second, through the accompaniment of acknowledgments of the facts or official apologies with abusive statements on the other hand at all times, Japan has revealed its true intentions in a bizarre manner.

2. The Japanese Government's Position as Expressed in UN Documents

In the international community, the Japanese government has consistently stated that it only feels moral responsibility for the victims but has no legal obligation to them whatsoever.

1) Detailed Explanation of the Issue of Japanese Military Sexual Slavery

In a report submitted to the UN Commission on Human Rights in 1996, the Japanese government stated that it had conducted an investigation of documentary materials and testimonies, both at home and abroad, on the issue of military sexual slavery since 1991 and announced the results in 1993. The gist of the reports is as follows (Permanent Mission of Japan to the United Nations, 1996):

① Comfort stations were established and managed at the request of the Japanese military authorities during the period.

② The Japanese armed forces directly and indirectly intervened in the establishment and management of comfort stations and the transportation of sex slaves.

③ The recruitment of sex slaves was performed mainly by private operators at the request of the military. In many cases, however, these women were mobilized against their wishes through specious promises or coercion, some directly mobilized by officials or soldiers as well.

In other words, as is clear here, in its report submitted to the UN in 1996, Tokyo admitted the direct intervention of the Japanese government and armed forces alike in the establishment and operation of military comfort stations and the recruitment and transport of sex slaves and the use of coercion in the mobilization of the victims.

2) The Issue of the Violation of International Law

Citing various passages from substantive laws, the Japanese government nevertheless has strongly denied its legal responsibility. Based on a report submitted by Tokyo to the UN Commission on Human Rights in 1996, Special Rapporteur McDougall of the UN Sub-Commission on Human Rights has thus summarized the position of the Japanese government (McDougall, 1998). Discussions on international law have already made it clear that Tokyo's arguments are untrue. In this section, the Japanese government's arguments will be summarized, and discussions on them in terms of international law will be presented in the footnotes:

① The latest developments or progress in international criminal law cannot be applied retroactively. Because the Geneva Convention of 1949 [i.e., Convention Relative to the Protection of Civilian Persons in Time of War; henceforth "4th Geneva Convention"] and other international laws did not yet exist during World War II, Japan does not need to assume responsibility for violations of international humanitarian laws. For example, the crime of slavery cannot accurately explain the comfort station system,[6] and the prohibition on slavery was not established as a customary norm in terms of international law that was applicable during the war.[7]

② In addition, the act of rape during armed conflict likewise was prohibited by neither regulations attached to the 4th Hague Convention of 1907 [i.e., Convention Respecting the Laws and Customs of War on Land; henceforth "4th Hague Convention"] nor international customary norms that were effective and applicable during World War II.[8]

---

6 Regardless of the situation concerning remuneration for money tickets, the fact that Japanese military sex slaves, who were deprived of freedom and recruited against their will, lost autonomy to a considerable degree and were treated like objects agrees with the definition of slavery as the "status or condition of a person over whom any or all of the powers attaching to the right of ownership are exercised," as described in the Geneva Convention on Slavery of 1926 (McDougall, 1998).

7 Slavery and slave trade were prohibited far before the creation of Japanese military comfort stations, and, in particular, the prohibition of slavery was clearly elevated to the status of an enforced law. The 4th Hague Convention (1907) includes an important clause protecting civilians and soldiers from slavery and forced labor. Following World War II, the Charter of the International Military Tribunal at Nuremberg stipulated that "[w]ar crimes… shall include… ill-treatment or deportation to slave labor or for any other purpose of civilian population of or in occupied territory" (McDougall, 1998).

8 Documents on regulations regarding war (including the Instructions for the Government of Armies of the United States in the Field, or the Lieber Code, of 1863) clearly prohibit rape and the cruel treatment of women during war. The Hague Convention of 1907 stipulates that "[f]amily honor and rights… must be respected," and Article 27 of the 4th Geneva Convention, succeeding to the spirit of the Hague Convention and created following World War II, stipulates, "[w]omen shall be especially protected against any attack on their honour, in particular against rape, enforced prostitution, or any form of indecent assault." As these stipulations show, the prohibition of rape and forced prostitution was already a well-established principle in international customary law at the time of the creation of Japanese military comfort stations. In addition, Japanese military sex slaves did not fall within the category of forced labor permitted by international law (ILO Forced Labour Convention) and were

③ Because laws of war apply only to acts of the Japanese armed forces committed against the peoples of belligerent powers, they do not apply to Korea and Formosa, which were Japanese colonies then.[9]

It is noteworthy that, since 1995, the ILO Committee of Experts has defined the issue of Japanese military sexual slavery as a violation of the Forced Labour Convention (ILO Convention No. 29) and that the Japanese government has not refuted this, only saying that it has satisfied its legal responsibility according to diverse international conventions, thus implicitly admitting its own violation of the Forced Labour Convention.

3) The Legal Responsibility for the Issue of Reparation

Regardless of the issue of the violation of international law above, the Japanese government has argued that individual sex slaves have no right to claim legal compensation for the following reasons:

① The Japanese government has faithfully fulfilled its legal obligation according to the relevant international conventions. Peace treaties and international conventions signed between or among Japan and other Asian countries following World War II have completely resolved the issue of individuals' right to claim legal compensation.[10]

---

clearly raped and held within war zones. Consequently, the crimes against military sex slaves are easily determined as rape and forced prostitution prohibited by laws on war (McDougall, 1998).

9 The prohibition of slavery is not applied solely to war crimes. In fact, as a crime against international customary law, which can be applied to wartime and peacetime, and against humanity, the virtual enslavement of Japanese military sex slaves was clearly prohibited as a cruel violation of international customary law at the time that it was committed regardless of the territorial status of Korea (McDougall, 1998).

10 This argument has been determined to be wrong by numerous international law experts based on the following grounds (International Commission of Jurists, 1994; Coomaraswamy, 1996; and McDougall, 1998):
First, when the San Francisco Treaty, South Korean-Japanese Claims Agreement (1965), and other postwar treaties were signed, the Japanese government's intervention in the establishment of military comfort stations was concealed. In terms of this decisive fact, any and all of Japan's attempts to avoid its responsibility based on these

② No civil or criminal case whatsoever can be raised regarding the issue of military comfort stations during World War II due to a temporal restriction stemming from the application of regulations on the statute of limitations.[11]

③ Because laws on international conventions regulate relationships between nations instead of those between nations and individuals, individual comfort women cannot make any claim to the Japanese government.[12]

---

treaties must be prohibited in the spirit of equity. In addition, judging from the fact that the Japanese government has concealed its intervention in this crime for a long time and actually continues to deny its legal responsibility for it, it is inappropriate for the Japanese government to argue that its settlement agreements or other postwar treaties were intended to settle all rights of claim for compensation for damages to military sex slaves.

Second, the word "claim" does not include the right of claim based on illegal acts. Nor do the Agreed Minutes and the Additional Protocols of the South Korean-Japanese Claims Agreement define this term. It is self-evident that the South Korean-Japanese Claims Agreement is an economic treaty aimed at resolving the right of claim regarding property between the two nations and therefore did not address human rights issues. Likewise, the overview of the claims made by the South Korean delegates clearly is unrelated to acts of violation of individual rights stemming from war crimes, crimes against humanity, or violations of slave conventions, Protocol to Prevent, Suppress and Punish Trafficking in Persons, Especially Women and Children (also known as "Palermo Protocol"), or norms of international customary law. In addition, while Japan clearly apologized and agreed to compensate for individual damages in its treaties with Western nations, it did not do so in the South Korean-Japanese Claims Agreement. In other words, the South Korean-Japanese Claims Agreement only annulled the right of claim regarding the economy and property between the two countries and not individuals' right of claim, and Japan still must assume the responsibility for its acts.

Third, regardless of international treaties, Article 3 of the Hague Convention stipulates that each nation is obliged to prevent, investigate, and punish grave human rights violations and violations of basic freedom. Consequently, the Japanese government is independently responsible for its failure to prevent evils committed against military sex slaves and to punish the relevant criminals.

11 There is no statute of limitations on crimes against humanity and war crimes. In addition, when new and grave facts have been discovered recently, statute of limitations cannot be applied. As has been discussed above, the crime against Japanese military sex slaves is a crime against humanity and a war crime, and it was only in 1993 that the Japanese government finally admitted the role of the Japanese armed forces in the establishment and management of military comfort stations (McDougall, trans. Cho Si-Hyun, 1998a: 94).

12 Many international laws (4th Hague Convention of 1907, Treaty of Versailles of 1919, UN Charter, Universal Declaration of Human Rights (UDHR), Charter of the International Military Tribunal for the Far East, etc.) acknowledge that not only states but also individuals are the subjects of the rights and obligations granted and imposed

Apart from its report submitted to the UN Commission on Human Rights, the Japanese government has submitted a report to the ILO as well and presents the same arguments here (Permanent Mission of Japan to the United Nations, 1996; International Labour Organization, 1997a; and McDougall, 1998). Such a position on the part of Tokyo has been repeated without changing at all. Although the UN Committee on Economic, Social, and Cultural Rights strongly recommended the Japanese government promptly to make appropriate compensation to former military sex slaves in its second regular report adopted in August 2001, Tokyo submitted a divergent opinion on this issue to the committee in August 2002. It stated that the Japanese government could not follow the decision of the UN Committee on Economic, Social, and Cultural Rights because it had faithfully fulfilled its legal responsibility in accordance with numerous international conventions (UN Doc. E/C. 12/2002/12).

4) The Japanese Government's Moral Solution

The Japanese government claims that it has apologized for its past conduct on many occasions on the level of the prime minister for the sake of morality even though it has no legal responsibility, actively supported the Asian Women's Fund, and been in charge of the victims' medical and welfare concerns (International Labour Organization, 1999). In a report submitted to the UN, it stated that Prime Minister Miyazawa Ki'ichi, Chief Cabinet Secretary Kono Yohei, and Prime Minister Murayama Tomi'ichi had extended deeply felt apologies for military sexual slavery, which had seriously damaged the honor and dignity of the victims, in 1992, 1993, and 1994, respectively, and that Prime Minister Hashimoto Ryutaro had sent a letter of apology during the Asian Women's Fund's presentation of consolation money to the survivors in 1996.[13]

---

by international law. In particular, during the latter half of the 1920s, international law acknowledged that when one nation inflicted damage on the people of another nation, it was liable for damages to the violated individuals (Coomaraswamy, 1996; and McDougall, trans. Cho Si-Hyun, 1998a: 96).

13 Prime Minister Hashimoto Ryutaro's letter states that it records "[his] personal feelings," thus indicating that it is an apology only from the premier himself and not from the Japanese state, and admits the fact neither of forced mobilization nor of Japan's violation of international law (Coomaraswamy, 1996).

Tokyo avers that, on the other hand, it actively supported the establishment of the Asian Women's Fund in order to promote mutual understanding with Asian victim nations and to present former military sex slaves with consolation money raised from Japanese citizens (Permanent Mission of Japan to the United Nations, 1996). It has repeatedly stressed its moral solution such as this also to the ILO (International Labour Organization, 1997a) and argued that numerous victims in Asia and the Netherlands have received consolation money from the Asian Women's Fund (International Labour Organization, 1999; and United Nations Committee on Economic, Social and Cultural Rights, 2002).[14] However, this is far from the actual situation. Because the Asian Women's Fund was rejected in South Korea and Taiwan alike on the government level, it is well-known that the personnel from the fund approached individual survivors and had the latter receive the money. Even in the Philippines, the country with the largest number of recipients of the Asian Women's Fund, the payment of money from the fund was implemented amid extreme confusion in civil society between those who accepted the fund and those who rejected it, with certain survivors refusing to receive money from the fund to the end. In the cases of the Netherlands and Indonesia, which both lacked a system where the government validated the victims, money from the fund was received in the form of medical aid in support projects implemented by the Stichting Project Implementation Committee in the Netherlands (also known as "Project Implementation Committee in the Netherlands"; PICN) in the former and financial support for senior citizen welfare projects implemented by the government in the latter, respectively. As for other victim nations, the payment of money from the Asian Women's Fund was not even attempted.

The Japanese government has pointed out the overall inappro-

14 Based on the following grounds, discussions in terms of international law have repeatedly pointed out that the Asian Women's Fund cannot be legal compensation (Coomaraswamy, 1996; International Labour Organization, 1997a and 1999a; and McDougall, trans. Cho Si-Hyun, 1998a: 102). First, this fund does not reflect the Japanese government's intention to admit its legal responsibility. Second, it does not satisfy the victims' expectations. International organs therefore have recommended that the Japanese government "promptly" take official and legal measures satisfying the survivors' expectations.

priateness of the reports of the UN Commission on Human Rights, UN Sub-Commission on Human Rights, and ILO Committee of Experts on military sexual slavery. First, Tokyo argues that because the institution was implemented before the creation of the UN, it is wrong for the latter to address it. Second, it complains that the UN and the ILO have one-sidedly taken into consideration the claims only of NGOs and minority labor unions, not heeding the Japanese government's opinion in a balanced manner (International Labour Organization, 1997 and 2002).

3. The Perspective of Right-wing Public Opinion in Japan

Seeming to step forward, one at a time, while repeating abusive statements and apologies, the Japanese government ultimately returned to the starting point, as if to mock five years of efforts by survivors and NGOs in South Korea. What, then, made this possible? It was due to none other than the awareness of the majority of the Japanese people. The history of Japanese nationalism (statism) goes back to prewar days and became extreme during World War II. Although weakened with Japan's defeat in the war, this nationalism has secretly continued to recover since the war, to be considerably boosted in the early 1990s, when the issue of the country's war responsibility was raised. Strongly opposed to prime ministers' admission of Japan's war as a war of aggression and the revision of textbooks in the mid-1990s, this movement, the supporters of which have been called by various names including the "right wing," "conservatives," and "neo-nationalists," has not only grown in number but also bridged the gap between the right wing, which was seen as a rather extreme group immediately after the war, and the comparatively moderate conservative faction, which existed separately, thereby expanding as a clear and widespread nationalistic movement (Chung Chinsung, 2001c: 129-202).

While it is impossible to encompass all discussions by this extensive group of figures, who have been dubbed "neo-nationalists" (Hata Nagami, 1996: 7), these people's discussions, when narrowed down to those on the issue of Japanese military sexual slavery based mainly on their submissions to conservative magazines such as *Seiron*, *Bungei Shunju*, *Jiyu*, and *Shokun!* can be summarized into the following several arguments. These magazine article contributors are mostly university professors, with journalists and writers included as well.

1) Criticism of the Raising of the Issue of Japanese Military Sexual Slavery

Let us first examine these right-wing intellectuals' discussion on Japanese military sexual slavery itself. They argue that military sexual slavery was not only a necessary evil but also an outstanding institution. Established to mitigate the sexual desire, which is an "inevitable" instinct, of men who were away from home, this institution was a necessary evil according to these right-wing intellectuals because it soothed the soldiers' mental and physical health, prevented the abuse of local women, and forestalled misfortunes such as the births of illegitimate children. Without asking why sex slaves were women from Japan's colonies and occupied territories instead of Japanese ones, these right-wing intellectuals claim that sexual slavery was an excellent institution because it stressed the management of the women's health (Kamisaka Fuyuko, 1992: 216-219; Arai Sawako, 1992a: 20 and 1992b: 14-17; Sato Kazuhide, 1993: 198; Uesugi Chitoshi, 1994: 63; and Konno Torisuke, 1998: 24).

One of the points argued emphatically by these right-wing intellectuals is that there was no forced taking. This claim, in turn, is linked to a general mistrust of testimonies. Arguing that historical facts must be viewed based on objective materials, these figures categorically brand all testimonies on forced taking as lies. According to them, the testimony of Yoshida Seiji that he forcibly took women as military sex slaves from Jeju Island in the name of the "Volunteer Corps" is fiction (Uesugi Chitoshi, 1992a: 63; Hata Ikuhiko, 1992; Itakura Yoshiaki, 1992; and Kuroda Katsuhiro, 1993),[15] and Senda Kakou's pioneering work on

15 They also conducted direct investigations on Jeju Island, which were endeavors to prompt the locals to recall Yoshida Seiji's forced taking. According to the investigations, the people of Jeju Island stated to these Japanese investigators that there had never been such incidents. In fact, the investigations conducted by the Korean Research Group likewise yielded the same results, and members of the research group were

Japanese military sexual slavery likewise is groundless (Uesugi Chitoshi, 1992c). According to these right-wing intellectuals, South Koreans nevertheless claim vehemently that there was forced taking because they would lose face as an ethnic group if sex slaves volunteered, in the absence of forced taking, and the Japanese government has admitted forced taking out of political consideration in order to arrive at a diplomatic settlement (Kuroda Katsuhiro, 1993: 123; and Uesugi Chitoshi, 1994: 63). Likewise, these right-wing intellectuals make the following claims without any evidence. They aver that Japanese military sex slaves, who had the oldest profession in the world, were recruited in Japan's war zones through free contracts and provided with stupendous wages so that volunteers rushed from impoverished colonial Korea and contracts were concluded mostly by these women's own parents. Because recruitments were consigned mostly to private operators, these right-wing intellectuals argue, it is unreasonable to argue for forced taking by the military. Moreover, they continue, it is preposterous to call comfort women "sex slaves" because their working conditions were favorable and many of these women even married Japanese soldiers (Takeda Tatsuo, 2001: 98-99).

In addition, these right-wing intellectuals strongly insist that the issue of military sexual slavery has been completely resolved through the Japanese government's numerous postwar treaties with other nations. In other words, because apologies and compensations have already been made, statements that still shackle Japan to the past must end (Ito Takashi, et al., 2001: 130). Moreover, conservative Japanese figures claim, South Korea initiated its current economic development with the money provided by Japan in compensation for its past actions at the time of the conclusion of the South Korean-Japanese Claims Agreement (1965; Nishioka Tsutomu, 1992: 314). Consequently, they argue, there is no need for Tokyo even to respond to cases in Japanese courts including the Tokyo District Court and international arenas of judgment such as the UN, International Court of Justice, and Permanent Court of Arbitration.

---

strongly impressed because the locals were highly guarded and seemed to be concealing something. Such a tendency among victims to maintain silence on their experiences has struck scholars conducting research on the Jeju Island April 3 Struggle 濟州四·三抗爭 as well. This attitude among survivors deserves persistent, in-depth, and repeated investigations.

These conservative figures claim that it was therefore a betrayal for former sex slaves to reject the Asian Women's Fund, which was proposed and financed by the Japanese government and fundraised by the Japanese people, and that the verdict of the 2000 Women's Tribunal was all wrong because it was based on inadequate evidence (Nishioka Tsutomu, 1992: 310-312; Tanaka Akira and Sato Katsumi, 1992: 135-137; Takeda Tatsuo, 2001: 94-103; Hata Ikuhiko, 2001a: 98-102, etc.). They have also expressed strong disapproval of the compensation to sex slaves sentenced by the Yamaguchi District Court in 1996 (Konno Torisuke, 1998: 21-22).

These conservative opinion leaders refer to the act of raising the issue of Japanese military sexual slavery as the "comfort women fiasco," which has simply caused noise without any ground, and urge the prompt investigation of this "comfort women fiasco" (Takeda Tatsuo, 2001).

2) Position on the War and Colonial Rule

Conservative public opinion in Japan basically denies that there was anything wrong with the nation's colonial rule and war. In other words, according to these people, to define the Asia-Pacific War as a war of aggression and to reflect on and apologize for it is tantamount to the destruction of "forefathers'" efforts and honor and a grave insult to the 2,300,000 war dead (*Sankei Shimbun*, August 11, 1993; *Hankyoreh*, August 12, 1993; and *Chosun Ilbo*, February 4, 1995).

3) The Revisionist View of History

These conservative figures' view of history is importantly based on an interpretation of history dubbed the so-called revisionist view of history. In other words, according to them, all historical facts must be understood within their contemporary contexts. Although the definition of "justice" changes in each era, they claim, a lack of such historical consciousness has brought about the unnecessary theory of Japan's war responsibility. They aver that Japan's colonial rule over Korea was a natural historical trend at the time because Japan had no choice but to occupy Korea for self-protection, not as an invasion, in an age characterized by the law of the jungle (Kamisaka Fuyuko, 1992: 217; and Kuroda Katsuhiro, 1993: 123) and that the issue of Japanese military sexual slavery likewise must not be judged based on today's perspective on human rights (Takeda Tatsuo, 2001: 99). They go on to claim that whenever the evaluation of the past is debated, the consciousness that arises in the context of current politics must be understood without fail. In other words, past issues are raised from ulterior motives so that historical issues are used as political tools (Nakanishi Terumasa, 2000: 30-43). Viewing Japanese progressives' stance on peace museums constructed around the nation, military sexual slavery, and Japanese textbooks as all being based on a misguided, masochistic, and apologetic views of Japanese history, conservative public opinion in Japan has urged the termination of this apologetic view of history (Sakamoto Takao, et al., 2000: 48; and Shoji Jun'ichiro, 2001: 158-167).

Established in 1996 by right-wing Japanese intellectuals, the Japanese Society for History Textbook Reform published ultra-rightist history textbooks through a publisher named Fusosha Publishing, Inc. and implemented a campaign to delete statements regarding Japanese military sexual slavery from the nation's textbooks. Descriptions of the institution, which began to be featured in Japanese middle school history textbooks in 1992 and were included in nearly all textbooks by 1996, all disappeared by 2005, with the exception of some high school textbooks.

4) A Defensive Stance

These conservative figures seem to be mindful of activities regarding Japanese military sexual slavery in international arenas including the UN. Expressing conservative opinions on numerous occasions, Uesugi Chitoshi argues that it is racially discriminatory of the UN to address the issue while sidestepping the wrongdoings of many Western nations. He also stresses that the Japanese people must prevent a second International Military Tribunal for the Far East by submitting their own opinions to the UN Special Rapporteur on "military comfort women," who has been "brainwashed" by activist groups such as the Korean Council (Uesugi Chitoshi, 1994: 60-62). In particular, such conservative public opinion argues that it is inappropriate for the UN to address military sexual slavery, which occurred even before even before the organization's establishment in 1945 (Kase Hideaki, 1997: 18). It criticizes that a viewpoint based on human rights leads one to understand things from a binarism of good versus evil and hence causes arrested thought, the UN is dominated by America, and the diplomacy of human rights advocated by the United States is cultural imperialism (Kawakami Takashi, 1999: 24-26; and Takubo Tadae, 2000: 30).

Most of the Japanese right wing's responses to the issue of military sexual slavery consist of the complaint that only their nation is blamed. According to them, the former Soviet Union committed even greater war crimes, Germany also established comfort stations in areas under its occupation, the United States set up comfort stations in Japan following World War II, and South Korea likewise established comfort stations for its own soldiers during the Vietnam War—why, then, should Japan be the only country to be blamed, they ask (Takeda Tatsuo, 2001: 98-100). These figures retort that recent discussions on the issue of postwar responsibility, where solely Japan is criticized, are tantamount to "Japan's second defeat at the hands of multiple nations."[16] Crying out to Japanese audiences that they themselves are the victims, the right wing tries to convince the Japanese people that Japanese national interest is being damaged. It is domestic interference for South Korea and China to demand Japan to face its supposed war responsibility and to mention Japanese textbooks and Japanese leaders' worship at Yasukuni Shrine, these right-wing figures claim, and Japanese politicians who not only fail to respond appropriately to such interference but also admit that Japan was the victimizer are pro-South Korean and pro-Chinese politicians unmindful of national interest, lamentably leaving a cause of contention for a century to come (Takeda Tatsuo, 2001: 99; Ito Takashi, et al., 2001, 135-136; and Nakanishi Terumasa, 2001: 25-36).

The right wing has voiced its strong opposition whenever Tokyo has admitted historical facts and reflected on and apologized for them. When the latter admitted partial forced taking in its second report in 1993, members of the Japanese right wing criticized this as a major blunder on the government's part. Likewise, they strongly criticized Prime Minister

16 According to these figures, if Japan's first defeat was due to American control, this second defeat was due to concerted attack by diverse Asian and Western nations (Eto Jun, 1998: 102).

Hosokawa Morihiro's admission that the Asia-Pacific War had been a war of aggression. The right wing criticized Prime Minister Miyazawa Ki'ichi's apology in Seoul as an ungrounded and irresponsible political compromise and even stated that it was no longer possible to rely on the government, which, in their eyes, lacked the correct view of Japanese nationhood, to resolve the situation (Uesugi Chitoshi, 1994: 60-61; Kawamoto Hiroshi, 1997: 144; and Takeda Tatsuo, 2001: 99). Not only the conservative media but also many ordinary citizens have submitted letters and articles to newspapers and magazines and appeared on television and radio shows, urging Tokyo to make its position clear without heeding Asian countries' sensibilities.

In addition to criticizing the Japanese government, right-wing figures have criticized left-wing intellectuals as well for supposedly overlooking or inciting the issue of Japanese military sexual slavery.[17] Arguing that their compatriots have led many activities including not only the raising of the issue and relevant lawsuits but also news coverage, they claim that the issue has evolved to such an extent that there is a "perverse situation in which the Japanese themselves now criticize what the former Japanese armed forces did in the past, thus accusing the current Japanese government" (Nishioka Tsutomu, 1992: 300-302). These conservatives define groups that discuss the nation's postwar responsibility as "anti-Japanese Japanese," "masochistic Japanese," and "anti-Japanese spies" and attack supporters of such groups as embodying "faceless collectivism" and "totalitarianism" (Nishio Kanji, 2001b: 140).

As has been discussed above, according to the right wing of Japan, victim nations have raised the issue of military sexual slavery without objective evidence and based on vindictiveness, thus making cool-headed and rational rebuttal and discussion impossible (Ito Takashi, et al., 2001: 100). These conservatives are especially antipathetic to South Korea and China when the latter raise the issue. In their view, South Korea brings up the issue of sexual slavery "as an anti-Japanese campaign that, repeated like a geyser, has a political motive." This is "a way of bypassing economic recession and also fodder for North-South Korean reunification

---

17 One piece of writing specifically points out Yoshimi Yoshiaki as the theoretical pillar of the party arguing for national compensation (Hata Ikuhiko, 1997).

by establishing [Japan's war responsibility] as a theme common to both Koreas now, after 50 years [of national division]" (Kamisaka Fuyuko, 1992: 216-219). The Japanese right wing is at once disdainful and hopeful because, in its view, South Korea actually and always depends mentally on Japan despite its purported anti-Japanese sentiments (Tanaka Akira and Sato Katsumi, 1992: 140). It finally presents the threat that if South Korea thus continues to raise issues, anti-South Korean sentiments will spread among Japanese citizens (Kamisaka Fuyuko, 1992: 219; and Nishioka Tsutomu, 1992: 300). Japanese conservatives also scornfully add that South Korea, the epicenter of the issue of sexual slavery, cannot even distinguish between "comfort women 慰安婦" and the "Volunteer Corps 挺身隊"[18] (Takeda Tatsuo, 2001: 99).

As for China, which began to take part in raising the issue of military sexual slavery slightly later than did South Korea, the Japanese right wing points out that this country has changed the tone of its attitude toward Japan since the war according to its own social changes (Ishihara Hoki, 1998) and claims that China's current reckless nationalism must be guarded against (Kase Hideaki, 1997; and "Special Feature," 2002: 192). Largely based on a consciousness of the recent rise of China, such criticism of the nation is closely linked to the defensiveness discussed above.

4. Responses to the 2007 Passage of the US House of Representatives' "Comfort Women Resolution"

After Congressman Lipinski (Illinois) of the Democratic Party first proposed a resolution on Japanese military sexual slavery in the House of Representatives in 1997 and continued to make efforts, Congressman Honda (California) presented a bill to the Subcommittee on Asia, the

18 As has been discussed in Chapter 1, because the mobilization of women as military sex slaves implemented by Japan in colonial Korea was generally executed in the names of the "supply of unmarried women to the government 處女供出," "Patriotic Corps 報國隊," "Volunteer Corps," and others, the public was not aware of the term "comfort women 慰安婦" at the time, and even the term "Volunteer Corps" was known only to some educated people. Consequently, such criticism from the Japanese stems from their ignorance of the wartime social situation.

Pacific and the Global Environment under the House of Representatives Committee on Foreign Affairs in January 2007. This bill was officially adopted by the committee on June 26 of the same year and, at last, passed unanimously in the lower house on July 30 (H. Res. 121; see Chapter 5).

1) The Responses of the Japanese Government and National Diet Members

In this process, the Japanese government exhibited a stance that was a wholesale repetition of its gradual change upon each discovery of new evidence regarding military sexual slavery in the early 1990s. As the resolution was successively passed in the House of Representatives Subcommittee on Asia, the Pacific, and the Global Environment and the House of Representatives Committee on Foreign Affairs and as the number of Congressmen supporting it increased, Tokyo's attitude actually regressed. Of course, there was no change in its basic position. When Congressman Honda submitted the bill in January 2007, Prime Minister Abe Shinzo argued that, regarding Japanese military sexual slavery, there had been no "coercion in the narrow sense" in terms of direct recruitment by the Japanese armed forces. In fact, he had maintained the stance that there had been no "coercion in the narrow sense" from early on (*Choson Sinbo*, March 20, 2007).[19]

At a session of the House of Councilors Committee on Budget in 2007, Prime Minister Abe Shinzo stated, "We will not apologize just because there is a resolution. The resolution was not based on objective facts" (*Yomiuri Shimbun*, March 5, 2007) but subsequently receded somewhat, saying that he supported Chief Cabinet Secretary Kono Yohei's position at the time. While visiting the US Congress and meeting with 11 leaders of both houses on April 26, the first day of his visit to the country, Abe Shinzo stated that he had a "sense of apology" and felt "sympathy" for former Japanese military sex slaves for having been placed in difficult situations (Yonhap News Agency, Washington, DC, April 27, 2007). This

19 His remarks at a subcommittee of the Committee on Budget, House of Representatives on May 27, 1997; his written contribution to the Group of National Diet Members Who Consider the Future of Japan and History Education in December 1997; his remarks at the House of Representatives Committee on Budget on December 6, 2006, etc.

was after 101 members of the House of Representatives had already and openly expressed their support for the resolution.

In addition, there were statements such as that of Chief Cabinet Secretary Shiozaki Yasuhisa that the "alliance between the two nations [i.e., Japan and the United States] [was] solid and [would] be so in the future. The mass media had better not cause a commotion" (*Sankei Shimbun*, June 27, 2007), and Tokyo is said to have dispatched figures such as the Special Adviser to the Prime Minister for National Security to the United States to engage in lobbying.

The Group of National Diet Members Who Consider the Future of Japan and History Education 日本の前途と歷史教育を考える議員の會 under the Liberal Democratic Party of Japan began to be active in earnest at the end of January, and Nakayama Yasuhide, the chair of the same party's Subcommittee to Address the Wartime Comfort Women Issue, made it clear at the group's meeting held on February 10 that the "Liberal Democratic Party of Japan plan[ned] to dispatch a group of National Diet members to the United States to stop the adoption [of the resolution]" (*Asahi Shimbun*, February 10, 2007). The group convened again on March 8 and submitted to the prime minister a proposal, together with the signatures of 130 members, demanding from the Japanese government diplomatic efforts to broaden the correct understanding of the issue of Japanese military sexual slavery including another fact-finding investigation, disclosure of the outcome, and arrest of the adoption of this resolution regarding Japan currently submitted to the US House of Representatives (*Sankei Shimbun*, March 8, 2007). National Diet members from the Democratic Party of Japan likewise initiated the Group for Verifying the Truth behind the Issue of Comfort Women and the Nanking Incident 慰安婦問題と南京事件の眞實を檢證する會 and established a plan to prompt the Japanese government to state a new stance that would include the awareness that there had been no fact of forced taking using government power (*Sankei Shimbun*, March 9, 2007).

On June 14, 60 individuals including 29 members of the Liberal Democratic Party of Japan, 13 members of the Democratic Party of Japan, two independent National Diet members, eight university professors, four political commentators, and three journalists jointly published in the *Washington Post* a one-page advertisement titled "The Facts" denying the

THE FACTS

FACT 1

FACT 2

FACT 3

FACT 4

FACT 5

Assentors

The Japanese right wing's *Washington Post* advertisement to stop the passage of the US House of Representatives resolution (Jun. 14, 2007)

forced mobilization of military sex slaves. When the resolution was passed on July 30, these National Diet members strongly objected, arguing, "The resolution is one-sided and not grounded on facts and thus can never be allowed."

Japanese and Japanese-American politicians in the United States assisted as well. According to a report by the Kyodo News, at a meeting with Japanese journalists held on February 13, Kato Ryozo, the Japanese ambassador to the United States, thus criticized: "concerning a groundless matter, the comfort women resolution will have a negative effect on Japanese-American relations" (*Hankook Ilbo*, February 16, 2007). In July, he repeatedly appealed to several members of the US House of Representatives including its speaker for opposition to the sex slave resolution, warning that, if adopted in the plenary session of the lower house, the resolution "[would] almost certainly have lasting and harmful effects on the deep friendship, close trust and wide-ranging cooperation our two nations now enjoy[ed]" (*Washington Post*, July 18, 2007). In March, Senator Daniel Ken Inouye sent letters to the chairs of the

House of Representatives Committee on Foreign Affairs and the House of Representatives Subcommittee on Asia, the Pacific, and the Global Environment as well as Congressman Honda, requesting them to refrain from processing the resolution. In April, Prime Minister Abe Shinzo met with the speaker of the House of Representatives during his visit to the United States and expressed his view that the "the effect on Japanese-American relations and the timing of the adoption of the resolution [were] not favorable" (*Dong-A Ilbo*, April 27, 2007). In addition, many right-wing intellectuals in Japan criticized the resolution, engaging in activities such as sending letters of protest to the American ambassador to Japan.

2) The Responses of the Japanese Press

Newspapers such as the *Asahi Shimbun*, *Mainichi Shimbun*, and *Tokyo Shimbun* expressed strong criticism of negative reactions to the resolution. In its editorial, the *Asahi Shimbun* criticized the argument that there had been no direct and forced taking by officials as turning one's attention away from the essence of the issue of Japanese military sexual slavery, thus expressing its stance: "How were comfort women gathered, taken to battlefields, and managed? The reality differed by area and time. However, overall, there is no mistake that women from [Japan's] colonies and occupied territories were taken against their will and serviced Japanese officers and soldiers… Rather than insisting on narrow facts and only presenting excuses, it befits a nation with dignity to understand [Japanese military sexual slavery] as an issue of ethnicity or the human rights of women and to face one's history squarely… Japan has appealed to the international community regarding kidnappings [of Japanese citizens] by North Korea as violations of human rights. If we turn a blind eye to violations of human rights in our own past, we will lose persuasiveness" (*Asahi Shimbun*, March 10, 2007). Regarding Prime Minister Abe Shinzo's statement that he was "shamefaced before comfort women" during his summit meeting with President George Walker Bush on April 26, the *Asahi Shimbun* and the *Tokyo Shimbun* thus criticized: "Is the recipient of the apology the United States?" (Yonhap News Agency, Tokyo, May 2, 2007). When the resolution was passed, the *Asahi Shimbun* stated, "The resolution is not without doubts… However, it must be accepted earnestly." In editorials respectively titled "The Prime Minister must be aware of the seriousness [of the passage of the resolution]" and "Do not turn the comfort women resolution into a hindrance to Japanese-American relations," the *Mainichi Shimbun* and the *Tokyo Shimbun* argued that Japan's responsibility for the violation of the honor and dignity of many women must be accepted (J-CAST News, June 28, 2007).

However, most of the Japanese press, especially the *Sankei Shimbun*, *Yomiuri Shimbun*, and *Seiron* under the *Sankei Shimbun* (Hata Ikuhiko, Nishio Kanji, et al.) presented the following argument. Regarding Congressman Honda, the Japanese press reported that he was related to an anti-Japanese organization in the United States or heavily relied on donations from Chinese-Americans (*Sankei Shimbun*, March 23, 2007; and *Yomiuri Shimbun*, March 16 and August 1, 2007). As for the resolution itself, they argued that it and the awareness of certain American Congressmen clearly went against facts, that the contents were slipshod and full of errors (*Sankei Shimbun*, February 21 and June 27, 2007), and that the resolution had no legal binding power (*Sankei Shimbun*, February 21 and August 1, 2007).

Focusing on "coercion," these newspapers argued that the heart of the issue of military comfort women was whether there had been forced taking by officials. Even according to the Japanese government's investigation, they claimed, there was no document proving this. Even among historians, they argued, the established view was that there had been no such thing (*Yomiuri Shimbun*, March 5 and August 1, 2007). Concern was expressed also: "If misunderstandings and exaggerations of historical facts are left alone as they are, they will remain sources of misfortune to posterity" (*Sankei Shimbun*, March 10, 2007). Consequently, demands to Tokyo were made, too: "As the resolution is full of distortions, the [Japanese] government must accurately explain the facts and stop its adoption… the government must not repeat the diplomatic error surrounding the resolution of the US House of Representatives (*Yomiuri Shimbun*, March 7, 2007).

Some also protested why Japan had to be the sole target of attacks. Their arguments ran thus: "While, in the over 2,000 years of human history, governments and armed forces have committed countless evil acts, criticizing only some specific cases from among them is linked to the danger of lessening the gravity of other evil acts" (*Sankei Shimbun*, February 25, 2007) and "Comfort facilities were not unique to the former Japanese military" (*Yomiuri Shimbun*, August 1, 2007).

As in the 1990s, the claim that Japanese military sexual slavery was a past incident continued to be raised. Those of this stance stated, "Those who actually implemented the plan are no longer alive. No one must be made to be responsible for one's ancestors' wrongful actions" (*Sankei Shimbun*, February 25, 2007). The argument that the Japanese government had apologized countless times already was added also.

Some predicted that discussions on this resolution in the US Congress would negatively affect American-Japanese relations. *The Sankei Shimbun* even more aggressively pointed out that "it [was] beyond foolish that one should teach a method of apology for a historical error to a friendly foreign government" (ibid.). The Japanese press also criticized South Korean citizens' activities as being based on nationalism and reported, "they ceaselessly play the comfort women card" and "South Korea day after day criticizes Japan and relishes it with nationalistic pleasure" (*Sankei Shimbun*, March 14 and July 30, 2007).

That such a stance on the part of the Japanese government and conservative organizations has continued without change for some 20 years since the issue of Japanese military sexual slavery was first raised and that, in the end, the United States and the international community have nevertheless and repeatedly confirmed this historical fact perhaps shows the paradox and progress of history at the same time.

5. From the Review of the Kono Statement to the December 28, 2015 Announcement of the Agreement on Japanese Military Sexual Slavery by the South Korean and Japanese Foreign Ministers

Tokyo's will actively to resolve Japanese military sexual slavery continued to weaken following the return of the Liberal Democratic Party of Japan to power in 1996, only to regress considerably during 2006-2007 under the Abe Shinzo administration. His reelection in 2012 further aggravated such a tendency. Tokyo's stance that legal responsibility had been performed and forced taking was not a historical fact became increasingly adamant so that, following Abe Shinzo's return to power, various incidents occurred in succession. Encompassing the Japanese government's review of the Statement by Chief Cabinet Secretary Kono Yohei on the Result of the Study on the Issue of "Comfort Women" 慰安婦關係調査結果發表に關する河野內閣官房長官談話 (河野談話; henceforth "Kono Statement") and the *Asahi Shimbun's* apologies for its past articles related to Yoshida Seiji, they finally culminated in the agreement regarding Japanese military sexual slavery between the South Korean and Japanese foreign ministers on December 28, 2015.

1) The Review of the Kono Statement

On June 21, 2014, the Abe Shinzo administration disclosed "Details of Exchanges between Japan and the Republic of Korea (ROK) Regarding the Comfort Women Issue: From the Drafting of the Kono Statement to the Asian Women's Fund 慰安婦問題を巡る日韓間のやりとりの經緯~河野談話作成からアジア女性基金まで~." As has been discussed above, this statement is the one made by Chief Cabinet Secretary Kono Yohei upon Tokyo's 1993 announcement of its second investigation on military sexual slavery. The gist of this statement was that the victims had been mobilized against their wishes and that though mobilization had been committed mostly by civilians, Japanese officials had taken part in some cases as well, and it expressed apologies and reflection on the level of the Japanese government for the deep injury to the honor and dignity of numerous women under the intervention of the former Japanese armed forces. At a discussion held on September 15, 2012 during the presidential election of the Liberal Democratic Party of Japan, Prime Minister Abe Shinzo claimed, "Due to the Kono Statement, Japan has been saddled with the dishonor that the Japanese armed forces supposedly kidnapped women and forcibly turned them into comfort women. It is therefore necessary once more to consolidate the revision of the Kono Statement [made by the first Abe Shinzo cabinet (2006-2007)]." Empowered by the creation of public opinion by organizations and media such as the Japan Restoration Party and the *Sankei Shimbun*, the Abe Shinzo administration established a review panel of five members and implemented the review.

The review process, which involved only one historian—Hata Ikuhiko, a representative right-wing scholar—focused on the prior coordination between the South Korean and Japanese governments in the process through which the Kono Statement had been drawn up. However, the results of this review, which did not review the historical truth of Japanese military sexual slavery and violated the convention of deferring the disclosure of diplomatic documents for 30 years, sank without much impact both in Japan and abroad.[20]

The entire Japanese society's climate of seeking to annul the issue of Japanese military sexual slavery grew stronger. In relation to testimonies by Yoshida Seiji that he, as the Labor Conscription Manager in the Shimonoseki branch of the Patriotic Labor Society in Yamaguchi Prefecture in Japan during the Pacific War, had forcibly taken many Korean women from Jeju Island in order to turn them into military sex slaves, the *Asahi Shimbun* published a total of 16 articles during 1982-1997. Following Hata Ikuhiko's problematization of Yoshida Seiji's testimonies in 1992, the newspaper company judged that the testimonies were partly problematic and therefore did not deal with them after 1992. Nevertheless, struck with a sense of crisis by the Abe Shinzo administration's review of the Kono Statement and the conservatization of the entire Japanese society, the *Asahi Shimbun* published a series of articles under the heading of "Thinking about the comfort women issue 慰安婦問題を考える" during August 5-6, 2014 and retracted its earlier articles on Yoshida Seiji's testimonies. On October 9, 2014, at the request of the representative of the newspaper company, a third-party committee was created in order to investigate the process and results of the *Asahi Shimbun's* coverage of Japanese military sexual slavery, problems, and devisement of measures for correction. In relation to the results of the investigation by the third-party committee, there was a presentation by Professor Hayashi Kaori from the University of Tokyo on her research that the newspaper's coverage of military sexual slavery had had little effect on Japan's international relations including Japanese-South Korean relations (Hayashi Kaori, 2015).

In October 2014, the Japanese government's Ambassador for

20 For details, see the Northeast Asian History Foundation, ed., 2014.

Human Rights and Humanitarian Affairs Sato Kuni personally visited Coomaraswamy, who had written a report on Japanese military sexual slavery in 1996 for the UN Commission on Human Rights, and demanded her to revise her report, which quoted Yoshida Seiji's report.[21] In fact, Coomaraswamy's report encompassed both Yoshida Seiji's testimonies and Hata Ikuhiko's rebuttal, pointing them out as materials for future research (Totsuka Etsuro, 2015: 8).

2) The December 28, 2015 Agreement by the South Korean and Japanese Foreign Ministers

Amid the crisis where South Korean-Japanese relations cooled down in diverse fields including the economy and national defense and the already elderly former military comfort women were passing away in increasing numbers, the governments of the two nations suddenly came to an agreement on Japanese military sexual slavery on December 28, 2015. As has been mentioned earlier, according to the joint press release regarding the South Korean and Japanese foreign ministers' talk published by the press, the Japanese side stated: (1) Prime Minister Abe Shinzo was to make apologies and to express remorse; (2) a foundation for South Korean victims was to be created; and (3) the agreement was to be the final and irreversible resolution of the issue. The South Korean side stated: (1) the agreement was to be the final and irreversible resolution; (2) there was concern about the prospects of the Statue of Peace; and (3) both countries were to refrain from mutual criticism.[22]

Even after this bilateral agreement stipulating that the two nations would refrain from mutual criticism in the international arena, Tokyo has continued to issue statements such as denials of the forced taking of women as Japanese military sex slaves. For example, in response to recommendations from the UN Committee on the Elimination of Discrimination against Women (UN Doc. CEDAW/C/JPN/CO/7-8, paras. 28-29), the Japanese government replied on February 16, 2016 that the forced taking of the victims had not occurred.

---

21 Sankei News, October 16, 2014. Requoted from Totsuka Etsuro, 2015: 27-28.

22 *Dong-A Ilbo*, Internet edition, December 28, 2015.

Chapter 10

The Movements of Japanese NGOs

1. Raising the Issue of Japanese Military Sexual Slavery in Japan

After South Korean women's movements raised Japanese military sexual slavery at the end of the 1980s, the Japanese movements for the resolution of the issue, keeping in step with the social movements that were spreading successively in South Korea, rapidly expanded as civic movements that included not only women but also men. Although thus incited by the movement in South Korea, they were formed as successors to the peace movement, which had formed an important current in social movements in postwar Japan and permeated diverse other social movements. In addition, these movements were based on the "new" women's movements, which had begun to bud in the 1970s and became prominent in the 1990s, and on Korean residents' movements, which had come into being amid changes in postwar Japanese society, and encompassed Christian, labor, and even conservative local movements as well. Firmly standing in Japanese society, which is dominated by a government that continues to maintain a threatening pose and public opinion that bears animosity against the issue of Japanese military sexual slavery, these movements were examples of Japanese conscience. However, they broke up regarding the implementation of the Asian Women's Fund, which the Japanese government had pursued since the latter half of 1994 and officially announced in June 1995, and this rupture failed to heal even in the process of preparing for the 2000 Women's Tribunal, which was held in Tokyo in December 2000. With the 2007 passage of the US House of Representatives resolution on Japanese military sexual slavery (see Chapter 5) as the occasion, efforts were made to create a new coalition group encompassing all figures who hitherto had participated in activism and research regarding the issue but do not seem to have been very successful.

Why, then, have Japanese NGOs participated in these movements, whose object of criticism is the Japanese government itself? Which organizations have been engaged in the movements and with what orientations? Why, in the end, did many of them collaborate with Tokyo's implementation of the Asian Women's Fund? Why have they failed to be united, and what are their differences from South Korean activist groups in their perspectives? These constitute the problematics raised in this chapter.

For this chapter, I have made use of the following three research methods. The first is literature research, which consists of collecting and analyzing not only existing studies but also publications by Japanese activist groups including pamphlets, newsletters, and sourcebooks. Second, the results of a survey of Japanese activist groups that I conducted in January 1997 have been used. Although I sent questionnaires to over 50 organizations verified to be participating in these movements, only 20 of them sent back replies. However, the majority of the organizations that completed and returned the survey, which consisted mostly of open-ended questions, described in detail their activities and standpoints. Finally, an important basis of this chapter are interviews with and personal participation in and observation of the activities of the working-level staff members of the many organizations that I have encountered during the past 25 years while being engaged with the issue of Japanese military sexual slavery.

2. The Awareness of the Issue and the Formation of the Movements: 1988-1991

When the Korea Church Women United 韓國教會女性聯合會 and Professor Yun Chung-Ok of South Korea first conducted field investigations in

Japan in order to unearth Japanese military sexual slavery in 1988, the Japan Anti-Prostitution Association 賣買春問題ととりくむ會, which had been engaged in a movement against Japanese men's sex tourism abroad, seems to have begun to realize the implications of the issue while providing assistance (Takahashi Kikue, 1992: 36). However, Japanese organizations had yet to start full-fledged activities to resolve the issue.

Those in Japan who officially raised Japanese military sexual slavery for the first time were members of the National Diet. This is an interesting fact demonstrating the relationship between social movements and politics in Japan.[1] In early 1990, Takemura Yasuko, a National Diet member of the Social Democratic Party of Japan, posed questions regarding the issue at a session of the National Diet. On June 6, 1990, Moto'oka Shoji, a National Diet member of the same party, likewise requested the Japanese government to investigate Japanese military sexual slavery at a session of the House of Councilors Committee on Budget. The questions, however, were snubbed with the answer that these women had been taken to become military sex slaves by civilians (Chung Chinsung, 1995: 179). South Korean organizations continued to engage in activism directed at the Japanese government by conducting investigations in Japan, presenting open letters of inquiry to Tokyo, and strongly raising the issue to Japanese premier Kaifu Toshiki during his visit to South Korea in 1991. Amid such a situation, National Diet member Moto'oka Shoji once more raised the issue at a session of the National Diet in April 1991. Again, Tokyo clearly stated that it had not intervened in Japanese military sexual slavery at the time and that the South Korean-Japanese Claims Agreement of 1965 had resolved all relevant problems. Although not publicized much, the issue nevertheless continued to be raised on the levels of the National Diet and local governments.

Starting in 1990, Japanese activist groups began to engage in activities such as inviting South Korean activists and victims to give lectures and demanding the Japanese government to take appropriate measures. Subsequently, instead of thus being addressed as an incidental issue by existing organizations, Japanese military sexual slavery came to

1 The fact that social movements in Japan are closely linked to politics is elucidated in Chung Chinsung, 2000.

stand on its own, with the establishment by female Korean residents of new, organizations solely for the purpose of resolving it. In May 1991, the Group for Considering the Issue of Korean Military Comfort Women 朝鮮人從軍慰安婦問題を考える會 was founded in Osaka, and, in November of the same year, the Military Comfort Women Issue Network Uri Yosong 從軍慰安婦問題ウリヨソンネットワ-ク was founded. These groups focused on the issue through activities including publications and lectures.

3. The Development of Full-fledged Movements for the Resolution of the Issue of Japanese Military Sexual Slavery: End of 1991-1993

1) The Impetus for the Movements

With the establishment of the Korean Council in South Korea in November 1990 and the gradual publicization of the issue of Japanese military sexual slavery in Japan, full-fledged movements began. Serving as occasions for the development of movements in earnest in Japan were the first testimony by a victim in August 1991, the creation of a hotline in September of the same year, both in South Korea, and the discovery of relevant military documents in the United States in November 1991 and in Japan in January 1992, respectively, which greatly aroused public opinion.

2) The Participation of Existing Organizations and the Formation of New Organizations

Beginning with existing organizations such as the Japan Woman's [*sic*] Council 日本婦人會議 (present-day IJoseikaigi I女性會議), YWCA, and Asian Women's Association アジアの女たちの會, the movements spread to broader NGOs such as the National Christian Council in Japan 日本キリスト教協議會, diverse organizations for postwar compensations, churches, labor unions, and teachers' groups. Also numerous were newly established organizations: those founded with a focus on special, historic locations such as the Executive Committee to Preserve the Matsushiro Korean "Comfort Women"

Station 松代·朝鮮人「慰安婦」の家を殘そう實行委員會 (founded in June 1991; subsequently renamed the Matsushiro Memorial Museum of Untold History Management Committee「もうひとつの歴史館·松代」運營委員會); the Association to Clarify the Post-war Responsibility of Japan (Hakkiri-kai) 日本の戰後責任をハッキリさせる會 (ハッキリ會; founded in December 1991), which was deeply involved in Japanese military sexual slavery even though it addressed postwar compensations in general; and organizations newly launched on special occasions amid activities by local organizations such as the Fukuyama Group for Considering the Issue of Japanese Military "Comfort Women" 日本軍「慰安婦」問題を考える會·福山 (founded in December 1992). Serving as an important impetus for such formation of new organizations were activities in South Korea, South Korean activists' and victims' visits to and lectures in Japan, and relevant films and performances. Also created were the Balloon Flower Society ききょうの會 and organizations focused on assisting former Japanese military sex slaves in the Philippines.

In addition, many existing Japanese organizations, though not focusing on Japanese military sexual slavery as an important agenda for activism, nevertheless became interested and held one-time events or participated in support amid their main activities. They were the Japan Asia Africa Latin America Solidarity Committee 日本アジア·アフリカ·ラテンアメリカ連帶委員會, sectors of labor unions, and local organizations.

3) The Formation of a Coalition Organization and the Establishment of a Hotline

Noteworthy among such activities and trends was the formation of the Action Network for the Resolution of the Japanese Military "Comfort Women" Issue 從軍「慰安婦」問題行動ネットワ-ク, a coalition organization, in January 1992 by diverse activist organizations (16 organizations) that had hitherto engaged in sporadic movements for the 1st Asian Solidarity Conference, which was held in Seoul in August 1992. Although a coalition of many different organizations like the Korean Council of South Korea, this was less a council engaged in a united movement than an organization created to enable diverse groups to exchange information and to communicate smoothly with their foreign (mainly South Korean) counterparts while being independently engaged in their respective movements.[2] However, this umbrella organization gradually weakened in the subsequent development of the movements due to the participating organizations' differences of opinions.

Another notable event was the creation of a hotline, as in South Korea, in order to receive reports by victims and victimizers. With the four organizations of the Group for Considering the Issue of Korean Military Comfort Women, Association to Clarify the Post-war Responsibility of Japan, Association of Democratic Korean Women in Japan 在日韓國民主女性會, and Military Comfort Women Issue Network Uri Yosong as the sponsors, in January 1992, Military Comfort Women #110 從軍慰安婦110番 (hotline) was established. With the cooperation of the National Christian Council in Japan, Japan Christian Women's Organization (also known as "Japan Women's Christian Temperance Union" and "Japan Woman's [*sic*] Christian Temperance Union"; JWCTU; Kyofukai) 日本キリスト教婦人矯風會, YWCA of Tokyo, Japan Woman's Council, Group of Men Who Oppose Prostitution in Asia アジアの賣買春に反對する男たちの會, members of the Executive Committee to Preserve the Matsushiro Korean "Comfort Women" Station, college student volunteers, and others, telephone reports by victims and experiencers of Japanese military comfort stations were received. As for the callers, they consisted more of former soldiers than victims and provided testimonies of the situations surrounding Japanese military sexual slavery. These reports were subsequently published as a book titled *Military Comfort Women #110: The Voice of History from across the Telephone* 從軍慰安婦110番—電話の向こうから歴史の聲が (Editorial Board of *Military Comfort Women #110*, ed., 1992).

2 Such Japanese coalitions in the form of a liaison group were generally created on the occasion of international conferences. Examples are the International Women's Year Liaison Group (IWYLG) 國際婦人年連絡會, which was formed for participation in the World Conference on Women held in 1975 in order to commemorate the International Women's Year, and the Japan Accountability Caucus for the Beijing Conference (also known as "Beijing-Japan Accountability Caucus" and "Beijing JAC") 世界女性會議ロビイングネットワ-ク北京JAC, which was established during the 4th UN World Conference on Women (Beijing) held in 1995.

4) The Expansion of the Participation of Intellectuals Including Researchers and Lawyers

Yet another aspect that merits attention is the participation of professional researchers in the process through which the movements expanded. Those including Yoshimi Yoshiaki early on made important accomplishments in the discovery of new materials, and, subsequently, numerous researchers including historians, sociologists, journalists, and women scholars endeavored to shed light on and to interpret academically the reality of Japanese military sexual slavery. A Korean-Japanese scholar who gathered and published a sourcebook of Japanese military and government documents on military sexual slavery in 1992 even before Tokyo disclosed its own materials on the issue in July of the same year, Geum Byeongdong likewise can be evaluated as an important figure in activism and research in this period. Scholars' creation of organizations, close relations with the movements, and research activities served greatly to activate the movements. The Fact-finding Team on the Truth about Forced Korean Laborers in Japan 朝鮮人强制連行眞相調査團, a pro-North Korean organization of Korean-Japanese scholars that from early on had investigated the reality of Japan's mobilization of Koreans for labor and war, began to focus on this issue. As for newly formed organizations, representative is the Center for Research and Documentation on Japan's War Responsibility 日本の戦争責任資料センタ-, which was created by historians including Yoshimi Yoshiaki and Arai Shin'ichi and many young members in July 1993. Although established to resolve Japanese military sexual slavery, this organization has addressed broader Japanese war crimes including the issues of prisoners of war, poison gas, and bacteriological warfare. In addition, the organization played a key role also in the movements for the resolution of Japanese military sexual slavery by holding joint seminars on the issue with the Korean Council in August and December 1993 and collaborating with the Korean Council in filing a lawsuit to the Permanent Court of Arbitration besides actively conducting research such as the publication of the quarterly *Report on Japan's War Responsibility* 季刊戰爭責任研究 (Center for Research and Documentation on Japan's War Responsibility, ed., 1993-2018).[3] In addition, existing organizations such as the Group for Considering Gender and the Emperor

South Korean survivors' testimonies in Japan demanding Tokyo's official apology and reparation (1995)

System グル-プ·性と天皇制を考える and the Group of Women Who Do Not Condone the Path to War 戦争への道を許さない女たちの會 came to study Japanese military sexual slavery in earnest, and newly created organizations likewise developed seminar groups.

In addition to the Korean Council-Center for Research and Documentation on Japan's War Responsibility joint seminars mentioned above, many symposia that included researchers' presentations of their studies and victims' testimonies were held in Japan and attended by numerous citizens. Besides academic symposia solely on Japanese military sexual slavery, many symposia on postwar compensations or the oppression of women also included the issue as an important agenda. On the other hand, innumerable single-volume works as well as so-called *minikomi* ミニコミ (zines)[4] including pamphlets, activity reports, and sourcebooks were published in the names of individual researchers or

3 [TN] Though the organization continues to engage in activities, it suspended the publication of the monthly after the December 2018 issue. See http://japanwarresp.g1.xrea.com (in Japanese).

4 A compound of the English words "mini" and "communication," *minikomi*(*shi*) ミニコミ(誌) are not official publications but are pamphlets and brochures independently produced by and circulated among activist organizations. They began to spread during the latter half of the 1960s in the processes through which social movements in Japan developed.

organizations.

In the process through which the movements thus expanded, the participation of lawyers was of significant help to the legal resolution of Japanese military sexual slavery. Indeed, even more lawyers participated in the movements to file a lawsuit to the Permanent Court of Arbitration, and noteworthy above all was the participation of the Japan Federation of Bar Associations. The Japan Federation of Bar Associations participated in the UN World Conference on Human Rights, held in Vienna in June 1993, and stressed the necessity of correctly resolving the issue and, in October of the same year, also held a symposium on Japan's postwar compensations (First Satellite Session Executive Committee of the Symposium during the 36th JFBA Convention on the Protection of Human Rights, ed., 1993).

5) The Expansion of Attention to the Issue of Postwar Compensations in General

Beginning with continued research by the pro-Pyongyang Korean residents' groups mentioned above and a handful of Japanese scholars, interest in postwar compensations in Japan developed into a more active movement during the latter half of the 1970s, with Korean-Japanese organizations at the center (National Council for Combating Discrimination against Ethnic Peoples in Japan, 1989). However, such efforts mainly centered on battling with the daily discrimination and disadvantages suffered by Korean residents in Japan, and postwar compensations therefore seem to have been an object of interest as a broader legal basis for the resolution of those issues.[5] It was in the 1990s that a full-fledged movement for postwar compensations emerged, in the forms of research and specific legal cases. Although it, of course, was a development of research and movements from previous eras, this movement had been significantly stimulated by the transformation of the issue of Japanese military sexual slavery into social movements.

Although the Research Society for the Issue of Postwar Compensations 戰後補償問題硏究會, which was founded in November 1989, states that

5 Since the mid-1970s, movements by Korean residents in Japan have clearly established coexistence with the Japanese in the nation as their premise.

South Korean survivors taking part in a rally demanding Tokyo's official apology and reparation outside the Japanese National Diet (1994)

it was created on the occasion of the legislation in the United States in 1988 of apologies and compensations to Japanese-Americans forcibly interned during World War II, judging from the fact that Japanese military sexual slavery is included in its studies as an important agenda (Research Society for the Issue of Postwar Compensations, 1990: 4), the organization was obviously affected by the transformation of the issue into a social one. In the 1990s, activities concerning postwar compensations in general, especially actions to help lawsuits in Japan such as the Group for Demanding Postwar Compensations and Supporting the Shimonoseki Court Case (also known as "Group for Supporting the Shimonoseki Court Case," "Association Supporting the Kanpu Trial Case and Facing Japan's Post-war Responsibility," and "Association for Supporting the Kanpu Lawsuit")[6] 戰後責任を問う·關釜裁判を支援する會 (關釜裁判を支援する會; April 1993) and the Group for Supporting a Korean Resident's Comfort Women Lawsuit 在日の慰安婦裁判を支える會 (1993), expanded even

6 [TN] This organization closed in 2013 but has maintained its homepage at http://kanpusaiban.bit.ph (in Japanese) for future reference, and its members have been active in the Fukuoka Network Addressing the "Comfort Women" Issue 「慰安婦」問題にとりくむ福岡ネットワーク.

further. These trials were held in diverse locations such as Tokyo and Fukuoka and encompassed not only the issue of former Japanese military sex slaves but also those of mobilization for labor and war and of postal savings and were supported by the abovementioned Association to Clarify the Post-war Responsibility of Japan, Action Network for the Resolution of the Japanese Military "Comfort Women" Issue, and numerous lawyers in addition to new organizations (Fukushima Mizuho, 1992: 43-45).

In addition, going beyond Japanese military sexual slavery, research and interest expanded considerably to the issues of Unit 731 部隊, Labor Volunteer Corps 勤勞挺身隊, and mobilization for labor and war as well as comparative studies on postwar compensations worldwide,[7] and the issue of Japanese history textbooks, which had hitherto been raised consistently, came to be raised even more actively thanks to that of military sexual slavery.

4. The Weakening of the Movements and the Search for Alternative Methods: End of 1993-August 1994

As the Japanese government suddenly became conservative, in contrast to its hitherto positive changes, and conservative public opinion in Japan increased in strength on one hand and as the movement regarding Japanese military sexual slavery in South Korea expanded to complaints and charges for the punishment of the parties responsible and the movements for a lawsuit to the Permanent Court of Arbitration on the other hand, the movements of Japanese NGOs weakened somewhat, in contrast to their hitherto full-fledged expansion, and began to reveal signs of division among activist groups as well.

1) Conservative Changes in the Japanese Government's Attitude and the Deterioration of Public Opinion

With the completion of its second report on Japanese military sexual

7 Studies by organizations such as the Center for Research and Documentation on Japan's War Responsibility and the Research Society for the Issue of Postwar Compensations address diverse issues related to postwar compensations.

slavery in August 1993 as the final action, Tokyo established its ultimate position that there was no legal responsibility on the state level and, as the concluding measure regarding the issue, announced in August 1994 a bill for the Asian Women's Fund, which was to be consolation money on moral and humanitarian levels instead of a legal compensation. At the same time, abusive remarks on Japanese military sexual slavery by figures including Minister of Justice Nagano Shigeto, Director-General of the Environmental Agency Sakurai Shin, Minister of International Trade and Industry Hashimoto Ryutaro, and Chief Cabinet Secretary Igarashi Kozo continued, and conservative public opinion gained great force. Published in nearly all major Japanese magazines during this period, conservative opinions basically started from the premise that Japan was utterly blameless in its past colonial rule and wars and even claimed that military sexual slavery had been a necessary evil of the era and, moreover, an outstanding institution aimed at protecting women in occupied territories. In addition, they argued that the issue had been completely resolved with the South Korean-Japanese Claims Agreement of 1965 and, furthermore, that the money South Korea had received from Japan then as a price for the settlement of the past had had started the country's current economic revival and that it was due to a political motive that South Korea was now raising the issue (see Chapter 9).

2) New Strategies for the Movement in South Korea and Signs of Division among Japanese Activist Organizations

As the situation thus deteriorated and victims began to despair as well, South Korean NGOs presented new strategies for the movement regarding Japanese military sexual slavery. These consisted of turning public attention, which hitherto had focused on the issue of compensations, to that of the punishment of the liable parties, thus expanding the scope of activism. South Korean NGOs therefore began to consider complaints and charges against the liable parties to the Japanese Public Prosecutors Office and lawsuits against these parties to the Permanent Court of Arbitration. This was also an alternative plan brought about by the lack of binding force on the part of international organs such as the UN and the ILO. However, chances of success were slim from the start because all such measures required Tokyo's consent. In February 1994, the Korean Council and survivors submitted a petition to the Japanese Public Prosecutors Office demanding the punishment of the liable parties but were rejected. In addition, although numerous South Korean and Japanese lawyers made efforts to file a lawsuit against the liable parties to the Permanent Court of Arbitration, in the end, the Japanese government officially announced in January 1995 its refusal to consent to the lawsuit to the court.

Thus faced with the criminal issue of specifically punishing the parties responsible, Japanese activist organizations and individuals, which hitherto had cooperated out of a somewhat abstract criticism of the issue of compensations to victims and Japan's criminality, began to disunite. National Diet member Shimizu Sumiko, who belonged to the Japan Woman's Council, a pro-Social Democratic Party of Japan organization, and had actively cooperated with the movements regarding Japanese military sexual slavery from the beginning, warned that not a few Japanese organizations would secede from the movements if South Korea continued to insist on punishing the liable parties. In addition, the bill for the Asian Women's Fund was gaining ground among Japanese public opinion and citizens. Amid such circumstances, Japanese organizations that hitherto had worked to resolve military sexual slavery came to be divided largely into those agreeing and collaborating with the fund and those opposing it. Organizations against the Asian Women's Fund were further divided into: those categorically opposing the fund; those seeking to create a genuine citizen's fund in opposition to the Asian Women's Fund; and those seeking to legislate the portion of the fund contributed by Tokyo. Meanwhile, as tedious debates on the Asian Women's Fund continued, efforts were made, with a focus on Japanese Christians and academics, also to change the nature of the fund by differentiating between government contributions and private donations in the fund. These three positions can be said to demonstrate the circumstances surrounding Japanese citizens' perceptions of not only the Asian Women's Fund itself but also Japanese military sexual slavery and Japan's overall war crimes.

(1) Organizations That Favored and Cooperated with the Asian Women's Fund

Conscientious Japanese citizens and South Koreans were shocked by the participation in the Asian Women's Fund, as active activists, of Japanese intellectuals including Wada Haruki and Onuma Yasuaki, who had been active as conscientious intellectuals regarding Japan's relations with South Korea such as the issue of Korean residents in Japan and Sakhalin even though they had not actively contributed to the resolution of Japanese military sexual slavery. In addition, Takagi Ken'ichi, a lawyer who had aided lawsuits regarding not only former Japanese military sex slaves but also former members of and civilian employees of the Japanese military 軍屬 held at district courts in Japan, and the Association to Clarify the Post-war Responsibility of Japan, which had been active since the early days of the movements, began actively to work for the Asian Women's Fund. The Japan Woman's Council, which was sympathetic to the Social Democratic Party of Japan, likewise switched to the Asian Women's Fund. The All-Japan Prefectural and Municipal Workers Union (AJPMWU) 全日本自治團體勞動組合 (自治勞; henceforth "Jichiro"), a labor union of staff workers of local governments nationwide that belonged to the Rengo 日本勞動組合總聯合會, participated in the Asian Women's Fund as an active member. Consisting of over a million labor unionists, this is an influential organization. However, not a few subordinate organizations are known to have opposed the decision of the Jichiro, their ruling organ, to participate in the Asian Women's Fund.[8]

The opinion of those who aided the creation of and actively participated in the implementation of the Asian Women's Fund was that, considering the current situation in Japan, the fund was the best resolution for the time being. According to them, consolation money must be transmitted as soon as possible because victims were aged, and the measure must be taken swiftly because it was only possible, in most likelihood, under the current Social Democratic Party of Japan administration. There was also a view that compensations through such private organizations could promote compensations on the state level (results of interviews that I conducted). Their deeper motive, however, seems to have been to mitigate mounting global public opinion and to

8 The hierarchy of the Jichiro is as follows: central headquarters-47 prefectural headquarters-regional liaison councils-municipal unions-labor unions of employees of individual wards.

restore Japan's damaged international image. After presuming that the Asian Women's Fund was the "best method for now," a major activist for the Asian Women's Fund whom I interviewed complained, "Though major Western countries like the United States and the Soviet Union overlook their more serious crimes of human rights violations, Japan alone has become a target of international public opinion." Such figures criticized South Korean NGOs as largely putting the "cause" before the victims themselves and emphasized that the prompt implementation of the Asian Women's Fund was the correct path for the survivors. Proposed by the Social Democratic Party of Japan, this bill for the Asian Women's Fund broadly expanded its support base as a kind of a compromise between the ultra-conservative forces, which denied all postwar responsibilities including compensations, and conscientious citizens' activist groups, which were increasingly losing ground.

(2) Positions Categorically against the Asian Women's Fund

① Positions Arguing for the Dissolution of the Asian Women's Fund

A handful of Japanese groups that, like South Korean NGOs, saw the Asian Women's Fund as an attempt by Tokyo to avoid its legal responsibilities and therefore sought to halt its implementation kept alive the movements to resolve Japanese military sexual slavery. Many of the Japanese Christian women's organizations, female Korean residents' organizations, and Japanese women's organizations examined above continued to maintain strong opposition to the fund. They also created a solidarity organization called the Executive Committee for Crushing the "Asian Women's Fund" つぶせ「國民基金」實行委員會 and engaged in an anti-Asian Women's Fund movement through activities such as protesting against the Japanese government for its secretive payment of the fund to former sex slaves, having signature campaigns, and holding international conferences. In addition, Japanese organizations that generally had continued to work together with South Korean NGOs individually engaged in activism against the fund. Arguing that the payment of the Asian Women's Fund to victims was an insult to them, these organizations urged Tokyo to stop the action immediately and to assume official

A rally held in Japan against the Asian Women's Fund (1996). Song Sin-do, a Korean survivor living in Japan, took part.

responsibilities for Japanese military sexual slavery on a government level. Newly created, too, were organizations such as the Group for Questioning the Sexual Violence of the Japanese Military "Together with the Malaya Lolas" 「マラヤ·ロラズとともに」日本軍の性暴力を問う會, which consisted of former Filipina victims and activists who were against the Asian Women's Fund. Although they were unable to lead strongly the movements against the Asian Women's Fund, these organizations nevertheless were significant to the movements because they clearly expressed their principle and direction of opposition.

② Movements for the Establishment of the Citizens' Fund and Legislation for the Investigation of the Truth

Although fundamentally identical in its position to organizations arguing for the dissolution of the Asian Women's Fund, there was also a movement that not only was against the fund but also sought to create, in opposition, a genuine citizens' fund based on private donations. Begun in August 1995 as the Citizens' Fund 市民基金, this movement was a part of a civic movement called the Campaign for the Realization of Postwar Compensations 戰後補償實現キャンペ-ン, which also encompassed demands for the discontinuation of the Asian Women's Fund and the prompt legislation of the Postwar Compensation Act 戰後補償法, and its participants included: Japanese organizations for the resolution of military sexual slavery such as the Group for Supporting Korean-Japanese Comfort Women 在日の慰安婦裁判を支える會, Chogakpo—Association for Walking with Grandmothers ハルモニと共に歩む會·チョガッポ, Fukuyama Group for Considering the Issue of Japanese Military "Comfort Women," and Lunas—Let's Walk Hand in Hand Filipina Former "Comfort Women" フィリピン人元「慰安婦」と共に·ルナス; organizations for Korean residents in Japan such as the Group for Supporting Mr. Kim Kyong-sok's Lawsuit against Nihon Kokan Co. 金景錫さんの日本鋼管訴訟を支える會, Group for Supporting Former Drafted Laborers' Lawsuits against Japan Iron & Steel Co. 日本製鐵元徵用工裁判を支援する會, and Japan-Philippines Solidarity Movement of Tokyo 日比連帶運動東京; and organizations for broad postwar compensations, and other relevant organizations as well as their individual members. In addition to collecting donations, these organizations engaged in activities including field investigations of damages and exchange with victims. When the Asian Women's Fund aggressively took the offensive by placing massive advertisements in South Korean newspapers (January 7, 1998), these organizations sought to place citizens' advertisements as a countermeasure. As has been mentioned above, their position is identical to the standpoint of categorical opposition to the Asian Women's Fund examined earlier, which strongly demands the Japanese government to stop the fund and to compensate victims individually, and can be evaluated as even more active for its endeavors to go one step further and to collect a citizens' fund. Such efforts did not lead to much success, however, just as the Citizens' Coalition against the Asian Women's Fund and for the Resolution of the Issue of Forcibly Taken Japanese Military Comfort Women 日本國民基金을 反對하는 强制連行當한 日本軍慰安婦問題解決을 爲한 市民連帶, a South Korean attempt against the fund, failed to be very successful, and the donations were mostly used to support victims in Asia.

Reflecting on the fact that the movements for the resolution of Japanese military sexual slavery were being narrowed down to a struggle against the Asian Women's Fund, these organizations sought to return to the original struggle against Tokyo, and one of their actions was a movement for the creation of a law for the investigation of the truth.

(3) Movements Based on a Partial Acknowledgement of the Asian Women's Fund

① Movements for Legislation Regarding the Japanese Government's Contributions to the Asian Women's Fund

Focusing on the fact that the Asian Women's Fund included Tokyo's contributions in addition to private donations, some interpreted these contributions actively as compensations to former Japanese military sex slaves and attempted to formalize them through legislation. At the same time, they pursued the enactment of a bill for the investigation of the truth that would prompt the Japanese government to express its will for continued investigation of the issue. This movement was propelled by several Japanese groups with differing opinions and without dialogue, however, and also failed to win support from South Korean NGOs.[9]

② Attempts to Change the Nature of the Asian Women's Fund

Japanese organizations came to face a situation where the struggle against the Asian Women's Fund continued tediously and international public opinion, too, swerved in favor of the fund due to Tokyo's lobbying.[10] Moreover, from early 1997, when the collection of funds in opposition to the Asian Women's Fund attempted in both Japan and South Korea did not proceed smoothly so that survivors were deeply frustrated, there began to emerge a quiet movement among Japanese intellectuals who hitherto had not been actively involved in the issue and were now expressing grave concern. In other words, their problematics was that a situation where the Japanese government, the party responsible for war crimes,

9 While a kind of a compromise that inserted the phrase "on humanitarian grounds" in the bill on Tokyo's investments instead of acknowledging the same government's crimes was rejected in South Korea, it was accepted in Taiwan, where this movement won some support.

10 In February 1997, the Working Group on Contemporary Forms of Slavery within the Sub-Commission on Human Rights under the UN Commission on Human Rights saw Japan's implementation of the Asian Women's Fund as a "positive step," and many NGOs that previously had expressed interest in Japanese military sexual slavery likewise evaluated the fund positively.

hid behind while the Asian Women's Fund, a civilian organ in form, was the object of victims' and citizens' activism had to be corrected no matter how. This stemmed also from an awareness of the circumstances that it was no longer possible categorically to deny the Asian Women's Fund, which had been established and existed so far. Consequently, consisting of figures including pastors and professors, this group planned to urge the Asian Women's Fund to separate the Japanese government's investments and private donations and to pay the former as official compensations to former Japanese military sex slaves through legal compensation procedures and, at the same time, also to distribute the private donations to victims while stressing that these were from a genuine civilian fund.[11]

5. The Downfall of the Asian Women's Fund, Movements for Legislation, the 2000 Women's Tribunal, and Research Activities

The Asian Women's Fund was not implemented so as to support victims, as publicized by Tokyo in the international community. As is well known, South Korea and Taiwan rejected the fund on the government level so that the Asian Women's Fund approached individual survivors in order to provide money. Even in the Philippines, the victim nation with the largest number of recipients of the fund, extreme confusion arose in civil society between positions for and against the Asian Women's Fund so that money was distributed amid some survivors' rejection of the fund to the end. As for the Netherlands and Indonesia, both lacked a system whereby the government could certify those claiming to have been victims of Japanese military sexual slavery. Consequently, money from the Asian Women's Fund was provided in the form of medical aid in support projects implemented by the Project Implementation Committee in the Netherlands in the former. In the latter, this was done in the form

11 Based on the awareness that the implementation of such a proposal amid both a failure to collect enough donations and attacks from the Asian Women's Fund could somewhat delay the forced implementation of this fund, the Korean Council passively accepted this bill.

of financial support for senior citizen welfare projects implemented by the government (see Chapter 9). With steady movements waged by South Korean and Japanese NGOs in the international community, global public opinion on the Asian Women's Fund once again deteriorated considerably.[12] Consequently, the standpoint in Japan that sought partly to acknowledge or to use the Asian Women's Fund abated unawares. Meanwhile, at the 5th Asian Solidarity Conference held in Seoul in 1998, it was decided that the 2000 Women's Tribunal would be established (see Chapter 8). Subsequently, the Japanese movements for resolving Japanese military sexual slavery divided into two currents: the movements for legislation, which had continued steadily; and the movements for the 2000 Women's Tribunal. However, these two sets of movements coexisted without being able to cooperate with each other.

1) Movements for Legislation

Forming a complex topography with the participation of not a few organizations and political parties, the Japanese movements for legislation created a steady yet very slow current. Briefly put, the movements for legislation, whose topography was highly complex, were as follows. The first was the movement for the legislation of a society for the National Diet's investigation of the issues not only of Japanese military sexual slavery but also of war responsibility in general. As of 2001, over 110 National Diet members including those who belonged to the Democratic Party of Japan, Social Democratic Party of Japan, Japanese Communist Party, and even the Liberal Democratic Party of Japan agreed with the legislation, and the Komeito joined them soon as well. Also active were NGOs, and 18 organizations[13] including the Center for Research

12 The UN and the ILO have repeatedly stressed that the Asian Women's Fund cannot be the correct solution desired by the victims.

13 The Support Group for Ex-Korean BC Class War Criminals Who Were Held Responsible in Place of Japanese 日本の戰爭責任を肩代わりさせられた韓國·朝鮮BC級戰犯を支する會, "Poison Gas Exhibition" Committee 「毒ガス展」實行委員會 (present-day ABC Project Committee ABC企劃委員會), Citizens' Council for the Issue of Atomic Bomb Victims in South Korea 在韓被爆者問題市民會議, Japan Catholic Council for Justice and Peace 日本カトリック正義と平和協議會, Shinjuku Group for Considering the Issue of Women 新宿·婦人問題を考える會, etc.

and Documentation on Japan's War Responsibility, VAWW-Net Japan, Group for Supporting Korean-Japanese Comfort Women, and Group of Jurists and Intellectuals Advocating the Legislation of Postwar Settlement 戰後處理の立法を求める法律家·有識者の會 combined to form the Citizens' Convention for the Realization of the Law of the Society for the Investigation of War Damages 戰爭被害調査會法を實現する市民會議, thus actively engaging in activities including a nationwide signature campaign. Although this organization originally started to work for the legislation of the Bill of the Establishment of Investigation Section for Permanent Peace 恒久平和調査局設置法案, it then shifted its goal to the establishment of the investigation society through the revision of the National Diet Library Act (known formally and later as "Bill of the Partial Amendment of the National Diet Library Act 國立國會圖書館法の一部を改正する法律"). The second was the Promotion of Resolution for Issues Concerning Victims of Wartime Sexual Coercion Bill 戰時性的强制被害者問題の解決の促進に關する法律案 (known earlier as "Bill of the Establishment of Special Organization for Investigation of Wartime Sexual Coercion 戰時性的强制被害者問題調査會設置法案"), which focused on Japanese military sexual slavery and was submitted jointly to the National Diet by the Democratic Party of Japan, Japanese Communist Party, and Social Democratic Party of Japan in 2000 following their respective submissions earlier. Afterwards, National Diet members both from the Japan New Party and without party affiliations also took part, and the bill continued to be submitted until 2008 but was subsequently discarded. Bills thus created mainly by National Diet members constituted an indirect method because they would search for ways to succor and apologize to victims by establishing an investigation society or committee within a Japanese government organ. Meanwhile, the Council of Defense Counsels Demanding the Legislation of Compensations to Former Comfort Women[14] 元「慰安婦」の補償立法を求める辯護團協議會, an organization established mainly by seven lawyers' groups supporting lawsuits regarding former military sex slaves,[15] engaged in a movement for the legislation of a

14 This organization supported the Shimonoseki trial, which, conducted in 1996, was the first trial in Japan to hold the Japanese government responsible for not having legislated laws for compensations to victims and to prompt it to compensate 300,000 yen per plaintiff for damages.

bill that would allude to apology and compensations more directly.

Numerous were Japanese NGOs that directly participated in or aided such activities for legislation. These included the Japan Network against Wartime Sexual Violence (WSV Network) 戰時性暴力問題連絡協議會 (development of the Japan Action Network for the Military Sexual Slavery Issue), Postwar Compensation Network 戰後補償ネットワ-ク, Advocacy Group for Legislation Settlement on "Comfort Women" Issue 「慰安婦」問題の立法解決を求める會, Japan All Solidarity Network for the Settlement of the "Comfort Women" Issue (also known as "All Solidarity Network for the Resolution of the 'Comfort Women' Issue," "All Solidarity Network," and "All Rentai") 「慰安婦」問題解決オ-ル連帯ネットワ-ク (オ-ル連帯), Liaison Group for the Legislation of the Promotion of Resolution for Issues Concerning Victims of Wartime Sexual Coercion Act 「戰時性的强制被害者問題解決促進法」の立法を求める連絡會議, Kansai Network for the Issue of Japanese Military "Comfort Women" (also known as "Japanese Military 'Comfort Women' Issue, Kansai Network") 日本軍「慰安婦」問題·關西ネットワ-ク, Citizens' Network in Fukuoka Demanding Redress Measures for the Former "Comfort Women" (also known as "Let's Make It Quick! Fukuoka-Net for Early Enactment of Law for the Settlement of the Military Comfort Women Issue") 早よつくろう!「慰安婦」問題解決法·ネットふくおか (present-day Fukuoka Network Addressing the "Comfort Women" Issue), and National Council of the Group for Supporting Prisoners of Conscience in South Korea 韓國良心囚を支援する會全國會議.

Such bills and movements for legislation were pursued under the Liberal Democratic Party of Japan administration in a somewhat indirect and weakened manner. With the establishment of the Democratic Party of Japan administration in 2009, the view that activities must turn in the direction of promoting legislation more directly and strongly by bringing

15 The defense counsel in the Shimonoseki court case, defense counsel in the lawsuit seeking state compensation to Filipina former military sex slaves, defense counsel in the lawsuit seeking apology and compensation to Korean-Japanese former military sex slaves, defense counsel in the lawsuit seeking compensation for damages to Dutch former prisoners and civilian internees, defense counsel in the lawsuit seeking state compensation to Chinese former sex slaves, defense counsel in the lawsuit seeking compensation for damages, etc. to victims of sexual violence in Shanxi Province, China, and defense counsel in the lawsuit seeking compensation and apology to Taiwanese former sex slaves.

about the creation of a new, relevant department within the Japanese government became dominant.[16]

2) Movements for the 2000 Women's Tribunal, the Construction of the Women's Active Museum on War and Peace, and Research Activities

Unlike the movements for legislation, which largely centered on NGOs including lawyers and men, the movements for the 2000 Women's Tribunal were conducted by women's organizations. In the over two years of the preparatory process, with the VAWW-Net Japan, which was established in 1998, as the secretariat, and the massive participation of diverse Japanese women's organizations including female Korean residents' organizations as well as organizations in victim nations such as the two Koreas (Korean Council, etc.), Philippines, Taiwan, Indonesia, Netherlands, and China, the cooperation of organizations within Japan and the development of international solidarity were accomplished, which are important achievements. Indeed, in the process of preparing for the 2000 Women's Tribunal, most Japanese women's organizations joined the movements. On the other hand, however, there is no trace of cooperation from those participating in the legislation and lawsuit movements, which were dispersed.

Held during December 8-12, 2000, the 2000 Women's Tribunal served as a very important occasion for the interim evaluation of the movements regarding Japanese military sexual slavery, which had developed since the end of the 1980s. Through it, activist organizations in Asian victim nations and the Netherlands forged systematic solidarity, and, through the Public Hearing held during the tribunal, organizations addressing current wartime violations of women's human rights such as those in the former Yugoslavia likewise gathered, with the tribunal as the center. The tribunal made it possible to settle hitherto accumulated

16 I have referred to the Korean Council for the Women Drafted for Military Sexual Slavery by Japan, "1st Policy Discussion for Responses to the Issue of Japanese Military 'Comfort Women' under the Hatoyama Coalition Government in Japan 日本鳩山聯立政權에서의 日本軍'慰安婦'問題對應을 爲한 一次政策懇談會" (October 8, 2009).

judgments in terms of international law, prompted activists to turn their attention to the future issue of actual praxis, and enabled small Japanese organizations, which up to then had been dispersed without solidarity, to cooperate with one another within a single system. In terms of the situation surrounding the movements that had hitherto been conducted in Japan, it was phenomenal indeed.

The significance of the 2000 Women's Tribunal was covered in detailed by the media in numerous countries including South Korea and China. However, the *Yomiuri Shimbun*, the newspaper with the greatest readership in Japan, did not publish any article on this people's tribunal whatsoever. Even Japan Broadcasting Corp. (NHK) did not fulfill its responsibility as a public broadcaster, producing a distorted program on the tribunal instead. Consequently, the VAWW-Net Japan filed a civil lawsuit against the broadcasting station. At last, in 2007, the Tokyo High Court acknowledged the charge that NHK had distorted its program on Japanese war criminals linked to military sexual slavery due to pressure from both Prime Minister Abe Shinzo and National Diet member Nakagawa Shoichi, declared the broadcasting company guilty, and ordered it to pay a compensation of 2 million yen to the VAWW-Net Japan, the plaintiff.

After gathering for a rally upon the final judgment in the Hague in December 2001, the organizations that had prepared the 2000 Women's Tribunal invited participants from victim nations to Tokyo and held a gathering in order to discuss follow-up work for the execution of the verdict in May 2002. Subsequently, they focused on memorializing victims and established the Women's Active Museum on War and Peace アクティブ·ミュ-ジアム女たちの戦争と平和資料館 in 2005.[17]

Meanwhile, the VAWW-Net Japan, established in 1998 in order to prepare the 2000 Women's Tribunal, was renamed the VAWW RAC in 2011 and went on to devote itself to research.[18] In 2013, it created a website named "Fight for Justice: The Japanese Military 'Comfort

17 Http://wam-peace.org.

18 Https://vawwrac.blogspot.com (in Japanese). [TN] The VAWW RAC stopped activities as an organization in September 2021, even though its executive members continue to engage in activities to resolve the issue of Japanese military sexual slavery.

As the fruit of a 4-year-long collaborative project by South Korean and Japanese women, a joint Korean-Japanese textbook on women's history was published in October 2005. The photographs show the cover of the book (Korean version) and the press conference.

Women'—Resistance to Forgetting & Responsibility for the Future Fight for Justice 日本軍「慰安婦」—忘却への抵抗·未來の責任" together with the Center for Research and Documentation on Japan's War Responsibility, which hitherto had focused on conducting research on and unearthing materials on Japanese military sexual slavery, and thereby has collected and publicized materials on the institution.[19]

Centering on the Association for Research on the Impacts of War and Military Bases on Women's Human Rights「女性·戰爭·人權」學會, Japanese scholars across diverse fields including Nakahara Michiko have devoted themselves to research. Especially noteworthy following the 2000 Women's Tribunal was the compilation of a joint textbook on women's history in Korea and Japan headed by women scholars from both nations. This was an effort directly challenging Japanese history textbooks, which had been a serious issue between South Korea and Japan since the latter half of the 1990s, seeking to define modern Japanese history as a history of war and the oppression of women and to create a history textbook accordingly. In 2001, South Korean, Japanese, and

19 Http://fightforjustice.info.

Korean-Japanese women scholars agreed to create a modern history textbook that could be read jointly by the Koreans and the Japanese at the juncture of the histories of the two nations and, after over three years of mutual exchange and research, published the work in both countries in 2005. In other words, except for inevitable and minimal differences between the two nations, a book of identical contents was published in South Korea as *Gender Perspective on Modern and Contemporary History of Korea and Japan* 女性의 눈으로 본 韓日近現代史 (Hanul) and in Japan as *Gender Perspective on Modern and Contemporary History of Japan and Korea* ジェンダ-の視點からみる日韓近現代史 (Nashi-no Kisha), respectively. Following the publication of the book, Suzuki Yuko, the person in charge on the Japanese side, created the Group for Considering the Women and Histories of Japan and Korea 日韓の女性と歴史を考える會, which succeeds the tasks of the textbook project, and has continued to compile history.

6. Attempts at a Nationwide Coalition

When the resolution on Japanese military sexual slavery was passed in the US House of Representatives in 2007 and interest in the issue was newly aroused worldwide, the Japan All Solidarity Network for the Settlement of the "Comfort Women" Issue was founded in the nation by encompassing those who hitherto had engaged in research and activities in order to resolve the issue. Under the goal of implementing measures such as public hearings in the National Diet, the passage in the Japanese legislature of a resolution for an apology, compensations through legislation, and the prevention of recurrence through history education, this organization saw the participation of countless individuals including researchers, activists, and jurists from groups discussed above such as the VAWW-Net Japan and the Center for Research and Documentation on Japan's War Responsibility. As such, it was an attempt at a coalition unprecedented in Japan. Without any noteworthy activity since 2009,[20] the organization presented a written request for compensations and apologies that would

20 Http://ameblo.jp/all-rentai. [TN] On another blog at http://blog.livedoor.jp/allrentai, this organization was more active during 2015-2021.

allow Tokyo, while maintaining its stance, to accept the legal responsibility demanded by South Korean victims and support groups in the forms of an acknowledgment of the facts and the provision of compensations to the Japanese prime minister and foreign minister in November 2015 (*Hankyoreh*, November 18, 2015).

Meanwhile, in 2010, yet another coalition was attempted. It was the Japan Nationwide Action for the Resolution of the Japanese Military "Comfort Women" Issue 日本軍「慰安婦」問題解決全國行動. Created by gathering groups and individuals hitherto active throughout the nation in order to resolve the issue, as with the earlier Japan All Solidarity Network for the Settlement of the "Comfort Women" Issue, this organization has engaged in activities to this day while forging close relations with the Korean Council.[21]

7. The Characteristics and Points of Contention of Activist Organizations in Japan

1) The Characteristics of the Major Activist Organizations

When examined in terms of their organizational characteristics, the Japanese activist groups mentioned above reveal many differences from their South Korean counterparts. As for the period in which they were established, these organizations can be divided into those that already existed before Japanese military sexual slavery was first raised and those that were newly created during 1991-1993 in order to address the issue. As can be expected, while existing organizations were large-scale national organizations or councils with numerous members, the newly founded ones were mostly small groups with memberships ranging from a few dozen to hundreds at most. Generally, as for existing organizations, they weakened considerably as the circumstances surrounding the movements became delicate, and, especially regarding the Asian Women's Fund, some came to support the fund while even those against it came to be more

21 Http://www.restoringhonor1000.info.

passive in expressing their opinions. On the contrary, nnewly created small groups have continued the movements amid growth and stagnation and mutual solidarity and conflict. Consequently, the de facto subjects of these movements, then, can be seen as new groups that have emerged in the currents of social movements including local, women's, labor, and peace movements.

While the South Korean movement has been conducted with a focus on the Korean Council, which is a coalition of existing organizations, the movements in Japan have consisted of innumerable small groups' coexistence and independent activities. Indeed, Japanese activist groups are unique not only in the scales of their organizations but also in their methods of organization. Not a few are groups that lack chairs or representatives and formal organizational divisions, thus engaging in activities solely through members' voluntary participation. Although such organizational forms can prompt democratic decision-making and members' autonomous activities, they can also lead to somewhat lower efficiency in many cases. This is because there is no overall system through which these small groups can effectively communicate with one another.

Nor, for that matter, have the small groups above never attempted to form a united coalition for the mutual coordination of opinions and efficient international solidarity. As has been examined above, at the initial stage of the movements, organizations related to Japanese military sexual slavery gathered in order to form the Action Network for the Resolution of the Japanese Military "Comfort Women" Issue, but the coalition dissipated without much effect. Since the implementation of the Asian Women's Fund, organizations such as the Executive Committee for Crushing the "Asian Women's Fund" and the Campaign for the Realization of Postwar Compensations have garnered the strength of dispersed small groups, but the scale itself is small, and it is difficult to say that the opinions of the small participating groups are coordinated well. Though attempts were made to create a new coalition following 2007, the movements still seem to center on small groups.

2) The Points of Contention in the Movements

Japanese military sexual slavery is simultaneously an issue concerning the violation of women's human rights, superpowers' violation of the human rights of the peoples of weaker nations, and the state's wartime violation of the human rights of citizens. Because the issue is thus complex, no less complex are the orientations of those who work to resolve it. In other words, the movements have been propelled with the convergence of and conflict among diverse standpoints regarding Japanese military sexual slavery including those of feminism, opposition to superpowers' hegemonism, pacifism against wars, criticism of oppressive states, and more universal humanism. In the case of Japan, such orientations of the movements are even more complicated.

(1) The Issues of Gender/Ethnicity and Human Rights/Ethnicity

When South Korean women's organizations raise Japanese military sexual slavery, their consciousness of both the issue of women's human rights and anti-Japanese nationalism coexists inseparably. In terms of the movements in Japan, however, this issue is rather delicate. When South Korean organizations make an issue of the exploitation of women from Japan's former colonies in relation to Japanese military sexual slavery, their Japanese counterparts problematize the danger of diluting the issue of Japanese women mobilized as military sex slaves in thus stressing the issue of women from the colonies. For example, at the 1st Asian Solidarity Conference held in 1992, one Japanese woman activist stated that if South Korea strongly raised the issue of ethnicity, it would be difficult to forge solidarity. In addition, in a commentary on Tokyo's announcement, in August 1993, of the results of its second investigation on Japanese military sexual slavery, the Korean Council pressed the same government's motive behind its neglect of discriminatory and forced mobilization and exploitation of women from former colonies and occupied territories, to which Japanese women's organizations did not respond favorably. Similarly, Japanese studies on this issue sensitively allude to the issues of gender and ethnicity (Kim Puja, 1994, etc.).

Related to this is the frequent disagreement of Japanese participants in the movements regarding Japanese military sexual slavery with South Korean activists and scholars on when the latter mention the issue of ethnicity in general during the Japanese colonial era in relation to that of military sexual slavery. For example, at a symposium jointly held in 1993 by the Korean Council and the Center for Research and Documentation on Japan's War Responsibility, when the South Korean participants gave a presentation arguing that the mobilization of Korean women as military sex slaves had been a part of the Japanization 皇國臣民化 policy implemented by Japan in colonial Korea from the end of the 1930s and had ultimately aimed at ethnic genocide, the Japanese participants disagreed by claiming that such an argument was overreaching in interpreting the mobilization as cultural genocide 民族文化抹殺 and therefore equating it with ethnic genocide.

Such examples can then be interpreted as the somewhat different standpoints of South Korean and Japanese participants in the movements on the issues of gender and ethnicity.

(2) The Punishment of the Liable Parties and the Issue of the Emperor System

It was when the issue of punishing the liable parties was raised that initially cooperative Japanese organizations began to waver. Indeed, in addition to organizations that actively expressed their opposition to the punishment of the liable parties, many participants in the movements were of the opinion that, in order to secure popular support for the movements, it would be compromising to stress the punishment of the liable parties. This is because the most certain and serious party responsible was none other than the Japanese emperor himself. It is well known that, in Japanese society, the emperor occupies a very special place.

Some Japanese have seen an ultimate link between the considerable weakening of the movements with respect to the Asian Women's Fund and the emperor system. In other words, the Asian Women's Fund won support because the majority of organizations saw it as an appropriate compromise evading both state compensations and the punishment of the liable parties. Indeed, according to this view, if state compensations were acknowledged, they would raise in succession countless issues regarding Japan's postwar responsibilities, which, in turn, not only would be an economic blow but also could shake the emperor system.

In response to the question "What is the correct solution?" Japanese organizations that responded to my survey and expressed their opposition to the Asian Women's Fund pointed out many issues including state compensations, the inclusion of Japanese military sexual slavery in Japanese textbooks, government apology, and the investigation of the truth. However, not a single one of them alluded to the punishment of the liable parties. This reveals that even the most conscientious Japanese participants were unconsciously excluding the issue of punishing the liable parties.

(3) The Potential for "Progressive" Nationalism

In the end, not only the Japanese government and conservative public opinion but also Japanese groups that endorsed the Asian Women's Fund can be said to have been based on nationalism. Indeed, when I asked one Japanese intellectual who was actively intervening in the Asian Women's Fund and, early on, had engaged in activism for Korean residents in Japan the reason for taking interest in the issue of Korean residents, this person answered, "Why, of course, to make Japanese society a better one." However, it is worth noticing that many of the most progressive Japanese figures who were actively engaged for the resolution of Japanese military sexual slavery and opposed the Asian Women's Fund were active ultimately from the same motive and for the same reason: to make Japan a better society. When I asked, "Why are you so deeply involved in this issue, which exposes a shameful secret of Japan?" a Japanese intellectual who was one of the most progressive figures regarding Japanese military sexual slavery and was very familiar with the movement in South Korea immediately answered, "To turn Japan into a more elevated society ethically." While this may be a very natural phenomenon, the question is how much potential such "progressive" nationalism holds. Even progressive Japanese intellectuals who, at first, had earnestly participated in the issue of Japanese military sexual slavery partly turned their backs regarding the issue of punishing the liable parties and then seceded *en masse* from the movements with respect to the Asian Women's Fund perhaps because they had not yet overcome nationalism in one way or another.

Part IV

The Nature of the Issue of Japanese Military Sexual Slavery

Chapter 11

The Nature of the Issue of Japanese Military Sexual Slavery

1. The Issue of Japanese Military Sexual Slavery as One of Multilayered Human Rights Violation

The issue of Japanese military sexual slavery began to reveal itself after prolonged silence in the 1990s, 50 years after the end of the war, above all, because of strengthened awareness of human rights, especially of women's human rights. As is well known, this issue was raised by women's activist groups in South Korea and soon won the attention of Japan, Asian victim nations, and global organizations that advocate human rights and seek to prevent war crime.

Organizations such as the UN Commission on Human Rights, UN Sub-Commission on Human Rights, and International Commission of Jurists define Japanese military sexual slavery as a violation of the categories of war crime and crime against humanity in major human rights-related international laws (see Chapter 6). The ILO has determined the issue as a violation of the Forced Labour Convention (ILO Convention 29), which is one of the organization's main human rights-related conventions (see Chapter 7). The international community thus concurs in viewing Japanese military sexual slavery as a serious human rights violation.

More specifically, victims of Japanese military sexual slavery suffered from human rights violations as women, as peoples from weak nations, as citizens powerless before state power, and in the extreme situation of war. While cases of human rights violations caused by such an overlap of diverse social conditions are rare, these conditions in themselves each create circumstances of human rights violations, and some of them overlap to give rise to even more serious human rights violations at times as well. Consequently, though Japanese military sexual slavery is a particular issue, it also exhibits the universal aspect of having a common base with other situations of human rights violations. This chapter will shed light on the social conditions behind each of such human rights violations.

1) The Issue of Women's Human Rights

Above all, Japanese military sexual slavery was a violation of women's human rights. In other words, the most important social condition that both caused and concealed this issue was the social situation of the denigration of women in not only Japan but also Asian victim nations including South Korea. Lying in the background against which Japan devised and managed military sexual slavery was the patriarchy implemented by modern Japan in mainland Japan and the colonies alike and a culture of denigrating women ensuing from that system. Accordingly, the country established institutions to prevent women from becoming legal subjects and created the licensed prostitution 公娼制 amid a sexual double standard that emphasized chastity only in the case of women. The pretext was that, in order to protect ordinary women sexually and to manage male society efficiently at the same time, the existence of prostitutes 娼妓 was a necessary evil.

Meanwhile, the silence of both the victims and the witnesses around them in Asian victim countries including South Korea and Taiwan and the difficult lives led by the victims amid serious mental and physical aftereffects since the end of the war can be seen as stemming from a social atmosphere based on Confucian patriarchy, which stresses women's chastity. According to a study examining the lives of the victims following the Liberation, these women, while holding a grudge not against males but against the state of Japan, viewed their inability to get married, to bear children, and to lead peaceful domestic lives as the most regretful of the damages from which they suffered (Yi Sang-Hwa, 1993).

It was women researchers and activists in South Korea who salvaged the issue of Japanese military sexual slavery from the dark recesses of history 50 years later, and, in other Asian victim nations such as the Philippines, women's organizations likewise played a central role in the development of the movement. In addition, many women's organizations in Japan, too, participated in the movement actively. In other words, a consensus was reached: in the end, the issue had been a product of a system that had oppressed women. This point served right away as a basis for uniting women's organizations worldwide as well. Numerous women's organizations cooperated with their South Korean counterparts at the UN, and women from a number of countries focused on the issue as a major violation of women's human rights at events including the World Conference on Human Rights held in Vienna in 1993 and the World Conference on Women held in Beijing in 1995. The UN Commission on Human Rights had a Special Rapporteur on Violence against Women investigate and report on Japanese military sexual slavery, and when a report demanding the Japanese government for rightful compensations was presented in 1996, 58 organizations centering on women's organizations created a group in support of it (International Alliance Supporting Radhika Coomaraswamy's Report on Military Sexual Slavery in Wartime).

All such efforts were based on the concern that, unless social conditions oppressing women changed, human rights violations like the issue of Japanese military sexual slavery would continue in different forms.

2) The Issue of the Violation of the Human Rights of the Peoples of Weak Nations by Strong Nations

The fact that, in mobilizing women as military sex slaves, Japan restricted the victims mainly to existing prostitutes in mainland Japan but mostly mobilized ordinary women in colonial Korea and Formosa as well as occupied territories demonstrates that this issue includes the important level of the issue of the human rights of the peoples of weak nations.[1]

1 There are many records that, even at Japanese military comfort stations, Japanese women were given preferential treatment in the fee rates and the ranks of the soldiers to whom they were to provide sexual services.

In other words, the oppression of both women and weak countries was imposed on the victimized women.

Japan implemented the mass mobilization of human power such as conscription and the draft 徵用 in colonial Korea in the 1930s-1940s, and the mobilization of women as Japanese military sex slaves, implemented in the context of such oppression of the entire Korean people by Japan, led to the most wretched case even among various forms of human rights violations. In other Asian countries including China and the Philippines, women were forcibly mobilized under the circumstance of occupation.

From the end of the war to more recent years, when the issue of Japanese military sexual slavery was raised, while no measure has been taken regarding victims in weak Asian countries, in contrast, the liable parties have been punished in cases of the mobilization of Dutch women as military sex slaves in the Netherlands East Indies (see Chapter 3). This shows that power relations among nations have had a strong effect on not only the conditions under which the issue arose but also the process through which it came to be buried. As is well known, Japan has adopted a stance of justifying its past colonization of Korea and Formosa and invasion of the Asian continent and avoided rightful resolution including compensations and the punishment of the liable parties.

Human rights violations suffered by weak nations increasingly worsened with the worldwide expansion of imperialism, and, with the further implementation of globalization in recent years, numerous issues including those of the human rights of ethnic minorities and migrant workers have become visible. Here, violations of the human rights of the peoples of weak countries, especially of women, who constitute a vulnerable group from among them, are becoming even more serious.

3) The Issue of the Violation of the Human Rights of Citizens by State Power

Japan was able to mobilize and systematically manage military sex slaves throughout the Asia-Pacific region during the 15 years in which it started and waged war because the system was implemented by the state through the use of official power. The Japanese state established military comfort stations as a national policy; the police, armed forces, and even administrative organs intervened in the process of mobilizing women as sex slaves; and the military performed the transport and allotment of the victims. In addition, the state systematically conducted regular medical examinations of military sex slaves and controlled military comfort stations. Such circumstances surrounding Japanese military sex slaves show an extreme case of sexual violence committed by the state. Japan continuously strengthened militarism following the establishment of the Meiji government and, to achieve that goal, established a powerful state system called the Japanese emperor system. During wartime in the 1930s-1940s, the state based on the emperor system suspended citizens' rights in mainland Japan and the colonies alike, implementing a controlled economy and the mobilization of both goods and human power. Social movements proceeded under the state initiative, and existing voluntary organizations likewise were forcibly turned into administrative organs. In other words, it was under such a system of mobilizing citizens that sexual exploitation in the colonies and occupied territories was committed very strongly.

4) The Issue of War and Human Rights

Damages due to Japanese military sexual slavery were severe because the system was implemented during wartime. War causes serious human rights violations, and people from vulnerable groups are victimized especially easily. It goes without saying that women constitute the main victims. All wars are accompanied by rape by soldiers, and women on the "enemy" side are targeted in particular. A case of the wartime violation of women's human rights, "ethnic cleansing" in Bosnia is one of the most tragic experiences undergone in world history in recent years. Unlike the mobilization of women in occupied territories as Japanese military sex slaves, the mobilization of women from Korea and Formosa exhibits special aspects different from other problems that arose in wartime. Though cases where the armed forces exploited women as comfort women are occasionally discovered, not to be found are those where systematic sex slave policies were implemented, as with Japan during the 1930s-1940s, and the forced mobilization of colonized women *en masse* here demonstrates an extreme example of the wartime violation of women's human rights. With this extreme historical fact not properly brought to account, the violation of women's human rights continue during wars and armed conflicts even today.

5) The Movement to Resolve the Issue of Japanese Military Sexual Slavery as a Human Rights Movement

Raised by South Korean women's organizations at the end of the 1980s and actively joined by women's groups and human rights organizations both in Asia and around the globe afterwards, the movement to resolve Japanese military sexual slavery has become an international civic movement based on cooperation transcending class, gender, and ethnicity. While the motive for joining this movement may be different for each individual, the participants have been able to forge solidarity because of both anger at this human rights violation and the goal of preventing such human rights violation from ever recurring anywhere in the world. Consequently, the first goal of the movement is the restoration of the victims' human rights.

The victims were mobilized to battlefields where bullets crisscrossed, without even knowing that they would be turned into sex slaves made to serve dozens of soldiers each day. They were subjected to subhuman treatment at comfort stations, the locations of which were concealed so that they could not even escape. After the war, they were simply discarded at these facilities while soldiers fled. The subsequent 50 years of leading hidden lives, denigrated as "fallen" women, were even more wretched. Most of the survivors were physically ill and mentally devastated as well.[2]

How, then, were these women's violated human rights to be restored? The first thing to which organizations in South Korea, Japan, and other Asian victims nations devoted their energy was support for the survivors. These groups encouraged the victims to disclose hitherto hidden stories, forged exchange among survivors with similar experiences, and provided economic aid through donations. Individuals and organizations other than activist groups providing assistance to the victims increased,[3] and

---

2 As for Korean victims' lives at comfort stations and postwar abandonment, see Shin Young-sook and Cho Hye-ran, 1996. As for these women's lives after the Liberation, see Yi Sang-Hwa, 1993.

the South Korean government likewise passed a special law in 1993 and has provided systematic livelihood aid ever since. As for survivors in the Philippines, because of the country's economic hardships, many support groups were formed in Japan. Such assistance has served as not only material aid but also considerable emotional support to the victims. Receiving this kind of public attention in itself signifies a process of recovery from damages for the survivors, who have lived in isolation and with strong self-blame. Moreover, as they come to realize that blame for their suffering lies not in themselves but in distorted society and history and that they were victimized, these women can gradually recover destroyed self-esteem. As long as the victimizers' denial of the facts continues, however, the victims' human rights cannot be restored. What the survivors want is their experiences to be publicized accurately, the victimizers to be unearthed, and compensations to be made for all the humiliation. That way, their honor can be restored. Consequently, restoring the victims' human rights equals correcting distorted history and holding the liable parties accountable.

Ultimately, the important historical significance of the correct resolution of Japanese military sexual slavery is the prevention of the recurrence of such human rights violations anywhere around the globe. Indeed, a major reason for the participation of human rights organizations worldwide in this movement can be seen as such progress for the international community. In other words, as with any other crime in society, the perpetrators of this particular crime must be appropriately convicted in order to prevent recurrence. The victims and activist groups have demanded from the Japanese government: the provision of appropriate compensations to each survivor; and the discovery and punishment of the liable parties. International organs such as the UN and the ILO, too, have recommended Tokyo to compensate the victims

3 The Korean Council started to receive victims' reports in 1990. The Buddhism Human Rights Committee 佛教人權委員會 established the House of Sharing, collective housing for survivors, and the Museum of Sexual Slavery by Japanese Military 日本軍慰安婦歷史館. In addition, many citizens and organizations including Seoul Jungang Hospital in Seoul and Kwak's Hospital in Daegu provided support. Support from abroad continued as well, with civilian groups and individuals in Japan taking up an important share.

appropriately.

2. The Historical Structure of the Oppression of Women

1) The Formation of a Structure Oppressing Women as a Result of Japanese Colonial Rule

In addition to directly violating women's human rights, Japanese military sexual slavery strengthened social conditions that distorted the formation of women's subjectivity in the processes of mobilization and responses to it, of concealment and problematization. In other words, damages due to the institution resulted in long-term and structural effects that aggravated the societywide conditions for oppressing women besides extreme violation of the victims' human rights.

The oppressive social environment surrounding colonized women that stemmed from Japan's colonial rule served as the backdrop against the massive mobilization of these women as Japanese military sex slaves. It is a well-known fact that colonial exploitation destroyed the rural economy, which, in turn, led to a massive rural exodus. The fact that economically productive age groups, impoverished people, and women took up a greater share of these migrants from the countryside demonstrates that, in the case of indigent farming households, daughters bore the burden of earning money for their male siblings' education. This was also because women's labor in rural areas was forcibly destroyed and reorganized. In order to ensure and boost the sales of Japan's textile products in colonial Korea, the Japanese authorities forcibly prohibited women's domestic weaving, even confiscating looms from farming households. In place, they dragged women to outdoor labor, which had been traditionally avoided in Korea, implemented communal cultivation through women's associations 婦人會, village advancement associations 村落振興會, or the police, and forced side jobs such as sericulture on women (Kim Jeongmi, 1980: 104). This situation surrounding women's labor in rural communities not only accelerated migration from the countryside but also served as a background facilitating employment fraud.

Korean women who thus left rural communities were absorbed first by low-wage factories. In particular, in the 1930s, women took up over 30% of total factory workers. The absolute reason for factories' absorption of women, however, was the low wages paid to this population group. In other words, Korean women were paid half of Korean men's wages and a quarter of Japanese men's wages, respectively, and Korean female factory workers aged below 16 were paid wages only one-fifth of those of Japanese men (Government-General of Korea, 1933: 233-243). Most of women factory workers (97%) were low-ranking (Government-General of Korea, 1934) and had to work longer than did men.[4] Moreover, they were faced with the dangers of male supervisors' patriarchal control and sexual violation. While women were gradually absorbed as work force at mines, they suffered from low wages and dangerous working conditions here, too. In particular, the Japanese colonial government lifted the existing prohibition on women's work in mine shafts in 1941, thus worsening the working conditions for women in mines (Miya Koichi, 1945: 43). Meanwhile, along with industrialization, occupations in the service industry increased in cities. A large number of Korean women were absorbed into work usually limited to women such as the provision of hospitality and housekeeping (Government-General of Korea, 1930: 258-262). Prospering amid the circulation of products and the movement of people, hospitality establishments such as lodging, restaurants, and bars were places where women directly faced the danger of prostitution (*Dong-A Ilbo*, June 29, 1925). In addition, the lives of Korean maids in the homes of Japanese settlers in the colony were most wretched, with traditional class discrimination compounded by ethnic discrimination. Besides these occupations, many women came to work as shop clerks and peddlers, and their situations were similar.

Such working conditions made it difficult to view the expansion of women's participation in the labor market simply as a "modern" change and strongly hindered women's formation of subjectivity. In addition, these very circumstances formed the condition enabling the mobilization

---

4 In 1938, the *Dong-A Ilbo* reported that the average working time per day was 9 hours 30 minutes for adult male factory workers, 10 hours 30 minutes for juvenile male factory workers, 10 hours 40 minutes for adult female factory workers, and 10 hours 18 minutes for juvenile female factory workers, respectively (*Dong-A Ilbo*, August 16, 1936).

of many women even in cities as Japanese military sex slaves. Indeed, testimonies show that the victims were sold or deceived from not only rural communities but also urban areas through means including employment agencies.

In addition, under Japan's modern system of licensed prostitution 公娼制, women's subjectivity was inevitably oppressed. Having permitted brothels 遊廓 since the Edo period, the Japanese government completed modern licensed prostitution by reorganizing this brothel system after the Meiji Restoration. Consequently, it came to place weight on contractual relations between procurers and prostitutes 娼妓, to make their payment of taxes mandatory, and to stipulate medical examinations for STDs and restrictions on outings from brothels in the case of prostitutes. The government claimed that, unlike Edo-era courtesans 遊女 placed under seizure of person, prostitutes in modern Japan could thus conclude or cancel contracts on prostitution "according to their wishes." Brothels were legally called *kashizashiki* 貸座敷 under modern licensed prostitution, and this term, meaning "facilities rented out" to prostitutes, likewise was a neologism coined by the Japanese government in order to stress that engagement in prostitution was based on the choices of prostitutes themselves.

However, in that women could not easily become the subjects of legal contracts within the structure of the patriarchal *ie* 家 (household) system of the times and that it allowed a cash advance provision whereby prostitutes inevitably incurred substantial debts, modern licensed prostitution was tantamount to the legal guarantee of the subjection of prostitutes to seizure of person. In addition, business by prostitute brokers was permitted, thus leaving room for the human trafficking of women. Indeed, the situation was such that the League of Nations, which investigated human trafficking in Japan in 1931, even pointed out, "One of the most surprising things upon arriving in Japan is the official licensing of professional entertainer and prostitute brokerage"[5] (Park Jung-ae, 2009: 119).

Following the initiation of the legislation of the relevant laws in

5 [TN] Though this is a back translation of a Korean translation of the English original, it reflects the essential meaning.

1873, modern Japanese licensed prostitution was completed in 1900 with the proclamation of the Regulations on the Regulation of Prostitutes 娼妓取締規則, which applied nationwide. Furthermore, licensed prostitution began to be introduced into Japanese concessions, occupied territories, and colonies in the process of the nation's imperialistic expansion. Its purpose was to prevent Japanese soldiers' infection with STDs in the process of carrying out wars of aggression and to promote Japanese citizens' immigration abroad, thus developing colonial settlements.

As for Korea, which was forcibly opened up to the world in 1876, licensed brothels 公娼 began to be introduced into the nation, with a focus on Japanese settlements in treaty ports. After installing the Residency-General of Korea[6] in the country in 1906 and expanding its dominance, Japan implemented licensed prostitution also in Korean communities, centering on Seoul. In 1916, by which the Government-General of Korea ruled this former empire, the Japanese authorities proclaimed the Regulations on the Regulation of Brothels and Prostitutes 貸座敷·娼妓取締規則, thus implementing licensed prostitution throughout the colony. In other words, Japan constructed licensed prostitution as it proceeded with the colonization of Korea.

Licensed prostitution in Korea had clauses more disadvantageous to prostitutes than did their counterparts in Japan. The permitted age for prostitution was 17 or above in Japan proper but 16 or above in the colony. The clause protecting prostitutes, which stipulated that prostitutes' names were to be deleted immediately from rosters of prostitutes if and when these women stopped engaging in the profession, did not even exist in Korea, unlike in Japan. Laws regulating brokers, too, were mere formalities so that, it the colony, there was much more room to commit human trafficking within the legal framework.

Waging a war of aggression for 15 years starting in 1931, the Japanese empire implemented the military comfort women system under the

6 [TN] Also known popularly but inaccurately as 韓國統監府, this agency partly ruled Korea, now a protectorate of Japan, until it was replaced by the Government-General of Korea, the full-fledged colonial administrative organ, with the annexation of the realm in 1910.

pretext of preventing STDs among its troops. The systematic mobilization of women and girls as military sex slaves through the use of brokers and the management of military comfort stations under the management of the Japanese government and armed forces were all possible because of modern Japan's experience with licensed prostitution.

As a general mobilization system was constructed following the initiation of the Second Sino-Japanese War and a cultural genocide policy 民族文化抹殺 was implemented in the colonies in the name of so-called Japanization 皇國臣民化, structures oppressing women intensified even further. The mobilization of women for war was implemented in Japan proper, too. However, the mobilization of women in the colonial metropolis was the mobilization of motherhood on one hand and labor mobilization on the other hand. Here, the mobilization of motherhood refers to the emphasis on women's motherhood starting in the 1930s and the consequent imposition on Japanese women of the role of bearing children and raising them into loyal imperial subjects. At the time, Japan saw the publication of numerous books with titles such as *The Mother of Japan* 日本の母 and *The Mother of the Military State* 軍國の母, which appealed to women's motherhood. In 1940, women's organizations under the Imperial Rule Assistance Association 大政翼贊會 likewise stressed women's responsibility to bear and rear children as imperial subjects (Suzuki Yuko, 1989: 21-60). Meanwhile, Japanese women were also mobilized for labor in order to supplement insufficient labor force. Even then, the Japanese government devoted considerable attention to the protection of motherhood. It mobilized women's labor through a series of policies such as the Labor Mobilization Plan 勞務動員計劃 of 1939, Women's Patriotic Labor Corps 女子勤勞報國隊 of 1941, and the Ordinance on Women's Voluntary Labor 女子挺身勤勞令 of 1944. At the same time, it continuously emphasized, as a special precaution, that because women had the crucial mission to raise children and to perform domestic chores in the home as an established custom of the family system, care must be taken so that the mobilization of women would not clash with this mission (Yeo Soon-joo, 1994: 17-19). Indeed, any plan to mobilize women as Japanese military sex slaves, which destroyed motherhood, was unthinkable in the case of Japanese women. On the other hand, colonized women were excluded from this policy of protecting motherhood, with the exception of some upper-class women, and became the main objects of the systematically implemented mobilization of women as military sex slaves.

2) Distorted Responses to Mobilization

The circumstances of the violation of Japanese military sexual slavery victims' human rights suppressed the formation of women's sense of subjectivity. In order to avoid being mobilized as military sex slaves, which was implemented in colonial Korea from the 1930s to the end of the war in 1945, all Korean women resorted to a gamut of methods, and numerous problems arose in the process. The majority of the victims were mobilized at ages ranging from 11 at least to the first half of the 20s at most (see Chapter 3). Because mainly unmarried women and girls were thus mobilized as military comfort women, not rare are testimonies that, in the colony at the time, young women married any men so as "not to be taken as [members of] the Volunteer Corps 挺身隊"[7] in a situation where men were already insufficient due to the draft and conscription. According to testimonies, the majority of parents sought quickly to marry off their daughters even before the latter were of marriageable ages in a social climate where employment fraud and human trafficking for the mobilization of women as military sex slaves were rampant, even in cases where physical and forced mobilization was not committed. In other words, due to the mobilization of women as military sex slaves, many women in Korea ended up choosing loveless marriages irrespective of their own wishes and burying themselves in the home.

Meanwhile, while the mobilization of women as Japanese military sex slaves was indiscriminately imposed on all Korean women (see Chapter 3), it was implemented first in impoverished rural areas and low-income districts in cities. This is why attention is paid to the issue of

7 At the time in colonial Korea, members of the "Volunteer Corps 挺身隊" seem to have been considered equivalent to "comfort women." However, this cannot be viewed merely as conceptual confusion. In addition to employment fraud and human trafficking, the mobilization of women as prospective military comfort women by government officials, police officers, and soldiers seems to have been implemented in the name of this institution (see Chapter 1).

class as an important characteristic of Japanese military sexual slavery. Such differences in women's experiences per class can be said to have served as a major occasion for oppressing the formation of women's self-awareness as subjects. In addition to this, however, elite Korean women's collaboration with the Japanese authorities' mobilization created great fissures in Korean women's self-awareness overall. In other words, elite women such as Maria Park 朴瑪利亞, Mary Ann Moh (Moh Youn-sook 毛允淑), Ko Hwanggyeong 高凰京, Noh Cheonmyeong 盧天命, Helen Kim 金活蘭, Heo Habaek 許河伯, and Bae Sangmyeong 裵祥明 raised their voices, arguing that the sons and daughters of Korea must proceed to the battleground and sacrifice their lives in order to repay the Japanese emperor's "grace" (Institute for Research in Collaborationist Activities, 1994: 114-126).

In Japan, so-called women leaders' collaboration with the war as principal members of the Imperial Rule Assistance Association deeply scarred the formation of women's sense of subjectivity (Ueno Chizuko, 1996). It can be said that similar collaboration in colonial Korea, committed amid the very existence of victims of extreme damages, further deepened the wounds.

3) Women's Consciousness Overwhelmed by Ethnic Consciousness

Due to and during the Japanese colonial era, Korean women were unable to form subjective consciousness and, instead, were overwhelmed by ethnic consciousness. Of course, this need not necessarily be viewed only in a negative way. On the contrary, it is possible to say that, as in many other colonial societies, women participating in nationalistic movements created an important stage in the formation of women's consciousness by bolstering their social consciousness and political acumen.[8] However, the

8 Women's unique nationalistic movements in Korea from the 19th century and onwards such as the Praise Society 讚揚會, National Debt Redemption Movement 國債報償運動, and Women's Righteous Army Corps 女子義兵團 show that, as in most former colonies worldwide, nationalistic movements constituted the first arena in which women formed a single group and engaged in political activities. Major social movements in Korean society during the Japanese colonial era, nationalistic movements and socialist

experiences of ruthless sexual exploitation by the Japanese armed forces and of discrimination with respect to Japanese women[9] prompted ethnic consciousness to take the deepest root, above all, in Korean women's formation of subjectivity, thus preventing women's consciousness from being perceived as such or, at least, from serving as an occasion for subjective formation as important as ethnic consciousness. Consequently, it cannot be overlooked that, to a certain extent, (South) Korean women have facilely relied only on ethnic consciousness as their oppositional consciousness. While aware that the heart of their damages lies in the annihilation of both women's human rights and motherhood and that the ensuing scars have continued to this day, they all too easily perceive their victimizer(s) as Japan itself, not accurately as Japanese men (Korean Council for the Women Drafted for Military Sexual Slavery by Japan, ed., 1993).

3. Nationalism and Feminism in the Issue of Japanese Military Sexual Slavery

In addition to patriarchy, there are many social variables that affect women's circumstances. They include the class circumstances, industrialization levels, labor market, and culture. Numerous conditions surrounding an ethnic group, its relations with other ethnic groups, and nationalistic discourse, too, are among important variables that determine women's circumstances. While other social variables have already been discussed to a considerable degree in women's studies, it is only in the 1980s that women's studies in the West began to turn its attention to the objective circumstances and discourses surrounding ethnicity. Initiated by non-white women scholars in the West, discussions on ethnicity and nationalism have been highlighted as a more important topic in the postcolonial women's studies of the Third World. Taking note of the

movements likewise can be seen as having contributed considerably to the formation of women's subjectivity (Jayawardena, 1986: 8 and 258).

9 Most Japanese women were assigned to military comfort stations catering to officers, and the official fee rates, though not properly implemented in practice, were higher for Japanese women than for Korean ones (see Chapter 4).

issue of women arising from ethnic relations between developed and developing nations, international feminism, too, has started to make theoretical efforts (Choi Chungmoo, 1999).

The issue of ethnicity is more important in South Korean society, which experienced a period of forced occupation by the Japanese empire, than in any other nation. Likewise, women's studies in the country has conducted research that naturally encompasses not only studies on women's history but also the concept of ethnicity from even before the introduction of Western discussions on the issue of ethnicity in the 1990s. With the acceptance of Western discussions on the ethnic issue in the 1990s, more theoretical research on the relationship between nationalism and feminism, too, has accumulated. Multifaceted research likewise has been conducted on the issue of Japanese military sexual slavery, which began to gain public interest in this period, and discussions on several points of contention surrounding the relations between the issue of ethnicity and that of women have been held.

1) Ethnicity, Nationalism, and Feminism

Probably rare are concepts that encompass complex contents on diverse levels as do those of ethnicity and nationalism. As with the relationship between class and class consciousness or between gender and feminism, ethnicity and nationalism are concepts on two levels that must be separated during analysis even though they are intertwined in reality. This is a point that must be premised first when summarizing points of contention regarding nationalism and feminism in discussions on Japanese military sexual slavery. As with class/class relations and gender/gender relations, ethnicity/ethnic relations are social conditions or variables that explicate social phenomena. Like class consciousness and feminism (or patriarchy), nationalism refers to social consciousness.

Discussions on ethnicity and nationalism seem to have developed in a very complex manner due to the difficulty not only of defining "nation," or ethnicity, but also of analyzing nationalism and the movements for the independence of nation-states, which newly emerged after the demise of the Eastern Bloc in the 1990s. Though there are debates on whether ethnicity is a cultural thing that has existed since before the modern era, a product of modernity, or a (re)constructed thing on the spectrum of the premodern and modern eras (Lee Na-Young, 2015), it is difficult to devise a definition of ethnicity that applies to all cases because countries differ from one another in history and culture. While an ethnic group can be defined as a "historically evolved, stable community of people, formed on the basis of a common language, territory, economic life and psychological make-up manifested in a common culture" (Hobsbawm, trans. Kang Miongsei, 1994: 21) or as a "population sharing a historic territory, common myths and historical memories, a mass public culture, a common economy" (Smith, 1995: 56), it is, in fact, difficult to find an ethnic group that matches this. However, an ethnic group becomes a social reality when it is linked to a particular type of territorial state, or the nation-state, and when a state comes to consist of a single ethnic group, that is the most natural condition (Hobsbawm, trans. Kang Miongsei, 1994: 25; and Kedourie, 1994: 52). It is in states unlike this that the issue of ethnicity, or ethnic groups, arises.

While it is a fact that most states consist of multiple ethnic groups, because the world since the modern era has changed with this nation-state as the unit, numerous conflicts have arisen from unequal relations among these nation-states. Consequently, the boundaries of nation-states are comparatively clear. This fact shows that ethnicity must be analyzed as an objective social phenomenon or variable that clearly affects many aspects of society. In comparison with the West, which experienced a complex process of the formation of ethnic groups until the rise of nation-states, in most Asian countries, which have long histories, the degree of the agreement between ethnicity and the nation-state is relatively higher.

Because the agreement between the definition and the reality is thus difficult, Western scholars have also argued that ethnic identity or the concept of nationalism as an ideology is closer to the reality than is ethnicity itself. Representative is the view that considers an ethnic group as an "imagined community," an ideological construct stemming from nationalism (Anderson, 1983). On the other hand, however, more persuasive is the argument that ethnicity must be analyzed in terms of a general aspect that is "far less nationalistic" (Hobsbawm, trans. Kang Miongsei, 1994: 26). Moreover, it is all the more difficult to understand nationalism as a single reality, just as it is difficult to define ethnicity, because its nature differs even further according to ethnic groups and according to the strata of members including class even within the same ethnic group.

Above all, the imperialism and colonialism of powerful nations and the resistant nationalism of weak countries and colonies have fundamental differences and therefore cannot be understood in the same name of "nationalism." Because the period of the formation of modern nation-states consisted of core ethnic groups' contention against one another, rule over the periphery, and formation of the structure of the world economy, and all modern ethnic groups can be seen as products of colonization (Balibar and Wallerstein, 1995: 89). Here, the nationalism of ethnic groups who were subjected to colonial rule and that of ethnic groups who imposed colonial rule cannot be identical. On the other hand, there exist nationalism as it manifests itself externally in terms of consciousness and actions and nationalism as it reveals many effects internally including dictatorship and the oppression of women. In addition, there coexist nationalism as formed by the state or the ruling forces (official nationalism) and popular nationalism (Moon Seungsook, 1998). Nationalisms on such diverse levels combine with one another and produce yet other, numerous forms of nationalism. For example, cases where the defensive nationalism of ethnic groups who have experienced colonial rule combines with official nationalism will surely differ considerably from those where it combines with popular nationalism. It goes without saying that the relationship between feminism and nationalism, too, must be seen amid such complex configurations.

Such discussions demonstrate the fact that the situations of ethnic groups as objective conditions and nationalism as a consciousness or a discourse must be separated analytically and that the situation of women is affected by the objective situations of ethnic groups so that, on the other hand, nationalism and feminism are not placed in a simple relationship.

Considerations of ethnicity within feminism started with the proposal by minority women in the United States and women in the Third World for diverse feminisms stemming from their unique histories and experiences with respect to Marxist feminism, which has been dubbed "second-wave" feminism, and radical feminism (Gluck, et al., 1991). This was an awareness that the situation of women was determined by not only gender (gender relations) but also its encounter with conditions such as ethnicity and class. While discussing the divergent experiences of these minority and Third World women, feminist research naturally came to take note of the relationship between colonialism and women. Newly opened up in discussions were the dimensions of not only the aggravation of the oppression of women by the ethnic oppression of imperialism but also the relations between women in the colonial metropolis and their counterparts in the colonies. Such studies discussed not only the issue of the double oppression imposed on women in the colonies but also women, gender, and sexuality as represented by colonialism. As the expression "virgin land" shows, examples include the representation of the colonies as female bodies and the colonists as male invaders (McClintock, 1995: 1-74).

Feminists influenced by discussions on Orientalism by figures such as Edward Said have criticized that, in thus shaping the image of the East at will, Western imperialists mystified colonies as veiled women and imaged them as beings desirable of being raped, simultaneously turning colonies and women into passive beings. In other words, here, colonized women are subjected to double displacement (Yegenoglu, 1998: 39-67).

While absorbing discussions on postcolonialism, feminism has also developed an extremely negative perspective on nationalism. Generally embracing the concept of "ethnic groups" as the "imagined communities" mentioned above, these scholars have argued that, in the process of creating ethnicity in resisting colonial rule, Third World countries have fixed women as passive, sacred, and subordinate beings (Chatterjee, 1993). Most feminists' view on nationalism is that ethnicity is thus a historical product and has "always" created unequal gender relations. In other words, according to them, ethnicity is a reproduction of the development of modernism in the West in the form of patriarchal discourse (Yegenoglu, 1998: 5). They argue that "all" nationalisms depend on strong gender organization and that women have participated in nationalistic movements only under the leadership and upon the invitation of men (McClintock, 1995: 352-388). Well known as a researcher on militarism and women, Cynthia Enloe likewise argues that nationalism has been forged from masculinized memory and hope (Enloe, 1989: 44).

While Third World feminism showed first signs of life in its rejection of a "single" feminism, it has returned to a focus on nationalism and come to insist, once again, only on a single nationalism, thus ironically turning women into passive objects in the historical process in the end. However, it is necessary also to note that criticism of this point has begun on one hand. Madhu Dubey has pointed out that feminists' criticism of the study of Algeria conducted by Frantz Fanon retains in its entirety the very viewpoint that they criticize—i.e., one that fails to see women as historical subjects. Furthermore, she stresses that such scholars must overcome the Western dichotomy of tradition/modernity (Dubey, 1998: 1-29). In addition, research demonstrating that the relationship between nationalism and feminism can manifest itself in diverse ways according to an ethnic group's conditions has been conducted. Taking note of the process through which women's consciousness budded with their participation in nationalistic movements in colonies, these studies show the historical process through which nationalistic movements and women's movements have cooperated mutually instead of being in a mutually oppressive relationship (Jayawardena, 1986; Mohanty, et al., eds., 1991; West, ed., 1997; Evans, trans. Chung Hyun Back, et al., 1997, etc.).

2) The Points of Contention Surrounding the Relationship between Ethnicity/Nationalism and Feminism in the Issue of Japanese Military Sexual Slavery

As the issue of Japanese military sexual slavery was raised in the early 1990s, research on the victims' awareness, too, was conducted along with the illumination of the facts, and these women were discovered to feel pent-up resentment at both patriarchy and ethnic discrimination (Yi Sang-Hwa, 1993). There also are studies that, in analyzing the social movements to resolve this issue, explain in a comparatively neutral manner the process through which nationalism (within South Korean society) and feminism (women's solidarity in the international arena) have forged tension and union (Shin Heisoo, 1994; and Lee Hyo Chae, 1997). It must be noted that, together with earlier research on social history, the bulk of these studies are by researchers who have been in close contact with the victims and personally participated in the movement.

On the other hand, research that emphasizes the priority of the variable of gender in the awareness of such historical facts and, based on this viewpoint, criticizes the studies discussed above has been presented as well. A study that seeks to grasp the issue of Japanese military sexual slavery from a "women's studies perspective" (Kang Sun-Mi and Yamashita Yeong-Ae, 1993) argues that "[t]his issue is one stemming from the gender contradiction, which is a manifestation of the entanglement of the ethnic contradiction and the class contradiction" and goes on to define itself as "research for elucidating the relationship between sexual violence and the state." Notwithstanding such a declaration of its limits, however, the study is problematic because it, seeing the structure of sexual violence as the relationship of the state-military-capitalism-patriarchy, grasps the Japanese policy on military sexual slavery as an "extension of licensed prostitution 公娼制." Judging from the clear fact that the policy on military comfort stations, which were on an immense scale, was planned from the beginning to be implemented on women in the colonies mostly through coercion—and not on Japanese women, on whom motherhood was forced—it cannot be an accurate analysis to exclude the variable of ethnicity.

There has also been criticism that the investigations of testimonies conducted by the Korean Research Group lack the perspective of women's studies (Kim Seong-Nae, 1994). Concentrating more on the ethnic discourses created following the emergence of the issue of Japanese military sexual slavery than on the objective facts related to the ethnic variable that gave rise to it, one study sees as the heart of these ethnic discourses "the forcible draft of Korean women and the destruction of their morality by the Japanese military" and criticizes that the discourses, "by placing greater symbolic significance on the signifier of sexual violation, deny the particularity of the women's experiences and universalize them as an ethnic issue (Kim Eun-Shil, 1994: 40-41). Similarly, another study (Yang Hyun-Ah, 1998) points out that the issue has been interpreted in South Korea not as the victimized women's stories but as nationalistic discourses spreading from the wounded pride of Korean men with respect to norms concerning chastity. In these studies, "ethnicity" is identical to the position of men, and the point that women's sexuality is reified into a property of male ethnicity is adopted, as in earlier research.

(1) Differences among the Victimized Women per Ethnicity

Women mobilized as Japanese military sex slaves consisted of Koreans, Japanese, natives from occupied territories, and Europeans from occupied territories. There were great disparities among these women, above all, in the scale of mobilization according to their ethnic origins, and disparities emerged also in the mobilization patterns, class composition, treatment, and postwar settlement. Depending on how these differences are seen, differences have arisen among movement participants and researcher groups as well.

As discussed above, women's studies in the West has already expressed skepticism that the argument of Virginia Woolf, who said, "As a woman I have no country… my country is the whole world"—i.e., "women's united voice"—may be an expression of feminist cultural imperialism. Location as a locus where the complexity of regional and temporal tension is adequately reexamined, differences that are recognized through the processes of such historical struggles, and the ensuing deconstruction of the hitherto fixed and universalized concept of gender have been discussed (Kaplan, 1994: 137-150). Just as black and ethnic minority women have urged the deconstruction of the middle class-centered feminism of the West, a Japanese feminist scholar has criticized the imperialistic feminism of her own country, which lacks both self-objectification as the dominant ethnic group and an awareness of female Korean residents in Japan (Fujime Yuki, 1998: 35). When viewed from such a perspective, ethnic disparities among women victimized by Japanese military sexual slavery must not be concealed, and an awareness of these differences is natural as well. It will be possible for solidarity among women to be even stronger when it is founded on such disparities.

What has been the greatest point of contention in relation to ethnicity in terms of the issue of Japanese military sexual slavery is the disparities among the victims according to their ethnic origins. Based on the male-centered idea that male sexual desire is "natural," the issue of military sexual slavery is, above all, an issue of sexuality. However, it is clear that the policy on military sexual slavery, planned to satisfy the entire Japanese armed forces, which were massive in number, would not have been feasible without considering women in the colonies as objects of mobilization. Meanwhile, it is possible to recall that, as for

Japanese women, motherhood was emphasized. Consequently, though the issue of Japanese military sexual slavery is one of gender, it cannot be elucidated without the perspective of the ethnic issue at the same time. On the battlefields, especially with the prolongation of the war, native women were mobilized when women from colonial Korea could not be replenished. Disparities in postwar settlement between women from the colonies and occupied territories and European women from the occupied territories[10] prompt us to raise the issue of racism.

Pointing out such differences in itself has been criticized as a nationalistic tendency as well. The passage from the Japanese government's announcement regarding its second report on Japanese military sexual slavery (1993) that, "Apart from Japanese, many of the comfort women transferred to the war areas were from the Korean Peninsula" can be viewed as a major distortion glossing over both the taking of most victims from colonial Korea and important disparities based on ethnic discrimination in the mobilization and management of military sex slaves.

Ethnic disparities among Japanese military sex slaves are significant because they point out that this sexual crime committed by the state encompassed a multifaceted structure of oppression, or of the issue of relations between strong/weak nations and between empires and colonies and, as such, can be an important topic of international feminism. It can be said that the task of women's studies is to analyze them in a theoretically appropriate manner, rather than overlooking them as harmful to solidarity among women.

(2) Licensed Prostitution and the Japanese Military Comfort Station Policy

Licensed prostitution is the historical background of the policy on Japanese military comfort stations. The basic notion and many of the operational techniques of the policy on military comfort stations originated from licensed prostitution, which was an institutional device

10 The punishment of Japanese soldiers who had forcibly mobilized Dutch women as military sex slaves by the Batavia War Criminal Court held in the Netherlands East Indies in 1948 forms a contrast to the thorough condonement of crimes committed against far more numerous Asian women.

established by the Japanese government in order to authorize both the commercialization of sex developing simultaneously with capitalism and men's licentious desire. However, licensed prostitution and the policy on military comfort stations are strictly distinct from each other. This is because Japanese military sexual slavery was based on a policy whereby the state forcibly mobilized *en masse* and turned into sex slaves women from the colonies and occupied territories in accordance with a total plan during the specific period of war. These characteristics make it impossible to equate military sexual slavery and licensed prostitution, even when the coerciveness and servility of the latter are amply acknowledged, and the ethnic issue is central even among these characteristics. The movement and most research in South Korea to resolve Japanese military sexual slavery start form this perception of military comfort station policy.

However it is erroneous logic to argue that such analysis stems from a perspective denigrating women in licensed brothels and to criticize the analysis as "discrimination against the victims where damages are seen as insignificant when the victims were prostitutes and are seen as crimes when the victims were virgins."

(3) The Ethnic Consciousness of the Victims and Women's Movements in South Korea

Research on victims in South Korea has illuminated, in the victims' minds, a mixture of anger at Japan and resentment at the damages suffered as women (Yi Sang-Hwa, 1993). With the Korean Council at the center, the movement in South Korea, too, consists basically of women's organizations only and is based on a feminist consciousness but also is aware of the importance of ethnic discrimination. In other words, the starting point of the movement is that Japanese military sexual slavery is an issue simultaneously of women and the Korean people. This movement was begun from the encounter of: numerous women's movement organizations in South Korea including church women's movements and the Korea Women's Associations United 韓國女性團體聯合, which had expanded considerably in scope and awareness alike in the 1990s; and a professor and graduate students in the Department of Women's Studies at Ewha Womans University who had continued to maintain an interest in the issue. Concerned that its own consciousness and strength as a women's movement would become dull, the movement adopted a strategy of limiting organizations that included men as cooperating organizations, excluding them from key decision-making, and of creating new, temporary organizations when support from the entire nation was necessary for donations or special international activities.[11] Efforts and policy to avoid the pitfall of the exclusiveness of regarding the entire Japanese people with hostility, as the other, are a noteworthy characteristic of this movement as well. Indeed, problematizing violence inflicted by the Japanese *state* but not indiscriminately directing responsibility for it at Japanese citizens was a clear policy from the initial stage of the movement. Stern rejection of the Asian Women's Fund was due to Japan's relegation of state responsibility to the entire civilian sector. On the other hand, however, there is no particular disagreement that Japanese military sexual slavery is an ethnic issue, and there does not seem to be much tension between nationalism and feminism within the movement. The criticism from certain quarters that the Korean Council, created under the specific activist goal of resolving Japanese military sexual slavery, perceives this issue solely as an ethnic one in some aspects has been debunked as this movement has transformed the victims into subjects and expanded to the provision of support for victims of wartime sexual violence around the world, as has been discussed in Chapter 5. Since 2010, a type of revisionist interpretation of Japanese military sexual slavery that purportedly calls for reconciliation with Japan has been raised and won full support in Japanese society and gained some supporters in South Korea as well.[12] However, it constitutes a denunciation of the victims and support groups that is not based on strict historical facts related to the issue and has caused confusion to the resolution of the issue. Falsely painting an awareness

---

11 For example, organizations called the Headquarters of the National Movement for the Collection of Living Allowances for Former Members of the Volunteer Corps 挺身隊할머니生活基金募金國民運動本部 and the Citizens' Coalition against the Asian Women's Fund and for the Resolution of the Issue of Forcibly Taken Japanese Military Comfort Women 日本國民基金을 反對하는 强制連行當한 日本軍慰安婦問題解決을 爲한 市民連帶, both of which included men as well, were temporarily formed in 1992 and during 1996-1997, respectively, for nationwide fundraising and dissolved later. For the 2000 Women's Tribunal, the Korean Organizing Committee was created with the participation of numerous male historians and international law experts.

12 For example, Park Yu-ha, 2013, etc.

regarding the objective fact of ethnic discrimination as nationalism that must be overcome, too, has been one reason for such confusion.

(4) Patriarchal Nationalism in South Korea

When Japanese military sexual slavery was raised as a social issue in the early 1990s, the response of South Korean society was intense. Responses to it were diverse, ranging from women's organizations active about resolving the issue to conservative positions that complained why a shame of the Korean people was being exposed voluntarily. Such diverse responses, in turn, encompassed diverse forms of nationalism at the basis. As has been discussed already, the victims and organizations for the movement likewise harbor a brand of nationalism. Nationalism does not signify a single form in a single voice. The problem is that discourses based on *patriarchal* nationalism weaken and, furthermore, denigrate the female aspect of this issue. As is well known, the movement to resolve the issue of Japanese military sexual slavery has won broad support from members of South Korean society including men because of nationalistic sympathies. It has been possible both for strong public opinion to form and for donations to be collected because this issue is one of the Korean people. At the same time, however, it was patriarchal nationalism that suppressed the correct resolution of the issue. Arguments such as "Demands for compensation have the danger of turning damages from sexual violence into prostitution" and a climate where "wounded national pride" suppressed individual victims' pain contained the danger of covering up this issue. Precaution against ethnic discourses (Kim Eun-Shil, 1994; Yang Hyun-Ah, 1998; and Yamashita Yeong-Ae, 1999) was against none other than such patriarchal nationalism. However, it must be pointed out that this was only a part of the diverse positions within nationalism in South Korean society, not their entirety. In addition, what must be criticized is patriarchal nationalism, not nationalism itself.

Another aspect that must be pointed out is that positions based on these diverse forms of nationalism have changed unceasingly instead of being static. In the process through which the issue of Japanese military sexual slavery was raised, the extreme patriarchal nationalism of the early stage seems to have changed considerably. Consciousness such as "Don't speak of it because it's shameful" and "We failed to protect our daughters" has changed, and more recent years have seen wide dissemination of the awareness that a large part of the pain suffered by the victims stemmed from the patriarchal climate of post-Liberation South Korean society. It would not be far-fetched to evaluate such progress as having been influenced by the feminism and a consciousness of human rights that emerged in the developmental process of the movement.

(5) The Issue of the Spread of Nationalism in Japan

Also found among the numerous Japanese organizations that either participate in or oppose the movement for the resolution of the issue of Japanese military sexual slavery are various forms of nationalism. Begun in South Korea, the movement spread at first not to other Asian victim nations but to Japan. Also important was the participation of Korean residents in Japan. The positions of the Japanese taking part in this movement, of course, are diverse, ranging from feminism to human rights and pacifism. The various currents in the movement bespeak such diverse value orientations (see Chapter 5). However, found among these people is the basic motivation of "to make Japan a better society." In addition, they have at times expressed strong antipathy toward the United States and other Western nations. This brand of nationalism on their part has emerged as considerable conflict in the course of the movement. When the punishment of the individuals responsible for Japanese military sexual slavery was newly raised in addition to demands for apologies and compensations, many of the Japanese organizations seceded from the movement. The reason was that because most of the individuals responsible at the time of the implementation of military sexual slavery were once again active in key positions in the Japanese government after the war, the punishment of these individuals would have an immense impact on Japanese society. Surrounding the Asian Women's Fund, even more Japanese organizations and individuals became enemies of the movement. They were ones who thought that the Asian Women's Fund would be an appropriate resolution that also demonstrated the Japanese society's conscience to a certain extent (see Chapter 10).

An even more serious problem is that, with this movement as the occasion, right-wing nationalism has spread rapidly in Japan. Indeed, spreading among the public with tremendous force have been: movements for the liberal view of Japanese history, which claims to stand for so-called healthy nationalism and seeks to reinterpret the issue of the previous war; movements among intellectuals including Kato Norihiro,[13] who claims to stand for the neutral ground between the conservatives and the progressives and strives to persuade the public into adopting a self-centered view of Japan as a war victim; and movements to spread such perspectives through comic books. Even within feminist discussions, there exists research from a nationalistic and conservative view of history, and the fact that this has acquired power over the public must be noted.

4. Conclusion

Japanese military sexual slavery is at once an issue of the universal violation of women's human rights that occurs during wars and armed conflicts and of the oppression of colonized women caused by imperial Japan's colonial rule based on ethnic, class, and gender discrimination. Consequently, a gender perspective that squarely faces this issue inevitably encompasses the issues not only of war and human rights but also of ethnic and class discrimination.

It is true that, in Korean history, nationalism has been used as an effective tool for oppressing the voices of women. On the other hand, however, as can be seen from the following, the diversity of both nationalism itself and its relationship with feminism possesses a complexity that cannot be treated so simplistically: a situation where ethnic relations with powerful countries including Japan aggravated women's suffering; the absolute influence of imperialism and colonialism, which are expressions of the ethnic issue, on women's lives; the processes through which women themselves have arrived at social awareness through ethnic consciousness; and the ways in which patriarchal nationalism has been changed by feminism.

---

13 Avoiding the extremes of the argument of responsibility for the war and the argument of non-responsibility for the war, Kato Norihiro has stressed the "neutral" position that Japan must reinterpret the war from the position of war victims. However, the criticism that this creates another ground for evading Japan's war responsibility is persuasive (Kato Norihiro, 1997).

Chapter 12

The Awareness of the International Community: The Universality and Historical Particularity of the Wartime Violation of Women's Human Rights

1. The Universality and Particularity of the Issue of Japanese Military Sexual Slavery

Following its publicization in the early 1990s in South Korea and Japan, Japanese military sexual slavery immediately began to expand in impact in the international community as well. First, NGOs in Asian victim countries quickly responded, and international human rights organs such as the UN and the ILO as well as international NGOs such as the International Commission of Jurists soon expressed interest. Groups in Asian victim nations then gathered to hold the Asian Solidarity Conference, which continues to this day. In December 2000, the 2000 Women's Tribunal, a people's tribunal led by these organizations, was held.

The issue thus gained the attention of the global community because of the widespread agreement that women were the most vulnerable and first victims during wartime. In particular, as the 1990s saw serious violence inflicted on women in interethnic conflicts in regions around the world including Eastern Europe, the international community came to see violence against women in wartime as one of the most important human rights issues. It was in this atmosphere that Japanese military sexual slavery thus came to be established in the perception of the international community as a historical root of wartime sexual violence in the contemporary era. Such problematization of and activities concerning the issue can be evaluated as very important moves expanding the theoretical and practical horizons of feminism in that they located the violation of women's human rights at the crossroads of the two disparate social conditions of patriarchy (discrimination against women) and war. The movement to resolve Japanese military sexual slavery has thus forged solidarity with those regarding diverse forms of wartime sexual violence that occur around the globe even today, prompted various international organs such as the UN to conduct and publish in-depth research and reports, and contributed to the accumulation of analytical research in the social sciences and women's studies.

On the other hand, however, in the process of constructing universal theory and solidarity regarding violence against women in wartime, this method of engaging in the movement has failed to historicize the differences both between Japanese military sexual slavery and other issues such as wartime sexual violence against women in the former Yugoslavia (macroscopic) and among the nations victimized by the institution (microscopic). In other words, it has failed to localize the particular positions of the victims in each country. That is, by stressing the commonality between problems experienced by the diverse groups of victims of Japanese military sexual slavery, each with its own particularity against the historical background of mobilization and exploitation, and those experienced by women victimized during wars today, this movement has blurred key aspects of military sexual slavery.

In the process of forging solidarity with women's organizations in Japan and around the world, the movement to resolve Japanese military sexual slavery has decisively overlooked the following points in its discursive structure: the crucial aspects of racism and the relationships between strong and weak nations in the case of all victim countries in Asia; and the context of imperialism/colonialism in the case of victims in Korea and Formosa. Such an oversight consequently has not only made it difficult accurately to grasp the particular nature of each victim group but also blocked in advance the possibility of important solidarity in the international community based on the issue of violence against women in terms of both the relationships between strong and weak nations and colonialism. Indeed, violence against women in the relationships between strong and weak countries is very general worldwide, and colonialism, which was inflicted systematically, methodically, and on a massive scale through the state bureaucracy, has left enduring traces around the globe.

These forms of violence against women can be said to be even more widespread than is the issue of violence against women in wartime because they occur in everyday life, which, in turn, leads to the wider possibility of solidarity based on them.

Examining both solidarity based on the universality of the movement to resolve Japanese military sexual slavery and the historical particularity of the issue, I have surveyed the international discussions that are both the fruits of this movement and the basis of solidarity. In the process, I have focused on reports published by NGOs and international organs since the early 1990s. Surprisingly, according to these documents from the global community, the movement for the resolution of Japanese military sexual slavery at first took into consideration the particular historical conditions of Asia but gradually established its solidarity and direction of activism based on the universality of the wartime violation of women's human rights. In addition, these reports position Japanese military sexual slavery above all within the larger framework of the wartime violation of women's human rights and, ultimately, as an issue of patriarchy but go one step further by carefully examining the particular historical conditions of each victim group and shedding light on the intersections of racism, imperialism, and colonialism with patriarchy. This chapter therefore will analyze such discussions in the international community and discusses why this historical consciousness has been overlooked in the processes of women's movements.

The documents from the international community mainly used in this chapter are as follows. As documents conveying the positions of the Asian victim countries as well as of Japan, there are materials from the Asian Solidarity Conference, which was begun in South Korea in 1992 and held up to the fifth session in 1998. Established based on solidarity among organizations in both the victim nations and Japan to respond to Japanese military sexual slavery, this conference agreed, during its fifth session held in Seoul, to create a legal court in 2000 (2000 Women's Tribunal). Also importantly used are materials from the UN World Conference on Human Rights, which was held in Vienna in 1993. At this conference, women's NGOs established the Global Tribunal on Violations of Women's Human Rights consisting of panels on the violation of women's bodily integrity including war crime, health, sexuality, and childbirth, women's social and economic rights, and political participation in order to address women's human rights intensively. Here, Japanese military sexual slavery was raised as an important agenda in war crime (Shin Heisoo, 1997: 382-383). A report by the International Commission of Jurists, which is highly respected as an international NGO, likewise is an important reference material. After visiting and conducting research in North and South Koreas, Philippines, and Japan, the International Commission of Jurists published a voluminous report titled *Comfort Women: An Unfinished Ordeal—Report of a Mission* in a book format in 1994. The first comprehensive report on Japanese military sexual slavery, this book includes at the end discussions in terms of international law that continue to be used as an important basis for discussions on the issue in terms of international law. Special reports of the UN Commission on Human Rights and the UN Sub-Commission on Human Rights have become the most authoritative materials on the issue. In 1994, the UN Commission on Human Rights newly created the post of the Special Rapporteur on Violence against Women and appointed Coomaraswamy to it. In her 1996 report, Coomaraswamy created a separate chapter titled "Report on the Mission to the Democratic People's Republic of Korea, the Republic of Korea and Japan on the Issue of Military Sexual Slavery in Wartime," where she discusses Japanese military sexual slavery in detail. Though a few additional reports were created subsequently, the 1996 report is the most detailed one. On the other hand, in 1995, the UN Sub-Commission on Human Rights appointed McDougall as the Special Rapporteur on Systematic Rape, Sexual Slavery and Slavery-like Practices during Armed Conflict, who submitted a report in 1998, where Japanese military sexual slavery is importantly discussed. In 1999, when Special Rapporteur McDougall's report was completed,[1] the UN Sub-Commission on Human Rights passed a resolution whereby the Office of the UN High Commissioner for Human Rights would annually submit a report to the UN Sub-Commission on Human Rights under the same title ("Systematic Rape, Sexual Slavery and Slavery-like Practices during Armed Conflict"), and, in accordance with this resolution, the Office of

1 Though it was completed in 1999, the final report was distributed in 2000 so that its actual submission year is the latter.

the UN High Commissioner for Human Rights began to issued reports in 2000. Although they mainly address the wartime violation of women's human rights today, these reports have important implications for Japanese military sexual slavery (see Chapter 6). An organization that continues to publish important reports on this issue, albeit from a slightly different perspective, is the ILO Committee of Experts. This committee sees and analyzes Japanese military sexual slavery as a violation of the Forced Labour Convention, which is ILO Convention No. 29 (see Chapter 7).

2. Japanese Military Sexual Slavery as an Issue of the Wartime Violation of Women's Human Rights

Amid the trend in international women's movements in the 1990s of examining women's human rights in terms of overall human rights and, at the same time, situating women's human rights in the mainstream of discussions on human rights,[2] Japanese military sexual slavery gained attention basically as an extreme case of violence against women stemming from both a mentality and social structures that denigrate women. Specifically, it came to be conceptualized as sexual slavery and forced labor and to be categorized as a wartime violation of women's human rights together with many current cases.

1) The Issue of the Extreme Denigration of Women

All parties concerned with Japanese military sexual slavery will agree

2 The issue of women has been marginalized throughout discussions on human rights. This may be due to the strategic error of feminism, which has insisted on the exclusive importance of gender. In other words, in order to elucidate the multiple forms of human rights violations from which women suffer, gender must be analyzed in its relationships with other factors such as ethnicity, race, and class. This is because most experiences of the violation of women's human rights are "gendered," and diverse forms of discrimination and human rights violations occur because the victims are women. The separation of women's human rights and discussions on human rights per se has relegated women's rights to a secondary status. In this respect, the reexamination of human rights from a feminist perspective can be seen as a development crucial to both international discussions on human rights and women's movements in the 1990s (Bunch, 1995: 11-17).

that the issue ultimately stemmed from a mentality and social structures that denigrated women. It is also on such a basis that the international community has understood this issue. The UN Commission on Human Rights and the UN Sub-Commission on Human Rights view the issue as an extreme form of violence against women. "Systematic Rape, Sexual Slavery and Slavery-like Practices during Armed Conflict," a report of the Office of the UN High Commissioner for Human Rights submitted annually to the UN Sub-Commission on Human Rights, very clearly and bluntly points out: "Gender-based violence is a consequence of the low status of women and girls in society... Armed conflicts exacerbate discrimination and violence directed at women... To end the cycle of violence, the equal rights of women to participate in the economic, social, political and cultural life of their societies must be promoted and protected" (Office of the United Nations High Commissioner for Human Rights, 2000: paras. 7 and 8; 2001: paras. 6 and 7). The reports of the UN Commission on Human Rights point out that a failure appropriately to condemn Japanese military sexual slavery, which thus was a major crime of both the denigration of women and sexual violence, has contributed to the strengthening of an overall social climate where violence is inflicted on women with impunity today (Coomaraswamy, 2001).

2) Japanese Military Sexual Slavery as Sexual Slavery

Most analyses conducted by the international community have concluded that Japanese military sexual slavery was a form of sexual slavery. Special Rapporteur Coomaraswamy of the UN Commission on Human Rights ascertains that, considering the forced prostitution, sexual pressure, abuse, daily repeated gang rape, and serious physical abuse from which the victims suffered, the term "military sex slaves" is far more accurate and appropriate than is "comfort women" (Coomaraswamy, 1996: 12). Calling military comfort stations "rape centres," Special Rapporteur McDougall of the UN Sub-Commission on Human Rights states that women undeniably were mobilized forcibly (i.e., taken against their will) and lived as slaves subjected to rape, forced prostitution, and sexual violence *en masse* at these facilities (McDougall, 1998). The verdict of the 2000 Women's Tribunal likewise points out that women were enslaved and subjected to repeated rape, bodily injury, and other forms of rape (Korean Council for the Women Drafted for Military Sexual Slavery by Japan, 2001: 123). In other words, Japanese military sexual slavery has been defined as an issue of victimization by the most ruthless sexual violence even within the broad category of patriarchy or the denigration of women.

3) "Comfort" as Forced Labor

Using a very concrete and intricate logic, the ILO Committee of Experts has clearly stated on numerous occasions that Japanese military sexual slavery was a violation of the Forced Labour Convention, which is ILO Convention No. 29.[3] The committee has clearly stated that this system violated the Forced Labour Convention overall and, more specifically, that compensations must be made according to Article 1 Clause 2, Article 14, and Article 15, and exceptions to the prohibition of forced labor stipulated in Article 2 Clauses 2a and 2d do not apply to Japanese military sexual slavery. In addition, it has stated that this illegal implementation of forced labor must be punished as a penal offence according to Article 25 of the convention and can be punished according to Articles 176 and 177 of the Japanese Penal Code (April 24, 1907; Act No. 45) as well (International Labour Organization, 1997a).[4] Such legal judgment by the ILO is highly respected in the international community and has been substantially

---

3 One of the most important basic conventions of the ILO, the Forced Labour Convention (Convention No. 29) has broadly affected the securement of basic human rights beyond labor. Influenced by international discussions on the issue of forced labor triggered by the abolition of slavery (Geneva Convention on Slavery was adopted in 1926), the ILO adopted this convention in 1930 (in effect since 1932), and 179 nations have ratified it as of present. Articles 1 and 11 of this convention prohibit women's forced labor, and Articles 14 and 15 stipulate the obligation to compensate for forced labor. Article 25 stipulates that those responsible for imposing forced labor must be punished according to criminal law. In addition, Article 2 stipulates the conditions of emergencies during which exceptions to the prohibition on forced labor are permissible (see Chapter 7).

4 While the ILO considers prostitution labor, it legally judges Japanese military sexual slavery as a violation of the Forced Labour Convention because the institution was forced prostitution. On this logical basis, the issue of forced labor during the colonial era was raised at the ILO in the same context. Consequently, as for the issue of Japanese military sexual slavery at the ILO, the unusual condition has been solidarity between South Korean women's organizations with labor unions both from the country and around the world, including those from Japan.

quoted in reports by the UN Commission on Human Rights and the UN Sub-Commission on Human Rights as well (see Chapter 7).

4) The Perception of the Issue as a Wartime Violation of Women's Human Rights

Based on this general awareness of the denigration of women, Japanese military sexual slavery, as a more specific category, has been established as an issue of the wartime violation of women's human rights. This is already clear from the fact that when the UN Sub-Commission on Human Rights was prompted to pass a resolution to appoint a Special Rapporteur on Japanese military sexual slavery in 1993, the first such occasion at the UN, the newly created post was to address "Systematic Rape, Sexual Slavery and Slavery-like Practices during Armed Conflict" (Shin Heisoo, 1997: 375).

Later, made public by the UN Commission on Human Rights in 1996, the report by Special Rapporteur on Violence against Women Coomaraswamy states that Japanese military sexual slavery is to be studied within the broader framework of violence against women. However, judging from the fact that, in defining this issue, she begins her discussion after pointing out that the expression "military sexual slavery" is more appropriate than is "comfort women [system]," Coomaraswamy likewise can be seen as narrowing down the issue to one of wartime or military sexual violence (Coomaraswamy, 1996). Her subsequent report from 1998 creates the subcategory of violence against women during armed conflict and, within it, addresses Japanese military sexual slavery along with the issues of Bosnia and elsewhere (Coomaraswamy, 1998). The 2001 report narrows down its topic to "Violence against women perpetrated and/or condoned by the State during times of armed conflict" and discusses Japanese military sexual slavery together with the issue of current violence against women in places with armed conflict such as Afghanistan, Timor-Leste, and Myanmar (Coomaraswamy, 2001).

While the regular reports of the Office of the UN High Commissioner for Human Rights on "Systematic Rape, Sexual Slavery and Slavery-like Practices during Armed Conflict" mentioned above mainly concern current issues only, they do occasionally and briefly mention

Japanese military sexual slavery (see Chapter 6). With such discussions at the UN on the issue within the category of the wartime violation of women's human rights, this view seems to have come to be established as the general perception of the international community. These reports point out that occupation forces' violence against women during wars has been a widely accepted practice and that violence against women has been rampant due to the domination of the armed forces by masculinity (Coomaraswamy, 1998).

Moreover, it is noteworthy that the global community has started to realize that violence against women not only occurs in the process of and as a result of war but also is used as a weapon of war. In 1999, the UN High Commissioner for Human Rights stated at the UN Security Council: "Civilians are no longer just victims of war today. They are regarded as instruments of war" (Office of the United Nations High Commissioner for Human Rights, 2000: para. 5). The reports of the Office of the UN High Commissioner for Human Rights on violence against women in wartime, submitted to the UN Sub-Commission on Human Rights since 2000, have further developed this view and pointed out that systematic rape is used to destroy the society under attack and that the trauma of such sexual violence not only makes individual recovery difficult but also threatens the reconstruction of that society at large after the conflict.[5] The International Criminal Tribunal for the Former Yugoslavia, which was established within the UN and delivered its first judgments in 2001, pointed out that "rapes were used by members of the... armed forces as an instrument of terror" (International Criminal Tribunal for the Former Yugoslavia, 2001).

However, these reports only present Japanese military sexual slavery together with many other forms of wartime sexual violence under the same category of wartime sexual violence without analyzing the differences among them. In other words, there is no analysis that takes note of the fact that, unlike many recent wartime women victims, Japanese military sex slaves neither were primary victims as a result of

5 "During past, recent, and ongoing conflicts, sexual violence has been used as a weapon of war; a method of threatening populations... systematic rape is often being used to humiliate civilians and military, to destroy the society and ruin all possibilities of a peaceful resolution of the conflict..." (Office of the United Nations High Commissioner for Human Rights, 2000: para. 4; and 2001: para. 5).

war nor were used as instruments of war. Although the reports of the UN Sub-Commission on Human Rights, which have attempted the most systematic analysis of the issue to date, define the situation of the military sex slaves at comfort stations as one of continuous gang rape (McDougall, 1998), they fail to proceed to a more in-depth analysis of the fact that Japanese military sexual slavery was not a result of war or a tool of invasion but, rather, a process of forced mobilization and enslavement implemented as a part of war from the very stage of planning war itself.

3. The Issue of Historical Particularity

Because Japanese military sexual slavery is sexual violence inflicted by the Japanese armed forces in the course of their war in Asia, it can amply and logically be addressed within the category of and be linked in solidarity to the issue of sexual violence that frequently occurs during armed conflict among states, ethnic groups, or tribes around the world today. At the same time, however, Japan's instigation of war and forced mobilization of military sex slaves are different from current issues and particular as well. This is because that war was an imperialistic war where Japan, an overwhelmingly stronger nation then, occupied weak Asian countries, and the sexual violence inflicted by Japan was systematic and organized mobilization planned by the state. Likewise, there exist differences even among the nations that were thus subjected to sexual violence. While Formosa and Korea were already Japanese colonies, China remained in a semi-colonial state, and some regions were more like occupied territories. The mobilization and conditions of sex slaves therefore differed considerably according to such regional particularity. Consequently, the nature of Japanese military sexual slavery becomes clear only when it is analyzed in terms not only of the problematics of gender-war-state-ethnicity (tribalism) but also of the issue of strong/weak nations and the perspective of colonialism, combining all these factors in the historical context. Such a view can be found in discussions in the international community.

1) The Awareness of the Issues of Relationships between Strong/Weak Nations and Racial Discrimination

South Korean women's movements first came to publicize Japanese military sexual slavery as a social issue against the important backdrop of the Korea Church Women United's 韓國敎會女性聯合會 earlier movement against Japanese men's sex tourism in the country. In other words, this organization rediscovered Japanese military sexual slavery as a historical root of the current issue of Japanese men's sex tourism in South Korea. In addition, such an awareness was shared by the Japan Anti-Prostitution Association 賣買春問題ととりくむ會 in Japan, which forged solidarity with the Korea Church Women United. An interesting fact is that the Philippines, which came to focus on Japanese military sexual slavery after South Korea and Japan, likewise began its movement when a group that was striving to redress the exploitation of Asian women laborers abroad today came to take an interest in this issue. Presented at the 1st Asian Solidarity Conference, which was held in Seoul in August 1992, the report by the Philippine group declared, "We will collect and widely disseminate to you information on the Japanese military sex slaves of Asia, women laborers in Kuwait, and other cases of violence against women and firmly engage in activities…"[6] (Sancho, 1992).

According to an exposé by a Thai women's organization that participated in the 1st Asian Solidarity Conference, 330,000 Asian workers were mobilized in the construction of a 415 km-long railroad (Thai-Burma Railway 泰緬連接鐵道) connecting Kanchanaburi, Thailand and Thanbyuzayat, Burma, led and completed by the Japanese government in October 1943, 80,000 of whom died in the process, and military comfort stations were built along this railroad. As with its counterparts in South Korea, Japan, and Philippines, this women's organization links the domestic and international trafficking of Asian women for prostitution and the violation of women's human rights by Japanese men's systematic sex tourism alike to Japanese military sexual slavery.[7]

6 [TN] Though this is a back translation of a Korean translation of the English original, it reflects the essential meaning.

7 As of 1992, approximately 1 million women were engaged in prostitution in Thailand,

Asian women's organizations thus came to participate in this movement in the initial period because of the awareness that Japanese military sexual slavery stood at the junction of the issues of the denigration of women and strong/weak countries. In particular, these women's organizations in Asia are seriously concerned about Japan's aggressive stance toward the region today.

Most wartime violations of women's human rights occur among disparate states, races, or ethnic groups. In that respect, the wartime violation of women's human rights can be seen as an issue where ethnic/racial conflict and sexism overlap, and this issue of ethnicity/race is taken for granted in the issue of the wartime violation of women's human rights, thus failing to gain particular attention in terms of either theory or social activism. The case of Japanese military sexual slavery, however, encompasses a mentality of ethnic/racial discrimination that cannot be simply termed ethnic/racial conflict. Citing the 1998 verdict of the Shimonoseki branch of the Yamaguchi District Court in Japan on the Japanese government's responsibility for military sexual slavery, a report by the UN Sub-Commission on Human Rights emphasizes that, "[u]pon examination of facts presented in this case, the [military] comfort women system was extremely sexist and racist [or ethnically discriminatory]" (McDougall, 1998). This is corroborated also by the fact that while there was not a single instance of punishment for crime against countless Asian women, nine Japanese soldiers were punished by the Batavia War Criminal Court in the Netherlands East Indies in 1946 for having forcibly drafted Dutch women as military sex slaves (McDougall, 1998).

2) An Examination of Forced Colonial Sexual Mobilization

All reports discuss in detail the colonial and historical conditions of the mobilization of Japanese military sex slaves. The earliest of these documents, the International Commission of Jurists report describes in its first chapter the historical background of the mobilization of military sex slaves in each country. As for Korea, it describes in detail the overall

with 800,000 of them estimated to be aged 16 or below (Mahissaya, 1992: 71-73).

illegality of colonial exploitation stemming from the illegality of the Japan-Korea Treaty of 1905 韓日協商條約[8] as well as the situations surrounding forced labor and the draft 徵用, discusses the mobilization of women as laborers, and stresses, "It is within this context that the taking of women for the [military] comfort stations has to be understood."[9] In the case of the Philippines, the report likewise discusses the historical context in which labor and women's sexuality were forcibly mobilized through fraud and violence in an unwanted war (International Commission of Jurists, 1994: 25-27).

Coomaraswamy of the UN Commission on Human Rights, too, makes it clear that, in the process through which the Koreans were mobilized *en masse* with the reinforcement of the National Mobilization Law 國家總動員法 during the Japanese colonial era, the mobilization of military sex slaves occurred through fraud and violence. In particular, according to her analysis of the forced draft and transportation of sex slaves, in which the Japanese armed forces and bureaucracy were involved, Japanese military sexual slavery was implemented in the historical context of colonial rule and therefore was under a category separate from that of general violence against women in wartime (Coomaraswamy, 1996).

Interestingly, the Japanese government, while admitting this very colonial nature of Japanese military sexual slavery, has argued, "the laws of war would only apply… to conduct committed by the Japanese military against nationals of a belligerent State and would not, therefore, cover the actions of the Japanese military with respect to… Korean nationals, since Korea was annexed to Japan" (McDougall, 1998). In response, NGOs in both North and South Koreas have maintained the stance that because the colonization of Korea itself was illegal and forced occupation (Coomaraswamy, 1996), laws of war can be appropriately applied to the country instead.[10] Considering that China and the Philippines likewise

8 [TN] Also known as the Eulsa Forced Treaty 乙巳勒約 in Korean, the Japan-Korea Protectorate Treaty 日韓保護條約 in Japanese, and the Yisi Treaty 乙巳條約 in Chinese, among other names.

9 International Commission of Jurists, 1994: 21-24.

10 At the 2000 Women's Tribunal, the joint North-South Korean prosecution team argued for the application of laws of war to the Japanese imperial authorities' mobilization of Korean women (see Chapter 8).

were in a semi-colonial state rather than being Japan's direct opponents in war, Japanese military sexual slavery overall must be understood as the forced and colonial mobilization of sex during wartime.

4. The Reasons for the Oversight of Historical Particularity in the Internationalization Process of the Movement

In the international community, the particular historical condition of Japanese military sexual slavery was thus discussed very specifically and carefully. Similarly, when this issue was first raised at international organs such as the UN, the more specific historical context of Japan's war crimes was seen as important. It was for these reasons that the Korean Council collaborated with Canadian prisoners of war organizations when it first raised the issue at the UN in 1992.

With increasing limitations to solidarity among women's organizations, however, activities in the international community for the resolution of this issue have come to be positioned as those for the issue of the wartime violation of women's human rights. After establishing Japanese military sexual slavery as a major international issue related to women's human rights by participating in the Global Tribunal on Violations of Women's Human Rights held at the UN World Conference on Human Rights, which was held in Vienna in 1993, the Korean Council cooperated with international rallies of women related to recent wartime violations of women's human rights such as those committed in the former Yugoslavia, at the same time beginning to draw public attention in South Korea to the issue of war and women together with those such as women during the Jeju Island April 3 Struggle 濟州四·三抗爭 (1947-1954) and the Gwangju Democratization Struggle 光州民主化抗爭 (1980) as well as women in military camp towns.[11] The reports of the UN Commission

11 In 1998, the study group on Japanese military sexual slavery within the South Korean National Assembly held a symposium at which the issue of sexual violence during armed conflict such as those of sexual violence in areas including Sri Lanka and Thailand during civil wars as well as of the Jeju Island April 3 Struggle and military camp towns in South Korea were discussed.

on Human Rights and the UN Sub-Commission on Human Rights were highlighted only as discussions on the issue of the wartime violation of women's human rights, and, held on the last day of the 2000 Women's Tribunal, the Public Hearing established Japanese military sexual slavery as an issue of the wartime violation of women's human rights along with many other current international issues.

Although all these efforts have played a role in making the international community become aware of Japanese military sexual slavery, they have also restricted the issue to one of the wartime violation of women's human rights and overlooked colonialism, which is its important historical nature. The reasons for such oversight can be found in the several aspects below.

1) The Issue of Solidarity

Women's movements in South Korea, which first raised Japanese military sexual slavery, have agreed that this issue is basically one of the denigration of women and, at the same time, one of colonial rule by the Japanese empire, which exploited and mobilized the Koreans *en masse*. In fact, in South Korea, women's movements have partly forged solidarity with NGOs that are primarily interested in the issue of ethnicity. In the international arena, other NGOs addressing Japan's war crime as well as labor unions both in Japan and around the globe that are seriously concerned with forced labor can become important allies. Nevertheless, such solidarity in the international community has been forged only partly per agenda, and South Korean organizations concerned with Japanese military sexual slavery overall have focused on solidarity with women's organizations that see the issue as one of the wartime violation of women's human rights. For example, although the South Korean movement to resolve the issue does forge solidarity with labor unions at the ILO and with groups of lawyers and intellectuals in court battles in Japan and the United States, such solidarity has been restricted only to the specific issues at hand.

Japanese military sexual slavery has come to be positioned as an issue of the wartime violation of women's human rights because, that way, solidarity with women's organizations can be broader and more lasting. In particular, solidarity with women's organizations in Japan is indispensable to the movement to resolve the issue so that, in the process, discussions on the colonial situation in Korea have had to be overlooked for the sake of solidarity.[12] The considerable difficulty of transcending the regional particularity mentioned above in forming solidarity regarding the issue of colonial rule, too, has ended up limiting solidarity to women. It is amid such a situation that organizations in Asian victim nations likewise have come to stop in their awareness of the damages at the word "wartime" instead of further exploring their own historical conditions—i.e., they had been semi-colonial occupied territories rather than belligerent powers.

2) The Importance of Turning the Issue into a Current One

One of the most important reasons for restricting Japanese military sex slaves to an issue of the wartime violation of women's human rights has been the effort to make current this issue, which occurred over 50 years ago. It is necessary to clarify why this issue lay buried for over five decades and to note that such silence and concealment are the products of the combination of conditions in the social structure—i.e., the vestiges of Japanese colonial rule and war—and patriarchy. In other words, the conditions for the rise and the subsequent concealment of this issue are one and the same. Nevertheless, such a historical axis has been sacrificed in order to position Japanese military sexual slavery as an issue among innumerable cases of the violation of women's human rights that continue to occur even today, thus leaving only the horizontal axis to be stressed. Furthermore, the issue has been simplified into one of the violation of women's human rights during armed conflict among ethnic and tribal groups, which have become frequent especially since the 1990s. Indeed, the verdicts of the International Criminal Tribunal for the Former Yugoslavia confirm similar forms of the enslavement of women committed in the area.[13] In thus turning Japanese military sexual slavery

12 For example, at the 1st Asian Solidarity Conference held in 1992, one lawyer on the Japanese side said that they could no longer forge solidarity if the South Korean side were to mention ethnic issues. Subsequently, whenever ethnic discrimination in the mobilization and other treatment of military sex slaves in and from colonial Korea and Japan were mentioned, the Japanese side likewise reacted sensitively in many cases.

into a current issue, solidarity in the international community such as the abovementioned UN World Conference on Human Rights held in Vienna in 1993, the UN World Conference on Women held in Beijing in 1995, and the Public Hearing at the 2000 Women's Tribunal has been crucial, and this solidarity, in turn, has led to the view that Japanese military sexual slavery is an issue of the wartime violation of women's human rights and a historical root of such recent issues.

3) The Issue of International Law

In fact, vestiges of damages inflicted by colonialism exist to a critical degree everywhere even today. However, the issue of Japanese military sexual slavery has failed to forge solidarity based on an awareness of this continued influence of the past also because the international community has yet to discuss the issue of the damages of colonialism in terms of international law. International laws and conventions on laws of war, slavery, forced prostitution, and forced labor have been created, and such crimes have been actively discussed despite the difficulty of actually implementing these laws and treaties. On the contrary, however, international law on colonial rule and its damages themselves still does not exist. The fact that international law is Eurocentric and therefore overlooks the issue of colonial rule, which is mostly a one-sided crime committed by the West, can be seen as the reason.

At a 2000 session of the UN Sub-Commission on Human Rights, mainly African members raised the damages of colonial rule as an issue of crime against humanity, problematized the prolonged failure to condemn this, and requested the UN Secretary-General to investigate the matter (United Nations Sub-Commission on the Promotion and Protection of Human Rights, 2000). The issue was passed in the form of a decision and reported as a note from the UN Secretary-General in 2001.[11] While there

---

13 For example, "girls were physically and psychologically detained, because even if they had managed to flee... they would have had nowhere to go" (International Criminal Tribunal for the Former Yugoslavia, 2001).

14 This report comprehensively and mainly discusses crime against humanity but does not specially allot space to colonial rule. However, it is nevertheless unprecedented because it makes possible the questioning of diverse criminal acts that were committed during

may be a possibility of newly expanding solidarity by linking the issue of Japanese military sexual slavery and that of colonial rule in the future, the question of how to address the historical context of Africa, which includes slave trade as well as the segregation and forced integration of tribes and differs from that of Asia, is a problem, too.[15]

5. Conclusion

Women's movements around the world have already started to reject uniformity. In other words, they have begun to realize that, even within the West, the feminism of middle-class women and that of impoverished working-class women differ from each other and that the historical contexts and demands of women of Latin American heritage and those of women of Asian heritage differ from one another. Moreover, women's movements in Asia, Africa, and Latin America differ from one another, and the situations in the Arab world, India, and East Asia inevitably differ from one another even within Asia. Indeed, it is no exaggeration to say that an awareness of such disparity, the recovery of commonality for solidarity, and the issue of resolving this theoretical dilemma are the greatest difficulties facing women's movements and women's studies worldwide today. In other words, the very same difficulties invariably and likewise lie before the specific issue of Japanese military sexual slavery. Whether the movement for the resolution of Japanese military sexual slavery, which is one of the civil movements that have most effectively forged international solidarity while focusing on a specific issue, can once again forge new solidarity while maintaining this tension between universality and historical particularity, and how theoretical work on such a question can be developed are other tasks facing the movement. More

the colonial era (United Nations Secretary-General, 2001).

15 In fact, as South Korean representatives including myself expressed willingness to form solidarity, an African member of the UN Sub-Commission on Human Rights who played a leading role in raising the issue of colonialism exhibited wariness, telling us not to make use of the issue of the damages that they had sustained due to colonial rule when it was just beginning to receive international attention for the first time (my own experience at a 2001 session of the UN Sub-Commission on Human Rights).

specifically, this issue concerns a close analysis of the hitherto neglected historical context of colonialism, the theoretical elucidation of the mutual determination of colonialism and violence against women during wars, and the search for the new direction of the movement.

Supplements

I

Research on Japanese Corporate Sexual Slavery

During the era of the wartime system, not only the armed forces but also the corporations of Japan mobilized sex slaves with the logic of the "improvement of productivity." Light was already shed on the issue of corporate sexual slavery 企業性奴隷制 long ago, albeit piecemeal, and the issue was once again discussed in earnest in the early 1990s. However, because public interest in South Korea overwhelmingly inclined toward the issue of military sexual slavery, research failed to be activated. Consequently, existing studies on the issue of corporate sexual slavery are nearly absent, and testimonies are very difficult to obtain as well. This is because the survivors advanced in age and public interest including the South Korean government's support has been weak. This chapter can be seen as a task of tracking the faint reality of the issue of corporate sexual slavery in such a situation.

Research on corporate sexual slavery is a task that very importantly includes policy and practical implications for the recovery of victims' human rights and, above all, seeks to unearth a piece of forgotten or unknown history. While the issue of military sexual slavery has been discussed as one formed under the complex social conditions of the state, class, gender, and war and thus made significant theoretical contributions to the understanding of women, that of corporate sexual slavery presents yet another form of the mechanism of exploitation through state-corporation collaboration where corporations, a sector of civil society, mediated between the state and the women victims.

Although it has been steadily conducted since the Liberation and, in particular, continued as a minute part of studies on forcibly taken laborers, which have been active since the 1970s (Fact-finding Team on the Truth about Forced Korean Laborers in Japan, 1974), research on corporate sexual slavery has failed to gain public attention. During 1991-1992, when in-depth research on Japanese military sexual slavery began to be conducted, piecemeal studies by researchers and activists in areas in Japan previously populated by many Korean forced laborers such as Fukuoka and Hokkaido were made public in the country (Higuchi Yuichi, 1992; Ogino Fujio, 1994; and Nishida Hideko, 2003), and research on military sexual slavery partly touched on this issue, but in-depth research was not forthcoming. However, scholars in both South Korea and Japan have resumed research on corporate sexual slavery in more recent years because of the discovery and awareness that not only the Japanese government and military but also Japanese private corporations collaborating with the war were responsible for the forced taking of laborers and the mobilization of sex slaves.

Because the primary purpose of the research in this chapter lies in unearthing a piece of forgotten or unknown history, emphasis has been placed, above all, on the discovery of materials. Although direct Japanese government documents on the taking of Korean women as corporate sex slaves have yet to be discovered, I have found documents on Chinese corporate sex slaves and comfort stations at coal mines, which make it possible to surmise the circumstances of Korean corporate sex slaves. In addition, I have obtained documents issued by Japanese corporations that established corporate comfort stations, memoirs by experiencers of such facilities, and materials compiled by local researchers interested in the issue. However, I have failed to obtain victims' testimonies, which are the most crucial materials for reconstructing historical facts. This is because, amid the prolonged oblivion regarding the issue of corporate sexual slavery and the absence of policy support, no one has yet revealed herself to the world to have been a victim of the institution. Consequently, in the research for this chapter, I have been able only to interview forcibly taken laborers who still remember corporate comfort stations and those who lived near these facilities. On the other hand, field research in Fukuoka and Hokkaido has been conducted as well.

1. The Names for Corporate Sex Slaves

Before proceeding to the main body, the term "corporate comfort women 企業慰安婦" must be discussed first. Since the existence of these sex slaves—who were taken for the purpose of "comforting" laborers forcibly taken to destinations such as corporations and coal mines in Japan to increase the latter's labor morale—first gained researchers' attention, the terms used to describe them have proliferated. This is because, as in the case of military sexual slavery, wartime policy documents from the Japanese government and materials from Japanese corporations did not use an established official term. Indeed, the terms used to describe these women in Japanese government documents are diverse, including: "prostitutes 娼婦" (Department of War Preparation, Bureau of Maintenance, Ministry of War, 1940); "comfort women" and "special women 特殊婦女" (Planning Board, Ministry of Greater East Asia, 1942b and 1943); and "bar girls 酌婦" (Institute for Science of Labour, 1943). Amid this absence of an official name, the terms used in more recent years by scholars have varied as well. They include "industrial comfort women 産業慰安婦" (Higuchi Yuichi, 1992; and Han Jeonghui, 1998), "workplace comfort women 事業場慰安婦" (Yoshimi Yoshiaki and Hayashi Hirofumi, eds., 1995), "coal mine comfort women 炭鑛慰安婦" (Nishino Rumiko, 1992), "labor comfort women 労務慰安婦" (Ogino Fujio, 1994; and Nishida Hideko, 2003), and "corporate comfort women" (Chung Chinsung, 1994) and have been used without much explanation as to the reasons for using them.

This chapter will call these women "*corporate* comfort women" to stress the fact that they were mobilized and exploited for corporate productivity in contrast to "*military* comfort women," who were mobilized and exploited for the Japanese armed forces. Because the establishment of corporate comfort stations and the mobilization of sex slaves were basically made possible by the Japanese government's policy-based intervention, the Japanese government is primarily responsible. At the same time, however, the term "*corporate* comfort women" can be seen as valid because corporations were the official and actual agents of the entire process and it stresses the responsibility of corporations in addition to that of the Japanese government. However, in the context of the problematics pointed out in the introduction and Chapter 1 that the term "sex slaves" should be established instead of "comfort women," I propose the use of the term "corporate sexual slavery" to refer to this issue from now on. In this section, the terms "corporate sexual slavery" and "corporate sex slaves" will be used interchangeably with "corporate comfort women system" and "corporate comfort women."

2. The Prehistory of Corporate Comfort Stations: Naturally Formed Korean "Restaurants"

It is difficult to find clear official documents regarding when and on the basis of which policy corporate comfort stations, which were established to raise the labor efficiency of Korean workers forcibly taken to coal mines and other workplaces in Japan during the war, were initiated. Nevertheless, several studies conducted so far, records and reports from the South Korean government and NGOs, and the Japanese government's documents on the introduction of Chinese sex slaves into Japan all reveal that Korean "restaurants 料理屋," which actually functioned as brothels as well and centered on ethnic Korean communities in Japan amid social conditions in Japan in the 1920s-1930s including an increase in the number of Korean residents and ethnic discrimination in licensed Japanese brothels 公娼, were closely linked to wartime corporate comfort stations. That is, in terms of their human resources such as managers and sex slaves, management methods whereby they doubled as comfort stations, and their building structures, already existing Korean "restaurants" became important resources for corporate comfort stations. In Under Japan's licensed brothel system prostitution 公娼制, ethnic Korean women were barred from becoming prostitutes 娼妓, who were licensed prostitutes, and the role of unlicensed prostitutes 私娼 was forced on them in the form of bar girls or waitresses 女給 instead. Japan's policy of regulating unlicensed prostitution was to implement examinations for STDs strictly in order to manage unlicensed brothels on the same level as licensed brothels rather than to prohibit unlicensed brothels altogether. In other words, amid strong criticism of licensed prostitution both at home and abroad, Japan adopted a policy of reducing licensed brothels externally (Commission on Verification and Support for the Victims of Forced Mobilization under Japanese Colonialism in Korea, 2011: 29-33). Consequently, Korean "restaurants" were treated as unlicensed brothels on the legal level but were managed by the police as venues of open prostitution. In addition, they came to be included in the category of de facto licensed brothels managed by the Japanese government in accordance with the government's policy of strengthening the prevention of STDs, which was implemented as a part of the National Spiritual Mobilization Plan 國民精神總動員計劃 put in motion throughout Japan in 1938, before the full-fledged establishment of corporate comfort stations.

However, despite the close relationship between Korean "restaurants" and corporate comfort stations, corporate comfort stations fundamentally differed from earlier Korean "restaurants" because they were established through a government policy based on collaboration between the state and corporations. In this respect, the expansion of Korean "restaurants" must be seen as the prehistory of the establishment of corporate comfort stations.

1) The Definition and Reality of "Restaurants"

(1) The Definition of "Restaurants"

According to the *History of the Hokkaido Prefectural Police* published in 1938, the Japanese government clearly distinguished between "restaurants 料理屋" and "eating houses 飲食店," as in <Supplementary Table 1-1>:

〈Supplementary Table 1-1〉 The distinction between restaurants and eating houses

Business Type	Classification	Business Practices	Permitted/ Reported
Restaurants	Traditional Japanese restaurants 割烹料理屋	Japanese-style rooms are installed, and professional entertainers 藝妓 or bar girls await by the tables, providing food, alcoholic beverages, and entertainment to clients	Permitted businesses
	Restaurants	Japanese-style rooms are installed, and only bar girls await by the tables, providing food, alcoholic beverages, and entertainment to clients	

⟨Supplementary Table 1-1⟩

Business Type	Classification	Business Practices	Permitted/ Reported
Eating houses	Cafés カフェ-	Western-style tables are installed, and waitresses serve food to clients	Reported businesses
	Eating houses	Japanese-style or Western-style rooms or tables are installed, and food is served to clients without the use of waitresses or similar types of female servers 給仕婦	
	Teahouses 喫茶店[1]	Western-style tables are installed, and food is served to clients without the use of waitresses or similar types of female servers, but alcoholic beverages are not sold	

Source: Editorial Board of the *History of the Hokkaido Prefectural Police*, ed., 1968: 309.

1 [TN] Touted and popular as "modern" social venues serving Western(ized) foods and drinks including coffee and black tea, Western-style "teahouses," "coffeehouses," and "cafés" began to be established in earnest in Japan in the early 1910s, excluding alcoholic beverages in certain cases. Though some businesses differed from their Western counterparts in employing young female servers, these women were not initially perceived or presented as the establishments' main—i.e., eroticized—"attractions" and performed regular duties such as serving and bussing. Following the Great Kanto Earthquake of 1923, however, waitresses as well as alcoholic drinks became the primary focus of one type of such businesses, with female servers engaging in conversation with and receiving tips from (male) clients at their tables. Moreover, illicit sexual activities between clients and waitresses, both on and off premises and often under the owners' tacit approval or even encouragement, became a social problem so that the Guidelines on the Regulation of Cafés, Bars, Etc. カフェ-・バ-等取締要項 (1929) and the Regulations on the Regulation of the Operation of Special Eating Houses 特殊飲食店営業取締規則 (1933) came to be legislated, thus placing such establishments under police control. With these laws, the distinction between the two types of businesses became official: "pure" teahouses 純喫茶, "ordinary" teahouses 普通喫茶店, teahouses 喫茶店, and "ordinary" eating houses 普通飲食店 on one hand; and "new" teahouses 新興喫茶, "social(izing)" teahouses 社交喫茶, "special" teahouses 特殊喫茶, "special" eating houses 特殊飲食店, and "cafés" カフェ- on the other. At least before the enactment of these laws, a "teahouse" or a "café" therefore could refer to various things depending on the context, with even the general survey provided in this footnote differing somewhat from the definitions of these business types in the supplementary table itself. Such changing yet overlapping terms and practices were perhaps motivated, in part, by a desire to avoid government restrictions or public criticism. See Murata Mizuho 村田瑞穂, "'Cafe' Culture in Modern Japan 近代日本におけるカフェ-の變遷," ed. Association of Historical Studies 史學會, Kyoto Women's University, *Kyoto Women's University Journal of Historical Studies* 史窗 64 (2007): 45-53; Asaba Yuiko 麻場友姫胡, "The Arrival of Tango in Japan: Allure, Fear, and Morality in Early 20th Century Japan," ed. Japan Society, *Japan Society Proceedings* 155 (2018): 106-123, etc.

入道の半島労務者たちに
同郷女性の慰めを
各地に朝鮮料理屋新設

An article on a plan to introduce corporate sex slaves in the *Otaru Shimbun,* a local newspaper in Hokkaido (Oct. 13, 1939)

Numerous materials prove that these "restaurants," in fact, served as unlicensed brothels where clandestine prostitution occurred. In early 1938, the Sapporo Municipal Police pointed out that the over 50 Korean "bars バ-" (i.e., "restaurants") in downtown Sapporo where ethnic Korean "bar girls" worked were "bars" in name only and were, in reality, brothels (*Hokkai Times*, March 7, 1938). Even the Fact-finding Team on the Truth about Forced Korean Laborers in Japan, which, for decades, has investigated the forced taking of Koreans, likewise has pointed out that the Korean "bars" in Hokkaido simply were unlicensed brothels (Fact-finding Team on the Truth about Forced Korean Laborers in Japan, 1974: 438).

(2) The Police Licensing of the Establishment and Operation of "Restaurants"

Considering that their establishment required police permission, these "restaurants" evidently engaged in prostitution behind closed doors, with tacit approval from the police. Consequently, due to such close links between the managers of these "restaurants" and the police, it was of no use when women working at such establishments, most of whom had been lured by fraud, filed reports to the police.

(3) The Reality of Korean "Restaurants"

In March 1938, the *Hokkai Times* reported that over 150 ethnic Korean "bar girls" were working at approximately 50 Korean "bars" (i.e., "restaurants") distributed in the districts of Sapporo including Shiroishi and Toyohira (*Hokkai Times*, March 7, 1938) while the daily *Otaru Shimbun* reported that there were 52 Korean "restaurants" and 80 Korean "bar girls" in Sapporo (*Otaru Shimbun*, March 19, 1938). However, as in <Supplementary Table 1-2> and <Supplementary Table 1-3>, according to <Tables of the Occupations of Korean Residents per Gender> announced by the Hokkaido Government 北海道廳 in July 1928, there were 80 "restaurant employees 料理屋雇傭人" (11 of them male), 88 "bar girls," and two "professional entertainers" (Hokkaido Government, 1928), thus showing that the number of Korean "bar girls" did not increase noticeably in the 1920s-1930s:

〈Supplementary Table 1-2〉 The number of employees of Korean "restaurants" in Hokkaido (1928)

(Unit: No. of people)

	Men		Women		
Total	Restaurant employees	Total	Restaurant employees	Bar girls	Professional entertainers
6,765	11	213	69	88	2

Source: Hokkaido Government, 1928.

〈Supplementary Table 1-3〉 The number of Korean "bar girls" in Fukuoka (Kanmon District;[2] 1929)

(Unit: No. of people)

Classification	No. of Korean Men	No. of Korean Women	No. of Professional Entertainers/Bar Girls
Shimonoseki	2,191	763	21
Moji	115	380	12
Wakamatsu	889	335	27
Yahata	1,961	645	18

Source: Fukuoka Prefectural Bureau of Employment Brokers, *The Situation of Korean Resident Laborers within the Jurisdiction*, 1929; requoted from Higuchi Yuichi, 1992: 16.

2 [TN] Though lumped together in the source material under "Fukuoka [Prefecture]," this comprises what are now the neighboring cities of Shimonoseki in Yamaguchi Prefecture and Kitakyushu in Fukuoka Prefecture, respectively. The latter was created after the war by combining the three areas in the table besides Shimonoseki.

2) The Social Conditions of the Formation of Korean "Restaurants"

Amid international criticism that the courtesan 遊女 system in existence since the Edo period constituted slavery, the Meiji government, which was unable to relinquish its management of prostitution in the name of preventing STDs among soldiers, started to reorganize Japan's modern licensed prostitution in 1873. The primary condition of the formation of Korean "restaurants" in terms of social structures was the development of licensed prostitution in Japan. However, licensed Japanese brothels were nearly inaccessible to ethnic Koreans, who began to increase in number in the 1920s. Consequently, the social structure and conditions by which Korean "restaurants" came to be formed were the increase in the number of ethnic Koreans in Japan, licensed Japanese prostitution, and ethnic discrimination.

With the formation of ethnic Korean communities in Japan following the Great Kanto Earthquake of 1923, Korean "restaurants" began to spread from those areas, with Kanagawa Prefecture and Osaka being the most representative of them. Numerous Korean "restaurants" were also established outside these ethnic Korean communities, close to licensed Japanese brothels, and catered to Japanese users. With names such as "Korean Pavilion 朝鮮亭," "Korean Restaurant 朝鮮屋," "Pyongyang Restaurant 平壤屋," and "Busan Restaurant 釜山屋," these Korean "restaurants" were usually two-storied, with each story divided into many small rooms (Higuchi Yuichi, 1992: 18). In the case of Sapporo, Korean "restaurants" began to open in numbers near licensed Japanese brothels in the early 1920s and spread throughout the city.

According to the testimonies of those who had experience with them, these Korean "restaurants" began to increase noticeably following the Manchurian Incident of 1931, when many laborers came from colonial Korea to the numerous mines near Sapporo, with their number amounting to approximately 20 in locations such as Toyohira, Minami Ichi-jo, and Susukino.[3] According to the testimonies of their experiencers,

3 [TN] All three are areas within the city.

these establishments engaged in forced prostitution despite their names ("restaurants") (Fact-finding Team on the Truth about Forced Korean Laborers in Japan, 1974: 441). Their number rose to over 100 by 1935, with the users including the Japanese as well. For ease of control, the Japanese police therefore designated areas in which Korean "restaurants" could operate, which were called Korean "markets 朝鮮場." In contrast, Korean "restaurants" in Hakodate and Otaru are said to have catered to the Japanese. Later, some of the "bar girls" and managers who had to leave these "restaurants" in accordance with the wartime policy of business closure or change relocated to comfort stations at coal mines and corporations (Higuchi Yuichi, 1992: 24; and Sapporo Municipal Workers Union Committee for the Establishment of the Research Institute for Local Autonomy and Local Government, et al., eds., 1987: 38).

3) The Process of Mobilizing "Bar Girls" and the Situation in "Restaurants"

While Higuchi Yuichi (Higuchi Yuichi, 1992: 16) states, somewhat weakly, that some of the women working at Korean "restaurants" were deceived by fraudulent promises of "good" workplaces, Professor Yun Chung-Ok, who has conducted a meticulous field survey of women at Korean "restaurants" in Sapporo (Yun Chung-Ok, 1991b: 21-23), describes in greater detail the process through which these women were forcibly mobilized. According to her, Korean women led harsh lives in contemporary Korea so that they ended up coming to Japan, deceived by Japanese *shusen-ya* 周旋屋 (work brokers) who promised an ample diet and wages. However, these *shusen-ya* supposedly would confine these women to their own houses to prevent search for other jobs, feed them well, show them around the town, and then sell them at high prices. Mostly aged 15-20, these girls and women committed suicide in droves, singly or collectively, when forced into prostitution. Because articles on such women were frequently published in Japanese newspapers, the Japanese government prohibited the press from covering the suicides of ethnic Korean women in 1943.[4]

4 According to Ikeda Haruo 池田晴男, a local civilian researcher whom Professor Yun Chung-Ok interviewed in Sapporo, these women often threw themselves from Cape

According to the *History of the Hokkaido Prefectural Police*, in 1939, the prefecture's Division of Police 警察部 established the Guidelines on the Regulation of Restaurants and Eating Houses 料理屋飲食店取締要綱, which included the following clause: "Do not traffic in women including professional entertainers, bar girls, and waitresses in collusion with brokers." This proves just how widespread the trafficking of these women was (*Asahi Shimbun*, 13th prefectural edition, March 17, 1992).

According to the testimonies of those who lived in Hokkaido at the time, Korean "restaurant" managers would travel to rural communities in colonial Korea, promise "good" jobs in Hokkaido, and take away girls and women at a debt of approximately 10 yen to the parents. The suffering that these women had to undergo while working as de facto prostitutes at these "restaurants" was dire indeed. They had to accost prospective clients in the streets even on cold late nights, their debt steadily increased from approximately 10 yen, most of them suffered from STDs, and they received mercury injections, only to have their health completely ruined in just 2-3 years. Nor was there any way of escaping. Even when these women sought refuge with the police, the latter, already bribed by the "restaurant" managers, would briefly preach to these women and return them to the "restaurants." In fact, according to many testimonies, the lives of women at such Korean "restaurants" were even more wretched than those of women at licensed Japanese brothels. The Fact-finding Team on the Truth about Forced Korean Laborers in Japan thus describes the situation of these Korean women: "The policy of [ethnic] discrimination was implemented even in hell" (Fact-finding Team on the Truth about Forced Korean Laborers in Japan, 1974: 441-442).

Tachimachi 立待岬 (*Tachimachi-misaki*), a cliff in present-day Hakodate, so that the roar of the waves breaking against the cliff sounded like the cry "Mother, mother" to the local residents (Yun Chung-Ok, 1991b: 21-22).

3. The National Mobilization Plan and the State Control of Korean "Restaurants" (Transformation into Licensed Brothels): 1938

Korean "restaurants," which expanded while thus functioning as de facto comfort stations in such diverse social conditions, came under state control as they were included in the larger framework of the National Mobilization Plan 國家總動員計劃 of 1938. This, in fact, was a transition period preparing for the establishment of corporate comfort stations, which soon occurred as a result of collaboration between the Japanese government and corporations around 1939, and paved the way for the government's intervention in corporate comfort stations. The inclusion of control over Korean "restaurants" in the National Mobilization Plan also shows just how the mobilization of sex occurred in the context of general mobilization.

1) Measures against STDs as a Part of the National Mobilization Plan

Following entry into full-scale war with its invasion of China in 1937, Japan established the National Mobilization Plan and began to reorganize not only politics and military affairs but also the economy under a system of wholesale government control. At the same time, starting in October 1937, it initiated the National Spiritual Mobilization Movement 國民精神總動員運動, thus deeply infiltrating even into the daily lives and minds of the people. The Guidelines on the Regulation of Businesses Related to Public Morals 風俗ニ關スル營業ノ取締要綱 and the Measures against Venereal Diseases 花柳病ニ關スル對策 were implemented in such a context, and because both were applicable to Korean "restaurants," these establishments began to be directly regulated by the Japanese government.

In particular, this policy on STDs had the more direct purpose of preventing the spread of STDs among soldiers at the front. As will be discussed later, it is worth noting that while those mainly subjected to diagnosis for STDs were women working at "restaurants" and "eating houses," the policy itself was called the Venereal Disease *Prevention* Law 花柳病豫防法. In other words, the focus of this law was on males. The

Japanese Ministry of Health and Welfare 厚生省 thus describes the reason for revising the Venereal Disease Prevention Law: "The development of the heavy industries as a result of war has led to a munitions boom so that the number of youths frequenting brothels has increased, which has increased the number of those suffering from STDs. Consequently, preventive measures are urgently needed" (Editorial Board of the *50-Year History of the Ministry of Health and Welfare*, ed., 1988: 456).

"Eating houses" and "restaurants" thus came to require business licenses, and their managers and female employees such as "bar girls" likewise were subjected to a license system. Now, these women had to undergo examination and testing for STDs as well. In other words, through measures on STDs, the Japanese government was, in fact, officializing "eating houses" and "restaurants," which hitherto had been semi-recognized brothels, as new institutions of prostitution in addition to the existing licensed brothels, which the government had regulated. This can be seen as the most important heart of the policy.

(1) The Guidelines on the Regulation of Businesses Related to Public Morals

The Hokkaido Government Division of Police established the Guidelines on the Regulation of Businesses Related to Public Morals in July 1938 because of the "need to reinforce the reformation and purification of social mores in response to the National Spiritual Mobilization Movement." As for main clauses on "restaurants," these guidelines stipulate in principle: the new opening, relocation, extension, and remodeling of such businesses are not to be permitted; business hours must be shortened to 12 PM; and "restaurants" in farming, fishing, and mountain villages must be guided to close or change business. There were some exceptions to the prohibition on the new opening or relocation of these "restaurants" for several areas including places with a sudden population increase (Editorial Board of the *History of the Hokkaido Prefectural Police*, ed., 1968: 303-305), which can be seen as having served as the legal basis for the subsequent establishment of corporate comfort stations for forcibly taken laborers (Nishida Hideko, 2003: 23).

(2) The Venereal Disease Prevention Law

According to the Japanese Ministry of Health and Welfare, "[Proclaimed in 1927,] the Venereal Disease Prevention Law was implemented only partly due to financial reasons, and the establishment of clinics, the heart of the law, had yet to be implemented. However, because the issue of venereal diseases (VDs) was an important part of the National Mobilization Plan and preventive measures were strongly needed, the 73rd session of the National Diet in 1938 approved of the budget necessary for the establishment of these clinics so that the Venereal Disease Prevention Law was fully implemented on April 20, 1938 by an imperial edict" (Editorial Board of the *50-Year History of the Ministry of Health and Welfare*, ed., 1988: 456-457). In other words, the Venereal Disease Prevention Law, previously enforced with a focus on the punishment of infectees to the exclusion of the treatment of STDs under the pretext of insufficient budget, came to be fully implemented, to include treatments, on April 20, 1938 (Park Jung-ae, 2016: 314-315). This led to not only the establishment of such clinics themselves but also support for medical examination fees by the Japanese government, and the clinics provided counseling as well.

Having been ordered by the Minister of Health and Welfare on June 7, 1938 to establish a clinic in accordance with the Venereal Disease Prevention Law and received permission, at the same time, from the chief of the Hokkaido Government Division of Police regarding the location and design of the clinic, Sapporo completed the construction of a municipal clinic on December 19, which cost 12,000 yen including a government subsidy of 6,000 yen.[5]

(3) The Establishment of Unions

In such a situation, to strengthen its regulation even further in

5 Located at Nishi Go-chome, Minami Roku-jo, Sapporo and owned by Nippon Seishu Co., Ltd. 日本清酒株式會社, the site had been the location of Café March Salon カフェ-三月サロン but was subsequently purchased at 8,000 yen (Sapporo City Hall, 1938: 102; and *Hokkai Times*, September 1, 1938). However, this clinic functioned as a hospital treating all kinds of diseases instead of restricting itself to STDs and, according to 1939 statistics, examined and treated five inpatients and 118 outpatients. These figures were but a minute fraction of the total number of inpatients and outpatients, which amounted to 42,619 (Sapporo City Hall, 1939: 46-47).

accordance with the Measures against Venereal Diseases, the Sapporo Municipal Police established a policy by which it would reorganize restaurant and eating house unions 料理屋飲食店組合 throughout the city into six unions (those for restaurants, cafés, "pure" teahouses, *soba* (buckwheat noodle) eateries 蕎麥屋, Korean "bars," and Nakanoshima[6] restaurants, respectively) and completely integrate and unionize all other some 550 smaller establishments without union membership under either the Eating House Union 飲食店組合 (mostly for establishments selling food such as *oden* (fishcake stew) eateries 御田屋 and *sushi* eateries 壽司屋) or the Restaurant and Eating House Union (mostly for establishments providing entertainment with "bar girls" and other such women) (*Hokkai Times*, April 10 and 14, 1938). In particular, the police planned to enforce medical examinations on the 330 "bar girls," 230 "professional entertainers," 762 "waitresses," and 1,420 "female employees 雇女" working at other "restaurants" and "eating houses" throughout Sapporo before the establishment of the clinic (*Hokkai Times*, June 12 and 15, 1938).

2) Control over Korean "Restaurants" and the Formation of a Korean "Restaurant" Union

Among the main objects of such STD prevention measures on the part of Hokkaido were Korean "restaurants." Already in March 1938, the Sapporo Municipal Police reported: grasping that Korean "restaurants" were hotbeds of STDs and had deplorable morals and hygiene, the police attempted but failed, in response, to gather them in a particular location to monitor them together. It therefore gathered the ethnic Korean managers of these establishments, urging them to provide health counseling and medical examinations to the "bar girls." As with other "eating houses," Korean "restaurants" were prohibited from newly opening or relocating (*Hokkai Times*, March 7, 1938; and *Otaru Shimbun*, March 19, 1938).

Here, it is necessary to note that, out of the six unions reorganized above, the Korean Restaurateurs' Self-Governing Union 朝鮮人料理店自治組合 constituted a separate, single union. Indeed, according to

6 [TN] The name of a neighborhood in Sapporo.

contemporary press coverage (*Otaru Shimbun*, April 1, 1938), "[i]n accordance with demand from the Sapporo Municipal Police and the need for a regulatory union, 49 managers of Korean restaurants and eating houses in Sapporo have created the Sapporo Self-Governing Union 札幌自治組合 consisting solely of Koreans, established the union leader, officers, and regulations on March 30, 1938, and reported this to the Sapporo Municipal Police on [March] 31. As a result of this organization of a union, Korean women will acquire health and hygiene information from diverse experts... receive medical examinations twice a month as a part of the union's business, and be provided with travel expenses for return to Korea upon the cancellation of their contracts."

Although Korean "restaurants" did not suffer particularly severely from the problem of STDs, they seem to have been made to form an independent union for the ease of regulation. This also shows that Korean "restaurants" were apart from mainstream Japanese society because they catered almost exclusively to ethnic Koreans and employed Korean women. Such separate control over Koreans seems to have served as an important condition for the establishment of Korean corporate comfort stations in the succeeding period.

4. The Establishment of Corporate Comfort Stations: 1939-1945

1) The Purpose behind the Establishment of Corporate Comfort Stations and the Ethnic Separation Policy

On July 4, 1939, the Japanese government decided through a Cabinet council the forced taking of laborers from colonial Korea.[7] The establishment of corporate comfort stations precisely coincided with this forced taking of laborers. In other words, it was in October 1939 that the Hokkaido Coal Mining Industry Association 北海道石炭鑛業會

7 Initially, under the expression of "volunteer recruitment," de facto forced taking was implemented. The intensity of coercion increased as the name of the policy changed to "official mediation 官斡旋" in 1942 and "the draft 徵用" in 1944, respectively.

requested the Hokkaido Government newly to establish no fewer than 26 Korean "restaurants" at 18 coal mines. According to press coverage from this period, the association felt that "[a]lthough, within the year, 8,000 Peninsulars [i.e., Koreans]… are to come, the method of consoling these laborers from the [Korean] Peninsula has become a problem so that… in the end, relief by a group of Peninsular women has been demanded…" and therefore requested the Department of Security 保安課 in the Hokkaido Government for the establishment of Korean "restaurants" (*Otaru Shimbun*, October 13, 1939). That is, the establishment of corporate comfort stations was a part of the forced taking of laborers to Japan.

Just as one of the purposes behind the establishment of military comfort stations lay in promoting soldiers' battle morale, likewise, these corporate comfort stations were established basically to boost workers' labor morale. Indeed, a 1942 report on the inspection of coal mines in Hokkaido by the Planning Board 企劃院 under the Ministry of Greater East Asia 大東亞省 (Planning Board, Ministry of Greater East Asia, 1942a) clearly stated that, as of July 1942, 16,460, or 27%, out of a total of 60,262 miners were Koreans and pointed out that increasing productivity and preventing abscondence were important issues. The number of Koreans continued to rise so that, according to a 1945 report by the Hokkaido Institute for Work Sciences 北海道立勞動科學研究所, 37.5%, or 38,364, of all coal mine workers throughout Hokkaido were Koreans. As for Chinese laborers, there were 4,058, or 4%, out of total coal mine workers (Hokkaido Institute for Work Sciences, 1945). The working conditions of laborers forcibly taken from colonial Korea and China were very adverse, and labor accidents, too, were rampant so that injuries and deaths continued unabated. In such a situation, workers' labor efficiency could hardly improve (Shirato Hitoyasu, 1992). This was because the Japanese government and corporations decided, without improving the working conditions themselves, that labor efficiency would improve if they could satisfy laborers' sexual desire even slightly. In other words, the ultimate goal of corporate comfort stations lay in improving labor efficiency (*Asahi Shimbun*, 13th prefectural edition, March 13, 1992), and, as such, comfort stations were used as a tool of labor management (*Asahi Shimbun*, 13th prefectural edition, March 17, 1992). This is proven by the fact that the

Department of Labor 勞務課 was in charge of these facilities. The greatest related problem that plagued the government and corporations of Japan in terms of the management of forcibly taken laborers was that of these workers' abscondence.[8] This is why the Japanese government established, as a policy preventing laborers' abscondence, the policy of introducing sex slaves in addition to that of summoning laborers' families to Japan.

On the other hand, the numerous corporations at coal mines feared that STDs would lead to a decrease in the number of laborers who were willing thus to work abroad. This seems to have been a strong motive behind the establishment of corporate comfort stations as well. Indeed, most corporate comfort stations devoted attention to the possible infection of laborers by STDs, with coal mine hospitals or police physicians conducting hygiene inspections of sex slaves and corporations providing prophylactics (condoms) free of charge (*Asahi Shimbun*, 13th prefectural edition, March 16, 1992). Similarly, in reports on these migrant laborers, gonorrhea and syphilis were important categories under "Diseases" (Futase Mining Station, Nittetsu Mining Co., Ltd., 1946: 96), and one of the most important tasks at comfort stations following their establishment was the hygiene inspection of sex slaves, all of which show that the prevention of STDs was a crucial goal of comfort stations.

Judging from these purposes under which corporate comfort stations were established, it seems only obvious as to why these facilities were separately established per national origin for forcibly taken laborers, who had been separated, taken, and made to work by their respective national origins and even native regions.[9] In other words, Korean sex slaves were assigned to Korean laborers and Chinese sex slaves were assigned to Chinese laborers, respectively, to maximize the effect of "comfort" and to

---

8 In statistics from organizations such as the Institute for Science of Labour, the category "dismissal" actually meant abscondence in most cases (Shirato Hitoyasu, 1992: 37).

9 It is a well-known fact that forcibly taken laborers were housed and exploited for labor separately by national origin. Indeed, diverse policy plans created in the process of newly introducing Chinese laborers into Japan included the stipulation that these laborers were not to be mixed with their Japanese and Korean counterparts (Planning Board, Ministry of Greater East Asia, 1942b, etc.). In addition, the Japanese authorities implemented a policy of separating, as much as possible, even Korean laborers by the regions from which they had come. This was for both productivity increase and ease of control.

facilitate control.

2) The Process of Establishing Corporate Comfort Stations

(1) Corporations' Request for Permission to Establish Comfort Stations and Permission from the Hokkaido Government

In October 1939, the Hokkaido Coal Mining Industry Association, a coalition of numerous corporations, requested the Department of Security in the Hokkaido Government for permission to establish Korean "restaurants." The reason was to provide forcibly taken (Korean) laborers with "consolation" (*Otaru Shimbun*, October 13, 1939). When examined in greater detail, the number of these "restaurants" was to be: five establishments in Yubari[10] for Hokkaido Colliery & Steamship Co., Ltd. 北海道炭鑛汽船株式會社; three establishments each in Bibai and Yubetsu[11] for Mitsubishi Mining Co., Ltd. 三菱鑛業株式會社 (present-day Mitsubishi Materials Corp.); two establishments each in Utashinai and Ponbetsu[12] for Sumitomo Mining Co., Ltd. 住友鑛業株式會社 (present-day Sumiseki Materials Co., Ltd.); and one establishment each in Mojiri[13] (Yubetsu Colliery & Railway Co., Ltd. 雄別炭礦鐵道株式會社), Heiwa[14] (Hokkaido Colliery & Steamship), Mayachi[15] (Hokkaido Colliery & Steamship), Noborikawa[16] (Hokkaido Colliery & Steamship), Horonai[17] (Hokkaido Colliery & Steamship), Oyubari[18] (Mitsubishi Mining), Bibai (Mitsui Mining Co., Ltd. 三井鑛山株式會社 (present-day Nippon Coke & Engineering Co., Ltd.)), Showa[19] (Meiji Mining Co., Ltd. 明治鑛業株式會社), Uryu[20] (Asano Dozoku Co., Ltd. 淺野同族株式會社), Shinhoronai[21]

10 [TN] The city 市, not the identically named district 郡. All subsequent allusions to "Yubari" will refer to the city unless otherwise specified.
11 [TN] Located in the present-day city of Kushiro.
12 [TN] Located in the present-day city of Mikasa.
13 [TN] Also known as "Moshiri," located in the present-day city of Akabira.
14 [TN] Located in the present-day city of Yubari.
15 [TN] Also located in the present-day city of Yubari.
16 [TN] Also located in the present-day city of Yubari.
17 [TN] Located in the present-day city of Mikasa.
18 [TN] Located in the present-day city of Yubari.
19 [TN] Located in the present-day district of Uryu.
20 [TN] Also located in the present-day district of Uryu. The mine has been known as "Asano Uryu Coal Mine" and "Asano Coal Mine" as well.
21 [TN] Located in the present-day city of Mikasa. The mine has been known as

(Hokkaido Colliery & Steamship), and Higashihoronai[22] (Higashihoronai Coal Mining Co., Ltd. 東幌内炭礦株式會社). According to press coverage from the era, the Department of Security in the Hokkaido Government planned more or less to accommodate this request in cooperation with the Sapporo Bureau of Mine Superintendence 札幌鑛山監督局, and a comfort station opened in Yubari on January 7, 1940 (*Otaru Shimbun*, October 13, 1939 and January 7, 1940; and *Hokkai Times*, October 14, 1939 and April 3, 1940). The January 21, 1940 issue of the *Otaru Shimbun* thus reported in considerable detail: "The Department of Security in the [Hokkaido] Government has issued permission for the opening of Korean restaurants, with the number of restaurants restricted to one per 500 laborers and the number of waitresses restricted to three per restaurant" (*Asahi Shimbun*, 13th prefectural edition, March 17, 1992).

On the other hand, there were also cases in which individual corporations established comfort stations with official permission but without the mediation of the Hokkaido Coal Mining Industry Association. For example, in April 1940, Sorachi Mining Station[23] owned by Hokkaido Colliery & Steamship established a comfort station named "Rest Home 憩の家"[24] (*Ikoi-no Ie*) on the model of the one in Yubari, which had been established earlier by the same corporation (*Hokkai Times*, April 3, 1940). Likewise, another "Rest Home" was newly established near the Loyal Life Dormitory 忠生寮 (*Chuseiryo*), the Korean laborers' dormitory in Sakae-machi for Oyubari Mining Station owned by Mitsubishi Mining, on September 24, 1940 and had 20 women provide (sexual) services (*Yubari Times*, September 29, 1940).

(2) Police Intervention

The police not only regulated comfort stations after their establishment but also seems to have played a key and important role in their establishment. Indeed, in 1943, Teshio Mining Station owned by Nisso Mining Co., Ltd. 日曹鑛業株式會社 in Toyotomi-cho, Teshio

---

"Shinmikasa Coal Mine" as well.

22 [TN] Located in the present-day city of Iwamizawa. The mine has been known as "Nara Coal Mine," "Miruto Coal Mine," and "Hokusei Coal Mine" as well.

23 [TN] Located in the present-day city of Utashinai.

24 [TN] Also written as 憩いの家.

District, Hokkaido sent a letter to the chief of the Teshio Police Station, where they "express[ed their] appreciation for [the police's] special consideration in the establishment of the [Korean] Peninsular restaurant [朝鮮]半島人料理店" and "hope[d] for continued and adequate guidance as [this kind of establishments] differ[ed] from general restaurants."

5. The Forced Mobilization of Corporate Sex Slaves

Unlike the case of Chinese comfort stations, which were to introduce Chinese women at the same time that Chinese laborers were introduced, Japanese policy documents on the forced taking of Korean laborers do not mention the mobilization of Korean sex slaves. However, based on materials such as hitherto discovered newspaper articles and studies, the three following mobilization methods can be confirmed: mobilization and assignment from existing "restaurants"; employment fraud and human trafficking; and physically forced taking. All of these methods can be said to have been forms of forced mobilization by the Japanese government and corporations.

1) Mobilization and Assignment from Existing Korean "Restaurants"

When corporate comfort stations first began to be established in 1939, comfort station managers and sex slaves seem to have been mobilized from existing Korean "restaurants" in many cases. According to an article in a Hokkaido newspaper from 1939, "Because it will be difficult to bring from Korea women who are to work at comfort stations for Korean laborers, a plan has been established to relocate the 300 women who are working at approximately 130 existing restaurants dispersed among six cities as well as other towns and villages in Hokkaido to newly established restaurants. When the plan is implemented, Korean restaurants will disappear from the cities" (*Asahikawa Shimbun*, October 14, 1939).

On the other hand, according to press coverage, Hokkaido Colliery & Steamship established in March 1940 three comfort stations, each named "Rest Home," in the Takadai area in Fukuzumi, Yubari for the over 1,000

Korean laborers there, ten women to work at these facilities arrived as the first shipment, and five more were to arrive (*Yubari Times*, March 17 and 24, 1940). Meanwhile, the same corporation also set up, at its Sorachi Mining Station, a comfort station once again named "Rest Home," which, in fact, was a "restaurant" relocated from Sapporo so that the six women who worked at the latter establishment were to provide (sexual) services (*Hokkai Times*, April 3, 1940).

Such press coverage shows that the women who worked at corporate comfort stations were mobilized and assigned from existing Korean "restaurants" by the Japanese government and corporations.

2) Employment Fraud and Human Trafficking

In a testimonial investigation conducted by the Fact-finding Team on the Truth about Forced Korean Laborers in Japan 朝鮮人强制連行眞相調査團, Kang Myeongtae, who had been forcibly taken to Yubari by Hokkaido Colliery & Steamship in 1940, thus stated: "We [Korean laborers] were allowed to go out for recreation once a month… Even though there were places called 'Korean restaurants', I honestly didn't want to go there. This was because… bad people who were working at the coal mine would go to Korea and bring girls aged 17-18, promising them jobs at places like spinning factories, only to have them receive clients [and provide sexual services] on the night of their arrival" (Fact-finding Team on the Truth about Forced Korean Laborers in Japan, 1974: 435-436).

3) Forced Taking by the Japanese Government

As has been discussed above, the establishment of comfort stations, which was implemented in relation to the introduction of Korean laborers, often made use of existing Korean "restaurants." Even considering this situation, it would nevertheless have been difficult to meet the demand of the laborers, who drastically increased each year starting in 1939, for such women solely with the female employees of Korean "restaurants" already living in Japan. Consequently, there is ample possibility that the forced taking of women occurred at the same time that laborers were introduced into Japan. The Fact-finding Team on the Truth about Forced Korean

Laborers in Japan, which closely investigated the forced taking of Koreans to Hokkaido and published the results in a report in 1974, points out that a plan to take women forcibly for work at corporate comfort stations seems to have been actually implemented together with the forced taking of laborers, which was begun in 1939 (Fact-finding Team on the Truth about Forced Korean Laborers in Japan, 1974: 435).

As with the case of military sexual slavery, it is difficult to find documentary materials that clearly show the forced taking of women for corporations by or with aid from the Japanese government. The January 7, 1940 issue of the *Otaru Shimbun* thus reported of Yubari: "It has been decided that Row House 長屋 (*Nagaya*) No. 3 will be established near the Migrants' Harmony Dormitory 移住協和寮 (*Iju Kyowaryo*), where Korean laborers are housed, and rented to [Korean] restaurant managers, to which 45 Korean women will be mediated 斡旋" (*Asahi Shimbun*, 13th prefectural edition, March 13, 1992). Although the article is unclear as to what "mediated" signifies here, considering that "official mediation" meant forced taking in the case of laborers and the Women's Labor Volunteer Corps 女子勤労挺身隊 (see Chung Chinsung, 1997c), this term can be seen as designating the forced taking of women. The newspaper article also shows that corporations established comfort stations, hired managers, and took sex slaves on their own, without depending on the managers. Judging from the fact that the establishment of comfort stations was implemented after obtaining official permission, the "mediation" of women likewise may very well have relied on help from the government authorities.

A pioneering researcher on this issue, Japanese scholar Higuchi Yuichi categorically states that, among women who worked at corporate comfort stations, many had been newly brought from colonial Korea (Higuchi Yuichi, 1992: 28). Most of these cases can be seen as forced taking involving the Japanese government. Shiba Takeo 芝竹夫, who is one of the foremost experts on this issue and a civilian researcher in Tagawa District, Fukuoka, concludes that the women most likely were taken at the same time that the laborers were introduced into Japan (*Nishinippon Shimbun*, evening edition, February 21, 1992). According to the testimony of yet another civilian researcher, in most cases, when corporations requested the respective governments of the prefectures in which they were located for sex slaves, the prefectural governments would, in turn, request the military and the police for mobilization, then receive the women and hand them over to the corporations.

In addition, there are strong implications for the forced taking of Korean sex slaves by the Japanese government and corporations in the Japanese government's documents on the forced taking of Chinese laborers. The Japanese government ordered the introduction of Chinese sex slaves at the same time that Chinese laborers were introduced into the country. The taking of Chinese laborers occurred later than and was modeled on that of Korean laborers, to meet the increasing demand for laborers, which could not be fulfilled by Korean laborers alone. A policy established by the Department of War Preparation 戰備課 in the Bureau of Maintenance 整備局, Ministry of War 陸軍省 in 1940, "Policy on the Introduction of Coolies into Mainland Japan: Guidelines on the Recruitment of Coolies. Guidelines on the introduction and treatment of coolies are to be stipulated separately 苦力內地移入ニ關スル方針: 苦力募集要綱. 苦力移入取扱要領ハ別途規定セラルルモノトス" thus states: "As for wages, their payment categories, and working condition categories, wages are to be in proportion to those of the Korean laborers introduced; and the working conditions are to be in proportion to those of the Korean laborers." Consequently, the argument that the taking of Chinese sex slaves, too, was modeled on the case of Koreans is amply convincing. Next, let us briefly examine the Japanese government's discussions on Chinese sex slaves.

4) The Policy on Taking Chinese Sex Slaves in the Japanese Government's Documents

Although discussed in March 1940 in the Bureau of Fuels 燃料局 in the Ministry of Commerce and Industry 商工省 between the Japanese government and corporations and actively mediated by the Department of War Preparation in the Ministry of War, the introduction of Chinese laborers failed to be implemented due to issues such as labor management and public order. Later, faced with a serious shortage of miners, organs including the Planning Board reviewed the matter in diverse ways and established the Labor Mobilization Plan 勞務動員計劃 in 1942. However, the actual implementation even of this plan was delayed due to differences in language and customs as well as political schemes. Finally, a consensus among the army, navy, and Planning Board was reached, which, in turn, led also to discussions on specific issues such as introduction methods, usage, and conditions of use between the East Asia Development Board 興亞院 and the civilian sector. The eventual decision to introduce Chinese laborers into Japan proper came to be realized through a decision made at a Cabinet council on November 29, 1942 (Editorial Office of the *70-Year History of Hokkaido Colliery & Steamship Co., Ltd.*, ed., 1958: 399-400).

In this process, various ministries of the Japanese government drew up plans to introduce Chinese laborers. In 1940, the Department of War Preparation in the Ministry of War proposed the introduction of Chinese laborers and clearly recorded, under the "Health and Welfare Facilities" category, the "Introduction of Korean and Chinese prostitutes in consideration of sexual desire" (Department of War Preparation, Bureau of Maintenance, Ministry of War, 1940). The Planning Board dispatched the Chinese Labor Situation Inspection Team 華人勞動事情視察團 to China and discussed the question of whether to introduce comfort women simultaneously in addition to that of provisions and wages with the Japanese embassy in Peking (present-day Beijing) and local organizations such as the North China Labor Association (NCLA) 華北勞工協會 (Ogino Fujio, 1994: 64). Here, all of the plans to introduce Chinese laborers into Japan included items on sex slaves without exception: "Comfort facilities are to be established appropriately" (Planning Board, Ministry of Greater East Asia, 1942b); "40-50 comfort women per 1,000 laborers are to be brought into Japan; the work is to be contracted to the Chinese, and they [i.e., Chinese bringing in the women into Japan] are to be provided with round trip fare" (Planning Board, Ministry of Greater East Asia, 1942c); "Policies on comfort stations and recreational facilities are to be discussed" and "Though the establishment of comfort stations will be discussed among the separate relevant government organs, the expenses incurred are to be paid by the users" (Planning Board, Ministry of Greater East Asia, 1942d); and "Nine comfort women per 212 laborers are to be brought into Japan at once together [with the laborers]" and "The issue of comfort stations is to be decided on later" (Planning Board, Ministry of Greater East Asia, 1943).

In addition, the *Monthly Foreign Affairs Bulletin* 外事月報, which was published during 1943-1944 by the Foreign Affairs Section 外事係 in the Department of Security, Bureau of Police and Public Security 警保局, Ministry of Home Affairs, thus mentioned sex slaves in its report on the introduction of Chinese laborers. The detailed items for implementation discussed among various relevant ministries on the introduction of coal mine laborers from China state, "As for comfort stations, the establishment methods are to be stipulated separately." In addition, as for loading and unloading at the port of Fushiki (present-day Fushiki-Toyama), Toyama Prefecture, where a comfort station was actually established later, the contract signed between North China Transport Co., Ltd. 華北運輸株式會社[25] and Fushiki Kowan Unso Co., Ltd. 伏木港灣運送株式會社 (present-day Fushiki Kairiku Unso Co., Ltd. 伏木海陸運送株式會社) reads, "The recruitment methods, expenses, and transportation methods for [Chinese] comfort women: Under consideration by the North China Labor Association, and [the comfort women are] to be brought [to Japan] together [with Chinese laborers] as legally as possible (six expected to be needed)" and "The management methods for the comfort station: Under consideration" (*Monthly Foreign Affairs Bulletin*, March 1943). As for loading and unloading at the port of Kobe, where the introduction of Chinese laborers was newly implemented, women were to be brought, as a part of "comfort facilities," under the pretext of "laundresses" (*Monthly Foreign Affairs Bulletin*, September 1943). At a vice ministers' meeting held on February 28, 1944, the Policy on the Introduction of Chinese Laborers into Mainland Japan 華人勞務者內地移入ニ關スル方針 was decided on, and the full-fledged introduction of Chinese laborers into Japan was implemented immediately. As one of the conditions for using the laborers, this policy ordered that appropriate measures be taken at factories and workplaces regarding "comfort stations" and "recreational facilities" (*Monthly Foreign*

25 [TN] Known in Chinese at the time as 華北運輸股份有限公司, this corporation is not to be confused with the similarly named North China Transportation Co., Ltd. (NCTC)—華北交通株式會社 in Japanese and 華北交通股份有限公司 in Chinese, respectively—which was the mother company and, in turn, itself under North China Development Co., Ltd. (NCDC) 北支那開發株式會社. Even when they were nominally joint Sino-Japanese ventures, businesses in China involved in the provision of Chinese laborers and/or comfort women either were under de facto Japanese control or ultimately served Japanese national interest.

Affairs Bulletin, March 1944). In addition, there were discussions on sex slaves actually introduced by Fushiki Kowan Unso including conflict between the Japanese government and corporations regarding the cost of bringing in these women and treating their STDs.[26]

The Hokkaido Coal Mining Industry Association at the time created the Guidelines on the Introduction of Chinese Laborers into Mainland Japan 華人勞務者內地移入要領, which can be seen as a synthesis of the policies of diverse government organs above. As with the various policies mentioned earlier, these guidelines ordered the strict separation of the Chinese from the Koreans in workplaces and housing and stipulated, "Appropriate measures regarding comfort stations and recreational facilities are to be established; as for the establishment of comfort stations, separate relevant government organs are to be consulted, and the expenses are to be imposed on the users; and [the obtainment of] 40-50 comfort women (special women 特殊婦女) per 1,000 laborers is to be contracted to the Chinese" (Editorial Office of the *70-Year History of Hokkaido Colliery & Steamship Co., Ltd.*, ed., 1958: 400-407).

These documentary materials on Chinese sex slaves show that the government and corporations of Japan alike were deeply involved in the taking of sex slaves from China.

---

26 In Fushiki, 224 Chinese laborers began to work on April 18, 1943. On May 11, staff members of the Japanese embassy in Peking, chief of the Department of Guidance in the North China Industrial Association 華北工業協會, chief of the Department of Labor in North China Transport, and executive director of Fushiki Kowan Unso signed a labor contract. This was accompanied by a compromise on the cost involved in bringing in sex slaves. It was because the introduction of sex slaves had already been decided on by this time so that concrete move-in conditions had to be determined. There was disagreement here: while the Japanese embassy demanded eight sex slaves and an expenditure of 10,000 yen, Fushiki Kowan Unso complained that such demands did not take into consideration the actual conditions in Japan. More specifically, the embassy demanded the following as the conditions for the sex slaves' residence: a total of 1,000 yen per sex slave, consisting of a prepayment of 700 yen and travel expenses and other miscellaneous expenses of 300 yen (*Monthly Foreign Affairs Bulletin*, May and August 1943).

6. The Reality of Corporate Comfort Stations

1) The Number and Conditions of Sex Slaves

According to an investigation conducted in 1940 by the Japanese government, in Hokkaido, the number of Korean managers of "restaurants" and "eating houses" amounted to 32 (25 men and seven women) and that of Korean "professional entertainers," "prostitutes," and "bar girls" amounted to 333 (Bureau of Statistics, Cabinet, 1940: 60). It is unclear how accurate these figures are and how many of the sex slaves who worked at corporate comfort stations established in 1939 or later are included here. Nevertheless, the age distribution in such statistics amply reveals how young the women mobilized to corporate comfort stations at the time were (see <Supplementary Table 1-4>).

It is easy to guess that the circumstances of these women were quite wretched. During the war, Benten-cho, a street in Hakodate, had a row of comfort stations where Korean women were forced into prostitution. Indeed, locals have testified that they often saw women who had escaped from these facilities commit suicide by throwing themselves into the sea from around Mt. Hakodate (Fact-finding Team on the Truth about Forced Korean Laborers in Japan, 1974: 436). Because Korean women's suicides by throwing themselves into the sea were frequently reported in newspapers, there is a testimony that, in 1943, an official order even prohibited the press coverage of such incidents (Editorial Board of the *Report on the Investigation of the Reality behind the Forced Taking of Koreans* and the Sapporo Gakuin University Editorial Office of the Report on the

⟨Supplementary Table 1-4⟩ The age distribution of Korean "professional entertainers," "prostitutes," and "bar girls" in Hokkaido (1940)

Age	14	15	16	17	18	19	20	21	22	23
No. of people	6	13	27	40	30	34	36	22	21	20
Age	24	25	26	27	28	29	30	31	32	Total
No. of people	21	27	21	6	5	2	0	2	0	333

Source: Based on the Bureau of Statistics, Cabinet, "Koreans in Mainland Japan Classified According to Industry (Subcategory), Occupation (Subcategory), and Age" <Table 21>, *Original Tables in the National Census Statistics of 1940.*

A bird's-eye view of Mitsubishi Mining-owned Bibai Coal Mine. The horizontal line indicates the border between the mine site and the town (1935).

Investigation Commissioned by Hokkaido, eds., 1999: 227). Stressed by the heavy labor, Korean laborers seem to have acted violently at comfort stations at times. In 1941, two laborers working at Bibai Coal Mine, which was owned by Mitsubishi Mining, broke the equipment and facilities at the local comfort station and behaved violently and consequently had to write an apology as punishment (Sin Am'u and Ku Duyun, 1941).

According to an investigation by the Japanese government, the proportion of Korean sex slaves assigned to mines and mining stations was as follows: 16 per 651 laborers (1943; Sunagawa Coal Mine owned by Mitsui Mining); seven per 947 laborers (Bibai Coal Mine owned by Mitsubishi Mining); and six per 300 laborers (Mining Station E in Hokkaido). According to Nagayama Eitai 永山榮泰, a Korean who had been forced to adopt a Japanese name and who served as an interpreter for Korean laborers at a mining station owned by Hokkaido Colliery & Steamship in Fukuzumi in Yubari, five Korean comfort stations in this area each had five women so that a total of 25 women serviced 8,000-10,000 laborers. When the Japanese government established a policy to introduce both Chinese laborers and sex slaves, the proportion of Chinese sex slaves assigned to laborers was as follows: 20-30 sex slaves per 1,000 laborers (Planning Board, Ministry of Greater East Asia, 1942b); 40-50 sex slaves per 1,000 laborers (Planning Board, Ministry of Greater East Asia,

1942c); and eight sex slaves per 224 laborers (Bureau of Police and Public Security, Ministry of Home Affairs, May 1943). Considering these records and contemporary numbers of laborers, the number of sex slaves can be estimated to have been 10,000-30,000.

2) The Medical Examination of Sex Slaves

Because corporate comfort stations were established to raise laborers' productivity, the regular examination of sex slaves for STDs was an obligation of these facilities. However, those in charge of examining sex slaves differed according to the corporation and were diverse, including police physicians, designated hospitals, municipal clinics, and coal mine dispensaries. In all cases, the medical examination of sex slaves can be said to have been an obligation of comfort stations.

3) The Ticket System

The numerous reports mentioned above state that, at comfort stations, tickets (money tickets 金券) issued by corporations were used.[27] Although these money tickets seem to have been used throughout their respective corporations, tickets also seem to have been created especially for admission to comfort stations in some cases. For example, at Inakuraishi Mine, the corporation owning the mine supposedly created tickets and sold them to comfort station users. According to postwar reminiscences by former employees of this particular corporation, Korean comfort stations charged Korean laborers with 2 yen 50 sen and Japanese laborers with 5 yen 50 sen, respectively (Kitani Taka, 1969: 12). As for the Chinese comfort station of Fushiki Kowan Unso, the fee was 1 yen for tea only and 2 yen for "acts of comfort," all paid with tickets (*Monthly Foreign Affairs Bulletin*, May 1943). It is unclear, however, whether such regulations were

27 These money tickets were also called "coal tickets 炭券" or "tickets 切符." Such money tickets were used instead of cash from the early years of the development of coal mines because there were not enough funds and financial organs were deficient. As a result, even coal mine workers could not receive their wages in cash but were issued private paper money (tickets), which they were to exchange for cash on designated days. This is why the word "receipt" was written on the money tickets.

properly adhered to. According to Kato Hiroshi 加藤博史, Nagayama Eitai, who served as an interpreter for Korean laborers at Yubari Mine, has testified that comfort station managers received cash from laborers. Indeed, some of these managers even became rich after the war with the money left over from the building maintenance fees and the cost of provisions paid to their respective corporations.

7. The Forms of Comfort Stations

The forms of corporate comfort stations encompassed: the transformation of existing "restaurants" into corporate comfort stations, with their features generally left intact; corporations' construction of buildings and wholesale employment of managers and women from existing "restaurants" for work at these new establishments; and the construction of completely new buildings and the recruitment of completely new managers. Based on hitherto unearthed materials, a summary of these different forms of comfort stations is as follows.

1) The Designation of Existing Korean "Restaurants"

This applies only to "restaurants" that were already established in areas with a large concentration of (Korean) laborers. According to a 1943 report by the Institute for Science of Labour (ISL) 勞動科學研究所 (present-day Ohara Memorial Institute for Science of Labour (ISL) 大原記念 勞動科學研究所), Mitsui Mining, which owned Sunagawa Coal Mine, designated and managed three [Korean] Peninsular "restaurants" downtown and employed 16 Korean "bar girls." It also points out that Mitsubishi Mining, which owned Bibai Coal Mine, likewise permitted the establishment of [Korean] Peninsular Quality *Sake* Tavern [朝鮮]半島銘酒屋 (*Meishu-ya*) No. 1[28] downtown and employed seven Korean "bar girls." In addition, Sumitomo Mining, which owned Yubetsu Mining Station, similarly managed Peninsular Quality *Sake* Tavern No. 1

28 During the Meiji era, establishments that employed female attendants and made them engage in prostitution under the guise of taverns were called "quality *sake* taverns."

(2-3 Korean "bar girls") downtown.

2) The Relocation of Existing Korean "Restaurants"

In April 1940, at the early stage of the establishment of corporate comfort stations, a comfort station named "Rest Home" and established at Sorachi Mining Station, which was owned by Hokkaido Colliery & Steamship, had, in fact, been a "restaurant" in Sapporo originally, transplanted for the miners (*Hokkai Times*, April 3, 1940). There is also a testimony that, here, the manager was drafted by the corporation with help from the Japanese government (Sapporo Municipal Workers Union Committee for the Establishment of the Research Institute for Local Autonomy and Local Government, et al., eds., 1987: 38).

3) The Establishment of New Korean "Restaurants"

The January 7, 1940 issue of the *Otaru Shimbun* cited above reported, "It has been decided that Row House No. 3 will be established [in Yubari] near the Migrants' Harmony Dormitory, where Korean laborers are housed, and rented to a restaurant manager" (*Asahi Shimbun*, 13th prefectural edition, March 13, 1992). According to a 1943 investigation conducted by the Institute for Science of Labour, Toyosato Mining Station, which was owned by Showa Denko KK 昭和電工株式會社, similarly established a comfort station called the "Sun Hall 太陽館" (*Taiyo-kan*) and designated a merchant to manage it. The Korean "restaurant" in the testimony in the investigation by the Fact-finding Team on the Truth about Forced Korean Laborers in Japan mentioned above was "[established] not in a [residential] neighborhood but in the center of the area lined with company housing because it was a comfort station built in the name of a 'restaurant', to be enjoyed by those [laborers] who had been forcibly brought." Judging from the fact that the same testimony alludes to the women who were working at the "restaurant" in question as having been brought from colonial Korea to Japan by employment fraud, this comfort station can be understood as having been newly established and the women, accordingly, as having been newly brought from the colony (Fact-finding Team on the Truth about Forced Korean Laborers in Japan, 1974: 436).

8. The Managers of Corporate Comfort Stations

Most managers of corporate comfort stations were determined by being designated and entrusted with the management of these facilities by corporations.

1) The Nature of the Managers

According to the stipulation in the Guidelines on the Regulation of Restaurants and Eating Houses established by the Hokkaido Government Division of Police in October 1939, new businesses were to be permitted only to army or navy veterans or civilian employees of the military 軍屬 who had participated in war and who were currently without appropriate occupations or had returned home due to honorable discharge or injury (Editorial Board of the *History of the Hokkaido Prefectural Police*, ed., 1968: 305). If these guidelines were indeed adhered to, it is possible to say that most managers of new corporate comfort stations were formerly soldiers or civilian employees of the military. Even if they were not strictly observed, these guidelines can be seen as supporting the existence of a considerable number of Japanese managers.

Nevertheless, the managers of Korean "restaurants" seem to have been mostly Koreans. Because corporate comfort stations were established unlimitedly regardless of the Guidelines on the Regulation of Restaurants and Eating Houses above and under special protection by the Japanese government and employed only Korean sex slaves specifically for Korean laborers, their managers were mostly Koreans as well. Indeed, as has been examined earlier, there was even a case where the manager, like the sex slaves, had been drafted to Japan for labor (Sapporo Municipal Workers Union Committee for the Establishment of the Research Institute for Local Autonomy and Local Government, et al., eds., 1987: 38).[29]

---

29 According to Nagayama Eitai, a Korean who had been forced to adopt a Japanese name and who worked as a Korean interpreter at a mining station in Fukuzumi, Yubari owned by Hokkaido Colliery & Steamship at the time, the managers of the five Korean comfort stations in the area were all Koreans, with the following Japanized last names, respectively: Boku (i.e., Bak 朴), So (i.e., Song 宋), Ri (i.e., Yi 李), Kanamori 金森 (i.e., Kim 金), and Minami (i.e., Nam 南). According to his testimony,

Although, as with the discussion above on the ages of the women, the accuracy of the number of Korean managers is debatable, statistics on these managers' age and gender distribution are worth noting. Apparently, most of them were men in their 30s-40s (see <Supplementary Table 1-5>):

〈Supplementary Table 1-5〉 The age distribution of comfort station managers in Hokkaido (1940)

(Unit: No. of people)

Classification	Aged 25-29	Aged 30-34	Aged 35-39	Aged 40-44	Aged 45-49	Aged 50-54	Aged 55-59	Aged 60 or Above	Total
Men	1	4	5	7	4	2	0	2	25
Women	4	1	2	0	0	0	0	0	7

Source: Based on the Bureau of Statistics, Cabinet, "Koreans in Mainland Japan Classified According to Industry (Subcategory), Occupation (Subcategory), and Age," <Table 21>, *Original Tables in the National Census Statistics of 1940.*

2) The Management Methods

The respective Departments of Labor at corporations were responsible for comfort stations, with separate sections for Koreans under these departments. As for Hokkaido Colliery & Steamship, the hierarchy was organized into the Division of Labor 勤勞部 → Department of Labor → Korean Section 朝鮮人係, and those in charge of Koreans were, in turn, organized into dormitory superintendents 寮長 → assistants → male cooks 賄夫, all of whom were Japanese. There also were Koreans who worked as interpreters (Editorial Office of the *70-Year History of Hokkaido Colliery & Steamship Co., Ltd.*, ed., 1958). As for Chinese laborers, they apparently

the corporation provided the buildings for these comfort stations. Using the very fact that many of the comfort station managers thus were Koreans, the Japanese press has argued, "The victimizers [of Korean sex slaves at corporate comfort stations] were Koreans, too" and stated that this has led to insufficient research on the issue in South Korea (*Hokkaido Shimbun*, September 2, 2003). However, such an interpretation is inappropriate in light of the overall circumstances surrounding corporate comfort stations for Korean laborers including: the purposes of establishing these facilities; the process of establishing the comfort stations through 100% intervention by the Japanese government and corporations; and the intervention of the Japanese police. Moreover, the participation of some of the Korean comfort station managers in anti-Japanese independence movements, which will be mentioned later, shows that such interpretations on the part of the Japanese are biased.

were controlled and monitored directly by not only the Departments of Labor but also the North China Labor Association and government officials at the same time (Futase Mining Station, Nittetsu Mining Co., Ltd., 1946: 20).

According to most investigative reports and testimonies, corporations in principle provided comfort station managers with not only purchased or leased buildings but also items such as food and medicine. As for the comfort stations at Yubari Mine, which was owned by Hokkaido Colliery & Steamship, the corporation leased the buildings free of charge and the Department of Labor supplied and supervised the provisions (Institute for Science of Labour, 1943). According to Kato Hiroshi's testimony, because it was difficult for comfort station managers to go outside due to the location of most comfort stations inside coal mines, corporations would purchase items including food and alcoholic beverages requested by these Korean "restaurants," to be remunerated later.

3) The Managers as Monitors of Laborers

It has already been discussed above that corporate comfort stations were established as one means of preventing laborers' abscondence as well. Based on its investigation of corporate comfort stations in Hokkaido in 1941, the Institute for Science of Labour reported that the Hokkaido Government permitted (forcibly) taken laborers at most mines to bring their families over after the 3-month-long training, which was intended to resolve the issue of sexual desire and to prevent abscondence. In addition, dormitory superintendents often were former soldiers, which can be seen as having been for the effective surveillance of the laborers (Institute for Science of Labour, 1943). In addition, the mine authorities strictly guarded against any unwanted behavior on the part of the laborers by maintaining frequent contact with the police. At Yubari Mine owned by Hokkaido Colliery & Steamship, 14-15 Japanese guards worked on both day and night shifts, and guards were assigned to trains. Laborers were allowed to go out for recreation only to Yubari and strictly watched, required to carry the certificate of travel issued by dormitory superintendents or the chief of the Department of Labor during such outings (Institute for Science of Labour, 1943). In other words, comfort stations also functioned as organs monitoring the activities of Korean laborers (Nishida Hideko, 2003: 30). Likewise, the Chinese comfort station in Toyama Prefecture managed by Fushiki Kowan Unso was constantly monitored and regulated by the Mizukami-cho Police Station in Fushiki, and the corporation, in turn, received reports of this (*Monthly Foreign Affairs Bulletin*, August 1943).

4) The Managers as Anti-Japanese Korean Independence Movement Activists

Some Korean comfort station managers used these facilities as secret bases and sources of funds for anti-Japanese Korean independence movements. Issued in 1945 by the Division of Labor 労務部 at Yubari Mining Station, which was owned by Hokkaido Colliery & Steamship, a document titled "Dispute Relations" includes a report sent by the chief of the Department of Labor at the mining station to the Department of Labor in the Division of Labor at the company headquarters on April 5, 1944. The contents are as follows: "An item regarding the issue of the ideology of the Peninsular [i.e., Korean] laborers introduced [into Japan proper]: The present document reports a summary of the post-arrest interrogation of Hiranuma Shigeo, who, reported previously, worked at the comfort station [i.e., Korean "restaurant"] at our mining station. The present comfort station-eating house 慰安所飲食店 was opened in March 1940 by Son Bangju together with Hiranuma Shigeo. With his own assets amounting to over 300,000 yen, Son Bangju opened Korean 'restaurants' in Seoul, Osaka, and Sapporo as well. After graduation from a private university in Japan proper, Son Bangju's eldest son engaged in Korean independence movements, with systematic routes inherited from his father through Hiranuma Shigeo, numerous [mining station] dormitory interpreters (Bak Hyeong'in: interpreter for Dormitory No. 16; Kim Jeongnam: interpreter for Dormitory No. 4; An Jaeheon: former interpreter for Dormitory No. 17; and Yang Haryong: interpreter for Dormitory No. 12) under Hiranuma Shigeo's supervision, and Korean independence movement headquarters in Seoul and Manchuria."

Such facts surface again in Kim Heunggon's 金興坤 memoir, which was published in 1981. According to this book, Son Bangju, who was quite wealthy because he operated comfort stations and a rice mill, assisted anti-Japanese Korean independence movements (Kim Heunggon, 1981: 183-216). Nakagawa Shigeichi 中川繁市, who, as a member of the Labor Section 労務係 in the Division of Labor at Yubari Mining Station owned by Hokkaido Colliery & Steamship, was in charge of the Korean laborers, kept the *Log on Koreans' Activities after the End of the War* 終戰後ニ於ケル朝鮮人動向日誌 from September 1945 to January 5, 1946. In the entry for October 21, 1945, he records that, "[a]rrested at a comfort station for ideological problems involving the independence of Korea, those such as An Jaeheon, Bak Hyeong'in, Yang Haryong, and Hiranuma Shigeo have been freed from Sapporo Prison and returned to the mine" (Nakagawa Shigeichi, 1945-1946: 25).

9. The Post-Liberation Situation

Most comfort stations seem to have continued their business even after the war (Nakagawa Shigeichi, 1945-1946). However, as forcibly taken Korean laborers returned to Korea, these facilities came to face a variety of problems. For example, Korean laborers organized labor unions and demanded the liberation of comfort stations as well. At Yubari Mining Station owned by Hokkaido Colliery & Steamship, comfort station managers demanded payments for financial losses and were paid consolation money by the corporation because they had to close business in December 1945 due to the "bar girls'" demand for liberation and consequently were unable to retrieve investments (Hokkaido Colliery & Steamship Co., Ltd., 1945). On the other hand, according to Kato Hiroshi's study on Nagayama Eitai, who worked as an interpreter for Korean laborers at a coal mine in Fukuzumi, Yubari, comfort station managers even became rich after the war because of the comfort station buildings offered to them by the mines (interview with Kato Hiroshi).

It is a well-known fact that, after the war, drafted Korean laborers incited many violent incidents, giving vent to emotions hitherto suppressed in Japan. Amid such a situation, a civilian researcher has testified, these drafted laborers and corporate sex slaves were housed in the same location and the women were forced to provide sexual "comfort" to the men as a way of preventing the laborers' pent-up anti-

Japanese sentiments from exploding in mass uprisings. Indeed, in the case of Tagawa Coal Mine owned by Mitsui Mining, in a mining area in Fukuoka, women were taken from Sakae-machi, a district concentrated with comfort stations, to Hosenkaku ("Hosen Pavilion") 豊泉閣 and made to provide sexual gratification to drafted laborers in order to prevent the latter's insurrection.

10. Conclusion

Despite their absence from documentary materials, diverse other forms of practices related to corporate sexual slavery were, in fact, widespread as well. Testimonies have revealed that many women taken to factories were routinely subjected to rape by the managers, usually at night. In addition to coal mines and factories, munitions facilities and construction sites likewise mobilized sex slaves for the laborers. They included the Matsushiro Imperial General Headquarters construction site in Nagano Prefecture, Kashiwa Airfield in Chiba Prefecture, Yanagimoto Airfield in Nara Prefecture, and Kan'onji Naval Airfield in Kagawa Prefecture (Higuchi Yuichi, 1992: 28). In addition, comfort stations for laborers seem to have spread to war zones beyond Japan proper. There, women not only from Korea but also from other occupied territories were mobilized. Nippon Chisso Hiryo KK 日本窒素肥料株式會社 (present-day Chisso Corp.) introduced a large number of laborers into Hainan Island, China, to excavate iron ore. Comfort stations likewise were established on the island, and women supposedly were brought from Hong Kong by deception to serve as sex slaves (Takagi Ken'ichi, et al., eds., 1993: 55-57; and Yoshimi Yoshiaki and Hayashi Hirofumi, eds., 1995: 145). There is also a record that many sex slaves were taken from colonial Korea to Japan to provide sexual service to seamen (*Hokkaido Shimbun*, December 6, 1991).

As such facts of damages continue to come to light, it is all the more urgently necessary that various areas in Japan where many corporate comfort stations seem to have existed be continuously studied to reconstruct the total reality of corporate sexual slavery. An especially imperative and urgent task that cannot be delayed even for a day is the search for the few remaining former sex slaves and experiencers of comfort stations and the transcription of their testimonies.

The primary responsibility for the damage incurred by corporate sexual slavery lies with the Japanese government. In other words, all departments in the central government, local governments, and police were deeply involved. However, it was corporations, above all, that established comfort stations and exploited sex slaves. The issue of corporate sexual slavery is therefore a more complex one that cannot be explained with the simple scheme of "state-civil society" and, as such, demands a new theoretical perspective on the exploitation of women based on the dynamics of gender, state, corporations, and ethnicity. In addition, the Measures against Venereal Diseases, which were established as a part of the National Mobilization Plan, and corporate comfort stations, the resulting channels, have very clear theoretical implications for the close relationship between politics and sexuality.

Finally, it must be stressed that policy considerations allowing victims to reveal themselves to the world are necessary. In other words, the reception of reports from and the provision of livelihood support to survivors of Japanese military sexual slavery hitherto implemented by the South Korean government must be expanded to former corporate sex slaves also. Though such measures are urgently necessary primarily for the recovery of these victims' human rights and economic and mental support for them, they are indispensable also for research, for the rectification of concealment and distortions in Korean history as well. In addition, grasping the victims of corporate sexual slavery will greatly aid the legal activities of NGOs, which have been performed in multifaceted ways in order to demand that not only the government but also corporations of Japan assume their liability.

II

The Reality of the Women's Labor Volunteer Corps

The Japanese empire's exploitation of Korea during its colonial rule over the latter took diverse forms in a variety of fields. From among them, the exploitation of women can be summarized as labor and sexual exploitation, both of which took place within the overall framework of the Japanese empire's exploitation of the Korean people in the last years of colonial rule.

Initiated with the Japanese occupation of Manchuria, the exploitation of Korean women's labor intensified as Japan entered a wartime system following the Second Sino-Japanese War of 1937. Generally, it was after the proclamation of the National Mobilization Law 國家總動員法 in 1938 that women began to be mobilized *en masse* in the names of units such as the Patriotic Labor Corps 勤勞報國隊 and the Women's Promotion Corps 女子推進隊, and the Women's Labor Volunteer Corps 女子勤勞挺身隊 emerged in earnest in the 1940s. In addition to such overt mobilization, however, the exploitation of women's labor occurred on a wide scale in the form of strengthening existing working women's labor. Although it will focus mainly on the Women's Labor Volunteer Corps, this chapter will also examine diverse forms of labor exploitation that took place from the 1930s and onwards.

As with all other cases of damages, it is very difficult to find materials on the exploitation of women for labor. Even the remaining materials are mostly pro-Japanese newspapers and magazines so that it is not easy to grasp the contemporary reality objectively. The contents of this chapter will summarize such materials and the testimonies of former Women's

Labor Volunteer Corps victims reported to the Korean Council during 1990-1991.

1. The Mobilization of Women's Labor under the Quasi-wartime System

As it entered a quasi-wartime system with the Manchurian Incident of 1931 as the occasion, Japan began to mobilize labor from colonial Korea. In the case of the exploitation of Korean women's labor, it can be classified into the reinforcement of existing women's labor and mobilization both in Korea and abroad.

1) The Strengthening of Rural Women's Labor

With the implementation of the Parallel Promotion of Agriculture and Industry Policy 農工竝進政策 in colonial Korea in the 1930s and the consequent need for laborers, the Japanese colonial authorities sought to maximize the use of women's labor. This was especially marked in rural areas. Although a policy of actively mobilizing rural women for outdoor labor and side jobs had been implemented since the beginning of the Japanese colonial period, the implementation of the Agrarian Development Movement 農村振興運動 in the 1930s further reinforced such a tendency. Arguments such as the "eradication of evil customs that denigrate women's outdoor labor" had already been raised since the early years of the Japanese colonial era, and, in the 1930s, women were actively mobilized for outdoor labor and provided with day-care centers to promote increased rural labor productivity (Chung Chun-Sung, 1988: 86).

2) Domestic Mobilization

In the process of Japan's industrialization of Korea in the 1930s, the demand for laborers was especially high in the northern region of the colony. The Government-General of Korea had already sought, during the latter half of the 1920s, to move populations from southern Korea to construction areas in the north, which became full-fledged with the establishment of the Plan for the Mass Migration of Southern Korean Laborers 南鮮勞動者團體移民案 in 1934. This policy sought to relocate laborers *en masse*, in units of 20 people (Huh Soo Youl, 1983: 80-84).

Because areas in need of laborers were construction sites or mines, men would have been the main targets of such mobilization. It is unknown how many women were similarly mobilized domestically.

3) Overseas Mobilization

Having won control over Manchuria by inciting the Manchurian Incident, Japan needed laborers to develop this region. It therefore implemented an active policy of promoting Koreans' migration and, starting in 1936, of relocating farmers *en masse* from southern Korea. The Japanese authorities therefore established Manchuria-Korea Development Co., Ltd. 滿鮮拓植株式會社 in both Seoul and Manchuria[1] as well as a systematic plan. This plan intended to relocate thousands of independent and tenant farmers each year.[2] Although it failed to be implemented fully, the plan nevertheless demonstrates the fact that, due to it, countless farmers in southern Korea were forced to migrate to Manchuria (Chung Chinsung and Cho Sung Youn, 1994: 256-258).

Because the Manchurian emigration policy sought to use agricultural labor based on emigration in units of entire families, women thereby came to be mobilized along with men.

1 [TN] The enterprise established in Seoul was named Korea-Manchuria Development Co., Ltd. 鮮滿拓殖株式會社, to be exact. Formally, it was the parent or investment company of the one founded in Manchuria.

2 The numbers of independent farmers to be relocated were as follows: 2,000 households in the first year; 3,000 in the second year; 4,000 in the third year; 7,000 each in the next two years; 9,000 each in the next eight years; and 10,000 each in the next two years. As for tenant farmers, the figures were: 1,000 households each in the first three years; 2,000 households each in the next three years; and 3,000 each in the next six years (*Korean Economic Yearbook*, 1939: 369-376).

2. The Mobilization of Women's Labor under the Wartime System

1) The National Mobilization System

As is well known, Japan entered a wartime system following the Second Sino-Japanese War of 1937 and reorganized both the mainland and all of its colonies into a mobilization system. With the proclamation of the National Mobilization Law in May 1938 as the turning point, colonial Korea, too, entered a full-fledged mobilization system. Based on the National Mobilization Law, laws including the Ordinance on the National Declaration of Vocational Capacity 國民職業能力申告令 (1939) and the Ordinance on Employment Agencies in Korea 朝鮮職業紹介所令 (1940) were enacted.[3]

(1) The Organizations for Mobilization

To implement such mobilization more efficiently, an organization called the National League for Spiritual Mobilization in Korea 國民精神總動員朝鮮聯盟 was formed in July 1938.[4] Although actually led by the Government-General of Korea, this organization included civilian organizations such as schools, corporations, banks, and factories as well, thus possessing separate organizational forms that were broader and more effective. Vertically, the league created a network of branches in provinces, cities, counties, islands, towns, neighborhoods, and villages under the central organ and, as basal organs of praxis at the ends, the Patriotic Units 愛國班, each consisting of ten households. As of June 1939, the number

3 First implemented in Japan in April 1938 and later applied to colonial Korea, the National Mobilization Law was used to proclaim diverse ordinances regarding labor mobilization such as the Ordinance on the National Declaration of Vocational Capacity (Article 21 of the National Mobilization Law), Ordinance on Provisional Measures on Wages 賃金臨時措置令 (Article 6), Ordinance on the Control of Wages 賃金統制令 (Article 6), Ordinance Restricting the Employment of School Graduates 學校卒業者使用制限令 (Article 6), Ordinance on Employment Agencies in Korea (1940), and Ordinance on the National Draft 國民徵用令 (Article 4) (Kobayashi Hideo, 1975/1983: 277).

4 This was created on the basis of the Central Information Commission of Korea 朝鮮中央情報委員會, which was established in the Government-General of Korea in 1937, with added civilian participation (Government-General of Korea, 1940a: 25).

of the Patriotic Units across the colony reached 347,728, which shows the fact that most Koreans were under the control of these organizations. In addition, organizations including schools and corporations were made to establish their own leagues and, in turn, to join local city and town branches of the umbrella league (Government-General of Korea, 1940a: 29-31).

With the outbreak of World War II in 1939, mobilization became even more pressing so that the National League for Spiritual Mobilization in Korea was reorganized as the National League of Total Effort in Korea 國民總力朝鮮聯盟 in October 1940, now becoming a colony-wide organization that subsumed the military, bureaucracy, and civilians. This new organization likewise consisted of the central organ, which included both bureaucrats such as the Governor-General of Korea and influential figures in the military and civilian sectors, under which were local branches in neighborhoods and villages as well as the Patriotic Units. The number of the Patriotic Units rose to 380,000 by December 1940 (Government-General of Korea, 1941: 7-8).

In addition, when the Japanese colonial government assumed control over brokers with the legislation of the Ordinance on Employment Agencies in Korea in 1940, these organizations came to play a part in the mobilization of labor. In 1940, labor-related duties were separated from the Department of Social Affairs 社會課 in the Government-General of Korea and transferred to the newly created Department of Labor, which, in turn, was abolished in 1944 and further divided into the Department of Labor Adjustment 勤勞調整課, Department of Labor Mobilization 勤勞動員課, and Department of Labor Guidance 勤勞指導課. 1941 saw the creation of the Korean Labor Association 朝鮮勞務協會, which was intended to assist labor-related administrative organs and which enabled the police directly to mobilize labor (Yeo Soon-joo, 1994: 30-31 and 43).

(2) Spiritual Mobilization

Mobilization in this period could be classified largely into spiritual mobilization and the mobilization of materials and labor. Implemented as a part of the so-called Japanization 皇國臣民化 policy, spiritual mobilization can be seen as the basis of labor mobilization. The National League for Spiritual Mobilization in Korea was founded in 1938 under the goal of implementing Japanization and Japanese-Korean unity 內鮮一體 quickly and, as such, established and implemented a program of praxis that covered diverse items including obeisance in the direction of the Japanese imperial palace 宮城遙拜 each morning, promotion of worship at Shinto shrines 神社參拜, recitation of the Oath of Allegiance of the Imperial Subject 皇國臣民ノ誓詞 whenever possible, promotion of respect for and the hoisting of the Japanese flag, and promotion of the use of the Japanese language and frugality and industriousness (Government-General of Korea, 1940a: 35-36). The forced adoption of Japanese names 創氏改名 was implemented through the revision of the Civil Ordinance of Korea 朝鮮民事令 in November 1939. Seeing the deepening of Japanese-Korean unity and the Japanization of the Korean people as the most pressing task, the National League of Total Effort in Korea likewise created a practical plan for thoroughly inculcating Koreans with the Japanese spirit in 1940 (Government-General of Korea, 1941: 6-11).

(3) Labor Mobilization

The mobilization of materials and labor thus occurred on a wide scale. While human mobilization was implemented in the forms of military mobilization, labor mobilization, and sexual mobilization, this section will briefly examine the mobilization of labor only. Through diverse laws and organizations, the Japanese colonial authorities sought to inculcate the Koreans with the spirit of "patriotic labor 勤勞報國" and to reinforce labor. For the efficient mobilization of labor, Japan first set out to grasp the reality of the quantity, quality, and whereabouts of the labor force. Diverse vocational capacity studies 職業能力調査 were conducted based on Article 21 of the National Mobilization Law, which was legislated and proclaimed in Japan in April 1938 and implemented in Korea in May of the same year, and the Ordinance on the National Declaration of Vocational Capacity, proclaimed in Japan in January 1939, was implemented in the colony in June of the same year. The contents of this second ordinance were strengthened through numerous revisions, developing into the National Registration System for Youths and Younger Adults 青壯年國民登錄制 in October 1941 and the National Registration System 國民登錄制 in 1944. The aim of such laws lay in grasping overall individuals who were equipped with technical abilities especially needed by the national mobilization system.

During the Japanese colonial period, the actual mobilization of labor was implemented, in most cases, without being based on laws for a considerable time, only to be given a legal basis for already implemented mobilization in the form of the belated proclamation of the relevant laws. In such a context, the Ordinance on National Cooperation with Patriotic Labor 國民勤勞報國協力令 was proclaimed in 1941,[5] and the Ordinance on Students' Labor 學徒勤勞令 was proclaimed in October 1944, respectively.

The mobilization of labor by Japan became increasingly stronger in legal binding force, shifting from recruitment (September 1939-January 1942) to official mediation 官斡旋 (February 1942-August 1944) and the draft (September 1944-August 1945). There was little difference in the contents because all three stages mobilized and exploited people for labor through the exercise of compelling power (Jeong Hye Kyung, 2003: 19). However, many materials show that, regardless of such formal laws, labor mobilization was implemented under strong coercion by the Japanese authorities from the recruitment stage. Led by brokers and the Departments of Social Affairs in respective township offices 面事務所, official mediation, in fact, involved the wholesale restriction of Koreans' freedom of movement and occupational choice in order to mobilize them to Japan and therefore can be seen as the application of a de facto national draft ordinance to the Korean people (Kobayashi Hideo, 1975/1983: 281). Indeed, the Government-General of Korea authorities, too, explained that official mediation was, for all practical purposes, identical to the draft (National League of Total Effort in Korea, 1944: 49). Likewise, recruitment involved, from the start, participation in direct recruitment by the police and township office clerks under the control of the Japanese government

5 In October 1941, the National League of Total Effort in Korea notified all of its provincial branches of the Working Rules of the Patriotic Labor Corps 勤勞報國隊準則 and proclaimed the Ordinance on National Cooperation with Patriotic Labor in November. According to this ordinance, men aged 14-39 and unmarried women aged 14-24 were obliged to participate in the Patriotic Labor Corps and to cooperate for at least 30 days per year. The ordinance was revised in 1943 to raise the age limit and duration for men to 49 and 60 days and the duration for women to 50 days, respectively (Yeo Soon-joo, 1994: 33). In addition, it was revised once more in November 1944 so that the age ranges were expanded to 14-60 for men and 14-40 for women, respectively (*Maeil Sinbo*, November 25, 1944).

and the Government-General of Korea (Ichihara Hiroshi, 1992: 83-86). In addition, civilian employees of the Japanese military 軍屬 began to be drafted in 1939 and were dispatched to regions including Manchuria, China, and South Seas Mandate. Faced with very adverse working conditions, forcibly mobilized Korean laborers attempted escape and resistance on innumerable occasions.

Although the exact number of the laborers thus mobilized has yet to be determined accurately, according to official announcements, approximately 4,870,000 were mobilized from colonial Korea during 1934-1945 (Bureau of Management, Ministry of the Treasury, 1947: 71), with approximately 1,519,000 dispatched to Japan (Fact-finding Team on the Truth about Forced Korean Laborers in Japan, 1974: 88). In addition, 154,907 civilian employees of the Japanese military were mobilized (Public Security Intelligence Agency, 1953). It is easy to surmise that the actual numbers were larger than these figures.

2) The Mobilization of Women's Labor

As has been mentioned in the overall labor mobilization situation examined above, the entire colonial Korea was under a meticulous mobilization system, which would have made it difficult for women to escape from such control.

(1) The Strengthening of Women's Labor

The Japanese colonial government's efforts to promote women's labor were further reinforced under the wartime system. This led to a deluge of academic papers, studies, and investigations criticizing the traditional Korean contempt for women's labor, tendency of Korean women themselves to stay in the women's quarters 閨房, and old practice of early marriage in the colony (Miya Koichi, 1940: 712-719) as well as to the announcement of the Department of Labor Adjustment in the Government-General of Korea that a policy for strengthening women's labor, which would actively bring out women, must be established.[6]

6 Discussions on women's labor were widespread in Japan proper as well (Welfare Research Society, 1941, etc.).

The forms of labor in existing women's labor likewise came to be reinforced so that, on April 19, 1941, a system permitting women miners to be employed at mines was implemented, thus permitting women's labor in mine shafts, previously prohibited, to those aged 16 or above (*Maeil Sinbo*, April 19, 1941). Diverse plans were created to maximize the use of women's labor in rural areas as well. In the same year, the Government-General of Korea established the Policy on the Adjustment of Agricultural Manpower 農村勞動力調整方針 and transmitted it to provincial governors 道知事 throughout the colony. This policy included, among other things, the organization of women's work units 婦人作業班. Based on this basic policy, the Government-General of Korea went on to announce its policy on the adjustment of rural laborers annually and to force labor mobilization on the populace. As a result, cooperative agricultural work units 農業共同作業班 were organized, with 34% (1944) of the members being women. The Japanese authorities also established communal day-care centers to force women to work, and the number of day-care centers established in 1942 alone amounted to 34,711. To encourage and to promote communal cooking in addition to communal day care, women leaders were trained (*Bulletin of the Agricultural Association of Korea*, vol. 15, no. 5, 1941: 66; *Bulletin of the Agricultural Association of Korea*, vol. 15, no. 6, 1941: 77; *Monthly Investigation Bulletin of the Industrial Bank*, 1944: 58; and Kang Seong Eun, 1979: 650-653). Organizations such as the National League of Total Effort in Korea actively sought to establish day-care centers (*Bulletin of the Agricultural Association of Korea*, vol. 15, no. 11, 1941: 66; and *Monthly Investigation Bulletin of the Government-General of Korea*, vol. 13, no. 4, 1942: 11; requoted from Kang Jeong-sook, 1993: 12-13).

(2) The Patriotic Labor Corps, Mobilization of Students, Women's Promotion Corps, Etc.

The Patriotic Labor Corps encompassed women, too. In first mobilizing students, the Japanese authorities included female students as well. In June 1938, the labor mobilization of students *en masse* was instructed to respective provincial governors and the principals of schools under direct government control through a notification from the Inspector-General of Political Affairs 政務總監 of the Government-General of Korea titled "Item Regarding the Implementation of Labor Service Work by Pupils and Students 學生生徒ノ勤勞奉仕作業實施ニ關スル件," which, in turn, was defined by the Guidelines on the Implementation of the Students' Patriotic Labor Corps 學徒勤勞報國隊實施要綱.[7] Consequently, male students were mobilized for public works and female students were mobilized for cleaning Japanese Shinto shrines and sewing military supplies, respectively.[8] The Japanese authorities thus implemented student mobilization first not only because students were easy to mobilize immediately and could easily be made to internalize mobilization by making it a compulsory part of the curriculum but also because coercion could be concealed (Jeon Sung-Hyun, 2015: 260-261).

Beginning with students, the objects of labor mobilization were expanded to the general public, and mobilization came to have legal binding force with the legislation of the Ordinance on National Cooperation with Patriotic Labor in November 1941. Policies whereby students would be mobilized directly and in diverse ways without the mediation of the Patriotic Labor Corps were also implemented. One method was to turn schools into factories and to have students work at factories outside. As for the mobilization of female students, school facilities were turned into factories as much as possible. When these girls had to work at factories outside, they were made to commute as much as possible. When they had to stay overnight at those factories, teachers were made to be on night duty. In addition, regulations stipulated that female students were not to engage in late-night work, thus revealing a protective perspective in mobilizing girls' labor (Ichimura Shuji, 1944: 117-118, 130, and 138), but it is uncertain just how much these regulations were adhered to. Besides such tasks, female students were exploited also for work including the composition of letters of sympathy to members of the Japanese military dispatched to diverse regions, creation of comfort kits,

7 [TN] Implemented in the same year, they are occasionally referred to, presumably erroneously, as "Guidelines on the Implementation of the School Patriotic Labor Corps 學校勤勞報國隊實施要綱" in some sources.

8 In 1938, in Gyeonggi Province alone, approximately 6,000 students from 32 schools were mobilized and made to work for ten days, six hours per day. In July 1940, over 4,000 students from 19 girls' schools in Gyeonggi Province organized the Patriotic Labor Corps (*Dong-A Ilbo*, June 23, 1938; and *Maeil Sinbo*, April 17, 1941).

and laundering of military uniforms.[9]

While the Patriotic Labor Corps and the mobilization of students were legally grounded, the Women's Promotion Corps proceeded in the form of recruiting members through official mediation and recommendation (*Maeil Sinbo*, August 26, 1944). That is, in most cases, provincial branches of the National League of Total Effort in Korea selected women who were aged 20-30 and had diplomas from primary schools or higher-level schools and organized them into the Women's Promotion Corps for each town. These corps seem to have been used to implement movements encouraging women's labor or the Japanization policy.[10]

In April 1944, the Special Women's Training Centers 女子特別練成所 for all Korean females were established throughout the colony, over 250 in Gyeonggi Province alone. The purpose of these training centers lay in preparing unmarried Korean girls aged 15 or below for mobilization in war by having prominent Japanese women or teachers in the colony assume leadership and train these girls spiritually and teach them labor methods (*Maeil Sinbo*, April 19, 1944; and Higuchi Yuichi, 1990: 3).

During the war, the Korean Headquarters of the Japanese Red Cross Society recruited military nurses and dispatched them to battlefields, but the number of recruitees was insufficient so that it even recruited them under the title of "temporary relief nurses" in 1943 (Higuchi Yuichi, 1990: 4).

(3) The Characteristics of the Mobilization of Women's Labor

The following characteristics of the mobilization of women can be derived from the discussion above. The mobilization of women was implemented within the framework of the overall mobilization system as well. Although some clauses seeking to protect motherhood were apparent, what is more noteworthy is that this period saw a drastic shift

9 There are records that, in May 1944, students from Incheon Girls' High School and Incheon Sohwa Girls' High School entered the Incheon Army Armory 仁川陸軍造兵廠 and that students at 19 public and private girls' secondary schools in Gyeonggi Province were ordered to process mica every day, one hour per day (*Maeil Sinbo*, May 9 and 13, 1944).

10 There are records that the Women's Promotion Corps were organized by the National League of Total Effort in Gyeonggi Province 國民總力京畿道聯盟 in 1942 and in Kaesong in 1944, respectively (*Maeil Sinbo*, August 2, 1942 and March 9, 1944).

from existing protective practices regarding women's labor to its active mobilization.

The mobilization of women's labor was implemented in a way that not only reinforced existing women's labor but also newly mobilized their labor. Such new mobilization for labor occurred through schools or the compelling power of government organs and sought out educated women as much as possible. This is in contrast to the mobilization of women as military sex slaves.

The Labor Volunteer Corps system can be seen as an institution that developed in the context of this new mobilization of labor and sought to mobilize educated women for labor by further stressing voluntariness on the surface.

3. The Women's Labor Volunteer Corps

1) The Concept of the Women's Labor Volunteer Corps

The Volunteer Corps 挺身隊 included both men and women and covered diverse fields including press reportage, medicine, and labor. The terms "Women's Volunteer Corps 女子挺身隊" and "Women's Labor Volunteer Corps 女子勤勞挺身隊" seem to have been used both interchangeably[11] and from before the proclamation of the Ordinance on Women's Voluntary Labor 女子挺身勤勞令 in 1944. However, it is uncertain whether the Women's Volunteer Corps and the Women's Labor Volunteer Corps were identical. In other words, "Women's Volunteer Corps" was the broader term, and the possibility that it encompassed other categories as well as the "Women's Labor Volunteer Corps" cannot be ruled out. Out of these other categories, an especially sensitive and problematic one is that of Japanese military comfort women. Suspicion grows even stronger because, unlike the Women's Labor Volunteer Corps, military sexual slavery was an arbitrary concept without a legal basis.[12]

11 Article 1 of the Ordinance on Women's Voluntary Labor thus stipulates: "henceforth to be called the 'Women's Volunteer Corps 女子挺身隊.'"

12 As for the concepts of "Labor Volunteer Corps 勤勞挺身隊" and "military comfort

2) The Establishment of the Women's Labor Volunteer Corps System

(1) The Ordinance on Women's Voluntary Labor

In August 1944, the Ordinance on Women's Voluntary Labor was proclaimed in Japan, and there was an announcement that this law would be implemented in Korea as well (*Maeil Sinbo*, August 26, 1944). In reality, however, the mobilization of women for the Women's Labor Volunteer Corps had already been implemented in the colony regardless of this ordinance.

In Japan, a Cabinet council held on January 20, 1943 decided on the Guidelines on Emergency Measures for Increasing Production 生産增强緊急對策要綱, which initiated the reinforcement of the mobilization of women's labor. This then led to the decision on the Item Regarding the Promotion of the Mobilization of Women's Labor 女子勤勞動員ノ促進ニ關スル件 at a vice ministers' meeting held on September 13, 1943, to be followed by the Guidelines on Measures for Strengthening the Women's Volunteer Corps System 女子挺身隊制度强化方策要綱, passed at yet another Cabinet council held on March 18, 1944, which, in turn, was met with the Guidelines on Measures to Be Taken by Parties Receiving the Women's Volunteer Corps 女子挺身隊受入側措置要綱 on June 21, 1944, finally to result in the proclamation of the Ordinance on Women's Voluntary Labor (see Higuchi Yuichi, et al., 2005).

In Korea, as with other cases of labor mobilization examined above, this last law was proclaimed in such a way to provide legal grounds belatedly to mobilization practices that had actually been in effect for considerable time. In addition, according to the ordinance, the objects of the Women's Labor Volunteer Corps were those who needed to report themselves for national registration, a qualification that applied to an extremely small number of women in the colony. Women who could be and were indeed nationally registered were "only technicians aged 12-39 who have graduated from mining or engineering schools that are on par with secondary schools, or have previously worked or are

women 軍慰安婦," see Chapter 1.

currently working as mining technicians, electric technicians, electric communication technicians, mechanical technicians, aviation technicians, shipbuilding technicians, chemical technicians, ceramics technicians, woodworking technicians, civil engineering technicians, architectural technicians, or meteorological technicians based on their expertise and experience" (National League of Total Effort in Korea, 1944: 66; and *Maeil Sinbo*, August 26, 1944). Consequently, neither August 1944, the point in time, nor this ordinance in itself is an indicator of the precise date and grounds of the mobilization of the Women's Labor Volunteer Corps, which, in fact, was widely implemented in colonial Korea.

(2) The Period of Mobilization

It is certain that the mobilization of the Women's Volunteer Corps was implemented from before the proclamation of the Ordinance on Women's Voluntary Labor in 1944. Tahara Minoru, a junior official in the Government-General of Korea Department of Labor 勞務課, thus stated in 1944: "All Women's Volunteer Corps in Korea have been [mobilized] through official guidance and mediation and dispatched to airplane factories with the best labor management and facility maintenance in Japan" (National League of Total Effort in Korea, 1944: 66). In the same year, the chief of the Bureau of the Mining Industry 鑛工局 in the Government-General of Korea stated, "The duration of the service of the Women's Volunteer Corps through official mediation is generally two years, whereas that in the present ordinance [i.e., Ordinance on Women's Voluntary Labor] is one year" (*Maeil Sinbo*, August 26, 1944).

However, it is uncertain when exactly mobilization in the name of the "Women's Volunteer Corps" began. Information in the daily *Maeil Sinbo* 每日申報,[13] which is nearly the only extant material that can be referred to with respect to the Women's Labor Volunteer Corps, is as follows. On September 21, 1943, the Government-General of Korea introduced a "system whereby the Women's Labor Volunteer Corps [would] be made to

13 As is well known, in this period, all civilian Korean-language newspapers including the *Dong-A Ilbo* and the *Chosun Ilbo* were discontinued by the Japanese colonial authorities and only the *Maeil Sinbo* and the *Keijo Nippo* (in Japanese only), both official newspapers of the Government-General of Korea, remained so that the credibility of the latter publications is an important issue.

be independently and newly established… and to go to work collectively over extended periods" included in the policy on the promotion of the mobilization of women's labor, which had been established in Japan, and announced that it would implement this policy of promoting the mobilization of women's labor in full consideration of the situation in colonial Korea (*Maeil Sinbo*, September 23, 1943). The chief of the Department of Labor in the Government-General of Korea Bureau of Audit and Inspection 司政局 stated on October 7 that full use would be made of idle middle-class manpower (*Maeil Sinbo*, October 7, 1943) and, on the following day, decided on the Guidelines on Labor Reinforcement Measures for Increasing Production 生産增强勞務强化對策要綱, which were announced as an ordinance on the mobilization, literally, of all 25 million Koreans regardless of gender. Among other things, these guidelines included a policy stating that means of actively controlling women's labor, hitherto left outside (official) control in principle, would now be devised and that men's labor would be restricted in occupations without hindrances to women's labor. In particular, they indicated the establishment of a system that would make full use of new school graduates and unmarried women aged 14 or above (*Maeil Sinbo*, October 8, 1944). Subsequently, from the latter half of 1943 to the first half of 1944, the Women's Labor Volunteer Corps of Japan received frequent press coverage (*Maeil Sinbo*, October 14 and November 25, 1943 and February 3 and March 4 and 19, 1944, etc.).

In November 1943, the monthly magazine *Morning Light* 朝光 offered the following explanation: "The Women's Labor Volunteer Corps are independently organized by those including new graduates and alumnae and guided by school principals and seniors. Through these Volunteer Corps, women wish voluntarily to sacrifice the time between graduation and marriage to the nation…" In addition, records from 1944 on the budget of the Government-General of Korea mention questions and answers on expenditure for the Women's Volunteer Corps (Yu Gwangnyeol, November 29, 1943; and Kondo Ken'ichi, ed., 1961: 47; requoted from Yeo Soon-joo, 1994: 54). All of this shows that mobilization in the name of the "Women's Labor Volunteer Corps" was already under way in colonial Korea as well, even before the proclamation of the Ordinance on Women's Voluntary Labor.

However, on April 19, 1944, the *Maeil Sinbo* thus reported: "The Pyongyang Women's Volunteer Corps 平壤女子挺身隊, the first and second units of which left for the ___ Armory ○○廠 in Pyongyang on March 20 and April 4, respectively, was the first case of the collective mobilization of women's labor [in colonial Korea]." There are also reports that, on May 9, the Women's Labor Volunteer Corps were dispatched from Pohang and Daegu to factories owned by Fujikoshi Steel Industry Co., Ltd. 不二越鋼材工業株式會社 (present-day Nachi-Fujikoshi Corp.) in Japan (*Maeil Sinbo*, October 28, 1944) and that, in May, approximately 300 Korean girls were taken from locations including Yeosu and Mokpo in South Jeolla Province to the Nagoya Aircraft Works (present-day Nagoya Aerospace Systems Works), owned by Mitsubishi Heavy Industries, Ltd. 三菱重工業株式會社, in Dotoku, Japan.

From June 1944 and onwards, articles more actively publicizing the mobilization of the Women's Labor Volunteer Corps began to appear in the press. One published on June 3 and titled "Go Forth, the Women's Volunteer Corps" reported that the Women's Labor Volunteer Corps had been organized in Seoul and Incheon, the first time for administrative units within Gyeonggi Province, and would be dispatched to major factories in Japan (*Maeil Sinbo*, June 3, 1944). This was followed by an advertisement from the head of Seoul Prefecture urging "unmarried women aged 17-20 who are graduates of primary schools or higher-level schools [to] volunteer" (*Maeil Sinbo*, June 7, 1944) and reports on the continued deluge of volunteers (*Maeil Sinbo*, June 12, 20, 23, 26, and 28, 1944) as well as articles on the considerable number of applicants through primary schools in Seoul, advertisements of factories in Japan owned by Fujikoshi Steel Industry, and articles and editorials urging parents' understanding (*Maeil Sinbo*, June 13, 15, and 23, 1944 and July 5, 1944). Finally, an article reported that the Women's Labor Volunteer Corps had departed for the factories of Fujikoshi Steel Industry on July 2 and arrived on July 6 (*Maeil Sinbo*, July 4, 1944). Government-General of Korea Inspector-General of Political Affairs 政務總監 Tanaka Takao made a statement to the effect that "The Women's Volunteer Corps will be organized, and, if there are requests, these corps will be dispatched to mainland Japan as well" on June 10. In the same month, the Women's Volunteer Corps were dispatched from South Chungcheong Province

Women's Labor Volunteer Corps members at a Fujikoshi Steel Industry factory after the Liberation, before returning to Korea (photographed by the US military; Oct. 19, 1945)

and South Jeolla Province to factories in Nagoya (*Maeil Sinbo*, August 15, 1944) and from Jinju to Japanese factories owned by Fujikoshi Steel Industry on June 8 (*Maeil Sinbo*, October 28, 1944).

It was thus with the mobilization of the Women's Labor Volunteer Corps already in practice that the Ordinance on Women's Voluntary Labor was proclaimed on August 23, 1944. A newspaper article from this period states that, later, Korean women were mobilized as the Labor Volunteer Corps in Osaka as well (*Maeil Sinbo*, August 28, 1944). There are also records on the second recruitment of Volunteer Corps 挺身隊 members in Seoul and Incheon (January 24, 1945), dispatch from Kaesong (February 22), the second recruitment of the Women's Volunteer Corps in Kaesong (February 24), dispatch of the Women's Volunteer Corps from Seoul (February 25), the second dispatch of the Women's Volunteer Corps from South Jeolla Province (February 27), and the third dispatch of the Women's Volunteer Corps from Gyeonggi Province (March) (*Maeil Sinbo*, August 28, 1944 and February 26 and 27 and April 5, 1945).

Judging from the discussions above, the Women's Labor Volunteer Corps seem to have been implemented in Korea at the same time that the plan to implement the Women's Labor Volunteer Corps system was announced in Japan in September 1943. However, there is also an ample possibility that these corps were implemented in the colony even earlier.

(3) The Objects of Mobilization

The qualifications of the objects of mobilization differ somewhat according to the document. The first of its type to remain on records, the Pyongyang Women's Volunteer Corps were reported to be "organized with unmarried women aged 16-22 with primary school diplomas" (*Maeil Sinbo*, April 19, 1944). In Seoul and Incheon, "The qualification for applicants [was] established as unmarried women aged 17-20 with educational levels on par with graduation from a primary school" (*Maeil Sinbo*, June 3, 1944), but a newspaper article published some days later stated, "aged 16-20" (*Maeil Sinbo*, June 13, 1944). Advertisements for the "Recruitment of Members of the Women's Labor Volunteer Corps" published by Seoul Prefecture in the *Maeil Sinbo* on June 29 (page 2) and 30 (page 3), 1944 restrict the qualification to "[educational levels] on par with the completion of the elementary program in a primary school (unmarried women aged 14-21)." However, other advertisements published by Seoul Prefecture in the January 24 (page 1) and 26 (page 2), 1945 editions of the same newspaper titled "Recruiting the Women's Volunteer Corps" restrict the qualification to "[educational levels] on par with the completion of a primary school, women aged 13-21."

While such records generally agree with the actual situations recounted in testimonies by victims of the Labor Volunteer Corps, there, of course, are many differences as well. When these records and the testimonies of experiencers of the system are synthesized, the characteristics of the objects of mobilization can be summarized as the following several aspects. First, with the exception of women in rural areas, working at factories, or currently engaged in labor, idle urban women generally were the objects. Second, while the objects of mobilization were unmarried young women approximately in the 13-22 age range, this range increasingly widened, actually to mobilize women regardless of age. Third, women with the educational attainment of at least upper classes in primary school were preferred. While this was due first to the fact that, in general, women with less education were already engaged in labor, it also reflects the need for those with enough proficiency in Japanese to be able to work at Japanese factories and, as will be apparent later, the greater facility of imposing Japanization education on this class of women. Nevertheless, despite such objectives of mobilization, it is also clear that women were mobilized regardless of their educational levels, which is proven by newspaper coverage of a woman who volunteered for the Volunteer Corps while working as an errand girl at someone else's home (*Maeil Sinbo*, October 6, 1944) and the testimony of a victim who volunteered together with her friend, a housemaid (Yeo Soon-joo, 1994: 67). Fourth, although the Japanese colonial authorities sought to mobilize women from the middle and upper classes (*Maeil Sinbo*, October 7, 1943), in reality, primary school students and graduates who were impoverished or had disadvantages such as participation in anti-Japanese Korean independence movements were mobilized.

3) The Mobilization of the Women's Labor Volunteer Corps

In terms of the form, the mobilization of the Labor Volunteer Corps could be classified into several categories: official mediation; recruitment; mobilization through schools; and coercion. As will be discussed in detail later, these mobilization methods generally consisted of forced mobilization by the Japanese government, much like the overall mobilization of labor examined above, with only slight differences in the forms of coercion. However, unlike the overall mobilization of labor, which became increasingly forced with the passage of time, shifting from recruitment to official mediation to the draft, the mobilization of women's labor generally employed diverse methods and was implemented based on coercion at the same time in indistinguishable ways until the completely forced mobilization that was practiced in the last years of the war.

(1) Official Mediation

The first method of mobilization that began to be employed was that of official mediation. Official mediation meant "guiding and encouraging, through administrative measures, those deemed appropriate for manual labor to volunteer for manual labor" (National League of Total Effort in Korea, 1944: 12). As has been cited above, the Government-General of

Korea stated that, in the colony, all members of the Women's Volunteer Corps had been mobilized through the colonial government's guidance and mediation from before the proclamation of the Ordinance on Women's Voluntary Labor and that this would be continued (National League of Total Effort in Korea, 1944: 66). Indeed, many victims of the Labor Volunteer Corps have testified that they joined these corps because their village leaders 區長, neighborhood association 町內會 heads, and township office 面事務所 clerks told them that they had to join these Volunteer Corps, visiting each household. At times, such official mediation was accompanied by threats that, unless women joined the Volunteer Corps, their entire families would be harmed (Yeo Soon-joo, 1994: 67). Continued until the end of the Japanese colonial period, official mediation seems to have been the most widely used method for mobilizing members of the Women's Labor Volunteer Corps.

(2) Recruitment/Volunteering

Advertisements recruiting members of the Women's Labor Volunteer Corps were made through newspaper advertisements and articles by departments in the Government-General of Korea such as the Departments of Labor in Seoul Prefecture, Incheon Prefecture, and Gyeonggi Province, respectively. After the proclamation of the Ordinance on Women's Voluntary Labor, the recruiting organs expanded to include ward offices 區役所 and police stations as well (Yeo Soon-joo, 1994: 71-72). The fact that, in these cases, the agent of recruitment was the Government-General of Korea fundamentally differs from the recruitment methods used in the overall mobilization of labor discussed above. These Government-General of Korea departments specified the applicants' qualifications and application deadlines, publicized the factories and working conditions of the Labor Volunteer Corps, and accepted volunteers. Due to advertisements such as the following ones, there supposedly were many volunteers (*Maeil Sinbo*, June 12, 1944): "Contrary to popular misunderstanding, the Labor Volunteer Corps differ utterly in nature from the drafting of women but signify women's voluntary sacrifice of their strength to momentous tasks of the nation as a manifestation of not only their own but also their parents' fervent imperial devotion [i.e., devotion to the Japanese empire]" (*Maeil Sinbo*, June 3,

1944); and the factories in which these women would be working were so splendid that "when they first step[ped] inside the corporations, [the women would be impressed with] the greatness of the corporations and the largeness of the factories' scales, and… the premises of the factories and corporations are clean and orderly… and everything is disciplined" (*Maeil Sinbo*, October 28, 1944).

(3) Mobilization through Schools and Organizations

In October 1943, the chief of the Department of Labor in the Bureau of Audit and Inspection, Government-General of Korea announced that, for the mobilization of the Women's Labor Volunteer Corps, the principals of schools from which potential candidates had graduated would be consigned to promote active mediation and that the Patriotic Units, women's organizations, and other organizations closely linked to the National League of Total Effort in Korea would be made use of (*Maeil Sinbo*, October 7, 1943). Introduced by the *Maeil Sinbo* as the first Women's Volunteer Corps to be organized in colonial Korea, the Pyongyang Women's Volunteer Corps were said to have been organized on the basis of the Young Women's Associations 女子青年團 in disparate districts of Pyongyang (*Maeil Sinbo*, April 19, 1944), and many survivors of the Volunteer Corps have reported that they joined these corps at the recommendation of homeroom teachers or principals at their respective schools. According to these reports, in general, homeroom teachers would summon and urge a few students from their respective classes who were from economically or politically vulnerable families to join the Volunteer Corps. Considering that, in this period, the authority of schoolteachers and schools alike was subsumed under mobilization organizations including the National League of Total Effort in Korea, it is clear that such "recommendation" was tantamount to coercion. Mobilization through schools is easy to confirm because school registers recorded young women who had left to join the Labor Volunteer Corps.

(4) Forced Taking

Though coercion in practice, the methods of mobilization above formally went through procedures such as persuasion, volunteering, and parents' permission. In contrast, toward the last years of Japanese colonial rule, completely forced mobilization seems to have been implemented. Though this is not found in records, victims have testified that, by August 1945, government officials and police officers mobilized women from both urban and rural areas, without any procedure whatsoever.

4) The Destinations of the Women's Labor Volunteer Corps

The destinations to which members of the Women's Labor Volunteer Corps were mobilized and taken seem to have been mostly factories in regions including colonial Korea, Japan, and Manchuria. Those most well elucidated to date were munitions factories in Japan. As for a factory belonging to Fujikoshi Steel Industry in Toyama Prefecture, records say that there were 1,089 Korean members of the Women's Labor Volunteer Corps as of the end of May 1945 (Fujikoshi Steel Industry, 1953: 35). Likewise, at the Nagoya Aircraft Works owned by Mitsubishi Heavy Industries, there were 272 Korean members of the Women's Labor Volunteer Corps at the end of the war (Aircraft Division, United States Strategic Bombing Survey, 1947; and Yeo Soon-joo, 1994: 78). In addition, the Women's Labor Volunteer Corps were mobilized also to other areas in Japan, Manchuria, and numerous locations in colonial Korea. As has been discussed above, the Women's Volunteer Corps from Pyongyang was mobilized to the ___ Armory within the city, and one of the victims has testified that she was mobilized to a factory belonging to Kanegafuchi Spinning KK 鐘淵紡績株式會社 (present-day Kracie Holdings, Ltd.) in Gwangju. It is difficult, however, to obtain accurate information on the degree and the destinations to which such domestic factory mobilization of the Women's Labor Volunteer Corps occurred.

From among former Japanese military sexual slavery victims who have reported their cases to the Korean Council, one has testified that she was mobilized for the Labor Volunteer Corps but taken to a Japanese military comfort station in the South Seas Mandate. Similarly, another has testified that she was mobilized for the Labor Volunteer Corps, only to be taken to a military comfort station in Japan. Such cases must be investigated more closely.

5) The Reality of the Transportation, Training, Lives, and Labor of the Women's Labor Volunteer Corps

After being forcibly mobilized, Labor Volunteer Corps victims were placed under even stricter surveillance and control.

(1) Transportation

The girls thus mobilized then generally underwent procedures such as farewell parties organized by their respective schools or send-off banquets organized by their respective cities or provinces (*Maeil Sinbo*, June 14 and July 4, 1944). Those mobilized to Japan were chaperoned by officials from their respective towns, counties, or provinces, schoolteachers or principals, or representatives from their respective Japanese corporations to Busan or Yeosu and transferred to their corporations. Then they would take ferries or battleships to get to Shimonoseki, finally to arrive at their final destinations, the factories, by train. In this process, individual freedom was prohibited and, it was impossible to escape or to break away.

Korean Women's Labor Volunteer Corps members leaving for the Mitsubishi Heavy Industries-owned Nagoya Aircraft Works (Jun. 1944)

(2) Spiritual Training

Once they arrived at the factories, these women were subjected to collective training, which consisted of both spiritual and vocational training. Spiritual training included Japanization education and acculturation to military-style orders. The contents and duration of the training differed for each factory and period. In the case of a factory owned by Fujikoshi Steel Industry in Toyama Prefecture, collective training lasted for no fewer than six months, with the first two months consisting of Japanization education and collective action training and the latter four months consisting of employment guidance training. The initial stage of spiritual training consisted mainly of lectures that involved questions such as why these women were working in Japan, far away from home, why the "Greater East Asia War 大東亞戰爭" was being continued, and why Japan had to win (*Maeil Sinbo*, October 31, 1944).

In addition to labor, these women had to begin each day with obeisance in the direction of the Japanese imperial palace and the recitation of the Oath of Allegiance of the Imperial Subject early in the morning and, again, to worship at Shinto altars 神殿拜禮 at night before going to bed (*Maeil Sinbo*, October 30, 1944).

(3) Dormitory Life

Korean women mobilized to Japan were housed in dormitories according to the regions from which they had come. At a factory owned by Fujikoshi Steel Industry, each dormitory room accommodated 10-11 women (*Maeil Sinbo*, October 13, 1944), separated from the men's dormitory (*Maeil Sinbo*, September 5, 1944). In addition to the mobilized women, these dormitories had dormitory superintendents 寮長, correctional officers, company commanders, and housemothers 寮母, out of whom dormitory superintendents and company commanders were men (*Maeil Sinbo*, October 30, 1944). Such personnel regulated and supervised dormitory life and also selected squad leaders and platoon leaders from among the dormitory residents, to have them monitor their own colleagues (Sasagi Masanori, 1942; requoted from Yeo Soon-joo, 1994: 82). Residents who stole away from dormitories or did not follow the strictly structured daily schedules were punished severely.[14]

Although the food was publicized to be excellent, in fact, all victims have testified that they were always very hungry.[15]

(4) Labor

The women laborers worked for 10-12 hours per day and wore uniforms. According to testimonies or reports, there hardly was break time, and laborers were unable to rest even when ill. A record that the non-absentee rate amounted to 96-100% (*Maeil Sinbo*, October 30, 1944) betrays the intensity of control imposed on these laborers. According to victims' testimonies, Japanese men called "foremen" oversaw the work, either punishing or rewarding, with certificates of commendation, the women laborers according to the latter's work output, and even lured these women with promises of girls' school diplomas for diligence (Yeo Soon-joo, 1994: 93-95). Due to intensive labor, many workers were injured or even killed (*Maeil Sinbo*, December 7 and 20, 1944 and June 7, 1945, etc.). Amid such a situation, wages were hardly paid. Indeed, the demand for the remittance of wages that were not paid under pretexts such as forced savings continues even to this day.

There are also testimonies according to which the women were made to sing and dance around their factories in addition to working itself, and some victims were made to work as factory laborers by day and as military sex slaves by night. Most were sexually abused despite the strict control. While some were taken to military comfort stations after being shown around the factories, others have testified that they were taken to military comfort stations after the destruction of the factories due to bombing. Although the credibility of such testimonies must be closely reviewed, it is nevertheless a fact that there was some overlap between women's labor as members of the Labor Volunteer Corps and women's sexual exploitation

14 5:00 AM: reveille, cleanup, clothes change, wash-up; 5:40 AM: roll call, calisthenics; 6:30 AM: obeisance in the direction of the Japanese imperial palace, recitation of the Oath of Allegiance of the Imperial Subject, breakfast; 6:50 AM: movement to the factory; 7:00 AM-5:00 PM: work, cleanup of the machinery; 5:20 PM: return to the dormitory, bath, dinner; 7:40 PM: cleanup, roll call, worship at the Shinto altar, sleep (*Maeil Sinbo*, October 29, 1944).

15 A former victim, Kim Deok-gyeong 金덕경 has testified that she worked at a factory belonging to Fujikoshi Steel Industry in Toyama Prefecture as a member of the Labor Volunteer Corps but escaped out of hunger, only to be caught and taken to a military comfort station (Kim Mi-Hyun, 2008: 127-129).

as military sex slaves.

4. Conclusion

Regarding the exploitation of women's labor during the Japanese colonial period, much still remains unknown. In particular, even more vague are the Women's Volunteer Corps, which were etched in the minds of contemporaries as a representative system used for the exploitation of both sex and labor.

What diverse contemporary Japanese laws and policies reveal is that, in the mobilization of women for labor, educated women from the middle and upper classes were sought out as much as possible. This is similar to the fact that the Japanese government sought out men from the middle and upper classes in the case of military mobilization to increase the degree of the Koreans' Japanization. In reality, however, this class aspect was insignificant. Because most women from the middle and lower classes consisted of both those in rural communities and urban laborers and therefore had already been mobilized for labor, they, too, were being exploited under the pretext of reinforced labor. In addition, just as military mobilization was, in fact, expanded to include all men regardless of their respective classes, the mobilization of women's labor likewise was expanded regardless of their respective classes.

Although the mobilization of women undeniably occurred in the context of the mobilization of the entire Korean people, it, at times, exhibited characteristics different from those of the mobilization of men for labor as well. In the case of Japan itself, there were debates on the wartime mobilization of women and the protection of motherhood. While a perspective of protecting motherhood such as defining the characteristics of the labor involved in the mobilization of women was apparent in colonial Korea, too, it is difficult to find evidence that such considerations were especially put into practice. It is worth noting, instead, that the process of exploiting women's labor often entailed their sexual victimization. This is very important for determining the nature of the exploitation of women's labor.

Bibliography

1. Works in Korean

Ahn, Byung Jik [安秉直], trans. and commentary. 2013. *The Diary of a Japanese Military Comfort Station Manager* [日本軍慰安所管理人의 日記]. Written by Bak [朴; forename unknown]. Seoul: Esoop Publishing [이숲].

Association for the Pacific War Victims [太平洋戰爭犧牲者遺族會]. 1999. "Communication of Duties" [業務連絡事項] (May 1).

Baek, Jaeye [白재예]. 2016. "Recognition of the Allied Powers on the 'Comfort Women' during the Pacific War" [아시아·太平洋戰爭期聯合國의 日本軍'慰安婦'認識에 關한 研究—ATIS, NEFIS審問報告書를 中心으로]. Master's thesis. Department of Sociology [社會學科], Seoul National University [서울大學校].

Bak, Duseok [朴斗錫]. 1977. "A War without Prisoners of War" [捕虜 없는戰爭]. *A True Record: The Korean People's Resistance 3* [實錄—民族의 抵抗3]. Seoul: Hansaem Books [한샘出版社].

Chang, Edward Taehan [張泰翰]. 2003. "The Management of Japanese Military Comfort Stations in the Philippines and Korean Sex Slaves: Based on Materials in the National Archives and Records Administration" [필리핀에서의 日本軍慰安所運營과 朝鮮人性奴隸—美聯邦政府記錄保存所資料에 根據하여]. Ed. Women's Rights Planning Division [權益企劃課], Ministry of Gender Equality [女性部] and the College of Social Sciences [社會科學大學], Seoul National University [서울大學校]. *Investigative Research on Overseas Materials on the Issue of Japanese Military Comfort Women (II)* [日本軍慰安婦問題에 關한 國外資料調査研究 (II)]. Research Report 2004-01 [研究報告 2004-01]. Seoul: Ministry of Gender Equality. 511-584.

Chang, Wan-Ick [張完翼]. 2001. "The Significance of the North-South Joint Written Indictment at the Women's International War Crimes Tribunal on Japan's Military Sexual Slavery in 2000" [2000年日本軍性奴隷戰犯女性國際法廷에서 南北共同起訴狀이 갖는 意義]. Ed. Legal Committee [法律委員會], Women's International War Crimes Tribunal on Japan's Military Sexual Slavery in 2000 [2000年日本軍性奴隷

戰犯女性國際法廷], Korean Council for the Women Drafted for Military Sexual Slavery by Japan [韓國挺身隊問題對策協議會]. *The Prospects of the Legal Resolution of the Issue of Japanese Military Comfort Women* [日本軍慰安婦問題에 對한 法的 解決의 展望]. Seoul: Pulbit [풀빛].

Chinkin, Christine Mary. Trans. Chang Bok-Hee [張福姬]. 2001. "A Legal Consideration of the Women's International War Crimes Tribunal on Japan's Military Sexual Slavery in 2000" [2000年日本軍性奴隸戰犯女性國際法廷의 法律的 考察]. Ed. Legal Committee [法律委員會], Women's International War Crimes Tribunal on Japan's Military Sexual Slavery in 2000 [2000年日本軍性奴隸戰犯女性國際法廷], Korean Council for the Women Drafted for Military Sexual Slavery by Japan [韓國挺身隊問題對策協議會]. *The Prospects of the Legal Resolution of the Issue of Japanese Military Comfort Women* [日本軍慰安婦問題에 對한 法的 解決의 展望]. Seoul: Pulbit [풀빛].

Cho, Hyo-Je [趙孝濟]. 2000. *The Age of NGOs* [NGO의 時代]. Seoul: Changbi [創作과 批評社].

Cho, Joo-hyun [曺珠鉉]. 1996. "Gender Identity Politics: The Case of Women's Liberation Movement in Korea in 80s and 90s" [女性正體性의 政治學—1980~1990年代韓國女性運動을 中心으로]. Ed. Korean Association of Women's Studies [韓國女性學會]. *Journal of Korean Women's Studies* [韓國女性學] 12.2.

Cho, Seiyoung [趙世暎]. 2014. *50 Years of South Korean-Japanese Relations, Footprints of Conflict and Cooperation* [韓日關係50年, 葛藤과 協力의 발자취]. Korean Contemporary History Ser. 9 [韓國現代史敎養叢書9]. Seoul: National Museum of Korean Contemporary History [大韓民國歷史博物館].

_____. 2015. "The Details of Diplomatic Responses and the Direction of Future Reactions to the Issue of Japanese Military 'Comfort Women'" [日本軍'慰安婦'問題의 外交的 對應經緯와 向後對處方向]. Ed. Northeast Asian History Foundation [東北亞歷史財團]. *Thinking about the Issue of Japanese Military "Comfort Women" with Former Prime Minister Murayama* [무라야마前總理와 함께 日本軍'慰安婦'問題를 생각한다].

Cho, Uhn [曺恩], and Yoon Taek-Lim [尹택림]. 1995. "New Women under Japanese Colonial Rule and Patriarchy" [日帝下新女性과 家父長制]. *Festschrift in Commemoration of the 50th Anniversary of the Liberation* [光復五十周年紀念論文集]. Seoul: Korea Research Foundation [韓國學術振興財團].

Cho, Youn Soo [趙胤修]. 2014. "Japanese Military Comfort Women and South Korea-Japan Relations: With a Focus on the 1990s" [日本軍'慰安婦'問題와 韓日關係—1990年代韓國과 日本의 對應을 中心으로]. Ed. Korean Association for Political and Diplomatic History [韓國政治外交史學會]. *Journal of Korean Political and Diplomatic History* [韓國政治外交史論叢] 36.1.

Choi, Chungmoo [崔貞茂]. 1999. "Colored Feminism and the Postcolonial Problem" [有色女性主義와 植民後期問題]. Presented at the symposium in commemoration of the foundation of the Gender Studies program [女性學協同過程] at Seoul National University [서울大學校] "Feminism in History, Feminism Next to Us" [歷史 속의 페미니즘, 우리 곁의 페미니즘] (Oct. 29).

Choi, Jong-Gil [崔鍾吉]. 2015. "The Establishment and Management of the Japanese Military 'Comfort Women' System as Seen through the Reconstruction of Administrative Documents" [行政文書再構成을 通해 본 日本軍'慰安婦'制度의 成立과 運用; 行政文書再構成から見た日本軍'慰安婦'制度の成立と運用]. Ed. Korea-Japan Historical Society [韓日關係史學會]. *Korea-Japan Historical Review* [韓日關係史研究] 51.

Chosun Ilbo [朝鮮日報]. 1995.

Chung, Chinsung [鄭鎭星]. 1987. "Ethnic Communities as Class: With a Focus on Korean Communities in Japan during the Japanese Colonial Era" [階級으로서의 民族共同體—日帝時期의 在日朝鮮人社會를 中心으로]. Ed. Research Society for Sociology [社會學研究會], Seoul National University [서울大學校]. *Contemporary Capitalism and the Theory of the Community: A Festschrift in Commemoration of Professor Choe Hong-Kee's 60th Birthday* [現代資本主義와 共同體理論—崔弘基教授回甲論文集]. Seoul: Hangilsa [한길社].

_____. 1988. "Women's Labor Participation in Colonial Korea" [植民地資本主義化過程에서의 女性勞動의 變貌]. Ed. Korean Association of Women's Studies [韓國女性學會]. *Journal of Korean Women's Studies* [韓國女性學] 4.

_____. 1994. "The Essence of the Japanese Military 'Comfort Women' Policy" [日本軍'慰安婦'政策의 本質]. Ed. Korean Social History Association [韓國社會史研究會]. *Social Ideologies and Social Movements in the Last Years of the Empire of Korea and during the Japanese Colonial Period* [韓末日帝下의 社會思想과 社會運動] (*Korean Social History Association Journal* [韓國社會史研究會論文集] 42).

_____. 1995. "An Unsettled Debt from the Colonial Era, the Volunteer Corps: With a Focus on the Responses of the Japanese Government and Public Opinion" [清算되지 못한 植民地時期의 負債, 挺身隊—日本政府와 與論의 對應을 中心으로]. Ed. Social Science Research Institute [社會科學研究所], Daegu Hyosung Catholic University [大邱曉星가톨릭大學校]. *Ilbon Pyongnon* [日本評論] 10. Seoul: Ulchi Sojok [乙支書籍].

_____. 1996a. "The Tradition of Mechanisms for the Oppression of Women and the Modern Era" [女性抑壓機制의 傳統과 近代]. *Quarterly Changbi* [創作과 批評] 94.

_____. 1996b. "Foreigner Movement in Japan" [日本의 外國人運動—가와사키地域의 參政權獲得運動에서의 在日韓國人과 行政의 만남]. Ed. Institute of Social Science Research [社會科學研究所], Duksung Women's University [德成女子大學校]. *Duksung Journal of Social Sciences* [社會科學研究] 3 (Aug.).

_____. 1997a. "The Establishment and Development of Japanese Military Comfort Station Policies" [日本軍慰安所政策의 樹立과 展開]. Ed. Korean Council for the Women Drafted for Military Sexual Slavery by Japan [韓國挺身隊問題對策協議會].

The Truth about "Comfort Women" in the Japanese Military [日本軍'慰安婦'問題의 眞相]. Seoul: Yuksa Bipyongsa [歷史批評社].

_____. 1997b. "Tendency of Social Integration in Japanese Women's Movements" [日本女性運動의 社會統合的 性格]. Ed. Korean Social History Association [韓國社會史學會]. *Society and History* [社會와 歷史] 51.

_____. 1997c. "The Reality behind the Women's Labor Volunteer Corps during the Japanese Colonial Era" [日帝時期女子勤勞挺身隊의 實狀]. Ed. Korean Chongshindae Research Group [韓國挺身隊硏究會]. *Unresolved Issues between Korea and Japan* [韓日間의 未淸算課題]. Seongnam: Asian Culture Press [亞細亞文化社].

_____. 1998a. "Japanese Peace Movement: Social Movement for the Resolution of the Problem of Military Sexual Slavery by Japan" [日本의 平和運動—軍慰安婦問題解決을 爲한 運動을 中心으로]. Ed. Institute of International Affairs [國際學硏究所], School of International and Area Studies [國際地域院], Seoul National University [서울大學校]. *RIAS: Review of International and Area Studies* [國際·地域硏究] 7.1.

_____. 1998b. "Neo-nationalist Movement in Japan: Focusing on the Movement of 'Liberalist View of History'" [日本의 新民族主義運動—'自由主義史觀'運動을 中心으로]. Ed. Institute of International Affairs [國際學硏究所], School of International and Area Studies [國際地域院], Seoul National University [서울大學校]. *RIAS: Review of International and Area Studies* [國際·地域硏究] 7.3.

_____. 1998c. "Forced Mobilization of Korean Military Sex Slaves by the Japanese Government" [軍慰安婦强制連行에 關한 硏究]. Ed. Academy of Korean Studies [韓國精神文化硏究院]. *Korean Studies Quarterly* [精神文化硏究] 21.4 (vol. 73).

_____. 1999. "Changes in South Korean Patriarchy and Women's Formation of Subjectivity" [韓國家父長制의 變化와 女性의 主體形成]. Kim Il-Chul [金一鐵], et al. *A Structural Understanding of South Korean Society* [韓國社會의 構造論的 理解]. Seoul: Arche [아르케].

_____. 2000. "The Universality and Particularity of Human Rights" [人權의 普遍性과 特殊性]. Ed. Korea Human Rights Foundation [韓國人權財團]. *Human Rights in the 21st Century* [21世紀의 人權]. Vol. 1. Seoul: Hangilsa [한길社].

_____. 2001a. "The Background and Significance of the Women's International War Crimes Tribunal on Japan's Military Sexual Slavery in 2000" ['2000年日本軍性奴隸戰犯女性國際法廷'의 背景과 意義]. Ed. Korea Women's Studies Institute [韓國女性硏究會]. *Women and Society* [女性과 社會] 12 (Mar.).

_____. 2001b. "The Structure of Problem Raising at the ILO" [國際勞動機構(ILO)에의 問題提起의 構造—强制勞動條約(ILO Convention 29)/專門家委員會를 通한 軍慰安婦問題提起]. Ed. Institute of International Affairs [國際學硏究所], School of International and Area Studies [國際地域院], Seoul National University [서울大學校]. *RIAS: Review of International and Area Studies* [國際·地域硏究] 10.1.

_____. 2001c. *A Theory of Social Movements in Contemporary Japan* [現代日本의 社會運動論]. Seoul: Nanam [나남].

_____. 2003. "The Internationalization of Human Rights Norms: The Problem of Japanese Military Comfort Women at the UN Sub-Commission on the Promotion and Protection of Human Rights" [人權規範의 國際化—UN人權小委員會에서의 日本軍慰安婦問題]. Ed. Committee for the Publication of a Festschrift in Commemoration of Professor Hwayang Shin Yong-Ha's Retirement [禾陽愼鏞廈教授停年記念論叢刊行委員會]. *A Study of the Development of South Korean Society* [韓國社會發展研究]. Seoul: Nanam [나남].

_____. 2015. "Korea's Colonial Experience and the Issue of Japanese Military 'Comfort Women'" [韓國의 植民地經驗과 日本軍'慰安婦'問題]. Presented at the international symposium in commemoration of the 70th anniversary of the Liberation "Rethinking Women in an Age of War and Violence: The Issue of Japanese Military 'Comfort Women' and Colonial Damages and Responsibilities for Them" [戰爭과 暴力의 時代, 다시 女性을 생각하다—日本軍'慰安婦'問題와 植民地被害, 그 責任].

Chung, Chinsung [鄭鎭星], and Cho Sung Youn [趙誠倫]. 1994. "A History of Koreans' Immigration to China: With a Focus on Immigration to Manchuria during the Japanese Colonial Era" [朝鮮族의 中國流移民史—日帝時期滿洲移民을 中心으로]. Ed. Korean Association for Political and Diplomatic History [韓國政治外交史學會]. *The Formation and Transformation of the Southeast Asian Order* [東南亞秩序의 形成과 變動]. Seoul: Gwahak Jeongbosa [科學情報社].

Chung, Hye-Kyung [鄭惠瓊]. 2003. *The History of the Forced Taking of Koreans at the End of the Japanese Colonial Period: A Documentary Study* [日帝末期朝鮮人强制連行의 歷史—史料研究]. Kyungin Koreanology Research Ser. 22 [景仁韓國學研究叢書22]. Seoul: Kyungin Publishing [景仁文化社].

Chung, Hyun Back [鄭鉉柏]. 1998. "Globalization, Nationalism, and Feminism in Korea" [地球化, 民族主義 그리고 韓國의 페미니즘]. Presented at the Korea Women's Studies Institute [韓國女性研究所] symposium "The Lives of Women in an Era of Crisis and Feminism in South Korea" [危機時代의 女性의 삶과 韓國의 페미니즘].

Chung, Jae-Chul [鄭在哲]. 1985. *A History of Japanese Imperial Rulers' Colonial Education Policies Regarding Korea* [日帝의 對韓國植民地教育政策史]. Seoul: Ilchisa [一志社].

Commission on Verification and Support for the Victims of Forced Mobilization under Japanese Colonialism in Korea [對日抗爭期强制動員被害調查 및 國外强制動員犧牲者等 支援委員會]. 2011. "An Investigation of Facts Concerning 'Corporate Comfort Stations' and Korean 'Corporate Comfort Women' in Japan during the War: With a Focus on the Hokkaido and Kyushu Regions" [戰時下日本地域의 '企業慰安所'와 朝鮮人'企業慰安婦'에 對한 眞相調查—北海道와 九州地域을 中心으로]. Seoul: Commission on Verification and Support for the Victims of Forced Mobilization under Japanese

Colonialism in Korea.

Compilation Committee of the *20-Year History of the Korean Council for the Women Drafted for Military Sexual Slavery by Japan* [『韓國挺身隊問題對策協議會二十年史』編纂委員會], ed. 2014. *The 20-Year History of the Korean Council for the Women Drafted for Military Sexual Slavery by Japan* [韓國挺身隊問題對策協議會二十年史]. Seoul: Hanul Academy [한울아카데미].

Coomaraswamy, Radhika. 1996. "Addendum: Report of the Special Rapporteur on Violence against Women, Its Causes and Consequences, Ms. Radhika Coomaraswamy, in Accordance with Commission on Human Rights Resolution 1994/45: Report on the Mission to the Democratic People's Republic of Korea, the Republic of Korea and Japan on the Issue of Military Sexual Slavery in Wartime" (UN Doc. E/CN. 4/1996/53/Add. 1; Jan. 4). Trans. National Assembly Library overseas resource officer [國會圖書館海外資料官]. "A Special Report of the UN Commission on Human Rights Regarding the Issue of Military Sexual Slavery in Wartime" (Apr. 1996. 52nd Session) [戰時軍性奴隸制問題에 關한 UN人權委員會特別報告(1996. 4. 第五十二次會議)]. Lee Mikyung [李美卿], ed. 1997. *Sourcebook on Assemblyperson Lee Mikyung's Legislative Activities 1* [李美卿議員議政資料集1] (Feb.).

Daegu Court of Review [大邱伏審法院]; Daegu District Court [大邱地方法院]; Miryang Branch [密陽支廳], Busan District Court [釜山地方法院]; Ganggyeong Branch [江景支廳], Daejeon District Court [大田地方法院]; Jangheung Branch [長興支廳], Gwangju District Court [光州地方法院]; Jeongju District Court [定州地方法院]; Gwangju District Court, etc. 1938-1944. Rulings.

Dong-A Ilbo [東亞日報]. 1925, 1927, 1936, 1938, 1992, 2007, and 2015.

Donnelly, Jack. 1996. "The Universality of the Concept of Human Rights and Asian Values" [人權概念의 普遍性과 아시아的 價値]. Ed. Institute of Social Sciences [社會科學院]. *Kyegan Sasang: The Growth of East Asia and Human Rights* [季刊思想—東아시아의 成長과 人權] (winter).

Evans, Richard J. 1977. *The Feminists: Women's Emancipation Movements in Europe, America and Australasia, 1840-1920.* London: Croom Helm. Trans. Chung Hyun Back [鄭鉉柏], et al. 1997. *The Feminists* [페미니스트]. Seoul: Changbi [創作과 批評社].

Federation of Korean Trade Unions [韓國勞動組合總聯盟]. 1995a. "A Letter from the ILO Director-General: August 11, 1995" [ILO事務總長書翰—一九九五年八月十一日] (Aug. 11).

_____. 1995b. "ILO Sub-Committee Discussions on the Federation of Korean Trade Unions' Petition on Comfort Women: November 11, 1995" [ILO小委員會韓國勞總의 慰安婦陳情論議: 一九九五年十一月十一日] (Nov. 11).

_____. 1996. "A Report on the 83rd ILO General Conference" [第八十三次ILO總會報告書].

Fujiwara, Akira [藤原彰]. 1987. *Japanese Military History, Vol. 1: Prewar Period* [日本軍事史—上卷戰前篇]. Tokyo: Nippon Hyoron Sha Co., Ltd. [日本評論社]. Trans. Eom Suhyeon [嚴秀鉉]. 1994. *Japanese Military History* [日本軍事史]. Seoul: Sisa Ilbonosa [時事日本語社].

Fukushima, Mizuho [福島瑞穗]. 1992. "A Report on the Trial Struggle" [裁判闘爭에 關한 報告]. Ed. Korean Council for the Women Drafted for Military Sexual Slavery by Japan [韓國挺身隊問題對策協議會]. *A Report on the Asian Solidarity Conference for the Issue of Military Sexual Slavery by Japan* [挺身隊問題아시아連帶會議報告書].

Han, Hye-In [韓惠仁]. 2013. "Act of Employment under the General Mobilization and Mobilization of Japanese Military Sexual Slave: Focused on Discriminative Operating System between Japan Empire and Colonial Chosun" [總動員體制下職業紹介令과 日本軍慰安婦動員—帝國日本과 植民地朝鮮의 差別的 制度運營을 中心으로]. Ed. Soosun Historical Association [首善史學會]. *Historical Journal* [史林] 46.0 (2013): 371-413.

_____. 2015. "Japan's Rule over the 'South Seas Mandate' and the Installation of Japanese Military 'Comfort Stations' during the War" [日本의 '南洋群島'支配와 戰爭期日本軍'慰安所'設置]. Presented at the 2015 Historical Society of Korea [韓國史學會] conference "The Concept and Categories of Japanese Military 'Comfort Women' as Seen through Cases of Local Damages during the Asia-Pacific War" [아시아太平洋戰爭時期地域被害事例를 通해 본 日本軍'慰安婦'의 概念과 範疇] (Sept. 4).

Han, Jeonghui [韓정희]. 1998. "Unmarried Korean Women Taken to Coal Mines in Hokkaido" [北海道炭鑛에 끌려간 朝鮮人處女들]. *Wolgan Sahoe Pyongnon Kil* [月刊社會評論 길] (Aug.).

Han, Woosung [韓우성]. 2000. "An Unfinished War: A Report on the Lawsuits Regarding 'Japanese Military Comfort Women' and the Labor Draft in Progress in the United States" [끝나지 않은 戰爭: 美國에서 進行中인 '日本軍慰安婦' 및 徵用訴訟에 對한 報告書]. *Dangdae Bipyeong* [當代批評] 13 (winter).

Hankook Ilbo [韓國日報]. 1981, 1992, 1998, 2007, and 2016

Hankyoreh [한겨레新聞]. 1990, 1993, 1998, 2014, 2015, 2016, and 2017.

Higashizawa, Yasushi [東澤靖]. 2001. "The Contributions of the Women's International War Crimes Tribunal on Japan's Military Sexual Slavery in 2000 to the International Commission of Jurists" [2000年日本軍性奴隸戰犯女性國際法廷의 國際刑事裁判所에 對한 寄與]. Ed. Legal Committee [法律委員會], Women's International War Crimes Tribunal on Japan's Military Sexual Slavery in 2000 [2000年日本軍性奴隸戰犯女性國際法廷], Korean Council for the Women Drafted for Military Sexual Slavery by Japan [韓國挺身隊問題對策協議會]. *The Prospects of the Legal Resolution of the Issue of Japanese Military Comfort Women* [日本軍慰安婦問題에 對한 法的 解決의 展望]. Seoul: Pulbit [풀빛].

Hobsbawm, Eric J. 1990. *Nations and Nationalism since 1780: Programme, Myth, Reality*. Cambridge: Cambridge University Press. Trans. Kang Miongsei [姜明世]. 1994. *Nations and Nationalism since 1780* [1780年以後의 民族과 民族主義]. Seoul: Changbi [創作과 批評社].

Hoopes, James. 1979. *Oral History: An Introduction for Students*. Chapel Hill: University of North Carolina Press. Trans. Yu Byeong'yong [유병용]. 1995. *An Introduction to Testimonial History* [證言史入門]. Seoul: Hanul Academy [한울아카데미].

Huh, Soo Youl [許粹烈]. 1983. "A Study of the Nature of Colonial Industry in Korea under Japanese Colonial Rule" [日帝下韓國에 있어서 植民地的 工業의 性格에 關한 一研究]. Doctoral dissertation. Department of Economics [經濟學科], Seoul National University [서울大學校].

Ichihara, Hiroshi [市原博]. 1992. "The Reality of Koreans' Labor in Coal Mines during the War: A Supplementary Discussion" [戰時下朝鮮人の炭鑛勞動の實態—補論]. Ed. Center for Research on Korean-Japanese Issues [日帝三十六年史研究所]. *International Symposium on the Forced Taking of Koreans: With a Focus on the Hokkaido Region* [朝鮮人强制連行에 關한 國際심포지엄—北海道地域을 中心으로].

Im, Jongguk [林鍾國], ed. and trans. 1981. *Veritable Records of the Volunteer Corps* [挺身隊實錄]. Irwol Ser. [日月叢書] 1. Seoul: Irwol Sogak [日月書閣] [posthumously revealed to have been a translation of Kim, Il-myon [or Kimu, Irumyoun [金一勉]]. 1976. *The Emperor's Armed Forces and Korean Comfort Women* [天皇の軍隊と朝鮮人慰安婦]. Tokyo: San-Ichi Shobo Publishing Inc. [三一書房]].

Institute for Research in Collaborationist Activities [反民族問題研究所]. 1994. *Unresolved History 2* [清算하지 못한 歷史 2]. Seoul: Chungnyunsa [青年社].

Jeon, Sung-Hyun [全盛賢]. 2015. "A Study on Changes to the School Fleet Organization and Mobilization of Collective Labor Force during the Wartime Period" [戰時體制期學校隊組織의 變化와 集團勞動力動員—朝鮮總督府의 學生動員政策을 中心으로]. Ed. Seokdang Academy [石堂學術院], Dong-A University [東亞大學校]. *Journal of Seokdang Academy* [石堂論叢] 62.

Joo, Sungsoo [朱聖秀], and Seo Yeongjin [徐영진]. 2000. *United Nations, NGOs, and Global Civil Society* [UN, NGO, 글로벌市民社會]. Seoul: Hanyang University Press [漢陽大學校出版部].

Kang, Jeong-sook [姜貞淑]. 1993. "Policies on Korean Women at the End of Japanese Colonial Rule (1937-1945)" [日帝末(1937~1945) 朝鮮女性政策]. Ed. Institute of Asian Culture Studies [아시아文化研究所], Hallym University [翰林大學校]. *Asian Culture* [아시아文化] 9.

_____. 1997. "The Geographical Distribution and Characteristics of Japanese Military Comfort Stations" [日本軍慰安所의 地域的 分布와 그 特徵]. Ed. Korean Council for the Women Drafted for Military Sexual Slavery by Japan [韓國挺身隊問題對策協議

會]. *The Truth about "Comfort Women" in the Japanese Military* [日本軍'慰安婦'問題의 眞相]. Seoul: Yuksa Bipyongsa [歷史批評社].

_____. 2010. "A Study for Colonialism Characteristics of Japanese Military 'Comfort Women' System: Focusing on Korean 'Comfort Women'" [日本軍'慰安婦'制의 植民性研究—朝鮮人 '慰安婦'를 中心으로]. Doctoral dissertation. Department of History [史學科], Sungkyunkwan University [成均館大學校].

Kang, Man-gil [姜萬吉]. 1993. "A Historiographical Approach to the Issue of Japanese Military Sex Slaves" [日本軍性奴隸問題의 歷史學的 接近]. Presented at the 2nd Joint Symposium by the Center for Research and Documentation on Japan's War Responsibility and the Korean Council for the Women Drafted for Military Sexual Slavery by Japan [日本의 戰爭責任資料센터·韓國挺身隊問題對策協議會 共同심포지엄; 日本の戰爭責任資料センタ-·韓國挺身隊問題對策協議會共同シンポジウム] (Dec.).

_____. 1997. "The Issue of the Concept and Names of Japanese Military Sexual Slavery" [日本軍性奴隸制의 概念과 呼稱問題]. Ed. Korean Council for the Women Drafted for Military Sexual Slavery by Japan [韓國挺身隊問題對策協議會]. *The Truth about "Comfort Women" in the Japanese Military* [日本軍'慰安婦'問題의 眞相]. Seoul: Yuksa Bipyongsa [歷史批評社].

Kang, Sun-Mi [康宣美], and Yamashita Yeong-Ae [山下英愛]. 1993. "The State under the Emperor System and Sexual Violence" [天皇制國家와 性暴力]. Ed. Korean Association of Women's Studies [韓國女性學會]. *Journal of Korean Women's Studies* [韓國女性學] 9.

Kang, Sunghyun [康誠賢]. 2016. "The Current Status and Tasks of the Excavation of American Materials on Japanese Military "Comfort Women" [日本軍'慰安婦'美國資料發掘現況과 課題]. *The Accomplishments and Tasks of Research on Japanese Military "Comfort Women"* [日本軍'慰安婦'研究成果와 課題]. Northeast Asian History Foundation [東北亞歷史財團] international academic conference sourcebook.

Kim, Chang-Rok [金昌祿]. 2015. "The Responsibility of Colonization—Message from Korea" [植民地支配의 責任—韓國으로부터의 發信]. Presented at the international symposium "Thinking of Women in the Era of War and Violence—Japanese Military 'Comfort Women' and Colonization: Responsibility & Accountability" [戰爭과 暴力의 時代, 다시 女性을 생각하다—日本軍'慰安婦'問題와 植民地被害, 그 責任의 方法] sponsored by the Ministry of Gender Equality and Family [女性家族部] and the Women's Human Rights Commission of Korea [韓國女性人權振興院].

Kim, Dae Sang [金大商]. 1978. "The Tragedy of the Women' Volunteer Corps under Japanese Colonial Rule" [日帝下女子挺身隊의 悲劇]. *Shindonga* [新東亞] (Apr.).

Kim, Eun-Shil [金恩實]. 1994. "Ethnic Discourse and Women" [民族談論과 女性]. Ed. Korean Association of Women's Studies [韓國女性學會]. *Journal of Korean Women's Studies* [韓國女性學] 10.

Kim, Mi Hyun [金美賢]. 2008. "An Investigation on Labor Mobilization through the 'Korean Women's Labor Volunteer Corps' Method" ['朝鮮女子勤勞挺身隊'方式에 依한 勞務動員에 關한 調査]. Ex Officio Investigation Report 2 [職權 調査 報告書 2]. Seoul: Truth Commission on Forced Mobilization under the Japanese Imperialism [國務總理所屬日帝强占下强制動員被害眞相糾明委員會].

Kim, Min-Young [金旻榮]. 1995. *A Study of the Japanese Colonial Authorities' Exploitation of Korean Manpower* [日帝의 朝鮮人勞動力收奪硏究]. Seoul: Hanul Academy [한울 아카데미].

Kim, Seong-Nae [金成禮]. 1994. "Oral History: A Methodology for Women's History" [口述史—女性史方法論]. Korean Association of Women's Studies [韓國女性學會] workshop materials.

Kim, Yoon Mi [金潤美]. 2008. "The Labor Corps for Repaying Country's Favor (LCRC) in the National Mobilization System: The Early Management of [LCRC (1938-1941)" [總動員體制와 勤勞報國隊를 通한 '國民皆勞'—朝鮮에서 施行된 勤勞報國隊의 初期運用을 中心으로(1938~1941)]. Ed. Association of Korean-Japanese National Studies [韓日民族問題學會]. *Journal of Korean-Japanese National Studies* [韓日民族問題硏究] 14.

Korea Times [美洲韓國日報]. 2007.

Korean Broadcasting System [韓國放送公社]. *Special Program on the 70th Anniversary of the Liberation: Girls Taken away Disappear at the Burma Front* [光復七十周年特輯—끌려간 少女들 버마戰線에서 사라지다]. Broadcast on KBS1 TV, August 9, 2015 (documentary; in Korean).

Korean Council for the Women Drafted for Military Sexual Slavery by Japan [韓國挺身隊問題對策協議會], ed. 1991-1995. *A Sourcebook on the Issue of the Volunteer Corps* [挺身隊問題資料集] I-V.

_____. 2001. "The Summary Verdict of the Women's International War Crimes Tribunal on Japan's Military Sexual Slavery in 2000" [2000年日本軍性奴隸戰犯女性國際法廷—略式判決文]. *A Report on the Women's International War Crimes Tribunal on Japan's Military Sexual Slavery in 2000* [2000年日本軍性奴隸戰犯女性國際法廷報告書].

_____. 2009. "1st Policy Discussion for Responses to the Issue of Japanese Military 'Comfort Women' under the Hatoyama Coalition Government in Japan" [日本鳩山聯立政權에서의 日本軍'慰安婦'問題對應을 爲한 一次政策懇談會] (Oct. 8).

Korean Council for the Women Drafted for Military Sexual Slavery by Japan [韓國挺身隊問題對策協議會], and the Korean-Japanese PCA Defense Counsel [PCA韓日辯護人團]. 1995. "A Report on a Forum of the Korean-Japanese Defense Counsel for the Lawsuit to the Permanent Court of Arbitration (PCA): For the Resolution of the Problem of Japanese Military Comfort Women through International Law" [國際仲裁裁判所(PCA)提訴를 爲한 韓日辯護人團討論會報告書—日本軍慰安婦問題의 國際法的解決을 爲하여].

Korean Council for the Women Drafted for Military Sexual Slavery by Japan [韓國挺身隊問題對策協議會], and the Korean Chongshindae Research Group [韓國挺身隊硏究會], eds. 1993. *Forcibly Taken Korean Military Comfort Women* [强制로 끌려간 朝鮮人軍慰安婦들], vol. 1. Seoul: Hanul [한울].

_____, eds. 1995. *Stories of the Korean Comfort Women Brought into China: Testimonies after 50 Years* [中國으로 끌려간 朝鮮人軍慰安婦들—50年後의 證言]. Seoul: Hanul [한울].

_____, eds. 1997. *Forcibly Taken Korean Military Comfort Women* [强制로 끌려간 朝鮮人軍慰安婦들], vol. 2. Seoul: Hanul [한울].

Korean Womenlink [女性平友會], ed. 1985. *Third World Women's Labor* [第三世界女性勞動]. Seoul: Changbi [創作과 批評社].

Lee, Hyo Chae [李效再]. 1976. "A Study on Korean Women's Labor Problems under the Japanese Rule" [日帝下의 韓國女性勞動問題]. *Journal of Korean Studies* [韓國學報] 2.3.

_____. 1989. *Women's Movements in Korea* [韓國의 女性運動]. Seoul: Chong'usa [正宇社].

_____. 1997. "The Developmental Processes of the Movements for the Resolution of the Issue of Japanese Military Comfort Women" [日本軍慰安婦 問題解決을 爲한 運動의 展開過程]. Ed. Korean Council for the Women Drafted for Military Sexual Slavery by Japan [韓國挺身隊問題對策協議會]. *The Truth about "Comfort Women" in the Japanese Military* [日本軍'慰安婦'問題의 眞相]. Seoul: Yuksa Bipyongsa [歷史批評社].

Lee, Jeong-Seon [李正善]. 2015. "Colonial Japan's Korean-Japanese Intermarriage Policy" [日帝의 '內鮮結婚'政策]. Doctoral dissertation. Department of Korean History [國史學科], Seoul National University [서울大學校].

Lee, Jung Ok [李貞玉]. 1990. "Segmentation by Nationality and Gender in Industrial Wage Labour Sector in Korea under the Japanese Rule, 1910-1945" [日帝下工業勞動에서의 民族과 性]. Doctoral dissertation. Department of Sociology [社會學科], Seoul National University [서울大學校].

Lee, Na-Young [李나영]. 2015. "Nationalism and Gender: Critical Mapping on Theoretical Debates and Feminist Challenges" [民族主義와 젠더—挑戰과 變形을 爲한 理論的 地形圖그리기]. Ed. Korean Association of Women's Studies [韓國女性學會]. *Journal of Korean Women's Studies* [韓國女性學] 31.2.

Lee, Seung-hee [李承姬]. 1990. "The Women's Movements of the '80s for Human Liberation and Women's Liberation" [人間解放·女性解放을 向한 80年代 女性運動]. Ed. Cho Hee-youn [曺喜昖]. *A History of Social Movements in Korea* [韓國社會運動史]. Seoul: Chuksan [竹山].

Maeil Sinbo [每日申報]. 1938 and 1940-1945.

Mahissaya, Somkid. 1992. "The Forced Labor Corps of the Thailand-Burma Railway and Comfort Women" [타이-버마鐵路의 勞役勤勞隊와 慰安婦]. Ed. Korean Council for the Women Drafted for Military Sexual Slavery by Japan [韓國挺身隊問題對策協

議會]. *A Report on the Asian Solidarity Conference for the Issue of Military Sexual Slavery by Japan* [挺身隊問題아시아連帶會議報告書].

Matsui, Yayori [松井やより]. 2003. *Love and Anger, the Courage to Fight: A Woman Journalist's Record of Life* [愛と怒り闘う勇氣—女性ジャ-ナリスト命の記錄]. Tokyo: Iwanami Shoten [岩波書店]. Trans. Kim Sunmi [金선미]. 2014. *Love, Be Angry, Fight with Courage: Journalist and Woman Activist Matsui Yayori's Record of Life* [사랑하라 憤怒하라 勇氣있게 싸워라—저널리스트이자 女性運動家 마츠이 야요리의 生命의 記錄]. Seoul: Mosineun Saramdeul [모시는 사람들].

McCormack, Gavan. 1997. "The True Identity of the Japanese 'Liberal View of History'" [日本'自由主義史觀'의 正體]. *Quarterly Changbi* [創作과 批評] 98.

McDougall, Gay Johnson. Trans. Cho Si-Hyun [曺時顯]. 1998a. "McDougall Report: Systematic Rape, Sexual Slavery and Slavery-like Practices during Wartime, Including Internal Conflict (1)" [맥두갈報告書: 武力衝突中의 體系的 强姦, 性奴隸制와 奴隸制와 다름없는 慣行 (1)]. Ed. Lawyers for a Democratic Society (Minbyun) [民主社會를 爲한 辯護士會(民辯)]. *Legal Defense for Democratic Society* [民主社會를 爲한 辯論(民辯)] 24 (Oct.).

_____. 1998b. "McDougall Report: Systematic Rape, Sexual Slavery and Slavery-like Practices during Wartime, Including Internal Conflict (2)" [맥두갈報告書: 武力衝突中의 體系的 强姦, 性奴隸制와 奴隸制와 다름없는 慣行 (2)]. Ed. Lawyers for a Democratic Society (Minbyun) [民主社會를 爲한 辯護士會(民辯)]. *Legal Defense for Democratic Society* [民主社會를 爲한 辯論] 25 (Nov./Dec.).

Miyoshi, Masao [三好將夫], and Harry D. Harootunian. 1989. "Introduction." Ed. Harootunian and Miyoshi. *Postmodernism and Japan*. Durham: Duke University Press. Trans. Gwak Donghun [郭동훈], et al. 1996. *Postmodernism and Japan* [포스트모더니즘과 日本]. Seoul: Sigak-kwa Ono [視覺과 言語].

Munhwa Broadcasting Corporation [文化放送]. *MBC Newsdesk* [MBC뉴스데스크]. "A photograph and a record of a scene where Japanese soldiers shot Korean comfort women *en masse* to death in 1944" [1944年, 日本軍이 韓國慰安婦를 集團銃殺한 場面 寫眞과 記錄]. Broadcast on MBC TV, August 15, 1997 (in Korean).

Nam, Sanggu [南相九]. 2014. "A Critical Review of the Japanese Government's Report on the Results of the Verification of the Kono Statement" [日本政府의 고노談話檢證結果報告에 對한 批判的 檢討]. Presented at the "Emergency Expert Discussion in Relation to the Verification of the Kono Statement" [고노談話檢證關聯緊急專門家討論會] sponsored by the Northeast Asian History Foundation [東北亞歷史財團] (Jun. 23).

National Assembly Group for the Issue of Japanese Military Comfort Women [國會日本軍慰安婦問題硏究모임]. 1998. *Women's Human Rights in Asia: Armed Conflict and Sexual Violence* [아시아의 女性人權—武力葛藤과 性暴力]. Symposium sourcebook.

Northeast Asian History Foundation [東北亞歷史財團], ed. 2014. *Sourcebook on the "Emergency Expert Discussion in Relation to the Verification of the Kono Statement"* [고노談話檢證關聯緊急專門家討論會資料集].

Pak, Myongok [朴明玉]. 1998. "To Co-representatives of the Korean Council for the Women Drafted for Military Sexual Slavery by Japan Mses. Lee Hyo Chae and Yun Chung-Ok" [韓國挺身隊問題對策協議會共同代表 李效再, 尹貞玉先生 앞]. Vice Chair Pak Myongok [副委員長 朴明玉] of the Committee on Measures for Compensation to the "Former Comfort Women for Japanese Army" and Pacific War Victims ['從軍慰安婦' 및 太平洋戰爭被害者補償對策委員會] (Aug. 20).

Pang, Sun-joo [方善柱]. 1992. "An Examination of Korean 'Military Comfort Women' in American Materials" [美國資料에 나타난 韓人'從軍慰安婦'의 考察]. Ed. National Institute of Korean History (National History Compilation Committee) [國史編纂委員會]. *Treatises on Korean History* [國史館論叢] 37.

_____. 1997. "The Return of Japanese Military Comfort Women: An Interim Report" [日本軍慰安婦의 歸還—中間報告]. Ed. Korean Council for the Women Drafted for Military Sexual Slavery by Japan [韓國挺身隊問題對策協議會]. *The Truth about "Comfort Women" in the Japanese Military* [日本軍'慰安婦'問題의 眞相]. Seoul: Yuksa Bipyongsa [歷史批評社].

Park, Hong Kyu [朴洪圭]. 1991. *South Korea and the ILO* [韓國과 ILO]. Seoul: Hyongsongsa [形成社].

Park, Hyun-Ok [朴현옥]. 1994. "Women, Nation, and Class: Differences and Collective Agency" [女性, 民族, 階級: 다름과 集合的 行爲]. Ed. Korean Association of Women's Studies [韓國女性學會]. *Journal of Korean Women's Studies* [韓國女性學] 10.

Park, Jung Ae [朴貞愛]. 2009. "A Study on State-regulated Prostitution and Unlicensed Prostitute Management of Japanese Imperialism" [日帝의 公娼制施行과 私娼管理研究]. Doctoral dissertation. Department of History [史學科], Sookmyung Women's University [淑明女子大學校].

_____. 2010. "The Structure and Nature of Human Trafficking during the Period of Imperial Japan's Invasion" [日帝侵略期人身賣買의 構造와 性格]. Ed. Compilation Committee of Collections of Research Papers on the History of Korean-Japanese Relations [韓日關係史研究論集編纂委員會]. *The Ideology of Description in South Korean and Japanese History Textbooks* [韓日歷史教科書敍述의 理念]. Collections of Research Papers on the History of Korean-Japanese Relations [韓日關係史研究論集] 19. Seoul: Kyungin Publishing [景仁文化社].

_____. 2015. "An Essay on the Category and Concept of 'Comfort Women' Drafted into the Japanese Forces through Damage Status" [被害實態를 通해 본 日本軍'慰安婦'의 概念과 範疇試論]. Ed. Historical Society of Korea [韓國史學會]. *Review of Korean History* [史學研究] 120.

_____. 2016. "Venereal Disease Prevention Policy of Joseon Government-General of Korea and <Venereal Disease Prevention Ordinance>" [朝鮮總督府의 性病豫防政策과 <花柳病豫防令>]. Ed. Soosun Historical Association [首善史學會]. *Historical Journal* [史林] 55.

Park, Kyung-Sik [朴慶植]. 1981. *Materials on the Korean Problem Series 2: Wartime Forced Taking and Labor Management Policy* [朝鮮問題資料叢書2—戰時强制連行·勞務管理政策]. Tokyo: Asia Research Institute [アジア問題研究所]. Trans. Editorial Board [編輯部]. 1998. Seoul: Kookhak Charyowon [國學資料院].

_____. 1986. *The Japanese Colonial Rule over Korea* [日本帝國主義의 朝鮮支配]. Seoul: Chung-A Publishing Co., Ltd. [菁莪出版社].

Park, Won Soon [朴元淳]. 1993. "The Essence of and Solution to the Issue of the Volunteer Corps" [挺身隊問題의 本質과 解決方案]. Unpublished paper.

_____. 1995. "The Issue of Military Comfort Women and Forced Labour Conventions" [從軍慰安婦問題와 强制勞動條約]. Presented at a Federation of Korean Trade Unions [韓國勞動組合總聯盟] seminar (Feb. 9).

_____. 1997. "The Prospects of the Resolution of the Issue of Japanese Military Comfort Women" [日本軍慰安婦問題解決의 展望]. Ed. Truth Investigation and Research Committee [眞相調査研究委員會], Korean Council for the Women Drafted for Military Sexual Slavery by Japan [韓國挺身隊問題對策協議會]. *The Truth about "Comfort Women" in the Japanese Military* [日本軍'慰安婦'問題의 眞相]. Seoul: Yuksa Bipyongsa [歷史批評社].

Park, Yong-ock [朴容玉]. 1984. *A Study of the History of Modern Women's Movements in Korea* [韓國近代女性運動史研究]. Seongnam: Academy of Korean Studies [韓國精神文化研究院].

Sancho, Nelia. 1992. "A Letter to the Asian Solidarity Conference" [아시아連帶會議에 부치는 書信]. Ed. Korean Council for the Women Drafted for Military Sexual Slavery by Japan [韓國挺身隊問題對策協議會]. *A Report on the Asian Solidarity Conference for the Issue of Military Sexual Slavery by Japan* [挺身隊問題아시아連帶會議報告書].

Senda, Kakou [千田夏光]. 1973. *Military Comfort Women: Indictment by 80,000 "Voiceless Women"* [從軍慰安婦—"聲なき女"八萬人の告發]. Tokyo: Futabasha Publishers, Ltd. [雙葉社]. Trans. Yi Songhui [李송희]. 1991. *Military Comfort Women* [從軍慰安婦]. Seoul: Paek Sobang [柏書房].

Seo, Hyun-ju [徐賢珠]. 2015. "The Colonial Character of Japanese 'Comfort Women' System" [日本軍'慰安婦'制度의 植民性: 紹介營業取締規則을 中心으로]. Presented at the International Conference on Historical Challenges and Prospects for Resolving the Japanese Military "Comfort Women" Issue [光復70周年紀念韓中日國際學術會議日本軍'慰安婦'問題의 解決을 爲한 歷史的 課題와 展望], Northeast Asian History Foundation [東北亞歷史財團], Seoul, South Korea (Nov. 17).

Seoul Shinmun [서울新聞]. 1946 and 1970.

Shim, Young-Hee [沈英姬]. 2001a. "The Courtroom in 2000 Was Not Over Yet" [2000年法廷은 아직 끝나지 않았다: 2000年日本軍性奴隸戰犯女性國際法廷參觀記]. Ed. Korea Women's Studies Institute [韓國女性硏究會]. *Women and Society* [女性과 社會] 12 (Mar.).

_____. 2001b. "The Final Verdict and Report to International Conferences" [最終判決 및 國際會議報告]. Ed. Korean Council for the Women Drafted for Military Sexual Slavery by Japan [韓國挺身隊問題對策協議會]. *A Report on the Women's International War Crimes Tribunal on Japan's Military Sexual Slavery in 2000* [2000年日本軍性奴隸戰犯女性國際法廷報告書].

Shin, Heisoo [申蕙秀]. 1994. "Nationalism and Feminism: Their Combination and Tension as Seen through the Issue of Japanese Military Comfort Women" [民族主義와 페미니즘: 日本軍慰安婦問題를 通해 본 그 結合과 緊張]. Presented at the Korean Association of Women's Studies [韓國女性學會] fall symposium.

_____. 1997. "The Accomplishments and Tasks of International Activities to Resolve the Issue of Japanese Military Comfort Women" [日本軍慰安婦問題解決을 爲한 國際活動의 成果와 課題]. Ed. Korean Council for the Women Drafted for Military Sexual Slavery by Japan [韓國挺身隊問題對策協議會]. *The Truth about "Comfort Women" in the Japanese Military* [日本軍'慰安婦'問題의 眞相]. Seoul: Yuksa Bipyongsa [歷史批評社].

Shin, Young-sook [申榮淑]. 1989. "A Study on the Korean Women's Society in the Period of the Japanese Dominations" [日帝下韓國女性社會史硏究]. Doctoral dissertation. Department of History [史學科], Ewha Womans University [梨花女子大學校].

Shin, Young-sook [申榮淑], and Cho Hye-ran [조혜란]. 1996. "A Study of the Reality and Characteristics of Korean 'Military Comfort Women' during the Japanese Colonial Era" [日帝時期朝鮮人'軍慰安婦'의 實態 및 特性에 關한 硏究]. Ed. Korean Chongshindae Research Group [韓國挺身隊硏究會]. *Unresolved Issues between Korea and Japan* [韓日間의 未清算課題]. Seongnam: Asian Culture Press [亞細亞文化社].

Shirato, Hitoyasu [白戶仁康]. 1992. "Bibai Coal Mine during World War II: With a Focus on the Issue of Koreans" [第二次世界大戰期美唄炭鑛—朝鮮人問題를 中心으로]. Ed. Center for Research on Korean-Japanese Issues [日帝三十六年史硏究所]. *International Symposium on the Forced Taking of Koreans: With a Focus on the Hokkaido Region* [朝鮮人强制連行에 關한 國際심포지엄—北海道地域을 中心으로].

Sin, Gyeong'a [신경아]. 1985. "Export-Oriented Industrialization and Female Labour in Korea" [韓國의 輸出指向的 工業化와 女性勞動]. Master's thesis. Department of Sociology [社會學科], Seoul National University [서울大學校].

Song, Eoun-ok [宋連玉]. 1998. "Japanese Colonization and the Introduction of Licensed

Prostitution" [日帝植民地化와 公娼制導入]. Master's thesis. Department of Korean History [國史學科], Seoul National University [서울大學校].

Sugihara, Yasuo [杉原泰雄]. 1992. *A History of Human Rights* [人權の歷史]. Tokyo: Iwanami Shoten [岩波書店]. Trans. Seok In Sun [석인선]. 1995. *A History of Human Rights* [人權의 歷史]. Seoul: Hanul [한울].

Takagi, Ken'ichi [高木健一]. 1992. "Regarding Japan's 'Postwar Compensations'" [日本의 '戰後補償'에 對해서]. Ed. Korea Women's Institute for Peace Studies [基督教女性平和研究院]. *Women Making Peace* [平和를 만드는 女性] 12.

_____. 1994. *The Logic of Postwar Compensations: How Are the Victims' Voices to Be Heard?* [戰後補償の論理—被害者の聲をどう聞くか]. Tokyo: Rengashobou-shinsha Publishers [れんが書房新社]. Trans. Choe Yonggi [崔용기]. 1995. *The Logic of Postwar Compensations* [戰後補償의 論理]. Seoul: Hanul [한울].

Takahashi, Kikue [高橋喜久江]. 1992. "Activities in Japan" [日本에서의 活動]. Ed. Korean Council for the Women Drafted for Military Sexual Slavery by Japan [韓國挺身隊問題對策協議會]. *A Report on the Asian Solidarity Conference for the Issue of Military Sexual Slavery by Japan* [挺身隊問題아시아連帶會議報告書].

Team for the Investigation and Annotation of American Materials on Japanese Military "Comfort Women" [日本軍'慰安婦'美國資料調查解題팀], Human Rights Center [人權센터], Seoul National University [서울大學校]. 2016. *Sourcebook on Forced Mobilization and Human Rights: The Project for the Investigation and Annotation of American Materials Related to Japanese Military "Comfort Women"* [强制動員과 人權資料集—日本軍'慰安婦'關係美國資料調查 및 解題事業].

Totsuka, Etsuro [戶塚悅朗]. 2015. "The Way of Historical Awareness and Reconciliation between Korea and Japan: In Order to Resolve the Japanese Military 'Comfort Women' Issue" [日本軍慰安婦問題の解決に向けた歷史と法の課題]. Presented at the International Conference on Historical Challenges and Prospects for Resolving the Japanese Military "Comfort Women" Issue [光復70周年紀念韓中日國際學術會議 日本軍'慰安婦'問題의 解決을 爲한 歷史的 課題와 展望], Northeast Asian History Foundation [東北亞歷史財團], Seoul, South Korea (Nov. 17).

Um, Kwang-Sup [嚴光燮]. 1946. "A Diary of Return" [歸還日記]. *Our Literature* [우리 文學] 1 (Feb.).

Van Boven, Theodoor "Theo" Cornelis. 1982. "Distinguishing Criteria of Human Rights." Ed. Karel Vasak. Trans. Philip Alston. *The International Dimensions of Human Rights*. Vol. 1. Paris/Westport: UNESCO/Greenwood Press. "Distinguishing Criteria of Human Rights" [人權의 分類基準]. 1986. Trans. Park Hong Kyu [朴洪圭]. *A Theory of Human Rights* [人權論]. Seoul: Silcheon Munhaksa [實踐文學社].

Women's Rights Planning Division [權益企劃課], Ministry of Gender Equality [女性部], and the College of Social Sciences [社會科學大學], Seoul National University [서

울大學校], eds. 2002. *Investigative Research on Overseas Materials on the Issue of Japanese Military Comfort Women* [日本軍慰安婦問題에 關한 國外資料調査研究]. Research Report 2002-27 [研究報告 2002-27]. Seoul: Ministry of Gender Equality.

Working Group on the Issue of Military Sexual Slavery [挺身隊問題實務對策班], Ministry of Foreign Affairs [外務部]. 1992. "Investigations on the Reality of Military Comfort Women under Japanese Colonial Rule: Interim Report" [日帝下軍隊慰安婦實態調査—中間報告書] (Jul. 31).

Yamashita, Yeong-Ae [山下英愛]. 1991. "A Study of the Implementation of Licensed Prostitution in Modern Korea" [韓國近代公娼制度實施에 關한 硏究]. Master's thesis. Department of Women's Studies [女性學科], Ewha Womans University [梨花女子大學校].

_____. 1997. "A Timeline of Activities Related to the Issue of Japanese Military Comfort Women" [日本軍慰安婦問題關聯活動年表]. Ed. Korean Council for the Women Drafted for Military Sexual Slavery by Japan [韓國挺身隊問題對策協議會]. *The Truth about "Comfort Women" in the Japanese Military* [日本軍'慰安婦'問題의 眞相]. Seoul: Yuksa Bipyongsa [歷史批評社].

_____. 1999. "The Comfort Women Issue in Korea and Nationalism" [韓國의 慰安婦問題와 民族主義]. Ed. Kang Deoksang [姜德相], Chung Chinsung [鄭鎭星], et al. *Modern and Contemporary Korean-Japanese Relations and Korean Residents in Japan* [近現代韓日關係와 在日同胞]. Seoul: Seoul National University Press [서울大學校出版部].

Yeo, Soon-joo [余舜珠]. 1994. "A Study on the Korean *Joshikinroteishintai* (女子勤勞挺身隊) in the Late Japanese Colonization" [日帝末期朝鮮人女子勤勞挺身隊에 關한 實態研究]. Master's thesis. Department of Women's Studies [女性學科], Ewha Womans University [梨花女子大學校].

_____. 1997. "A Study of the Everyday Lives of Military Comfort Women" [軍慰安婦生活에 關한 硏究]. Ed. Korean Council for the Women Drafted for Military Sexual Slavery by Japan [韓國挺身隊問題對策協議會]. *The Truth about "Comfort Women" in the Japanese Military* [日本軍'慰安婦'問題의 眞相]. Seoul: Yuksa Bipyongsa [歷史批評社].

Yi, Mahn-yol [李萬烈]. 1997. "The Historical Background in Colonial Korea of the Formation of Japanese Military Comfort Women Policies" [日本軍慰安婦政策形成의 朝鮮側歷史的 背景]. Ed. Korean Council for the Women Drafted for Military Sexual Slavery by Japan [韓國挺身隊問題對策協議會]. *The Truth about "Comfort Women" in the Japanese Military* [日本軍'慰安婦'問題의 眞相]. Seoul: Yuksa Bipyongsa [歷史批評社].

Yi, Sang-Hwa [李相和]. 1993. "A Study of Military Comfort Women's Experience—Centering on Changes of Their Consciousness" [軍慰安婦經驗에 關한 硏究—結婚過程에서 나타나는 認識變化를 中心으로]. Master's thesis. Department of Women's

Studies [女性學科], Ewha Womans University [梨花女子大學校].

Yi, Yeoseong [李如星], and Kim Se-yong [金世鎔]. 1931. *A Numerical Study of Korea: Vol. 1* [數字朝鮮硏究第一輯]. Seoul: Segwang Chulpan [世光出版].

_____. 1933. *A Numerical Study of Korea: Vol. 4* [數字朝鮮硏究第四輯]. Seoul: Segwang Chulpan [世光出版].

Yokota, Yuichi [橫田雄一]. 2001. "The Women's International War Crimes Tribunal on Japan's Military Sexual Slavery in 2000 as Seen from the Perspective of Civil Trials" [民事裁判에서 본 2000年日本軍性奴隸戰犯女性國際法廷]. Ed. Legal Committee [法律委員會], Women's International War Crimes Tribunal on Japan's Military Sexual Slavery in 2000 [2000年日本軍性奴隸戰犯女性國際法廷], Korean Council for the Women Drafted for Military Sexual Slavery by Japan [韓國挺身隊問題對策協議會]. *The Prospects of the Legal Resolution of the Issue of Japanese Military Comfort Women* [日本軍慰安婦問題에 對한 法的 解決의 展望]. Seoul: Pulbit [풀빛].

Yonhap News Agency [聯合뉴스]. 2001 and 2007.

Yoon, Hyaesin [尹惠信]. 2006. "The Discourse of 'Degraded *Gisaeng*' in Japanese Occupied Korea" [日帝時代'妓生의 低級化談論'에 對한 硏究]. Master's thesis. Gender Studies program [女性學協同過程], Seoul National University [서울大學校].

Yoon, Taek-Lim [尹택림]. 1994. "Nationalist Discourse and Women: Toward Feminist Historiography" [民族主義談論과 女性—女性主義歷史學(Feminist Historiography)에 對한 試論]. Ed. Korean Association of Women's Studies [韓國女性學會]. *Journal of Korean Women's Studies* [韓國女性學] 10 (Jan.).

Yoon, Young Mo [尹英模]. 1999. "A Report on the Korean Confederation of Trade Unions' Participation in the ILO General Conference" [民主勞總ILO總會參加報告書]. Seoul: Korean Confederation of Trade Unions [全國民主勞動組合總聯盟].

Yoshida, Seiji [吉田淸治]. 1983. *My War Crimes: The Forced Transport of Koreans* [私の戰爭犯罪—朝鮮人强制連行]. Tokyo: San-Ichi Shobo Publishing Inc. [三一書房]. Trans. Modern Korean History Research Society [韓國現代史硏究室]. 1989. *I Kidnapped Koreans like This: Confession of My War Crimes* [나는 朝鮮사람을 이렇게 잡아갔다—나의 戰爭犯罪告白]. Seoul: Cheonggye Yeon'guso [淸溪硏究所].

Yoshimi, Yoshiaki [吉見義明]. 1993. "A Historical Study of the Issue of Military Comfort Women" [從軍慰安婦問題の歷史學的究明]. Presented at the 2nd Joint Symposium by the Center for Research and Documentation on Japan's War Responsibility and the Korean Council for the Women Drafted for Military Sexual Slavery by Japan [日本의戰爭責任資料센터·韓國挺身隊問題對策協議會共同심포지엄; 日本の戰爭責任資料センタ-·韓國挺身隊問題對策協議會共同シンポジウム] (Dec.).

_____. 1995. *Military Comfort Women* [從軍慰安婦]. Tokyo: Iwanami Shinsho [岩波新書]. Trans. Yi Gyutae [李圭泰]. 1998. *Japanese Military Comfort Women* [日本軍軍隊慰安婦]. Seoul: Sowha [小花].

_____. 2010. *What Is the Japanese Military "Comfort Women" System?* [日本軍「慰安婦」制度とは何か]. Iwanami Booklet [岩波ブックレット] No. 784. Tokyo: Iwanami Shoten [岩波書店]. Trans. Nam Sanggu [南相九]. 2013. *The Historical Truth behind Japanese Military "Comfort Women": What Is the Japanese Military "Comfort Women" System?* [日本軍'慰安婦' 그 歷史의 眞實—日本軍'慰安婦'制度란 무엇인가?]. History Lectures for Cultured People [教養人을 爲한 歷史講座] Ser. No. 1. Seoul: Yeoksa Gonggan [歷史空間].

Yu, Gwangnyeol [柳光烈]. 1943. "The Strengthening of Domestic Battle Preparations at the Zero Hour" [決戰國內態勢의 强化]. *Morning Light* [朝光] (Nov.).

Yun, Chung-Ok [尹貞玉]. 1991a. "What Is the Problem with the Volunteer Corps?" [挺身隊, 무엇이 問題인가]. Ed. Korean Council for the Women Drafted for Military Sexual Slavery by Japan [韓國挺身隊問題對策協議會]. *A Sourcebook on the Issue of the Volunteer Corps* [挺身隊問題資料集] I.

_____. 1991b. "A Record of the Collection of Materials on the Traces of the Wretched Volunteer Corps" [挺身隊冤魂 서린 발자취取材記]. Ed. Korean Council for the Women Drafted for Military Sexual Slavery by Japan [韓國挺身隊問題對策協議會]. *A Sourcebook on the Issue of the Volunteer Corps* [挺身隊問題資料集] I.

_____. 1997. "Japanese Military Comfort Women as a Part of Colonial Policies in Korea" [朝鮮植民政策의 一環으로서 日本軍慰安婦]. Ed. Korean Council for the Women Drafted for Military Sexual Slavery by Japan [韓國挺身隊問題對策協議會]. *The Truth about "Comfort Women" in the Japanese Military* [日本軍'慰安婦'問題의 眞相]. Seoul: Yuksa Bipyongsa [歷史批評社].

Yun, Myungsuk [尹明淑]. 2003. *Japan's Military Comfort Station System and Korean Military Comfort Women* [日本の軍隊慰安所制度と朝鮮人軍隊慰安婦]. Tokyo: Akashi Shoten [明石書店]. Trans. Choe Minsun [崔민순]. 2015. *Korean Military Comfort Women and the Japanese Military Comfort Station System* [朝鮮人軍慰安婦와 日本軍慰安所制度]. Seoul: Ehaksa [而學社].

2. Works in Japanese

2nd Company [第二中隊], 2nd Independent Heavy Siege Artillery Battalion [獨立攻城重砲兵第二大隊]. 1938. *Field Diary* [陣中日誌] (Jan. 1-Apr. 30).

2nd Independent Heavy Siege Artillery Battalion [獨立攻城重砲兵第二大隊]. 1938. "Regulations on the Use of Comfort Stations" [慰安所使用規定]. "Regulations on Internal Duties during the Occupation of Changchow" [常州駐屯間內務規定] (Government Announcement Materials: Material No. 41 [政府公表資料41番資料]; Mar. 16).

3rd Torpedo Boat Unit [第三魚雷艇隊]. 1944. *The Wartime Diary of the 3rd Torpedo Boat Unit* [第三魚雷艇隊戰時日誌] (Japan Defense Agency National Institute for Defense

Studies Materials: Material No. 85 [防衛廳防衛研究所資料—85番資料]; Jul.).

6th Garrison Construction Labor Company [要塞建築勤務第六中隊]. 1944. *Field Diary* [陣中日誌] (May-Jun.).

9th Infantry Brigade [歩兵第九旅團]. 1938. *Field Diary* [陣中日誌] (Jul. 1-31).

35th Independent Defense Infantry Battalion [獨立守備歩兵第三十五大隊]. 1942a. *Field Diary* [陣中日誌] (Apr. 1-Jun. 30).

_____. 1942b. *Information Thrice-monthly* [情報旬報]. No. 19. *Field Diary* [陣中日誌] (Dec.).

48th Division [第四十八師團]. 1946. *War History Materials and Postwar Conditions of the 48th Division* [第四十八師團戰史資料竝終戰狀況] (Jul.).

3475th Yama Unit [山第三四七五部隊 [i.e., 32nd Infantry Regiment [歩兵第三十二連隊]]]. 1944. "Regulations on Soldiers' Clubs" [軍人俱樂部ニ關スル規定] (Dec.).

Agricultural Association of Korea [朝鮮農會], ed. 1941. *The Bulletin of the Agricultural Association of Korea* [朝鮮農會報] 15.5, 15.6, and 15.11. Seoul: Agricultural Association of Korea.

Arai, Sawako [新井佐和子]. 1992a. "A Consideration of the Issue of Military Comfort Women" [従軍慰安婦問題に思う]. Ed. Contemporary Korea Research Institute [現代コリア研究所]. *Contemporary Korea* [現代コリア] (Jan.).

_____. 1992b. "The Heart of the 'Comfort Women Issue' That No One Has Written about" [だれも書かなかった'従軍慰安婦'問題の核心部分]. *Shukan Jiji* [週刊時事] (Feb. 1).

Arai, Shin'ichi [荒井信一], et al., eds. 1997. *Military Comfort Women and Historical Consciousness* [従軍慰安婦と歴史認識]. Tokyo: Shinko Shuppansha Keirinkan [新興出版社啓林館].

Asahi Shimbun [朝日新聞]. 1992. 13th prefectural edition.

_____. 1992, 2007, 2013, and 2014. Evening edition.

Asahikawa Shimbun [旭川新聞]. 1939.

Aso, Tetsuo [麻生徹男], 2nd Lt. [少尉]. 1939. "Methods for the Active Prevention of Venereal Diseases" [花柳病ノ積極的豫防法] (Jun. 26).

Bureau of Management [管理局], Ministry of the Treasury [大藏省]. 1947. *A Historical Investigation on the Overseas Activities of the Japanese* [日本人の海外活動に關する歴史的調査]. Vol. 10. 9th book on Korea.

Bureau of Police and Public Security [警保局], Ministry of Home Affairs [內務省]. 1923. "Notification by Order on the Item Regarding the Recruitment of Korean Laborers" [朝鮮人勞動者募集ニ關スル件依命通牒] (May 14).

_____. 1926-1942. *The State of Social Movements* [社會運動の狀況].

_____. 1943-1944. *The Monthly Foreign Affairs Bulletin* [外事月報].

_____. 1944. *The Monthly Bulletin of the Special Higher Police* [特高月報].

Bureau of Printing [印刷局], Ministry of Finance [大藏省], ed. 1944. *The Official Gazette List* [官報目錄] (Aug.).

Bureau of Statistics [統計局], Cabinet [內閣], ed. 1940. *National Census Statistics* [國勢調査統計]. Tokyo: Bureau of Statistics, Cabinet.

Cabinet Councilors' Office on External Affairs [內閣外政審議室], Cabinet Secretariat [內閣官房]. 1992. "On the Issue of the So-called Wartime Comfort Women from the Korean Peninsula" [朝鮮半島出身のいわゆる從軍慰安婦問題について] (1st report; Jul. 6).

_____. 1993. "On the Issue of 'Comfort Women'" [いわゆる從軍慰安婦問題について] (2nd report; Aug. 4).

Center for Research and Documentation on Japan's War Responsibility [日本の戰爭責任資料センタ-], ed. 1993. *Report on Japan's War Responsibility* [季刊戰爭責任研究] 1 (fall).

Chiba, Hoichi [千葉奉一], Chief, Division of Foreign Affairs [外事部長], Government-General of Taiwan [臺灣總督府]. 1940. "Item Regarding the Treatment of Travelers to Opposite Areas Acknowledged as Impossible to Regulate through Certificates of Purpose of Travel to China, Etc." [渡支事由證明書等ノ取奇不能ト認メラレル對岸地域ヘノ渡航者ノ取扱ニ關スル件].

Chief, Bureau of Police Affairs [警務局長], Government-General of Korea [朝鮮總督府]. 1942. "Item Regarding the Regulation of Japanese Nationals Traveling to China" [渡支邦人ノ取締ニ關スル件] (Material Nos. 24 [24番資料] and 25 [25番資料]; Mar. 19 and Aug. 29).

Chief, Bureau of Police and Public Security [警保局長], Ministry of Home Affairs [內務省]. 1938. "Item Regarding the Treatment of Women Traveling to China" [支那渡航婦女ノ取扱ニ關スル件] (Material No. 5 [5番資料]; Feb. 23).

Choson Sinbo [朝鮮新報]. 2007.

Commander, 2nd Independent Heavy Siege Artillery Battalion [獨立攻城重砲兵第二大隊長]. 1938. "A Report on the State of Affairs" [狀況報告] (Jan. 20).

Commander, Hantsungho Unit [寒蔥河隊長], Suiyang County Border Police Corps [綏陽縣國境警察隊]. 1941. "Suiyang County Border Police Corps Suifenho-Hantsungho Top Secret No. 890" [綏國警綏寒特秘第八九零號] [also titled "Item Regarding the Installation of Korean Restaurants Exclusively for the Japanese Military" [日軍專用鮮人料理店開設ニ關スル件]] (Oct. 20; housed in the Heilongjiang Province Archives Administration [黑龍江省檔案局]).

Department of Hygiene [衛生課], Bureau of Medical Affairs [醫務局], Ministry of War [陸軍省]. 1942. "Item Regarding the Treatment of the Sexually Transmitted Diseases of Soldiers Related to the Greater East Asia War" [大東亞戰爭關係將兵ノ性病處置ニ關スル件] (Jun. 18).

Department of Military Affairs [兵務課], Bureau of Military Affairs [兵務局], Ministry of War [陸軍省]. 1938. "Item Regarding the Recruitment of Female Workers for

Military Comfort Stations, Etc." [軍慰安所従業婦等募集ニ關スル件] (Mar. 4).

Department of War Preparation [戰備課], Bureau of Maintenance [整備局], Ministry of War [陸軍省]. 1940. "Policy on the Introduction of Coolies into Mainland Japan: Guidelines on the Recruitment of Coolies. Guidelines on the introduction and treatment of coolies are to be stipulated separately" [苦力內地移入ニ關スル方針: 苦力募集要綱. 苦力移入取扱要領ハ別途規定セラルルモノトス].

Division of Investigation [調查部], Chosen Industrial Bank [朝鮮殖産銀行]. 1944 and 1947. *The Monthly Investigation Bulletin of the Industrial Bank* [殖銀調查月報].

Division of Labor [勞務部], Yubari Mining Station [夕張鑛業所], Hokkaido Colliery & Steamship Co., Ltd. [北海道炭鑛汽船株式會社]. 1945. "Dispute Relations" [爭議關係]. Yubari: Hokkaido Colliery & Steamship Co., Ltd.

Division of Literature [文學部], Bibai Coal Mine Labor Union [美唄炭鑛勞動組合], Mitsubishi Mining Co., Ltd. [三菱鑛業株式會社], ed. 1954a. *A History of Everyday Life in Coal Mines* [炭鑛の生活史].

_____. 1954b. *A History of Everyday Life in Coal Mines: Revised Edition* [炭鑛の生活史: 改訂版].

Division of Medical Officers [軍醫部], 15th Division [第十五師團]. 1942-43. "A Summary Report on Hygiene Duties" [衛生業務要報] (Dec. 1942-Feb. 1943).

Division of Special Affairs [特務部], Ro Group [呂集團] [i.e., 11th Army [第十一軍]]. 1940. *The Monthly Bulletin of the Ro Group Division of Special Affairs* [呂集團特務部月報].

Editorial Board of *Military Comfort Women #110* [『從軍慰安婦110番』編輯委員會], ed. 1992. *Military Comfort Women #110: The Voice of History from across the Telephone* [從軍慰安婦110番—電話の向こうから歷史の聲が]. Tokyo: Akashi Shoten [明石書店].

Editorial Board of the *50-Year History of the Ministry of Health and Welfare* [『厚生省五十年史』編輯委員會], ed. 1988. *The 50-Year History of the Ministry of Health and Welfare* [厚生省五十年史]. Health and Welfare Research Society [厚生問題硏究會].

Editorial Board of the *History of the Hokkaido Prefectural Police* [『北海道警察史』編輯委員會], ed. 1968. *The History of the Hokkaido Prefectural Police, Vol. 2: The Showa Era—Hokkaido Prefectural Police Headquarters* [北海道警察史(二): 昭和編—北海道警察本部]. Sapporo: Hokkaido Prefectural Police Headquarters.

Editorial Board of the *History of the War in Nanking* [『南京戰史』編輯委員會], ed. 1989. *A Sourcebook on the History of the War in Nanking* [南京戰史資料集]. Tokyo: Kaikosha [偕行社].

Editorial Board of the *Report on the Investigation of the Reality behind the Forced Taking of Koreans* [『朝鮮人强制連行實態調查報告書』編輯委員會], and the Sapporo Gakuin University Editorial Office of the Report on the Investigation Commissioned by Hokkaido [札幌學院大學北海道委託調查報告書編輯室], eds. 1999. *Hokkaido and Korean Laborers: A Report on the Investigation of the Reality behind the Forced*

Taking of Koreans [北海道と朝鮮人勞動者—朝鮮人强制連行實態調査報告書]. Sapporo: Social Aid Section [保護課], Health and Welfare Department [保健福祉部], Hokkaido Government [北海道].

Editorial Office of the *70-Year History of Hokkaido Colliery & Steamship Co., Ltd.* [『北海道炭鑛汽船株式會社七十年史』編輯室], ed. 1958. *The 70-Year History of Hokkaido Colliery & Steamship Co., Ltd.: Labor—From 1938 to 1945* [北海道炭鑛汽船株式會社七十年史勤勞編: 自昭和十三年至同二十年]. Tokyo: Hokkaido Colliery & Steamship Co., Ltd.

Eto, Jun [江藤淳]. 1998. "Japan's Second Defeat" [日本第二の敗戰]. *Bungei Shunju* [文藝春秋] (Jan.).

Fact-finding Team on the Truth about Forced Korean Laborers in Japan [朝鮮人强制連行眞相調査團]. 1974. *A Record of the Forced Taking and Forced Labor of Koreans: Hokkaido, Kuril Islands, Sakhalin* [朝鮮人强制連行·强制勞動の記錄: 北海道, 千島, 樺太]. Tokyo: Gendaishi Shuppankai [現代史出版會].

First Satellite Session Executive Committee of the Symposium during the 36th JFBA Convention on the Protection of Human Rights [日本辯護士聯合會第三十六回人權擁護大會シンポジウム第一分科會實行委員會], ed. 1993. *Keynote Report: Japan's Postwar Compensations—In Search of Recovery from Human Rights Violations during War* [基調報告書: 日本の戰後補償—戰爭における人權侵害の回復を求めて]. Tokyo: Japan Federation of Bar Associations.

Fujikoshi Steel Industry Co., Ltd. [不二越鋼材工業株式會社], ed. 1953. *Fujikoshi 25 Years* [不二越二十五年]. Toyama: Fujikoshi Steel Industry Co., Ltd.

Fujime, Yuki [藤目ゆき]. 1998. *A Historiography of Sexuality* [性の歷史學]. Tokyo: Fuji Shuppan Co., Ltd. [不二出版].

Fujinaga, Takeshi [藤永壯]. 1998. "The Russo-Japanese War and the Transplantation of Licensed Prostitution in Manchuria by Japan" [日露戰爭と日本に依る滿洲への公娼制度移植]. Ed. Katsuragawa Mitsumasa [桂川光正]. *Pleasure and Regulation: The Course of Recreation in the Modern Era* [快樂と規則—近代に於ける娯樂の行方]. Osaka: Institute for Industrial Research [産業硏究所], Osaka Sangyo University [大阪産業大學].

Fukada, Masuo [深田益男], Major [少佐]. 1941. "A Report on the Inspection of the Hygiene Situation in the Netherlands East Indies by Medical Officer Major Fukada" [深田軍醫少佐蘭印衛生狀況視察報告] (Jul.).

Fukae, Masako [深江誠子]. 1989. "Prostitution and the Emperor System" [賣春制度と天皇制]. Ed. Suzuki Yuko [鈴木裕子] and Kondo Kazuko [近藤和子]. *Women, the Emperor System, and War* [女, 天皇制, 戰爭]. Tokyo: Origin Shuppan Center [オリジン出版センタ-].

Fukuoka Prefectural Bureau of Employment Brokers [福岡地方職業紹介事務局]. 1929. *The*

Situation of Korean Resident Laborers within the Jurisdiction [管內 在住朝鮮人勞動事情].

Futase Mining Station [二瀨鑛業所], Nittetsu Mining Co., Ltd. [日鐵鑛業株式會社]. 1946. *A Report on the Course of the Employment of Chinese Laborers* [華人勞務者就勞顚末報告書].

General Headquarters [總司令部], China Expeditionary Army [支那派遣軍]. 1942. "Opinions, Questions, and Answers from Meetings of Adjutants (General Affairs Officers) in September 1942 (Addenda)" [昭和十七年九月副官(庶務將校)會同席上意見, 質疑及回答(追加)] (Sept.).

Geum, Byeongdong [琴秉洞]. 1992. *A Sourcebook of Top Secret Materials on Military Comfort Women as Seen through Battlefield Diaries* [戰場日誌に見る從軍慰安婦極秘資料集]. Tokyo: Ryokuin Shobo [綠陰書房].

Government-General of Korea [朝鮮總督府]. 1930. *A Report on the National Census of Korea: Entire Korea* [朝鮮國勢調査報告—全鮮篇]. Seoul: Government-General of Korea.

_____. 1933. *An Investigation of the State of Factory and Mine Laborers* [工場及鑛山ノ勞動者狀況調查]. Seoul: Government-General of Korea.

_____. 1934. *The Annual Statistical Bulletin of the Government-General of Korea* [朝鮮總督府統計年報]. Seoul: Government-General of Korea.

_____. 1938. *Written Reply to the Consultation of the Government-General of Korea Investigative Meeting for Plans against the Present Situation* [朝鮮總督府時局對策調査會諮問答申書]. Seoul: Government-General of Korea. 1998. Seoul: Minsokwon [民俗苑].

_____. 1940a. *National Spiritual Mobilization in Korea* [朝鮮ニ於ケル國民精神總動員]. Seoul: Government-General of Korea.

_____. 1940b. *A Summary of the Results of the National Census of Korea in 1940* [朝鮮昭和十五年國勢調査結果要約]. Seoul: Government-General of Korea.

_____. 1940c. "Government-General of Korea Ordinance on South Jeolla Province No. 39: Regulations on the Regulation of Brokerage" [朝鮮總督府全羅南道令第三十九號紹介營業取締 規則]. *The Official Gazette of the Government-General of Korea* [朝鮮總督府官報]. Seoul: Government-General of Korea (Jun. 11).

_____. 1941. *The National Total Effort Movement on the Peninsula* [半島ノ國民總力運動]. Seoul: Government-General of Korea.

_____. 1942. *The Monthly Investigation Bulletin of the Government-General of Korea* [朝鮮總督府調査月報]. Seoul: Government-General of Korea.

Hamamura, Ikusaburo [濱村幾三郎]. 1987. *From the Big Dipper to the Southern Cross* [北斗七星から南十字星まで]. Tokyo: Sanbunsha [讃文社].

Hata, Ikuhiko [秦郁彦]. 1992. "In Pursuit of the Riddle of the History of the Showa Period" [昭和史の謎を追う]. *Seiron* [正論] (Jun.).

_____. 1997. "The Instigator of the Union of Comfort Women and Unit 731 [慰安婦と731部隊合體の仕掛人]. *Shokun!* [諸君!] (Mar.).

_____. 1999. *Comfort Women and Sex in the Battle Zone* [慰安婦と戰場の性]. Shincho Selected Books [新潮選書]. Tokyo: Shinchosha Publishing Co., Ltd. [新潮社].

_____. 2000. "History and Historical Consciousness" [歴史と歴史認識]. *Shokun!* [諸君!] (Feb.).

_____. 2001a. "A Record of Personal Observation of the Women's International War Crimes Tribunal" [女性國際戰犯法廷見聞記]. *Shokun!* [諸君!] (Mar.).

_____. 2001b. "A Way to Avoid the Japanese-South Korean Textbook War" [日韓教科書戰争を避ける法]. *Bungei Shunju* [文藝春秋] (Jul.).

Hata, Nagami [波田永實]. 1996. "The Activities and Logic of the Anti-War Responsibility Camp" [戰争責任不正派の動向と論理]. Ed. Center for Research and Documentation on Japan's War Responsibility [日本の戰争責任資料センタ-]. *Report on Japan's War Responsibility* [季刊戰争責任研究] 11 (spring).

Hayashi, Chiyo [林千代]. 1992. *The Postwar History of Homes for Mothers and Children: Another Life for Women* [母子寮の戰後史—もう一つの女たちの暮らし]. Tokyo: Domesu Publishers, Inc. [ドメス出版].

Hayashi, Hirofumi [林博史]. 1993. "Regarding Japanese Military Comfort Stations on the Malay Peninsula" [マレ-半島に於ける日本軍慰安所について]. Ed. Society of Liberal Arts [教養學會], College of Economics [經濟學部], Kanto Gakuin University [關東學院大學]. *Nature, People, Society* [自然·人間·社會] 15 (Jul.).

_____. 1994. "Japanese Military Comfort Stations in Singapore" [シンガポ-ルの日本軍慰安所]. Ed. Center for Research and Documentation on Japan's War Responsibility [日本の戰争責任資料センタ-]. *Report on Japan's War Responsibility* [季刊戰争責任研究] 4 (summer).

_____. 1999. "The Japanese Military during the Siberian Intervention and 'Overseas Japanese Prostitutes'" [シベリア出兵時に於ける日本軍と'からゆきさん']. Ed. Center for Research and Documentation on Japan's War Responsibility [日本の戰争責任資料センタ-]. *Report on Japan's War Responsibility* [季刊戰争責任研究] 24 (summer).

_____. 2005. *Tribunals on Class B and C War Criminals* [BC級戰犯裁判]. Tokyo: Iwanami Shinsho [岩波新書].

_____. 2014a. "Presentation of Materials: Sexual Coercion Incidents Such as 'Comfort Women' and the Armed Forces' Schemes at Concealment" [資料紹介:「慰安婦」など性的强制事件と軍による隱蔽工作]. Ed. Center for Research and Documentation on Japan's War Responsibility [日本の戰争責任資料センタ-]. *Report on Japan's War Responsibility* [季刊戰争責任研究] 82 (summer).

_____. 2014b. "Presentation of Materials: Coercion Incidents Such as Japanese Military 'Comfort Women' on Java Island—The Case of the Military Police in Djember" [資

料紹介: ジヤワ島における日本軍「慰安婦」等强制事件—ジョンベル憲兵隊ケ-ス]. Ed. Center for Research and Documentation on Japan's War Responsibility [日本の戰爭責任資料センタ-]. *Report on Japan's War Responsibility* [季刊戰爭責任研究] 83 (winter).

Headquarters [司令部], 14th Mixed Brigade [混成第十四旅團]. 1933. "Guidelines on the Implementation of the Medical Examination of Professional Entertainers and Prostitutes and Bar Girls" [藝娼妓酌婦健康診斷實施要領]. *Hygiene Duties Thrice-monthly* [衛生業務旬報] (May 1-10).

Headquarters [司令部], 21st Army [第二十一軍]. 1939. *Wartime Thrice-monthly (Rear Relations)* [戰時旬報(後方關係)] (Apr. 11-20).

Headquarters [本部], Gunnery Unit [砲銃隊]. 1940. "Measures for Arousing Soldiers' Morale as Observed in the Experience of the Second Sino-Japanese War" [支那事變ノ經驗ヨリ觀タル軍氣振作對策] (Sept. 19).

Headquarters [司令部], Nami Group [波集團] [i.e., 23rd Army [第二十三軍]]. 1939. *Wartime Thrice-monthly (Rear Relations)* [戰時旬報(後方關係)] (Apr. 11-20).

Higuchi, Keishichiro [樋口敬七郎], Chief of Staff [參謀長], Taiwan Army [臺灣軍]. 1942. "Taiwan Army Telegram No. 935" [臺電九三五號] (Jun. 13).

Higuchi, Yuichi [樋口雄一]. 1990. "Regarding the Forced Taking of Korean Girls to Japan: A Memorandum for Investigations of the Actuality" [朝鮮人少女の日本への强制連行について—實體調査のための覺え書き]. Ed. Society for Research on the History of Korean Residents' Movements in Japan [在日朝鮮人運動史研究會]. *A Study of the History of Korean Residents in Japan* [在日朝鮮人史研究] 20.

_____. 1992. "Women at Korean Restaurants and Industrial Comfort Women" [朝鮮料理店女性と産業慰安婦]. Ed. Research Society for the Korean Issue [朝鮮問題研究會]. *Kaikyo* [海峡] 16.

Higuchi, Yuichi [樋口雄一], et al. 2005. *The Wartime Labor Mobilization of Koreans* [朝鮮人戰時勞動動員]. Tokyo: Iwanami Shoten [岩波書店].

Hokkai Times [北海タイムス]. 1938-1940.

Hokkaido Colliery & Steamship Co., Ltd. [北海道炭鑛汽船株式會社]. 1945. *Trips to and from the Head Office in 1945* [昭和二十年度本店往復]. Tokyo: Hokkaido Colliery & Steamship Co., Ltd.

Hokkaido Government [北海道廳]. 1903. *A Handbook of the Standing Decrees of the Hokkaido Government in 1902* [明治三十六年北海道廳現行布令便覽]. Sapporo: Hokkaido Government.

_____. 1928. *Statistical Tables on Koreans* [朝鮮人統計表]. Sapporo: Hokkaido Government.

Hokkaido Institute for Work Sciences [北海道立勞動科學研究所]. 1945. *A Collection of Statistical Data on Coal Mines in Hokkaido II: Labor* [北海道炭鑛統計資料集成II—

勞動篇]. Research Investigation Report No. 12 [研究調査報告第十二號]. Sapporo: Hokkaido Institute for Work Sciences.

Hokkaido Shimbun [北海道新聞]. 1991-1992 and 2003.

Hong, Yunshin [洪玧伸]. 2016. *The Battle of Okinawa and "Comfort Stations" in Memory* [沖縄戦場の記憶と「慰安所」]. Tokyo: Impact Shuppankai [インパクト出版會].

Hu, Shuisheng [戸水昇], Governor [知事], Taipei Prefecture [臺北州]. 1939. "Item Regarding the Regulation of [Japanese Nationals'] Travel to China" [渡支取締方ノ件] (Mar. 2).

Hyogo Society for Research on Korean Issues [兵庫朝鮮關係研究會]. 1990. *Underground Factories and the Forced Taking of Koreans* [地下工場と朝鮮人强制連行]. Tokyo: Akashi Shoten [明石書店].

Ichikawa, Yasuto [市川靖人]. 1989. *Oh, the Navy: The Great Story* [ああ, 海軍ばか物語]. Tokyo: Banyusha [萬有社].

Ichimura, Shuji [市村秀志]. 1944. *A Factory Reader* [工場讀本]. Tokyo: Keijo Shobo [京城書房].

Igeta, Jun [井下田純]. 1992. "Diverse Issues Surrounding Korean Military Comfort Women" [朝鮮人従軍慰安婦をめぐる諸問題]. *The Bulletin of the Ageo City Medical Association* [上尾市醫師會報] 60.

Ikeda, Norihiko [池田憲彦]. 1997. "The Relationship between the Individual and History: Memory and Healing" [個人と歴史の關わり—記憶と癒し]. *Jiyu* [自由] (Jul.).

Iloilo Office [イロイロ出張所], Visaya Branch [ビサヤ支部], Philippines Military Administration [比島軍政監部]. 1942. "Item Regarding the Forwarding of Regulations on Comfort Stations (Asia Hall, Comfort Station No. 1)" [慰安所(亞細亞會館第一慰安所)規定送付ノ件] (Nov. 22).

Inaba, Masao [稲葉正夫], ed. 1970. *General Okamura Yasuji Materials, Vol. 1: Reminiscences of the Battlefield* [岡村寧次大將資料上卷—戰地回想篇]. Tokyo: Hara Shobo [原書房].

Inspectorate-General of Military Training [教育總監部], ed. 1938. "Wartime Service Manual" [戰時服務提要] (May 25).

Institute for Science of Labour [勞動科學研究所]. 1943. *Part 1. Industrial Labor and Labor Management: Vol. 8. A Report on the Investigation of the Labor Conditions of Peninsular Laborers* [第一部. 工業勞動及勞務管理—第八冊. 半島勞務者勤勞狀況ニ關スル調査報告]. Tokyo: Institute for Science of Labour.

Ishihara, Hoki [石原崩記]. 1998. "Changes in the Tone of Postwar China toward Japan" [戰後中國の對日論調の變遷]. *Jiyu* [自由] (Aug.-Dec.).

Itakura, Yoshiaki [板倉由明]. 1992. "Verification: The Truth behind the Repentant 'Comfort Women Hunter'" [檢證—'慰安婦狩り'懺悔者の眞相]. *Shokun!* [諸君!] (Jul.).

Ito, Takashi [伊藤隆], et al. 2001. "Questioning Japan's Mettle as an Independent Nation"

[日本獨立國家の氣概を問う]. *Shokun!* [諸君!] (Nov.).

J-CAST News [J-CAST ニュース]. 2007.

Japan Anti-Prostitution Association [賣買春問題ととりくむ會]. 1996. "Activities against Prostitution and Sexual Exploitation in Japan" [日本に於ける賣買春·性的搾取反對活動] (zine).

Japan Mining Association [日本鑛山協會]. 1940. *A Report on the Investigation of Peninsular Laborers* [半島人勞務者ニ關スル調査報告]. Tokyo: Japan Mining Association.

Japanese Consulate-General in Nanking [在南京日本總領事館]. 1938. "Decisions of the Meeting of the Personnel from the Ministry of War, Ministry of the Navy, and Ministry of Foreign Affairs Regarding the Permission and Regulation of Diverse Business Operations of Japanese Nationals Abroad" [在留邦人ノ各種營業許可及取締ニ關スル陸海外三省關係者會同決定事項] (Apr. 16).

Japanese Consulate-General in Shanghai [在上海日本總領事館]. 1932. "Diverse Businesses of Japanese Nationals as of the End of December 1932" [昭和七年十二月末調邦人ノ諸營業].

Kamisaka, Fuyuko [上坂冬子]. 1992. "Isn't Newspaper Coverage of 'Military Comfort Women' Strange?" [新聞の'從軍慰安婦'報道っておかしくありませんか]. *Weekly Post* [週刊ポスト] (Feb. 28).

Kang, Seong Eun [康成銀]. 1979. "The Policies for the Exploitation of Manpower from the Rural Communities of Korea under Japanese Imperialism during the War" [戰時下日本帝國主義下の朝鮮農村勞動力收奪政策]. *Rekishi Hyoron* [歷史評論] 355 (Nov.).

Kase, Hideaki [加瀨英明]. 1997. "Asia and Japan in the 21st Century" [21世紀のアジアと日本]. *Jiyu* [自由] (Jan.).

Kato, Norihiro [加藤典洋]. 1997. *A Post-Defeat Theory* [敗戰後論]. Tokyo: Kodansha [講談社].

Kawakami, Takashi [川上高司]. 1999. "A Theory on the International Culture of Human Rights" [人權の國際文化論]. *Jiyu* [自由] (Oct.).

Kawamoto, Hiroshi [河本弘]. 1997. "A Japan Lacking a View of Nationhood" [國家觀缺如の日本]. *Jiyu* [自由] (Jul.).

Kawashima, Takeyoshi [川島武宜]. 1950. *The Familial Constitution of Japanese Society* [日本社會の家族的構成]. Tokyo: Nippon Hyoron Sha Co., Ltd. [日本評論社].

Kichisaburo, Nomura [野村吉三郎], Minister of War [外務大臣], and Hanawa Yoshitaka [花輪義敬], Consul-General in Hankow [在漢口總領事]. 1939. "Regarding the Travel to China of Women at the Comfort Station of the Amaya Unit of the Army in Hankow" [漢口陸軍天野[i.e., 天谷]部隊慰安所婦女渡支ノ件] (communication; Dec. 22 and 27).

Kim, Heunggon [金興坤]. 1981. "The Strait of Wrath" [怒りの海峽]. *Kikan Ningen Zasshi*

[季刊人間雜誌] 7.

Kim, Jeongmi [金靜美]. 1980. "Japanese Colonial Authorities' Policies on Rural Korean Women" [朝鮮農村女性に對する日帝の政策]. *Chosenshiso* [朝鮮史叢] 3.

Kim, Puja [金富子]. 1994. "The Issue of Military Comfort Women: The Movement and Its Significance" [從軍慰安婦問題—運動とその意味]. Ed. Hara Hiroko [原ひろ子], et al. *Gender* [ジェンダ-] 2.

Kimura, Kan [木村幹]. 2000. *The Nationalism and Small-Nation Consciousness of Korea: From a Tributary State to a Nation-State* [朝鮮-韓國のナショナリズムと小國意識—朝貢國から國民國家へ]. Tokyo: Minerva Shobo [ミネルバ書房].

Kinbara, Setsuzo [金原節三]. 1939-1941. *A Summary of the Main Points of the Work Logs of the Ministry of War* [陸軍省業務日誌摘錄]. Vol. I (Mar. 12, 1939-Nov. 19, 1941). Manuscript.

_____. 1941-1943. *A Summary of the Main Points of the Work Logs of the Ministry of War* [陸軍省業務日誌摘錄]. Vol. II (Nov. 20, 1941-Sept. 11, 1943). Manuscript.

Kitani, Taka [木谷孝]. 1969. *A History of the People at Inakuraishi Mine* [稻倉石鑛山人民の歷史]. N. p.

Kobayashi, Hideo [小林英夫]. 1975 and 1983. *The Formation and Collapse of the "Greater East Asia Co-Prosperity Sphere"* [「大東亞共榮圈」の形成と崩壞]. Tokyo: Ochanomizu Shobo [御茶の水書房].

Kondo, Ken'ichi [近藤釼一], ed. 1961. *Governance in Korea at the End of the Pacific War* [太平洋戰下終末期朝鮮の治政]. Modern Korean Historical Materials: Selection of Important Documents Related to the Government-General of Korea 2 [朝鮮近代史料—朝鮮總督府關係重要文書選集第二]. Tokyo: Korean Historical Material Compilation Committee [朝鮮史料編纂會]. 1984. Photographic edition. Seoul: Kookhak Charyowon [國學資料院].

_____, ed. 1964. *Korea during the Pacific War 5: The Period of the End of Governance—Production, Savings, Finance, Transport Capacity, and Labor Situation* [太平洋戰下の朝鮮第五—終政期=生産·貯蓄·金融·輸送力·勞動事情]. Modern Korean Historical Materials: Selection of Important Documents Related to the Government-General of Korea 8 [朝鮮近代史料—朝鮮總督府關係重要文書選集第八]. Tokyo: Korean Historical Material Compilation Committee [朝鮮史料編纂會] and the Friendly Nation Society [友邦協會]. 1984. Photographic edition. Seoul: Kookhak Charyowon [國學資料院].

Konno, Torisuke [今野取介]. 1998. "In Criticism of the Verdict of Compensation for Damages to Comfort Women" [慰安婦損害賠償判決を批判する]. *Jiyu* [自由] (Jul.).

Korean Branch [朝鮮支部], Coalition of National Economic Investigation Organs [全國經濟調查機關聯合會], ed. 1939. *Korean Economic Yearbook* [朝鮮經濟年譜]. Tokyo: Kaizosha [改造社].

Kurahashi, Masanao [倉橋正直]. 1994. *A Historical Study of the Issue of Military Comfort Women* [從軍慰安婦問題の歷史的研究]. Tokyo: Kyoei Shobo [共榮書房].

Kurasawa, Susumu [倉澤進], and Akimoto Ritsuro [秋元律郎]. 1991. *Neighborhood Associations and Regional Groups* [町內會と地域集團]. Tokyo: Minerva Shobo [ミネルバ書房].

Kuroda, Katsuhiro [黑田勝弘]. 1993. "The Inside Information on the 'Political Settlement' of Comfort Women through Joint Japanese-South Korean Collaboration" [日韓合作慰安婦'政治結着'の內幕]. *Shokun!* [諸君!] (Oct.).

Lawsuit seeking compensation for the Korean victims of the Asia-Pacific War [アジア太平洋戰爭韓國人犧牲者補償請求事件]. 1992. *Petition* [訴狀]. 2nd ed.

Mainichi Shimbun [每日新聞]. 2007. Morning edition.

Manabe, Motoyuki [眞鍋元之]. 1981. *One Day, the Red Paper Came: The Last of the Imperial Army as Seen by a Conscriptee* [ある日, 赤紙が來て—應召兵の見た帝國陸軍の最後]. Kojinsha NF Library [光人社NF文庫]. Tokyo: Kojinsha [光人社].

Maruyama, Masao [丸山眞男]. 1964. *The Ideas and Actions of Contemporary Politics* [現代政治の思想と行動]. Tokyo: Miraisha [未來社].

_____. 1976. "Modern Thought, 1945" [近代的思惟一九四五]. *Between the War and the Postwar Era, 1936-1957* [戰中と戰後の間—1936~1957]. Tokyo: Misuzu Shobo [みすず書房].

Matsumura [松村], Chief, Division of Medical Officers [軍醫部長], Nami Group [波集團] [i.e., 23rd Army [第二十三軍]]. "A Report by the Chief of the Nami Group Division of Medical Officers Matsumura" [松村波集團軍醫部長報告]. 1939. Kinbara. 1939-1941. 1-I (Mar. 12-May 30).

Ministry of Foreign Affairs [外務省]. 1939. "Item Regarding Reporting on Population Statistics on Japanese Nationals Abroad per Occupation" [在留邦人人口統計職業別報告ノ件] (Apr.-Sept.).

Ministry of Home Affairs [內務省]. 1940. "Points of Consultation on 'Item Regarding the Provisional Treatment of Japanese Nationals Traveling to China'" [「渡支邦人暫定處理ノ件」打合事項] (May).

Ministry of War [陸軍省]. 1943. *Great Log of Army Secrets in China in 1942, No. 39* [昭和十七年陸支密大日記第三十九號]. Tacloban Military Police Squad Leader Tohei Ken [タクロバン憲兵分隊長東平健]. "Reply to 'Item Regarding the Investigation of the State of Military Comfort Stations and Recreation'" [軍慰安所竝娛樂狀況調査ノ件回答] (Aug. 14).

Miya, Koichi [宮孝一]. 1940. *The Laborers of Korea* [朝鮮の勞動者]. Tokyo: Toto Shoseki [東都書籍].

Miyachi, Masato [宮地正人]. 1988. "The Function of the [Japanese] Emperor in Political History" [政治史に於ける天皇の機能]. Ed. Historical Science Society of Japan [歷史

學研究會]. *In Consideration of the Emperor and the Emperor System* [天皇と天皇制を考える]. Tokyo: Aoki Shoten [青木書店].

Miyata, Setsuko [宮田節子], ed. 1989. *A Brief History of the Chosen Army* [朝鮮軍概要史]. Top Secret Sourcebook on the 15-year War, Vol. 15 [十五年戰爭極秘資料集 15]. Tokyo: Fuji Shuppan Co., Ltd. [不二出版].

Nagai, Kazu [永井和]. 2000. "A Consideration of the Establishment of Army Comfort Stations and the Recruitment of Comfort Women" [陸軍慰安所の創設と慰安婦募集に關する一考察]. Ed. Editorial Committee of Twentieth Century Studies [『二十世紀研究』編集委員會], Graduate School of Letters [大學院], Faculty of Letters [文學研究科], Kyoto University [京都大學]. *Twentieth Century Studies* [二十世紀研究] 1. http://nagaikazu.la.coocan.jp/works/iansho.pdf.

_____. 2004. "Regarding Japanese Military Policies on Comfort Stations" [日本軍の慰安所政策について]. *A Report at the Seminar Jointly Organized by the Institute for Gender Research at Seoul National University and the Research Society for Social History* [ソウル大學校女性研究所·社會史研究會共催セミナ-報告書]. http://nagaikazu.la.coocan.jp/works/guniansyo.html.

Nakagawa, Shigeichi [中川繁市]. 1945-1946. *Log on Koreans' Activities after the End of the War* [終戰後ニ於ケル朝鮮人動向日誌] (Sept. 25, 1945-Jan. 5, 1946).

Nakane, Chie [中根千枝]. 1983. "The Structure of the Household" [家の構造]. Ed. Okouchi Kazuo [大河內一男], et al. *University of Tokyo Public Lecture 11: Home* [東京大學公開講座<11>家]. Tokyo: University of Tokyo Press [東京大學出版會].

Nakanishi, Terumasa [中西輝政]. 2000. "How Is History to Be Faced?" [歷史とどう向き合うか]. *Shokun!* [諸君!] (Feb.).

_____. 2001. "The Lost National Interest" [喪われた國益]. *Shokun!* [諸君!] (Oct.).

Nakasone, Yasuhiro [中曾根康弘]. 1978. "The Supreme Commander of 3,000 at the Age of 23" [二十三歲で三千人の總指揮官]. Ed. Matsuura Takanori [松浦敬紀]. *The Endless Navy: Wish to Convey It, Leave It to Young Generations* [終りなき海軍—若い世代へ傳えたい殘したい]. Tokyo: Bunka Hoso Shuppanbu [文化放送出版部].

National Council for Combating Discrimination against Ethnic Peoples in Japan [民族差別と鬪う連絡協議會]. 1989. *The Compensation of Korean Residents in Japan and Human Rights Laws: Toward Postwar Compensations Related to People in Japan from Former Colonies and the Legislation of Laws Ensuring Human Rights* [在日韓國·朝鮮人の補償·人權法—在日舊植民地出身者に關する戰後補償および人權保障法制定をめざして]. Tokyo: Shinkansha [新幹社].

National League of Total Effort in Korea [國民總力朝鮮聯盟]. 1944. *An Explanation on the National Draft* [國民徵用ノ解說].

Ni'imi, Takashi [新美隆]. 1994. "Judgment on the Case of Forced Dutch Comfort Women by the Temporary Court Martial Tribunal of Batavia" [オランダ女性慰安婦强制事件

に關するバタビア臨時軍法會議判決]. Ed. Center for Research and Documentation on Japan's War Responsibility [日本の戰爭責任資料センタ-]. *Report on Japan's War Responsibility* [季刊戰爭責任研究] 3 (spring).

Nishida, Hideko [西田秀子]. 2003. "The Formation and the Reality of Korean Labor Comfort Women in Hokkaido during the War: In Terms of the Relation to Forced Taking" [戰時下北海道に於けるる朝鮮人勞務慰安婦の成立と實態—强制連行との關係性において]. Ed. Sapporo Research Society for Women's History [札幌女性史研究會]. *Women's History in Hokkaido* [女性史研究ほっかいどう] 1

Nishinippon Shimbun [西日本新聞]. 1992. Evening edition

Nishino, Rumiko [西野留美子]. 1992. "Testimonies from Chikuho: Coal Mine Comfort Women" [筑豊からの提言—炭鑛慰安婦]. *MILE: Korean Information Magazine* [ミレ: Korean Information Magazine] 33.

_____. 1995. *Following Japanese Military Comfort Women* [日本軍慰安婦に追いて]. Tokyo: Mass Communication Information Center [マスコミ情報センタ-].

Nishio, Kanji [西尾幹二]. 2001a. "The Distorted Debate on History Textbooks" [歪められた歷史教科書論爭]. *Bungei Shunju* [文藝春秋] (May).

_____. 2001b. "Fascism amid Peace" [平和のなかのファシズム]. *Shokun!* [諸君!] (Nov.).

Nishioka, Tsutomu [西岡力]. 1992. "What Was the 'Comfort Women Issue'?" ['慰安婦問題'とは何だったのか]. *Bungei Shunju* [文藝春秋] (Apr.).

Oe, Shinobu [大江志乃夫], ed. 1988. *The Russo-Japanese War from Soldiers: From 500 Military Letters* [兵士からの日露戰爭—500通の軍事郵便から]. Asahi Shinsho [朝日新書] Vol. 349. Tokyo: Asahi Shimbun Co. [朝日新聞社].

Ogino, Fujio [荻野富士夫]. 1994. "Regarding Labor Comfort Women in Toyama Prefecture" [富山縣に於ける勞務慰安婦について]. Ed. Center for Research and Documentation on Japan's War Responsibility [日本の戰爭責任資料センタ-]. *Report on Japan's War Responsibility* [季刊戰爭責任研究] 6 (winter).

Okabe, Naozaburo [岡部直三郎], Chief of Staff [參謀長], North China Area Army [北支那方面軍]. 1938. "Notification on the Item Regarding Caution with the Behavior of Soldiers and Units to Locals" [軍人軍隊ノ對住民行爲ニ關スル注意ノ件通牒] (Jun. 27).

_____. 1982. *The Diary of General Okabe Naozaburo* [岡部直三郎大將の日記]. Tokyo: Fuyo Shoten [芙蓉書店].

Omata, Yukio [小俣行男]. 1967. *A Reporter on the Battlefield* [戰場の記者]. Tokyo: Tojusha [冬樹社].

Otaru Shimbun [小樽新聞]. 1938-1940.

Park, Kyung-Sik [朴慶植]. 1975. "Introduction" [序文]. Ed. Park. *A Compilation of Materials Related to Korean Residents in Japan 1* [在日朝鮮人關係資料集成1]. Tokyo: San-Ichi Shobo Publishing Inc. [三一書房].

Planning Board [企劃院], Ministry of Greater East Asia [大東亞省]. 1942a. "A Report on the Inspection of Coal Mines in Hokkaido in August 1942: Labor Conditions and Opinions" [昭和十七年八月北海道炭鑛視察報告—勞務狀況ト所見]. Tokyo: Division 3 [三部], Planning Board, Ministry of Greater East Asia.

_____. 1942b. "Top Secret: Item Regarding Coolies" [極秘—苦力ノ件]. Eastern Branch, Association for the Control of Coal [石炭統制會東部支部] (Oct.).

_____. 1942c. "Top Secret: Guidelines on the Use of Coolies" [極秘—苦力使用ノ要領] (Oct.).

_____. 1942d. "Item Regarding the Introduction of Chinese Laborers into Mainland Japan: Guidelines on the Implementation of the Introduction of Chinese Laborers into Mainland Japan Based on Measure 3" [華人勞務者內地移入ニ關スル件: 第三措置ニ基ク華北勞務者內地移入實施要領]. Tokyo: Division 3 [三部], Planning Board, Ministry of Greater East Asia (Nov. 27).

_____. 1943. "The Particulars of the Implementation of the First Supply (Introduction) of Chinese Laborers to Japan" [華人勞務者第一次對日供出(移入)實施稅目].

Public Security Intelligence Agency [公安調查廳]. 1953. *The Overall Conditions of Korean Residents in Japan* [在日朝鮮人の概況]. Tokyo: Public Security Intelligence Agency.

Research and Executive Bureau [研究事務局], Center for Research and Documentation on Japan's War Responsibility [日本の戰爭責任資料センタ-]. 2007. "Presentation of Materials: The Japanese Military Comfort Women System, Adjudged at the Tokyo Tribunal" [資料紹介: 東京裁判で裁かれた日本軍慰安婦制度]. Ed. Center for Research and Documentation on Japan's War Responsibility [日本の戰爭責任資料センタ-]. *Report on Japan's War Responsibility* [季刊戰爭責任硏究] 56 (summer).

Research Society for the Issue of Postwar Compensations [戰後補償問題硏究會], ed. 1990. *A Sourcebook on the Issue of Postwar Compensations: Vol. 1* [戰後補償問題資料集—第一集] (zine). Tokyo: Research Society for the Issue of Postwar Compensations.

Research Society for Women's History [女性史總合硏究會], ed. 1982. *A History of Japanese Women* [日本女性史]. Vols. 3-5. Tokyo: University of Tokyo Press [東京大學出版會].

Saito, Yasuaki [齊藤泰明]. 1964. "The Mobilization and Assignment of Soldiers and Laborers" [兵力·勞動力の動員とその配置]. Ed. Ohara Institute of Social Research [大元社會問題硏究所]. *The Conditions of Laborers during the Pacific War* [太平洋戰爭下の勞動者狀態]. Tokyo: Toyo Keizai, Inc. [東洋經濟新報社].

Sakamoto, Takao [坂本多加雄], et al. 2000. "History and Historical Consciousness" [歷史と歷史認識]. *Shokun!* [諸君!] (Feb.).

Sankei News. 2014.

Sankei Shimbun [產經新聞]. 1993 and 2007.

Sapporo City Hall [札幌市役所]. 1938. *Sapporo City Administrative Report, 1938: Vol. 1* [昭和十三年札幌市事務報告上]. Sapporo: Sapporo City Hall.

_____. 1939. *Sapporo City Administrative Report, 1939: Vol. 1* [昭和十四年札幌市事務報告

上]. Sapporo: Sapporo City Hall.

Sapporo Municipal Workers Union Committee for the Establishment of the Research Institute for Local Autonomy and Local Government [札幌市職自治研推進委員會], Research Society on Foreign Residents in Japan and Self-governing Bodies [在日外國人と自治体研究會], and Group for Considering Sapporo, an International City [國際都市札幌を考える會], eds. 1987. *Jichiken Sapporo Extra: "The City Administration of Sapporo and Korean Residents—In Search of Inner 'Internationalization'"* [自治研さっぽろ號外:「札幌市政と韓國·朝鮮人—内なる"國際化"を求めて」]. Sapporo: Sapporo Municipal Workers Union [札幌市役所職員組合].

Sasagi, Masanori [佐佐木正制]. 1942. *The Management of Factory Dormitories* [工場寄宿舍管理]. Tokyo: Toyo Shokan [東洋書館].

Sato, Kazuhide [佐藤和秀]. 1993. "Comfort Women and World History" [慰安婦と世界史]. *Seiron* [正論] (Oct.).

Senda, Kakou [千田夏光]. 1978. *Military Comfort Women: The Main Part* [從軍慰安婦—正篇]. Tokyo: San-Ichi Shobo Publishing Inc. [三一書房].

Shimada, Toshihiko [島田俊彦]. 1965. *The Kwantung Army: The Arbitrary Actions of the [Imperial Japanese] Army in Manchuria* [關東軍—在滿陸軍の獨走]. Chuko New Books [中公新書] 81. Tokyo: Chuokoron-Shinsha, Inc. [中央公論新社].

Shoji, Jun'ichiro [庄司潤一郎]. 2000. "Historical Consciousness as Seen from the Peace Museum" [平和博物館から見た歷史認識]. *Shokun!* [諸君!] (Oct.).

Sin, Am'u [申岩又], and Ku Duyun [具斗潤]. 1941. *Written Account* [始末書]. Bibai Mining Station [美唄鑛業所], Mitsubishi Mining Co., Ltd. [三菱鑛業株式會社].

Society for Research on the History of Women in Donan [道南女性史研究會], ed. 1991. *Research on the History of Women in Donan* [道南女性史研究] 8.

Society for the Investigation of Hygiene in the Rural Society of Korea [朝鮮農村社會 衛生調査會]. 1949. *Hygiene in the Rural Villages of Korea* [朝鮮の農村衛生]. Tokyo: Iwanami Shoten [岩波書店].

"Special feature" [特輯]. 1992. "The Instigator of the Comfort Women Problem Is the Instigator Who Is Duped by 'This Man'" [慰安婦問題の煽動者は'この男'に乗る煽動者]. *Shukan Shincho* [週刊新潮] (Dec. 24-31).

_____. 2002. "22 Frightening Plots That Are Pervading Japan" [日本を覆う怪しい謀群22]. *Shokun!* [諸君!] (Feb.).

Special Service Ship Unit [特設艦船部隊]. 1940. "File of the 8th Summary Table of Achievements in the Second Sino-Japanese War, Investigation of the Meritorious Service of the Navy" [支那事變第八回功績概見表綴, 海軍武功調査] (Apr.-Nov.).

Squad [分隊], Tacloban Military Police [タクロバン憲兵], and Squad, Baguio Military Police [バギオ憲兵]. 1943. *The Monthly Military Police Bulletin of the 14th Army Military Police Corps* [第十四軍憲兵隊軍事警察月報].

Squad Leader [分隊長], Cebu Military Police [セブ-憲兵], and Squad Leader, Tacloban Military Police [タクロバン憲兵]. 1943. "Item Regarding the Investigation of the State of Military Comfort and Recreation Facilities" [軍慰安竝娯樂設備狀況調査ノ件] (Material No. 72 [72番資料]; Aug.).

Sub-committee to Address the Wartime Comfort Women Issue [從軍慰安婦問題等小委員會], Ruling Parties' Project to Deal with Issues Fifty Years after the War [與黨戰後五十年問題プロジェクト]. 1994. "The First Report on the So-called Wartime Comfort Women Issue" [與黨 戰後五十年問題プロジェクト·從軍慰安婦問題等小委員會第一次報告] (Dec. 7).

Suzuki, Yuko [鈴木裕子]. 1988. *Feminism and War* [フェミニズムと戰爭]. Tokyo: Marge-sha [マルジュ社].

_____. 1989a. "Mr. Hirohito and the History of the Showa Era and Women" [ヒロヒト氏と昭和史と女]. Ed. Suzuki and Kondo Kazuko [近藤和子]. *Women, the Emperor System, and War* [女, 天皇制, 戰爭]. Tokyo: Origin Shuppan Center [オリジン出版センタ-].

_____. 1989b. *Pioneering Women's History 2* [女性史を拓く2]. Tokyo: Miraisha [未來社].

_____. 1991a. "The Issue of Military Comfort Women and Japanese Women" [從軍慰安婦問題と日本女性]. Ed. Korean Council for the Women Drafted for Military Sexual Slavery by Japan [韓國挺身隊問題對策協議會]. *A Sourcebook on the Issue of the Volunteer Corps* [挺身隊問題資料集] I. Trans. Group for Considering the Issue of Korean Military Comfort Women [朝鮮人從軍慰安婦問題を考える會]. Osaka: Group for Considering the Issue of Korean Military Comfort Women.

_____. 1991b. *Korean Military Comfort Women* [朝鮮人從軍慰安婦]. Iwanami Booklet [岩波ブックレット] 229. Tokyo: Iwanami Shoten [岩波書店]

_____. 1992. *Military Comfort Women and Japanese-Korean Marriage: Considering Sexual Invasion and Postwar Responsibilities* [從軍慰安婦·內鮮結婚—性の侵略· 戰後責任を考える]. Tokyo: Miraisha [未來社].

Taiwan Army [臺灣軍]. 1942. "Item Regarding Travelers Dispatched to the South" [南方派遣 渡航者ニ關スル件] (Mar.).

Takagi, Ken'ichi [高木健一]. 1992. *Military Comfort Women and Postwar Compensations* [從軍慰安婦と戰後補償]. Tokyo: San-Ichi Shobo Publishing Inc. [三一書房].

Takagi, Ken'ichi [高木健一], et al., eds. 1993. *Hong Kong and Postwar Compensations* [香港と戰後補償]. Tokyo: Akashi Shoten [明石書店].

Takahashi, Kikue [高橋喜久江]. 1992. "The Prostitution Problem Today" [今日の 賣買春問題]. Ed. Tachikawa Group for the Transcription of Women's Lives [立川·女の暮らし聞き書きの會]. *Tsumugu* [つむぐ] 8.

Takashima Mining Station [高島鑛業所], Mitsubishi Mining Co., Ltd. [三菱鑛業株式會社], ed. 1953. *Investigation Report on Chinese Laborers* [華人勞務者に關する調査報告書]. N. p.: Mitsubishi Mining Co., Ltd.

Takayama, Akane [高山明根], Assisting Police Officer [警補], Special Operations Section [特務係]. 1941. "Item Regarding the Installation of Restaurants Designated for Units of the Japanese Armed Forces" [日本軍部隊指定料理店開設ニ關スル件] (Oct. 30; housed in the Heilongjiang Province Archives Administration [黑龍江省檔案局]).

Takeda, Tatsuo [武田龍夫]. 2001. "An Investigation of NHK's View of History" [NHKの歴史認識を糾す]. *Shokun!* [諸君!] (Apr.).

Takubo, Tadae [田久保忠衛]. 2000. "The First Step of American Imperialism" [米帝國主義の第一步]. *Jiyu* [自由] (Sept.).

Tanaka, Akira [田中明], and Sato Katsumi [佐藤勝巳]. 1992. "Japanese-Korean Relation Worsens the More We Apologize [謝罪するほど惡くなる日韓關係]." *Bungei Shunju* [文藝春秋] (Mar.).

Teshio Mining Station [天鹽鑛業所], Nisso Mining Co., Ltd. [日曹鑛業株式會社]. 1943 and 1944. "Guidelines on the Treatment of Peninsular Laborers Introduced" [移入半島勞務者取扱要綱].

"The Proceedings of [the Meeting of] Bureau Chiefs on July 30, 1942" [昭和十七年七月三十日局長[會同]會報]. Kinbara Setsuzo. 1941-1943. 4-Ro (Jul. 30, 1942).

Totsuka, Etsuro [戸塚悅朗]. 1995. "An Essay: Ethnic Discrimination in Japanese Society and the International Community" [漫筆—日本社會による民族差別と國際社會]. *Roudou Hanrei* [勞動判例] (Sept. 10).

_____. 1997. "The War Responsibility That Japan Does Not Know" [日本が知 らない戰爭責任]. *Hougaku Semina* [法學セミナ-] 509 (May) and 512 (Aug.).

_____. 1999. *The War Responsibility That Japan Does Not Know: The Human Rights Activities of the UN and the Issue of Japanese Military Comfort Women* [日本が知らない戰爭責任: 國聯の人權活動と日本軍慰安婦問題]. Tokyo: Gendai Jinbunsha [現代人文社].

Toyo Keizai, Inc. [東洋經濟新報社], ed. 1980. *A Comprehensive Survey of the National Census during the Showa Era* [昭和國勢總覽]. Tokyo: Toyo Keizai, Inc.

Tsunoda, Yukiko [角田由紀子]. 1989. "Sexual Violence and the Emperor System" [性暴力と天皇制]. Ed. Suzuki Yuko [鈴木裕子] and Kondo Kazuko [近藤和子]. *Women, the Emperor System, and War* [女, 天皇制, 戰爭]. Tokyo: Origin Shuppan Center [オリジン出版センタ-].

Ueno, Chizuko [上野千鶴子]. 1996. "The Nation-State and Gender" [國民國家とジェンダ-]. *Gendai Shiso* [現代思想] (Oct.).

_____. 1998. *Nationalism and Gender* [ナショナリズムとジェンダ-]. Tokyo: Seidosha [青土社].

Uesugi, Chitoshi [上杉千年]. 1992a. "Police OBs Enraged" [警察OB大いに怒る]. *Shokun!* [諸君!] (Aug.).

_____. 1992b. "Beheading Senda Kakou's *Military Comfort Women*" [千田夏光著『從軍慰

安婦』を斬る]. *Getsuyo Hyoron* [月曜評論] (Sept. 28).

_____. 1992c. "Summary: The Made-up Story of Comfort Women Hunting" [總括—従軍慰安婦の狩りの作り話]. *Jiyu* [自由] (Sept.).

_____. 1994. "A Written Statement to the UN Special Rapporteur" [國連·特別報告者 への意見書]. *Jiyu* [自由] (May).

Van Poelgeest, Bart, Ministry of Interior [*Ministerie van Binnenlandse Zaken*]. 1993. *Forced Prostitution of Dutch Women in the Former Netherlands East Indies* [*Gedwongen Prostitutie van Nederlandse Vrouwen in Voormalig Nederlands-Indië*]. Presented to the House of Representatives of the Dutch States-General [*Tweede Kamer der Staten-Generaal*], session 1993-1994, 23 607, no. 1. Hague: Sdu Uitgeverij Plantijnstraat. Trans. Yasuhara Keiko [安原桂子] and comment. Yoshimi Yoshiaki [吉見義明]. 1994. "[Material] Report of a Study of Dutch Government Documents on the Forced Prostitution of Dutch Women in the Dutch East Indies during the Japanese Occupation" [[資料] 日本占領下蘭領インドにおけるオランダ人女性に對する强制賣春に關するオランダ政府所藏文書調查報告]. Ed. Center for Research and Documentation on Japan's War Responsibility [日本の戰爭責任資料センタ-]. *Report on Japan's War Responsibility* [季刊戰爭責任研究] 4 (summer).

Weekly Post [週刊ポスト]. 1992.

Welfare Research Society [厚生研究會], ed. 1941. *Universal Labor: Labor Mobilization during the War* [國民皆勞—戰時下ノ勞務動員]. Tokyo: Shinkigensha [新紀元社].

Women's Association of Greater Japan [大日本婦人會]. 1942a. "Three Patriotic Platforms for the Home" [家庭報國三綱領].

_____. 1942b. "13 Main Points for Practice" [實踐十三要目].

Yamada, Shoji [山田昭次]. 2005. "A Comparative Review of the Mobilization of the Korean Women's Labor Volunteer Corps and the Wartime Mobilization of Korean Men to the Steel Industry: Regarding the Characteristics of Methods of the Wartime Mobilization of Koreans to Industrial Fields in Mainland Japan" [朝鮮女子勤勞挺身隊の動員と鐵鋼業への朝鮮人男子の戰時動員との比較檢討—日本內地の工業分野への朝鮮人戰時動員方式の特徵について]. Ed. Association of Korean-Japanese National Studies [韓日民族問題學會]. *Journal of Korean-Japanese National Studies* [韓日民族問題研究] 9.0.

Yokogawa, Teruo [横川輝雄]. 1990. "Coal Mines in Chikuho and Military Comfort Women" [筑豊の炭鑛と従軍慰安婦].

Yomiuri Shimbun [讀賣新聞]. 1992 and 2007. Evening edition.

Yoneda, Karl Gozo [カ-ル·ゴ-ゾ-·ヨネダ; 米田剛三]. 1989. *A Nikkei M. I. S. Soldier's Diary: 1942-1945* [アメリカー情報兵士の日記]. Tokyo: PMC Shuppan [PMC出版].

Yoshida, Seiji [吉田清治]. 1977. *Korean Comfort Women and the Japanese People: The Memoir of the Former Labor Conscription Manager of the Shimonoseki Patriotic*

Labor Society [朝鮮人慰安婦と日本人—元下關勞報動員部長の手記]. Tokyo: Shin-Jinbutsuoraisha [新人物往來社].

Yoshida, Yutaka [吉田裕]. 1996. "Discussions of the National Diet Surrounding the Consciousness of the War 4" [戰爭認識をめぐる國會論議4]. Ed. Center for Research and Documentation on Japan's War Responsibility [日本の戰爭責任資料センタ-]. *Report on Japan's War Responsibility* [季刊戰爭責任研究] 14 (winter).

Yoshimi, Yoshiaki [吉見義明]. 1992a. *The Issue of Military Comfort Women* [從軍 慰安婦問題]. Tokyo: Akashi Shoten [明石書店].

_____. 1992b. *A Sourcebook on Military Comfort Women* [從軍慰安婦資料集]. Tokyo: Otsuki Shoten [大月書店].

_____. 1994. "The Dispatch Abroad of Military Comfort Women and the Government-General of Korea" [從軍慰安婦の送出と朝鮮總督府]. Ed. Center for Research and Documentation on Japan's War Responsibility [日本の戰爭責任資料センタ-]. *Report on Japan's War Responsibility* [季刊戰爭責任研究] 5 (fall).

_____. 1995. *Military Comfort Women* [從軍慰安婦]. Tokyo: Iwanami Shinsho [岩波新書].

_____. 2007. "A Reconsideration of Coercion Regarding the Issue of Japanese Military Comfort Women" [日本軍慰安婦問題に於ける强制性再論]. Presented at the symposium organized by the Korean Research Institute for the Women Drafted for Military Sexual Slavery by Japan [韓國挺身隊硏究所] "What Is Coercion?" [强制性이란 무엇인가] (May 4).

Yoshimi, Yoshiaki [吉見義明], and Hayashi Hirofumi [林博史], eds. 1995. *Joint Study: Japanese Military Comfort Women* [共同硏究: 日本軍慰安婦]. Tokyo: Otsuki Shoten [大月書店].

Yubari Times [夕張タイムス]. 1940.

Yun, Myungsuk [尹明淑]. 2003. *Japan's Military Comfort Station System and Korean Military Comfort Women* [日本の軍隊慰安所制度と朝鮮人軍隊慰安婦]. Tokyo: Akashi Shoten [明石書店].

Yutaka, Shuichi [豊秀一]. 2015. "Thinking about the Issue of Comfort Women and the Media Situation in Japan: From the Perspective of a Newspaper Reporter" [慰安婦問題と日本のメディア狀況を考える—新聞記者の觀點から]. Presented at the seminar "Never Having to Say I Am Sorry? The Issue of Comfort Women and Post-War Japan" [Never Having to Say I Am Sorry? 慰安婦問題와 戰後日本] sponsored by the Asia Center [아시아硏究所], Seoul National University [서울大學校] (Oct. 16).

3. Works in English

Aircraft Division, United States Strategic Bombing Survey. 1947. *The United States Strategic Bombing Survey: Corporation Report No. 1 (Airframes and Engines): Mitsubishi Heavy Industries, Ltd. (Mitsubishi Jukogyo K K)*, Reports: Pacific War,

No. 16, Washington, DC: Aircraft Division, United States Strategic Bombing Survey (Jun.).

Allied Translator and Interpreter Section, [General Headquarters,] Supreme Commander for the Allied Powers. 1945. "Research Report No. 120: Amenities in the Japanese Armed Forces" (Record Group 165, Entry 79, Box 342; and Record Group 407, Entry A1-427, Box 913) (Nov. 15).

Allied Translator and Interpreter Section, South West Pacific Area. 1943a. "Interrogation Report No. 28, Terada, K." (serial no. 40; Jan. 30).

_____. 1943b. "Interrogation Report No. 37 Kumagae, S." (serial no. 55; Feb. 23).

_____. 1943c. "Interrogation Report No. 47, Yoshikawa, S." (Record Group 3, Box 111, Records of Headquarters South West Pacific Area, 1942-1945; serial no. 79; Apr. 1).

Amnesty International. 2005. "Still Waiting after 60 Years: Justice for Survivors of Japan's Military Sexual Slavery System."

Anderson, Benedict. 1983. *Imagined Community: Reflections on the Origin and Spread of Nationalism*. London: Verso.

Apodaca, Clair, et al. 1998. "Moving Norms to Political Reality: Institutionalizing Human Rights Standards through the UN System." Ed. Chadwick F. Alger. *The Future of the United Nations System: Potential for the Twenty-first Century*. New York: United Nations University Press.

Balibar, Etienne, and Immanuel Wallerstein. 1995. *Race, Nation, Class: Ambiguous Identities*. London and New York: Verso.

Brown, Chris. 2001. *Understanding International Relations*. New York: Palgrave.

Bunch, Charlotte. 1995. "Transforming Human Rights from a Feminist Perspective." Ed. Julie Peters and Andrea Wolper. *Women's Rights, Human Rights*. New York: Routledge.

Chan, Won-Loy. 1986. *Burma: The Untold Story*. Novato, CA: Presidio Press.

Chang, Yunshik [張윤식]. 1967. "Population in Early Modernization: Korea." Doctoral dissertation. Princeton University.

Chatterjee, Partha. 1989. "Colonialism, Nationalism, and Colonized Women: The Contest in India." *American Ethnologist* 16.4.

_____. 1993. *The Nation and Its Fragments: Colonial and Postcolonial Histories*. Princeton: Princeton University Press.

Chavez, Linda Lou. 1995. "Working Paper on the Situation of Systematic Rape, Sexual Slavery and Slavery-like Practices during Wartime, Including Internal Armed Conflict, Submitted by Ms. Linda Chavez in Accordance with Subcommission Decision 1994/109" (UN Doc. E/CN. 4/Sub. 2/1995/38; Jul. 13).

_____. 1996. "Preliminary Report of the Special Rapporteur on the Situation of Systematic Rape, Sexual Slavery and Slavery-like Practices during Periods of

Armed Conflict, Ms. Linda Chavez" (UN Doc. E/CN. 4/Sub. 2/1996/26; Jul. 16).

Chen, Edward I-te [陳以德]. 1968. "Japanese Colonialism in Korea and Formosa: A Comparison of Its Effects upon the Development of Nationalism." Doctoral dissertation. University of Pennsylvania.

Chinkin, Christine Mary. 2001. "Women's International Tribunal on Japanese Military Sexual Slavery." *American Journal of International Law* 95 (Apr.).

Choi, Chungmoo [崔貞茂]. 1998. "Nationalism and Construction of Gender in Korea." Ed. Elaine H. Kim [金惠經] and Choi. *Dangerous Women: Gender and Korean Nationalism*. New York: Routledge.

Chung, Chinsung [鄭鎭星]. 1984. "Colonial Migration from Korea to Japan." Doctoral dissertation. University of Chicago.

Cohen, Jerome B. 1949. *Japan's Economy in War and Reconstruction*. Minneapolis: University of Minnesota Press.

Combat Intelligence Center, South Pacific Area Command. 1942. "Translation of Captured Japanese Document: Regulations Governing the Use of the Special South Sector Brothel and Regulations Governing the Operation Thereof," item no. 1033 (Record Group 165, Entry 79, Box 404; Dec. 10).

Congressional Research Service Memorandum. 2007. "Japanese Military 'Comfort Women' System" (Apr. 3).

Conroy, Hilary. 1960. *The Japanese Seizure of Korea: 1868-1910*. Philadelphia: University of Pennsylvania Press.

Coomaraswamy, Radhika. 1996. "Addendum: Report of the Special Rapporteur on Violence against Women, Its Causes and Consequences, Ms. Radhika Coomaraswamy, in Accordance with Commission on Human Rights Resolution 1994/45: Report on the Mission to the Democratic People's Republic of Korea, the Republic of Korea and Japan on the Issue of Military Sexual Slavery in Wartime" (UN Doc. E/CN. 4/1996/53/Add. 1; Jan. 4).

_____. 1998. "Report of the Special Rapporteur on Violence against Women, Its Causes and Consequences, Ms. Radhika Coomaraswamy, Submitted in Accordance with Commission Resolution 1997/44" (UN Doc. E/CN. 4/1998/54; Jan. 26).

_____. 2001. "Report of the Special Rapporteur on Violence against Women, Its Causes and Consequences, Ms. Radhika Coomaraswamy, Submitted in Accordance with Commission on Human Rights Resolution 2000/45: Violence against Women Perpetrated and/or Condoned by the State during Times of Armed Conflict (1997-2000)" (UN Doc. E/CN. 4/2001/73; Jan. 23).

Crowley, James B. 1966. *Japan's Quest for Autonomy*. Princeton: Princeton University Press.

Donnelly, Jack. 1989. *Universal Human Rights in Theory and Practice*. Ithaca: Cornell

University Press.

_____. 1990. "Traditional Values and Universal Human Rights: Case in India." Ed. Claude E. Welch, Jr. and Virginia A. Leary. *Asian Perspectives on Human Rights*. Boulder: Westview Press.

_____. 1993. *International Human Rights*. Boulder: Westview Press.

Dubey, Madhu. 1998. "The 'True Lie' of the Nation: Fanon and Feminism." *Differences* 10.2.

Enloe, Cynthia. 1989. *Bananas, Beaches and Bases: Making Feminist Sense of International Politics*. Berkeley: University of California Press.

Eriksen, Thomas Hylland. 1993. *Ethnicity and Nationalism: Anthropological Perspectives*. London: Pluto Press.

Executive Committee of the International Public Hearing [國際公聽會實行委員會]. 1993. *War Victimization and Japan: International Public Hearing Report*. Osaka: Toho Shuppan, Inc. [東方出版].

Federation of Korean Trade Unions [韓國勞動組合總聯盟]. 1995. "Letter to Director-General, ILO: 20 March 1995" (Mar. 20). Korean Confederation of Trade Unions [全國民主勞動組合總聯盟], and the Federation of Korean Trade Unions. 2000. *Observations Submitted to the ILO Committee of Experts on the Application of Conventions and Recommendations*.

Gluck, Sherna, et al. 1991. "Whose Feminism, and Whose History?" Ed. Gluck, et al. *Women's Words: The Feminist Practice of Oral History*. New York: Routledge.

Gold, T. B. 1981. "Dependent Development in Taiwan." Doctoral dissertation. Harvard University.

Halliday, Jon. 1975. *A Political History of Japanese Capitalism*. Pantheon Asia Library Vol. 25. New York: Pantheon Books.

Hannum, Hurst. 1965. *Guide to International Human Rights Practice*. Philadelphia: University of Pennsylvania Press.

Harada, Shuichi [原田脩一]. 1969. *Labor Conditions in Japan*. New York: Columbia University Press.

Hayashi, Kaori [林香里]. 2015. "Never Having to Say I Am Sorry? *Asahi's* Comfort Women Reporting Scandal amid the Abe Administration." Presented at the seminar "Never Having to Say I Am Sorry? The Issue of Comfort Women and Post-War Japan" [Never Having to Say I Am Sorry? 慰安婦問題와 戰後日本] sponsored by the Asia Center [아시아硏究所], Seoul National University [서울大學校] (Oct. 16).

Headquarters, 1st Corps, Office of the Assistant Chief of Staff, G-2 (Intelligence), 163rd Language Detachment, APO 301. 1945 (Record Group 338, Box 443; May 21).

Headquarters, United States Naval Military Government, Okinawa. 1945. "Pictorial Supplement to Report of Military Government Activities for November 1945"

(Record Group 313, Entry P31, Box 19; Nov.).

International Commission of Jurists. 1994. *Comfort Women: An Unfinished Ordeal—Report of a Mission.*

International Labour Organization. 1995. *Handbook of Procedures Relating to International Labour Conventions and Recommendations.*

_____. 1996a, 1997a, 1999a, 2001a, 2002a, and 2003a. *Report of the Committee of Experts on the Application of Conventions and Recommendations.*

_____. 1996b, 1997b, 1999b, 2001b, 2002b, and 2003b. *Report of the Committee on the Application of Standards.*

International Labour Organization's Database on International Labour Standards. 1997. CEACR: Individual Observation Concerning Convention No. 29, Forced Labour, 1930 Japan (ratification: 1932).

_____. 1999. CEACR: Individual Observation Concerning Convention No. 29, Forced Labour, 1930 Japan (ratification: 1932).

International Tribunal for the Prosecution of Persons Responsible for Serious Violations of International Humanitarian Law Committed in the Territory of the Former Yugoslavia since 1991. 2001. "Press Release: Judgement of Trial Chamber II in the Kunarac, Kovač and Vuković Case" (JL/P. I. S./566-e). Hague (Feb. 22).

Jayawardena, Kumari. 1986. *Feminism and Nationalism in the Third World.* London: Zed Books.

Johnston, Bruce F. 1953. *Japanese Food Management in World War II.* Stanford: Stanford University Press.

Kaplan, Caren. 1994. "The Politics of Location as Transnational Feminist Critical Practice." Ed. Inderpal Grewal and Kaplan. *Scattered Hegemonies: Postmodernity and Transnational Feminist Practices.* Minneapolis: University of Minnesota Press.

Kedourie, Elie. 1994. *Nationalism.* Oxford and Cambridge: Blackwell.

Kiernan, V. G. 1975. *Marxism and Imperialism: Studies.* New York: St. Martin's Press.

Kim, Elaine H. [金惠經], and Choi Chungmoo [崔貞茂]. 1998. "Introduction." Ed. Kim and Choi. *Dangerous Women: Gender and Korean Nationalism.* New York: Routledge.

Korean Confederation of Trade Unions [全國民主勞動組合總聯盟]. 1998. *Observations Submitted to the ILO Committee of Experts on the Application of Conventions and Recommendations.*

Korean Confederation of Trade Unions [全國民主勞動組合總聯盟], and the Federation of Korean Trade Unions [韓國勞動組合總聯盟]. 1999 and 2000. *Observations Submitted to the ILO Committee of Experts on the Application of Conventions and Recommendations.*

Korean Council for the Women Drafted for Military Sexual Slavery by Japan [韓國挺身隊

問題對策協議會]. 2014 (Aug. 2).

Lawyers for a Democratic Society (Minbyun) [民主社會를 爲한 辯護士會(民辯)], and the Korean Council for the Women Drafted for Military Sexual Slavery by Japan [韓國挺身隊問題對策協議會]. 1993. "Human Rights and Japanese War Responsibility: Counter Report to the Human Rights Committee on the Japanese Government's Third Periodic Report Submitted under Article 40 of the International Covenant on Civil and Political Rights" (Oct.).

Lee, Hoon Koo [李勳求]. 1936. *Land Utilization and Rural Economy in Korea*. Chicago: University of Chicago Press.

MacKay, James. 1996. *Betrayal in High Places*. Stockport, UK: A Lane Publishing.

Manjoo, Rashida. 2010. "Report of the Special Rapporteur on Violence against Women, Its Causes and Consequences, Rashida Manjoo" (UN Doc. A/HRC/14/22; Apr. 23).

McClintock, Anne. 1995. *Imperial Leather: Race, Gender, and Sexuality in the Colonial Contest*. New York: Routledge.

McDougall, Gay Johnson. 1998. "Systematic Rape, Sexual Slavery and Slavery-like Practices during Armed Conflict: Final Report Submitted by Ms. Gay J. McDougall, Special Rapporteur" (UN Doc. E/CN. 4/Sub. 2/1998/13; Jun. 22).

_____. 2000. "Systematic Rape, Sexual Slavery and Slavery-like Practices during Armed Conflict: Update to the Final Report Submitted by Ms. Gay J. McDougall, Special Rapporteur" (UN Doc. E/CN. 4/Sub. 2/2000/21; Jun. 6).

Military Intelligence Service, United States Army, Department of War. 1945. "Special Questions for Korean PWS" (Apr. 4).

Mohanty, Chandra Talpade, et al., eds. 1991. *Third World Women and the Politics of Feminism*. Indianapolis: Indiana University Press.

Moon, Seungsook [文승숙]. 1998. "Begetting the Nation: The Androcentric Discourse of National History and Tradition in South Korea." Ed. Elaine H. Kim [金惠經] and Choi Chungmoo [崔貞茂]. *Dangerous Women: Gender and Korean Nationalism*. New York: Routledge.

Morris-Suzuki, Tessa. 2015. "You Don't Want to Know about the Girls? The 'Comfort Women', the Japanese Military and Allied Forces in the Asia-Pacific War." *Asia-Pacific Journal: Japan Focus* 13.31.2 (Aug. 3).

Nelson, M. Frederick. 1945. *Korea and Old Orders in Eastern Asia*. Baton Rouge: Louisiana State University.

Netherlands Forces Intelligence Service. 1944a. "Compilation of NEFIS Interrogation Reports Nos. 103, 106-138, 141-159, 161-171, 173, 175-178 and 193-194 (Not Issued [Separately])" (Aug. 28).

_____. 1944b. "Compilation of NEFIS Interrogation Reports Nos. 295, 330 and 334 (Not Issued Separately)" (Oct. 14).

_____. 1944c. "Compilation of NEFIS Interrogation Reports Nos. 418-425 Inclusive (Not Issued Separately)" (Oct. 23).

_____. 1944d. "Compilation of NEFIS Interrogation Reports Nos. 455 to 469 (Not issued separately)" (Nov. 6).

_____. 1944e. "Compilation of NEFIS Interrogation Reports Nos: 534, 552, 567, 568, 579, 586, 587, 588 and 592 (Not issued separately)" (Dec. 6).

_____. 1944f. "Compilation of NEFIS Interrogation Reports Nos. 661-669 (Not issued separately)" (Dec. 12).

_____. 1944g. "Interrogation Report No. 409" (Oct. 23).

_____. 1944h. "Interrogation Report No. 554" (Nov. 16).

_____. 1945. "Compilation of NEFIS Interrogation Reports Nos. 1590-1630 (Not Issued Separately)" (May 5).

_____. 1946a. "Affidavit of Interrogation: Summary of Examination of J. Beelman-v. Ballegooyen, 16 May, 1946" (IMTFE Exhibit No. 1725-A; May 16).

_____. 1946b. "Affidavit of Nguyen-thi-Thong" (IMTFE Exhibit No. 2120; Sept. 6).

_____. 1946c. "Report on Enforced Prostitution in Western Borneo, N. E. I. during Japanese Naval Occupation" [also known as "Report of Investigator Captain J. F. [*sic*] Heybroek, Royal Netherlands Indies Army"] (IMTFE Exhibit No. 1702; Jul. 5).

_____. 1946d. "Report on Interrogation of Hayashi Shuichi Dated March 13th 1946 on Pontianak Massacre" (IMTFE Exhibit No. 1701-A; Mar. 13).

_____. 1946e. "Statement by Lt. Ohara Seidai, 13 January, 1946" (IMTFE Exhibit No. 1794; Jan. 13).

_____. 1946f. "Summary of Examination of Lois Antonio Numes Rodreigues, 26 June, 1946" (IMTFE Exhibit No. 1792-A; Jun. 26).

New Delhi Television. 2015.

Norman, Herbert. 1940. *Japan's Emergence as a Modern State*. New York: Institute of Pacific Relations.

Office of Strategic Services. 1945. "Attached Memorandum: Korean and Japanese Prisoners of War in Kunming: 28 April, 1945." Kunming-REG-OP-3, Field Station Files, Records of the Office of Strategic Services (Record Group 226, Entry 154, Box 185; Apr. 28).

Office of the United Nations High Commissioner for Human Rights. 2000-2003. "Systematic Rape, Sexual Slavery and Slavery-like Practices during Armed Conflicts: Report of the High Commissioner for Human Rights" (UN Doc. E/CN. 4/Sub. 2/2000/20; Jun. 27, UN Doc. E/CN. 4/Sub. 2/2001/29; Jun. 29, UN Doc. E/ CN. 4/Sub. 2/2002/28; Jul. 18, and UN Doc. E/CN. 4/Sub. 2/2003/27; Jun. 17).

_____. 2016. "Japan/S. Korea: 'The long awaited apology to "comfort women" victims is yet to come'—UN rights experts" (Mar. 11). https://www.ohchr.org/en/press-releases/2016/03/japan-s-korea-long-awaited-apology-comfort-women-victims-yet-come-un-rights?LangID=E&NewsID=17209.

_____. 2014a. "Japan's Approach to the Issue of 'Comfort Women' Causing Further Violations of Victims' Human Rights - Pillay" (Aug. 6). https://www.ohchr.org/EN/NewsEvents/Pages/DisplayNews.aspx?NewsID=14920&LangID=E.

_____. 2014b. "Committee on the Elimination of Racial Discrimination Considers Report of Japan" (Aug. 21). https://www.ohchr.org/en/NewsEvents/Pages/DisplayNews.aspx?NewsID=14957.

Permanent Mission of Japan to the United Nations [國際聯合日本政府代表部]. 1996. "Note Verbale Dated 26 March 1996 from the Permanent Mission of Japan to the United Nations Office at Geneva Addressed to the Centre for Human Rights: Japan's Policy on the Issues of Violence against Women and 'Comfort Women'" (UN Doc. E/CN.4/1996/137; Mar. 27).

Psychological Warfare Team, United States Army Forces India-Burma Theater, APO 689, United States Office of War Information. 1944. "Japanese Prisoner of War Interrogation Report No. 49" (Record Group 208, Entry 366A, Box 231 [also classified as Record Group 208, Entry 378, Box 446 or Record Group 208, Box 226]; Oct. 1).

Quarton, Harold B. 1942. "Survey of Current Political Thought and Temper of the Korean People" (11d; Aug. 15). United States Department of State, Records of the Department of State Relating to the Internal Affairs of Korea (Chosen), 1940-1944 (Department of State Decimal File 895 (document 895.01/162 PS/ET [also classified as 895.01/157-1/2])).

"Samuel T. Shinohara: Trial by Military Commission at Agana, Guam, 28 July, 1945." 1945. Records of the Office of the Judge Advocate General (Navy), 1799-1950, Records of the Navy War Crimes Branch, Records Relating to Interrogations of Japanese Witnesses and Defendants in War Crimes Cases, 1945-1949 (Record Group 125, Entry A1-12, Box 7; Jul. 28) [also known as "Case of Samuel T. Shinohara," *Record of Proceedings of a Military Commission Convened at Agana, Guam, by Order of the Island Commander* (July 28, 1945), WWII Judge Advocate General (JAG) Case Files, Pacific-Navy].

Smith, Anthony D. 1995. *Nations and Nationalism in a Global Era*. Cambridge: Polity Press.

Son, Hijoo [孫희주]. 1997. "Report at the 1997 ILO" (Jun.)

United Nations. 1968. "Economic and Social Council Resolution 1296 (XLIV) on Consultative Arrangements" (UN Doc. ECOSOC 1296; May 23).

United Nations Committee against Torture. 2013. "Concluding Observations on the Second Periodic Report of Japan, Adopted by the Committee at Its Fiftieth Session

(6-31 May 2013)" (UN Doc. CAT/C/JPN/CO/2; Jun. 28).

United Nations Committee on Economic, Social and Cultural Rights. 2002. "Note by the Secretariat: Comments by States Parties on Concluding Observations" (UN Doc. E/C. 12/2002/12; Nov. 29).

_____. 2013. "Concluding Observations on the Third Periodic Report of Japan, Adopted by the Committee at Its Fiftieth Session (29 April-17 May 2013)" (UN Doc. E/C. 12/JPN/CO/3; Jun. 10).

United Nations Committee on the Elimination of All Forms of Discrimination against Women. 2009. "Concluding Observations of the Committee on the Elimination of Discrimination against Women: Japan" (UN Doc. CEDAW/C/JPN/CO/6; Aug. 7).

_____. 2016. "Concluding Observations on the Combined Seventh and Eighth Periodic Reports of Japan" (UN Doc. CEDAW/C/JPN/CO/7-8; Mar. 10).

United Nations Committee on the Elimination of All Forms of Racial Discrimination. 2014. "Concluding Observations on the Combined Seventh to Ninth Periodic Reports of Japan" (UN Doc. CERD/C/JPN/CO/7-9; Sept. 26).

United Nations Human Rights Committee. 2008. "Consideration of Reports Submitted by States Parties under Article 40 of the Covenant: Concluding Observations of the Human Rights Committee" (UN Doc. CCPR/C/JPN/CO/5; Dec. 18).

_____. 2014. "Concluding Observations on the Sixth Periodic Report of Japan" (UN Doc. CCPR/C/JPN/CO/6; Aug. 20).

United Nations Secretary-General. 2001. "Mass and Flagrant Violations of Human Rights Which Constitute Crimes against Humanity and Which Took Place during the Colonial Period, Wars of Conquest and Slavery: Note by the Secretary-General" (UN Doc. E/CN. 4/Sub. 2/2001/8; Jun. 28).

United Nations Sub-Commission on Prevention of Discrimination and Protection of Minorities. 1992. "Report of the Working Group on Contemporary Forms of Slavery: Draft Resolution" (UN Doc. E/CN. 4/Sub. 2/1992/L. 3; Aug. 13).

_____. 1993. "1993/Systematic Rape, Sexual Slavery and Slavery-like Practices during Wartime, Including Internal Conflict" (UN Doc. E/CN. 4/Sub. 2/1993/L. 12/Rev. 1; Aug. 20).

United Nations Sub-Commission on the Promotion and Protection of Human Rights. 1999. "Systematic Rape, Sexual Slavery and Slavery-like Practices during Armed Conflict, Including Internal Armed Conflict: Note by the Secretariat" (UN Doc. E/CN. 4/Sub. 2/1999/16; Jun. 17).

_____. 1999. "Systematic Rape, Sexual Slavery and Slaverylike Practices: Sub-Commission Resolution 1999/16" (UN Doc. E/CN. 4/Sub. 2/RES/1999/16; Aug. 26).

_____. 2000. "Globalization and Its Impact on the Full Enjoyment of Human Rights:

Preliminary Report Submitted by J. Oloka-Onyango and Deepika Udagama, in Accordance with Sub-Commission Resolution 1999/8" (UN Doc. E/CN. 4/Sub. 2/2000/13; Jun. 15).

_____. 2000. "Mass and Flagrant Violations of Human Rights Which Constitute Crimes against Humanity and Which Took Place during the Colonial Period, Wars of Conquest and Slavery: Sub-Commission on Human Rights Decision 2000/114" (UN Doc. E/CN. 4/Sub. 2/Dec/2000/114; Aug. 18).

_____. 2001. "The Rights of Non-citizens: Preliminary Report of the Special Rapporteur, Mr. David Weissbrodt, Submitted in Accordance with Sub-Commission Decision 2000/103" (UN Doc. E/CN. 4/Sub. 2/2001/20; Jun. 6).

_____. 2002. "Other Issues: Note by the Secretary-General" (UN Doc. E/CN. 4/Sub. 2/2002/29; Jun. 20).

_____. 2003. "Contemporary Forms of Slavery: Report of the Secretary-General on the Implementation of the Programme of Action for the Prevention of the Sale of Children, Child Prostitution and Child Pornography, Submitted Pursuant to Sub-Commission Resolution 1998/19" (UN Doc. E/CN. 4/Sub. 2/2003/26; May 30).

United States Office of War Information. 1944. "Investigation Reports, Directives and Other Records Relating to Captured Personnel and Materials, 1940-1946" (Record Group 165, Entry 177, Box 915, OWI Outpost Report No. WDC406; Apr. 18).

Van Poelgeest, Bart, Ministry of Interior [*Ministerie van Binnenlandse Zaken*]. 1993. *Forced Prostitution of Dutch Women in the Former Netherlands East Indies* [*Gedwongen Prostitutie van Nederlandse Vrouwen in Voormalig Nederlands-Indië*]. Presented to the House of Representatives of the Dutch States-General [*Tweede Kamer der Staten-Generaal*], session 1993-1994, 23 607, no. 1. Hague: Sdu Uitgeverij Plantijnstraat. Trans. anon. 1994. "Report of a Study of Dutch Government Documents on the Forced Prostitution of Dutch Women in the Dutch East Indies during the Japanese Occupation" (Jan. 24).

War Department. 1945a. "S-11414" (Record Group 457, Entry A1 9032, Box 900; Jun. 15). https://archives.seoul.go.kr/ item/17.

_____. 1945b. "S-12382" (Record Group 457, Entry A1 9032, Box 900; Jun. 29). https://archives.seoul.go.kr/item/46.

Washington Post. 2007.

West, Lois A., ed. 1997. *Feminist Nationalism*. New York: Routledge.

Yang, Hyun-Ah [梁鉉娥]. 1998. "Remembering the Korean Military Comfort Women." Ed. Elaine H. Kim [金惠經] and Choi Chungmoo [崔貞茂]. *Dangerous Women: Gender and Korean Nationalism*. New York: Routledge.

Yegenoglu, Meyda. 1998. *Colonial Fantasies: Towards a Feminist Reading of Orientalism*. Cambridge: Cambridge University Press.

Index

A

M

N

O

P

R